SURVEY OF ACCOUNTING

Cecily A. Raiborn
Loyola University New Orleans

Stephanie F. Watson
Louisiana State University

WILEY

www.wiley.com/college/raiborn

Acquisitions Editor *Jay O'Callaghan*
Marketing Manager *Keari Bedford*
Production Manager *Lari Bishop*
Designer *Jennifer Fisher*
Illustration Editor *Kris Pauls*
Indexer *Linda Buskus*
Cover Design *Benjamin Reece*
Cover Images Statue of Atlas, © Corbis; all other photos, © PhotoDisc Inc.

This book was set in Minion and printed and bound by R.R. Donnelly & Sons. The cover was printed by Phoenix Color Corp.

This book is printed on acid free paper.∞

ISBN 978-0-471-46711-3

Printed in the United States of America

10 9 8 7 6 5

This book is dedicated to all those from whom we have learned.

To Fred and Falba Watson and Theresa Simmons for their continuous support and enthusiasm throughout all my endeavors.
—Stephanie Watson

CONTENTS IN BRIEF

CONTENTS

PREFACE

This text is designed for use in a one-semester, introductory survey of accounting class, providing the basics of both financial and managerial accounting. Financial accounting provides primarily monetary information about business activities that result in the financial statements that are published for use by people outside the business. Managerial accounting provides monetary and nonmonetary information about business activities that result in supporting details for the financial statements; it also provides information for internal organizational users to plan, control, or make decisions about operations.

The text addresses a wide breadth of accounting issues and covers each in moderate depth, but the text is not intended to be a comprehensive volume in either financial or managerial accounting. Thus, supplementing the text with extended cases, on-line activities, and real-world discussions will provide greater breadth and depth of subject matter. To ease the inclusion of these items into course materials, the text is supported by access to a well-developed Web site.

Consequently, this text is *flexible* in its uses. It is appropriate for a one-semester course for **undergraduate non-accounting or non-business majors,** and with the addition of cases and current topics, it is ideal for **MBA students** who have had no prior exposure to accounting. The information contained in this text will benefit everyone going into the workforce because accounting is the language essential to economic activity worldwide. Decisions made daily use economic information and have economic consequences. Should I invest in the stock of a particular company? What will be the total cost if I take out a loan to pay for my car? How can I budget how much money I will need for the next year? All of these questions can be answered using accounting information.

Although personal questions such as the above can be answered using accounting information, the focus of this text will be on answering questions about business. Accounting is called "the language of business" because of its usefulness in all organizational functions. The goal of this text is to present accounting as a source of information. For example, financial accounting information is commonly used when bankers are deciding whether to loan money to a company or when people are making decisions about whether to invest or disinvest in stock and bonds. Managerial accounting information is commonly used when companies are trying to determine their advertising budget or when sales personnel are deciding how changes in sales prices will affect organizational profitability.

Technology has made the world much smaller and the introduction of Internet companies has created a global marketplace. Although all countries do not use the same accounting methods, there are basic similarities that exist. Learning these basics will provide a foundation for understanding financial statements of companies, regardless of their domestic base.

The expression "Money makes the world go around" is an accurate one. And accounting essentially provides a business representation of money: where it came from and where it went; what activities occurred and how they affected profitability; what belongs to the organization and what it owes; and how changes in organizational activities could or did affect a company's performance.

ORGANIZATION AND FEATURES OF THE TEXT

This text is divided into five main parts:

I **Accounting Fundamentals** encompasses the first three chapters and presents an introduction to business organizations, defines accounting, and discusses the role of accounting in business. Concepts and principles underlying the preparation of financial statements are explained and illustrated. Double-entry bookkeeping rules, which are necessary to provide the groundwork for the preparation of financial statements, are introduced and the activities necessary to start and complete the accounting cycle are covered.

II **Accounting for Assets**, the next three chapters, discusses the majority of short-term and long-term assets (cash, accounts receivable, inventory, plant assets, and intangibles).

III **Accounting for Liabilities and Ownership Interests** contains two chapters. The first covers corporate debt including short-term payables, contingent liabilities, bonds payable, and other long-term payables. The second addresses the corporate form of business organization and accounting for the various elements of stockholders' equity.

IV **Analysis of Accounting Data**, which includes the final two financial chapters, covers the composition of a corporate income statement, including discontinued operations, extraordinary items, changes in accounting principle, and differences between accounting and taxable income. Accounting for long-term investments in stocks and bonds is also discussed. Methods of analyzing financial statement data are discussed as well as the issue of earnings quality and earnings management. This section also addresses the preparation and use of a Statement of Cash Flows.

V **Managerial Accounting** contains four chapters on information for use by internal decision makers. Differences between financial and managerial accounting are discussed and managerial accounting terms are defined. Product costing systems and activity-based costing are introduced. Cost-volume-profit relationships, relevant costs in decision making, and the budgeting process (and its use of standard costs) are presented. The final chapter discusses organizational structure and how to measure and assess performance in differing organizational settings.

The text contains many features that make it friendly, flexible, and easy to understand:

In the Real World

Each chapter begins with a section entitled *In the Real World*, which presents chapter issues as illustrated by a business organization, persons within an organization, or a business activity. In Chapter 1, for example, the forms of organizations are introduced; *In the Real World* discusses the merger of a restaurant and grown-up arcade, both sole proprietorships, into Dave & Buster's, a national restaurant/entertainment company, now publicly traded. The statement of cash flows is the focus of Chapter 10, and *In the Real World* relates the cash flow problems encountered by United Airlines after September 11, 2001. These vignettes will be supplemented with updated information on the web site as necessary.

Visual Recaps

Some accounting topics are more easily understood by examining them graphically rather than through reading. Thus, wherever appropriate, *Visual Recaps* are provided to illustrate significant topics in a pictorial manner or summarized in a table. These recaps are intended to capture the "one picture is worth a thousand words" adage and help students comprehend and retain concepts. For example, in Chapter 9, accounting methods for long-term investments in other companies are summarized in a simple table that recaps accounting treatment for investments, dividends, and earnings at all ownership levels. In Chapter 11, costs associated with raw material, work in process, and finished goods inventories as well as other accounts are depicted in a flow diagram with descriptions of each cost flow and arrows showing direction.

Accounting Information for Decision Making

Most chapters include a section entitled Accounting Information for Decision Making. This section is designed to emphasize a user (rather than preparer) perspective of accounting information. These sections will address how external parties can analyze and interpret the types of information discussed in the chapter. For example, in Chapter 4 on Cash, Short-Term Investments, and Accounts Receivable, this section addresses issues such as the decision to extend credit to customers and how to calculate and determine the meaning of the accounts receivable turnover ratio and age of accounts receivable. These chapter sections will be very beneficial for students who will not *be* accountants, but are taking accounting to understand financial statement numbers.

End-of-Chapter Materials and Icons

Each chapter contains a summary, key terms list, and a variety of questions, exercises, problems, and short cases for in-class discussion or homework. Some of these end-of-chapter items are marked with icons to indicate that they will address writing, ethical, and teamwork skills. Other EOC items will provide faculty the option to have students use the Internet or work in groups. In addition, learning objectives are listed and numbered at the beginning of each chapter. End-of-chapter questions, exercises, problems, and cases are identified by learning objective number, making it simple to include or exclude end-of-chapter materials that pertain to topics covered or not covered in your course.

writing

ethics

Internet

Excel

group

Supplemental Materials for Instructors and Students

This text is accompanied by several supplements for use by instructors and/or students.

- **Solutions Manual**—The solutions manual gives solutions to all end-of-chapter questions, exercises, problems, and supplemental problems. Solutions are also given for the majority of cases, except those requiring students to select their own companies and make team analyses.

- **Instructors' Manual**—The manual contains sample syllabi, a listing of chapter terms, chapter lecture outlines, an assignment difficulty table indicating the level of difficulty of all end of chapter materials, and teaching tips for each chapter.
- **Test Bank**—The test bank provides true/false statements, multiple choice questions, and short exercises for each chapter. There are approximately 50 questions for each chapter.
- **Web Site**—A comprehensive web site containing chapter outlines, updates on applicable current events and news items, and short on-line tests will be available to instructors and students.

ACKNOWLEDGEMENTS

We would like to thank the many people who have helped us during the development of this text. The constructive comments and suggestions made by the following reviewers were instrumental in developing, rewriting, and improving the quality and readability of this book.

Robert Allen, University of Utah
Sandra Byrd, Arkansas State University
Thomas Gilday, Thomas More College
Leslie Fletcher, Georgia Southern University
R. Steven Flynn, Thomas More College
Jack Ruhl, Western Michigan University
Nancy Snow, University of Toledo
Eileen Taylor, University of South Florida
Larry Trussell, University of Nebraska at Omaha
Barbara Uliss, Metropolitan State Collge of Denver

Our gratitude goes to Chris and Carol Knapp, who worked tirelessly to produce a prior version of this text. Their work ethic and attention to detail in preparing the foundation financial accounting material is appreciated.

Special thanks to Tony Randazzo, who prepared the test bank that accompanies the text, and Kevin Breaux, who created the instructor's manual.

The terrific team of professionals at Leyh Publishing, LLC both initiated and managed the project through to completion. Special thanks to Rick Leyh, Lari Bishop, Benjamin Reece, and Jaye Joseph.

In addition, Susan Elbe, Jay O'Callaghan, and Keari Bedford of John Wiley & Sons, Inc. encouraged and supported the authors throughout the project.

ABOUT THE AUTHORS

Cecily A. Raiborn

Cecily A. Raiborn is a Professor of Accounting at Loyola University New Orleans (LUNO). She graduated from Louisiana State University with a Ph.D. in Accounting and has earned the CPA and CMA. She received the AICPA/Louisiana CPA Society Outstanding Educator Award in 1991, after being nominated by LUNO's Beta Alpha Psi chapter. Raiborn has co-authored several textbooks and has been published in a wide variety of professional journals, including *Journal of Business Ethics, Advances in Management Accounting, Journal of Developmental Entrepreneurship, Journal of Accounting Case Research,* and *Management Accounting* (now *Strategic Finance*). Professional and honorary memberships include the American Accounting Association (Management Accounting section), Institute of Management Accountants, Texas Society of CPAs, Beta Alpha Psi, Phi Delta Gamma, and Phi Kappa Phi. In addition to the academic setting, her work experience includes the manufacturing and not-for-profit sectors.

Stephanie F. Watson

Stephanie F. Watson is a doctoral student in the Accounting Department at Louisiana State University (LSU). She has taught introductory accounting for three years and has been recognized as an excellent teacher, receiving three teaching awards during that time (two at the department level and one at the college level) and positive student evaluations of her teaching. Watson considers herself a student of teaching and learning as well as accounting; she devotes considerable time to developing and refining teaching techniques designed to help students enjoy learning and understand the material, rather than memorize. Watson conducts research in the areas of management fraud and accounting education and passed the Certified Internal Auditor (CIA) exam in November 2001. She is a member of several professional organizations, including the American Accounting Association, Institute of Internal Auditors, and Association of Certified Fraud Examiners. Watson received her B.S. and M.S. in Accounting from LSU in 1991 and 1997, respectively. After earning her undergraduate degree, she worked in private accounting in the retail industry for seven years in her hometown of Little Rock, Arkansas.

PART I

ACCOUNTING FUNDAMENTALS

CHAPTER 1

An Introduction to the Role of Accounting in the Business World

LEARNING OBJECTIVES

1. Identify the major types of business entities, their principal legal forms, and their key internal functions.
2. Identify the primary means by which accountants communicate financial information to decision makers.
3. Briefly describe how financial data are collected by an organization's accounting system.
4. Define the nature, structure, and major segments of the accounting profession.
5. Discuss some key changes taking place in the accounting profession.

Dave & Buster's (www.daveandbusters.com)

The late 1970s found two young men in Little Rock, Arkansas, operating establishments that, while side by side in location, were worlds apart in concept. Situated in the Missouri Pacific Train Station, both enjoyed a rewardingly brisk trade. James W. "Buster" Corley opened Buster's. The restaurant's casually elegant style and warm, historic ambience made it a favorite watering hole and eatery among the locals. Buster's also offered one of the most wonderfully eclectic menus in town. Next door, Dave Corriveau ran a place called Slick Willy's World of Entertainment that featured games for grownups and a limited menu, consisting mainly of things that could be eaten with hands. The neighboring entrepreneurs became fast friends.

Dave and Buster soon discovered that they had spawned a unique traffic phenomenon. Patrons were frequently seen rotating between the two establishments. As this pattern became obvious, an idea was formed. What would happen if Dave and Buster put both establishments under one roof? After a year or so of scratching out a rough plan, Dave and Buster combined their resources and went in search of the right location to begin building a dream.

The men ended up at an empty 40,000 square-foot warehouse at the end of "Restaurant Row" in Dallas, Texas. Having already been proclaimed certifiably crazy by many in the restaurant industry, Dave and Buster still dove headlong into construction. By December 1982, the first Dave & Buster's opened its doors. The year 1988 saw the opening of a second Dallas location, and since then the D&B family has grown to include locations across the country and around the world.

Dave & Buster's became a proud member of the New York Stock Exchange in June 1999, under the ticker symbol DAB. Dave & Buster's had previously traded on the NASDAQ national market.

SOURCE: "History." In About D&B. Available from http://www.daveandbusters.com.

INTRODUCTION

Dave Corriveau and James W. "Buster" Corley are only two of the many individuals who have achieved success in the business world. Other well known names include Fred Smith (FedEx), Bill Gates (Microsoft), Mary Kay Ash (Mary Kay Cosmetics), Dave Thomas (Wendy's), and Sam Walton (Wal-Mart). Studying the case histories of such individuals uncovers several similar features, but probably the most important trait common to these people was their ability to make wise economic decisions. Faced with limited economic resources—money, land, equipment, and so on—these business icons had a knack for knowing how to allocate what little they did have wisely to maximize the profitability of their new ventures. Part of their ability to make wise choices stems from their reliance on accounting to provide necessary information for decision making. **Accounting** provides quantitative information about economic entities that is intended to be useful in making economic decisions.

This chapter provides an introduction to the business world, including the different types of businesses, their legal forms, and their key internal functions. Then, the accounting functions of business organizations are examined more closely. The means by which accountants communicate financial data to decision makers and accounting systems collect financial data for business organizations are discussed.

MAJOR TYPES OF BUSINESS ENTITIES

A **business** is an organization that attempts to earn a return over the cost of providing services or goods that satisfy the needs or wants of others.[1] Businesses are typically categorized into three broad groups: service, manufacturing, and merchandising companies. Service companies provide an activity that has value to their customers. Service businesses include dry cleaners, professional sports teams, theme parks, law firms, airlines, and advertising firms. Dave & Buster's is a service firm.

Alternatively, manufacturing firms convert one or more raw materials into finished products. These firms would include companies such as General Mills (www.generalmills.com), Intel (www.intel.com), and Ford (www.ford.com). The finished products made by manufacturers are typically sold to other manufacturers or merchandising companies rather than directly to customers.

There are two types of merchandising companies: wholesalers and retailers. An example of a wholesaler is United Stationers, Inc. (www.unitedstationers.com), the leading wholesale distributor of business products in North America. This company carries approximately 40,000 items from 500 manufacturers and sells to 20,000 resellers, including office products superstores, computer products resellers, office furniture dealers, mass merchandisers, and e-commerce merchants.

Retail merchandising firms, such as Sears (www.sears.com), J.C. Penney (www.jcpenney.com), and Wal-Mart (www.walmart.com), buy products principally from wholesalers and resell these products to the public from retail outlets. Retail merchandisers may also sell their goods by mail order, on a door-to-door basis, and/or on the Internet.

Common Forms of Business Organizations

Businesses in the United States operate in many different legal forms, including sole proprietorships, partnerships, and corporations. In the United States, the most common form of business organization is the sole proprietorship; however, as indicated in Exhibit 1-1, corporations account for the majority of the total annual business revenues and profits.
A **sole proprietorship** is a business owned by one individual, such as the separate establishments owned by Dave Corriveau (Slick's) and James W. "Buster" Corley (Buster's). This business form is the most common in the United States and, often, sole proprietorships are

[1] Some organizations exist as not-for-profits; these groups may provide services or goods to others but seek to do so without the underlying goal of generating profits.

EXHIBIT 1-1

Sole Proprietorships, Partnerships, and Corporations in the U.S.

	Sole Proprietorships	Partnerships	Corporations
Number	17,176,000	1,759,000	4,710,000
Sales (in billions)	$870	$1,297	$15,889
Profits (in billions)	$187	$1,686	$915

SOURCE U.S. Census Bureau, *Statistical Abstract of the U.S.* (2000), p. 536

service-oriented. A **partnership** is a business with two or more owners. Many large law and accounting firms are partnerships, with several hundreds or thousands of partners. Profits of sole proprietorships and partnerships are taxed to the owner(s) as individuals; the business organization itself pays no taxes.

A **corporation** is a legal "being" that exists separately from its owners, who are called **stockholders.** A corporation can have any number of stockholders, as long as that number is consistent with the laws of the state of incorporation. This type of business entity has some of the same rights (such as the ability to own and transfer property) and duties (such as the requirement to pay taxes) as individuals. Many corporations, such as Dave and Buster's, began as either sole proprietorships or partnerships.

A corporation has several advantages over a sole proprietorship or partnership, the most important of which is limited liability. In a corporation, the owners (or stockholders) have limited liability for the company's actions; that is, only a stockholder's current investment is at risk should the corporation owe more than it can pay. The same cannot be said for sole proprietorships and partnerships. In a lawsuit against a corporation, the plaintiffs can only recover any settlement or judgment from the corporation's assets, not from the personal assets of the firm's stockholders. If a sole proprietorship or partnership owes debts that cannot be paid from the holdings of the company, the owners are responsible for paying the debt, even if it must be paid out of the owners' personal assets. In fact, one partner could be forced to pay all the debts of a partnership if the other partners were unable to pay their "fair" share.

Three other forms of organizations are the LLP (limited liability partnership), LLC (limited liability corporation), and Subchapter S (Sub S) corporation. Each of these business forms is a hybrid between a partnership and a corporation, and provides limited liability to owners. However, the owners are taxed as individuals and the organization is not taxed as a separate legal entity.

This text concentrates on the accounting function of corporations. Most accounting issues faced by large corporations are similar, if not identical, to the accounting issues faced by smaller, unincorporated businesses. Visual Recap 1.1 summarizes the various forms of organizations.

VISUAL RECAP 1.1

Forms and Characteristics of Business Organizations

	Sole Proprietorships	Partnerships	Corporations
Ownership	1 Owner (Owner)	2+ Owners (Partners)	1+ Owners (Stockholders)
Legal Entity	Not separate from owner	Not separate from partners	A separate legal entity
Taxes	Business taxes paid with owner's personal taxes	Business taxes paid with partners' personal taxes	Business pays taxes directly; not combined with stockholders' personal taxes
Liability	Owner is responsible for the debts of the business	Partners are responsible for the debts of the business	Stockholders are not responsible for the debts of the business

Internal Functions of Business Organizations

Every large company has numerous internal functions that are necessary to make the firm grow and succeed. Most business owners recognize that they do not have all of the necessary skills; therefore, they hire individuals with specialized skills and training. Management, marketing, finance, and accounting are among the most commonly recognized fields of business. Within each of these fields, there is an array of "sub-specialties." For example, the management function includes production management, human resource management, and strategy. Marketing functions include advertising, consumer behavior, and distribution. A person in the finance area may plan bond and stock issuances or investments in other companies. An internal accountant may be involved with the preparation of financial statements, internal cost analyses, tax return preparation, or outsourcing decisions.

This course focuses on two primary areas of the internal accounting function of business organizations: financial accounting and managerial accounting. Every working person needs to be familiar with accounting functions because he or she will probably be affected by the information they provide. Effective sales managers, personnel specialists, or chief executive officers must thoroughly understand the organization's accounting functions to interpret accounting data and recognize the limitations of that data. People in the performing arts need to have a grasp of accounting information because engagements often hinge on the profitability of the performance. Advertising firms will be retained or released because of the sales, or lack thereof, generated from commercials and media blitzes. Certainly, anyone who decides to invest money in the stock market should understand the financial statements prepared by the companies in which investments are to be made. In other words, accounting is the language of business and most people interact on a daily basis in some way with business enterprises.

THE NATURE AND ROLE OF ACCOUNTING IN BUSINESS

To make wise decisions regarding the use of money, equipment, or people, business executives must have ready access to a wide array of financial information regarding their firms. For example, in the mid-1970s, Federal Express (www.fedex.com) was almost forced to file for bankruptcy. A sudden and significant increase in fuel prices resulting from a Middle Eastern oil crisis caused Federal Express to begin losing more than $1 million per month. Based on information supplied by the firm's accounting department, FedEx was able to quickly implement cost containment measures that saved the company from financial ruin, allowing it instead to become part of both the Fortune 500 and the Global 500 companies.[2]

In today's business world, accountants provide the majority of information needed by executives to make critical business decisions. In the current Information Age, accountants serve as information merchants for the business world.

First and foremost, accounting is a service activity. Its function is "to provide quantitative information, primarily financial in nature, about economic entities that is intended to be useful in making economic decisions—in making reasoned choices among alternative courses of action."[3] Thus, accounting is a means to assist a wide variety of parties in making economic decisions. Accountants generally segregate decision makers into two groups: internal and external decision makers. Internal decision makers are executives or employees of a given entity. External decision makers, on the other hand, are third parties (such as investors, suppliers, and bank loan officers) who do not have ready access to an organization's financial records or accountants.

---

[2] In 2001, FedEx's rankings were 112 and 268, respectively, for the Fortune 500 and Global 500.

[3] Accounting Principles Board, *Statement Number 4: Basic Concepts and Accounting Principles Underlying Financial Statements of a Business Enterprise* (NY: AICPA, 1970), para. 40.

Internal Decision Makers

Within an organization, accounting information is used by a variety of people for a number of purposes. CEOs use accounting information on the profitability of a division or a store to determine that manager's bonus. Sales staff use accounting information to assess a customer's credit payment history. Purchasing agents use accounting information to determine how many parts are needed to complete production for the upcoming period. Factory shop workers use accounting information to know how long it should take to make one unit of product.

The accounting information used by internal decision makers may be monetary or nonmonetary. Additionally, that information may be prepared in different formats to suit the needs of the individual decision maker. Some of this information may appear on the external financial statements, but much of it will not. It will merely help internal parties understand how to perform their tasks in an efficient and effective manner and how their operations generate and use money.

External Decision Makers

As indicated in Exhibit 1-2, there are numerous groups of people and institutions that comprise the category "external decision makers." External users employ financial statements as input to a wide range of decisions, including whether to invest in a given company, to grant credit to a company, or, in the case of a regulatory authority, whether a company is complying with specific regulations. **Financial statements** are the principal means that accountants use to communicate financial information to external decision makers.

Most large companies prepare an annual financial report that is distributed to the public. This report contains a set of financial statements that, taken together, provide information on the financial performance of the organization over a period of time or at a specific time. Companies now commonly include their financial statements and annual reports on their Web sites, usually in the category entitled Investor Relations.

FINANCIAL STATEMENT DEFINITIONS

The form and content of financial statements are specified by formal accounting rules, concepts, and principles called **generally accepted accounting principles** (GAAP). The phrase "generally accepted" is important because most accounting principles were established from general acceptance or usage over time.[4] Presently, the **Financial Accounting Standards Board** (FASB) is the principal accounting rule-making authority within the

[4] These principles are discussed in Chapter 2.

EXHIBIT 1-2

External Decision Makers

Type of Decision Maker	Use of Financial Statements
Stockholders and potential investors	Determine return on investment; estimate future returns and profitability
Bankers and suppliers	Determine ability to repay loans and pay for purchases
Securities and Exchange Commission and other regulatory agencies	Determine compliance with regulations
Internal Revenue Service	Determine reliability of amounts found on tax returns

United States. The FASB (www.fasb.org) is not a government agency; it is an independent, private sector body that receives more than half its funds from the public accounting profession and the rest from industry and the financial community.

An annual financial report is the primary communication of financial information to external users. Among other items, the annual report contains four financial statements and the related footnotes: a balance sheet, an income statement, a statement of cash flows, and a statement of stockholders' equity. Each of these statements is defined and discussed in the following sections.

Balance Sheet

A **balance sheet** is also known as a statement of financial position. This financial statement summarizes the assets (resources that the organization owns), liabilities (debts that the organization owes), and stockholders' equity (amounts owners have contributed and what the entity has earned for them) of an entity at a specific time. Because it is prepared for a specific moment, a balance sheet can be viewed as a financial "snapshot" of a company.

The title "balance sheet" is appropriate for this statement because the sum of an entity's assets must equal the sum of its liabilities and stockholders' (or owners') equity. Accountants refer to this equation as the **accounting equation,** or the balance sheet equation. Expressed in equation form for a corporation, this relationship appears as follows:[5]

Assets = Liabilities + Stockholders' Equity

The following simple examples illustrate this equation. Assume that a corporation's stockholders invest $100,000 in the company. The $100,000 of cash assets are equal to the $100,000 of stockholders' equity. Then the corporation decides to buy a piece of land that costs $45,000. To do so, the company pays $20,000 in cash and borrows the remaining $25,000 from the bank. After this transaction, assets of $125,000 ($100,000 + $45,000 – $20,000) equal the liabilities of $25,000 plus stockholders' equity of $100,000.

Income Statement

An **income statement** summarizes a business's revenues and expenses for a specific time period. **Revenues** generally result from selling the merchandise or providing the services that have been chosen for the company's primary business activity. More formally, revenues are increases in assets and decreases in liabilities resulting from an entity's profit-oriented activities. For instance, the primary revenue source for DaimlerChrysler (www.daimlerchrysler.com) comes from sales of manufactured automobiles. For Dollar Thrifty Automotive Group (www.dtag.com), the revenue comes from vehicle rentals. The Olive Garden's (www.olivegarden.com) primary revenue source is its food and beverage sales.

Expenses are legitimate costs of doing business. Expenses decrease assets or increase liabilities. The costs of salaries, rent, utilities, and insurance are common expenses. In addition, the cost of the products sold to customers is an extremely large expense in a merchandising company.

Like a balance sheet, an income statement also has a basic equation:

Revenues – Expenses = Net Income

People often use the phrase "the bottom line" to refer to the **net income** figure reported on an income statement. If revenues exceed expenses, the business has made a

[5] The balance sheet equation for a sole proprietorship and partnership is essentially the same as for a corporation except that there cannot be a stockholders' equity because there are no stockholders. Thus, the equation is Assets = Liabilities + Owner's (or Owners') Equity.

profit on its business activities. Because the profits belong to the owners, the net income for a fiscal year increases the stockholders' equity (ownership interest). Alternatively, a net loss decreases stockholders' equity because the organization's assets have been reduced. A net loss occurs when a company's expenses are larger than its revenues.

An entity's **fiscal year** is the twelve-month period covered by its annual income statement. The fiscal year of many companies often coincides with the calendar year (January 1 to December 31), but it may begin on any date. For instance, The Walt Disney Company (www.disney.go.com) has a September 30 fiscal year end. Thus, its fiscal year is from October 1 to September 30.

Notice that the time frame of an income statement is different from that of a balance sheet. Because it is prepared for a span of time, the income statement can be viewed as a financial "movie" rather than a "snapshot." The income statement summarizes revenues (selling prices) and expenses (costs of doing business) for the fiscal year only. For example, revenues generated from tickets to Disney World on October 1, 2002, will not be on Walt Disney Company's income statement for the fiscal year ended September 30, 2002. Instead the October 2002 revenues will appear on the income statement for the year ended September 30, 2003.

Statement of Cash Flows

The **statement of cash flows** reveals how a business generated and spent cash during a given accounting period. The accounting period covered by a statement of cash flows is the same period as that covered by the income statement. The statement begins with a summary of the cash inflows and outflows from three major types of activities engaged in by business entities: operating (earning money by providing a product or service), investing (buying and selling long-term assets), and financing (obtaining and repaying additional funds from creditors and investors). The final section of a statement of cash flows reconciles an entity's cash balance at the beginning of a period to its cash balance at the end of that period. The ending cash balance is also found on the balance sheet along with the other assets.

When decision makers review a company's statement of cash flows, the question foremost in their minds is "How do the company's cash flows from its profit-oriented (operating) activities compare to its net income?" Successful companies should, over the long run, generate the majority of their cash from their operating activities. However, in a given accounting period, the net cash flow from operating activities may not be closely correlated with its net income.

Just because a company earns large profits, does not mean that it is generating enough cash flows to sustain operations. A very profitable company may experience severe cash flow problems, including falling behind on its debt payments and being unable to replace inventory as it is sold. Several factors could account for such a circumstance, including slow paying customers and increasing prices for raw materials and other goods and services required in the firm's day-to-day operations.

Alternatively, a company that is experiencing losses may have positive cash flow from operations. To illustrate, for fiscal year 2000, Kmart Corporation (www.bluelight .com) reported a $244 million net loss on its income statement and a $1+ billion cash inflow from operating activities on its statement of cash flows. Obviously, the net loss was more indicative of the company's actual operations because Kmart filed for bankruptcy in early 2002.

Statement of Stockholders' Equity

The **statement of stockholders' equity** reconciles the dollar amounts of ownership equity components from the beginning to the end of an accounting period. The primary question answered by this statement is "What events or transactions accounted for the changes in a company's stockholders' equity over the previous year?" In part, through its inclusion of net income as a major component of the change for the period, the statement of stockholders' equity provides a link between the income statement and the balance sheet.

Financial decision makers often disagree as to which of the four primary financial statements is the most important or informative. However, most decision makers would agree that the statement of stockholders' equity is the least important financial statement.

This overview of the four primary business financial statements indicates that they are closely linked despite their differing structures, contents, and objectives. For example, many of the changes in a business's assets and liabilities (shown on the balance sheet) during a given period are a direct result of the entity's revenues and expenses (shown on the income statement) for that period. Additionally, the statement of cash flows accounts for the change in the amount of cash reported in a company's balance sheet at the beginning and end of a given period. These statements and their interrelationships are summarized in Visual Recap 1.2.

Financial Statement Footnotes

Besides the four financial statements, the annual report contains other important information about the company. One particularly informative section of an annual report is the **financial statement footnotes.** These footnotes assist decision makers in interpreting and drawing the proper conclusions from a business's financial statements. Footnotes to a

VISUAL RECAP 1.2

The Interrelationship of Financial Statements

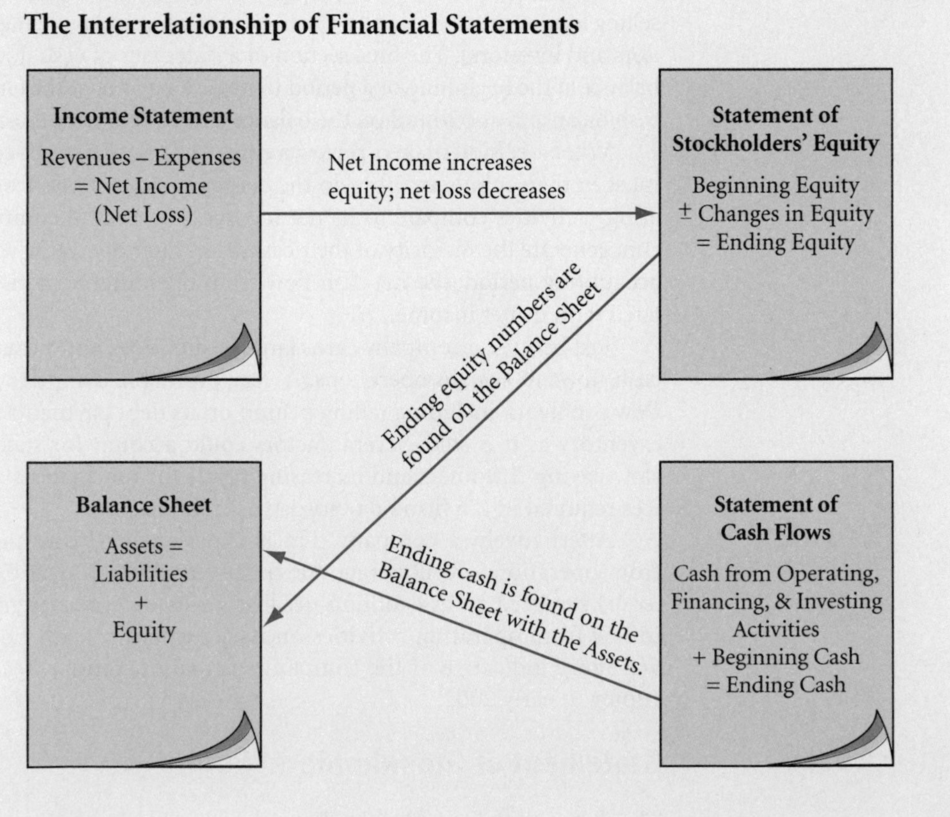

company's financial statements identify the specific accounting methods used, significant accounting policies, assumptions that underlie key financial statement amounts, financial data regarding major business segments, and descriptions of any pending lawsuits. For instance, a footnote in the 2000 annual report of Philip Morris Companies, Inc. (www.philipmorris.com) discusses one of that company's potential liabilities. The footnote says, in part: "In July 2000, a jury in a Florida smoking and health class action returned a punitive damages award of approximately $74 billion against PM, Inc." Obviously, by reviewing the footnotes, potential investors can gather significant details to help them make informed decisions. The footnotes often provide crucial information about the company and should not be ignored.

AN OVERVIEW OF THE ACCOUNTING PROFESSION

Most businesspeople think of the accounting profession as consisting of two segments: private accounting and public accounting.[6] These two sectors have completely different functions.

Private Accounting

Accountants in private industry are employed by businesses, not–for-profit organizations, and governmental agencies. Individuals in private accounting may have job titles such as controller, internal auditor, cost analyst, and tax accountant. Controllers (or chief financial officers) are the top accounting executives in organizations and their primary responsibility is to ensure that an entity's periodic financial statements are prepared on a timely and accurate basis. Internal auditors monitor the compliance of an organization's employees with operating policies and procedures. Cost analysts may have any number of accounting-related responsibilities within an organization: maintaining production cost records for manufacturing processes, analyzing variances from budgeted expenditures, or preparing customized reports that forecast expected costs for a new operating unit. Tax accountants in the private sector collect and process the data needed to file the employing entity's periodic federal, state, and local tax returns.

Public Accounting

Public accounting firms, like law firms, range in size from sole proprietorships to huge international partnerships that have hundreds of partners and thousands of employees. Among the services offered by public accounting firms are bookkeeping, tax preparation and advice, certain types of management consulting, and auditing.

Auditing is the most important professional service provided by public accounting firms. An audit performed by a public accounting firm differs from the service provided by internal company auditors because the public accounting firm is independent from the company that is being audited. A business entity hires a public accounting firm that has no financial interest in, or other important ties to, the entity. The external auditors' mission is to perform a review of the company's financial statements.

The principal objective of an independent audit is to determine whether an entity's financial statements have been prepared in accordance with GAAP. That conclusion is based on an examination of the audit client's financial statements and accounting records.

[6] A third sector does exist: academic accountants who teach at colleges and universities and research the effects of accounting information on financial systems and behavior.

If a company's financial statements have been prepared in accordance with GAAP, those statements are presumed to fairly reflect the company's financial affairs. Business executives might have economic incentives (such as higher salaries or improved stock values) to "window dress" financial statements to make their companies appear more profitable and financially stable than they actually are. In the absence of an independent audit, external financial statement users might not believe that a company's published financial statements are honest representations of its financial affairs. Preparation of the financial statements is the responsibility of the organization's controller; the responsibility of the external auditor is to give his or her opinion about the preparation of the statements.

By independently examining the financial statements and accounting records of companies, public accounting firms bolster the confidence that third parties have in the accuracy of those statements. This higher level of confidence in financial statements increases the likelihood that individuals will invest in, or loan funds to, business entities and thus keep the economy healthy and growing. Exhibit 1-3 shows the audit report for the 2000 financial statements of The Gap, Inc. (www.gapinc.com) by the public accounting firm of Deloitte & Touche LLP.

Although audits are designed to determine if financial statements have been presented fairly, there are occasions where that objective fails. The most common reason for the failure of an audit to uncover financial statement errors and irregularities is management fraud. There have been several highly notable recent cases of audited financial statements consisting of "bad" figures: Waste Management, Sunbeam, Rite Aid, and Enron, to name just a few. Unfortunately, the few cases that result in problems overshadow the thousands of cases in which the audited financial statements are "fairly presented" as per the attestation.

EXHIBIT 1-3

Independent Auditors' Report

To the Shareholders and Board of Directors of The Gap, Inc.:

We have audited the accompanying consolidated balance sheets of The Gap, Inc. and subsidiaries as of February 3, 2001 and January 29, 2000, and the related consolidated statements of earnings, shareholders' equity, and cash flows for each of the three fiscal years in the period ended February 3, 2001. These financial statements are the responsibility of the Company's management. Our responsibility is to express an opinion on these financial statements based on our audits.

We conducted our audits in accordance with auditing standards generally accepted in the United States of America. Those standards require that we plan and perform the audit to obtain reasonable assurance about whether the financial statements are free of material misstatement. An audit includes examining, on a test basis, evidence supporting the amounts and disclosures in the financial statements. An audit also includes assessing the accounting principles used and significant estimates made by management, as well as evaluating the overall financial statement presentation. We believe that our audits provide a reasonable basis for our opinion.

In our opinion, such consolidated financial statements present fairly, in all material respects, the financial position of the Company and its subsidiaries as of February 3, 2001 and January 29, 2000, and the results of their operations and their cash flows for each of the three fiscal years in the period ended February 3, 2001, in conformity with accounting principles generally accepted in the United States of America.

Deloitte & Touche LLP
San Francisco, California
February 28, 2001

Certifications

"Accountant" is a generic term that can be applied to anyone who works in the field of accounting. However, there are numerous certifications that may be held by accountants in the private and public sector. The three most common are certified public accountant (CPA), certified management accountant (CMA) and certified internal auditor (CIA). Becoming certified requires a candidate to pass a rigorous comprehensive examination, meet certain experience requirements, and agree to abide by continuing education and ethics rules. Obtaining any of these certifications does not limit where an individual may work; CPAs often work in private accounting. Additionally, a CPA may also be a CMA and/or CIA.

Regulation of the Accounting Profession

In the early 1930s, Congress established the **Securities and Exchange Commission** (SEC) to deter the abusive accounting and financial reporting practices that contributed to the 1929 stock market collapse. The SEC regulates the sale and subsequent trading of stocks and bonds by companies listed on stock exchanges. Companies that market their stocks, bonds, or other securities on an interstate basis are generally referred to as "publicly owned" companies. The SEC does not assess the investment quality of the securities issued by the companies that it regulates, nor does it prohibit the sale of highly speculative securities. Instead, the SEC ensures that publicly owned companies provide third parties with sufficient information to make informed economic decisions regarding the securities these firms sell. Thus, the SEC oversees the financial reporting and accounting practices of these publicly owned companies. "Full and fair disclosure" is the SEC's motto.

The SEC closely monitors the accounting profession's rule-making processes and has the authority to override any new rules issued by the FASB to the extent that those rules apply to publicly owned companies. However, in the past, the SEC has seldom interfered with accounting rule-making bodies.

Challenges Facing the Accounting Profession

The growing trend toward multinational business enterprises and international trade promises to complicate the work roles of public and private accountants in the future. Cultural differences in business practices, varying governmental regulations, and a lack of uniform international accounting rules create "global-sized" headaches for accountants of multinational companies.

Business organizations and the accounting profession face numerous challenges in the twenty-first century. For centuries, accountants have played an integral role in the economic success of business enterprises. Businesses that will thrive in this new century must have in their employ accountants who understand the organization, recognize the information needs of external and internal decision makers, and satisfy those needs on a timely basis with relevant and reliable data. Such individuals are essential in an era in which knowledge and information are key ingredients to success.

SUMMARY

The three major types of businesses are service, manufacturing, and merchandising companies. The most common legal forms of business organizations are sole proprietorships, partnerships, and corporations. The majority of U.S. businesses are sole proprietorships, although corporations account for most of the gross business revenues each year.

Large companies have several internal functions that are performed by individuals with specialized training and experience in a field of business. Management, marketing, finance, and accounting are the most commonly recognized specialized fields in business. The principal role of the accounting function of business entities is to provide financial information regarding those organizations to decision makers.

The manner in which accountants communicate financial data depends upon the type of decision maker who will use that data. Accountants communicate financial and nonfinancial data to internal decision makers using customized reports designed with specific objectives in mind. Financial statements (balance sheet, income statement, statement of cash flows, and statement of stockholders' equity) are the primary means accountants use to communicate financial information to investors, creditors, regulatory agencies, and others. These statements are prepared using concepts, guidelines, and rules known collectively as generally accepted accounting principles (GAAP).

Private accounting and public accounting are the two major segments of the accounting profession. Accountants in private accounting are employed by businesses, not-for-profit organizations, and other entities in various accounting-related work roles. Public accountants are employees, partners, or proprietors of accounting firms. Public accounting firms provide an array of professional services to the public including auditing, tax return preparation, and some management consulting.

The business world and the accounting profession face several challenges in this new century. Two of the most important challenges are globalization and business ethics. The first is important because the lack of uniform international accounting standards impairs the compatability comparability of financial data prepared in different countries. The second is important because the lack of personal, professional, or corporate ethics may be reflected in financial statement misrepresentations.

KEY TERMS

accounting
accounting equation
balance sheet
business
corporation
expense
Financial Accounting Standards Board (FASB)
financial statement
financial statement footnote
fiscal year
generally accepted accounting principles (GAAP)
income statement
net income (net loss)
partnership
revenue
Securities and Exchange Commission (SEC)
sole proprietorship
statement of cash flows
statement of stockholders' equity
stockholder

QUESTIONS

1. Identify the three general types of businesses and provide an example of each. *(LO 1.1)*
2. Identify the three common forms of business organizations. How do these forms differ? Which form of business organization is most common in the United States? *(LO 1.1)*
3. What is the primary purpose of a business's accounting function? *(LO 1.1)*
4. Identify the four major financial statements. What information is contained on each of these statements? Why do businesses issue financial statements? *(LO 1.2)*

5. "A company's fiscal year is always the same as a calendar year." Explain why this statement is false. *(LO 1.3)*
6. Businesses engage in three types of activities. List and define them. Which financial statement uses these three activities as section headings? *(LO 1.3)*
7. Define "generally accepted accounting principles" (GAAP). What is the primary purpose of GAAP? What body is currently charged with establishing GAAP? *(LO 1.3)*
8. Distinguish between private and public accounting. Briefly describe several work roles in private accounting. *(LO 1.4)*
9. What services do public accounting firms typically offer to the public? Which of these services is the most important and why? *(LO 1.4)*
10. What prompted the formation of the Securities and Exchange Commission (SEC), and what is its primary function? *(LO 1.4)*

EXERCISES

11. **True or False** *(all LOs)*

Following are a series of statements regarding topics discussed in this chapter.

Required:

Indicate whether each statement is true (T) or false (F).

(1) Financial statements are the principal means accountants use to communicate financial information regarding business entities to external decision makers such as bank loan officers and investors.

(2) A key advantage of the corporate form of business is that the personal assets of a corporation's owners are not at risk if the business is sued.

(3) The Securities and Exchange Commission issues most new accounting rules in this country.

(4) Sole proprietorships are the most common form of business organization in the United States and account for the majority of business revenues generated in this country each year.

(5) A trait common to most successful businesspeople is an ability to make wise decisions regarding the allocation of their business's economic resources.

(6) A business's fiscal year is the twelve-month period covered by its balance sheet

(7) A key objective of independent auditors is to bolster the confidence of third parties in a business entity's financial statements.

(8) Controller, internal auditor, and cost analyst are common job titles in private accounting.

(9) Because it is a service activity, accounting does not contribute significantly to the success of business organizations.

(10) The reported profits of multinational companies are not affected by their home country's accounting rules.

(11) LLPs, LLCs, and Subchapter S corporations pay taxes separately from their owners.

12. **Major Types of Businesses** *(LO 1.1)*

Businesses are often classified into three broad groups: service companies, manufacturing companies, and merchandising (retail) companies.

Required:

(1) Identify each of the following well-known firms as a service company (S), a manufacturing company (M), or a merchandising company (R).

(a) General Motors

(b) Kinko's

(c) Merrill Lynch

(d) Toys "R" Us

(e) Levi Strauss

(2) For the companies listed, identify a key business decision that each firm's management likely faces on a recurring basis. What type of data might the accountants for each firm provide to management to help make the decisions identified?

13. **Common Legal Forms of Business Organizations** *(LO 1.1)*

The text identified three common legal forms of business organizations: sole proprietorships, partnerships, and corporations.

Required:

(1) Compare and contrast what you believe would be key advantages and disadvantages of operating a business as a sole proprietorship versus a corporation.

(2) Compare and contrast what you believe would be key advantages and disadvantages of operating a business as a partnership versus a corporation.

(3) What other forms of business organizations were discussed in the chapter and what is (are) their distinguishing characteristics?

14. **Information Needs of External and Internal Decision Makers** *(LO 1.2)*

Each of the following items of information may be obtained from a company's accounting records:

(a) Net income

(b) Inventory cost per unit

(c) Total liabilities

(d) Total sales by geographical area of business operations

(e) Five-year trend in total sales

(f) Employee salaries by department

Required:

(1) Indicate a specific type of decision maker who would have a primary interest in each information item. The decision maker may be an external party or an internal party.

(2) Briefly explain why the decision maker identified in Part 1 would have a need for the given item of information.

15. **The Need for Financial Statements** *(LO 1.2)*

Jim's Bike Shop sells and repairs bicycles. The owner, Jim Hardy, took several accounting courses in college and has decided to maintain his business's accounting records. Although the shop has been in operation for longer than three months, Hardy has not yet prepared any financial statements for the business. Although several of Hardy's friends who are business owners prepare monthly financial statements for their businesses, Hardy has decided that it is too much of a hassle to prepare monthly financial statements for Jim's Bike Shop.

Required:

Write a memo to Hardy explaining why financial statements would help him operate his business more efficiently and effectively.

16. **Analyzing Business Transactions** *(LO 1.3)*

All business transactions affect assets (resources owned), liabilities (amounts owed), stockholders' equity (ownership interest), or some combination of these items. Following is an analysis of the equal dollar effects of two transactions.

Transactions	**Assets**	=	**Liabilities**	+	**Equity**
(a) Purchased $1,000 of office supplies on credit	+$1,000	=	+ $1,000	+	$0
(b) Purchased a set of tires for $200 cash	+$200 – $200	=	$0	+	$0

Required:

Using the format above, analyze the effects of each of the following transactions for Fuente & Demond Realtors, Inc. on the firm's assets, liabilities, and stockholders' equity.

(1) Purchased equipment for $12,500 cash.

(2) Fuente and Demond bought an additional $17,000 of stock in the firm.

(3) Paid $1,500 owed to an office supply store for a purchase made the previous month.

(4) Purchased supplies for $4,000 on credit.

PROBLEMS

17. **Use of Income Statement Information** *(LO 1.2)*

The following condensed income statement is for CJ's, a fast-food restaurant chain operating in the western United States. Amounts are expressed in thousands.

CJ's Fast-Food Restaurant Chain
Condensed Income Statement

REVENUES	
Sales by Company-Operated Restaurants	$ 381,700
Revenues from Franchised and Licensed Restaurants	78,600
Other Income	6,100
EXPENSES	
Operating Expenses	(449,900)
Interest Expense	(10,400)
Income Tax Expense	(1,800)
Other Expenses	(800)
Net Income	$ 3,500

Required:

(1) Describe how the following three groups of decision makers might use CJ's income statement data:

(a) company stockholders (its owners)

(b) company executives
(c) bankers

(2) Also identify additional information regarding this company's income statement data that each group of decision makers might request.

18. **Analyzing Financial Statement Data** *(LO 1.2)*

The following table lists the net income of three large companies from 2000 to 2002.

	2000	2001	2002
Lifestyle Manazines	$207,300,000	$246,300,000	$264,000,000
BigWin Hotel & Casino	$ 10,649,000	$ 15,966,000	$ 18,745,000
Quick & Yummy Foods, Inc.	$ 80,517,000	$ 97,432,000	$110,070,000

Required:

(1) Which of these companies was most profitable over the given three-year period?

(2) Which company's profitability improved the most over this period?

(3) What business trends, economic variables, or other factors likely influence the profitability of each of these firms? When responding to this question, consider the nature of each firm's principal line of business.

19. **Financial Statement Information** *(LO 1.2)*

The financial information of three companies is listed below with some numbers omitted.

	Alpha Co.	Bravo Inc.	Charlie LLP
Assets	$510,000	(c)	$950,000
Liabilities	(a)	$430,000	367,000
Equity	318,000	320,000	(e)
Revenues	510,000	870,000	(f)
Expenses	320,000	(d)	678,000
Net Income	(b)	$210,000	331,000

Required:

For each of the three companies listed above, find the missing numbers.

20. **Effects of Industry Accounting Practice** *(LO 1.5)*

During the 1980s, a special set of accounting rules was in effect for the savings and loan industry. These accounting rules allowed companies in that industry to record losses on sales of certain securities over a several-year period. For example, suppose that a savings and loan sold a security for $1 million that had originally cost $3 million. Rather than immediately reporting the loss on this sale, the company could have spread the loss over several years in its income statement.

Required:

(1) In the example just given, how much loss would the savings and loan have reported in the year of sale had the special accounting rules not been in effect?

(2) Assume now that the savings and loan spread the loss on the sale of the security over a five-year period, recognizing an equal portion of that loss in each of those years. What portion of the loss did the savings and loan report in the year of sale?

(3) How was this special accounting treatment for losses on the sale of certain securities misleading to financial statement users?

CASES

21. **Annual Reports** *(LO 1.2, Internet)*

The annual financial report is the primary communication of financial information to external users.

Required:

Use the annual report of Carnival Corporation for the 2001 fiscal year to answer the following questions. The annual report can be found at www.carnival.com /aboutCCL; follow the links to investor relations.

(1) On what days does Carnival Corporation's fiscal year begin and end?

(2) How many years of balance sheet information are presented?

(3) How many years of income statement information are presented?

(4) How many years of cash flow information are presented?

(5) How many years of shareholders' equity information are presented?

(6) List two places in the annual report that each of the following pieces of information can be found (list the statement and the year):

- (a) 2001 ending balance of Cash
- (b) 2001 beginning balance of Cash
- (c) 2001 ending balance of Retained Earnings
- (d) 2001 Net Income
- (e) 2001 ending balance of Common Stock

(7) What public accounting firm audited the financial information of Carnival Corporation?

22. **Financial Accounting Standards Board** *(LO 1.4 and 1.5, Internet)*

Presently, the Financial Accounting Standards Board (FASB) is the principal accounting rule-making authority within the United States.

Required:

Use FASB's Web site (www.fasb.org) to answer the following questions.

(1) What organization has statutory authority to establish financial accounting and reporting standards?

(2) How long has FASB been the designated organization for establishing standards?

(3) What is the mission of FASB?

(4) Who is the current Chairman of FASB?

(5) List several ways that topics are added to the FASB's agenda.

(6) What is an exposure draft?

(7) Does FASB list any exposure drafts on its homepage? What is the topic of the exposure draft(s)? [Don't read the entire draft; just look at the title.]

CHAPTER 2

Concepts and Elements Underlying Accounting

LEARNING OBJECTIVES

1. Describe the nature, purpose, and content of each of the four primary financial statements.
2. Recognize the three financial reporting objectives of business entities.
3. Discuss the key attributes or characteristics that accounting information should possess.
4. Discuss the fundamental concepts that underlie accounting and financial reporting rules and practices.
5. Define an accounting system and identify its principal elements.

Financial Literacy

Late 2001 and early 2002 saw the collapse of Enron Corp., an energy-trading giant and darling of the financial investment community. One of the more unusual but important responses to this situation came from Federal Reserve Chairman Alan Greenspan. In early February 2002, Greenspan stated that studies point "to a critical need to improve financial literacy, the lack of which leaves millions of Americans vulnerable to financial losses from unscrupulous business practices." He also indicated that "competency in mathematics, both in numerical manipulation and in understanding its conceptual foundations, enhances a person's ability to handle the more ambiguous and qualitative relationships that dominate our day-to-day financial decision making."

Although Chairman Greenspan was specifically addressing knowledge of mathematics, his comments are equally applicable to knowledge of accounting. It was not mathematics that contributed to the downfall of Enron, but rather a variety of concealed losses, inflated earnings, related party transactions, and other accounting "trickery" in the financial statements.

Samuel Taylor Coleridge said, "The worth and value of knowledge is in proportion to the worth and value of its object." Some additional accounting knowledge might certainly have been valuable in retrospect, considering the loss of billions of dollars by people and firms in the Enron debacle.

SOURCE: Martin Crustsinger, "Greenspan to Schools: Do the Math," (San Francisco) *The Examiner*, 2 February 2002.

INTRODUCTION

The primary objective of financial accounting and accountants is to provide useful information to external decision makers. Chapter 1 introduced the primary document for communicating this information, the annual report, which contains four financial statements: the balance sheet, the income statement, the statement of cash flows, and the statement of stockholders' equity. This chapter begins by expanding on the elements that comprise the financial statements. Next, the financial reporting objectives of business entities, qualitative attributes that should be possessed by financial accounting information, and fundamental concepts that underlie accounting and financial reporting practices are discussed. The last part of the chapter describes the principal elements of an accounting system.

COMPOSITION OF FINANCIAL STATEMENTS

Financial statements present monetary information by listing accounts and showing their balances. Accounts can be thought of as tabulations of one's financial interests. For example, your checking account (the money you have on deposit at the bank) is one account; your Visa account (the money you owe on your credit card) is another. While both accounts are a summary of monetary interests, they are kept separate because they are of a different nature. Businesses use dozens of accounts to keep track of their financial interests. As summarized in Visual Recap 2.1, there are six types of accounts:

- **Assets**—the property or belongings of a business
- **Liabilities**—the debts of a business
- **Stockholders' Equity**—the ownership interest in the business (includes owner contributions and profits from operations)
- **Dividends**—the distributions of business profits to stockholders
- **Revenues**—the selling prices of the business's goods or services
- **Expenses**—the costs of doing business and generating revenues

This chapter describes the content of the balance sheet and the income statement relative to the account types found on each statement. Chapter 9 provides more in-depth discussion of the income statement, and Chapters 8 and 10 discuss the two other primary financial statements.

Balance Sheet

As indicated in Chapter 1, the balance sheet provides a snapshot of a corporation's assets, liabilities, and stockholders' equity at a specific time. (If a balance sheet were to be prepared for a sole proprietorship or a partnership, stockholders' equity would be renamed as either owner's equity or owners' equity as appropriate.) A balance sheet provides answers to many questions that external decision makers may have regarding a business's financial status. Examples of these questions include: "How much cash does the company have?"; "Is the cash balance large enough to allow the company to pay off the debts that are coming due in the next few months?"; and "How much inventory does the company have?" A simplified balance sheet is presented in Exhibit 2-1 and the key components of a balance sheet are discussed next.

Assets

The accounting definition of assets are "probable future economic benefits obtained or controlled by a particular entity as a result of past transactions or events."[1] A non-accountant

[1] Financial Accounting Standards Board, *Statement of Financial Accounting Concepts No. 6: Elements of Financial Statements of Business Enterprises* (Stamford, CN: FASB, 1985).

VISUAL RECAP 2.1

Account Types and Their Components

Assets (future economic benefits)	**Liabilities (debts to 3rd parties)**	**Equity (owners' interest)**
Current Assets	Current Liabilities	Paid-In Capital
Long-term Investments	Long-term Liabilities	Additional Paid-In Capital
Property, Plant & Equipment		Retained Earnings
Intangible Assets		

Revenues (earnings)	**Expenses (cost of doing business)**	**Dividends (distributions to owners)**
Operating Revenues	Cost of Goods Sold	Cash Dividends
Nonoperating Revenues	Operating Expenses	Stock Dividends
	Nonoperating Expenses	

EXHIBIT 2-1
Balance Sheet

Kirtley, Inc. Balance Sheet December 31, 2002			
ASSETS			
Current Assets			
Cash			$ 900
Short-Term Investments			1,500
Accounts Receivable			4,800
Inventory			12,200
Prepaid Assets			100
Total Current Assets			$19,500
Long-Term Investments			15,000
Property, Plant and Equipment			
Land		$ 10,000	
Building	$ 50,000		
Accumulated Depreciation	(12,000)	38,000	48,000
Intangible Assets			
Patent			4,000
Total Assets			$86,500
LIABILITIES			
Current Liabilities			
Notes Payable			$ 1,200
Accounts Payable			600
Accrued Wages Payable			250
Unearned Revenue			120
Total Current Liabilities			$ 2,170
Long-Term Liabilities			
Bonds Payable			20,000
Total Liabilities			$22,170
STOCKHOLDERS' EQUITY			
Common Stock (20,000 shares; $1 par value)		$ 20,000	
Additional Paid-In Capital		15,000	
Retained Earnings		29,330	64,330
Total Liabilities and Stockholders' Equity			$86,500

might simplify this definition to "things that a company owns." Notice that Kirtley, Inc.'s assets in Exhibit 2-1 are classified into four groups: current assets; long-term investments; property, plant and equipment; and intangible assets.

Current Assets Current assets are typically listed first in a balance sheet. A **current asset** is cash or any other asset that will be converted into cash, sold, or used up within the next year or the normal business operating cycle, whichever is longer. A business's **operating cycle** is the average time a company takes to buy inventory, sell that inventory, and collect cash from customers. The operating cycle of a restaurant chain, such as Luby's Cafeterias (www.lubys.com), is usually just a few days. Luby's buys unprocessed raw materials (such as flour, fruit, meats, and vegetables), converts those materials into ready-to-eat food items, and sells the food items to its customers for cash or allows them to charge their purchases on national credit cards, such as VISA or MasterCard. Alternately, the operating cycle of a manufacturing firm such as McIlhenny Company (www.tabasco.com) can be several months or longer, in part because of the aging process of the hot sauces.

The most common current assets are cash, short-term investments, accounts receivable, inventory, and prepaid assets. Current assets are listed in descending order of liquidity or "nearness to cash"; thus, cash is the first current asset reported in a balance sheet. Short-term investments (sometimes called marketable securities) generally include investments in another company's stocks or bonds that the company expects to sell and, thereby convert into cash, within a short period of time. For example, Kirtley, Inc. might decide to invest some of its excess cash in a bond issued by AOL Time Warner (www.aoltimewarner.com) so that the cash would earn interest until it is needed.

Many small retailers allow customers to only pay cash for products or services. In other instances, customers may charge their purchases on national credit cards. Retailers allowing this type of payment usually collect the credit card charges, less a service fee, daily from the credit card companies. The customers owe the purchase price to the company that issued the national credit card, *not* the merchandiser that sold the goods to the customer. Other companies, such as Dillard Department Stores, Inc. (www.dillards.com) offer "in-house" credit cards to their customers. Amounts owed to a company by its customers are referred to as accounts receivable. In general, accounts receivable between businesses and accounts receivable from a business to a customer, if paid by the first statement's due date, do not carry interest charges. To illustrate, assume you made two purchases at Dillard's, one for $150 on your Wells Fargo Visa card and one for $80 on your Dillard's card. Wells Fargo would pay Dillard's $150 less a service fee and record a $150 account receivable from you. Dillard's would also have an $80 account receivable from you.

In a retail company, inventory refers to the goods the company intends to sell to its customers. Manufacturing companies such as Bethlehem Steel Corp. (www.bethsteel.com) also have supplies, raw materials, and in-process (semi-finished) inventories; these items will be converted during the operating cycle into saleable goods available to wholesalers or, possibly, directly to customers.

Businesses often pay for costs such as rent, insurance, and advertising in advance of their due dates. For example, a company may pay for twelve months of insurance at the beginning of a year. These amounts are reported as "prepaid assets" in the current asset section of a balance sheet. These expenditures are considered assets rather than expenses because they still have future economic benefit.

By definition, all assets other than current assets are long-term assets. Most companies have several categories of long-term assets, including long-term investments, property, plant and equipment, and intangibles. "Other assets" may also be used as a balance sheet "catch-all" classification for miscellaneous long-term assets of an insignificant amount.

Long-term Investments In addition to short-term investments, companies may purchase the debt or ownership securities of other companies and hold these investments for an extended period. Such investments in corporate bonds and stocks are made to generate an on-going stream of additional income (interest or dividends) for the company. Additionally, the companies may want to exercise some degree of control over or form an alliance with another organization. For example, as of the end of 2000, DaimlerChrysler (www.daimlerchrysler.com) owned 34 percent of Mitsubishi Motors Corporation (www.Mitsubishi-Motors.co.jp); the reason given for such an investment was that DaimlerChrysler could gain direct Asian access and gain technology related to more fuel-efficient cars.

Another type of long-term investment is land or another asset that is not currently being used in business operations. For instance, assume that a company purchased land at a bankruptcy auction. If the company intended to hold the land for future resale rather than use, that land would be considered a long-term investment.

Property, Plant and Equipment Generally, the largest category of noncurrent assets is property, plant and equipment (PP&E). This category includes land, buildings, machinery, furniture, and other such assets used in the normal operating activities of a business. To illustrate the size of this category, Aluminum Company of America (Alcoa) (www.alcoa.com) had total assets of $31,691,000,000 at the end of 2000; of that, $12,850,000,000 or 40.5 percent, was included in PP&E.

Most PP&E assets have limited useful lives and are called depreciable assets. Accounting requires that the costs of depreciable assets be recorded as expenses over the time periods benefited by those assets. **Depreciation** is the accounting term used to describe this write-off process. For example, assume that a company pays $25,000 for a new automobile for one of its salespeople. The salesperson is expected to use the car for three years, at which time it will have an estimated value of $13,000. The easiest way to calculate accounting depreciation is to subtract the $13,000 estimated value at the end of three years of use from the $25,000 original cost; divide the $12,000 of "depreciable cost" by three years; and arrive at a depreciation expense of $4,000 per year.

Accumulated depreciation is the total amount of depreciation that has been recorded on a depreciable asset since its acquisition. In other words, it is the amount of the asset that has been "used up" by the company. For balance sheet purposes, the accumulated depreciation for PP&E is subtracted from the cost of the depreciable assets to obtain **book value.** For instance, the accumulated depreciation at the end of the second year on the salesperson's automobile would have been $8,000 or $4,000 for each of two years, and the book value would have been $25,000 minus $8,000 or $17,000.

Note that the accounting and general usages of the term *depreciation* differ. Depreciation, as used in general conversation, refers to the decline in market value of an item. Continuing the example above, assume that the salesperson quit after one year and the company decided to sell the car. The dealer might give the company only $18,000 for the car because it had "depreciated," or declined in market value, $7,000 in one year. In most situations, the fastest loss of market value for most assets is in the first year of use, but accounting presumes that PP&E items were bought for long-term use rather than short-term resale.

Land is another common property, plant and equipment asset. However, because land does not have a limited useful life, land is not depreciated and is generally carried on the balance sheet at its original purchase price.

Intangible Assets Intangible assets are long-term assets that do not have a physical form or substance; examples include copyrights, trademarks, and goodwill. A patent is an intangible that represents an exclusive right (granted by the United States Patent Office) to manufacture a specific product or to use a specific process. Many pharmaceutical companies, such as La Jolla Pharmaceutical Company (www.ljpc.com), own important product patents that prohibit other firms from producing or selling those products or their generic substitutes. However, some pharmaceutical companies such as Eli Lilly (www.lilly.com) do not show any amounts for patents on the financial statements because the cost of generating those patents was expensed during the development period. Only amounts used to purchase patents from external sources can be recorded as assets. This concept is discussed more in Chapter 6.

Liabilities

Amounts owed by businesses to third parties are called **liabilities.** These amounts represent "probable future sacrifices of economic benefits arising from present obligations of a particular entity to transfer assets or provide services to other entities in the future as a result of past transactions or events."[2] Like assets, liabilities may be current or long-term.

Current Liabilities A **current liability** is a debt or obligation that will be eliminated by giving up current assets or incurring another current liability. Current liabilities are listed first in the liabilities section of a balance sheet. The most common types of current liabilities are notes payable, accounts payable, accrued liabilities (such as salaries payable and interest payable), and unearned revenues.

Companies frequently borrow money from banks or other parties on a short-term basis by signing promissory notes. Such notes are legally binding commitments to repay borrowed funds as well as interest for the use of these funds. If the notes are due within the upcoming year or operating cycle, they are listed as current liabilities on a company's balance sheet.

Accounts payable are amounts owed by a business to its suppliers. Essentially, an account payable represents the buyer's side of a seller's account receivable. For example, when Home Depot (www.homedepot.com) buys cabinets from Thomasville Cabinetry (www.thomasvillecabinetry.com) to stock as inventory in its 1,100+ stores, Thomasville Cabinetry's balance sheet would show an account receivable from Home Depot and Home Depot's balance sheet would show an account payable to Thomasville Cabinetry.

At the end of an accounting period, a company must determine if there are any amounts that it currently owes but has not yet recorded. These amounts typically relate to obligations incurred near the end of an accounting period and often must be estimated. For instance, at the end of an accounting period, a company may need to estimate its liability for electricity usage since the last electric bill was received. When such an obligation is determined, the company will record an **accrued liability** for the amount. However, because of the time lag in preparing end-of-period financial statements, many of these amounts become known before the financial statements are actually issued.

Companies may also receive money in advance of selling a product or performing a service. At the time that such money is received, the company would record a liability account for **unearned revenue.** These amounts are considered debts of the company because it must either provide the customer the product or service desired or return the money. For example, when Gannett Co., Inc. (www.gannett.com) receives payment from you for a one-year subscription to *USA Today,* the company owes you 12 months of papers or a refund. Only as issues are sent to you does the magazine earn revenue. Another example is Ticketmaster's (www.abouttmcs.com) sale of concert tickets. The service charge that is paid for the ticket is a nonrefundable amount that is revenue upon the sale of the ticket; however, Ticketmaster does not earn the concert fee until the concert occurs.

Long-term Liabilities Long-term liabilities are the debts of a business other than those classified as current liabilities. Examples of long-term liabilities include long-term notes payable, mortgages payable, and long-term accrued liabilities. When a long-term liability of a company will be paid within the next year or operating cycle, it is reclassified from the long-term to the current liability section of the balance sheet. Quite often, a company

[2] Financial Accounting Standards Board, *Statement of Financial Accounting Concepts No. 6: Elements of Financial Statements of Business Enterprises* (Stamford, CN: FASB, 1985).

reports the collective amount of several long-term liabilities on one balance sheet line item entitled "long-term debt" or simply "long-term liabilities."

Stockholders' Equity

Stockholders' equity represents the owners' interest in the company. The three most common components of stockholders' equity are paid-in capital (often called common stock), additional paid-in capital, and retained earnings. The total dollar amount of stockholders' equity represents the owners' claims on assets of the corporation.

A corporation's common stock represents that firm's ownership interest that is sold in single units, or shares. The amount shown on the balance sheet for **common stock** is the total par value of the number of shares of stock that the corporation has issued. **Par value** is merely the specific dollar amount per share that is printed on each stock certificate. Most companies are now establishing very small par values for common stock shares. The par value of La-Z-Boy Incorporated's (www.la-z-boy.com) common stock is $1 per share; $0.01 per share is the par value of Lillian Vernon Corporation's (www.lillianvernon.com) common stock.

Generally, the par value has little, if any, relationship to the initial selling price of the share of stock. When stock shares are first sold, the amount received by the company is more than the par value. Any amounts over par or stated value will be recorded in an account entitled **Additional Paid-in Capital.**[3]

The total amount of profits generated by a company and not distributed as dividends to stockholders is accumulated in **Retained Earnings.** Profits, because they benefit stockholders, increase Retained Earnings. Dividends, on the other hand, are no longer kept in the business; thus, they decrease Retained Earnings. It is important to realize that there is no cash in Retained Earnings: cash is a current asset on the balance sheet and *not* a part of stockholders' equity.

Income Statement

The two primary types of accounts on an income statement are revenues and expenses. Exhibit 2-2 presents an income statement for Kirtley, Inc. for the year ended December 31, 2002. The following discussion covers the key elements that create the net income (or net loss) on an income statement.

Revenues Revenues represent inflows of new assets into the business. Revenues may be operating or nonoperating, depending on how they were generated. Generally, **operating revenues** reflect the sales prices of the products sold or the services performed from the primary operations of the company. **Nonoperating revenues** are commonly generated from "side-line" activities. For example, the interest a bank charges its customers is an operating revenue because lending money is a primary operating activity of the bank. A retail store that earns interest by extending credit to customers would classify the interest as nonoperating revenue.

Expenses Expenses are costs of doing business. There are three basic categories of expenses: cost of goods sold, operating expenses, and nonoperating expenses. In a merchandising or manufacturing company, one of the largest expenses is Cost of Goods Sold or the price that the company paid for the inventory that it sells to its customers. For

[3] There are many other acceptable titles for this account, including Paid-in Capital in Excess of Par (Stated) Value and Contributed Capital in Excess of Par.

EXHIBIT 2-2
Income Statement

Kirtley Inc.
Income Statement
For Year Ended December 31, 2002

Sales Revenue		$190,000
Cost of Goods Sold		(75,000)
Gross Profit		$115,000
Operating Expenses		
Salaries and wages	$52,000	
Rent	12,000	
Utilities	25,900	
Depreciation	6,000	(95,900)
Operating Income		$ 19,100
Nonoperating Revenues and Expenses		
Interest Expense		(1,800)
Income Before Income Taxes		$ 17,300
Income Tax Expense (20%)		(3,460)
Net Income		$ 13,840
Earnings Per Share (20,000 shares)		$ 0.692

example, a store that sells an item of inventory to a customer for $150 (operating revenue) might have purchased that item for $70 (cost of goods sold).

Costs, other than cost of goods sold, incurred for a company's principal business operations are known as **operating expenses.** Common operating expenses include salaries and wages, sales commissions, advertising costs, rent, utilities, and depreciation. The remaining expenses listed on an income statement are nonoperating expenses that result from an entity's nonprincipal business operations. For example, the interest expense that is incurred because of borrowing money from a bank is a nonoperating expense.

Gross Profit Gross profit is a very important and informative figure for financial statement users. This amount is the difference between sales (operating) revenue and cost of the goods sold during the period. The **gross profit percentage** (gross profit divided by sales) can be viewed as the profit margin earned on the sale of products. This percentage may differ dramatically between companies or within segments of a company, depending on the type of business in which the companies or segments are engaged. Quite often, an early sign that a company's profitability is declining is a decrease in its gross profit percentage. When gross profit percentage declines, a company often has to compensate by cutting its operating expenses.

Exhibit 2-3 provides a two-year summary of the gross profits for the three primary segments of Recoton Corporation (www.recoton.com), a manufacturing and marketing company of consumer electronics. Notice the impact on the segment's income as the gross profit percentages change between the two years. The changes in income for the segment will, naturally, affect the net income for the company.

Operating Income The difference between gross profit and a company's operating expenses is **operating income,** also called income from operations. This figure is an

EXHIBIT 2-3
Gross Profit Percentages—Recoton Corp. (Amounts in Thousands)

	Accessory		Audio		Gaming	
	1999	2000	1999	2000	1999	2000
Gross Profit Percentage	37.8%	43.6%	29.8%	34.8%	43.5%	34.9%
Segment Income	$7.6	$30.8	[$5.3]	$17.3	$9.3	[$13.1]

important one because a company's eventual success or failure hinges on the profitability of its principal line, or lines, of business.

Net Income

Exhibit 2-2 shows that "income before income taxes" is determined by adding or subtracting the net amount of other revenues and expenses to or from operating income. Subtracting income tax expense from income before income taxes provides the net income (or net loss) for the period. Because corporations pay taxes, an income tax expense amount is shown on Kirtley, Inc.'s income statement. Corporate income tax expense is computed using a graduated scale: higher amounts of income are taxed at higher tax rates.

Earnings per Share

A corporation also reports an earnings per share (EPS) figure on its income statement. In its most simplistic form, EPS is computed as net income divided by number of shares of common stock held by stockholders. Corporations report earnings per share each period to assist stockholders in determining the profit that period that is attributable to their ownership interest in the firm.

OBJECTIVES OF FINANCIAL REPORTING

Determining a consistent manner in which items on the balance sheet and income statement (as well as the other primary financial statements) should be presented is an important issue to the Financial Accounting Standards Board (FASB). To integrate the current, and guide the development of future, financial accounting and reporting standards, the FASB established a conceptual framework project. Some of the primary outputs of this project are discussed in the following sections.

To make sound economic decisions, external parties need a wide array of financial information about business enterprises. The FASB decided that the starting point of its conceptual framework project should be to determine the primary objectives of financial reporting by businesses. The outcome of this process was to state that businesses have the following three financial reporting objectives, each of which directly or indirectly reflects the need for a business entity's financial statements to assist external parties in making rational and informed economic decisions.[4]

[4] Financial Accounting Standards Board, *Statement of Financial Accounting Concepts No. 1: Objectives of Financial Reporting by Business Enterprises* (Stamford, CN: FASB, 1978).

1. Financial reports should provide information that is useful in making investing, lending, and other economic decisions.
2. Financial reports should provide information that is useful to decision makers in predicting the future cash flows of businesses and future cash dividends from those businesses.
3. Financial reports should provide information about the assets and liabilities of businesses and the transactions and other events that have resulted in changes in those assets and liabilities.

These three objectives provide assistance in determining the types of financial statements that a business should present as well as the types of information that should be included on those financial statements. For example, objective number two focuses on the distinct need of external parties to have information about a business's cash situation—providing direct support for the Statement of Cash Flows. Objective number three indicates that a business should provide information about events that caused changes in assets and liabilities; some items that cause such changes, however, do not necessarily involve cash. Thus, these two objectives indicate a need for both cash-based and non-cash-based (income statement) information.

KEY ATTRIBUTES OF ACCOUNTING INFORMATION

Because of the quantitative nature of accounting, financial statement users often overlook important qualitative features of accounting information. Therefore, the FASB decided that the conceptual framework needed to define and describe the qualitative attributes that accounting information should possess.[5] If financial statement accounting data do not exhibit the following attributes, information needs of decision makers are unlikely to be satisfied, and the statements are unlikely to be useful. In fact, usefulness in the decision making process was determined to be *the* most important qualitative characteristic that accounting information should possess. To qualify as useful to decision makers, accounting information should be understandable, relevant, and reliable.

Understandability

Because so many people have access to financial statements, the accounting profession has long debated the "audience" to whom the financial statements should be directed. Should financial statements be understandable or comprehensible to everyone, even the most naive or unsophisticated users? Or should financial statements be principally directed toward people who have an in-depth understanding of financial reporting and accounting issues? The FASB settled this debate by stating that financial reports should be comprehensible to individuals who have a "reasonable understanding of business and economic activities and who are willing to study the information with reasonable diligence."[6]

Thus, it is not necessary that financial statements be understandable to "everyone," but they should be understandable to a broad range of users. In addition, the Securities and Exchange Commission (SEC) decided to require that companies filing certain documents with the Commission must use "plain English principles" in the writing of those documents. Although the SEC rules do not apply at this time to all financial reports or statements, plain

[5] Financial Accounting Standards Board, *Statement of Financial Accounting Concepts No. 2: Qualitative Characteristics of Accounting Information* (Stamford, CN: FASB, 1980).

[6] Financial Accounting Standards Board, *Statement of Financial Accounting Concepts No. 2: Qualitative Characteristics of Accounting Information* (Stamford, CN: FASB, 1980).

English (rather than legalistic or overly complex wordings) is becoming more and more the norm in financial reporting. Exhibit 2-4 provides some of the plain English guidelines.

Relevance

For accounting information to be useful, it must possess a high degree of relevance by being timely and having feedback and/or predictive value. If information is provided too late to influence decisions, then it is not relevant. Feedback value enables decision makers to confirm or correct earlier expectations about, for instance, a business's operating results. Predictive value allows a user to forecast future occurrences from current information. For example, a banker considering a company's loan application should be able to use financial statements to help predict whether the company will be able to repay the loan.

Reliability

To be useful to decision makers, accounting information must also be reliable and, thus, must possess the following traits: verifiability, neutrality, and representational faithfulness. Verifiability means that multiple persons can validate the information; it does not mean that accounting data are necessarily exact or precise. The majority of financial data are not exact amounts, but rather approximations based on underlying supportable details. For example, the presentation by International Paper (www.internationalpaper.com) of all its financial statements in the millions of dollars could hardly be considered precise—but the information underlying those rounded amounts could be verified by different parties.

To be neutral, accounting data must be presented without bias. Thus, accountants should not consciously attempt to influence the decisions of the users of accounting data. This characteristic is one reason that financial statements are said to be "general purpose" in nature.

Finally, "representational faithfulness" implies that accounting data should portray, to the greatest extent possible, the true nature of a business's economic resources, obligations, and transactions. The necessity of this characteristic can be understood in reference to a map: leaving Atlanta off a map of Georgia would not be considered "representationally faithful" for most users; leaving off Riddleville, Georgia, probably would not create difficulties...unless, of course, that was where the user was headed.

Attributes of Accounting Information: A Few Other Issues

In certain situations, accounting data do not have to satisfy the understandability, relevance, and reliability criteria. For example, accounting data do not have to be perfectly reliable if imprecision in the data would not "matter" to decision makers. **Materiality** refers to the relative importance of specific items of accounting information. An item is

EXHIBIT 2-4

Six Basic "Plain English" Principles

1. Use short sentences.
2. Use definite, concrete, everyday words.
3. Use the active voice.
4. Use tabular presentations or bullet lists for complex material whenever possible.
5. Do not use legal jargon or highly technical business terms.
6. Do not use multiple negatives.

SOURCE: Securities and Exchange Commission, *Securities Act of 1933*, 1998, Rule 421(b).

deemed material if it is significant enough to influence a financial statement user's decision. For example, the expensing of a $15 trashcan rather than depreciating it over a useful life of five years would not create a material misstatement of any of the five years' income amounts.

Usefulness of accounting data is enhanced by **comparability,** which refers to the ease with which the accounting information of an entity can be compared with its similar prior period information and with similar information reported by other business entities. The failure of an entity to use the same accounting rules from period to period is a major threat to comparability. Therefore, if a company changes an accounting principle that will significantly affect comparability of period-to-period financial statements, the effect of that change must be highlighted in the financial statements and disclosed in the financial statement footnotes.

FUNDAMENTAL ACCOUNTING CONCEPTS

Accounting rules have evolved over several centuries on an industry-by-industry basis. At one time, there was a set of accounting rules that were considered generally accepted by merchants, while another set of accounting rules was generally accepted within the shipbuilding industry. Eventually, accountants decided that allowing accounting rules to be validated strictly by general acceptance was not necessarily a good idea.

Today's changing business environment continually creates new types of transactions and new variations of routine or familiar transactions. For instance, the question of whether the cost of developing a company Web site should be shown as an asset or an expense would never have been an issue in the 1980s.

Properly recording new types of transactions and analyzing financial statements require consideration of fundamental **generally accepted accounting principles** (GAAP). GAAP refer to the collection of concepts, guidelines, and rules that are used in applying double-entry bookkeeping to the task of recording and reporting financial information. Financial statement preparers and users can both benefit greatly from understanding the basic concepts that dictate how accounting information is recorded and reported. Such an understanding provides a grasp on both the uses and limitations of accounting data. Exhibit 2-5 provides a list of the key concepts that underlie the accounting and financial reporting rules, procedures, and practices that are important to understanding accounting information. Each of these items is discussed separately.

Accounting Period Concept

Determining the profitability of a business cannot be truly assessed until it ceases operations. However, decision makers demand financial information about business entities on a regular basis. The **accounting period concept** allows accountants to prepare meaningful financial reports for ongoing businesses by dividing their lives into reporting intervals of equal length. As a result, businesses typically release financial statements to external decision makers at the end of each fiscal year. Publicly owned companies regulated by the Securities and Exchange Commission must issue financial statements on both a quarterly and an annual basis. These documents are called the 10-Q and the 10-K and can be

EXHIBIT 2-5

Key Accounting Concepts and Principles

- Accounting Period Concept
- Historical Cost Principle
- Unit-of-Measurement Concept
- Going Concern Assumption
- Entity Concept
- Revenue Recognition Rules
- Expense Recognition Rules
- Full Disclosure Principle

Acronym: A HUGE REF

found online at the SEC's EDGAR (Electronic Data Gathering, Analysis, and Retrieval) Web site (www.sec.gov/edgar.shtml).

Historical Cost Principle

In the United States, the **historical cost principle** dictates that most assets are shown on the financial statements at their original cost to a company. For instance, assume a company acquires a tract of land for $500,000. That historical cost will be reported on the balance sheet three years later even if, by that time, nearby urban development has caused the appraised value of the land to skyrocket to $2 million.

Historical costs are used as the primary valuation basis for assets because such costs are more verifiable and less subject to estimation or opinion than current values. The land cost referred to in the previous paragraph can be found on the purchase contract. Alternatively, determining the land's current value is much more subjective and would need to be established using a real estate appraisal or market comparison. Commonly, however, appraised values are subject to errors and may differ among appraisers.

It is important to note that use of the historical cost principle can cause the values of assets that have been held for a long time to be significantly undervalued. Alternatively, liabilities are generally current amounts. This differentiation in valuations causes a net "book value" that borders on meaningless. Unfortunately, an alternative would be to allow companies to set their own values on assets each reporting period, which would conflict with the principles of verifiability and comparability.

There are, however, several exceptions to the general rule of valuing assets for accounting purposes at historical cost. First, some investments in corporate stocks and bonds may be reported in financial statements at current values rather than historical costs. Second, if an asset's value has permanently declined below its historical cost, that asset should be written down to its current value. For example, if land value were reduced because a hurricane uprooted all the trees, then the book value would be reduced. This exception is based on the **conservatism principle** which states that, when alternative valuations are possible, assets and revenues should be not be overstated and liabilities and expenses should not be understated. This principle does *not,* however, indicate that assets and revenues should be understated and liabilities and expenses should be overstated. Such choices would violate the reliability characteristic discussed earlier in the chapter.

Unit of Measurement Concept

The **unit of measurement concept** mandates that businesses use a common unit of measurement in accounting for their transactions. This concept allows financial data to be quantified, summarized, and reported in a uniform, timely, and consistent manner. In the United States, the appropriate unit of measurement is a "constant" dollar—that is, the dollar that is not restated for the effects of inflation or deflation.

Going Concern Assumption

Unless there is evidence to the contrary, accountants use the **going concern assumption** to reflect a belief that a business will continue to operate "long enough to use its longest-lived asset." Because businesses continuously replace old assets with new ones, this presumption often indicates that the business will continue indefinitely. The going concern concept allows firms to book PP&E at cost and depreciate them over their useful lives.

Since PP&E assets will eventually be used up by the firm, they are not required to be written down to fair market value each year.

The going concern assumption has significant implications for the accounting and financial reporting decisions rendered by and about business enterprises. For example, a company that has severe financial problems and has filed for bankruptcy may not show its property, plant and equipment assets at book value on the balance sheet, but rather at the fair value that could be received in liquidation. When a company's status as a going concern is seriously in doubt, this fact should be disclosed in the firm's financial statements.

Entity Concept

Regardless of its legal form (sole proprietorship, partnership, or corporation), a business enterprise is treated, for accounting purposes, as a distinct and independent entity. Thus, the **entity concept** requires that the transactions of a business should be accounted for separately from the personal transactions of its owners. This concept is particularly important for sole proprietorships. A sole proprietor will not be able to prepare financial statements that accurately depict the financial status of his or her company if personal and business assets and liabilities are commingled.

Revenue Recognition Rules

One of the most important accounting issues that businesses face is when to record revenues and expenses in the accounting records. The accounting profession has established some general rules to dictate the timing of revenue recognition. These rules limit the ability of management to misrepresent a firm's operating results by being able to selectively choose the accounting periods in which to record revenues.

The FASB established a two-part **revenue recognition rule** to follow in deciding when to record revenues. Before being recorded in a business's accounting records, a revenue should be both realized and earned. Revenues are realized when assets have been exchanged for cash or a claim to cash. Revenues are earned when the company has, or has substantially, provided the product or performed the service that was required for the transaction to be complete (that is, for the company to be entitled to the revenue). For most merchandising and service companies, both of these requirements are usually satisfied at the point of service or sale. It is not necessary for cash to change hands when recognizing revenues. For example, when Dillard's sells a tie and the customer uses his Dillard's charge account, Dillard's should recognize the revenue even though no cash has been involved.

There are instances in which the point of sale rule is improper. For example, many construction projects create economic impacts over multiple years. In such cases, revenues may need to be spread over several accounting periods rather than being recorded totally at the end of the project. For example, when Horizon Offshore, Inc. (www.horizonoffshore.com) provides its numerous construction services to the oil and gas industry, revenues are recognized in proportion to the costs incurred to date on the projects. Thus, if the company incurs 30 percent of the total estimated cost on a project, 30 percent of the expected revenues would be recorded. This method of recognizing revenues is called the percentage-of-completion method.

Expense Recognition Rules

As discussed in the previous section, two rules exist relative to recognizing revenues in the financial statements. These rules also affect expense recognition, in that costs of doing business should be recognized as expenses in the accounting period in which they provide economic benefit to the business. Typically, this rule means that the **matching principle** should apply: an expense should be recognized in the accounting period when the related revenue is recorded.

In many cases, the matching principle is simple to apply because there is a corresponding cause-and-effect relationship between a cost and the subsequent revenue that it generates. To illustrate, the cost of inventory sold should be recorded as Cost of Goods Sold expense in the period in which the Sales Revenue is recognized. Similarly, a commission paid to a salesperson should be recorded as an expense in the same accounting period that the related sale was recorded as revenue.

In other situations, there is difficulty in seeing a relationship between a cost and a revenue. Thus, two other possibilities exist for expense recognition. First, when a cost, such as an equipment purchase, provides an economic benefit to several accounting periods, that expenditure should be recorded as an asset and gradually written off to expense over the time that benefit is provided. In the case of equipment, that time would be the asset's useful life and the write-off is called depreciation expense. Second, when no direct cause and effect can be determined and no clear expected benefit time frame can be identified, the cost should be recorded immediately as an expense. Consider the case of pharmaceutical companies that engage in long-term research programs to develop new products. Because such companies seldom know which research efforts will result in viable products, the costs are recorded as expenses when they are incurred.

Similar to accounting for revenues, cash need not be exchanged for an expense to be recognized. For example, assume that a company does not need to pay for its Mother's Day sale newspaper advertisement until June. Advertising expense should be recognized in May even though the company has not yet paid for the ad.

Companies using the revenue and expense recognition rules just discussed are using the **accrual basis of accounting.** Under this accounting basis, the economic impact of a transaction is recognized whether or not the transaction involves cash. Some business entities (usually very small ones) use the **cash basis of accounting;** they record revenues when cash payments are received from customers and expenses when disbursements of cash are made to suppliers, employees, and other parties. As a result, the reported net income of a cash basis business for a given period may not be a reliable indicator of its true profitability for that period. The cash basis is not a generally accepted accounting principle. Consider the potential manipulation that could be involved if management were able to recognize revenues and expenses only when cash was received or paid.

Full Disclosure Principle

The **full disclosure principle** requires that all information for a thorough understanding of a company's financial affairs be included in its financial statements or accompanying narrative disclosures, such as footnotes. Examples of information that users may need but which is not part of the four primary financial statements are management's plans for the future, information about employee pension plans, business risks, and details of major transactions with related parties.

Related party transactions may be structured to economically benefit one party to the transaction at the expense of the other. Disclosure of related party transactions allows decision makers to assess the reliability of a given firm's reported financial results. Enron, the company mentioned at the start of this chapter, was heavily involved in related party transactions with its 3,000+ subsidiaries and partnerships. Many of these relationships were specifically designed to allow Enron to transfer assets at highly inflated prices and record massive amounts of profits. Many of these transactions were not even disclosed by Arthur Andersen LLP, Enron's auditing firm.[7]

[7] Daniel Fisher, "Shell Game," *Forbes* (January 7, 2002), pp. 52-54.

AN INTRODUCTION TO THE ACCOUNTING SYSTEM

The objectives, concepts, and principles discussed in the previous sections of the chapter create the framework for the basic accounting system. An accounting system is a systematic approach to collecting, processing, and communicating financial information to decision makers in an orderly, effective, and efficient manner. Such systems have varying degrees of complexity and sophistication. Manual, or "pen and paper," accounting systems are still used by some small businesses to process financial data. However, most businesses have integrated computer accounting systems. The accounting concepts and methods in this text apply equally well to manual and computer-based accounting systems. All accounting systems comprise of similar elements: accounts, a general journal, and a general ledger.

Accounts

The basic storage units for financial data in an accounting system are called **accounts.** Financial data related to the assets, liabilities, and other financial statement items of a business are recorded and stored, either electronically or manually, in accounts. Accounts are designed to show increases, decreases, and a balance for each type financial statement element.

A **chart of accounts** is a numerical listing of all the accounts of a business. A chart of accounts can be thought of as an address book. When recording a transaction, an accountant refers to the chart of accounts to identify the proper address for each account affected by the transaction. Instead of being listed alphabetically, though, a chart of accounts is listed in financial statement order: assets, liabilities, stockholders' equity, revenues, and expenses. In this way, all similar "types" of accounts are grouped together. Each account in the chart of accounts is given a number based on the type of account it is. This numbering system helps minimize errors that might occur in the accounting process.

The General Journal and General Ledger

The two principal accounting records for most business enterprises are journals and ledgers. Each transaction of a business is initially recorded, or journalized, in a **general journal.** This journal is considered the book of original entry and is kept in chronological order. Essentially, a journal can be viewed as a financial diary in which the dollar amounts of transactions that affect the financial status of a business are recorded. Most transactions are recorded individually, but some might be recorded as a total amount. For instance, a small grocery store would probably record a single amount for its cash sales at the end of each day rather than individually for each customer.

The **general ledger** is the accounting record that contains all of the individual accounts for a business. Although the general journal establishes a historical record of the transactions and events affecting a business, it would be very difficult to prepare financial statements directly from the hundreds, thousands, or even millions of journal entries recorded for a business during a given accounting period. Thus, the accounting data are transferred, through a process called **posting,** from the general journal to the individual accounts in the general ledger. Posting can be performed daily, weekly, or monthly. In a computerized accounting system, journalizing and posting transactions usually occur simultaneously.

At the end of an accounting period, accountants prepare a listing, or **trial balance,** of the general ledger account balances of a business. These account balances are incorporated into the appropriate financial statements. For financial statement purposes, similar account balances are often consolidated into one line item. For example, a company having ten cash accounts would add their balances together and report the total as Cash on the balance sheet.

This section provides a very condensed summary of the **accounting cycle** or the set of recurring accounting procedures that must be performed in a business each accounting period. This cycle contains the following actions:

1. Financial data for transactions and other events affecting a business are journalized.
2. These data are posted to the appropriate general ledger accounts.
3. The period-ending general ledger account balances are organized into a trial balance.
4. The account balances are consolidated and incorporated into the appropriate financial statements.

The next chapter will discuss the activities that occur in the accounting cycle at greater length.

SUMMARY

The two primary financial statements discussed in this chapter are the balance sheet and income statement. A balance sheet summarizes a business's assets, liabilities, and stockholders' equity at a specific time. The asset section of the balance sheet is classified into current assets, long-term investments, property, plant and equipment, and intangibles. Liabilities can be current or long-term. The three primary components of stockholders' equity are common stock, additional paid-in capital, and retained earnings.

An income statement reports on a business's profitability for a stated period of time, usually the entity's fiscal year. Gross profit is the difference between a company's sales revenue and its cost of goods sold. Nonoperating revenues and expenses are deducted from gross profit to obtain income before income taxes. Income taxes for a corporation are computed on an upwardly sliding tax rate. Net income (or net loss) is the total difference between a business's revenues and expenses. Earnings-per-share is also shown on the face of the income statement.

During the mid-1970s, the FASB began developing a conceptual framework to guide the development of future accounting standards. Three financial reporting objectives for business enterprises were detailed, each of which concerns the need to assist third parties in making rational and informed economic decisions. Business enterprises satisfy these reporting objectives by preparing the four primary financial statements for distribution to interested third parties.

The key attribute that accounting information should possess is decision usefulness and, therefore, the information should be understandable, relevant, and reliable. Numerous concepts and principles underlie accounting practices. Knowledge of these items is useful both for accountants to develop proper accounting procedures for new types of transactions and for users to understand how the information on the financial statements was created. These principles include the accounting period concept, historical cost principle, unit of measurement concept, going concern assumption, entity concept, revenue recognition principles, expense recognition principles, and full disclosure principle.

The accounting cycle is the time it takes for a business to make or acquire inventory, sell it, and collect cash from customers. During this cycle, numerous transactions occur and these are first recorded in a general journal. The information in the journal is then posted to the accounts in a general ledger for use in preparing a trial balance. From the trial balance information, the company's financial statements can be developed.

KEY TERMS

account
accounting period concept
accrual basis of accounting
accrued liability
accumulated depreciation
asset
book value (of a PP&E asset)
cash basis of accounting
chart of accounts
comparability
common stock
conservatism principle
current asset
current liability
depreciation
dividend
entity concept
full disclosure principle
generally accepted accounting principles (GAAP)
general journal
general ledger
going concern assumption
gross profit
gross profit percentage
historical cost principle
intangible asset
liability
matching principle
materiality
nonoperating revenue
operating cycle
operating expense
operating income
operating revenue
par value
posting
retained earnings
revenue recognition rule
unearned revenue
unit of measurement concept

QUESTIONS

1. The principal focus of financial accounting is serving whose information needs? Why was this group chosen? *(LO 2.1)*
2. What is the balance sheet equation? Discuss the components of a balance sheet. *(LO 2.1)*
3. What is an operating cycle and how does it affect the classification of items on a balance sheet? *(LO 2.1)*
4. Does the Retained Earnings account contain cash? Explain your answer. *(LO 2.1)*
5. Is the income statement a "specific time" statement or a "period-of-time" statement? Discuss the difference between these two perspectives. *(LO 2.1)*
6. Briefly describe or define the following three items: revenues, gross profit, and net income. *(LO 2.1)*
7. Choose a company with which you are familiar and provide examples of an operating revenue, a nonoperating revenue, and an operating expense for that company. *(LO 2.1)*
8. What is the common theme of the three financial reporting objectives of business entities? Why is this "theme" so important? *(LO 2.2)*
9. To qualify as "reliable," accounting information should have what three traits? Provide an example of each of these traits. *(LO 2.3)*
10. What is the principal justification for using historical costs instead of current values as the primary valuation basis for assets? Could the use of historical costs create any difficulties for users? Explain the rationale for your answer. *(LO 2.4)*
11. What two conditions must be met for a company to recognize revenue from a transaction or event in its accounting records? *(LO 2.4)*
12. What information is contained in a general journal? Why would a business need both a general journal and a general ledger? *(LO 2.5)*

EXERCISES

13. **True or False** *(all LOs)*

Following are a series of statements regarding topics discussed in this chapter.

Required:

Indicate whether each statement is true (T) or false (F).

(1) The revenue and expense recognition rules limit the ability of business executives to freely choose the accounting periods in which to record their firm's revenues and expenses.

(2) A key advantage of using historical costs for asset valuation purposes is that historical costs are more objective, or verifiable, than current values.

(3) Common current assets include cash, short-term investments, prepaid expenses, and intangible assets.

(4) The entity concept requires that all information needed to obtain a thorough understanding of a company's financial affairs be included in its financial statements or accompanying narrative disclosures.

(5) The conceptual framework of the Financial Accounting Standards Board provides a foundation for developing accounting pronouncements.

(6) The unit of measurement concept suggests that accountants can prepare meaningful financial reports for ongoing business enterprises by dividing their lives into reporting intervals of equal length.

(7) One purpose of an income statement is to reconcile a business's cash balance at the beginning of a period to its end-of-period cash balance.

(8) To qualify as "reliable," accounting information should be timely and have feedback value and/or predictive value.

(9) Examples of operating expenses include sales commissions, advertising costs, and the salaries of a firm's top executives.

14. **Balance Sheet Equation** *(LO 2.1)*

Rick Francis & Son, Inc., has assets equal to twice the amount of its liabilities.

Required:

(1) Assuming Francis & Son's total stockholders' equity is $1,000,000, determine the company's total assets and total liabilities.

(2) Assuming $750,000 of the company's stockholders' equity consists of common stock and additional paid-in capital, determine Francis & Son's retained earnings.

15. **Classification of Balance Sheet Items** *(LO 2.1)*

Following are items that can be found in a balance sheet:

- Accounts payable
- Inventory
- Retained earnings
- Notes payable (due in ten years)
- Prepaid expenses
- Common stock
- Intangible assets
- Cash
- Accounts receivable
- Notes payable (due in six months)

- Additional paid-in capital
- Property, plant & equipment

Required:

Determine the correct balance sheet classification for each item listed. Choices are current assets, long-term assets, current liabilities, long-term liabilities, and stockholders' equity.

16. **Current Asset Classification** *(LO 2.1)*

Following are current assets of Nunez Enterprises, Inc.:

- Accounts Receivable
- Inventory
- Cash
- Prepaid Expenses
- Short-term Investments

Required:

(1) In what order would you usually find these accounts listed in the current assets section of a balance sheet?

(2) Explain the significance of the ordering of these accounts.

17. **Liability Classification** *(LO 2.1)*

For the past several years, Farewell Distributors reported a long-term debt of $100,000 in its balance sheet. Next year, the company will begin paying off this debt in four annual installments of $25,000 each.

Required:

(1) How should Farewell's $100,000 debt be reported in the company's balance sheet at the end of the current year?

(2) Why is the proper balance sheet classification of a company's liabilities important to the firm's creditors and potential creditors?

18. **Interpreting Gross Profit** *(LO 2.1)*

Company A and Company B operate in the wholesale shoe industry in New Mexico. In 2002, Company A had a gross profit of $400,000, while Company B had a gross profit of $120,000. Both companies had approximately $1.2 million in sales.

Required:

(1) Identify at least two factors that could account for the large difference in the two companies' gross profits.

(2) If you were the president of Company B, what strategies might you implement to increase your firm's gross profit?

19. **Operating and Nonoperating Items** *(LO 2.1)*

The following items might be seen on the income statement of a large retail "super-store."

- Income tax expense
- Sales revenue
- Interest revenue
- Cost of goods sold expense
- Utility expense
- Revenue from cafeteria food sales to employees

- Shipping expense to obtain inventory items
- Property tax expense

Required:

Indicate whether each of the above items would be considered an operating or a nonoperating item. If you are uncertain, provide a brief reason for your selection.

20. **Gross Profit and Gross Profit Percentage** *(LO 2.1)*

The August 2002 income statement for LeAnn Co. contains the following items:

Wages expense	$145,000
Sales revenue	550,000
Interest expense	12,000
Cost of goods sold	380,000

Required:

(1) Determine LeAnn's gross profit for August 2002.

(2) Determine LeAnn's gross profit percentage.

(3) What are your perceptions of LeAnn Co.'s financial status based on the information given and calculated?

21. **Qualitative Characteristics of Accounting Information** *(LO 2.3)*

The following items refer to various qualitative characteristics of accounting information:

(a) The relative importance of information

(b) Timeliness, predictive value and/or feedback value

(c) Continuity over time

(d) Clearness

(e) Verifiability, neutrality, and representational faithfulness

Required:

Match each narrative item with one of the following terms: understandability, relevance, reliability, materiality, comparability.

22. **Operating Cycle** *(LO 2.4)*

Khalid, Inc. manufactures furniture for sale to department stores. On average, 90 days elapse between Khalid's payment for raw materials and the sale of furniture produced from those raw materials. On average, the firm's customers pay for the goods they purchase in 45 days. (All of Khalid's sales are on credit.)

Required:

(1) What is the length of Khalid's operating cycle?

(2) How does the length of a company's operating cycle affect the classification of items in its balance sheet?

23. **Accrued Liabilities** *(LO 2.4)*

BioTechnica International, an agricultural seed distribution company based in Peoria, Illinois, reported accrued liabilities of $2,847,000 at the end of a recent fiscal year.

Required:

Provide two examples of transactions or events that could result in a company recording accrued liabilities in its accounting records at the end of an accounting period.

PROBLEMS

24. Preparing an Income Statement *(LO 2.1)*

Following are the line items, presented in random order, that were included in a recent income statement of Malenski Corporation:

Selling, General and Administrative Expenses	$ 45,050
Operating Income	?
Cost of Goods Sold	65,750
Net Income	?
Income Tax Expense	1,500
Net Sales	115,000
Income Before Income Taxes	?
Gross Profit	?
Interest Revenue	5,000

Required:

(1) Compute each missing amount.

(2) Prepare an income statement for Malenski Corporation.

25. Computing Depreciation Expense *(LO 2.1)*

Assume that Tankersley Enterprises purchased a piece of machinery for $18,000 in early January 2001. The machinery's estimated useful life is five years, and it will have no value at the end of its useful life.

Required:

(1) Using the straight-line depreciation method discussed in this chapter, compute the annual depreciation expense on this asset.

(2) At the end of 2003, what amount of accumulated deprecation will be shown for this machine on the balance sheet?

(3) What accounting principle or principles require companies to depreciate long-term assets over their useful lives instead of expensing their total cost in the year of purchase?

26. Computing Gross Profit and Net Sales *(LO 2.1)*

In 2001, Doolan Company sold 10,000 units of inventory at twice their purchase price of $27.50 each. In 2002, Doolan had a gross profit of $200,000 and cost of goods sold of $225,000.

Required:

(1) What were Doolan's net sales in 2001?

(2) What was Doolan's gross profit in 2001?

(3) What were Doolan's net sales in 2002?

(4) What was Doolan's gross profit percentage in 2002?

27. Statement of Stockholders' Equity *(LO 2.1)*

Following is a recent statement of stockholders' equity for Tucson Company.

	Common Stock	Paid-in Capital	Retained Earnings
Balances, January 1, 2002	$1,000,000	$200,000	$800,000
Sale of Common Stock	240,000	300,000	
Exercise of Employee Stock Options	10,000	15,000	—
Net Income	—	—	125,000
Balances, December 31, 2002	$1,250,000	$515,000	$925,000

Required:

(1) How does a company's statement of stockholders' equity articulate with, or relate to, the firm's balance sheet?

(2) What transaction or event accounted for the largest increase in Tucson's stockholders' equity during 2002?

28. **Analyzing Balance Sheet Data** *(LO 2.1)*

Following is the asset section of a recent balance sheet of First Union Real Estate Investments. This company owns and manages real estate properties throughout the United States. Amounts are expressed in thousands.

Investments in Real Estate:	
Land	$ 44,594
Buildings and Improvements	391,800
	$436,394
Less: Accumulated Depreciation	(111,972)
Total Investments in Real Estate	$324,422
Mortgage Loans Receivable	35,761
Other Assets	
Cash	2,975
Accounts Receivable and Prepayments	4,594
Miscellaneous Assets	8,437
Total Assets	**$376,189**

Required:

(1) First Union's balance sheet is unusual in that it begins with *Investments in Real Estate* instead of *Current Assets.* Why do you believe the company uses this format for the assets section of its balance sheet?

(2) If most real estate companies use this format for the assets section of their balance sheets, what accounting principle would First Union violate by using a different format?

29. **Financial Reporting Objectives** *(LO 2.2)*

Wagner Company operates a small chain of department stores. Thea Wagner, the owner of Wagner Company, has decided to open two additional stores next year, but the company does not have sufficient cash to finance this expansion project. To raise the needed funds, Thea has asked several friends to consider investing in the firm. She has provided these individuals with audited financial statements for Wagner's most recent fiscal year.

Required:

(1) Besides the audited financial statements, what additional information do you believe the potential investors would want to obtain regarding Wagner Company before deciding whether to invest in the firm? Be specific.

(2) Which financial reporting objective or objectives will Wagner's audited financial statements help satisfy in this context?

(3) Which of Wagner's financial statements do you believe the potential investors will find most useful? Defend your answer.

30. Ethics and Financial Reporting *(LO 2.4, ethics)*

Tim Michael, the chief executive officer of Kokomo Corporation, is very concerned about his company's profitability. In the next few weeks, Kokomo will apply for a large loan from a local bank. This loan is needed to replace several pieces of outdated equipment on the company's production line. Michael is worried that the loan will be rejected because Kokomo's profits have been declining over the past two years. Profits are declining because Kokomo's products cost more to produce than the comparable products of the company's primary competitor. In turn, these higher production costs are due to Kokomo's inefficient production equipment.

To ensure that Kokomo receives the loan, Michael decides to overstate the company's sales and net income for its most recent fiscal year. In his own mind, Michael believes this decision is justified because if Kokomo obtains the loan and purchases the new equipment, he is almost certain that the company will generate sufficient profits and positive cash flows to repay the bank loan. "Besides," Michael reasons, "if we don't get this loan, the company may go under, leaving more than one hundred people without jobs."

Required:

According to Tim Michael's way of thinking, the "end justifies the means." What would you do if you found yourself in Michael's shoes? If you were almost certain that your company would be able repay the loan if granted, could you justify being dishonest to protect the jobs of the company's employees? Do you believe that any other factors have entered into Michael's decision to misrepresent Kokomo's financial data? Explain.

31. Applying Accounting Concepts *(LO 2.4)*

The following situations involve the application of accounting concepts or principles. In some cases, more than one concept or principle may be involved.

(a) Whitecotton Enterprises recently changed its method of computing depreciation for the third time in three years.

(b) Hethcox Distributors sold two of its five divisions immediately after the close of its most recent fiscal year. Company executives included information regarding the sale of these two divisions in the footnotes to the company's financial statements.

(c) Inventory is the largest asset of Still Gardening Company. Last year, Still's inventory was reported at its historical cost in the company's balance sheet. This year, the company intends to report its inventory at market value because the inventory's market value is significantly below its historical cost.

(d) A footnote to the recent financial statements issued by Mason, Inc. lists the cash payments that the company is required to make over the next several years under its long-term lease agreements.

Required:

(1) Identify the accounting concepts or principles involved in each of these situations.

(2) Indicate whether the given accounting concept or principle has been properly applied in each case. Explain your reasoning.

CASES

32. **Annual Reports** *(LO 2.1 and 2.3, Internet)*

Use the annual report of Carnival Corporation for the 2001 fiscal year to answer the following questions. The annual report can be found at www.carnival.com /aboutCCL; follow the links to investor relations.

Required:

(1) Using Carnival's November 30, 2001, Income Statement (titled Consolidated Statement of Operations), answer the following questions.

 (a) Why is Interest Income separated from Revenues?

 (b) Does Carnival Corporation primarily provide a service or a product? How does this information affect the company's Cost of Goods Sold?

 (c) List several sources from which Carnival obtains its operating revenues.

(2) Using Carnival's November 30, 2001, Balance Sheet, answer the following questions.

 (a) How much does Carnival list in total assets?

 (b) Excluding the "Fair Value of Hedged Firm Commitments," segregate the total assets into four classifications: Current Assets, Long-term Investments, Property, Plant & Equipment, and Intangible Assets. (Hint: Note number 11 to the Financial Statements may help you.)

 (c) Carnival lists its Property and Equipment as "net," which means that depreciation has been subtracted from the original cost. How much did Carnival pay for its PPE and how much has it been depreciated? (Hint: You will find this information in the Notes to the Financial Statements.)

 (d) Why does Carnival list its Property and Equipment at historical cost rather than fair market value?

 (e) Why are customer deposits listed as liabilities instead of revenues?

 (f) Did Carnival estimate an amount owed but not yet recorded? If so, what was the amount and what was it for?

 (g) How much has Carnival generated in profits and not distributed to its stockholders?

33. **Annual Reports and the Objectives of Financial Reporting** *(LO 2.2 and 2.3, Internet)*

In its annual report for the 2001 fiscal year, Carnival Corporation lists Note 8, entitled Contingencies, in the Notes to the Financial Statements. This note explains three different situations with uncertain outcomes. Read Note 8 and answer the questions below. (The annual report can be found at www.carnival.com/aboutCCL; follow the links to investor relations).

Required:

(1) Is the information contained in Note 8 relevant? Why or why not?

(2) Is the information contained in Note 8 material? Why or why not?

(3) List the three objectives of financial reporting.

(4) If Carnival chose to omit Note 8, would these three objectives still be met? Why or why not?

CHAPTER 3

The Mechanics of Double-Entry Accounting

LEARNING OBJECTIVES

1. Analyze business transactions to determine account effects.
2. Understand the rules of debit and credit.
3. Prepare general journal entries.
4. Post general journal entries to a general ledger.
5. Prepare a trial balance.
6. Develop end-of-period adjustments to general ledger account balances.
7. Prepare an income statement, a statement of stockholders' equity, and a balance sheet.
8. Perform the closing process.
9. Prepare a post-closing trial balance.

Knowing Accounting Helps

Sometimes not knowing why things are done makes people uncomfortable and distrustful. Or so Denise Bredfelt believed when she worked on the shop floor of an engine remanufacturing plant in Springfield, Missouri. However, then she learned about the "financial underpinnings of a business" and she "understood how her work contributed to her company's survival." She now teaches financial basics to a variety of front-line employees: "What blows me away is that if you didn't take an accounting class in high school or college, you don't have a prayer of knowing this stuff because you don't learn it anywhere else." Having an understanding of the financial basics makes employees much more valuable to the company for which they work, and cultivates a skill that is "portable" to other jobs.

SOURCE: Eric Krell, "Learning to Love the P&L," *Training,* September 1999, 66–72.

INTRODUCTION

Chapters 1 and 2 covered the four financial statements prepared for external users. These statements present the balances of different accounts to external users. This chapter is designed to help understand how the balances of accounts are created and changed. First, an overview is provided about how an accounting system converts individual economic transactions into financial statements. Next, the chapter discusses the three basic steps in bookkeeping: record (journalize) transactions in a general journal, post transactions to a general ledger, and prepare a trial balance.

This chapter examines the mechanics of accounting by focusing on manual, rather than computer-based, accounting systems. The computer does not change the fundamental nature of how transaction data are collected, processed, and assimilated into a set of financial statements. The computer merely increases the speed with which transaction data are processed and enhances the reliability of accounting records.

The final section of this chapter focuses on the **accounting cycle,** or set of recurring accounting procedures, that must be completed for a business each accounting period. People who understand the process that takes place at the end of the accounting period are better able to gain information from the financial statements and to perform internal managerial tasks such as budgeting.

CAPTURING ACCOUNTING DATA

Preparation of financial statements requires that information about an organization's economic events be captured and recorded in a rational and systematic manner. Financial record keeping, in one form or another, has existed for thousands of years. However, the origins of modern accounting can be traced to a mathematics book written in 1494 by Luca Pacioli, a Franciscan monk living in what is now Italy.

In his book, Pacioli discussed the mechanics of **double-entry bookkeeping,** a record keeping system that had been used for several decades in and around Venice. Although

Pacioli did not invent the "Method of Venice," his book did formalize and document this system that allowed merchants to maintain financial records summarizing the operating results and financial condition of their businesses in a logical and easily understood manner. More importantly, double-entry bookkeeping permitted merchants to make informed and timely decisions regarding their business affairs. Economic historians attribute the rapid spread of commerce across Europe during the sixteenth century in large part to the availability of this record keeping system.

The key premise underlying double-entry bookkeeping is that financial transactions must be recorded as if they consist of two equal and opposite effects. A brief example may be helpful. Assume that Blanchard & Wood, Attorneys At Law, purchases $1,000 of supplies on credit from Office Depot. From the law firm's perspective, this transaction can be reduced to two parts: the company obtains office supplies (assets) valued at $1,000 and assumes a debt (liability) in the same amount.

An accountant can reduce every business transaction, regardless of size, into at least two equal effects expressed in dollars. If a company properly records the dual nature of each transaction, the entity's financial records will be "in balance" at any given time. Failure to apply the basic premise of double-entry bookkeeping results in an "unbalanced" set of financial records—an unacceptable situation.

RECORDING TRANSACTIONS: DOUBLE-ENTRY BOOKKEEPING

As explained in Chapter 1, the basic accounting equation requires that assets of a business equal the sum of its liabilities and stockholders' equity.

$$\text{Assets} = \text{Liabilities} + \text{Equity}$$

Every transaction of a business must be recorded in such a way that the accounting equation for that business remains in balance.

The accounting cycle begins with the occurrence of an economic transaction. Most information about a business transaction is found in a **source document** that provides the underlying support for, and the key features of, the transaction. Common types of source documents include invoices, sales slips, legal contracts, checks, and purchase orders. Next, the transaction is analyzed to identify which accounts were affected by the transaction, in what amounts, and whether the accounts were increased or decreased.

The following discussion considers the first two transactions of Snow Mountain Retreat, a small corporation. These examples illustrate how to analyze business transactions.

1. April 1 Stockholders purchased 4,000 shares of Snow Mountain Retreat's $10 par value common stock. Checks totaling $40,000 were received from stockholders.

   Source documents: Checks received from investors and stock shares issued to investors.

   Analysis: The corporation's cash increased by $40,000 and, because 4,000 shares were issued, stockholders' equity in the form of common stock increased by $40,000.

2. April 1 Purchased furniture costing $12,000, paying $5,000 in cash and signing a 12% note payable for the balance. The note and interest are due in one year. The furniture is expected to have a two–year useful life with no salvage value.

   Source documents: Invoice for furniture purchase; note payable to furniture seller; advertisement about furniture and its characteristics.

Analysis: The corporation's furniture increased by $12,000; the corporation's cash decreased by $5,000; and the corporation's liabilities, in the form of notes payable, increased by $7,000.

As shown in Exhibit 3-1, the accounting equation format could be used to record these business transactions and their effects on Snow Mountain Retreat's assets, liabilities, and stockholders' equity items. This format would contain a column for each financial statement item affected by these transactions. Think of these columns as simple accounts. After the two transactions, balances are computed to prove the equality of the balance sheet equation.

Notice that for each transaction, there is a true mathematical statement. In the first transaction, two accounts increased, but because they are on opposite sides of the equal sign, the statement $40,000 = $40,000 is true. In transaction (2), three accounts changed; two increased and one decreased. However, the mathematical statement $12,000 – 5,000 = $7,000 is true.

Theoretically, the process illustrated in Exhibit 3-1 could be used for an actual business. However, such a system would become extremely cumbersome as the number of transactions (rows) and their related accounts (columns) increased. In fact, as discussed in Chapter 2, businesses enter financial data in accounting records known as journals and ledgers. However, before illustrating those records, it is important to understand debits and credits as well as the rules of double-entry bookkeeping, which dictate how financial data are recorded in the accounting records.

Debits and Credits

Debits and credits are accounting terms with specialized, but uncomplicated, meanings. Essentially, the terms *debit* and *credit* mean, respectively, left and right. A T-account is used to illustrate the use of debits and credits. A **T-account** is not really part of any formal accounting system; it is a device used for illustrative or analytical purposes, whose name is derived from its shape. Following is a T-account for Snow Mountain Retreat's Cash account.

Cash	
Debit	Credit

When **debit** is used as a noun, it refers to an amount entered on the left-hand side of an accounting record, such as a T-account. Debit can also be used as a verb, meaning to enter a given amount on the left-hand side of an accounting record, such as a T-account. The term **credit** refers to an amount entered on the right-hand side of an accounting record or to enter an amount on the right-hand side of an accounting record.

EXHIBIT 3-1

Snow Mountain Retreat Transactions

Account Types:	Assets		=	Liabilities	+ Stockholders' Equity
Accounts	Cash	Furniture		Notes Payable	Common Stock
(1)	$ 40,000				$40,000
(2)	$ (5,000)	$12,000		$7,000	
	$ 35,000	$12,000		$7,000	$40,000

For example, in the following T-account, cash is debited for $1,000, debited for $300, and credited for $600.

Cash	
Debit	Credit
$1,000	$600
$ 300	

If the debit side of a T-account is larger than the credit side, the account has a **debit balance.** If the credit side is larger, the account has a credit balance. The Cash account above has debits totaling $1,300 and a credit of $600; therefore, it has a debit balance of $700.

Cash	
Debit	Credit
$1,000	$600
$ 300	
$1,300	$600
$ 700	

Accountants use debits and credits to define the rules of double-entry bookkeeping. The debit/credit rules can be correlated with the accounting equation. Assets appear on the left-hand side of the accounting equation. To increase an asset, it must be debited, with the appropriate dollar amount being entered on the left-hand side of the account. Liabilities and stockholders' equity appear on the right-hand side of the accounting equation. An increase in one of these accounts means that the appropriate dollar amount is credited or entered on the right-hand side of the account.

As a business begins normal operations, three additional account types are used: revenues, expenses, and dividends. Revenues cause stockholders' equity to increase and, because increases in stockholders' equity are shown as credits, revenues also increase with credits. Alternatively, expenses and dividends cause stockholders' equity to decrease, and decreases in stockholders' equity are shown as debits. The more expenses a business has or the more dividends that a business distributes, the smaller stockholders' equity becomes. Thus, expenses and dividends increase with debits. The expanded accounting equation, incorporating all six account types follows:

$$\text{Assets} + \text{Expenses} + \text{Dividends} = \text{Liabilities} + \text{Equity} + \text{Revenue}$$

The normal balance of each account is on the side on which increases are recorded. Thus, assets, expenses, and dividends normally have debit balances; liabilities, stockholders' equity, and revenues normally have credit balances. The rules of debit and credit and for normal balances are summarized in Exhibit 3-2.

These rules are summarized graphically in Visual Recap 3.1, which employs the expanded accounting equation. Notice that for the left-side accounts, increases and normal

EXHIBIT 3-2

Rules of Debit and Credit

	Assets	Liabilities	Stockholders' Equity	Dividends	Revenues	Expenses
Increases are	Debits	Credits	Credits	Debits	Credits	Debits
Decreases are	Credits	Debits	Debits	Credits	Debits	Credits
Normal balance is	Debit	Credit	Credit	Debit	Credit	Debit

VISUAL RECAP 3.1

Remembering Debits and Credits

Left-side accounts			Right-side accounts	
Assets + Expenses + Dividends		=	Liabilities + Equity + Revenues	
debit	*credit*		*debit*	*credit*
increase (+)	decrease (-)		decrease (-)	increase (+)
normal balance				normal balance

balances are on the left side of the T-account (the debit side). For right-side accounts, debits and normal balances are on the credit, or right side of the T-account.

Using Debits and Credits

The first two transactions for Snow Mountain Retreat provide simple illustrations of debit and credit rules using the company's Cash T-account. Transaction (1) increased cash (an asset) by $40,000; thus, that amount is shown as a debit. Transaction (2) decreased cash (an asset) by $5,000; thus, that amount is shown as a credit. Since the debit amount was greater than the credit amount, there is a $35,000 debit (normal) balance in the cash account after the two transactions.

Cash	
(1) $40,000	$5,000 (2)
Balance $35,000	

A fundamental rule of double-entry bookkeeping is that debits must equal credits. (This requirement is similar to the rule that states assets must always equal liabilities plus stockholders' equity.) To prove this rule, the four accounts affected by Snow Mountain Retreat's first two transactions are presented next in T-account form. Notice that for each transaction, and in total, debits are equal to credits.

	Cash		+	Furniture		=	Notes Payable		+	Common Stock	
(1)	$40,000										$40,000
(2)		$5,000		$12,000				$7,000			
	$35,000			$12,000				$7,000			$40,000

When an account has a balance on the "wrong" side, it may need to be reclassified. For example, assume that Snow Mountain Retreat's next transaction was a purchase of kitchen equipment costing $38,000. The company inadvertently wrote a check to pay for the equipment. The $38,000 would be recorded as a credit in the Cash account, resulting in a $3,000 credit balance. In such a situation, the company would have overdrawn its checking account and would now owe the bank the $3,000, thereby creating a liability (a credit-balanced account) for Snow Mountain Retreat.

In contrast to this situation, there are a few accounts that actually have balances on the "wrong" side based on their financial statement classifications. These accounts are discussed next.

Contra-Accounts

In a few circumstances, accounts are designed to show offsets to, or reductions in, other related accounts. Such accounts are called **contra-accounts**. An example of a contra-account is Accumulated Depreciation, which was discussed briefly in Chapter 2. Accumulated Depreciation is a contra asset account because, for balance sheet purposes, its balance is subtracted from an asset account such as Equipment.

From a bookkeeping perspective, the normal account balances and bookkeeping rules for contra-accounts are exactly the reverse of those for the related type of account. For instance, contra-asset accounts have credit balances and are increased by credits and decreased by debits. Contra-liability accounts have debit balances and are increased by debits and decreased by credits. As the text continues, all contra-accounts will be distinctly noted.

THE ACCOUNTING CYCLE

Accounting is a cyclical process. When one cycle ends at the close of an operating period, another cycle begins for the next period. There are four steps to the accounting cycle.

1. Collect, examine and process transactions.
   a. Record transactions in the general journal.
   b. Post transactions to the general ledger.
   c. Prepare a trial balance.
2. Adjust account balances as necessary.
   a. Record adjustments in the general journal.
   b. Post adjustments to the general ledger.
   c. Prepare an adjusted trial balance.
3. Prepare financial statements.
   a. Income Statement
   b. Statement of Stockholders' Equity
   c. Balance Sheet
   d. Statement of Cash Flows
4. Close temporary accounts.
   a. Record closing entries in the general journal.
   b. Post closing entries to the general ledger.
   c. Prepare a post-closing trial balance.

Step 3, which was discussed in Chapters 1 and 2, is the only step that is seen by external users. Steps 1, 2, and 4, are all internal processes that are used to create and adjust the balances of financial statement accounts. Notice that steps 1, 2, and 4 all involve journal entries. Also notice that, after every recording of transactions in a journal, they are posted to the ledger and, after posting is completed, a trial balance is prepared.

Step 1: Collect, Examine, and Process Transactions

Step 1a: Record Transactions in the General Journal

The Snow Mountain Retreat example is continued through this chapter. As indicated earlier, business transactions must be analyzed to determine the accounts affected and the

EXHIBIT 3-3

The General Journal

General Journal					
Date		Description	PR	Debit	Credit

amounts of those effects. A transaction is analyzed to gather the information needed to prepare a general journal entry.

The process of journalizing a transaction relies on the rules of debit and credit. A general journal has two monetary columns: one for debit amounts and one for credit amounts. Exhibit 3-3 shows a blank general journal for Snow Mountain Retreat.

Mechanically, the following steps are required to prepare a general journal entry:

1. Enter the transaction date in the Date column of the general journal. Typically, the year and month are recorded only at the top of each general journal page.
2. Refer to the chart of accounts to identify the appropriate titles for the accounts affected by the transaction.
3. Enter the title(s) of the account or accounts to be debited in the description column on the first line of the entry. Insert the transaction amount related to this account in the debit column.
4. On the following line, indent and enter the title(s) of the account(s) to be credited. Insert the transaction amount related to this account in the credit column.
5. Write a brief explanation of the transaction in the description column below the title of the account credited.

The following transactions for Snow Mountain Retreat took place in April 2003. The two entries provided earlier in the chapter are provided again. Each entry is first analyzed as to its debit and credit effects. Next, the items are shown as they would be recorded in the general journal, using the appropriate account titles from the company's chart of accounts (Exhibit 3-4). Gaps are left in the numbering system to allow additional accounts to be inserted.

April 1 Stockholders purchased 4,000 shares of Snow Mountain Retreat's $10 par value common stock. Checks totaling $40,000 were received from stockholders.

Analysis:

- Cash, an asset account, increased by $40,000. Assets are increased with debits.
- Common Stock, a stockholders' equity account, increased by $40,000. Stockholders' equity is increased with credits.

General Journal					
Date		Description	PR	Debit	Credit
Apr	1	Cash		40,000	
		Common Stock			40,000
		Initial investment by stockholders in business			

April 1 Purchased furniture costing $12,000, paying $5,000 in cash and signing a 12% note payable for the balance. The note and interest are due in one year. The furniture is expected to have a two-year useful life with no salvage value.

Analysis:

- Furniture, an asset account, increased by $12,000. Assets are increased with debits.

EXHIBIT 3-4

Snow Mountain Retreat Chart of Accounts

Account Number	
	Assets
101	Cash
103	Accounts Receivable
120	Supplies
125	Prepaid Rent
150	Furniture
151	Accumulated Depreciation—Furniture
	Liabilities
201	Notes Payable
203	Accounts Payable
206	Wages Payable
210	Interest Payable
225	Unearned Rental Revenue
280	Income Tax Payable
	Stockholders' Equity
305	Common Stock
350	Retained Earnings
	Dividends
405	Dividends
	Revenues
510	Rental Revenue
	Expenses
603	Wages Expense
605	Rent Expense
607	Supplies Expense
609	Utilities Expense
650	Depreciation Expense
670	Interest Expense
680	Income Tax Expense
700	*Income Summary (discussed later in the chapter)*

- Cash, an asset account, decreased by $5,000. Assets are decreased with credits.
- Notes Payable, a liability account, increased by $7,000. Liabilities are increased with credits.

General Journal

Date		Description	PR	Debit	Credit
Apr.	1	Furniture		12,000	
		Cash			5,000
		Notes Payable			7,000
		Purchase of furniture with a cash downpayment and by signing a note payable			

This type of entry is known as a **compound journal entry** because it affects more than two accounts. Compound journal entries may have several debits and one credit, several credits and a single debit, or multiple debits and multiple credits. Like all journal entries, the dollar amount of debits and the dollar amount of credits in a compound journal entry must be equal.

April 1 Signed a one-year lease on a large, partially furnished house in Castle Rock, Colorado, to be operated as a bed and breakfast establishment. Rent of $18,000 for one year was paid by check.

Analysis:

- Prepaid Rent, an asset account, increased by $18,000. Assets are increased with debits. This amount is an asset because Snow Mountain Retreat has the right to use the house for the next 12 months or to have its lease payment returned.
- Cash, an asset account, decreased by $18,000. Assets are decreased with credits.

General Journal					
Date		Description	PR	Debit	Credit
Apr.	1	Prepaid Rent		18,000	
		Cash			18,000
		Signed a 12-month lease for the B&B and paid cash for the rental			

April 3 Purchased $500 of supplies on credit.

Analysis:

- Supplies, an asset account, increased by $500. Assets are increased with debits.
- Accounts Payable, a liability account, increased by $500. Liabilities are increased with credits.

General Journal					
Date		Description	PR	Debit	Credit
Apr.	3	Supplies		500	
		Accounts Payable			500
		Bought supplies on account			

April 8 Received $5,000 for two one-week rentals: April 22–28 and May 20–26. This payment is fully refundable if the reservations are canceled. Revenue received before it is earned is recorded in a liability account. In this case, an appropriate title for such a liability account is Unearned Rental Revenue.

Analysis:

- Cash, an asset account, increased by $5,000. Assets are increased with debits.
- Unearned Rent Revenue, a liability account, increased by $5,000. Liabilities are increased with credits.

General Journal					
Date		Description	PR	Debit	Credit
Apr.	8	Cash		5,000	
		Unearned Rental Revenue			5,000
		Received payment for two weeks, one in April and one in May			

As discussed in Chapter 2, when customers pay for products or services before receiving them, the company has incurred liability—in this case, Unearned Rental Revenue. Thus,

Snow Mountain Retreat owes the customers one of two things: occupancy of the rooms for the specified weeks or the return of the $5,000 cash.

April 19 Rented four rooms for the weekend for $1,500 cash.

Analysis:

- Cash, an asset account, increased by $1,500. Assets are increased with debits.
- Rental Revenue, a revenue account, increased by $1,500. Revenues are increased with credits.

General Journal					
Date		**Description**	**PR**	**Debit**	**Credit**
Apr.	19	Cash		1,500	
		Rental Revenue			1,500
		Earned revenue from room rentals			

April 24 Rented two rooms for one week for $3,250 cash.

Analysis:

- Cash, an asset account, increased by $3,250. Assets are increased with debits.
- Rental Revenue, a revenue account, increased by $3,250. Revenues are increased with credits.

General Journal					
Date		**Description**	**PR**	**Debit**	**Credit**
Apr.	24	Cash		3,250	
		Rental Revenue			3,250
		Earned revenue from room rentals			

April 26 A part-time maintenance person began working on April 8. He was paid $800 for two-weeks' wages: April 8–19.

Analysis:

- Wages Expense, an expense account, increased by $800. Expenses are increased with debits.
- Cash, an asset account, decreased by $800. Assets are decreased with credits.

General Journal					
Date		**Description**	**PR**	**Debit**	**Credit**
Apr.	26	Wage Expense		800	
		Cash			800
		Paid maintenance worker wages for two weeks			

April 26 Rented two rooms for weekend for $750 to be paid by May 15. Even though the cash has not yet been received, Snow Mountain has earned the rental revenue because the resort provided the rooms.

Analysis:

- Accounts Receivable, an asset account, increased by $750. Assets are increased with debits.

- Rental Revenue, a revenue account, increased by $750. Revenues are increased with credits.

General Journal					
Date		Description	PR	Debit	Credit
Apr.	26	Accounts Receivable		750	
		Rental Revenue			750
		Earned revenue from room rentals			

April 30 Paid $250 of the $500 owed on account for the supplies purchased on April 3. Snow Mountain is paying for the supplies purchased on April 3. No new supplies are acquired on April 30; therefore, the Supplies account is not affected.

Analysis:

- Accounts Payable, a liability account, decreased by $250. Liabilities are decreased with debits.
- Cash, an asset account, decreased by $250. Assets are decreased with credits.

General Journal					
Date		Description	PR	Debit	Credit
Apr.	30	Accounts Payable		250	
		Cash			250
		Paid an account payable			

April 30 Received and paid the $390 electricity bill for April.

Analysis:

- Utilities Expense, an expense account, increased by $390. Expenses are increased with debits.
- Cash, an asset account, decreased by $390. Assets are decreased with credits.

General Journal					
Date		Description	PR	Debit	Credit
Apr.	30	Utilities Expense		390	
		Cash			390
		Paid the utility bill for April			

April 30 Stockholders declared and paid themselves a dividend of $500.

Analysis:

- Dividends, a dividend account, increased by $500. Dividends are increased with debits.
- Cash, an asset account, decreased by $500. Assets are decreased with credits.

General Journal					
Date		Description	PR	Debit	Credit
Apr.	30	Dividends		500	
		Cash			500
		Paid dividends to company stockholders			

Remember that, although a dividend account has the same debit and credit rules as an expense, dividends paid by a corporation to its stockholders are *not* expenses. Whereas expenses will decrease net income, dividends have no impact on net income and only affect the amount of a corporation's Retained Earnings.

Step 1b: Post Transactions to the General Ledger

After a transaction has been journalized, the information is then posted (again using the debit and credit rules) to accounts in the general ledger. Each account in the ledger has three monetary columns: one for debits; one for credits; and one for the account balance. Other information is also recorded in the general ledger as will be discussed later. A blank general ledger is shown in Exhibit 3-5.

1. For each account listed in a general journal transaction, determine the appropriate general ledger account number in the chart of accounts. Find that account in the general ledger.
2. In the general ledger account, record the transaction date and brief description of the transaction as provided in the general journal.
3. In the posting reference column of each affected account, indicate the journal and page number from which the amount was posted. In this example, "GJ1" is inserted in the post reference (PR) column to indicate that each amount was posted from page 1 of the general journal.
4. Enter the transaction amount in the appropriate debit or credit column in the account.
5. Compute the new balance of each account and enter that amount in the balance column.
6. After posting each element of the transaction to the general ledger, return to the general journal and record the general ledger account number to which the debit or credit amount was posted in the posting reference column.

Posting financial data from the general journal to the general ledger summarizes the data by specific account. Journal entry data may be posted daily, weekly, or even monthly in a manual accounting system. In computer-based accounting systems, transaction data are typically posted to general ledger accounts simultaneously with the journalizing process. As transaction data are keyed into a computerized accounting system by a data entry clerk or captured electronically by the system, a chronological record (journal entry) of the transaction is prepared. At the same time, the dollar amounts involved in the transaction are electronically routed (posted) to the computer files (accounts) of the financial statement items affected by the transaction. Programming instructions automatically indicate whether the computer should debit or credit the dollar amounts to the individual accounts to correctly update their balances.

EXHIBIT 3-5

General Ledger

Account Name						Account No.
Date		Explanation	PR	Debit	Credit	Balance

Exhibits 3-6 and 3-7 show, respectively, the completed general journal and general ledger accounts for the above April transactions for Snow Mountain Retreat. Note that the PR column in the general journal indicates where the information was posted; in the general ledger, this column is indicates where the information came from.

Step 1c: Prepare a Trial Balance

The **trial balance** is a two-column (one debit and one credit) listing of general ledger account balances. Each general ledger account that has a monetary balance is listed in order, with that balance being appropriately entered in either the debit or credit column of the trial balance. The primary purpose of a trial balance is to determine that the accounting system is "in balance," in that the total debits and total credits entered in the general ledger accounts during the period are equal.

If a trial balance does not balance, there are one or more errors in the accounting records. Those errors must be found and corrected before the accounting cycle can continue. Unfortunately, even if a trial balance has equal debits and credits, there may be errors in the accounting records. For example, if the debits and credits of a journal entry were posted to incorrect accounts, the debit and credit columns of the trial balance would be equal even though at least two of the accounts would be incorrect. Exhibit 3-8 (see page 62) is the trial balance for Snow Mountain Retreat.

Step 2: Adjust Account Balances as Necessary

As previously discussed, there are two principal methods of accounting: cash basis and accrual basis. Under the cash basis of accounting, businesses generally record transactions *only* if they involve the payment or receipt of cash. Under the accrual basis of accounting, the economic impact of a transaction is recorded *whether or not* the transaction involves cash. Most business entities use the accrual basis of accounting since it better represents the economic reality of their operations and financial condition.

When the accrual basis of accounting is used, a special category of journal entries is needed at the end of an accounting period: adjusting entries. **Adjusting entries** are prepared to ensure that the revenue and expense recognition rules, discussed in Chapter 2, are properly applied each accounting period and that revenues and expenses have been appropriately recorded in the accounting period to which they relate. For example, adjusting entries are required to recognize expenses that a business has incurred, but has not yet paid or recorded, at the end of an accounting period.

Step 2a. Record Adjustments in the General Journal

The specific circumstances that require adjustments to a business's general ledger account balances at the end of each accounting period must be identified. This identification process occurs through talking to management, scanning accounting records, reviewing prior periods' adjusting entries, and, most importantly, using intuition and accounting expertise. Computerized accounting systems may automatically scan the accounting records and produce a tentative list of adjusting journal entries. However, such a list will need to be reviewed for completeness.

Deferrals and Accruals Before developing period-ending adjustments, the concepts of deferrals and accruals must first be defined and illustrated. As shown in Visual Recap 3.2 (see page 63), a deferred item is one for which the cash has been paid or received, but the expense or revenue has not yet been recognized. An accrued item is one for which the cash

EXHIBIT 3-6

Snow Mountain Retreat General Journal

General Journal

Date		Description	PR	Debit	Credit
Apr.	1	Cash	101	40,000	
		Common Stock	305		40,000
		Initial investment by stockholders in business			
	1	Furniture	150	12,000	
		Cash	101		5,000
		Notes Payable	201		7,000
		Purchase of furniture with cash downpayment and by signing a note payable			
	3	Prepaid Rent	125	18,000	
		Cash	101		18,000
		Signed a 12-month lease for the B&B and paid cash for the rental			
	3	Supplies	120	500	
		Accounts Payable	203		500
		Bought supplies on account			
	8	Cash	101	5,000	
		Unearned Rental Revenue	225		5,000
		Earned revenue from room rentals			
	19	Cash	101	1,500	
		Rental Revenue	510		1,500
		Earned revenue from room rentals			
	24	Cash	101	3,250	
		Rental Revenue	510		3,250
		Earned revenue from room rentals			
	26	Wage Expense	603	800	
		Cash	101		800
		Paid maintenance worker wages for two weeks			
	26	Accounts Receivable	103	750	
		Rental Revenue	510		750
		Earned revenue from room rentals			
	30	Accounts Payable	103	250	
		Cash	510		250
		Paid an account payable			
	30	Utilities Expense	609	390	
		Cash	101		390
		Paid the utility bill for April			
	30	Dividends	400	500	
		Cash	101		500
		Paid dividends to company stockholders			

EXHIBIT 3-7

Snow Mountain Retreat General Ledger (1 of 2)

Cash — Account No. 101

Date		Explanation	PR	Debit	Credit	Debit Balance
Apr.	1	Sold stock	GJ1	40,000		40,000
	1	Made furniture downpayment	GJ1		5,000	35,000
	1	Prepaid 12-month lease	GJ1		18,000	17,000
	8	Received rent in advance	GJ1	5,000		22,000
	19	Earned rental revenue	GJ1	1,500		23,500
	24	Earned rental revenue	GJ1	3,250		26,750
	26	Paid maintenance wages	GJ1		800	25,950
	30	Paid account payable	GJ1		250	25,700
	30	Paid utilities	GJ1		390	25,310
	30	Paid divided	GJ1		500	24,810

Accounts Receivable — Account No. 103

Date		Explanation	PR	Debit	Credit	Debit Balance
Apr.	26	Rental	GJ1	750		750

Supplies — Account No. 102

Date		Explanation	PR	Debit	Credit	Debit Balance
Apr.	3	Bought supplies	GJ1	500		500

Prepaid Rent — Account No. 125

Date		Explanation	PR	Debit	Credit	Debit Balance
Apr.	1	Prepaid 1-year lease	GJ1	18,000		18,000

Furniture — Account No. 150

Date		Explanation	PR	Debit	Credit	Debit Balance
Apr.	26	Bought furniture	GJ1	12,000		12,000

Notes Payable — Account No. 201

Date		Explanation	PR	Debit	Credit	Credit Balance
Apr.	1	Issued 12%, 1-year note	GJ1		7,000	7,000

Accounts Payable — Account No. 203

Date		Explanation	PR	Debit	Credit	Credit Balance
Apr.	3	Bought supplies	GJ1		500	500
	30	Paid accounts payable	GJ1	250		250

Unearned Rental Revenue — Account No. 225

Date		Explanation	PR	Debit	Credit	Credit Balance
Apr.	8	Received rent in advace	GJ1		5,000	5,000

EXHIBIT 3-7
Snow Mountain Retreat General Ledger (2 of 2)

Common Stock — Account No. 305

Date		Explanation	PR	Debit	Credit	Credit Balance
Apr.	1	Issued stock	GJ1		40,000	40,000

Dividends — Account No. 400

Date		Explanation	PR	Debit	Credit	Debit Balance
Apr.	30	Declared a cash dividend	GJ1	500		500

Rental Revenue — Account No. 510

Date		Explanation	PR	Debit	Credit	Credit Balance
Apr.	19	Earned revenue	GJ1		1,500	1,500
	24	Earned revenue	GJ1		3,250	4,750
	26	Earned revenue	GJ1		750	5,500

Wages Expense — Account No. 603

Date		Explanation	PR	Debit	Credit	Debit Balance
Apr.	26	Maintenance wages 4/8–4/19	GJ1	800		800

Utility Expense — Account No. 609

Date		Explanation	PR	Debit	Credit	Debit Balance
Apr.	30	April electricity	GJ1	390		390

EXHIBIT 3-8
Snow Mountain Retreat Trial Balance

Snow Mountain Retreat
Trial Balance
April 30, 2003

	Debit	Credit
Cash	$24,810	
Accounts Receivable	750	
Supplies	500	
Prepaid Rent	18,000	
Furniture	12,000	
Notes Payable		$ 7,000
Accounts Payable		250
Unearned Rental Revenue		5,000
Common Stock		40,000
Dividends	500	
Rental Revenue		5,500
Wage Expense	800	
Utilities Expense	390	
Totals	$57,750	$57,750

VISUAL RECAP 3.2

Deferrals and Accruals

DEFERRAL	ACCRUAL
Cash	
EXPENSE REVENUE	REVENUE EXPENSE

has not yet been paid or received, but the expense or revenue has already been recognized. End-of-period adjusting entries may create or affect deferred and accrued items.

A **deferred expense** is an asset that represents a prepayment of an expense item. When an expense is prepaid, an asset account is debited and the Cash account credited. For example, when Snow Mountain Retreat prepaid its $18,000 one-year lease amount on April 1, the company debited Prepaid Rent, an asset account, and credited Cash. Over the lease term, the economic benefit provided by the asset (prepayment) will be gradually used up. As a result, by the end of the one-year lease term, the full amount of the rent prepayment will be debited to Rent Expense and credited to Prepaid Rent. Thus, a deferred expense is originally recorded as an asset, but will eventually be recognized, or written off, as an expense.

A **deferred revenue** is a liability that represents an amount received by a business for a service or product that will be provided or delivered in the future. The Unearned Rental Revenue account of Snow Mountain Retreat is a deferred revenue account. Upon receiving the funds, Snow Mountain Retreat owes its customers either the room that was paid for in advance or a refund. When the customers occupy the rooms, the earnings process is completed and the deferred revenue will be debited with an offsetting credit to a revenue account.

An **accrued asset** is a receivable resulting from revenue that has been earned but has not yet been received. An account receivable is the most common accrued asset. Another type of accrued asset is interest that has not yet been received on an amount loaned to a customer or another party.

A liability for an expense that has been incurred but has not yet been paid is called an **accrued liability.** A common accrued liability is salaries or wages payable. Typically, the end of a business's accounting period does not coincide with the end of a payroll period. Thus, at the end of most accounting periods, a business's employees have earned, but not been paid, some amount of salaries or wages. These amounts are recognized by debiting an expense account, such as Wages Expense, and crediting a liability account, such as Wages Payable.

Deferrals and accruals and their adjusting entries are summarized in Visual Recap 3.3. The XXX's in the graphic indicate a type of asset or liability account title. For example, if cash were paid in advance for insurance, the account titles to be used would be Prepaid

VISUAL RECAP 3.3

Adjusting Deferrals and Accruals

Deferred

Deferred Expense (Asset)

Cash is paid to vendor before service is received

- The cash is paid and an asset is established.

Prepaid XXX	$18,000	
Cash		$18,000
Prepaid one year's XXX		

- The expense is recorded when the asset is used up.

XXX Expense	$1,500	
Prepaid XXX		$1,500
Used one month of prepaid XXX		

Deferred Revenue (Liability)

Cash is received before service is provided to customers

- The cash is received and a liability is recorded.

Cash	$5,000	
Unearned XXX revenue		$5,000
Customer paid advance		

- The revenue is recorded when the liability is eliminated.

Unearned XXX Revenue	$2,500	
XXX Revenue		$2,500
Earned half of customer advance		

Accrued

Accrued Liability (Expense)

Service is received from vendor before cash is paid

- The service is received and payable is recorded.

XXX Expense	$700	
Accounts Payable		$700
Received XXX bill		

- The payable is eliminated when the cash is paid.

Accounts Payable	$700	
Cash		$700
Paid accounts payable		

Accrued Asset (Revenue)

Service is provided before cash is received

- The service is rendered and a receivable is recorded.

Accounts Receivable	$2,000	
XXX Revenue		$2,000
Billed customer for service		

- The receivable is eliminated when the cash is received.

Cash	$2,000	
Accounts Receivable		$2,000
Customer paid on account		

Insurance and Insurance Expense. Or if cash were received in advance for rent on a building, the account titles to be used would be Unearned Rent Revenue and Rent Revenue

Adjusting Journal Entries for Snow Mountain Retreat Following are seven circumstances requiring adjustments to Snow Mountain Retreat's general ledger account balances as of April 30, 2002. An analysis of each adjustment is provided.

Adjustment A: Expiration of Prepaid Rent On April 1, 2002, Snow Mountain Retreat prepaid one year's rent on the house to be used for the bed and breakfast. By the end of April, one-twelfth of this deferred expense had been used. The decrease in this asset should be recognized as an expense so that the company's assets are not overstated and expenses are not understated.

Analysis:

- Rent Expense, an expense account, increased by $1,500 ($18,000 ÷ 12). Expenses are increased with debits.
- Prepaid Rent, an asset account, decreased by $1,500. Assets are decreased with credits.

Adjustment B: Depreciation of Furniture On April 1, 2002, furniture was purchased for the B&B. This asset must be systematically depreciated over the accounting periods during which the furniture provides an economic benefit to the business. Snow Mountain Retreat uses the straight-line method of depreciation. Under this method, the asset's cost less any estimated salvage value at the end of the asset's useful life is written off in equal amounts over that useful life.

Because Snow Mountain Retreat's furniture has a zero salvage value at the end of its two-year life, the depreciation expense for the furniture is computed as $12,000 divided by 24 months or $500 per month. The decrease in this asset should be recognized as an expense so that the company's assets are not overstated and expenses are not understated.

Analysis:

- Depreciation Expense, an expense account, increased by $500. Expenses are increased with debits.
- Accumulated Depreciation, a contra-asset account, increased by $500. Contra-assets are increased with credits. By using the Accumulated Depreciation account to show the total amount of depreciation taken on the asset, the $12,000 historical cost of the furniture is preserved in the general ledger asset account.

Adjustment C: Recognition of Interest Expense on Note Payable By signing the $7,000 note payable on April 1, Snow Mountain Retreat promised to pay the seller of the furniture that amount plus interest at 12 percent in one year. However, even though the note principal and interest are not paid until April 1, 2003, Snow Mountain Retreat incurs interest expense for each day that the note is not paid. Thus, at the end of April, the company owes, but has not paid, one month's interest expense. The calculation of the amount of interest owed is:

$$\text{Interest} = \text{Principal} \times \text{Rate} \times \text{Time}$$

In this case, the principal is the $7,000 original amount of the note; the rate is 12 percent per year; and the time is one month.[1] Snow Mountain Retreat's interest expense for April is $(7{,}000 \times 0.12 \times 1/12)$ or $70. This expense should be recognized so that the company's expenses and liabilities are not understated.

Analysis:

- Interest Expense, an expense account, increased by $70. Expenses are increased with debits.
- Interest Payable, a liability account, increased by $70. Liabilities are increased with credits.

Adjustment D: Supplies Used At the end of April 2002, $420 of supplies remained of the $500 of supplies purchased earlier in the month. Thus, $80 of supplies had been used during April. The decrease in this asset should be recognized as an expense so that the company's assets are not overstated and expenses are not understated.

Analysis:

- Supplies Expense, an expense account, increased by $80. Expenses are increased with debits.
- Supplies, an asset account, decreased by $80. Assets are decreased with credits.

Adjustment E: Recognition of Revenue on Advance Rental Payment On April 8, 2002, an individual paid $5,000 to Snow Mountain Retreat for two rentals during the weeks of April

[1] Interest rates are always stated on an annual basis unless otherwise indicated. Therefore, fractions representing the passage of time should always represent a portion of a year. For example, 5 months would be shown as 5/12.

22–28 and May 20–26. When this amount was received, Unearned Rental Revenue (a deferred liability) was recorded. By the end of April, the customer had used her reservation for the week of April 22–28 and, thus, Snow Mountain Retreat had earned $2,500 (one-half of the $5,000 advance payment). The decrease in this liability should be recognized as revenue so that the company's liabilities are not overstated and revenues are not understated.

Analysis:

- Unearned Rental Revenue, a liability account, decreased by $2,500. Liabilities are decreased with debits.
- Rental Revenue, a revenue account, increased by $2,500. Revenues are increased with credits.

Adjustment F: Recognition of Unpaid Salary Expense Snow Mountain Retreat's part-time maintenance employee earns $800 every two weeks or $40 per day for Monday through Friday. (Payroll taxes and other deductions that affect the employee's take home pay are ignored at this point.) Payroll dates are one week after the end of the payroll period. Having started work on April 8, the employee received his first paycheck on April 26 and was scheduled to receive his second paycheck on May 3. As of April 30, the employee had worked seven days (4/22–26 and 4/29–30) for which he had not been paid. Thus, Snow Mountain Retreat owed wages of $280 to the maintenance man at the end of April. This expense should be recognized so that the company's expenses and liabilities are not understated.

Analysis:

- Wages Expense, an expense account, increased by $280. Expenses are increased with debits.
- Wages Payable, a liability account, increased by $280. Liabilities are increased with credits.

Adjustment G: Recognition of Estimated Income Tax Expense At the end of each year, Snow Mountain Retreat will be required to pay a corporate income tax on any earned profits. On April 30, 2002, Snow Mountain Retreat did not know how much would be earned for the year and, therefore, could not determine an exact amount of income tax that would need to be paid. Nevertheless, a business must estimate its income tax expense each accounting period because of the matching aspect of the expense recognition rule. After reviewing the tax rate schedule, Snow Mountain Retreat recorded a $200 accrued liability as an estimate of the corporate income tax would eventually be paid on the profit earned during April. This expense should be recognized so that the company's expenses and liabilities are not understated.

Analysis:

- Income Tax Expense, an expense account, increased by $200. Expenses are increased with debits.
- Income Tax Payable, a liability account, increased by $200. Liabilities are increased with credits.

These adjusting entries are journalized in the General Journal as shown in Exhibit 3-9.

Step 2b: Post Adjustments to the General Ledger

The journal entries from Exhibit 3-9 are posted to the general ledger (Exhibit 3-10). Notice that the balances in many of the accounts previously shown in Exhibit 3-7 have not changed in Exhibit 3-10; however, some additional accounts have been added.

EXHIBIT 3-9

Snow Mountain Retreat General Journal—Adjusting Entries

General Journal					
Date		**Description**	**PR**	**Debit**	**Credit**
Apr.	30	Rent Expense	605	1,500	
		Prepaid Rent	305		1,500
		One month of prepaid rent expired			
	30	Depreciation Expense	605	500	
		Accumulated Depreciation—Furniture	151		500
		Recorded one-month depreciation on furniture			
	30	Interest Expense	670	70	
		Interest Payable	210		70
		Recorded one month's interest on the note payable			
	30	Supplies Expense	607	80	
		Supplies	120		80
		Recorded supplies used in April			
	30	Unearned Rental Revenue	225	2,500	
		Rental Revenue	510		2,500
		Recorded the earning of revenue for the week of April 22–28			
	30	Wages Expense	603	280	
		Wages Payable	206		280
		Recorded maintenance worker wages for seven days			
	30	Income Tax Expense	680	200	
		Income Tax Payable	280		200
		Recorded estimated income taxes for April			

EXHIBIT 3-10

Snow Mountain Retreat General Ledger After Adjusting Entries (1 of 4)

Cash						**Account No. 101**
Date		**Explanation**	**PR**	**Debit**	**Credit**	**Debit Balance**
Apr.	1	Sold stock	GJ1	40,000		40,000
	1	Made furniture downpayment	GJ1		5,000	35,000
	1	Prepaid 12-month lease	GJ1		18,000	17,000
	8	Received rent in advance	GJ1	5,000		22,000
	19	Earned rental revenue	GJ1	1,500		23,500
	24	Earned rental revenue	GJ1	3,250		26,750
	26	Paid maintenance wages	GJ1		800	25,950
	30	Paid account payable	GJ1		250	24,700
	30	Paid utilities	GJ1		390	25,310
	30	Paid dividend	GJ1		500	24,810

EXHIBIT 3-10

Snow Mountain Retreat General Ledger After Adjusting Entries (2 of 4)

Accounts Receivable — Account No. 103

Date		Explanation	PR	Debit	Credit	Debit Balance
Apr.	26	Rental	GJ1	750		750

Supplies — Account No. 102

Date		Explanation	PR	Debit	Credit	Debit Balance
Apr.	3	Bought supplies	GJ1	500		500
	30	Used supplies in April	GJ2		80	420

Prepaid Rent — Account No. 125

Date		Explanation	PR	Debit	Credit	Debit Balance
Apr.	1	Prepaid 1-year lease	GJ1	18,000		18,000
	30	One month expired	GJ2		1,500	16,500

Furniture — Account No. 150

Date		Explanation	PR	Debit	Credit	Debit Balance
Apr.	1	Bought furniture	GJ1	12,000		12,000

Accumulated Depreciation—Furniture — Account No. 151

Date		Explanation	PR	Debit	Credit	Credit Balance
Apr.	30	Recorded 1 month's depreciation	GJ2		500	500

Notes Payable — Account No. 201

Date		Explanation	PR	Debit	Credit	Credit Balance
Apr.	1	Issued 12% 1-year note	GJ1		7,000	7,000

Accounts Payable — Account No. 203

Date		Explanation	PR	Debit	Credit	Credit Balance
Apr.	3	Bought supplies	GJ1		500	500
	30	Paid accounts payable	GJ1	250		250

Wages Payable — Account No. 206

Date		Explanation	PR	Debit	Credit	Credit Balance
Apr.	30	Owe 7 days wages	GJ1		280	280

Interest Payable — Account No. 210

Date		Explanation	PR	Debit	Credit	Credit Balance
Apr.	30	Owe one month interest on note	GJ2		70	70

EXHIBIT 3-10

Snow Mountain Retreat General Ledger After Adjusting Entries (3 of 4)

Unearned Rental Revenue						Account No. 225
Date		**Explanation**	**PR**	**Debit**	**Credit**	**Credit Balance**
Apr.	8	Received rent in advance	GJ1		5,000	5,000
	30	Earned one week rental revenue	GJ2	2,500		2,500

Income Tax Payable						Account No. 280
Date		**Explanation**	**PR**	**Debit**	**Credit**	**Credit Balance**
Apr.	30	Estimate for April	GJ2		200	200

Common Stock						Account No. 305
Date		**Explanation**	**PR**	**Debit**	**Credit**	**Credit Balance**
Apr.	1	Issued stock	GJ1		40,000	40,000

Dividends						Account No. 400
Date		**Explanation**	**PR**	**Debit**	**Credit**	**Debit Balance**
Apr.	30	Declared a cash dividend	GJ1	500		500

Rental Revenue						Account No. 510
Date		**Explanation**	**PR**	**Debit**	**Credit**	**Credit Balance**
Apr.	19	Earned revenue	GJ1		1,500	1,500
	24	Earned revenue	GJ1		3,250	4,750
	26	Earned revenue	GJ1		750	5,500
	30	Earned revenue	GJ2		2,500	8,000

Wages Expense						Account No. 603
Date		**Explanation**	**PR**	**Debit**	**Credit**	**Debit Balance**
Apr.	26	Maintenance wages 4/8–4/19	GJ1	800		800
	30	Maintenance wages for 7 days	GJ2	280		1,080

Rent Expense						Account No. 605
Date		**Explanation**	**PR**	**Debit**	**Credit**	**Debit Balance**
Apr.	30	For April	GJ2	1,500		1,500

Supplies Expense						Account No. 607
Date		**Explanation**	**PR**	**Debit**	**Credit**	**Debit Balance**
Apr.	30	For April	GJ2	80		80

Utility Expense						Account No. 609
Date		**Explanation**	**PR**	**Debit**	**Credit**	**Debit Balance**
Apr.	30	April electricity	GJ1	390		390

EXHIBIT 3-10
Snow Mountain Retreat General Ledger After Adjusting Entries (4 of 4)

Depreciation Expense					Account No. 650	
Date		Explanation	PR	Debit	Credit	Debit Balance
Apr.	30	For April on furniture	GJ2	500		500

Interest Expense					Account No. 670	
Date		Explanation	PR	Debit	Credit	Debit Balance
Apr.	30	For April on note	GJ2	70		70

Income Tax Expense					Account No. 680	
Date		Explanation	PR	Debit	Credit	Debit Balance
Apr.	30	Estimate for April	GJ2	200		200

Step 2c: Prepare an Adjusted Trial Balance

Exhibit 3-11 presents the adjusted trial balance for Snow Mountain Retreat as of April 30, 2002. The account balances listed in the trial balance were taken from the general ledger accounts shown in Exhibit 3-10. Only general ledger accounts that have nonzero balances are included in a trial balance. The debits and credits in the trial balance are summed and found to be equal. Thus, the next step of the accounting cycle, preparing the financial statements, can be performed.

Step 3: Prepare Financial Statements

After debits and credits of the adjusted trial balance are determined to be in balance, the company's financial statements can be prepared. Using the information from accounts listed in the adjusted trial balance, Snow Mountain Retreat's income statement (Exhibit 3-12), statement of stockholders' equity (Exhibit 3-13), and balance sheet (Exhibit 3-14) are developed.

Snow Mountain Retreat's statement of stockholders' equity at the end of April 2002 reconciles the beginning and end-of-period balances of the corporation's stockholders' equity accounts. Three items must be considered when computing a company's period-ending retained earnings: beginning balance, net income for the period, and dividends declared during the period.

Note that Snow Mountain Retreat's Retained Earnings account is *not* included in the firm's adjusted trial balance prepared on April 30, 2002, there was no balance in that account when the trial balance was prepared because the company began operations on April 1, 2002. However, all of the information needed to compute the firm's Retained Earnings as of April 30, 2002 is available in the adjusted trial balance. The April 30, 2002 Retained Earnings balance is computed by subtracting the $500 of dividends for April from the April net income of $4,180. In May 2002, the $3,680 will be included in the trial balance as the beginning balance of Retained Earnings.

In most computerized accounting systems, a set of financial statements can be generated electronically after adjusting the general ledger accounts. In fact, many large public companies both prepare their financial statements electronically and deliver them electronically to external users via the Internet. The EDGAR (Electronic Data Gathering, Analysis, and Retrieval) system Internet Web site (www.sec.gov/edgarhp.htm) maintained by the Securities and Exchange Commission provides investors and other interested parties timely access to hundreds of large companies' financial statements in an electronic format.

EXHIBIT 3-11

Snow Mountain Retreat Trial Balance

Snow Mountain Retreat
Trial Balance
April 30, 2002

	Debit	Credit
Cash	$24,810	
Accounts Receivable	750	
Supplies	420	
Prepaid Rent	16,500	
Furniture	12,000	
Accumulated Depreciation—Furniture		$ 500
Notes Payable		7,000
Accounts Payable		250
Wages Payable		280
Interest Payable		70
Unearned Rental Revenue		2,500
Income Tax Payable		200
Common Stock		40,000
Dividends	500	
Rental Revenue		8,000
Wages Expense	1,080	
Rent Expense	1,500	
Supplies Expense	80	
Utilities Expense	390	
Depreciation Expense	500	
Interest Expense	70	
Income Tax Expense	200	
Totals	$58,800	$58,800

EXHIBIT 3-12

Snow Mountain Retreat Income Statement

Snow Mountain Retreat
Income Statement
For Month Ended April 30, 2002

Rental Revenue		$ 8,000
Operating Expenses		
Wages	$ 1,080	
Rent	1,500	
Supplies	80	
Utilities	390	
Depreciation	500	(3,550)
Operating Income		$ 4,450
Other Revenues and Expenses		
Interest Expense		(70)
Income Before Income Taxes		$ 4,380
Income Tax Expense		(200)
Net Income		$ 4,180
Earnings Per Share (4,000 shares; rounded)		$ 1.05

EXHIBIT 3-13
Snow Mountain Retreat Statement of Stockholders' Equity

Snow Mountain Retreat
Statement of Stockholders' Equity
For the Month Ended April 30, 2002

	Common Stock	Retained Earnings
Balance, April 1, 2002	$ 0	$ 0
Sale of Common Stock	40,000	
Net Income		4,180
Dividends		(500)
Balance, April 30, 2002	$40,000	$3,680

EXHIBIT 3-14
Snow Mountain Retreat Balance Sheet

Snow Mountain Retreat
Balance Sheet
April 30, 2002

ASSETS		
Current Assets		
Cash		$24,810
Accounts Receivable		750
Supplies		420
Prepaid Rent		16,500
Total Current Assets		$42,480
Property, Plant and Equipment		
Furniture	$12,000	
Accumulated Depreciation	(500)	11,500
Total Assets		$53,980
LIABILITIES		
Current Liabilities		
Notes Payable		$ 7,000
Accounts Payable		250
Wages Payable		280
Interest Payable		70
Unearned Rental Revenue		2,500
Income Tax Payable		200
Total Current Liabilities		$10,300
STOCKHOLDERS' EQUITY		
Common Stock (4,000 shares; $10 par value)	$40,000	
Retained Earnings	3,680	43,680
Total Liabilities and Stockholders' Equity		$53,980

Step 4: Close Temporary Accounts

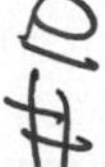

At the end of a period, a business will "close" its books so that it can start the new period with a "clean slate." Normally the closing process only takes place at the end of the company's fiscal year but, for illustrative purposes, it is assumed that Snow Mountain Retreat closes its books at the end of each month. Before discussing the closing process, the concept of permanent and temporary accounts must be addressed.

Every company's chart of accounts contains permanent and temporary accounts. Balance sheet accounts (assets, liabilities, and stockholders' equity) are called **permanent accounts** because their period-ending balances are carried forward to the next accounting period. Alternately, revenue, expense, and dividend accounts are referred to as **temporary accounts** because they begin each new accounting period with a zero balance. These temporary accounts all affect the balance of one permanent account: Retained Earnings.

Retained Earnings is a key stockholders' equity account because, at any time, the balance of this account represents the sum of all a corporation's net income (revenues minus expenses) since its inception minus all dividends distributed to the firm's stockholders. The dollar amounts associated with revenue, expense, and dividend transactions are stored in temporary accounts during an accounting period and are transferred to Retained Earnings at the end of a period with closing entries.

Step 4a: Record Closing Entries in the General Journal

The temporary accounts of a business can begin each accounting period with a zero balance because the balances of these accounts are transferred using **closing entries** to Retained Earnings. An account called Income Summary is often used to help close temporary accounts each accounting period. The Income Summary account is used to channel the balances of all temporary accounts into the Retained Earnings account through closing entries. The Income Summary account is also a temporary account.

Following are the four closing entries that businesses make at the end of an accounting period:

1. Transfer credit balances of income statement accounts to the Income Summary account.
2. Transfer debit balances of income statement accounts to the Income Summary account.
3. Transfer the balance of the Income Summary account to the Retained Earnings account.
4. Transfer the balance of the Dividends account to the Retained Earnings account.

The closing entry rules are depicted in Visual Recap 3.4.

Exhibit 3-15 presents the closing entries for Snow Mountain Retreat at April 30, 2002. The first entry closes the Rental Revenue account by bringing that account balance to zero and creating a credit-balanced Income Summary account. The second entry closes the debit-balanced expense accounts on the income statement. Following the posting of that entry, each of Snow Mountain Retreat's expense accounts will have a zero balance and the Income Summary account will have a credit balance of $4,180. This amount equals the company's net income for April. By transferring the period-ending balances of all revenue and expense accounts to Income Summary, a business can confirm that the proper net income amount was calculated on the Income Statement. The third entry closes the Income Summary account by transferring its balance to Retained Earnings.

The final closing entry for Snow Mountain Retreat transfers the balance of the Dividends account to Retained Earnings. If no dividends have been paid to stockholders during a period, this entry will not be necessary. However, it is important to notice that dividends are closed separately from the company's expenses. This separate entry emphasizes that dividends are not expenses of the business and also allows the confirmation of the net income amount.

VISUAL RECAP 3.4

Closing Entry Rules

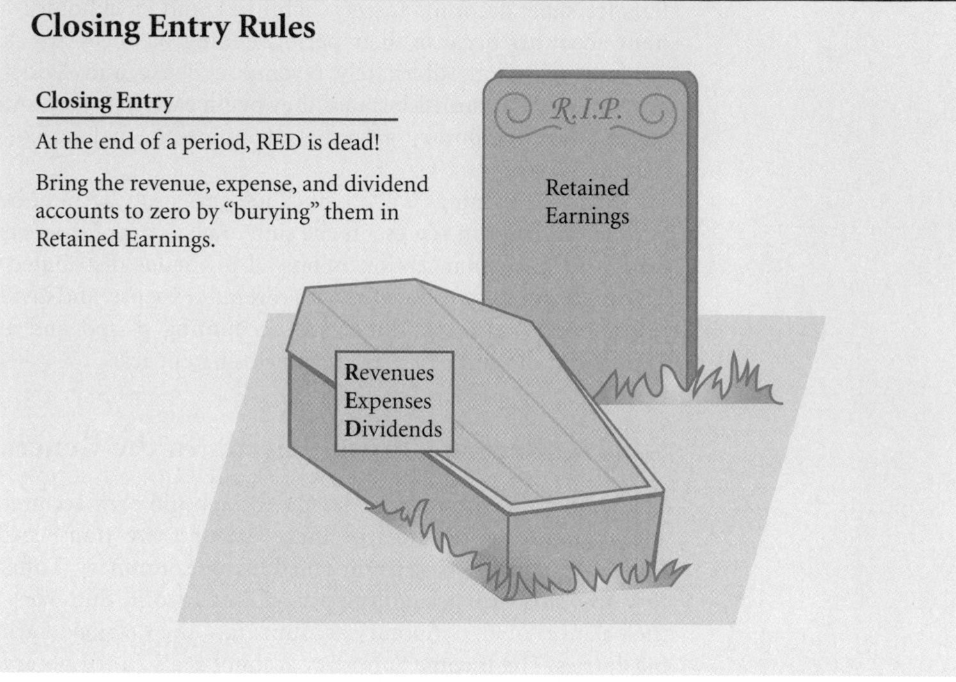

EXHIBIT 3-15

Snow Mountain Retreat General Journal—Closing Entries

General Journal					
Date		Description	PR	Debit	Credit
Apr.	3	Rental Revenue	510	8,000	
		Income Summary	700		8,000
		To close the revenue account			
	30	Income Summary	700	3,820	
		Wage Expense	603		1,080
		Rent Expense	605		1,500
		Supplies Expense	607		80
		Utilities Expense	609		390
		Depreciation Expense	650		500
		Interest Expense	670		70
		Income Tax Expense	680		200
		To close the expense accounts			
	30	Income Summary	700	4,180	
		Retained Earnings	350		4,180
		To close Income Summary and transfer net income to Retained Earnings			
	30	Retained Earnings	350	500	
		Dividends	400		500
		To close the dividends account			

Step 4b: Post Closing Entries to the General Ledger

The account numbers appearing in the post-reference column in Exhibit 3-15 indicate that the closing entries have been posted to the appropriate general ledger accounts. Only the general ledger accounts of Snow Mountain Retreat that have been affected by the closing entries are shown in Exhibit 3-16; all other account balances remain the same as they are in Exhibit 3-6.

EXHIBIT 3-16

Snow Mountain Retreat General Ledger After Closing Entries (1 of 2)

Retained Earnings						Account No. 350
Date		Explanation	PR	Debit	Credit	Credit Balance
Apr.	30	Net income for April	GJ3		4,180	4,180
	30	Dividends for April	GJ3	500		3,680

Dividends						Account No. 400
Date		Explanation	PR	Debit	Credit	Debit Balance
Apr.	30	Declared a cash dividend	GJ1	500		500
	30	Closing entry	GJ3		500	0

Rental Revenue						Account No. 510
Date		Explanation	PR	Debit	Credit	Credit Balance
Apr.	19	Earned revenue	GJ1		1,500	1,500
	24	Earned revenue	GJ1		3,250	4,750
	26	Earned revenue	GJ1		750	5,500
	30	Earned revenue	GJ2		2,500	8,000
	30	Closing entry	GJ3	8,000		0

Wages Expense						Account No. 603
Date		Explanation	PR	Debit	Credit	Debit Balance
Apr.	26	Mainenance wages 4/8–4/19	GJ1	800		800
	30	Maintenance wages for 7 days	GJ2	280		1,080
	30	Closing entry	GJ3		1,080	0

Rent Expense						Account No. 605
Date		Explanation	PR	Debit	Credit	Debit Balance
Apr.	30	For April on B&B	GJ2	1,500		1,500
	30	Closing entry	GJ3		1,500	0

Supplies Expense						Account No. 607
Date		Explanation	PR	Debit	Credit	Debit Balance
Apr.	30	For April	GJ2	80		80
	30	Closing entry	GJ3		80	0

EXHIBIT 3-16
Snow Mountain Retreat General Ledger After Closing Entries (2 of 2)

Utility Expense						Account No. 609
Date		Explanation	PR	Debit	Credit	Debit Balance
Apr.	30	April electricity	GJ1	390		390
	30	Closing entry	GJ3		390	0

Depreciation Expense						Account No. 650
Date		Explanation	PR	Debit	Credit	Debit Balance
Apr.	30	For April on furniture	GJ2	500		500
	30	Closing entry	GJ3		500	0

Interest Expense						Account No. 670
Date		Explanation	PR	Debit	Credit	Debit Balance
Apr.	30	For April on note	GJ2	70		70
	30	Closing entry	GJ3		70	0

Income Tax Expense						Account No. 680
Date		Explanation	PR	Debit	Credit	Debit Balance
Apr.	30	Estimate for April	GJ2	200		200
	30	Closing entry	GJ3		200	0

Step 4c: Prepare a Post-Closing Trial Balance

The accounting cycle concludes with the preparation of a post-closing trial balance to ensure that the general ledger is in balance. If the debit and credit column totals of this trial balance are equal, the adjusting and closing entries are assumed to have been entered correctly in the accounting records. The April 30, 2002, post-closing trial balance of Snow Mountain Retreat is shown in Exhibit 3-17. Notice that only the company's permanent or balance sheet accounts are listed in this trial balance. At this point, each of the temporary accounts has been closed and thus has a zero balance. Additionally, Retained Earnings is included with the same balance that was shown for that account in the statement of stockholders' equity (Exhibit 3-13), the balance sheet (Exhibit 3-14), and the general ledger account balance in Exhibit 3-16.

In a fully computerized accounting system, a company's accounting records may be closed and a post-closing trial balance prepared in a matter of seconds by activating the appropriate computer software instructions.

SUMMARY

A system of financial record keeping known as double-entry bookkeeping has been used for centuries by businesses to capture financial data regarding transactions and related events. This system requires that at least two elements of an economic event be recognized in recording that event.

Each accounting period, a set of accounting procedures called the accounting cycle must be completed for a business. These procedures convert financial data resulting from a business's transactions during an accounting period into a set of financial statements.

EXHIBIT 3-17

Snow Mountain Retreat Post-Closing Trial Balance

Snow Mountain Retreat
Post-Closing Trial Balance
April 30, 2002

	Debit	Credit
Cash	$24,810	
Accounts Receivable	750	
Supplies	420	
Prepaid Rent	16,500	
Furniture	12,000	
Accumulated Depreciation—Furniture		$ 500
Notes Payable		7,000
Accounts Payable		250
Wages Payable		280
Interest Payable		70
Unearned Rental Revenue		2,500
Income Tax Payable		200
Common Stock		40,000
Retained Earnings		3,680
Totals	$54,480	$54,480

The accounting cycle begins with an analysis of these transactions. Key information regarding business transactions is obtained from a variety of source documents.

The next step in the accounting cycle is the preparation of journal entries. In journalizing economic transactions affecting a business, the rules of double-entry bookkeeping must be followed. The key to understanding and applying these rules is the meaning and use of the terms "debit" and "credit." Debit refers to the left-hand side of a T-account, or to the process of entering an amount on the left-hand side of an account. Credit refers to the right-hand side of a T-account, or to the process of entering an amount on the right-hand side of an account. Asset, expense, and dividend accounts normally have debit balances; increases in these accounts are recorded as debits and decreases are recorded as credits. Liability, stockholders' equity, and revenue accounts normally have credit balances; increases in these accounts are recorded as credits and decreases are recorded as debits.

When analyzing a transaction for the purpose of preparing a journal entry, first identify the type of each account (asset, liability, and so on) affected by the transaction. Next, decide whether the account has been increased or decreased by the transaction. Then, determine whether these changes should be recorded as debits or credits. Finally, make certain that the transaction has equal debit and credit amounts.

The financial data recorded in the journals of a business are transferred or posted periodically to the appropriate general ledger accounts. At the end of each accounting period, a trial balance of the general ledger accounts is prepared to determine whether the total debits and total credits entered in the accounting records during a given accounting period are equal. Equality of the debit and credit totals in the trial balance does not, however, guarantee that transactions have been journalized and posted correctly.

At the end of each accounting period, the general ledger accounts are adjusted for certain accrual and deferral items. After journalizing and posting the adjusting entries, the firm's financial statements are prepared. Next, closing entries to bring revenue, expense, and dividend accounts to zero are journalized and posted. A post-closing trial balance is prepared to determine that the general ledger is in balance at the end of the period.

KEY TERMS

accounting cycle
accrued asset
accrued liability
adjusting entry
closing entry
compound journal entry
contra-account
credit
debit
deferred expense
deferred revenue
double-entry bookkeeping
journalize
permanent account
source document
T-account
temporary account
trial balance

QUESTIONS

1. List two examples of each of the following components of the accounting equation: assets, liabilities, and stockholders' equity. *(LO 3.1)*
2. What types of transactions affect the stockholders' equity of a business? Provide two examples. *(LO 3.1)*
3. Identify several source documents from which accountants obtain information needed to journalize business transactions. What types of transactions would be represented by each type of source document? *(LO 3.1)*
4. Why is information posted from the general journal to the general ledger? *(LO 3.4)*
5. What is a trial balance and what is its purpose? Does a trial balance being "in balance" mean that all transactions have been recorded correctly? Why or why not? *(LO 3.4)*
6. Define a deferred expense. Provide two examples of deferred expenses. Why are adjusting entries generally required at the end of an accounting period for deferred expenses? *(LO 3.6)*
7. Why is a deferred revenue a liability? Provide two examples of deferred revenues. Why are adjusting entries generally required at the end of an accounting period for deferred revenues? *(LO 3.6)*
8. Why is an accrued revenue an asset? Provide two examples of accrued revenues. Why are adjusting entries generally required at the end of an accounting period for accrued revenues? *(LO 3.6)*
9. How does a company's net income for a given accounting period affect its period-ending balance sheet? *(LO 3.7)*
10. Where is the Retained Earnings account presented in a set of financial statements? What is represented by this account? *(LO 3.7)*
11. What are dividends? Where are dividends shown in a set of financial statements? Are dividends considered expenses? Why or why not? *(LO 3.1 & 3.7)*
12. Define the terms *permanent* and *temporary* as related to types of accounts. Why are these terms appropriate? In which financial statement is each type of account found? *(LO 3.8)*
13. Briefly describe the nature and purpose of correcting entries, adjusting entries, and closing entries. *(LO 3.3, 3.6, & 3.8)*

EXERCISES

14. **True & False** *(All LOs)*

Following are a series of statements regarding topics discussed in this chapter.

Required:

Indicate whether each statement is true (T) or false (F).

(1) If a journal entry affects one asset account and two liability accounts, that journal entry must be out of balance in reference to the accounting equation.

(2) If a business's trial balance is "in balance," then the entity's accounting records are free of any errors.

(3) Contra-accounts are typically treated as offsets to related accounts for financial statement purposes.

(4) Every business transaction must be recorded so that the accounting equation for that business remains in balance.

(5) Journal entries may contain several debits and one credit, several credits and one debit, or multiple debits and multiple credits.

(6) A company that has consistently experienced net losses throughout its existence will have a credit balance in its Retained Earnings account.

(7) The initial step of the closing process is posting journal entry data to the appropriate general ledger accounts.

(8) An Income Summary account is a permanent account that is used during the preparation of period-ending adjusting journal entries.

(9) A primary purpose of period-ending adjusting journal entries is to avoid violations of the revenue recognition and expense recognition rules.

(10) Privately-owned companies typically prepare a formal set of financial statements for external users only once per year.

(11) The temporary accounts of a business must begin each accounting period with a zero balance.

(12) Most of the information needed by accountants to analyze business transactions is found in source documents.

(13) Double-entry bookkeeping is a financial record keeping system used only in the United States and a few European countries.

15. **Normal Account Balances** *(LO 3.2)*

Following are account titles taken from the financial statements of three large companies. Alcoa is the leading worldwide producer of aluminum; Honeywell produces a wide array of products including security systems; and Wendy's operates a chain of fast-food restaurants.

Alcoa	Honeywell	Wendy's
Short-Term Investments	Short-Term Debt	Income Taxes Expense
Accounts Payable	Receivables	Inventories
Retained Earnings	Cash and Cash Equivalents	Income Taxes Payable
Operating Expenses	Research & Development Expenses	General & Administrative Expenses
Sales Revenue	Property, Plant, & Equipment	Land

Required:

(1) For each account listed, indicate whether it is an asset (A), liability (L), equity (Q), revenue (R), expense (X), or dividend (D).

(2) For each account listed, indicate whether its normal account balance is a debit (D) or a credit (C).

16. **Analyzing General Journal Entries** *(LO 3.1 & 3.3)*

The following general journal entries (presented in a simplified format) were made recently by the bookkeeper of Chandlers' Hilltop Texaco:

General Journal

Account	Debit	Credit
Supplies	400	
Cash		400
Interest Expense	270	
Cash		270
Equipment	4,000	
Notes Payable		4,000

Required:

(1) Briefly describe the transaction that resulted in each of these journal entries.

(2) Suppose that the bookkeeper inadvertently recorded the third entry by debiting Notes Payable and crediting Equipment, each for $4,000. How would this error have affected the assets and liabilities of Chandlers' Hilltop Texaco?

(3) How would the error in Part 2 affect the trial balance prepared at the end of the period for Chandlers' Hilltop Texaco?

17. **General Journal Entries** *(LO 3.3)*

Following are two recent transactions of Grady Real Estate Company:

(a) Received $24,000 advance payment for one year's rent on an office building being leased to an accounting firm by Grady.

(b) Paid $6,000 in advance for six months of newspaper advertising.

Required:

(1) Prepare a general journal entry to record each of these transactions in Grady's accounting records.

(2) Prepare a general journal entry for each transaction from the point of view of the other party (company) to the transaction.

(3) Were Grady's total assets increased, decreased, or unchanged as a result of each of these transactions?

18. **Analyzing T-accounts** *(LO 3.4)*

Consider the following Cash and Accounts Payable T-accounts:

Cash		Accounts Payable	
14,000	10,000	4,000	6,000
$9,000	$600	5,000	8,200
$8,000	2,000	1,000	1,000

Required:

(1) How would each of these accounts be classified in a balance sheet?

(2) What type of balance should each T-account normally have?

(3) Compute the balance of each of these accounts.

(4) Identify two possible transactions that would have resulted in the $8,000 posting to the Cash account.

(5) Identify two possible transactions that would have resulted in the $5,000 posting to the Accounts Payable account.

19. **Posting General Journal Entries** *(LO 3.4)*
Following are several general journal entries of the Houseman Corporation during a recent month; journal entry descriptions have been omitted:

General Journal					
Date		**Description**	**PR**	**Debit**	**Credit**
2002					
Jan.	2	Office Supplies		320	
		Cash			320
	5	Inventory		7,500	
		Accounts Payable			7,500
	7	Cash		5,750	
		Accounts Receivable			5,750
	9	Accounts Payable		4,300	
		Cash			4,300
	12	Utilities Expense		2,000	
		Cash			2,000

Following are the account numbers and January 1 balances of the accounts affected by the listed journal entries:

	Account Number	January 1 Balance
Cash	101	$12,400
Accounts Receivable	111	9,300
Inventory	116	6,100
Office Supplies	121	840
Accounts Payable	201	14,200
Utilities Expense	505	0

Required:

(1) Prepare a T-account for each of the accounts affected by the general journal entries listed for the Houseman Corporation. Enter the January 1 balance in each of these accounts.

(2) Post the journal entries to the appropriate accounts.

(3) Determine the balance of each of the accounts after the transactions have been posted.

(4) What is the purpose of posting general journal entries to general ledger accounts?

20. **Adjusting Journal Entries for Balance Sheet Accounts** *(LO 3.6)*
Following are several December 31 account balances of Brookhaven Square, Inc. prior to the preparation of year-end adjusting journal entries:

Property, Plant & Equipment	$1,530,200
Cash	120,600
Unearned Rental Revenue	72,000
Common Stock	30,000
Prepaid Rent	5,400
Land	340,500
Note Payable	50,000
Retained Earnings	770,100

Required:

(1) Of the listed accounts, which ones will likely require year-end adjusting journal entries?

(2) Briefly describe the nature of the adjusting journal entries for the accounts identified.

(3) Why would adjusting entries not be needed for each of the nonaffected accounts?

21. **Adjusting Journal Entries for Liability Accounts** *(LO 3.6)*

Following is the liabilities section of a recent balance sheet of Thokeel Corporation. Amounts are expressed in millions.

CURRENT LIABILITIES		
Short-term Debt	$27.1	
Accounts Payable	40.3	
Accrued Compensation	46.4	
Other Accrued Expenses	28.9	
Income Taxes Payable	2.6	
Current Portion of Long-term Debt	0.1	
Total Current Liabilities		$145.4
NON-CURRENT LIABILITIES		
Long-term Debt	$87.9	
Accrued Retiree Benefits Other Than Pensions	76.0	
Deferred Income Taxes	16.9	
Accrued Interest and Other	89.8	
Total Non-current Liabilities		270.6
Total Liabilities		$416.0

Required:

(1) Identify the current liabilities in Thokeel's balance sheet that may have been recorded or affected by period-ending adjusting entries.

(2) What type of adjusting entry related to Long-term Debt may have been required in Thokeel's accounting records?

(3) Assume that the Accrued Compensation liability was recorded in a period-ending adjusting entry. Prepare that entry.

22. **Adjusting Journal Entries** *(LO 3.6)*

Montana Designs, Inc. is an interior-decorating firm. Customers must pay 50 percent of their estimated bill before any work is performed. On November 20 of the current year, Montana Designs received and recorded a $5,000 partial payment from a customer on a new job that was scheduled to begin on December 1. As of December 31, the job has been completed. No further payments have been received by December 31 from the customer, nor have any additional entries relating to this job been recorded in the accounting records of Montana Designs.

Required:

(1) Prepare the entry to record the November 20 partial payment.

(2) Prepare any necessary adjusting journal entry in Montana Designs' accounting records as of December 31.

23. **Failure to Record Year-End Adjusting Journal Entry** *(LO 3.6, ethics)*

Consider the following two situations:

(a) On December 1, 2002, Harsha's Cleaning Service, a new business, bought $6,500 of cleaning supplies. At the end of December, the business had $3,400 of supplies on hand.

(b) Silverman & Sachs is a large investment–banking firm. In December 2002, the firm earned fees of $4.1 million for investment banking services provided to three large clients. As of December 31, 2002, the firm had not been paid for these services.

Required:

(1) Record the December 1, 2002, entry for the purchase made by Harsha's Cleaning Service.

(2) Given the facts provided in each situation, prepare an appropriate adjusting journal entry as of December 31, 2002 for each company.

(3) Suppose the adjusting journal entries from Part 2 were not recorded. Which accounting principles or concepts would be violated by these oversights? Why are these violations important?

(4) As an investor in these companies, would you be concerned to find that the adjusting entries had been omitted? Why or why not?

24. The Accounting Equation *(LO 3.7)*

Following are the balance sheet accounts of a small business:

Cash	$2,500
Accounts Payable	?
Equipment	5,200
Supplies	?
Land	8,200
Owners' Equity (total)	9,000
Notes Payable	5,400

Required:

(1) Fill in the missing amounts assuming that the business has total assets of $18,000.

(2) Fill in the missing amounts assuming that the business has total liabilities and owners' equity of $19,900.

(3) Prepare a trial balance assuming the information in Part 1.

25. Closing Entries *(LO 3.8)*

Following are selected account balances from the December 31, 2002, adjusted trial balance of Hernandez Brothers Supply Company:

Cash	$ 2,000
Accounts Receivable	3,000
Unearned Rental Revenue	6,100
Utilities Expense	3,000
Income Taxes Expense	4,000
Accounts Payable	1,500
Sales Revenue	25,000
Selling Expenses	6,000
Prepaid Rent	4,500

Required:

(1) Assuming that all of the company's temporary accounts are included in the listed accounts, prepare the appropriate December 31 closing entries for Hernandez Brothers.

(2) How much net income did the company earn during the period?

(3) For any item not used in Part 1, indicate where that item would appear on the financial statements.

26. **Need for Adjusting and Closing Entries** *(LO 3.6 & 3.8, writing)*

Theo's Tailors is a small business operated by Alex Theodorius. The accounting records for this business are maintained by Markey & Michaels, CPAs. Recently, Alex questioned the monthly accounting bill submitted to him by the CPA firm. Included in the bill were the following line items, among others:

Adjustment of year-end account balances:
5 hours @ $60 per hour $300

Year-end closing of revenue and expense accounts:
1 hour @ $60 per hour 60

Alex does not understand why his accounting records must be adjusted at year-end. In a recent telephone conversation, he complained to a partner of Markey & Michaels, "If you guys did my accounting records right the first time, you wouldn't have to adjust them at year-end." Alex went on to protest the $60 charge for closing his business's revenue and expense accounts. "Why do you close those accounts every December 31? Don't you always use them again the next year? I think you're closing them just to run up my bill."

Required:

Write a memo to Alex Theodorius explaining the purpose of, and need for, period-ending adjusting and closing entries.

PROBLEMS

27. **Correction of Accounting Errors** *(LO 3.3)*

Jabbar Company's inexperienced bookkeeper places a question mark next to a journal entry if he is uncertain the entry is correct. Question marks appear next to each of the following entries in Jabbar's accounting records.

		Debit	Credit
(a)	Accounts Receivable	2,000	
	Cash		2,000
	To record collection of accounts receivable		
(b)	Office Equipment	800	
	Cash		800
	To record purchase of office supplies for cash		
(c)	Cleaning Supplies	100	
	Accounts Payable		100
	To record purchase of cleaning supplies on credit		

Required:

(1) Given each journal entry and its accompanying explanation, identify the nature of the error in the entry, if any, and how the entry should have been prepared.

(2) Given your responses in Part 1, prepare any necessary correcting entries.

(3) Analyze each of the errors you identified in Part 1 in reference to the accounting equation. How would these errors have affected the accounting equation of Jabbar Company, if at all?

28. **General Journal Entries** *(LO 3.3)*

Following are the December transactions of Cerullo Electrical Contractors.

December 1	Purchased supplies for $300.
December 3	Paid $250 electricity bill for November that had been properly recorded with an adjusting entry on November 30.
December 9	Paid employee salaries for first week of December, $1,200.
December 16	Received $600 for interest that had been earned in November on a bank account; an appropriate adjusting journal entry had been recorded for this item on November 30.
December 22	Received $1,700 from customer in payment of account receivable.
December 26	Paid January rent on leased office space, $400.
December 30	Received $2,500 advance payment from a customer for work to be performed in January.
December 31	Purchased equipment on credit for $3,000.

Required:

(1) Prepare general journal entries for these transactions.

(2) Identify which accounts affected by the journal entries prepared in Part 1 are deferred expenses, deferred revenues, accrued assets, or accrued liabilities.

29. **Journalizing and Posting Transactions** *(LO 3.3 & 3.4, writing)*

Orlando opened a hair salon recently, but did not maintain a formal set of accounting records during the first week of his business's operations. Instead, he simply maintained a checkbook for the business. Following are the entries included in Orlando's checkbook for the period January 2–January 8, 2002:

Date	Transaction	Deposits	Withdrawals
January 2	Bank loan	$20,000	
January 3	Rent to landlord		$ 500
January 3	Hair styling fees earned	650	
January 4	Bought inventory		7,000
January 4	Bought inventory		3,500
January 8	Hair styling fees earned	800	

Required:

(1) Prepare the necessary general journal entries for Orlando's Hair Salon for the period January 2–January8.

(2) Prepare T-accounts for Orlando's Hair Salon and post the journal entries for the period January 2–January 8 to these accounts. Determine the account balances as of January 8.

(3) Verify that the general ledger accounts are in balance.

(4) In a short memo to Orlando, explain why his current method of record keeping does not provide him with the information he needs to monitor and evaluate the financial status of his business. Be sure to indicate whether his checkbook will record all transactions that affect his business in any given period.

30. Trial Balance *(LO 3.5, writing)*

Following are the general ledger account balances of Baggett Construction Company, Inc. (BCCI), as of September 30, 2002:

Cash	$ 25,000
Accounts Receivable	150,000
Inventory	150,000
Office Equipment	425,000
Accumulated Depreciation, Office Equipment	55,000
Accounts Payable	350,000
Income Taxes Payable	50,000
Common Stock	45,000
Retained Earnings	50,000
Sales Revenue	300,000
Operating Expenses	100,000

Required:

(1) Prepare a trial balance for BCCI as of September 30, 2002. (Hint: Each account has a normal balance.)

(2) Even if a trial balance is in balance, one or more general ledger accounts of a business may contain errors. Provide three examples of accounting errors that would not cause a business's trial balance to be unbalanced.

(3) What steps could the management of BCCI take to help ensure that its accounts are error-free? Write a brief memo to the company's management listing your recommendations.

31. Adjusting Journal Entries *(LO 3.6, writing)*

The following information pertains to the operations of Story Investigating, a private detective agency, for December 2002.

(a) Story's employees earn $420 of salary collectively each day. The employees work Monday through Friday and are paid each Friday for the week just worked. December 31 falls on a Tuesday.

(b) On December 31, the owner estimates that December's electricity bill will be $240.

(c) The owner also estimates that the firm will have income tax expense of $800 for December. This amount will be paid in March 2003.

(d) On December 1, Story received and recorded a $300 payment from a customer for services to be rendered by Story evenly during December, January, and February. Story's principal revenue account is Fees Revenue.

(e) Story received $680 cash from a new client on December 28; this amount was properly recorded. No services had been provided to this client as of December 31.

(f) Bonocher, Inc. owes Story $1,400 for services provided during December. No entry pertaining to these services has been recorded in Story's accounting records.

Required:

(1) For items (a) through (f), prepare any necessary adjusting journal entry as of December 31 in Story's accounting records.

(2) Suppose that Story Investigating uses the cash basis of accounting instead of the accrual basis. Analyze items a through f and determine how Story's

revenues and expenses for December would be affected by using the cash rather than accrual basis of accounting.

(3) Write a brief memo indicating whether the cash basis or accrual basis of accounting provides a more appropriate measure of Story's net income each accounting period.

32. **"Window-Dressing" Financial Statements** *(LO 3.7, ethics)*

You are an accountant for Kelberg, Inc., an advertising agency and you are preparing to close Kelberg's accounting records for the current year since December 31 is only a few days away. The business owner is planning to apply for a loan from a local bank in early January. To make the financial statements more acceptable to the bank, the owner instructs you to credit a $31,000 advance payment received from a customer on December 27 to a revenue account. Kelberg will not provide the services paid for by this customer until March of next year. The owner also instructs you to not record a year-end adjusting entry for $7,500 of December rent owed to the real estate firm that leases office space to Kelberg.

Required:

(1) If you comply with the owner's instructions, how will Kelberg's December 31 balance sheet for the current year be affected? How will the company's income statement for the current year be affected?

(2) What accounting principles will be violated if you comply with the owner's instructions?

(3) What will you do in this situation? Identify the parties likely to be affected by your decision to comply or not comply with the owner's requests. Indicate how each of these parties may be impacted by your decision.

33. **Preparation of Financial Statements** *(LO 3.7)*

The following adjusted trial balance of Blackburn Consultants, Inc. was prepared for the year ended December 31, 2002.

	Debit	Credit
Cash	$ 24,000	
Accounts Receivable	71,000	
Interest Receivable	1,000	
Inventory	125,000	
Prepaid Insurance	6,000	
Equipment	242,000	
Accumulated Depreciation—Equipment		$ 31,000
Accounts Payable		17,000
Interest Payable		4,000
Income Tax Payable		90,000
Notes Payable (long-term)		67,000
Common Stock		15,000
Retained Earnings		91,000
Consulting Fees Revenue		460,000
Interest Revenue		3,000
Salaries Expense	176,000	
Advertising Expense	22,000	
Utilities Expense	6,000	
Interest Expense	5,000	
Depreciation Expense—Equipment	10,000	
Income Taxes Expense	90,000	
Totals	$ 778,000	$778,000

Required:

(1) Prepare an income statement for the year ended December 31, 2002.

(2) Prepare a Statement of Stockholders' Equity for the year ended December 31, 2002; assuming Blackburn Consultants, Inc. did not issue any new stock in 2002. (Hint: The January 1, 2002 balance for Retained Earnings is listed in the adjusted trial balance.)

(3) Prepare a classified balance sheet as of December 31, 2002.

34. **Closing Entries** *(LO 3.8)*

Random Access, Inc. is a small business that leases computer equipment. Following are several account balances that were included in the company's year-end adjusted trial balance:

Cash	$100,000
Interest Revenue	5,000
Accounts Payable	40,000
Accumulated Depreciation, Equipment	36,000
Rental Revenue	152,000
Dividends	15,000
Salaries Expense	45,000
Depreciation Expense	12,000

Required:

(1) Indicate which of the listed accounts are permanent accounts and which are temporary accounts.

(2) Given the information provided, prepare all appropriate closing entries for Random Access.

(3) What is net income for Random Access for the year?

(4) If the Retained Earnings account contained a balance of $47,000 prior to closing, what is the balance of this account after closing entries are prepared and posted?

CASES

35. **Recording and Posting Transactions** *(LO 3.3 & 3.4, Excel)*

The following transactions took place during the first two weeks of operations of Not So Taxing, Inc., a walk-in tax preparation service.

March 1	Issued common stock of the corporation in exchange for $100,000 cash.
March 3	Purchased $2,000 of supplies on account from Kidd Supply Company.
March 4	Paid $1,500 of office rent for March.
March 5	Completed tax work for Mr. East and billed him $850.
March 6	Received a total of $2,400 from customers for services provided during the week.
March 8	Received a $1,000 advance from Mr. West for tax services that have not yet been provided.
March 10	Placed a telephone order for a $550 laser printer.
March 11	Paid $1,000 to Kidd Supply Company.
March 12	Received $450 from Mr. East.
March 13	Paid an employee $700 for two weeks.

March 13 Received $3,700 cash from customers for services provided during the week.

Required:

(1) Enter the transactions into the general journal.

(2) Post the transactions to the general ledger and calculate balances for each account. Verify that the ledger is in balance.

36. **Annual Reports** *(LO 3.7, Internet)*

The financial statements of a company are prepared before the closing entries.

Required:

Use the annual report of Carnival Corporation for the 2001 fiscal year to answer the following questions. Specifically, look at the Income Statement (Consolidated Statement of Operations) and the Statement of Stockholders' Equity for the fiscal year ended November 30, 1999. The annual report can be found at www.carnival.com/aboutCCL/; follow the links to investor relations.

(1) Prepare Carnival's four closing entries for 1999. [Hint: Revenues are added and Expenses are subtracted on the Statement of Operations.]

(2) What was the balance of Retained Earnings at the beginning of the fiscal year (December 1, 1998)?

(3) Prepare the T-account for Retained Earnings (start with the balance on December 1, 1998) and post the closing entries you prepared in Part 1.

(4) Prepare the T-account for Income Summary to verify that its ending balance is zero.

(5) Verify that the ending balance of the T–account equals the ending balance of Retained Earnings shown on Carnival's Statement of Stockholders' Equity for 1999.

37. **Comprehensive Accounting Cycle Problem** *(LO 3.3, 3.4, 3.5, 3.6, 3.7, 3.8, & 3.9)*

During the summer of 2004, Terry Simmons began and incorporated a small lawn mowing service. The following information relates to the first two months of business.

Required:

(1) (a) Record the following transactions in Terry's General Journal:

6/1 Terry invested $600 in the business.

6/1 Terry borrowed $200 on a 7-month, 6% (annual rate) note payable. Principal and interest are due by January 1, 2005.

6/2 Mrs. Jones paid Terry $75 to mow her lawn once a month for 3 months.

6/2 Terry bought a $600 lawn mower that is expected to last 5 years.

6/3 Terry placed a telephone order for $50 of office supplies.

6/3 Terry bought $10 of gasoline.

6/3 The supplies ordered on 6/3 were received with an invoice for $50.

6/15 As of 6/15, Terry had mowed 30 lawns at $25 each. Twenty customers paid in cash and the rest were billed for their balances.

6/18 Terry bought $10 of gas.

6/20 Terry paid $50 to a mini–storage facility to store the lawnmower for one month.

6/30 Terry mowed 25 more lawns at $25 each. Twenty customers paid cash; the remainder were billed.

6/30 Terry received $150 from people billed.

6/30 Terry took $200 in salary.

7/2 Terry had to have the lawnmower repaired and received a bill for $100.

7/3 Terry bought $20 of gas.

7/10 Terry paid for half of the supplies received on 6/3.

7/20 Terry received $100 from customers billed.

7/31 Terry mowed 65 more lawns at $25 each. Forty customers paid cash; the remainder were billed.

7/31 Terry took $400 in salary.

7/31 Terry paid the $100 lawnmower repair bill.

(b) Create a general ledger and post the entries to it. Calculate ledger account balances.

(c) Prepare a trial balance. [Checkpoint: Trial Balance = $3,900]

(2) (a) Make the appropriate adjusting entries in the general journal given the information below.

7/31 Terry has $30 worth of supplies left.

7/31 Terry has $3 of gas left.

7/31 Terry has mowed Mrs. Jones' yard twice.

7/31 Determine whether any other adjustments are necessary.

(b) Post the adjusting entries to the general ledger and calculate account balances.

(c) Prepare an adjusted trial balance. [Checkpoint: Trial Balance = $3,922].

(3) (a) Prepare an income statement. [Checkpoint: Net Income = $2,221]

(b) Prepare a statement of stockholders' equity. [Checkpoint: Ending Retained Earnings = $2,221]

(c) Prepare a balance sheet. [Checkpoint: Total Assets = $3,073]

(4) (a) Prepare the closing entries in the general journal.

(b) Post the closing entries to the general ledger and calculate account balances.

(c) Prepare an adjusted trial balance. [Checkpoint: Trial Balance = $3,093]

SUPPLEMENTAL PROBLEMS

38. **Journalizing Transactions** *(LO 3.3, writing)* [Compare to Problem 28]

Jenonne's Gardening Supply had the following transactions involving cash during early August:

August 1 Purchased four lawnmowers for $300 each.

August 2 Purchased $320 of office supplies for cash.

August 4 Paid $400 of income taxes.

August 4 Received $450 for lawn care services provided.

August 5 Paid $500 of salaries.

August 7 Paid $1,000 of interest on a bank loan.

Required:

(1) Prepare general journal entries for the transactions.

(2) After reviewing the journal entries prepared in Part 1, the owner of Jenonne's Gardening Supply is convinced that each transaction has been "double-counted." Write a short memo to the owner explaining why each entry requires at least one debit and one credit and why this procedure does not double-count the transactions.

39. **Journalizing, Posting, and Preparing a Trial Balance** *(LO 3.3, 3.4, & 3.5)* [Compare to Problems 28, 29, and 30]

Georgian Enterprises uses the following general ledger accounts in its accounting system. Listed for each account is its account number and balance as of January 1, 2004.

	Account Number	Balance
Cash	101	$ 60,000
Supplies	121	10,000
Office Equipment	151	170,000
Accumulated Depreciation—OE	152	45,000
Accounts Payable	201	70,000
Common Stock	301	90,000
Retained Earnings	350	35,000
Fee Revenue	401	0
Selling Expenses	501	0
Salary Expense	511	0
Supplies Expense	531	0

In early January 2004, Georgian Enterprises engaged in the following transactions:

January 2 Paid $30,000 on accounts payable.

January 3 Purchased $1,100 of supplies for cash.

January 4 Purchased office equipment for $2,700 cash.

January 6 Earned and received fees (revenues) from customers of $16,400.

January 7 Paid selling expenses of $7,100.

January 7 Paid employee salaries of $5,200.

Required:

(1) Why do some of Georgian's accounts have zero balances at the beginning of January?

(2) Prepare a journal entry for each of the transactions listed.

(3) Prepare four-column general ledger accounts for Georgian Enterprises as of January 1, 2004. Post the January 2004 journal entries to these accounts.

(4) Prepare a trial balance for Georgian Enterprises as of January 7, 2004.

40. **Preparation of Financial Statements** *(LO 3.7)* [Compare to Problem 33]

Following is an adjusted trial balance for DGA & Associates for the year ended December 31, 2004.

	Debit	Credit
Cash	$112,500	
Accounts Receivable	95,000	
Supplies	12,000	
Prepaid Advertising	18,000	
Prepaid Rent	40,000	
Equipment	90,500	
Accumulated Depreciation—Equipment		$ 71,000
Accounts Payable		38,000
Salaries Payable		2,400
Unearned Fee Revenue		75,000
Common Stock		34,000
Retained Earnings		20,000
Fee Revenue		315,000
Interest Revenue		9,100
Rent Expense	69,500	
Income Taxes Expense	35,000	
Salaries Expense	75,000	
Depreciation Expense—Equipment	17,000	
Totals	$564,500	$564,500

Required:

(1) Prepare an income statement and a statement of stockholders' equity for DGA & Associates for the year ended December 31, 2004. [Hint: No stock was sold during 2004.]

(2) Prepare a classified balance sheet for DGA & Associates as of December 31, 2004.

(3) Identify three general classes of financial statement users who might make economic decisions based upon the financial statements of DGA & Associates. How might errors in the financial statements affect such decisions?

41. **Closing Entries** *(LO 3.8)* [Compare to Problem 34.]

Following is a list of certain account balances included in the adjusted trial balance of Sharon's Shoe Repair Shop as of December 31, 2004. This list includes all of the business's revenue and expense accounts as well as selected additional accounts.

Prepaid Rent	$ 4,500
Accounts Payable	8,200
Utilities Expense	1,000
Cash	12,000
Accounts Receivable	3,000
Shoe Repair Revenue	35,000
Prepaid Insurance	5,500
Unearned Repair Revenue	700
Salaries Expense	12,000
Salaries Payable	900
Bonds Payable	1,500
Income Taxes Expense	8,000

Required:

(1) Prepare all appropriate closing entries for Sharon's Shoe Repair Shop on December 31, 2004.

(2) What was the company's net income (loss) for 2004?

PART II

ACCOUNTING FOR ASSETS

CHAPTER **4**

Cash, Short-Term Investments, and Accounts Receivable

LEARNING OBJECTIVES

1. Account for the major types of transactions involving cash as well as accounts and notes receivable.
2. Prepare a bank reconciliation and related entries.
3. Estimate and record bad debts for accounts receivable.
4. Use ratios and other analysis techniques to make decisions about cash, short-term investments, and accounts receivable.

Bank Errors: They Can Be Your Problem!

Your bank statement arrives in the mail. Do you: (a) reconcile it with your transactions; (b) use it as a glass coaster; (c) throw it away; or (d) file it without a second glance? Cathy X normally opted for (d) until September 2000 when her mortgage payment bounced. After reviewing bank statements beginning in 1992, she found a $693 deduction that wasn't in her checkbook. Her belief is that a fraudulent check was drawn against her account. Unfortunately, the bank told her that she had waited too long to report the problem and refused to do anything. Cathy no longer uses that bank.

Cathy's bank, like most others, has customers sign agreements when accounts are opened. This bank gave its clients "30 days from the time the statement is mailed to notify the bank of any forgeries, unauthorized signatures, alterations or errors." Should no notification be given within that time frame, customers waive their rights to any claims. But commercial law (under the Uniform Commercial Code) provides a one-year statute of limitation on such problems.

Banks must provide a reasonable time for customers to review their bank statements and report errors. Cathy's six years cannot be considered reasonable. So, going back to the original question: the right answer is (a)!

SOURCE: "Read Your Bank Statement," *Money,* 30 January 2001; available online @ http://money.cnn.com/2001/01/30/banking/q_bankrate/index.htm.

INTRODUCTION

This chapter focuses on accounting issues for three important and closely related current assets: cash, short-term investments, and accounts receivable. Cash and cash equivalents are essential for an organization to pay its bills. However, companies do not want to have "too much" cash and may take some of the "excess" and make short-term investments. (Each organization's management makes its own determination of how much is "too much.") One factor that significantly influences a company's cash needs is the length of its operating cycle or time between cash use for normal operating activities and cash collections from customers. For instance, grocery stores have short operating cycles because inventory turns over quickly and most sales are for cash. Alternately, furniture stores and wine manufacturers have a much longer operating cycle. Accounts receivable are amounts that customers owe to the organization; these amounts are usually collected in cash within the company's established credit period.

CASH AND CASH EQUIVALENTS

Current assets are listed in order of decreasing liquidity on a balance sheet. **Liquidity** refers to how readily the asset can be converted into cash; therefore, cash or "cash and cash equivalents" is generally listed as the first line item. For example, at year-end 2001, Microsoft (www.microsoft.com) had approximately $3.9 billion in cash and cash equivalents on its balance sheet. This amount is significantly larger than the $842 million for The Walt

Disney Company (www.disney.com) or $683 million by PepsiCo (www.pepsico.com) at the same time.

Cash equivalents are highly liquid amounts such as certificates of deposit (CDs), money market funds, and United States treasury bills. To qualify as a cash equivalent, an item must be readily convertible into a specific amount of cash and have very little risk of a change in value from the time it is acquired to the time it is changed back into cash. Given these criteria, investments in the stocks or bonds of another company do not qualify as cash equivalents; there is always risk relative to the value of the investment.

To illustrate the difference between a cash equivalent and a short-term investment, consider the following. **Treasury bills** are short-term U.S. government obligations with a term of one year or less. These debt items are sold for less than their face value and do not pay interest before maturity. The difference between the purchase price of the bill and the amount that is paid at maturity is the interest earned on the bill. For instance, in the last quarter of 2001, a 91-day T-bill paid approximately 2.0 percent interest and, because it was backed by the U.S. government, there was certainty about getting the money at the 91-day maturity![1] Alternatively, the common stock of Delta Air Lines (www.delta.com) was trading at $39 per share on September 4, 2001; on September 17, it had plummeted to $20.61 per share because of the September 11th tragedy. Although the stock continued to rebound (trading at $29.19 on November 26), an investment in Delta shares would have resulted in vast differences in the amount of cash that could have been received from cashing in that investment.

Cash has long been considered one of the most important business assets because of its use in paying current debts. The sale of goods or services for cash and the collection of accounts receivable are probably the two most common cash transactions. Each of these was illustrated in Chapter 3. The other two most common accounting issues relative to cash are petty cash and bank reconciliations. The next two sections discuss these topics.

Petty Cash

Most organizations keep a limited amount of **petty cash** on hand (in a petty cash box, for example) to pay for small items. The size of the petty cash fund depends on business needs, but the size is usually small enough so that loss of the money in the fund would not be detrimental. One employee is designated as the custodian of the petty cash. The fund is established with a debit to an account called Petty Cash and a credit to Cash:

General Journal				
Date		**Description**	**Debit**	**Credit**
XXX		Petty Cash	50	
		Cash		50
		To establish a petty cash fund		

Usually one person is designated as the custodian of the petty cash fund. He or she uses petty cash to pay for small, but necessary, business expenses and should obtain a receipt for the expenditures. These receipts are considered source documents. At any time, the total of the cash and the receipts in the petty cash box should total the amount originally put in the fund.

Journal entries are not made when funds are expended. When the fund is low, the receipts are used as source documents to make the necessary journal entry. The expenses

[1] For more information about T-bills and other U.S. government securities, go to www.publicdebt.treas.gov.

that created the distributions from the petty cash fund are recorded and a check is written to obtain additional cash to replenish the petty cash fund. The resulting journal entry is a debit to several expenses and a credit to cash.

Assume that, over two weeks, $45 of petty cash was spent on the following items: overnight mail charges for a package, $16; overhead transparencies for a manager's presentation, $9; cab fare for an employee who worked overtime one evening, $13; and coffee creamer for the office coffee room, $7. At this time, there is a $5 bill left in the fund and $45 in receipts, totaling the original $50. The custodian would make the following entry:

General Journal				
Date		**Description**	**Debit**	**Credit**
XXX		Postage Expense	16	
		Office Supplies Expense	9	
		Transportation Expense	13	
		Miscellaneous Expense	7	
		Cash		45
		To replenish the petty cash fund		

The custodian would cash the check and replace the $45 of petty cash. After replenishing the petty cash fund, there is $50 in cash and no new receipts, so the total in the petty cash box is still $50.

Bank Reconciliations

A business's petty cash can be compared to the money that an individual has in his/her wallet. But most businesses, like most individuals, do not have a significant amount of cash on hand. Companies normally use checking accounts at banks (or other financial institutions) to pay the majority of large expenditures. A checking account provides a company a safe place to store money, some control over who has access to those funds, and source documentation (sequentially numbered checks, return of cancelled checks, and bank statements) of cash transactions.

A company may have multiple bank accounts for its cash balances; for instance, one account may be used for general business expenses and one for payroll. Although each bank account is contained in a separate general ledger account, all the bank accounts will be added together to find the "cash" line item that appears on the balance sheet.

Each month, depositors receive bank statements that summarize the activities that have occurred in the bank accounts for the period. Such activities include information about the physical and direct deposits, checks that have cleared, ATM transactions, direct withdrawals, payments made using debit cards, and (possibly) service charges or interest that has been earned on the account. By adding and subtracting the results of these activities, based on their nature, to and from the beginning account balance, the bank determines an ending balance in the depositor's account. However, this information is not normally in absolute agreement with the cash account contained in the depositor's general ledger because of one or more of the following items:

- ***Deposits Not Yet Recorded by Depositor***—The bank may have deposited an amount to the depositor's account without his/her knowing the amount. For example, a depositor's checking account may pay interest that is deposited directly into that account upon calculation at the end of the month. Thus, the bank records have included the addition of the amount, but the depositor's records have not. No adjustment needs to be made to the bank balance; the general ledger cash account needs to be increased.

- ***Deposits in Transit***—A depositor may have made a deposit to his/her checking account, but the bank has not yet been recorded that deposit. For example, if a deposit is made at 4:45 PM on a Friday afternoon, the bank will not record it until Monday morning. Thus, the book records have included this deposit as an addition to cash, but the bank records have not. No adjustment needs to be made to the general ledger cash account; the bank balance needs to be increased.
- ***Outstanding Checks***—A depositor may have written a check that has not yet cleared his/her checking account. Thus, the book records have included this reduction to cash, but the bank records have not. No adjustment needs to be made to the general ledger cash account; the bank balance needs to be reduced.
- ***Direct Bank Charges***—The bank may deduct amounts (such as check printing charges, service fees, and stop payment orders) from a depositor's account without his/her knowing the amount. Thus, the bank records have included this reduction, but the book records have not. No adjustment needs to be made to the bank balance; the general ledger cash account needs to be reduced.
- ***NSF (Not Sufficient Funds) Checks***—When a check is received from a customer, the company debits Cash for the amount of the check. If, however, the customer's checking account does not have the funds to cover that check, the company's bank will not record the increase to the company's checking account. Thus, the bank records will not include an increase, but the book records already did. No adjustment needs to be made to the bank balance; the general ledger cash account needs to be reduced for funds that did not really "exist."
- ***Errors***—Despite the best efforts of the depositor and bank, errors will occasionally occur. For a depositor, the most common mistakes are that amounts are added or subtracted incorrectly or not at all (such as ATM withdrawals or debit card payments). The bank may make a deposit to, or withdraw a check from, the wrong customer's account. The necessary adjustment on the reconciliation depends on which party (depositor or bank) made the error and what the erroneous transaction was. If the depositor made the error, the adjustment will be made to the general ledger cash account. If the bank made the error, its records need to be adjusted accordingly. Note: Depositors are more likely to make errors than banks. Bank errors (both positive and negative) should be communicated to the bank as soon as they are found.

Because of these items, the bank or the depositor may not know the actual cash balance at any particular moment. The differences can be explained by timing. Consider the example that follows. Assume you write a $100 check and mail it to the electric company. You will deduct $100 from your checking account. However your bank has no knowledge of that check until the utility company presents it for payment. A week or more could pass before your bank receives the $100 check, depending on the promptness of the mail service and the utility company's accounting department. If the bank prepared your month-end bank statement after you wrote the check but before the check was cashed, there would be a $100 difference between the bank's determination of your cash balance and your determination of your cash balance. However, given enough time, both sets of records would be the same (at least relative to that check).

Because of the differences that exist between the bank's and depositor's cash records, a **bank reconciliation** should be prepared whenever a bank statement is received. This reconciliation presents the differences between the bank statement and the cash account, so that an accurate balance of cash can be determined for a specific time.

When preparing a bank reconciliation, the first step should be to compare the bank's statement with the company's cash or bank account. The items that need to be included in the reconciliation are those that appear only on one record (either the bank statement or the company cash account). Each difference should be examined in two ways: whether it will increase or decrease the company's cash account and whether it was found on the bank statement or the cash ledger. Items that appear on the bank statement require an adjustment to the cash ledger. Items that appear on the cash ledger require an adjustment to the bank balance. Company errors and bank errors should be categorized as an increase or decrease depending on the effect of *correcting* the error. Visual Recap 4.1 depicts a 2 x 2 matrix for categorizing the reconciliation items.

The following example discusses the process of preparing a bank reconciliation for the Lily Corporation for the month ending on February 28, 2002. At this date, the company's general ledger cash account showed a balance of $13,450; the bank statement for this date showed a balance of $16,890. An analysis of the bank statement and Lily's cash account provided the following information; explanations on the reconciliation effects are shown in italics.

Bank Statement Information:

- The bank deposited $33 to Lily's account for interest on the checking account.[2] *Lily Corporation has earned the interest (a revenue) on the checking account and the bank has added those funds to the company checking account. But Lily didn't know the amount of interest until receiving the bank statement. Therefore, Lily needs to increase the general ledger cash account shown for cash by $33. The bank has already included the $33 as an increase in Lily's checking account balance.*

[2] When a bank deposits funds to a customer's account, the bank will prepare a credit memo; a reduction in a customer's account is shown on a debit memo. This situation seems odd because deposits to a customer's account increase that account and, therefore, should be debits. However, remember that on the bank records, a customer's checking account is an Account Payable of the bank and increases in liabilities are shown as credits; decreases are shown as debits. Thus, from the perspective of the preparer of the memos, the debit and credit notations are appropriate.

VISUAL RECAP 4.1

Categorizing Items for the Bank Reconciliation

	Found on Bank Statement (Adjust Cash Ledger)	Found in Cash Account (Adjust Bank Balance)
Increase	Interest Earned Direct Deposits Company Errors	Deposits in Transit Bank Errors
Decrease	Service Charges NSF Charges Drafts Company Errors (including unrecorded ATM or debit card amounts)	Outstanding Checks Bank Errors

- The bank charged Lily Corporation $20 for printing checks. *Lily Corporation has incurred a cost of doing business (an expense). Even though Lily ordered the checks, Lily didn't know the amount of the charge until receiving the bank statement. Lily needs to decrease the book balance shown for cash by $20. The bank has already included the $20 as a decrease in Lily's checking account balance.*
- The bank returned Henry Dow's check for $360 marked NSF. *When Lily Corporation received the check, Cash was debited (increased) by $360 and Accounts Receivable was credited (decreased) by $360. However, Dow really did not make a payment because his account had insufficient funds to cover the check; Dow still owes Lily the $360. Lily was made aware of the NSF upon receiving the bank statement. Now Lily needs to decrease the book balance shown for cash by $360. The bank never added the funds to Lily's account; therefore, the bank balance is correct. (NOTE: The bank will probably charge Lily a service fee related to this check.)*
- Included with Lily's cancelled checks, the bank returned a $250 check from Lali Corporation that had been charged in error against Lily Corporation's account. *The bank incorrectly removed funds from Lily Corporation's account, thereby making Lily's account balance too small. Thus, Lily needs increase the bank balance by $250. Lily's book balance was never affected, so that amount is correct. Until Lily informs the bank, it will not be aware of the error, and the correct amount will not be shown on the bank statement.*

Cash Account Information:

- The company had deposited $3,000 in the bank that did not appear on the current bank statement. *Lily's book balance is correct, but the bank balance needs to be increased by $3,000. When the bank statement was printed, the bank was unaware of the $3,000. No call is necessary to the bank because deposits in transit tend to clear very quickly.*
- The company had written four checks for a total of $1,580 that were outstanding at the end of the month. *Lily's book balance is correct, but the bank balance needs to be decreased by $1,580. At the time the bank statement was printed, these checks had not been presented to the bank.*
- The company had written a check for $320 to pay an account payable; however, the amount posted from the journal entry to both Cash and Accounts Payable was $230. *Lily's cash is overstated by $90 because too little was deducted in recording the check. Thus, the book balance needs to be decreased by $90. Lily's check cleared the bank at the proper amount of $320, so there are no problems with the bank statement. Lily didn't know there was an error until the bank statement arrived.*

Given the preceding explanations, Lily Corporation categorized the items where the bank and cash account differed as shown in Exhibit 4-1. Then Lily prepared a bank

EXHIBIT 4-1

Categorization of Lily's Items for the Bank Reconciliation

	Found on Bank Statement (Adjust Cash Ledger)	Found in Cash Account (Adjust Bank Balance)
Increase	Interest earned, $33	Deposits in transit, $3,000 Error—Lali check, $250
Decrease	Check printing, $20 NSF—Dow, $360 Error A/P, $90	Outstanding checks, $1,580

EXHIBIT 4-2

Bank Reconciliation

	Book Balance			**Bank Balance**	
As stated, 6/1		$6,450	As stated, 6/1		$4,343
Add:	Interest earned	33	Add:	Deposit in transit	3,000
				Error—Lali	250
Deduct:	Printing charge	(20)	Deduct:	Outstanding checks	(1,580)
	NSF check—Dow	(360)			
	Error—A/P amount	(90)			
Correct balance, 6/30		$6,013	Correct balance, 6/30		$6,013

reconciliation (Exhibit 4-2) to adjust both the bank's balance and Lily's ledger balance. After all the items are shown in the reconciliation, the balance on the book and bank balance side should agree. The amount shown is the actual amount of cash that Lily Corporation has available at the end of June.

The entries needed to adjust Lily Corporation's cash account balance are shown in Exhibit 4-3. Notice that no entries are made for anything on the "bank balance" side of the reconciliation: Lily Corporation cannot make journal entries to change another entity's accounting records. Lily does need to call and inform the bank of the error related to Lali's check and have the $250 redeposited to Lily's checking account.

One additional item needs to be mentioned in relation to the coverage of NSF checks. As discussed above, NSF refers to a check that has been given to a company by someone who does not have sufficient funds to cover it. If Lily Company writes a "bad" check, the cash account would have a credit balance and would be classified as a current liability. Additionally, the bank (as well as the company to whom the check was written) will charge Lily a NSF service fee for the bounced check. Nationally, the average fee for such checks is approximately $24.50.[3]

[3] Laura Bruce, "Average Fee for a Bounced Check Has Risen 2.4 Percent in the Last Six Months," *Money* (May 9, 2001); http://money.cnn.com/2001/05/09/living/q_bankrate/index.htm.

EXHIBIT 4-3

Journal Entries from the Bank Reconciliation

Necessary entries to correct Lily's cash account balance:

Date		**Description**	**Debit**	**Credit**
Feb.	28	Cash	33	
		Interest Revenue		33
		To record June interest on checking account		
	28	Miscellaneous Expenses	20	
		Cash		20
		To record bank charge for printing checks		
	28	Accounts Receivable	360	
		Cash		360
		To record Dow's NSF check		
	28	Accounts Payable	90	
		Cash		90
		To correct error in previously recording A/P payment amount		

SHORT-TERM INVESTMENTS

Companies need to hold an adequate amount of cash to meet current obligations, but do not generally want to hold significantly more cash than will be needed. Cash should be put to productive use and even cash that is deposited in an interest-bearing checking account would still generally be considered "idle." Therefore, companies often make short-term investments of excess cash in the stocks and bonds of other companies or **available-for-sale securities.** These investments are usually sold in the short term and are held only to generate a return on the investment greater than what could be earned on an interest-bearing checking account.

When preparing a balance sheet, short-term investments are shown at fair market value (FMV) rather than cost. Such an adjustment requires an end-of-period adjusting journal entry to record a loss or a gain relative to the investment cost. Such accounting violates the historical cost principle, but provides users with better information because the investments will generally be sold soon after the balance sheet date.

ACCOUNTS RECEIVABLE

Accounts receivable reflect amounts owed to a business by its customers from their purchases of goods or services on credit. This section addresses credit specifically granted by a business to its customers (such as Sears, Neiman Marcus, and Target) rather than national or bank credit cards (such as Visa, MasterCard, and American Express).

The nature of a business's operations significantly influences the proportion of total assets that is typically comprised by accounts receivable. Some companies, such as small service businesses, have a relatively small amount of accounts receivable on their balance sheets. Alternatively, manufacturers and department stores make extensive use of in–house credit. In these industries, a company that does not allow its customers to purchase merchandise on credit will find itself at a significant competitive disadvantage.

Accounting for Accounts Receivable

A company that has decided to allow credit purchases by customers will screen applicants for credit-worthiness. Different types of customers are commonly given different **credit terms.** Such terms express the agreement between buyer and seller regarding the timing of payment and any discount available to the buyer for early payment.

A credit term of "net 30" (expressed as n/30) requires the buyer to pay the full invoice amount within thirty days of the invoice date. This thirty-day period is known as the credit period and does not include the date of the invoice. For example, a customer who buys goods on May 1 with credit terms of n/30 would have until May 31 to pay for the goods.

Sales Discounts

To speed up the cash collection on credit sales, many companies offer **sales discounts** to customers so that they will pay their account balances prior to the end of the credit period. One of the most common credit terms allows a customer to subtract two percent from the invoice price if the bill is paid within ten days (expressed as 2/10). If payment is not made within the ten-day discount period, the full amount of the invoice is due 30 days following the invoice date. Thus, this credit term is expressed as 2/10, n/30.

To illustrate accounting for sales discounts, assume that Payne Company sells $400 of merchandise with credit terms of 2/10, n/30 to Brenda Joyner on March 1. At the time the sale is made, Payne Company does not know whether Ms. Joyner will take advantage of the discount. Consequently, the sales transaction is recorded in the general journal at the $400 shown on the sales invoice:

General Journal				
Date		**Description**	**Debit**	**Credit**
March	1	Acounts Receivabe—B.Joyner	400	
		Sales Revenue		400
		To record credit sale with terms 2/10, n/30		

Assume that Ms. Joyner chooses to take advantage of the available discount and pays her account receivable on March 11, the last day of the discount period. The following entry is made:

General Journal				
Date		**Description**	**Debit**	**Credit**
March	11	Cash	392	
		Sales Discounts	8	
		Accounts Receivable—B. Joyner		400
		To record payment on account within the discount period		

The Sales Discounts account reflects the reduction in selling price granted for prompt payment. Sales Discounts is a contra-revenue account and, as such, directly reduces the balance in the Sales Revenue account. As all contra-accounts do, Sales Discounts has the opposite balance of its related account. That is, Sales Revenue has a credit balance, so Sales Discounts has a debit balance. The use of this account allows the full amount of the sale to remain in revenue account (Sales Revenue) of the accounting records. Sales Discounts is shown on the income statement as a reduction of Sales Revenue.

If Ms. Joyner does not take advantage of the sales discount and pays her account receivable on March 31, the following entry is required:

General Journal				
Date		**Description**	**Debit**	**Credit**
March	31	Cash	400	
		Accounts Receivable—B. Joyner		600
		To record payment on account		

Customers should almost always take advantage of any prompt payment discounts that are offered—even if it means having to go to the bank and borrow the money to do so! Consider the above example. Ms. Joyner can either pay on the 10th day of the discount period (saving $8) or on the 30th day after the invoice. The 2 percent rate is essentially an interest charge for a 20-day period. There are approximately 18 20-day periods in a year (360 days ÷ 20 days). Thus, a 2 percent rate for 20 days translates into approximately a 36 percent annual rate of interest. Assume that Ms. Joyner can borrow money from the bank at 9 percent per year. She borrows $320 on March 11 and remits those funds to Payne Company. Twenty days later (when she would have had to pay Payne Company), Ms. Joyner repays the bank; her interest charge on the $320 she borrowed for 20 days is $1.60 ($320 × 0.09 × 20/360)—a savings of $6.40.

Sales Returns and Allowances

Most merchandising companies grant cash or credit customers a full refund if they need or want to return merchandise. Additionally, customers also may be granted a price reduction, called a **sales allowance,** to persuade them to keep damaged, defective, or out-of-season merchandise. Because these items may be fairly small in amount individually, such

EXHIBIT 4-4

Use of Contra-Revenue Accounts

Information:

On March 10, Dinah Company sold Glover's Shirt Shop 20 specially-monogrammed shirts at $35 each. Dinah grants Glover credit terms of 2/10, n/30. On March 12, Glover returns 1 shirt to Dinah Company because of a tear in the fabric. On March 14, Glover calls Dinah Company and asks for a price reduction of $38 on the remaining shirts because the logo was slightly smaller than ordered; Dinah Company agrees to the price reduction. On March 21, Glover remits half of the amount owed and remits the remaining amount owed on April 9.

General Journal

Date		Description	PR	Debit	Credit
Mar.	10	Accounts Receivable—Glover		700.00	
		Sales Revenue			700.00
		To record sale on account			
	12	Sales Returns and Allowances		35.00	
		Accounts Receivable—Glover			35.00
		To record return of shirt for credit			
	14	Sales Returns and Allowances		38.00	
		Accounts Receivable—Glover			38.00
		To record an allowance given for a monogramming error			
	21	Cash		307.23	
		Sales Discounts		6.27	
		Accounts Receivable—Glover			313.50
		To record partial payment on account receivable within the discount period A/R = $700 – $35 – $38 = $627; half = 313.50; .02 × $313.50 = $6.27			
Apr.	9	Cash		313.50	
		Accounts Receivable—Glover			313.50
		To record payment for remaining account receivable			

The revenue section of an income statement prepared using only the information about this transaction would appear as follows:

Sales Revenue		$700.00
Less: Sales Discounts	$ 6.27	
Sales Returns and Allowances	73.00	(79.27)
Net Sales		$620.73

refunds and price reductions are recorded together in another contra-revenue account entitled Sales Returns and Allowances.

The Sales Returns and Allowances account, like Sales Discounts, has a debit balance and is subtracted from Sales on the income statement. Reducing the sales revenue account by these two contra-accounts results in an amount called net sales, which is typically the first line item on a merchandising or manufacturing company's income statement. Exhibit 4-4 illustrates the use of the Sales Returns and Allowances, account as well as the Sales Discount account.

Uncollectible Accounts

There are two key activities associated with a credit sale: making the sale and collecting the resulting receivable. Occasionally, the latter task is the more challenging of the two. Whenever a business decides to extend credit to customers, there is the potential for bad debts. When it becomes apparent that a receivable will not be collected, businesses should eliminate, or write off, that receivable. Such a write-off is a legitimate cost of doing business and, as such, is an expense. There are two ways that bad debt write-offs could be treated: the direct write-off method and the allowance (or estimation) method.

Under the **direct write-off method,** a company simply waits until a particular account has been determined to be uncollectible and, at that time, writes-off the account. For example, assume that in November 2002, Dozier Company sold $300 of merchandise on credit to D. Ronaho. On September 18, 2003, after vigorous collection efforts had failed, Dozier decided to write off the $300 receivable using the direct write-off method. The following entry would be made:

General Journal				
Date		Description	Debit	Credit
Sep.	18	Uncollectible Accounts Expense	300	
		Accounts Receivable—D. Ronaho		300
		To write off account receivable		

Under these circumstances, the write-off entry is made in September 2003, while the related credit sale was recorded in November 2002. The matching principle states that a company should attempt to match expenses with their corresponding revenues. Businesses will almost certainly have some bad debts when credit sales are made and, in general, a reasonable estimate of such write-offs can be made. In most cases, businesses will spend many months trying to collect from customers; therefore, the write-off often does not occur until an accounting period after the credit sale. The direct write-off method violates the matching principle by ignoring the relationship between credit sales and the possibility of bad debts. Therefore, this method is not considered a generally accepted accounting principle and should not be used for financial reporting purposes.

To satisfy the matching principle, an estimate of future uncollectible accounts should be recorded as an expense in the period that credit sales are generated. Under the **allowance** (or estimation) **method,** a business makes an estimate of uncollectible accounts expense at the end of each accounting period. This estimate is recorded through an adjusting entry that includes a debit to Uncollectible Accounts Expense and a credit to a contra-asset account called Allowance for Uncollectible Accounts. The Allowance for Uncollectible Accounts reduces Accounts Receivable and has a credit balance; thus, increases are recorded as credits and decreases are recorded as debits. For balance sheet purposes, this account is subtracted from Accounts Receivable to reduce that asset to its approximate net realizable value. It is important to note that, at the time that the estimate is made, *no specific customers' receivables have been identified as uncollectible and Accounts Receivable cannot be affected.*

Numerous methods exist to estimate bad debts; one of the easiest is to use a percentage of credit sales, using historical or industry data. For example, assume that Onken Furniture Company had total sales in 2002 of $2,500,000. Of that amount, $1,800,000 was on credit. Onken's manager researches industry data and found that, given the company's business, customer profiles, and location, a reasonable estimate of bad debts is 1.5 percent ($1,800,000 × 0.015 = $27,000). The estimate is applied only to credit sales because the cash sales have already been collected. When adjusting entries are made on December 31, 2002, the company records the following entry:

General Journal				
Date		Description	Debit	Credit
Dec.	31	Uncollectible Accounts Expense	27,000	
		Allowance for Uncollectible Accounts		27,000
		To record an estimate for bad debts related to 2002 credit sales		

When an actual account is determined to be uncollectible, the Allowance for Uncollectible Accounts will be reduced (debited) and the customer's Account Receivable will be written off (credited). Suppose that Dan Quinn, a customer owing Onken Furniture Company $2,300, filed for personal bankruptcy in February 2003. Given this information, the company did not expect to collect Quinn's account. Under such circumstances, the following entry would have been appropriate to write off the receivable from Dan Quinn.

General Journal				
Date		Description	Debit	Credit
Feb.	18	Allowance for Uncollectible Accounts	2,300	
		Accounts Receivable—D. Quinn		2,300
		To write off an accounts receivable		

Note that the write-off entry does not include a debit to Uncollectible Accounts Expense. The December 31, 2002, adjusting entry for the estimated uncollectible accounts expense took into consideration the likelihood that a certain percentage of the company's year-end receivables would not be collected. That adjusting entry properly matched the bad debt expense associated with such receivables to Onken's 2002 fiscal year. When specific receivables from 2002 later prove to be uncollectible, they are debited to the allowance account.

If a previously written-off account is later collected, the account must be reestablished, but only for the amount collected. This is accomplished by reversing the write-off entry. The entry immediately following will depict the collection of the cash. For example, if Quinn makes restitution of 40¢ on the dollar on May 15, he would pay Onken $920 ($2,300 × $0.40). The entries to record his payment are shown below.

General Journal				
Date		**Description**	**Debit**	**Credit**
May	15	Accounts Receivable— D. Quinn	920	
		Allowance for Uncollectible Accounts		920
		To reestablish a previous write off		
May	15	Cash	920	
		Accounts Receivable— D. Quinn		
		To collect an account receivable		920

Credit Card Receivables

Increased sales and larger market shares await companies that allow customers to charge purchases of goods and services. Credit cards, such as VISA, MasterCard, and American Express, have become important fixtures in the national economy. Retailers realize several important benefits by having their customers make purchases with these types of credit cards. One of these benefits is that credit card companies absorb bad debt losses resulting from credit card sales. Credit card companies also relieve retail businesses of the need to check credit references of prospective customers. Finally, credit card companies generally pay amounts owed to retailers on a more timely basis than do individual customers.

A company that accepts credit cards is called a merchant. Merchants must wait for payment from the credit card company just like they wait for payment from their customers (but usually not for as long). Therefore, a receivable is still debited when a sale is made on a credit card. For example, if Langer Company makes $6,000 in Visa sales on February 20, 2002, the following journal entry would be made:

General Journal				
Date		**Description**	**Debit**	**Credit**
Feb.	20	Credit Cards Receivable	6,000	
		Sales Revenue		6,000
		To record Visa sales		

Credit card authorization machines at the merchant's place of business use the phone lines to immediately charge a customer's credit card. Because the charge is processed so quickly, the cash for the sale is usually directly deposited into the merchant's bank account the next business day. However, credit card companies charge for the services they provide. These companies typically deduct a 1 to 5 percent fee from the gross receipts they collect for retailers. (Such a fee can be viewed as a type of "prompt payment" discount given to company charge card customers.) Given the quantity of business that Langer does with Visa, that company charges Langer a 2.5 percent service fee. When the cash is deposited into Langer's account on February 22, Langer would make the following journal entry:

General Journal				
Date		Description	Debit	Credit
Feb.	22	Cash	5,850	
		Credit Card Expense	150	
		Credit Cards Receivable		6000
		To record purchase of inventory on account		

Notes Receivable

When unable to pay an account receivable by the due date, a customer may be asked to sign a promissory note, which is a legal document that formally recognizes a debt owed by one party to another. When such a note is signed, a customer's receivable balance is transferred from Accounts Receivable to Notes Receivable. Besides more formally documenting a customer's receivable account, a promissory note typically requires the customer to begin paying interest on his or her unpaid receivable balance.

Assume that Guzzardi Corp. sells $2,500 worth of merchandise to Dauterive Co. on July 1, 2002; credit terms are 2/10, n/30. On July 31, Dauterive Co. informs Guzzardi that the bill cannot be paid and requests that the account be transferred to a note. A $2,500, 8%, 3-month note receivable is prepared and exchanged. The note and the $50 ($2,500 × 0.08 × 3/12) of interest are paid on the due date. Exhibit 4-5 provides the journal entries for these transactions.

ACCOUNTING INFORMATION FOR DECISION MAKING

Cash and accounts receivable are particularly important assets because they provide the primary means by which a business can pay its debts as they come due. Declining cash or slow accounts receivable collections can leave a business searching for other ways to raise the funds needed to finance its day-to-day operations.

Decision makers need to be informed of any unusual characteristics or conditions associated with a company's accounts or notes receivable. For example, a company having a significant amount of receivables from related parties, such as company executives, should disclose that fact in the firm's financial statements. One reason such information is important is that management may not vigorously pursue collection efforts on such receivables or may "forgive" the loans even if the company is in poor financial condition. To illustrate the potential for problems, consider that WorldCom (www.worldcom.com) had loaned its founder and CEO $341 million in the late 1990s. The loans, still on the company books in 2002, carried interest rates at slightly over two percent and had no fixed due date.[4] WorldCom was the subject of a major fraud investigation as of July 2002.

A company can also borrow against (use as collateral) its accounts receivable for a loan. If a company defaults on such a loan, the lender can recover the amount it is owed from the subsequent cash collections on the receivables that were pledged in support of the loan application. Pledged accounts receivable should be disclosed in the firm's financial statement footnotes. Such disclosure alerts decision makers that the company has one less financing alternative available in the future.

[4] Joan S. Lublin and Shawn Young, "WorldCom Loan to CEO of $341 Million Is the Most Generous in Recent Memory," *Wall Street Journal* (March 15, 2002), p. A3.

EXHIBIT 4.5
Notes Receivable

General Journal				
Date		**Description**	**Debit**	**Credit**
July	1	Accounts Receivable—Dauterive	2,500	
		Sales Revenue		2,500
		To record sale on account		
	31	Notes Receivable—Dauterive	2,500	
		Accounts Receivable—Dauterive		2,500
		To record exchange of open account for a 90-day, 8% note		
Oct.	1	Cash	2,550	
		Notes Receivable—Dauterive		2,550
		Interest Revenue		50
		To record collection of note and interest		

Quick Ratio

Financial ratios are measures that express the relationship or interrelationships between, or among, two or more financial statement items. One key financial ratio involving cash is the quick ratio. The **quick ratio** is computed by dividing the sum of an entity's quick assets by the sum of its current liabilities. **Quick assets** generally include cash and cash equivalents, short-term investments, and the net amount of current notes and accounts receivable (receivables less any allowance accounts).

$$\text{Quick ratio} = \text{Quick assets} \div \text{Current liabilities}$$

If the firm has more quick assets than current liabilities, the quick ratio indicates the number of times a company can pay its current liabilities. For example, if Abbott Company has a quick ratio of 1.25 (or 125%), Abbott can pay all of its current liabilities and still have quick assets left. If quick assets are less than current liabilities, the quick ratio indicates the percent of current liabilities the company can pay. For example, if Babbin Company has a quick ratio of 0.92 (or 92%), the company can only pay 92% of its current liabilities with its existing quick assets.

The quick ratio is used to evaluate a business's liquidity Liquidity refers to an entity's ability to finance its day-to-day operations and to pay its liabilities as they mature. Liquidity is heavily influenced by the amount of cash a business has on hand and the amount of cash it can quickly raise, such as by selling short-term investments. As the quick ratio decreases, so does liquidity.

Insight on a company's liquidity can be gained by comparing the firm's quick ratios to key benchmarks. For example, Dun & Bradstreet (www.dnb.com), an investment advisory firm, suggests that businesses should generally maintain a quick ratio of at least 1.0. Another yardstick for evaluating a company's quick ratio is the industry norm for that ratio. Many companies have a strong liquidity position because they have recently obtained long-term loans from banks or sold stock to investors. To determine the source of a company's liquidity, the firm's recent cash flow data must be examined on the statement of cash flows.

Age of Accounts Receivable

Financial analysts often consider the quality of a company's accounts receivable, which is principally a function of their age. Determining the age of a company's receivables is a two-step process. First, the accounts receivable turnover ratio is computed as follows:

A/R turnover ratio = Net credit sales ÷ Average A/R

This ratio measures the number of times that a company "turns over" or collects its receivables each year. Companies want to convert their receivables into cash as quickly as possible. Consequently, a general rule is that high accounts receivable turnover ratios are better than low ratios. The average accounts receivable is equal to the beginning plus the ending balances of accounts receivable divided by two.

The **age of receivables** is computed by dividing 360 (the approximate number of days in a year) by the accounts receivable turnover ratio:

Age of receivables = 360 days ÷ A/R turnover ratio

This measurement indicates the average number of days that a company's receivables have been outstanding. Viewed another way, age of receivables indicates the average period required for a company to collect a receivable resulting from a credit sale. This age can be compared to the standard credit terms allowed to determine if the company is collecting its receivables in accordance with its credit policies. Exhibit 4-6 provides an illustration of the computation of the accounts receivable turnover ratio and the age of receivables.

Many financial ratios, including age of receivables, vary significantly from company to company and industry to industry. For example, at the end of its fiscal year, Starbucks' (www.starbucks.com) age of receivables was only about 11 days, while Pfizer's (a pharmaceutical company; www.pfizer.com) age of receivables was almost six times "older."

Starbucks (as of 9/30/01):
Average A/R = ($90,425,000 + $76,385,000) ÷ 2 = $83,405,000
A/R turnover = $2,648,980,000 ÷ $83,405,000 = 31.8
Age of receivables = 360 ÷ 31.8 = 11.3 days

Pfizer (as of 12/31/00):
Average A/R = ($5,638,000,000 + $5,489,000,000) ÷ 2 = $5,563,500,000
A/R turnover = 29,574,000,000 ÷ 5,563,500,000 = 5.3
Age of receivables = 360 ÷ 5.3 = 67.9 days

This comparison does not necessarily mean that Pfizer's receivables are of lower quality than Starbucks'. Among other factors, differing credit terms offered by the two companies

EXHIBIT 4-6

Accounts Receivable Turnover Ratio and Age of Receiviables

Net credit sales for 2002	$704,250
Accounts receivable, 1/1/02	$ 82,000
Accounts receivable, 12/31/02	$ 74,500

Average Accounts Receivable = ($82,000 + $74,500) ÷ 2 = $78,250
Accounts Receivable Turnover Ratio = $704,250 ÷ $78,250 = 9
Age of Receivables = 360 days ÷ 9 = 40 days

If normal credit terms are 2/10, n/30, the company is not doing a very good job of collecting its accounts receivable in the 30 days expected. On average, the accounts are 10 days overdue.

and varying economic conditions affecting each firm's industry may account for the large disparity in their age of receivables. The normal for the age of receivables in Starbucks' industry is about 16 days, while the corresponding norm for Pfizer's industry is 54 days. These industry data suggest that Starbucks collects its receivables a little more quickly than the typical company in its industry, while Pfizer's receivables could be considered "elderly" compared to the industry norm. This indicator might suggest that Pfizer faces a higher risk of bad debt losses than most firms in its industry.

SUMMARY

Cash typically does not pose complex accounting issues. Critical elements for cash are safekeeping and control over access. Companies handle such control, in part, by using financial institutions to store cash, and by dispersing most large cash payments by check (rather than using petty cash). Preparing a monthly bank reconciliation allows for a formalized review of cash transactions and helps determine the actual amount of cash on hand at the end of the bank statement period. Once that amount is found, journal entries will be needed to correct the general ledger account balance.

Accounts receivable are recorded at the sales prices of the items sold. Companies may provide credit terms, such as 2/10, n/30, to customers to entice them to pay earlier than the end of the credit period. Such prompt payment discounts are recorded in a contra-revenue account entitled Sales Discounts. The cost of returned goods from customers and price reductions offered to entice customers to keep defective or undesired merchandise are recorded in another contra-revenue account called Sales Returns and Allowances.

The key accounting issue for accounts receivable is arriving at a reliable estimate of uncollectible accounts expense. Businesses are generally required to use the allowance method to estimate the uncollectible accounts expense for financial reporting purposes. A common approach to estimating the amount of expected uncollectible accounts at the end of an accounting period is to take a percentage of credit sales for the period. The estimate is then recorded as an expense of the period and in a contra-asset account until the actual uncollectible accounts are known.

Notes receivable may be used when a company sells goods (or loans funds) for payment terms of longer than the normal 30-day credit period. Notes receivable typically require interest to be paid on the amount of the principal of the sale (or the loan).

Decision makers need information regarding the liquidity (or ability to pay debts as they mature) and collectibility of accounts receivable. Financial ratios can be used to assess the financial health of a business. The quick ratio measures the liquidity or ability to pay debts as they come due. A financial ratio used to monitor the collectibility of accounts receivable is the age of receivables. As the average age of a company's accounts receivable increases, the percentage of those receivables that must be written off as uncollectible generally increases as well.

KEY TERMS

accounts receivable turnover ratio
age of receivables
allowance method
available-for-sale securities
bank reconciliation
cash equivalent
credit term
direct write-off method
financial ratio
liquidity
petty cash
quick asset
quick ratio
sales allowance
sales discount
sales return

QUESTIONS

1. What is a "cash equivalent?" Why are cash equivalents combined with cash on a balance sheet? *(LO 4.1)*
2. Why might the length of a company's operating cycle affect its cash needs? *(LO 4.4)*
3. What is the purpose of a bank reconciliation? Why should it be prepared in a timely manner? *(LO 4.2)*
4. What are the most common situations that require adjustments on your personal bank reconciliation? Why do these items occur? *(LO 4.2)*
5. Why would a company choose to sell on credit rather than strictly on a cash basis? What problems would the decision to sell on credit create for a business? How would these problems differ if the business issued its own credit cards versus allowed the use of national credit cards? *(LO 4.4)*
6. What accounting concept requires businesses to estimate their uncollectible accounts expense each accounting period? Why will such estimations provide better information to decision makers than would the direct write-off method? *(LO 4.3)*
7. Define "liquidity." Why is liquidity important in preparing a balance sheet? *(LO 4.4)*
8. What types of decision makers are most interested in a company's liquidity and why? *(LO 4.4)*
9. How is the quick ratio computed? How do decision makers use a company's quick ratio? *(LO 4.4)*
10. How are the accounts receivable turnover ratio and age of receivables helpful in analyzing the collectibility of a company's accounts receivable? *(LO 4.4)*

EXERCISES

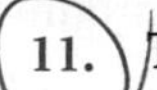

11. **True & False** *(All LOs)*

Following are a series of statements regarding topics discussed in this chapter.

Required:

Indicate whether each statement is true (T) or false (F).

(1) The risk of third-party (national) credit cards is greater than the risk of in-house credit.

(2) Sales Returns and Allowances is a contra-revenue account.

(3) Bank errors require an adjustment to the company's general ledger cash account.

(4) Collectibility of a business's accounts receivable is the key information need of decision makers.

(5) The direct write-off method results in an appropriate matching of sales revenue with bad debts expense.

(6) Inventory is a quick asset.

(7) Cash equivalents are funds that companies have invested in short-term securities that mature six months or less from the date of purchase.

(8) The credit terms for a sales transaction express the agreement between the buyer and seller regarding the timing of payment and any discount available to the buyer for early payment.

(9) Outstanding checks decrease the balance of the bank account.

(10) Notes receivable are always dated in one-year increments.

12. **Journal Entries for Accounts Receivable** *(LO 4.1)*

Following are recent transactions and other events involving Rodman's Rainbow, a company that markets hair-care products.

June 1	Customer purchased $400 of merchandise on credit with terms of n/60.
June 5	Wrote off an uncollectible account receivable of $350.
June 15	Customer purchased $1,200 of merchandise on credit with terms of 2/10, n/30.
June 17	Customer who purchased merchandise on June 1 returned $60 of that merchandise because it was defective.
June 25	Received amount due from customer who purchased merchandise on June 15.
June 29	Received payment in full from customer whose account balance was written off on June 5.
June 30	Received amount due from customer who purchased merchandise on June 1.

Required:

Prepare journal entries to record each of these transactions or events.

13. **Credit Card Sales** *(LO 4.1)*

The Magic Shoppe sells games, books, and party favors. Most customers charge their purchases to national credit cards. Following is a summary of The Magic Shoppe's total credit card sales for July and the service fee of each credit card honored by the business.

	PlasticCard	BanCard	BigCard
July credit card sales	$10,500	$22,000	$37,250
Service fee	3%	3%	5%

Required:

(1) Record these July credit card sales and the collection entries from the credit card companies in The Magic Shoppe's accounting records.

(2) Why do retail stores honor bank credit cards? Won't allowing customers to pay for their purchases with credit cards effectively reduce a business's profit because of the fees that these cards charge?

(3) Given the relatively high service fee charged by BigCard, what is one reason The Magic Shoppe may choose to honor that card?

14. **Recording Notes Receivable** *(LO 4.1)*

On October 1, 2002, Davidson Co. received a $3,000, 10%, 4-month note from Chris Spent in exchange for his open account receivable. Davidson's fiscal year ends on December 31.

Required:

(1) Prepare the entry to record the receipt of this note receivable for this company.

(2) Prepare the necessary year-end adjusting entry related to this note receivable. Why is this entry needed?

(3) Assume that Chris repaid the note and interest on the due date. Prepare the entry needed to record the funds received by Davidson Co.

15. **Estimating Uncollectible Accounts Expense** *(LO 4.3)*

Lernig Company had total sales of $1,350,000 for the year ended December 31, 2002; of that amount, $1,000,000 was on credit. The company had a balance of $16,300 in the Allowance for Uncollectible Accounts on January 1, 2002. During the year, $12,500 worth of bad debts was written off. On December 31, 2002, Lernig made an adjusting entry to record estimated uncollectible accounts at 2.5 percent of credit sales.

Required:

(1) Prepare the appropriate year-end adjusting entry to record the uncollectible accounts expense for this company at the end of 2002.

(2) What was the balance in Allowance for Uncollectible Accounts after making the entry in part (1)?

(3) What was the balance in Uncollectible Accounts Expense after making the entry in part (1)?

(4) Why are the answers to parts (2) and (3) different?

16. **Computing the Quick Ratio** *(LO 4.4, Excel)*

Macromedia, Inc. designs and markets computer software products. The following are the company's year-end current assets and current liabilities for two recent years.

	Year 1	Year 2
Accounts payable	$6,007	$11,364
Accounts receivable (net)	8,040	14,601
Accrued liabilities	3,492	8,956
Cash and cash equivalents	10,230	28,829
Inventory	1,601	1,568
Other current liabilities	347	331
Prepaid expenses	2,264	8,115
Short-term investments	23,751	87,833
Unearned revenue	2,767	1,235

Required:

(1) Compute Macromedia's quick ratios for Years 1 and 2. Did this ratio improve or weaken between the end of Year 1 and the end of Year 2? Explain your answer.

(2) Briefly discuss factors that may have accounted for the change in Macromedia's liquidity position between the end of Year 1 and the end of Year 2.

17. **Analyzing Accounts Receivable** *(LO 4.4)*

Consider the following financial information for a recent year for two fairly similar companies:

	Altizer Corporation	Bechtel Corporation
Cash sales	$20,000	$40,000
Net credit sales	80,000	60,000
Total sales	$100,000	$100,000
Average accounts receivable during the year	$60,000	$30,000

Required:

(1) Compute each company's accounts receivable turnover ratio and age of receivables.

(2) Which of these companies is better managing its accounts receivable? Explain.

PROBLEMS

18. Petty Cash *(LO 4.1)*

Maitland & Murphy, an advertising agency, established a petty cash fund to reduce the number of small checks that were written. On April 1, 2004, the fund was established for $400. On May 1, the petty cash envelope contained $187.23 in cash and coins and the following receipts:

Vendor	Amount	For
Dan's Doughnuts	$18.21	Staff meeting doughnuts
The Hardware Depot	27.54	Repairs
Jamie's Art Supply	87.54	Art supplies
U-Move Vanlines	30.75	Delivery truck rental
Texakon Gas Station	10.50	Gas for delivery truck
U.S. Postal Service	38.23	Stamps

Required:

(1) Record the April 1 journal entry to establish the petty cash fund.

(2) Record the entry to replenish petty cash on May 1.

(3) Assume that instead of $187.23, the amount of cash in the petty cash envelope was $185.02 on May 1 before replenishment. Provide two reasons why this situation could occur.

19. Credit Card Sales *(LO 4.1)*

Andee's Restaurant accepts three credit cards: Verra Express, United Card, and MacCard. Sales information for Andee's first three days in business is given below.

	Customer Paid With			
	Verra Express	United Card	MacCard	Cash
Sept. 1	$173	$181	$149	$778
Sept. 2	352	87	107	821
Sept. 3	128	144	60	668

The following payments were directly deposited into Andee's bank account on Sept 3:

(a) $514.50 from Verra Express for the sales on September 1 and 2.

(b) $257.28 from United Card for the sales on September 1 and 2.

(c) $143.79 from MacCard for the sales on September 1.

Required:

(1) Record the journal entries for the sales on September 1, 2, and 3.

(2) Record the journal entries for the direct deposits on September 3.

(3) What percent fee does each credit card company charge?

(4) How might Andee's employees encourage customers to use the credit card with the lowest service fee?

20. Sales of Merchandise *(LO 4.1)*

Cousins, Inc. sells ladies clothing. Customers may pay with (1) cash or check, (2) national credit card (which charges a 1% service fee), or (3) in-house credit with terms 2/10, n/30. The following are selected transactions from Cousins.

March 1	Ms. Leonard charged $450 to her in-house account.
March 4	Cash sales were $1,124 and sales on national credit cards were $1,643.
March 6	The credit card company deposited the appropriate amount to Cousins, Inc.'s bank account.
March 8	Ms. Leonard returned $50 of her March 1 purchases.
March 15	Ms. Adams charged $800 to her in-house account.
March 22	A customer returned merchandise and was given a $120 cash refund.
March 24	Ms. Adams paid her balance in full.
March 25	Ms. Leonard paid her balance in full.

Required:

Journalize the above transactions.

21. Notes Receivable *(LO 4.1)*

All sales for Ronnie Co. are made with credit terms of 2/10, n/30. If a customer is unable to pay by the end of the credit period, Ronnie Co. will exchange the account receivable for a 12%, 3-month note receivable. On October 1, 2002, Chandra Co. purchased $5,500 of merchandise from Ronnie Co. However, Chandra Co. could not pay for the merchandise on the due date.

Required:

(1) What was Chandra Co.'s original due date for payment for the merchandise?

(2) If Chandra Co. had been able to pay for the merchandise within the discount period, on what date and how much would Chandra Co. have paid?

(3) On what date is the note receivable due? What is the total amount that will need to be paid at that time?

(4) Prepare all necessary journal entries for Ronnie Co.'s transactions with Chandra Co., assuming that payment is made for the note on its due date.

(5) Given its terms of business, do you think that Ronnie Co. should make an estimate for uncollectible notes receivable? Provide rationale for your answer.

22. Bank Reconciliation *(LO 4.2, Excel)*

Xenon, Inc.'s August 31 bank statement had an ending cash balance of $2,567. On August 31, Xenon's general ledger showed a balance of $860. After comparing the general ledger to the bank statement, the following items were noted:

(a)	Outstanding checks	$2,250
(b)	Interest paid by the bank	12
(c)	An NSF check from one of Xenon's customers	32
(d)	Deposits in transit	1,900
(e)	Service fee charged by the bank	8
(f)	A direct deposit from a customer	1,400
(g)	Check 345, to Acme Insurance, was written for and cleared for $615. It was recorded in the general ledger for $600.	

Required:

(1) Prepare a bank reconciliation for Xenon, Inc.

(2) Make the required journal entries associated with the bank reconciliation.

(3) Discuss the benefits and drawbacks of maintaining a checking account at a financial institution rather than paying all bills in cash.

23. **Journal Entries for a Merchandising Company** *(LO 4.1 & 4.3)*

Jenkins, Inc., which sells household appliances, begins its fiscal year on June 1. A partial balance sheet for Jenkins is given below.

Jenkins, Inc.
Partial Balance Sheet
May 31, 2004

Accounts Receivable	$35,000
Allowance for Uncollectible Accounts	(3,500)
Net Realizable Value	$31,500

The following transactions took place during June 2004.

June 1	Cash sales for the day totaled $1,100.
June 4	Sold $2,000 of merchandise to another appliance retailer, JLK Company, with terms of 2/10, n/30.
June 6	Sold $300 of merchandise to Jae Lee, terms n/20.
June 8	Wrote off an uncollectible account receivable of $450.
June 12	JLK Company returned $500 of the merchandise purchased on June 4 because the merchandise was defective.
June 14	JLK Company paid Jenkins the amount due for the June 4 transaction.
June 20	Sold $950 of merchandise to Larissa Rodriguez with terms of n/20.
June 26	Received payment from Jae Lee for merchandise sold to him on June 6.
June 28	Received a check for $450 from customer whose account balance had been written off on June 8.

Required:

(1) Prepare general journal entries for the June transactions.

(2) Calculate Jenkins' net sales for June.

(3) Calculate Jenkins' balance in Accounts Receivable and Allowance for Uncollectible Accounts.

(4) Prepare a partial balance sheet as of June 30, 2004.

24. **Uncollectible Accounts Expense** *(LO 4.3, ethics)*

Following are the December 31, 2002, balances of Accounts Receivable and Allowance for Uncollectible Accounts of Easton Hammer Corporation (EHC).

Accounts Receivable	$3,200,000
Allowance for Uncollectible Accounts (credit balance)	112,500

During 2003, EHC wrote off the following accounts:

May 15	Jim Cantore	$1,425
July 6	Mike Bono	930

Required:

(1) Prepare the journal entries that were made to record the write-offs of the Cantore and Bono accounts.

(2) At year-end 2003, the company's accountant estimates that EHC has $363,000 of uncollectible accounts receivable. Prepare the appropriate adjusting journal entry to record uncollectible accounts expense at year-end.

(3) Suppose that the accountant in part (2) was too conservative in his estimate. Instead of uncollectible accounts receivable of $363,000, the company actually has uncollectible accounts of $278,000. How will the accountant's overstatement of year-end uncollectible accounts receivable affect EHC's income statement and balance sheet for the year in question? How may this overstatement affect the decisions of third parties, such as bankers and investors, who rely on those financial statements?

(4) Will the assumed overstatement referred to in part (3) affect EHC's financial statements for the following year? If so, explain how. If not, explain why not.

(5) Is it ever permissible to intentionally overstate expenses in a company's financial statements? Defend your answer and refer to related accounting concepts or principles from Chapter 2.

(6) Assume Mike Bono paid EHC $930 on August 14, 2004. How would this receipt be journalized by EHC?

25. **Analyzing Liquidity** *(LO 4.4)*

Year-end balance sheet data (shown in millions of dollars) for Calisto Soup Company follow.

	Year 1	Year 2
Cash and Cash Equivalents	$94	$63
Short-Term Investments	2	7
Accounts Receivable (net)	578	646
Inventories	786	804
Property, Plant & Equipment (net)	2,401	2,265
Current Liabilities	1,665	1,851
Long-Term Liabilities	1,338	1,343

Required:

(1) Explain the significance of the quick ratio. How do decision makers use this ratio when interpreting a company's financial statements?

(2) Compute Calisto's quick ratio for both years. Based strictly on these ratios, in which year was the company's liquidity position stronger?

(3) If the average quick ratio in Calisto's industry is 1.2, is the company's quick ratio better or worse than the industry norm?

(4) Identify at least three factors that could account for Calisto's quick ratio being significantly different from the industry norm.

26. **Analyzing Accounts Receivable** *(LO 4.4, Excel)*

QL Corporation sells computer peripherals, primarily on a credit basis. Following are selected financial data, expressed in thousands, for this firm for a recent three-year period. QL had net sales of $52,257,000 in the year 2000 and accounts receivable of $6,046,000 on January 1, 2001.

	2001	2002	2003
Net Sales	$44,902	57,675	$53,779
Year-End Accounts Receivable	6,007	9,358	7,003

Required:

(1) Compute QL's accounts receivable turnover ratio and age of receivables for Years 2001 through 2003.

(2) Did these ratios improve or weaken over this three-year period? Explain.

CASES

27. **Establishing a Credit Policy** *(LO 4.1, writing)*

Recently, Erica Lovell, owner of Erica's Electronics, decided to allow customers to purchase merchandise on credit. Credit customers will be given 60 days to pay for their purchases. No discounts will be granted for early payment. Erica believes this new policy will increase her store's sales because her principal competitor in town has a strict cash-only sales policy.

Required:

Write a brief memo to Erica describing some of the business benefits of, and problems with, the new credit policy. Include in your memo nonaccounting issues that Erica will confront following this policy's implementation.

28. **Annual Reports** *(LO 4.4, Internet, Excel)*

Use the annual report of Carnival Corporation for the 2001 fiscal year to answer the following questions. The annual report can be found at www.carnival.com/aboutCCL; follow the links to investor relations.

Required:

(1) Calculate Carnival's quick ratios for 2000 and 2001.

(2) What do the quick ratios calculated in part (1) indicate about Carnival's liquidity?

(3) All else being equal, what effects would each of the following have on the quick ratio?

(a) an increase in cash and cash equivalents

(b) a decrease in short-term investments

(c) an increase in current liabilities

(d) an increase in inventory

(e) an increase in sales revenue

(4) Comment on the change in the quick ratio from 2000 to 2001. What account(s) is (are) primarily responsible for this change?

(5) Does anything in Carnival's Notes to the Financial Statements help explain the change in the accounts comprising the calculation of the quick ratio? If so, what information is provided?

29. **Annual Reports** *(LO 4.4, Internet, Excel)*

May Department Stores Company is the parent company to several department store chains including Foley's, Lord & Taylor, and David's Bridal. Use May's annual report for the 2001 fiscal year to answer the following questions. The annual report can be found at www.mayco.com; follow the links to investor relations.

Required:

Answer each of the following questions for the fiscal year ended February 2, 2002.

(1) What is the net realizable value of May's accounts receivable?

(2) What is the balance in the following accounts on February 2, 2002:

(a) accounts receivable

(b) allowance for uncollectible accounts

(3) What is the average balance in accounts receivable?

(4) What is the total of May's net credit sales? [Hint: Net Retail Sales include both credit and cash sales. Net Credit Sales is only the portion sold on credit. Where might you find a discussion about what portion of sales are on credit?]

(5) Calculate the accounts receivable turnover ratio and the age of receivables ratios. Comment on the results.

30. **Comparing Companies** *(LO 4.4, group, Internet)*

Identifying the similarities and differences between companies is as crucial to making investment decisions as understanding a single company's financial statements. Form groups of at least four students. Each group should select a single industry. Each group member should locate a different annual report within that industry. (The industry and individual company may be assigned by your instructor.)

Required—individual group members:

(1) Calculate the following ratios for the company you selected for the two most recent fiscal years.

(a) quick ratio

(b) accounts receivable turnover

(c) age of receivables

(2) Does the company you chose have any short-term investments? What percentage of current assets do the short-term investment represent? What percentage of total assets do the short-term investments represent? Why might a company have short-term investments?

Required—groups:

(3) Compile the ratio calculations for each company prepared by the individual group members into one table.

(4) Compare the results from company to company in the same fiscal year. Include in your comparison a graphical analysis. Discuss reasons why these ratios might be similar or different within an industry.

(5) Compare the occurrence and percentage of short-term investments within your industry.

Required—class:

(6) Compare the ratios from each industry. Discuss reasons why these ratios might be similar or different between industries.

(7) Does one industry seem to be a better investment than another? Do you think this is constant over time?

SUPPLEMENTAL PROBLEMS

31. **Petty Cash** *(LO 4.1)* [Compare to Problem 17]

Theodore Bear, Inc. established a $200 petty cash account on January 2, 2000. On October 5, 2003, the account was increased to $500. On December 3, 2004, the petty cash drawer contained $219.04 in cash and coins and the following receipts:

Vendor	Amount	For
United Express Service	$ 79.42	Overnight shipping
Danielle's Restaurant	124.30	Client entertainment
Quick Print	46.49	Printing brochures
U-Move Van Lines	30.75	Delivery truck rental

Required:

(1) Record the January 1, 2000 journal entry to establish the petty cash fund.

(2) Record the October 5, 2003 journal entry to increase the amount of the petty cash fund.

(3) Record the entry to replenish petty cash on December 3, 2004.

(4) Assume that instead of $219.04, the amount of cash in the petty cash envelope was $120.75. Provide two possible situations that might cause the petty cash difference. What actions might you take to correct future instances of the two situations just discussed?

32. **Credit Card Sales** *(LO 4.1)* [Compare to Problem 18]

Credit card sales for TentRent, a party rental company, are given below for a one-week period. All payments from the credit card company are directly deposited into TentRent's bank account less a service fee.

Sale Date	Credit Card Sale Amount	Payment Date	Payment Amount
July 6	$520	July 8	$509.60
July 7	452	July 9	442.96
July 8	745	July 10	730.10
July 9	623	July 13	610.54
July 10	512	July 13	501.76
July 11	477	July 14	467.46

Required:

(1) Record the July 6 sales entry.

(2) Record the July 13 entry for the two receipts from the credit card company.

(3) What percent fee does the credit card company charge?

(4) What are the benefits and costs to TentRent for accepting third-party (national) credit cards?

(5) What are the benefits and costs to TentRent if it were offer in-house credit cards instead?

33. **Bank Reconciliation** *(LO 4.2)* [Compare to Problem 21]

Radon, Inc.'s February 28th bank statement showed an ending cash balance of $10,640. On February 28, Radon's general ledger cash account showed a balance of $10,869. After comparing the general ledger to the bank statement, the following items were noted:

(a)	Interest paid by the bank	$ 129
(b)	Deposits in transit	760
(c)	Draft of electric bill	620
(d)	Outstanding checks	1,227
(e)	Service fee charged by the bank	25

(f) Check 657, to Apple Long Distance, was written for and recorded in the journal for $796, but it cleared the bank for $976.

Required:

(1) Prepare a bank reconciliation for Radon, Inc.

(2) Make the required journal entries associated with the bank reconciliation.

(3) It would be possible (though not probable) for a small company do business without a checking account. Discuss the problems that attempting to operate in such a manner would create for the business.

34. **Uncollectible Accounts Expense** *(LO 4.3)* [Compare to Problem 23]

A partial balance sheet of Eatontown Steel is provided below.

Eatontown Steel
Partial Balance Sheet
December 31, 2003

Accounts Receivable	$105,000
Allowance for Uncollectible Accounts	(3,150)
Net Realizable Value	$101,850

During 2004, $1,450,000 was charged to accounts receivable and $1,375,000 was paid on the account by customers. Also during 2004, Eatontown wrote off the following uncollectible accounts:

March 18	Jimbo Builders	$1,000
June 22	Warehousing, Inc.	1,500
November 28	Dryer Contractors	900

Required:

(1) Record the journal entries to write off the three uncollectible accounts.

(2) Prepare a T-account for the Allowance account and calculate the balance on December 31, 2004. How should that balance be interpreted?

(3) Prepare a T-account for Accounts Receivable and calculate the balance on December 31, 2004.

(4) Eatontown estimates that 4 percent of the accounts receivable balance will be uncollectible. What amount is estimated to be uncollectible at the end of 2004? What amount would be considered the net realizable value of the receivables?

(5) Eatontown Steel wants to prepare an adjusting entry for uncollectible accounts that will make the net realizable value equal to the amount calculated in part (4). Prepare the journal entry to record the estimated uncollectible accounts. [Hint: The amount calculated as uncollectible will not be the amount used in the journal entry.]

35. **Ratio Analysis** *(LO 4.4, Excel)* [Compare to Problems 24 & 25]

Selected financial information for Harrison, Inc. is shown below (in thousands).

	Year 1	Year 2
Cash and Cash Equivalents	$ 104	$ 108
Short-term Investments	10	18
Accounts Receivable (gross)	654	611
Accounts Receivable (net)	622	580
Inventories	988	1,022
Prepaid Expenses	111	92
Current Liabilities	840	866
Long-Term Liabilities	1,181	1,304
Net Credit Sales	7,914	7,889

Required:

(1) What account creates the difference between gross and net accounts receivable? What does this account represent?

(2) Calculate the quick ratios for years 1 and 2.

(3) Calculate the accounts receivable turnover ratio and age of receivables for year 2.

(4) Why can the accounts receivable turnover ratio not be calculated for year 1?

(5) Assume that, in year 3, the economy took a downturn and interest rates rose substantially. What would you expect to happen to the accounts receivable turnover ratio and the age of receivables relative to those calculated in part (3)? Explain the rationale for your answers.

CHAPTER 5

Inventory

LEARNING OBJECTIVES

1. Account for common inventory transactions.
2. Use the four major inventory cost flow methods to calculate ending inventory and cost of goods sold.
3. Use the retail inventory method to calculate ending inventory and cost of goods sold.
4. Apply the lower-of-cost-or-market rule to inventory.
5. Determine the effects of inventory errors on financial statements.
6. Use ratios and other analysis techniques to make decisions about inventory.

Inventory Management at Tuesday Morning

Tuesday Morning, with its high-quality, name-brand household furnishings and gifts, and deeply discounted prices, is a company known to dedicated shoppers. The company has over 450 stores and eight "grand opening" events each year, with store closings in between for restocking inventory. According to one source, 40 percent of sales occur during the first five days of the opening events.[1] However, Tuesday Morning had two big inventory problems: bare shelves by the third week of an event and a huge stock of merchandise in distribution centers. Changes were made to improve the inventory management system. Now stores generally get alternate week deliveries except during the busiest four months, when deliveries arrive weekly. Inventory turnover was less than twice per year in 2000; in 2001, the turnover was 2.5 times. Less than 5 percent of the inventory is over a year old. Such impressive improvements allowed the company to reduce its debt by almost $89 million in one year.

The previous chapter focused on the assets (cash and accounts receivable) that businesses acquire as a result of sales transactions. This chapter addresses inventory, which is the asset that businesses exchange in making those sales transactions, and its related expense item, cost of goods sold.

SOURCE: Connie R. Gentry, "Keeping Tuesday Morning Stocked," *Chain Store Age* (January 2002), pp. 90, 100; http://www.tuesdaymorning.com, Investor Relations Overview.

INTRODUCTION TO INVENTORY

Inventory consists of all goods that businesses intend to sell to their customers, as well as, for a manufacturer, raw materials and in-process items that will be converted into saleable goods. Inventory is classified as a current asset on the balance sheet. The two primary types of inventory systems, some common inventory transactions, and terminology are discussed in the following sections.

Perpetual and Periodic Inventory Systems

There are two general types of inventory accounting systems: perpetual and periodic. The primary differences between these two systems are in the accounts used to record transactions, and the timing and manner in which cost of goods sold is determined. The choice to use either a perpetual or periodic inventory system is often associated with the nature of the inventory and the level of computerization of the business.

In a **perpetual inventory system,** a continuous record of inventory acquired and sold is maintained in the inventory asset account. When inventory is purchased, the inventory account is increased (debited) and either cash or accounts payable is credited. When inventory is sold, the inventory is removed from (credited to) the asset account and a cost of goods sold expense account is increased (debited). This entry recognizes the expense, and a second entry shows the increases in cash or accounts receivable and sales revenue. Thus, at any time (assuming away losses due to theft, breakage, or spoilage), the inventory account shows the actual quantity and cost of the inventory on hand and the cost of goods sold account shows the total cost of the goods sold to customers during the period. Having this information is a key advantage of using a perpetual inventory system.

In the past, perpetual inventory systems were typically used only when inventory items were unique or specifically identifiable. For example, an exclusive jewelry store could identify each Rolex watch sold by its serial number and antique dealers could identify pieces by style and period. The perpetual inventory system was more difficult to use in businesses with many identical items. Until the widespread usage of computers and bar coding technology, perpetual inventory systems were difficult and expensive to maintain; the cost and time of record keeping was not often worth the information provided.

As companies began selling a wider variety of products and a greater emphasis was placed on cost and inventory control, the information provided by a perpetual inventory system took on greater importance. Now, bar-coding of sales tags lets most retail businesses use perpetual inventory systems. Information on a product's cost (as well as size, color, and brand) can be included in the bar code; and scanning the tag not only updates inventory records, but often results in automatic indications of the need to reorder products.

Some companies, though, still cannot or do not use perpetual inventory systems. Smaller businesses and those that sell nondistinguishable or inexpensive items (such as nuts, bolts, and nails) often use periodic inventory systems. For example, a bakery may not want to determine the cost of each doughnut sold, and a florist may not care about the cost of each piece of flower wire included in a bouquet.

A **periodic inventory system** updates the inventory and cost of goods sold accounts only once a period rather than continuously. Instead of debiting and crediting inventory to reflect acquisitions and sales of merchandise, temporary accounts are used to record the transactions associated with acquiring inventory. The temporary accounts used in a periodic inventory system are as follows: Purchases, a debit-balanced account used for inventory purchases; Purchases Discounts, a credit-balanced contra-purchases account used for prompt payment discounts; Purchases Returns and Allowances, a credit-balanced contra-purchases account used for the return of merchandise to suppliers or reductions given by suppliers; and Freight-In, a debit-balanced account that will cause the cost of goods purchased to increase because of shipping charges. These accounts are all closed at the end of the accounting period.

Also in a periodic inventory system, no entry is made for cost of goods sold expense when a sale is made, although the revenue portion of the transaction is recorded. In these systems, the quantity of inventory on hand is determined at the end of each accounting period and that quantity is multiplied by the appropriate per unit cost to arrive at the dollar value of ending inventory. Subtracting that figure from the total cost of goods that the company had available for sale during the period provides the cost of goods sold expense for the period. Thus, no information is available on an ongoing basis regarding the quantity or cost of inventory on hand or sold. In addition, because no information is recorded as goods are sold, the periodic inventory system provides little internal control; at the end of a period, goods that are not on hand are assumed to have been sold.

Visual Recap 5.1 compares the perpetual and periodic inventory systems. Because of its common usage, however, this chapter focuses on the use of a perpetual inventory system.

Accounting for Common Inventory Transactions

There are six common transactions related to accounting for inventory: purchasing inventory from a supplier, paying for freight-in on purchases, returning inventory to a supplier, selling inventory to a customer, accepting returns of inventory from a customer, and paying on account for purchases of inventory. Marcia's Boutique, a small retail store with a perpetual inventory system, is used to illustrate these transactions.

VISUAL RECAP 5.1

Comparison of Perpetual and Periodic Inventory Systems

	Perpetual	Periodic
Provides good internal control	yes	no
Records Cost of Goods Sold at selling point	yes	no
Uses temporary accounts to record inventory transactions	no	yes
Information in Inventory account during the year is	current	beginning of the year balance
Information in Cost of Goods Sold account during the year is	current	nonexistent

Purchasing Inventory from a Supplier

On August 1, Marcia's purchased 12 dresses at $50 each from a supplier, Kwon, Inc. The purchase had credit terms of 2/10, n/30 and shipping terms of FOB shipping point. The credit terms indicate that Marcia's Boutique is entitled to a two percent discount if the invoice is paid within ten days of the invoice date. If payment is not made by August 11, Marcia's must pay the full amount of the invoice by August 31, the last day of the thirty-day credit period. As noted in the previous chapter, from the supplier's viewpoint, these terms are sales discounts; from the buyer's viewpoint, these prompt payment terms are called **purchase discounts.** The shipping terms for a transaction indicate whether the seller or buyer is responsible for paying the delivery cost of the goods. This topic is discussed relative to the entry on August 3.

To account for this transaction, Marcia's must increase its inventory (debit) and increase its accounts payable (credit) for the cost of the dress.

General Journal				
Date		Description	Debit	Credit
Aug.	1	Inventory	600	
		Accounts Payable—Kwon		600
		To record purchase of inventory on account		

Paying for Freight-In on Purchases

On August 3, Marcia's paid the freight charges on the shipment of dresses. When one business purchases goods from another, the two must agree on which party will be responsible for paying the delivery costs for the goods. The point at which the legal title to goods transfers from the seller to the buyer dictates the party responsible for paying the delivery charges, as well as when the legal title to goods transfers from seller to buyer. The two most common shipping terms are FOB shipping point and FOB destination.

Under terms of **FOB shipping point,** the seller delivers the goods free on board (FOB) to the shipping point, such as the seller's loading dock. There, a freight company usually takes possession of the goods and delivers them to the buyer. With these shipping terms, the buyer pays delivery charges since title to the goods transfers to the buyer at the shipping point. When goods are shipped **FOB destination,** the seller retains legal title to the goods until they reach the destination point. As a result, the seller is responsible for paying the transportation charges.

The shipping terms for the dresses purchased by Marcia's Boutique on August 1 were specified as FOB shipping point. Thus, the delivery charges increase the cost of the dresses to Marcia's Boutique. When Marcia's receives and pays the $22 freight bill on August 3, the cost of inventory is increased (debited). Had the goods been shipped FOB destination, the seller would have recorded the shipping charges (Freight Out, a selling expense) and Marcia's Boutique would have no entry.

General Journal				
Date		Description	Debit	Credit
Aug.	3	Inventory	22	
		Cash		22
		To record payment of FOB charges		

Returning Inventory to a Supplier

On August 5, Marcia's Boutique returned a dress to Kwon because the dress was found to have a fabric flaw. Merchandising companies, like their customers, are sometimes dissatisfied with goods purchased. Merchandise is occasionally received that was not ordered, is defective, or was damaged when packaged. Reductions in amounts owed to suppliers resulting from returned goods (**purchase returns**) or price concessions granted for defective or damaged goods (**purchase allowances**) are referred to collectively as purchase returns and allowances. Marcia's journalizes the reduction to inventory with a credit, and debits Accounts Payable to decrease the amount owned to Kwon.

General Journal				
Date		Description	Debit	Credit
Aug.	5	Accounts Payable—Kwon	50	
		Inventory		50
		To record return of a dress for credit		

Selling Inventory to a Customer

When Marcia's Boutique sells three dresses for cash on August 7, the perpetual inventory system requires two journal entries. The first entry records the revenue ($110 per dress) resulting from the transaction, while the second entry records the related amount paid for the inventory. Cost of Goods Sold is an expense account that accumulates, through debits, the cost of inventory sold to customers during an accounting period. The second journal entry also accounts for the reduction of inventory (credit) in the store at the original cost of $50 per dress.

General Journal				
Date		Description	Debit	Credit
Aug.	7	Cash	330	
		Sales Revenue		330
		Cost of Goods Sold	150	
		Inventory		150
		To record cash sales and the related cost of goods sold		

Accepting Returns of Inventory from a Customer

On August 8, one of the customers who bought a dress on August 7 returned it. The previous chapter indicated that companies establish a Sales Returns and Allowances account to record merchandise refunds and price concessions granted to customers. In a perpetual inventory system, a sales return requires two entries. The first entry records the return and the customer's refund (or account receivable reduction), while the second entry makes the necessary corrections to replace the merchandise into Inventory (debit) and reduce Cost of Goods Sold (credit).

General Journal				
Date		Description	Debit	Credit
Aug.	8	Sales Returns and Allowances	110	
		Cash		110
		Inventory	50	
		Cost of Goods Sold		50
		To record a customer's cash refund for the return of a dress		

Paying On Account for Purchases of Inventory

On August 11, Marcia's paid for the dresses purchased from Kwon. The credit terms from Kwon Fashions allow Marcia's Boutique to deduct 2 percent from the total amount owed if payment is made by August 11. Following the August 5 purchase return, the total amount owed to Kwon Fashions is \$550 (\$600 – \$50). Thus, Marcia's Boutique is entitled to an \$11 discount (\$550 × 0.02) when the company pays for the goods within the discount period. This purchase discount is credited to the Inventory account to reduce the cost of the goods acquired.

General Journal				
Date		Description	Debit	Credit
Aug.	11	Accounts Payable—Kwon	550	
		Cash		539
		Inventory		11
		To record payment within the discount period for dresses purchased		

The Marcia's Boutique example is simplistic first because it focused only on a single purchase of goods and the related sales of those goods. Businesses will generally have goods from many different vendors on hand and available for sale simultaneously. Second, all the dresses purchased in the example had the same acquisition cost. In most companies, purchases will be made throughout the period at a variety of costs. When products are being sold that have had different acquisition costs, a determination must be made of the inventory cost flow method to be used to record cost of goods sold. Third, the example did not attempt to attach the freight charges for the dresses to the dresses at point of sale. Realistically, since Marcia's paid $22 for freight and had 11 dresses to sell (because one was returned), the actual cost of each dress sold was $52 (the $50 purchase price plus $2 freight) rather than $50.

The six primary transactions used in a perpetual inventory system are summarized in Visual Recap 5.2.

INVENTORY COSTING METHODS

"Inventory cost flow" is a common business expression. A merchandiser begins an accounting period with a certain amount of inventory. During the period, additional purchases of inventory are made and some inventory may be returned to the supplier. Adding beginning inventory and net merchandise purchases (purchases minus purchase returns) gives the **cost of goods available for sale** for that period. The cost of merchandise sold during an accounting period flows out of inventory and into cost of goods sold, which is shown on the income statement. At the end of a period, the cost of unsold merchandise is shown as ending inventory on the balance sheet. This cost flow cycle is repeated each accounting period.

For inventory, as for most assets, cost is the primary valuation basis. Two important accounting issues faced by businesses are how to determine the cost of the goods that are sold and, as a result, the cost of ending inventory. At first, these calculations may not seem

VISUAL RECAP 5.2

Summary of Perpetual Inventory Transactions

Increases to Cost of Inventory			Decreases to Cost of Inventory		
Purchase			**Return of Purchase**		
Inventory	X		A/P (or Cash)	X	
A/P (or Cash)		X	Inventory		X
Freight In (FOB Shipping Point)			**Discount on Credit Purchase**		
Inventory	X		A/P	X	
Cash		X	Cash		X
			Inventory		X
Customer Return			**Sale to Customer**		
Sales R&A	X		A/R (or Cash)	X	
A/R (or Cash)		X	Sales Revenue		X
Inventory	X		Cost of Goods Sold	X	
Cost of Goods Sold		X	Inventory		X

to be a particularly challenging—and they would not be if all similar inventory units were purchased at the same price every time a purchase was made.

Some businesses can specifically identify which goods are being sold when sales take place. For example, an automobile dealership knows which car a customer has purchased because of the VIN; the exact invoice cost to the dealer of that automobile can be determined and moved from the inventory to Cost of Goods Sold. Other businesses have fairly readily identifiable physical flows of inventory. The three most common types of physical flow are FIFO (first-in, first-out), LIFO (last-in, first-out), and average.

When a grocery dairy case is restocked, the "old" milk is moved to the front and the "new" milk is placed in the back of the case. The intention is to create a first-in, first-out physical inventory flow. Items that are stacked (such as firewood) would typically be associated with a last-in, first-out physical flow. Under an average physical flow, all goods are mixed together and cannot be identified as to date of purchase; an example is gasoline in a storage tank.

The operations of University Bookstore are used to explore the topic of inventory costing. Exhibit 5-1 depicts inventory data for January for a *Principles of Marketing* textbook. The text is a paperback version and, thus, there are no used copies of the text available for sale. To simplify the example, it is assumed that University Bookstore only had sales on two days.

Given the exhibit information, the cost of goods available for sale in January is $3,000 + $14,000 + $2,730 or $19,730. Additionally, the bookstore has 30 (100 + 400 - 360 + 70 – 180) texts on hand at the end of January. Some very important information is, however, unknown at this time. First, what amounts should be recorded as Cost of Goods Sold (and a reduction in inventory) on January 14 and 22? Second, what amount should be shown for the ending inventory on the January 31 balance sheet? Thus, the Inventory and Cost of Goods Sold accounts are directly related to each other because, only after the cost of goods sold amounts are identified, can the cost of unsold items that comprise ending inventory be computed. The following sections illustrate four different inventory costing methods that can be used to assign the cost of goods available for sale amount to cost of goods sold and ending inventory.

Specific Identification Method

One costing method is **specific identification.** To use this method, a business must be able to identify the actual cost of each unit of inventory sold during an accounting period and the actual cost of each unsold unit at the end of an accounting period. Assume that University Bookstore electronically bar codes each inventory item with the date and price of purchase; these codes are scanned at point of sale to have access to the data needed to apply the specific identification method.

In a perpetual inventory system, a business maintains an inventory ledger that contains an account for each inventory item. Exhibit 5-2 provides the inventory record for the marketing text.

The perpetual inventory record reveals the cost of each textbook purchased or sold during the month as well as the cost of each book on hand during the month. For example, 70 of the books sold on January 14 had a per-unit cost of $30 (these books were from

EXHIBIT 5-1
University Bookstore Inventory Data

1/ 1	Beginning inventory	100 copies @ $30 each	$ 3,000
1/ 8	Purchased	400 copies @ $35 each	14,000
1/14	Sold	360 copies	
1/18	Purchased	70 copies @ $39 each	2,730
1/22	Sold	180 copies	

EXHIBIT 5-2

Perpetual Inventory Record, Specific Identification Method

Item: Principles of Marketing

	Purchases			Sold			Balance		
Date	#	Unit Cost	Total	#	Unit Cost	Total	#	Unit Cost	Balance
Jan. 1							100	$30	$ 3,000
Jan. 8	400	$35	$14,000				100	$30	$ 3,000
							400	35	14,000
							500		$17,000
Jan. 14				70	$30	$ 2,100	30	$30	$ 900
				290	35	10,150	110	35	3,850
							140		$ 4,750
Jan. 18	70	$39	$ 2,730				30	$30	$ 900
							110	35	3,850
							70	39	2,730
							210		$ 7,480
Jan. 22				20	$30	$ 600	10	$30	$ 300
				100	35	3,500	10	35	350
				60	39	2,340	10	39	390
							30		$ 1,040

the beginning inventory), while the remaining 290 books cost $35 each (these were from the purchase on January 8). Following the initial one-day opening, the University Bookstore had 140 copies of the marketing text on hand at a total cost of $4,750. These 140 copies were distributed across two layers: 30 books with a per-unit cost of $30 and 110 books having a per-unit cost of $35. University Bookstore's January specific identification inventory information is summarized as follows:

Ending Inventory	30 copies: 10 @ $30	$ 300	
	10 @ $35	350	
	10 @ $39	390	$ 1,040
Cost of Goods Sold	360 copies on 1/14	$ 2,100	
		10,150	
	180 copies on 1/22	600	
		3,500	
		2,340	18,690
Total cost of goods available for sale			$19,730

Companies not having the information technology to allow them to use specific identification or choosing not to use specific identification may select a FIFO, LIFO, or average cost flow assumption to calculate cost of goods sold and ending inventory. Visual Recap 5.3 depicts the assumptions. The calculations associated with these assumptions are discussed in detail in the following sections.

FIFO (first-in, first-out) Method

The **FIFO (first-in, first-out) method** of inventory costing assumes that the goods acquired first (the oldest, or first in, goods) are the ones sold first; thus, their costs are the first ones to be sent to Cost of Goods Sold (first out). In turn, the per unit costs of the most

VISUAL RECAP 5.3

Cost Flow

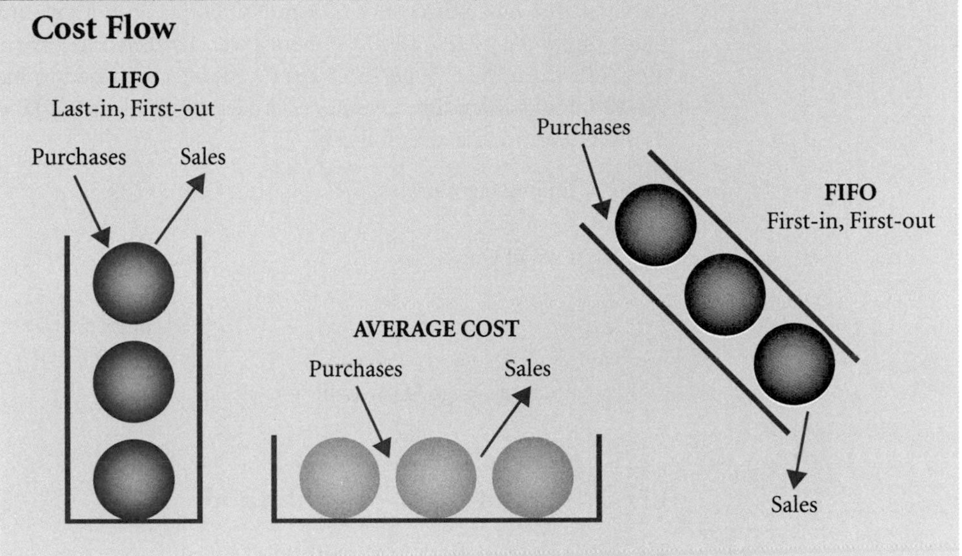

recently acquired goods (last in) are used to determine the cost of ending inventory under the FIFO method. The FIFO method is referred to as an inventory cost flow *assumption* because the business does not know whether the oldest units are actually being sold first unless there is only one layer of inventory in existence.

Exhibit 5-3 provides the inventory record for the *Principles of Marketing* text assuming that University Bookstore applies the FIFO inventory costing method. On January 8, after the purchase of 400 books at a per-unit cost of $35, there were two layers of inventory: 100 books at $30 and 400 books at $35. Applying the first-in, first-out concept to the 360 books sold on January 14, the bookstore assumed that all 100 of the oldest (first-in) books were sold. The remaining 260 books sold were assumed to have been purchased on January 8 at a cost of $35 per unit.

EXHIBIT 5-3

Perpetual Inventory Record, FIFO Method

Item: Principles of Marketing

	Purchases			Sold			Balance		
Date	#	Unit Cost	Total	#	Unit Cost	Total	#	Unit Cost	Balance
Jan. 1							100	$30	$ 3,000
Jan. 8	400	$35	$14,000				100	$30	$ 3,000
							400	35	14,000
							500		$17,000
Jan. 14				100	$30	$3,000	140	$35	$ 4,900
				260	35	9,100			
Jan. 18	70	$39	$ 2,730				140	$35	$ 4,900
							70	39	2,730
							120		$ 7,630
Jan. 22				140	$35	$4,900			
				40	39	1,560			
							30	$39	$ 1,170

Following the January 18 purchase, there again were two layers of inventory: 140 books with a per-unit cost of $35 and 70 books with a per-unit cost of $39. For the sales made on January 22, the 140 $35 books were assumed to have been sold first. Additionally, 40 books from the $39 per-unit layer were also assumed to have been sold, leaving 30 of the $39 books in ending inventory. University Bookstore's January FIFO inventory information is summarized as follows:

Ending Inventory	30 @ $39		$ 1,170
Cost of Goods Sold	360 copies on 1/14	$ 3,000	
		9,100	
	180 copies on 1/22	4,900	
		1,560	18,690
Total cost of goods available for sale			$ 19,730

LIFO (last-in, first-out) Method

The **LIFO (last-in, first-out) method** of inventory costing assumes that the most recently acquired goods (last in) are sold first, while the oldest acquired goods (first in) remain in inventory. Exhibit 5-4 provides the inventory record for the *Principles of Marketing* text assuming that University Bookstore applies the LIFO inventory costing method.

Similar to the FIFO example just discussed, the LIFO schedule indicates that there were two layers of books following the January 8 purchase: 100 books that cost $30 per unit and 400 books that cost $35 per unit. On January 14, the bookstore assumed that the 360 books sold were all books costing $35 each. This assumption left intact the original layer of 100 books, as well as a layer of 40 books at a cost of $35 each.

Following the January 18 purchase, there were three layers of books: 100 books costing $30 each, 40 books costing $35 each, and the newest layer of 70 books costing $39 each.

EXHIBIT 5-4

Perpetual Inventory Record, LIFO Method

Item: Principles of Marketing

	Purchases			Sold			Balance		
Date	#	Unit Cost	Total	#	Unit Cost	Total	#	Unit Cost	Balance
Jan. 1							100	$30	$ 3,000
Jan. 8	400	$35	$14,000				100	$30	$ 3,000
							400	35	14,000
							500		$17,000
Jan. 14				360	$35	$12,600	100	$30	$ 3,000
							40	35	1,400
									$ 4,400
Jan. 18	70	$39	$ 2,730				140	$30	$ 3.000
							40	35	1,400
							70	39	2,730
							120		$ 7,130
Jan. 22				70	$39	$ 2,730			
				40	35	1,400			
				70	30	2,100	30	$30	$ 900

Applying the last-in, first-out concept, the January 22 sale of 180 books eliminated the layers of 70 books costing $39 and 40 books costing $35 each as well as reducing the original layer to only 30 books. University Bookstore's January LIFO inventory information is summarized as follows:

Ending Inventory	30 @ $30		$ 900
Cost of Goods Sold	360 copies on 1/14	$12,600	
	180 copies on 1/22	2,730	
		1,400	
		2,100	18,830
Total cost of goods available for sale			$19,730

Moving-Average Method

Under the **moving-average method** of inventory costing, the average per unit cost for an inventory item is computed before each sale. The cost basis of ending inventory for an item is determined by multiplying the number of unsold units of that item by its moving-average per-unit cost at the end of the accounting period. Before the January 14 sale of 360 books, the average per-unit cost of the 500 books on hand was $34:

$$\begin{aligned}\text{Average price} &= [(100 \times \$30) + (400 \times \$35)] \div 500\\ &= (\$3{,}000 + \$14{,}000) \div 500\\ &= \$17{,}000 \div 500\\ &= \$34\end{aligned}$$

The 360 books sold on January 14 are expensed at $34 per unit.

Before the January 22 sale, the new moving-average cost was $35.67 per unit, computed as follows:

$$\begin{aligned}\text{Average price} &= [(140 \times \$34) + (70 \times \$39)] \div 210\\ &= (\$4{,}760 + \$2{,}730) \div 210\\ &= \$7{,}490 \div 210\\ &= \$35.67\end{aligned}$$

Thus, the total cost assigned to the 180 books sold during on January 22 was $6,420 (180 × $35.67, rounded to balance).

The moving-average inventory card is shown in Exhibit 5-5. Notice that no average cost is shown in the Balance column after each new purchase; there is no need to calculate such an average because, should another purchase take place before a sale, the average cost would change.

University Bookstore's January moving-average inventory information is summarized as follows:

Ending Inventory	30 @ $35.67		$ 1,070
Cost of Goods Sold	360 copies on 1/14	$ 12,240	
	180 copies on 1/22	6,420	18,860
Total cost of goods available for sale			$19,730

EXHIBIT 5-5

Perpetual Inventory Record, Moving-Average Method

Item: Principles of Marketing

	Purchases			Sold			Balance		
Date	#	Unit Cost	Total	#	Unit Cost	Total	#	Unit Cost	Balance
Jan. 1							100	$30	$ 3,000
Jan. 8	400	$35	$14,000						
							500		$17,000
Jan. 17				360	$34	$12,240			
							140	$34	$ 4,760
Jan. 18	70	$39	$ 2,730						
							210		$ 7,490
Jan. 22				180	$35.67	$ 6,420			
							30	$35.67	$ 1,070

Generally accepted accounting principles (GAAP) allow a business to use any rational and systematic method to assign costs to the inventory sold during an accounting period. Thus, a business may use an inventory cost flow assumption that is at variance with the actual physical flow of its goods. For example, although a company sells goods in a FIFO pattern, the firm may choose to use the LIFO inventory costing method. A business whose inventory flows in a LIFO pattern may elect to use the FIFO inventory costing method. Similarly, a merchandiser that can identify the actual per unit costs of the items in ending inventory may still use the FIFO, LIFO, or the moving-average inventory costing method.

Comparison of Income Statement Effects of Inventory Costing Methods

Exhibit 5-6 shows the gross profit amounts for the *Principles of Marketing* text under each of the four inventory costing methods. This schedule assumes that the bookstore sold the marketing text for $50 per unit throughout January. These gross profit figures range from $8,140 for the LIFO method to $8,440 for the FIFO method. In absolute terms, this $300 difference seems quite small; however, in a company that engages in hundreds of thousands of inventory transactions in a single year, the differences in total gross profit would be much more substantial.

Balance Sheet Valuation versus Income Determination

In an inflationary economic environment (that is, when the cost of purchases is rising), the FIFO method yields a higher net income (or lower net loss) than the LIFO method when these methods are applied to the same financial data.[1] The question of whether FIFO or LIFO is the most informative (or better) method of accounting for inventory has been debated for years. The problem in resolving this debate is that there are two important but conflicting questions that must be considered: Which method results in the more appropriate balance sheet valuation for ending inventory; and which method does a better job of matching a business's expenses with its revenues? The following discussion assumes inflation; thus, the effects would be reversed when prices are falling (deflation).

[1] The moving-average method typically yields a net income between the net income figures produced by the FIFO and LIFO methods. The specific identification method usually results in a net income figure that approximates the net income produced by applying the moving-average method.

EXHIBIT 5-6
Cost Flow Gross Profit and Inventory Amounts

	Specific Identification	FIFO	LIFO	Moving Average
Sales ($540 @ $50)	$27,000	$27,000	$27,000	$27,000
Cost of Goods Sold	18,690	18,560	18,830	18,860
Gross Profit	$ 8,310	$ 8,440	$ 8,170	$ 8,140
Inventory, 1/31	$ 1,040	$ 1,170	$ 900	$ 1,070

FIFO yields a higher net income because the more expensive goods (those purchased later in the period) are assumed to be in ending inventory, with the "cheaper" goods (beginning inventory or early purchases) expensed to Cost of Goods Sold. Under LIFO, the reverse is true: the goods assumed to be in ending inventory are the relatively low cost goods on hand at the beginning of, or acquired early in, the period, while the costs of higher-priced goods purchased later in the period are assigned to Cost of Goods Sold. For balance sheet purposes, FIFO and LIFO assign, respectively, the newest and the oldest per-unit costs of goods to ending inventory. For this reason, FIFO provides a more appropriate balance sheet valuation for ending inventory. For income statement purposes, FIFO and LIFO assign, respectively, the oldest and the newest per-unit costs of goods to cost of goods sold. For this reason, LIFO is generally perceived to better match current dollars of business revenues and expenses and, thereby, produces a profit figure that better reflects a business's economic reality.

Consider an extreme example. A company purchased one unit of inventory last year for $10 and one unit yesterday for $50. A sale of one unit is made today for $57. The company would need to spend $50 to replace the unit sold. Thus, after selling and replacing one unit of inventory, the company would be "better off" by $7 on the transaction, before considering other expenses such as income taxes. For accounting purposes, gross profit would be $7 on the transaction if the LIFO method were used. However, if FIFO is used for accounting purposes, the gross profit entered in the accounting records would be $47 ($57–$10).

In summary, most businesspeople maintain that LIFO does a better job of matching revenues and expenses than FIFO does. Consequently, when income determination is considered a more important issue than balance sheet valuation, LIFO is preferred over FIFO. Since most decision makers consider income determination a more critical issue than balance sheet valuation, they generally prefer businesses to use the LIFO method.

FIFO versus LIFO: Tax Consequences

Tax consequences are an important consideration when choosing an inventory costing method. Because LIFO yields lower profits than FIFO in a period of steadily rising prices, the LIFO method translates into lower income tax payments. Thus, from a taxation standpoint, LIFO is generally preferred by businesses over FIFO in a period of rising prices. During the highly inflationary period of the late 1970s and early 1980s, hundreds of firms switched from FIFO to LIFO to reduce their income taxes.

Valuing Inventory at Other Than Cost

Although cost is the primary valuation basis for inventory, businesses must occasionally depart from the cost basis of valuing inventory to prevent their financial statements from being misleading to decision makers. Two common departures from cost are the retail inventory method and the lower-of-cost-or-market rule.

Retail Inventory

The **retail inventory method** is often used in small businesses to estimate the amount of inventory on hand. To use this method, there should be a consistent relationship between the costs and the selling prices of a company's products. Information on individual purchases and sales do not need to be maintained because the retail method reflects a periodic inventory system. Retail inventory, however, does allow a level of internal control not commonly provided by a periodic inventory system. This method can be used with a FIFO, LIFO, or average cost flow assumption; the average cost flow assumption is illustrated in this text and all price changes after products are originally priced are ignored for simplicity.

Under the retail inventory method, as goods are received, information on both purchase cost and retail price is gathered. Sales are recorded at retail prices without a separate entry for Cost of Goods Sold. At the end of the period, the retail prices of the goods on hand are added and the cost of ending inventory is determined. The retail prices of the goods that should be on hand can be compared with the retail prices of the goods that are actually on hand to determine if theft or breakage occurred.

Kristi's Kollections, which sells Limoges china boxes, is used to illustrate the retail inventory method. The company began 2002 with inventory costing \$100,000 on hand; these goods had selling prices totaling \$145,000. During the year, Kristi's purchased \$219,600 of goods and marked them to sell for \$325,000. A close-of-business physical inventory was taken on December 31, 2002, with information being gathered on the *selling* (retail) *prices* of the inventory on hand. Since selling prices cannot be shown on the asset section of the balance sheet, this information needs to be converted to a cost amount through the use of a cost-to-retail percentage. Sales for the year totaled \$385,000. Exhibit 5-7 shows the calculations related to this retail inventory example.

No matter what amount of physical inventory exists at year-end, cost of goods sold for 2002 would be calculated as \$261,800 (\$385,000 × 0.68). If the December 31, 2002 inventory showed goods on hand marked at \$85,000, the cost of inventory for balance sheet purposes would be \$57,800. In this case, the amount of goods that should have been on hand was actually there: the \$470,000 of goods available to sell at retail prices minus the \$385,000 of goods that were actually sold at retail prices. However, if the inventory resulted in goods on hand totaling only \$75,000, Kristi's managers could conclude that \$10,000 of inventory in retail prices (or \$6,800 in cost amounts) had either been broken or stolen during the period. The \$6,800 would be shown as a loss for the year on the income statement; the balance sheet would show a year-end inventory of \$51,000 (\$75,000 × 0.68).

Lower-of-Cost-or-Market

The **lower-of-cost-or-market (LCM) rule** requires businesses to value ending inventories at the lower of cost (as determined by FIFO or some other costing method) and current

EXHIBIT 5-7
Retail Inventory Method

	Cost	Retail
Beginning inventory, 1/1/02	\$100,000	\$ 145,000
Purchases during 2002	219,600	325,000
Cost of goods available for sale*	\$319,600	\$ 470,000
Sales (at retail amounts)		(385,000)
Ending inventory at retail		\$ 85,000
Times cost-to-retail %		× 0.68
Ending inventory at cost	\$ 57,800	

*Cost-to-retail percentage = \$319,600 ÷ \$470,000 = 68%

market value. For purposes of this rule, market value is generally determined to be **current replacement cost** or the per-unit amount that must be paid for buy additional inventory items. As shown in Exhibit 5-8, the LCM rule can be applied on an item-by-item basis or a total inventory basis. An inventory write-down resulting from application of the LCM rule is typically debited to Cost of Goods Sold and credited to Inventory.

To apply the LCM rule on a total inventory basis, the total cost and total market value of a firm's inventory is computed and the lower figure is selected. For the information in Exhibit 5-8, the lower of total inventory cost and total inventory market value is $2,370. To apply the LCM rule on an item-by-item basis, the lower of cost or market value is identified for each inventory item. Then, these amounts are added to determine the dollar amount of ending inventory for financial reporting purposes. Using the item-by-item version of the LCM rule, the year-end inventory would be valued at $2,070, as shown in Exhibit 5-8.

Inventory Errors

In most merchandising businesses, inventory is one of the largest current asset accounts. Improper inventory calculations can significantly distort a company's balance sheet and income statement. Errors can be caused by miscounting or mispricing.

Because the sum of ending inventory and cost of goods sold need to equal the cost of goods available for sale, a misstatement of one amount creates a misstatement of the other. For example, assume that University Bookstore took a physical inventory of its marketing text at the end of January and counted only 29 books on hand rather than the 30 that should be there. Using the LIFO information in Exhibit 5-4, one text at $30 needs to be removed from the ending inventory cost to make that amount $870 (29 books at $30 each). The easiest way to adjust the inventory balance is for University Bookstore to add that $30 to Cost of Goods Sold. If the "missing" marketing text were later found in a stack of mathematics texts, it is clear that the ending inventory of marketing texts was understated and the Cost of Goods Sold for marketing texts was overstated for January.

Additionally, a misstatement in inventory at the end of one accounting period will automatically affect the following period's beginning inventory because inventory is a permanent account. Thus, an inventory error affects financial statement data for at least two consecutive accounting periods. The effects of inventory errors are shown in Visual Recap 5.4.

Note that ending inventory and CGS have an inverse relationship; that is, as more goods are sold, fewer goods are left in ending inventory. Therefore, an understatement of ending inventory creates an overstatement of cost of goods sold. However, beginning inventory and CGS have a direct relationship. Therefore, any effect on beginning inventory will have the same effect on cost of goods sold.

Cost of goods sold and net income also have an inverse relationship. In calculating net income, the CGS is subtracted from sales revenue; therefore, if CGS increases, net income decreases. Any effect on CGS resulting from a misstatement of beginning or ending inventory will have the opposite effect on net income.

EXHIBIT 5-8

Lower-of-Cost-or-Market Inventory

Item	Quantity	Unit Cost	Replacement* Cost	Total Cost	Total Market	Item-by-Item LCM
727 jeans	30	$14	$18	$ 420	$ 540	$ 420
757 jeans	20	24	17	480	340	340
Tank tops	50	15	20	750	1,000	750
Pullovers	40	18	14	720	560	560
				$2,370	$2,440	$2,070

*Replacement cost is determined at the fiscal year end.

VISUAL RECAP 5.4

Effects of Overstating and Understating Ending Inventory

If this year's ending inventory is overstated:	Effects on Current Year	Effects on Next Year
Inventory (Balance Sheet)	Beg. Inv. Overstated	Beg. Inv. Overstated
Cost of Goods Sold (Income Statement)	Beg. Inv. Understated	Beg. Inv. Overstated
Net Income (Income Statement)	Beg. Inv. Overstated	Beg. Inv. Understated

If this year's ending inventory is understated:	Effects on Current Year	Effects on Next Year
Inventory (Balance Sheet)	Beg. Inv. Understated	Beg. Inv. Understated
Cost of Goods Sold (Income Statement)	Beg. Inv. Overstated	Beg. Inv. Understated
Net Income (Income Statement)	Beg. Inv. Understated	Beg. Inv. Overstated

ACCOUNTING INFORMATION FOR DECISION MAKING

On the balance sheets of merchandising and manufacturing companies, inventory is the asset most likely to attract the attention of decision makers. Investors and other decision makers monitor business inventory levels, changes in inventory and cost of goods sold between periods, and related financial disclosures to evaluate the changing financial fortunes of those businesses.

Inventory Issues

An unusual or unanticipated change in inventory often provides definite clues regarding a company's future prospects. For example, Polaroid's (www.polaroid.com) inventories increased by 22 percent and sales decreased six percent from 1999 to 2000. Digital cameras were being introduced with more functions and lower prices, and Polaroid was apparently not keeping pace. In July 2001, the company reported a $16 million liquidation of discontinued models and product lines; in October 2001, Polaroid filed for Chapter 11 bankruptcy.

Sometimes inventory errors are unintentional, but sometimes they are intentional...better known as fraud! Numerous cases of fraud involving inventory have existed over the past half-century including McKesson & Robbins, Phar-Mor, and Leslie Faye. One 1999 study found that asset misstatements comprised nearly half of the cases of fraudulent financial statements and the majority of those misstatements involved inventory.[2]

[2] Joseph T. Wells, "Ghost Goods: How to Spot Phantom Inventory," *Journal of Accountancy* (June 2001), pp. 33-36.

One of the few areas in which the tax code requires consistency between tax reporting and financial accounting relates to the use of LIFO inventory valuation. If a company uses LIFO for federal tax purposes, LIFO must also be used for financial reporting. In periods of rising prices, LIFO would result in lower profits when used for financial reporting, than would FIFO. Because FIFO is the most widely used inventory costing method, it appears that many firms have decided that reporting higher income statement profits is more important than the tax savings produced by using LIFO. Higher profits are often tied to executive compensation—creating the question of whether LIFO was selected to reduce corporate tax payments or increase executive bonuses.

Companies include a summary of the accounting methods used for inventory, and other major accounts, in their financial statement footnotes. Decision makers should be aware of and understand the inventory accounting methods that a company uses because the choice of inventory method can dramatically affect a firm's reported inventory value and periodic earnings.

Inventory Ratios

Inventory also impacts several key financial ratios. Decision makers closely monitor the age of a business's inventory in addition to the monitoring of the age of accounts receivable. As a company's inventory "ages," it becomes more subject to valuation problems that can be created by spoilage, obsolescence, or related problems.

Determining the age of inventory is a two-step process. First, the inventory turnover ratio must be computed.

$$\text{Inventory Turnover Ratio} = \text{Cost of Goods Sold} \div \text{Average Inventory}$$

Average inventory refers to the beginning inventory plus the ending inventory divided by two.

The **inventory turnover ratio** indicates the number of times that a company sells or "turns over" its inventory each year. A business attempts to turn over its inventory as quickly as possible without running out of items to sell. A high rate of inventory turnover not only reduces the risk of inventory spoilage and obsolescence but also minimizes carrying costs for items such as insurance and handling.

The **age of inventory** is computed by dividing 360 days by the inventory turnover ratio.

$$\text{Age of Inventory} = 360 \text{ days} \div \text{Inventory Turnover Ratio}$$

Inventory age indicates the average period required to sell an item of inventory. As the inventory turnover ratio increases, the age of inventory is shortened. Lower is better when it comes to the age of inventory. Data for the Shapiro Clothing Company are given in Exhibit 5-9 to illustrate the computation of inventory turnover and the age of inventory.

If Shapiro's primarily restocks its inventory with every new season (four times a year, or every 90 days), the company has an extremely good turnover ratio and age of inventory.

EXHIBIT 5-9

Inventory Turnover Ratio and Age of Inventory

Inventory, 1/1/02	$232,000
Cost of Goods Sold for 2002	$791,920
Inventory, 12/31/02	$184,600

Average inventory = ($232,000 + $184,600) ÷ 2 = $208,300
Inventory turnover ratio = $791,920 ÷ $208,300 = 3.8
Age of inventory = 360 days ÷ 3.8 = 95 days

SUMMARY

Inventory is a focal point for decision makers analyzing a company's financial statements. Perpetual and periodic are two major types of inventory accounting systems. Perpetual inventory systems provide a continually updated record of inventory quantities and cost of goods sold. In recent years, two factors have caused many firms to switch from periodic to perpetual inventory systems: declining technology cost of employing the system and the growing importance of their information advantage.

Important accounting tasks facing merchandising and manufacturing firms each accounting period are determining the ending inventory cost and cost of goods sold. Cost is the principal valuation basis used for inventory and four primary inventory costing methods can be used by a business: specific identification, FIFO (first-in, first-out), LIFO (last-in, first-out), and moving-average. Some small businesses may use the retail inventory method, which focuses on the selling prices of goods and is a type of periodic inventory system. When inventory cost exceeds market value, the lower-of-cost-or-market (LCM) rule requires the inventory to be written down to market value. Generally, current replacement cost is defined as market value for purposes of the LCM rule.

Numerous issues are important to decision makers relative to inventory. The specific method or methods used to account for this asset can significantly affect the appearance of a business's financial condition and reported operating results. Also helpful to decision makers are disclosures indicating how a company's financial data would have been affected had a different inventory accounting method been used. Information on any significant changes in inventory levels can also be important in analyzing inventory. Decision makers closely monitor a business's age of inventory because, as inventory ages, it becomes more subject to spoilage, obsolescence, or related problems. Inventory age is calculated as 360 divided by the inventory turnover ratio (computed as cost of goods sold divided by average inventory).

KEY TERMS

age of inventory
cost of goods available for sale
current replacement cost
FIFO (first-in, first-out) method
FOB destination
FOB shipping point
inventory
inventory turnover ratio
LIFO (last-in, first-out) method
lower-of-cost-or-market (LCM) rule
moving-average method
periodic inventory system
perpetual inventory system
purchase allowance
purchase discount
purchase return
retail inventory method
specific identification method

QUESTIONS

1. Identify the key differences between a perpetual and a periodic inventory system. *(LO 5.1)*
2. Why is inventory always considered a current asset? *(LO 5.1)*
3. Describe what is meant by the phrase "inventory cost flow." *(LO 5.2)*
4. How is the cost of goods available for sale determined for a merchandising company for a given accounting period? *(LO 5.2)*
5. Identify and briefly describe the four most common inventory costing methods. *(LO 5.2)*
6. In a period of rising prices, which inventory costing method, FIFO or LIFO, generally yields the higher ending inventory value? Why? *(LO 5.2)*

7. Which inventory costing method, FIFO or LIFO, is generally considered the more appropriate method for balance sheet valuation purposes? Why? *(LO 5.2)*
8. Which inventory costing method, FIFO or LIFO, is generally considered the more appropriate method for income determination purposes? Why? *(LO 5.2)*
9. How does the choice to use LIFO or FIFO affect income taxes? *(LO 5.2)*
10. Explain how the retail inventory method helps managers know if goods have been broken or stolen during the year. *(LO 5.3)*
11. Briefly describe the lower-of-cost-or-market (LCM) rule. *(LO 5.4)*
12. What effect does an overstatement of ending inventory in 2003 have on the (a) 2003 balance sheet, (b) 2003 income statement, (c) 2004 balance sheet, and (d) 2004 income statement? *(LO 5.5)*
13. How do decision makers use the inventory turnover ratio and the age of inventory when analyzing a company's financial data? *(LO 5.6)*

EXERCISES

14. **True & False** *(All LOs)*

Following are a series of statements regarding topics discussed in this chapter.

Required:

Indicate whether each statement is true (T) or false (F).

(1) An error in a company's ending inventory balance automatically causes the following period's beginning inventory balance to be misstated.

(2) Companies may value inventory at current replacement cost if the historical cost of inventory is lower than current replacement cost.

(3) Under the LIFO method of inventory, the costs of the most recently acquired goods are sent to Cost of Goods Sold first, while the costs of the oldest goods remain in inventory.

(4) When goods are shipped FOB destination, the seller is responsible for paying the transportation charges.

(5) Merchandising companies want to maintain as low an inventory turnover ratio as possible.

(6) Generally accepted accounting principles require a company to select the inventory cost flow assumption that most closely matches the physical flow of its goods.

(7) If a company uses the LIFO method of inventory costing for federal tax purposes, it must also use LIFO for financial reporting purposes.

(8) In an inflationary economic environment, the FIFO inventory costing method typically yields a lower net income than the LIFO method when these methods are applied to the same financial data.

(9) As the inventory turnover gets smaller, days in inventory gets larger.

(10) Because they do not keep track of cost of goods sold during a period, periodic inventory systems cannot provide information to managers about theft losses during a period.

15. **Shipping Terms** *(LO 5.1)*

The following items were in transit to or from Dean Canning Company on December 31, 2002.

(a) Goods costing $2,000 were sent FOB shipping point from Dean Canning to a customer.

(b) Goods costing $1,580 were sent FOB destination to Dean Canning from a vendor.

(c) Goods costing $2,760 were sent FOB destination from Dean Canning to a customer.

(d) Goods costing $957 were sent FOB shipping point to Dean Canning from a vendor.

Required:

(1) Identify which of these items Dean Canning should include in its December 31, 2002, inventory.

(2) Explain the rationale for either including or excluding the items.

16. **Perpetual Inventory Accounting** *(LO 5.1)*

Several transactions from Olsen Corp. are listed below.

(a) Olsen Corp. purchased inventory from Johnson, Inc. on account.

(b) Olsen paid shipping for the merchandise to be shipped from Johnson, Inc to Olsen.

(c) Olsen Corp. returned one defective item of inventory to Johnson, Inc.

(d) Olsen Corp. purchased inventory from Anderson Wholesalers on account.

(e) Olsen Corp. sold merchandise to a Mrs. Adams on account.

(f) Olsen paid shipping for the merchandise to be shipped from Olsen to Adams.

(g) Olsen Corp. paid Johnson, Inc. for the inventory purchase in time to earn a discount.

(h) Olsen Corp. paid Anderson Wholesalers, but didn't receive a discount.

(i) Mrs. Adams returned merchandise to Olsen Corp.

(j) Mrs. Adams paid for the balance of the merchandise she purchased within the discount period.

Required:

(1) Assuming a perpetual inventory system, indicate for each transaction whether the Inventory account is increased or decreased.

(2) Would your answers to part (1) change if Olsen Corp. used a periodic inventory system? If so, how and why? If not, why not?

17. **Cost of Goods Available for Sale and Cost of Goods Sold** *(LO 5.2)*

Ederington Enterprises is a merchandising company using a perpetual inventory system. At each year-end, Ederington takes a physical inventory and adjusts its inventory records to agree with the results of the physical inventory. Following is selected financial information for 2002 for Ederington.

January 1 inventory	$150,000
Merchandise purchases	625,000
December 31 inventory	125,000

Required:

(1) Compute Ederington's cost of goods available for sale and Cost of Goods Sold for 2002.

(2) Assume that Ederington took a physical count of inventory at the end of 2002 and found only $110,000 of goods in inventory. What factors may be responsible

for the $15,000 difference between Ederington's perpetual inventory records and the dollar amount of inventory determined by the year-end physical count? How would Ederington treat the $15,000 for financial statement purposes?

(3) Provide four ways that a company could help prevent inventory shrinkage from theft by employees and by customers. Indicate whether your prevention method would relate to employees, customers, or both.

18. **Valuing Inventory** *(LO 5.2)*

On August 4, Big Luggage Super Store (BLSS) had eight identical black briefcases in stock. The cost of each briefcase is given below in the order that the briefcases were purchased. On August 4, BLSS sold two black briefcases for $200 each.

1st briefcase	$95	5th briefcase	$ 98
2nd briefcase	95	6th briefcase	101
3rd briefcase	98	7th briefcase	101
4th briefcase	98	8th briefcase	104

Required:

Complete the table below. For the specific identification method, assume that the two briefcases sold were the 3rd and 8th ones purchased.

	Specific ID	FIFO	LIFO	Moving Average
Cost of Goods Available for Sale				
– Ending Inventory				
= Cost of Goods Sold				
Revenues				
– Cost of Goods Sold				
= Gross Profit				

19. **Inventory Costing Methods** *(LO 5.2)*

The following schedule summarizes the inventory purchases and sales of Gregory, Inc. during February 2004:

	Units	**Per Unit Cost**
Beginning inventory	600	$4.00
February 1 purchase	650	4.50
February 7 sale	500	
February 8 purchase	750	5.00
February 12 sale	800	
February 15 purchase	840	5.40
February 19 sale	795	
February 22 purchase	745	5.75
February 28 sale	825	

Required:

(1) What is Gregory's cost of goods available for sale for February 2004?

(2) What cost flow method is Gregory using if the cost of sales for February 12 is $3,975? Show calculations.

(3) What cost flow method is Gregory using if the cost of sales for February 19 is $4,014.75? Show calculations.

(4) What cost flow method is Gregory using if the cost of sales for February 28 is $4,483? Show calculations.

(5) What cost flow method is Gregory using if February's ending inventory is (a) $3,591.00, (b) $3,823.75, and (c) $2,692.50? Show calculations.

(6) Assume that Gregory sells its product for $10.50 each. Calculate Gregory's gross profit for each cost flow method.

20. **Retail Inventory** *(LO 5.3)*

Brendon Co. sells a variety of Egyptian products. The company began 2003 with inventory having a cost of $136,000 and a retail value of $241,000. During 2003, Brendon purchased a total of $662,200 of goods; upon receipt of the goods, they were marked to sell at retail prices totaling $987,000. The company uses the retail inventory method and sales for 2003 were $1,040,000.

Required:

(1) What is Brendon's actual cost of goods available for sale during 2003?

(2) What is the cost-to-retail percentage for 2003?

(3) What is the estimated ending inventory at retail?

(4) What is the estimated ending inventory at cost?

(5) Will the actual ending inventory be equal to the estimates? Why or why not?

21. **Lower-of-Cost-or-Market** *(LO 5.4)*

Kidd's Shoes sells four styles of children's canvas tennis shoes. Information about Kidd's May 31 ending inventory of these four styles is given below.

	Units in Ending Inventory	Per Unit Cost	Current Replacement Cost
Style 456	50	$20	$18
Style 489	30	25	25
Style 591	40	28	26
Style 599	45	32	35

Required:

(1) How much did Kidd's Shoes pay for the shoes that are in its May 31 inventory?

(2) If Kidd's Shoes had to replace its ending inventory of tennis shoes, what would it cost?

(3) What entry should be made to adjust Kidd's Shoes to the lower-of-cost-or-market amount if LCM is applied on a total inventory basis? On an item-by-item basis?

(4) Explain the effect the adjustment has on the income statement and balance sheet.

22. **Income Statement Impact of Inventory Errors** *(LO 5.5, ethics)*

Robert Kincade owns and operates the Winterset Company. Following is the business's income statement for its most recent fiscal year.

Sales	$89,000
Cost of Goods Sold	(31,000)
Gross Profit	$58,000
Operating Expenses	(10,000)
Operating Income	$48,000
Income Taxes Expense (30%)	(14,400)
Net Income	$33,600

Shortly after the company's financial statements were issued, Kincade's accountant discovered that the company's ending inventory had been inadvertently overstated by $12,000. This error stemmed from an error on the part of the accountant, who double counted some items of ending inventory. The inventory balance was shown at $39,000, while the true inventory value was $27,000.

Required:

(1) Prepare a corrected income statement for Winterset Company.

(2) Suppose that Robert Kincade told his accountant to ignore the inventory error saying, "Why bother? The financial statements have already been issued, and besides it was an honest error." Evaluate Kincade's decision. Has he behaved unethically? Why or why not? What parties may be affected by Kincade's decision? Explain.

23. **Inventory Analysis** *(LO 5.6)*

Massoud Company has the following inventory balances for 2003: beginning, $156,000; ending, $148,000. The company's Cost of Goods Sold for the year was $1,456,800.

Required:

(1) What is Massoud Company's average inventory for 2003?

(2) What is the company's inventory turnover ratio?

(3) Calculate the average age of inventory for Massoud Company.

(4) Assume that Massoud Company is a retail toy company and its fiscal year-end is December 31. Would Massoud's inventory be at an annual high or low at the end of the year? In this situation, would the inventory turnover ratio provide valid information to a decision maker? Why or why not?

(5) Given the information in part (4), how might you obtain a better indication of the average amount of inventory that Massoud Company had on hand during the year?

PROBLEMS

24. **Journalizing Transactions in a Perpetual Inventory System** *(LO 5.1)*

House of Jeans uses a perpetual inventory system. All jeans, regardless of style, are sold for $35 per pair. Following are selected transactions of the House of Jeans for April 2002.

April 6	Purchased 30 pairs of 404 Jeans with terms of 2/10, n/30; the per unit cost was $22.
April 9	Returned ten pairs of the 404 Jeans purchased on April 6 due to fabric flaws.
April 13	Sold two pairs of 303 Jeans for cash; the per-unit cost of these jeans was $21.
April 16	Paid amount due to the supplier for jeans purchased on April 6.
April 17	Purchased 12 pairs of 606 Jeans with terms of 2/10, n/30; the per-unit cost was $18.
April 20	Sold one pair of 909 Jeans on credit; the cost of this pair was $24.
April 21	A customer returned a pair of 808 Jeans because they were the wrong size; the jeans, which cost $20, were returned to inventory.
April 27	Sold two pairs of 101 Jeans on credit; the per-unit cost of these jeans was $17.
April 27	Paid amount due to the supplier for jeans purchased on April 17.

Required:

Prepare the journal entries necessary to record these transactions for House of Jeans.

25. **Inventory Costing Methods** *(LO 5.2, Excel)*

The following schedule summarizes the inventory purchases and sales of Brooks Street Enterprises during January 2003:

	Units	Per Unit Cost	Per Unit Selling Price
Beginning inventory	400	$20	
January 2 purchase	200	22	
January 5 sale	300		$40
January 9 purchase	200	24	
January 14 sales	350		45
January 18 purchase	200	25	
January 21 sales	150		45
January 25 purchase	500	26	
January 31 sales	450		50

Required:

(1) Determine Brooks Street's ending inventory, cost of goods sold, and gross profit for January 2003 assuming the company uses a perpetual inventory system and the following inventory costing methods: (a) FIFO, (b) LIFO, and (c) moving-average.

(2) Which of the three inventory costing methods yields the most impressive financial results for Brooks Street? Explain.

(3) What factors should a company consider when choosing an inventory costing method? Should one of these factors be the inventory costing method preferred by the decision makers who will be using the company's financial statements?

26. **Retail Inventory** *(LO 5.3)*

Nicholas, Inc. uses the retail inventory method. The company's beginning inventory for 2003 had a cost of $125,300 and a selling price of $329,000. During the year, $621,160 of purchases was made; these goods were marked up for sale at $958,000. Actual 2003 retail sales for the company were $876,000.

Required:

(1) What was cost of goods available for sale at cost? At retail?

(2) What was the cost-to-retail percentage for 2003?

(3) Assume that the physical ending inventory showed goods on hand that would retail for $395,000. What is the cost of the ending inventory for balance sheet purposes?

(4) How much inventory loss should be shown on the income statement for 2003?

(5) Assume that Nicholas, Inc. is an art gallery, selling primarily paintings and sculptures. What is the most likely source of the inventory loss? Explain.

(6) What is meant by the term *bonded* when discussing employees? Is bonding an effective deterrent to employee theft? What other internal controls might be more effective?

27. **Lower-of-Cost-or-Market Rule** *(LO 5.4)*

Best Plumbing Supplies sells plumbing fixtures. The company had the following inventory quantities, per unit costs, and per unit market values (current replacement costs) at the end of a recent fiscal year.

	Unit	Per Unit Cost	Per Unit Market Value
Industrial Strength			
Item A	100	$160	$150
Item B	150	200	205
Medium Strength			
Item C	75	120	125
Item D	110	140	125
Low Strength			
Item E	80	80	80
Item F	130	75	70

Required:

(1) Compute Best Plumbing's ending inventory by applying the lower-of-cost-or-market rule on an item-by-item basis.

(2) Briefly describe how the application of the LCM rule will affect the financial statement data of Best Plumbing Supplies.

(3) In your view, which of the following inventory valuation methods would provide the most relevant and reliable accounting data for external decision makers: (a) valuing inventories strictly on a cost basis, (b) valuing inventories strictly on a market basis, or (c) valuing inventories on a lower-of-cost-or-market basis? Defend your choice.

28. **Analyzing Inventory** *(LO 5.6)*

Outer Reaches, Inc. is a leading firm in the aerospace and defense industries. The following selected financial data (in millions) are for three years. The company's fiscal year-end is September 30.

	2000	2001	2002
Net Sales	$1,311.7	$1,201.7	$1,643.9
Cost of Goods Sold	1,122.4	996.4	1,137.9
Net Income	63.0	63.8	72.0
Ending Inventory	146.0	118.4	169.9

Required:

(1) Compute the inventory turnover ratio and age of inventory for Outer Reaches, Inc. for each of the years listed. The company's inventory balance at the beginning of 2000 was $153 million.

(2) Would you expect companies in the aerospace and defense industries to normally have high or low inventory turnover ratios? Explain the rationale for your answer.

(3) Did Outer Reaches, Inc.'s inventory ratios improve or deteriorate between 2000 and 2003? Explain.

(4) For several years, many companies in the aerospace and defense industries were forced to "downsize." Is such downsizing evident in Outer Reaches, Inc.'s financial statements? Explain.

CASES

29. Accounting for Inventory *(LO 5.1, 5.2, and 5.4)*

Omega Sales uses the Internet to sell encyclopedias for $250 per set. All encyclopedia sets are purchased from Galaxy Encyclopedia for cash. On March 1, Omega had 20 sets of encyclopedias in inventory that cost $100 each. The following transactions occurred in March 2003.

March 1	Purchased 15 sets of encyclopedias at a cost of $95 each.
March 8	Sold 13 sets of encyclopedias.
March 9	Purchased 10 sets of encyclopedias at a cost of $94.
March 13	Sold 16 sets of encyclopedias.
March 16	Purchased 10 sets of encyclopedias at a cost of $92.
March 21	Sold 19 sets of encyclopedias.
March 23	Purchased 15 sets of encyclopedias at a cost of $90.
March 31	Sold 14 sets of encyclopedias.

Required:

(1) Record the March journal entries for Omega Sales, assuming the company uses LIFO.

(2) Prepare a partial income statement (through gross profit) for Omega Sales for March.

(3) What ending inventory balance would Omega show on its balance sheet?

(4) What would be the balance of Cost of Goods Sold if Omega used FIFO?

(5) Assuming LIFO, apply the lower-of-cost-or-market rule on March 31st and make the appropriate journal entry. How does the fact that encyclopedia prices are declining affect your answer? Would your answer change (and, if so, by how much?) if Omega used FIFO?

(6) Explain why Omega might choose to omit the LCM adjustment.

30. Inventory Systems *(LO 5.5, writing, ethics)*

Garcon Fashions tags its inventory with retail prices, but does not keep thorough inventory records. The lax system makes it very costly for Garcon to determine the cost of the inventory in its store. The cost of Garcon's merchandise is typically 40% to 60% of retail price, so Garcon determines cost of ending inventory by calculating retail price of ending inventory and dividing by 2 (to get 50%).

Required:

Write the CEO of Garcon a letter explaining the errors that might be created by the company's inventory system.

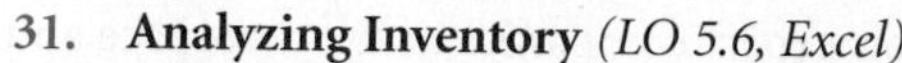

31. Analyzing Inventory *(LO 5.6, Excel)*

Good Eats is a Tennessee-based company that operates a large chain of restaurants. The following information is available for the company.

	2000	2001	2002
Net Sales	$400,577,000	$517,616,000	$640,898,000
Cost of Goods Sold	130,885,000	171,708,000	215,071,000
Net Income	33,943,000	46,652,000	57,947,000
Ending Inventory	23,192,000	28,426,000	41,989,000

Required:

(1) Compute Good Eats' inventory turnover ratio and age of inventory for 2000 through 2002. (The company's beginning inventory for 2000 was $15,746,000.)

(2) Comment on the ratios you computed in part (1). Are there any definite trends in these ratios? If so, are these trends favorable or unfavorable? Explain.

(3) Why do decision makers pay close attention to the age of inventory statistic for companies in the restaurant industry?

32. **Annual Reports** *(LO 5.6, Internet)*

May Department Stores Company (www.mayco.com) is the parent company to several department store chains including Foley's, Lord & Taylor, and David's Bridal. Use the annual report of May Department Stores, obtained at the company Web site, to answer the following questions.

Required:

Answer each of the following questions for the fiscal year that ended in February 2002.

(1) What is May's cost of sales?

(2) What is the average balance in inventory for the year?

(3) Calculate the inventory turnover ratio and the age of inventory. Comment on the results.

(4) What is the main method of cost flow valuation used by May?

(5) Does the company write its inventory down to lower-of-cost-or-market?

(6) From February 2001 to February 2002, what was the percent increase or decrease in (a) retail sales, (b) cost of goods sold, and (c) ending inventory? Comment on the relationship among these percentages.

33. **Comparing Companies** *(LO 5.6, group, Internet)*

Identifying the similarities and differences between companies is as crucial to making investment decisions as understanding a single company's financial statements. Form groups of at least four students. Each group should select a single industry. Each group member should locate a different annual report within that industry. (The industry and individual company may be assigned by your instructor.)

Required—individual group members:

(1) If you obtained the annual report of a company of which you had no previous knowledge, how would you determine whether the company sold a product as a primary means of generating income?

(2) Does the company you chose generate income primarily by selling a product?

(3) If you answered yes to part (2), calculate the following ratios for the company you selected for the two most recent fiscal years.

  (a) Inventory turnover ratio

  (b) Days in inventory

(4) If you answered yes to part (2), scan the notes to the financial statements and determine what cost flow assumption (LIFO, FIFO, or moving-average) the company uses and whether the cost of inventory is adjusted for lower-of-cost or market.

Required—groups:

(5) Compile the ratio calculations for each company prepared by the individual group members into one table. Compare the results from company to company in the same fiscal year. Include in your comparison a graphical analysis. Discuss reasons why these ratios might be similar or different within an industry. Why did some companies not have ratio calculations for part (3)?

(6) What are the differences in the financial statements between a company that sells inventory and one that does not? Is it possible to compare these two types of companies? If so, how? If not, why not?

Required—class:

(7) Compare the ratios from each industry. Discuss reasons why these ratios might be similar or different between industries. Does one industry seem to be a better investment than another? Explain. Do you think this situation is constant over time? Why or why not?

(8) Discuss the differences and similarities in the decision to invest in a company between a company that sells inventory and one that does not.

SUPPLEMENTAL PROBLEMS

34. **Perpetual Inventory Systems** *(LO 5.1)* [Compare to Problem 24]

During July of the current year, Art's Auto Repair engaged in the following transactions involving car mirrors purchased from Prisms, Inc.:

July 1	Purchased ten car mirrors from Prisms, Inc., for $25 each; terms 2/10, n/30.
July 5	Sold six car mirrors on credit for $40 each; terms 1/10, n/30.
July 7	Two car mirrors sold on July 5 were returned by the customers because the mirrors were flawed.
July 9	Returned the two flawed mirrors to Prisms, Inc. for credit.
July 11	Paid the amount due Prisms, Inc., for the car mirrors purchased on July 1.
July 15	Received the amount due from customers who purchased car mirrors on July 5.

Required:

Prepare the journal entry for each transaction listed, assuming that Art's Auto Repair uses a perpetual inventory system.

35. **Inventory Costing Methods** *(LO 5.2)* [Compare to Problem 25]

Top of the World (TOW) is a retail store on Campus Corner that sells baseball caps. TOW had the following inventory purchases and sales during May 2002:

	Number of Units	Per-Unit Cost	Selling Price Per-Unit
Beginning Inventory	1,000	$ 5	
May 3 purchase	300	6	
May 7 sales	400		$12
May 9 purchase	375	8	
May 14 sales	350		16
May 16 purchase	400	9	
May 22 sales	500		17
May 25 purchase	500	10	
May 31sales	700		20

Required:

Determine TOW's (a) ending inventory, (b) cost of goods sold, and (c) gross profit for the year in question assuming the company uses a perpetual inventory system and the following inventory costing methods:

(1) FIFO

(2) LIFO

(3) Moving-average

36. **Lower-of-Cost-or-Market Rule** *(LO 5.4)* [Compare to Problem 27]

Following is information regarding the year-end inventory of Madison County Steelworks.

Item	Quantity	Original Per-Unit Cost	Replacement Cost Per Unit
Exgots	125	$17	$14
Ingots	100	12	13
Ongots	200	15	13
Ungots	50	20	19

Required:

(1) Apply the lower-of-cost-or-market (LCM) rule to Madison County's ending inventory assuming that the company applies the rule on (a) an item-by-item basis and (b) a total inventory basis.

(2) What accounting concept or concepts dictate that businesses apply the LCM rule? Does this rule seem reasonable to you? Why or why not?

37. **Analyzing Inventory** *(LO 5.6)* [Compare to Problem 28]

Francesca Johnson owns and operates a sporting goods store. Following are selected financial data regarding Francesca's business over the past three years.

	2000	2001	2002
Sales	$280,000	$300,000	$330,000
Cost of Goods Sold	168,000	195,000	224,400
Net Income	37,100	38,500	39,600
Ending Inventory	80,000	110,000	130,000

Required:

(1) Compute the inventory turnover ratio and age of inventory for Francesca's store for each year listed. (Note: On January 1, 2000, the store's inventory was $60,000.)

(2) Given the data provided and the ratios you computed in part (1), evaluate Francesca's management of inventory over this three-year period.

(3) Francesca is concerned by the slow growth in her business's net income in recent years. Given the data provided, identify factors that may be adversely affecting the business's profitability.

CHAPTER 6

Long-Term Assets: Property, Plant & Equipment and Intangibles

LEARNING OBJECTIVES

1. Determine the acquisition cost of property, plant and equipment assets.
2. Compute depreciation expense using three depreciation methods.
3. Account for disposals of property, plant and equipment.
4. Identify major types of intangible assets and the key accounting issues related to these assets.
5. Identify the key information needs of decision makers regarding long-term assets.

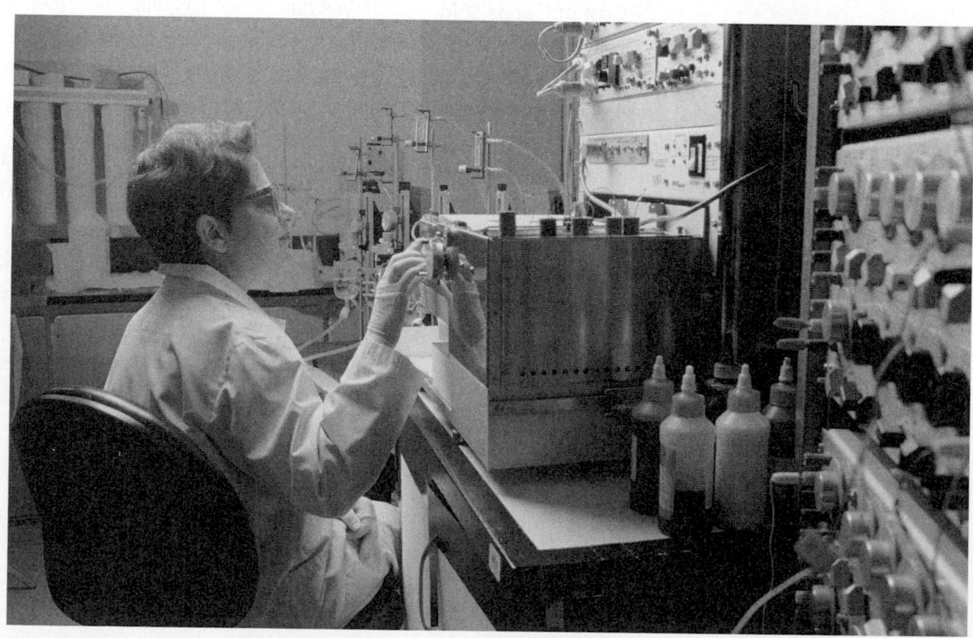

Old Machines?

Did you ever wonder about the age of the airplane that you just boarded? Or did you contemplate whether the medical equipment that was just used to diagnose your health had been properly maintained? We generally don't consider how old a company's assets are, or how well they have been maintained, when we use that company's products or services—but maybe that should be a consideration.

The Committee of the Radiological and Electromedical Industries (COCIR) in Europe is raising such points. The COCIR is concerned that medical equipment used throughout Europe may be too old; and malfunctioning equipment might result in a misdiagnosis for a patient. Asset age is not simply a concern for both patients and investors. COCIR expects that equipment which has been used for ten years or more will dramatically deteriorate within the next several years. Such deterioration will reduce the efficiency of healthcare treatment as well as raise the cost of healthcare because of higher maintenance costs. These problems will, in turn, lead to a reduction in customer satisfaction and loss of revenues. Thus, business investors should consider the age of a company's assets as an indication of potential future maintenance costs, future revenue changes, and future capital investment needs.

SOURCE: "Concern over Europe's Aging Electromedical Equipment," *Medical Device Business News* (November 1, 1996)

INTRODUCTION

Chapters 4 and 5 discussed accounting for current assets or items that provide economic benefits to a business over a twelve-month period or a business operating cycle, whichever is longer. In comparison, long-term assets typically provide benefits to a business for several years, if not several decades. This chapter addresses two specific types of long-term assets: property, plant and equipment (PP&E), and intangibles.

PROPERTY, PLANT & EQUIPMENT

The most common types of property, plant and equipment assets are land, buildings, machinery and equipment, furniture and fixtures, automobiles, and land improvements (such as parking lots and driveways). Generally accepted accounting principles require businesses to depreciate long-term assets, with the exception of land, over their useful lives. Because land improvements are depreciated, they must be recorded separately from land.

PP&E assets pose four general accounting issues. First, the asset acquisition cost must be determined. Second, depreciation expense must be computed for each accounting period. Third, following original acquisition of PP&E, additional related expenditures must be analyzed and recorded. Finally, disposals of PP&E must be accounted for. Each of these topics is discussed in the following sections.

Acquisition of PP&E

The acquisition cost of a PP&E asset includes all *reasonable* and *necessary* expenditures incurred in obtaining the asset and preparing it for use. Suppose that Elmer Co. purchases a large copier. The copier's suggested retail price is $40,000, but the vendor grants a 10 percent discount to Elmer Co. Freight charges to deliver the copier are $550, and installation expenses total $320. During installation, an employee at Elmer's accidentally damages the copier, resulting in a repair cost of $410. The total acquisition cost of the copier is determined as follows:

Net invoice cost ($40,000 – $4,000 discount)	$36,000
Freight charges	550
Installation cost	320
Total cost	$36,870

Note that the repair cost is not considered part of the copier's acquisition cost because the $410 was neither reasonable nor necessary to obtain the copier or to get it ready for use. The repair expenditure is recognized as an expense in the period incurred.

The following entries would be made to record the purchase of the copier. Included in the description for this entry is an asset number. For control purposes, an identification number is often assigned to each major PP&E asset of a business.

General Journal				
Date		**Description**	**Debit**	**Credit**
Apr.	1	Copier	36,870	
		Accounts Payable		36,000
		Cash		870
		Purchase of copier (asset #231-7) on credit and payment of charges for freight and installation		
Apr.	1	Repair Expense	410	
		Cash		410
		Repair copier		

Businesses often acquire several long-term assets in a single transaction. For example, a company may purchase a production facility that includes land, land improvements, buildings, and equipment. In such cases, the purchase price must be allocated to the specific, individual assets acquired; this allocation is usually based on the relative market values of the acquired assets. Suppose that Hodnett Company purchases land, a building, and a piece of equipment for $600,000 at a court-ordered auction of a bankrupt firm's assets. Exhibit 6-1 shows the allocation of the purchase price to the assets and the journal entry to record the acquisition.

Depreciation of PP&E

Depreciation is the process of allocating the cost of a long-term asset over its useful life in a rational and systematic manner. Useful life reflects the expected time that the asset will provide economic benefits to the business. Depreciating long-term assets is one method businesses use to match revenues recognized each accounting period with the expenses incurred to generate those revenues.

Three factors must be considered when computing depreciation expense: asset cost, useful life, and salvage (or residual) value. **Salvage value** is the estimated value of an asset at the

EXHIBIT 6-1
Allocation of Acquisition Cost to Multiple Assets

	Market Value	Proportion of Total Market Value	Total Cost	Allocated Cost
Land	$160,000	160 ÷ 800 = 20%	$600,000	$120,000
Building	400,000	400 ÷ 800 = 50%	$600,000	300,000
Equipment	240,000	240 ÷ 800 = 30%	$600,000	180,000
	$800,000			$600,000

Date	Account	Debit	Credit
May 10	Land	120,000	
	Building	300,000	
	Equipment	180,000	
	Cash		600,000
	Purchase of PP&E and allocation of purchase price.		

end of its useful life. When computing depreciation, the term **depreciable cost** is often used, which refers to the asset's acquisition cost less its salvage value. Thus, depreciable cost is the amount of asset cost that is expected to be consumed or "used up" over its useful life. #4

As shown in Chapter 5, a variety of methods can be used to calculate the cost of goods sold and ending inventory balance. The same situation exists for calculating the depreciation expense on property, plant and equipment. Three commonly used methods are the straight-line, units-of-production, and double-declining balance method. A company can select different methods for different PP&E assets or use the same method for all assets. Each method will result in a different amount of depreciation expense for an accounting period and, therefore, a different amount of net income.

Assume that Riverside Construction Company acquired a drill press on January 1, 2002. The following data are used to illustrate the three depreciation methods.

Equipment: Drill Press (Asset #14-27B)
Acquisition Date: January 1, 2002
Acquisition Cost: $68,000
Useful Life: 4 years or 30,000 units
Salvage Value: $8,000
Depreciable Cost: $68,000 – $8,000 = $60,000

Straight-Line Method

Under the **straight-line** (S-L) **method,** a business allocates an equal amount of depreciation expense to each full year of an asset's estimated useful life. The premise underlying this method is that an asset is equally productive each year that it is in service. The annual depreciation expense under the SL method is computed as:

Depreciation Expense = Depreciable Cost ÷ Useful Life in Years

Substituting the information on Riverside's drill press in this formula yields an annual depreciation expense of $15,000 (or $60,000 ÷ 4). The following adjusting journal entry (made on the last day of the fiscal year) is required to record depreciation expense at the end of the drill press's first year of service.

General Journal

Date		Description	Debit	Credit
Dec.	31	Depreciation Expense	15,000	
		Accumulated Depreciation—#1427B		15,000
		Record annual depreciation on drill press		

For each of the next four years, Riverside Construction Company will record the same amount of depreciation expense on the drill press. Remember from Chapter 3, accumulated depreciation is a contra-asset account and reflects the total amount of the asset's original cost that has been depreciated or charged off as an expense since the asset was acquired. The difference between an asset's cost and the balance of its related accumulated depreciation account is called book value.

After the four years of depreciation, the depreciable cost of the asset will have been completely written off to depreciation expense. The book value at that time will be equal to the salvage value of the asset. The machine will not necessarily be taken out of service at the end of four years. Unless the asset is unreliable or should be replaced for other reasons, it may be kept in service. If the asset continues to be used, additional depreciation may be taken, but only to the extent of the salvage value. An asset cannot be depreciated below its original cost.

If the drill press had been acquired during the year, rather than on January 1, Riverside would generally compute depreciation expense for 2002 by multiplying $15,000 by the fraction of the year the drill press was owned during 2002. For example, if the drill press had been purchased on March 1, the appropriate depreciation expense for 2002 would be $12,500 ($15,000 × 10/12). A full year's depreciation would be taken in 2003, 2004, and 2005. In 2006, only two months' depreciation or $2,500 ($15,000 × 2/12) would be taken. Thus, the total depreciation taken ($60,000) would still equal the depreciable cost of the drill press.

Units-of-Production Method

Under the **units-of-production method,** an asset's useful life is expressed in a number of units of production or use. Depreciation expense for any given period is a function of the asset's level of usage during that period. This depreciation method is well suited for assets for which wear-and-tear is a predominant cause of declining usefulness. For example, an industrial dishwasher may have a useful life of ten years when used in a restaurant that is open only during the evening for dinner business. However, if this dishwasher is used in a restaurant that is open 24-hours a day, it is unlikely to be in service ten years from its purchase date.

Suppose that Riverside applies the units-of-production method to its drill press. When the drill press is acquired, the manufacturer provided an estimate stating that the asset would probably be able to produce 30,000 units of product in its useful life. The per-unit depreciation expense is computed as follows:

Per-Unit Depreciation Expense = Depreciable Cost ÷ Useful Life in Units

Substituting the information on Riverside's drill press in this formula yields a per-unit annual depreciation expense of $2 (or $60,000 ÷ 30,000 units). For any given period, the asset's depreciation expense under the units-of-production method is determined by multiplying the per-unit depreciation cost by the number of units produced that period:

Depreciation Expense = Per-Unit Expense × Total Units Produced

The following adjusted journal entry would be required to record depreciation expense at the end of the drill press's first year of service, assuming that 11,000 units of product were completed using the drill press.

General Journal

Date		Description	Debit	Credit
Dec.	31	Depreciation Expense	22,000	
		Accumulated Depreciation—#1427B		22,000
		Record annual depreciation on drill press		

Each year, the amount of depreciation expense will vary, depending on the usage of the drill press. However, regardless of the quantity of use, depreciation stops at estimated usage unless the overuse would affect the salvage value.

Unlike under the straight-line method, the units-of-production method is not affected by when the asset was purchased. Depreciation is taken based on how much was produced, not how long the asset was in service during the period.

Double-Declining-Balance Method

Some companies use a depreciation method that allows larger amounts of depreciation to be taken in the early years of an asset's life compared to later years. The premise underlying this method is that proportionately more of a depreciable asset's economic benefit is consumed during the early years of the asset's useful life. Machinery, for example, generally becomes less productive over time due to increasing breakdowns and more extensive maintenance requirements.

Under the **double-declining-balance** (DDB) **method** of depreciation, annual depreciation expense is computed by multiplying an asset's book value at the beginning of a year by twice the straight-line rate of depreciation. For example, the annual straight-line depreciation rate for an asset with a ten-year useful life is 10 percent (100% ÷ 10); under DDB, the annual depreciation rate would be 20 percent (2 × 10%). Thus, the DDB depreciation calculation is as follows:

DDB Depreciation Expense = (2 × S-L rate)(Beginning of Year Book Value)

Note that book value, *not* depreciable cost, is used in this formula. Both the straight-line and units-of-production methods subtract salvage value from an asset's original cost to determine its depreciable cost; this amount is then expensed over the asset's useful life. Under the double-declining-balance method, an asset's salvage value is initially ignored when computing periodic depreciation expense. However, once the asset's book value is equal to its salvage value, no further depreciation is recorded.

For Riverside's drill press, the accelerated depreciation rate under the DDB method is twice the straight-line rate of 25 percent or 50 percent. At the beginning of 2002, the asset's book value is equal to its cost of $68,000. Depreciation expense for 2002 is $34,000 (50% × $68,000). At the beginning of 2003, the drill press's book value is $34,000 (cost of $68,000 less accumulated depreciation of $34,000). Thus, depreciation expense for 2003 is $17,000 (50% × $34,000). At the beginning of 2004, the drill press's book value is $17,000 (cost of $68,000 less accumulated depreciation of $51,000). Thus, depreciation expense for 2004 is $8,500 (50% × $17,000).

At the beginning of 2005, a total of $59,500 ($34,000 + $17,000 + $8,500) of depreciation has been taken on the drill press. The calculation for depreciation expense would normally be 50% times the book value of $8,500 ($68,000 – $59,500) or $4,250. However, taking that amount of depreciation would result in a total accumulated depreciation of $63,750. That amount of accumulated depreciation would cause the book value of the drill press to be $3,750 below its $8,000 salvage value. Therefore, so that the original salvage value estimate can be maintained, only $500 of depreciation can be taken in 2004.

Like the straight-line method, the DDB method of depreciation requires an adjustment to the depreciation calculation for the purchase of an asset during the year rather than at the beginning of the year. However, the partial-period adjustment is made only in the first year of the asset's life (rather than the first and last, as under the straight-line method). If Riverside had acquired the drill press on October 1, 2002, depreciation for 2002 would have been calculated as follows: (50% × $68,000) × 3/12 = $8,500. In 2003, depreciation expense for the year would have been $29,750, computed as follows:

[50% × ($68,000 – $8,500)] or (50% × $59,500). The asset would continue to be depreciated until book value is equal to salvage value.

Exhibit 6-2 provides a comparison of the full depreciation schedules for Riverside's drill press, using the original assumption of a January 1 date of acquisition.

Disposal of PP&E

When PP&E assets are no longer needed or no longer provide benefits, a company will remove those assets from service and either junk them, sell them, or exchange them for other assets. However, if a depreciable asset is disposed at any point other than year-end, an adjusting entry must be made to record depreciation expense on that asset before its disposal is recorded. This entry reflects the depreciation expense on the asset for the period since the last entry for depreciation expense was journalized.

EXHIBIT 6-2

Depreciation Schedules Under Three Methods

Asset cost	$68,000
Salvage value	(8,000)
Depreciable cost	$60,000

Life: 4 years or 30,000 units

Actual production: in 2002, 10,000 units; in 2003, 8,000 units; in 2004, 5,000 units; and in 2005, 7,000 units.

Straight-line

Year	Computation	Depr. Exp.	Yr. End Balance of Acc. Depr.	Yr. End Book Value*
1	$60,000 ÷ 4	$15,000	$15,000	$53,000
2	$60,000 ÷ 4	$15,000	$30,000	$38,000
3	$60,000 ÷ 4	$15,000	$45,000	$23,000
4	$60,000 ÷ 4	$15,000	$60,000	$ 8,000

Units of Production

Per unit expense = $60,000 ÷ 30,000 = $2

Year	Computation	Depr. Exp.	Yr. End Balance of Acc. Depr.	Yr. End Book Value*
1	$2 × 10,000	$20,000	$20,000	$48,000
2	$2 × 8,000	$16,000	$36,000	$32,000
3	$2 × 5,000	$10,000	$46,000	$22,000
4	$2 × 7,000	$14,000	$60,000	$ 8,000

Double-Declining Balance

S-L rate = 100% ÷ 4 year life = 25% per year; DDB rate = 50%

Year	Computation	Depr. Exp.	Yr. End Balance of Acc. Depr.	Yr. End Book Value*
1	0.5 × $68,000	$34,000	$34,000	$34,000
2	0.5 × $34,000	$17,000	$51,000	$17,000
3	0.5 × $17,000	$ 8,500	$59,500	$ 8,500
4	0.5 × $ 8,500	$ 500**	$60,000	$ 8,000

*Computed as: Original asset cost ($68,000) less year-end balance of accumulated depreciation.

**Cannot take the $4,250 as calculated because that amount would bring the book value to less than the salvage value of the asset.

Riverside Construction's drill press will be used to illustrate a simple retirement and a cash sale of a plant asset.[1] These examples assume that Riverside calculated depreciation on this asset using the straight-line method.

Simple Retirement

Suppose that, at the end of its third year of service, Riverside's drill press becomes obsolete because a new and more efficient model becomes available. The book value of the drill press at the end of Year 3 is $23,000 as indicated in Exhibit 6-2. Given the new technology available, Riverside cannot sell the drill press.

On January 2, 2004, the local junkyard removes the drill press for no charge in exchange for the scrap metal that can be recovered from the machine. No additional depreciation expense needs to be recorded on this item because Riverside Construction made an adjusting entry to record depreciation on December 31, 2003. The disposition of the drill press results in a loss equal to the asset's book value of $23,000. The following entry records the disposal of the drill press.

General Journal				
Date		Description	Debit	Credit
Jan.	2	Accumulated Depreciation—#1427B	45,000	
		Loss on Disposal of Asset	23,000	
		Equipment—#1427B		68,000
		To record the disposal of the drill press for junk		

This entry removes both the cost of the drill press and its accumulated depreciation from Riverside's accounting records. Gains and losses on the disposal of long-term assets are generally classified as "other items" on an income statement.

Cash Sale

When a long-term asset is sold for less than its book value, a loss must be recorded equal to the difference between the asset's book value and selling price. Assume that Riverside's drill press is sold for $10,000 on June 30, 2004.

On the date that the drill press is sold, six months have passed since the previous adjusting entry (December 31, 2003) for depreciation. Before recording the sale, Riverside would record one-half a year's depreciation expense or $7,500 ($15,000 × 6/12) to recognize use of the drill press for the first six months of 2004.

General Journal				
Date		Description	Debit	Credit
June	30	Depreciation Expense	7,500	
		Accumulated Depreciation—#1427B		7,500
		To record the depreciation on the drill press for partial year		

After this entry is made, the book value of the asset is calculated as follows:

Original cost			$68,000
Less:	Acc. Depreciation (as of 12/31/03)	$45,000	
	Adjusting entry, 6/30/04	7,500	(52,500)
Book value at 6/30/04			$15,500

[1] The entries for asset exchanges are not included because they are beyond the scope of this text.

Given the assumed selling price of $10,000 and the book value of $15,500, Riverside would record a loss of $5,500 on the sale of the drill press as reflected by the following entry.

General Journal				
Date		Description	Debit	Credit
June	30	Cash	10,000	
		Accumulated Depreciation—#1427B	52,500	
		Loss on Disposal of Asset	5,500	
		Equipment—#1427B		68,000
		To record the sale of the drill press		

The gain or loss on the sale is calculated as the cash received minus the asset's ending book value. If Riverside sells the drill press for more than its book value, a gain will be recognized. For example, suppose that the selling price of the drill press on June 30, 2004, had been $25,000 rather than $10,000. In this case, Riverside would record a gain of $9,500 ($25,000 cash received – $15,500 ending book value) as shown in the following entry.

General Journal				
Date		Description	Debit	Credit
June	30	Cash	25,000	
		Accumulated Depreciation—#1427B	52,500	
		Equipment—#1427B		68,000
		Gain on Disposal of Asset		9,500
		To record the sale of the drill press		

NATURAL RESOURCES

The most important PP&E assets of forestry, mining, and petroleum companies are natural resource properties. **Natural resources** include long-term assets that are extracted or harvested from or beneath the earth's surface; such assets would include tracts of standing timber, minerals, coal, oil, and natural gas.

Natural resources are often referred to as wasting assets. The value of these properties gradually declines as timber, gems, petroleum, and so on are extracted or harvested. Instead of depreciation, the term **depletion** is used to describe the allocation of the cost of natural resources to the periods of economic benefit to an entity. Firms in the extractive industries apply the units-of-production concept to record depletion expense on natural resource properties. To compute annual depletion, the following adaptation of the units-of-production depreciation equation is used.

$$\text{Annual Depletion} = \text{Per-Unit Depletion} \times \text{Total Units Recovered During Period}$$

Suppose Joyner Oil purchases, for $20 million, the oil rights for a property that has an estimated two million barrels of oil. The depletion cost per barrel of oil recovered is calculated as $20,000,000 ÷ 2,000,000 barrels or $10 per barrel. For simplicity, assume that Joyner Oil immediately sells all barrels of oil without any type of additional processing. Because Joyner Oil is in the business of selling oil, the oil is its inventory, and, as such, the cost of this product is sent to Cost of Goods Sold when the oil is sold. Assume that Joyner Oil recovers and sells 300,000 barrels from this property in 2002. The following entry would be made:

General Journal			
Date	**Description**	**Debit**	**Credit**
2002	Cost of Goods Sold	3,000,000	
	Accumulated Depreciation—Oil		3,000,000
	To record the recovery and sale of 300,000 barrels of oil		

Note that the cost of the oil is not, in this circumstance, charged to an account called Depletion Expense. Essentially, Joyner is converting natural resources into inventory, which was then sold (Cost of Goods Sold). If the barrels of oil had not been sold, the cost of the oil would have been recorded as Joyner's inventory. When inventory was sold, its cost would have been recorded in a Cost of Goods Sold account.

INTANGIBLE ASSETS

Long-term assets that do not have a physical form or substance are called intangible assets. These assets pose the same general types of accounting issues as long-term depreciable assets. For example, a cost must be assigned to an intangible asset and then this cost must be systematically allocated to the accounting periods to which the asset provides economic benefits to the business. This intangible asset allocation process is referred to as **amortization** instead of depreciation (property, plant and equipment) or depletion (natural resources).

The general rule is that an intangible asset should be amortized over the shorter of its legal life, its useful life, or forty years (which is an arbitrary period established for financial accounting purposes). Because their cost is generally not an extremely significant portion of the balance sheet, intangibles typically do not have related Accumulated Amortization accounts. The write-off of the cost of intangibles is made directly to the asset account. Amortization calculations are commonly identical to straight-line depreciation; however, salvage value is almost always zero.

For example, assume that a patent which had been purchased for $1,000,000 had an expected useful life of 10 years. At the end of each full year of that ten-year period, the owning company would make the following adjusting entry.

General Journal			
Date	**Description**	**Debit**	**Credit**
XXX	Amortization Expense	100,000	
	Patent		100,000
	To record the amortization of a patent		

Identifiable Intangibles

Patents, copyrights, trademarks, and leasehold improvements are the common types of identifiable intangible assets found on the balance sheets of businesses. Some of these intangibles have a useful life that is limited by federal statute or by a contractual agreement; other intangibles have indefinite useful lives.

Many companies engage in research and development (R&D) activities that hopefully produce patentable new products. The cost of the R&D must be expensed as it is incurred. New products or processes that result from the R&D can be granted a patent from the United States Patent Office. A **patent** grants the holder an exclusive right to manufacture a specific product or to use a specific process for 20 years. Given the pace at which knowledge is expanding, however, many patents will never be useful for their entire legal lives.

The federal government grants creators of songs, books, films, and other works of art a **copyright** or the exclusive right to produce and sell those items. Copyrights generally have a useful life of no more than a few years, although their legal lives extend fifty years beyond the life of the creator.

A **trademark** is a distinctive name, symbol, or logo used to identify a specific business entity or one of its products. A trademark familiar to personal computer users is the catchy two-word logo used by Intel Corporation: "Intel inside." This logo is printed on adhesive labels applied to millions of personal computers. Trademarks can be registered with the Patent Office and, unlike patents and copyrights, these rights can be renewed indefinitely. Companies must be extremely diligent about protecting their trademarks and trade names. Not adequately protecting these intangibles may allow them to fall into generic, or everyday, usage. For example, *aspirin* and *escalator* were once specific product names but now anyone is able to use these terms.

Many businesses lease rather than purchase long-term assets. The lessee (the party that leases an asset) acquires the legal right to use that asset for a specified period subject to any restrictions in the lease agreement. Companies that lease office buildings, retail stores, and production facilities often modify the leased properties to accommodate their operations. Expenditures for such modifications are referred to as **leasehold improvements.** Leasehold improvements revert to the property owner (the lessor) at the end of the lease term. The cost of leasehold improvements should be amortized over their useful life or the term of the lease, whichever is shorter.

Goodwill

To most individuals, goodwill represents that "warm, fuzzy feeling" that makes them shop at Grandma's Corner Grocery instead of Discount MegaMarkets USA. Superior service, excellent location, family ties to the community, and many other factors go into determining the goodwill associated with a business. However, just because Grandma's Corner Grocery has accumulated a considerable amount of goodwill does not mean that goodwill can be recorded for accounting purposes.

Goodwill can only be recorded when one business entity (or a large segment of a business) is acquired by another. In this context, **goodwill** is defined as the excess of the collective market value of a group of net assets (assets minus liabilities) over the collective book value. Suppose that Exxon pays $25 million for a company that operates a chain of service stations. If the collective market value of that company's net assets is only $20 million, the remaining $5 million of the purchase price would be attributed to goodwill.

Until 2001, goodwill was amortized as an expense over a period not to exceed forty years. In that year, the Financial Accounting Standards Board issued an accounting rule requiring that goodwill should not be amortized. Instead, the total amount assigned to the goodwill account would remain in the accounting records until the company determined that the goodwill had been impaired. **Impairment** of an asset exists when its carrying value exceeds its fair market value.

After issuance of this new rule, many companies began reviewing their goodwill accounts for possible impairment. The following goodwill write-offs in the first quarter of 2002 represent only a handful of companies affected: AOL Time Warner, $54 billion; Blockbuster, $1.82 billion; Coca-Cola, $926 million; and AT&T Wireless, $166 million.[2] Companies that booked goodwill relative to acquisitions of technology or telecommunications operations "may have to write off half or more" of the goodwill due to overly optimistic expectations of future earnings.[3] Important to note is that goodwill impairment

[2] Various annual reports and news articles.

[3] Richard Korman, "Write-Offs under Rule Change Could Hurt Some Companies," *ENR* (February 4, 2002), p. 13.

write-offs are shown on the income statement as cumulative effects of accounting changes and *not* as part of continuing operations. These topics are discussed in Chapter 9.

Disposal of Intangibles

Disposals of intangible assets are accounted for much like the disposals of depreciable assets. If an intangible asset is sold, the gain or loss on the asset is computed by subtracting the unamortized cost of the asset from the selling price. Because of their nature, intangible assets are prone to rapidly losing their value. For instance, a patent held by a company may become worthless because a competitor develops a technologically advanced product. In such a case, the unamortized cost of the patent should be immediately written off as a loss.

ACCOUNTING INFORMATION FOR DECISION MAKING

Of all the items appearing in financial statements, long-term assets may be responsible for the most misconceptions in the minds of financial statement users. For this reason, it is very important that "user-friendly" information concerning long-term assets and related accounting decisions be included in a business's annual report. This section identifies several important items of information that decision makers need regarding a business's long-term assets.

Valuation

Nearly all businesses in the United States report their long-term assets at historical costs less accumulated depreciation, depletion, or amortization because of the historical cost principle. However, as mentioned earlier, land is not depreciated. A key advantage of historical costs is objectivity: the historical cost of an asset is a "matter of record," while the current value of that same asset is a "matter of opinion."

Businesses occasionally must depart from historical cost in valuing long-term assets. The conservatism principle requires businesses to write down (reduce the amount carried in the accounting records) long-term assets when their value has been permanently impaired. An asset is considered to be impaired when its book value (cost less accumulated depreciation) is determined to be greater than the expected benefits (in terms of future cash flows) to be generated by the asset. This difference results in a loss that must be recognized in the period that the impairment is determined.

Many companies have reported asset write-downs in recent years. For example, in 2000 (prior to its 2001 merger with Chevron), Texaco (www.texaco.com/archive/investor/2000ar) reported a $232 million write-down of certain oil and gas properties in the Gulf of Mexico and the U.K. North Sea, as well as a $105 million write-down of a refinery in Panama because of impairment.

Increases in long-term asset values, however, are not considered in the preparation of the financial statements.

Capitalization versus Expensing

When a company makes an expenditure related to a long-term asset, the amount may be capitalized or expensed depending on the circumstances. Visual Recap 6.1 provides general rules for deciding which expenditures to capitalize (or include in the asset cost) and which to expense. An example of an expenditure after acquisition that should be capitalized because it has a life longer than one year is a building roof. A necessary after-acquisition

VISUAL RECAP 6.1

PP&E Expenditure Capitalization Rules

When?	Needed?	How Often?	Accounting Treatment
Before acquisition or beginning use	Yes	Once	Capitalize
	No	Once	Expense
After acquisition or beginning use	Yes	Once or life is greater than one year and cost is large	Capitalize
	Yes	Periodically or life is one year or less	Expense
	No	Once or periodically	Expense

expenditure that would be expensed (rather than capitalized) because of its short life span and insignificant cost would be an annual automobile registration.

PP&E, natural resources, and intangible assets are shown on the balance sheet; however, the related depreciation, depletion, and amortization affect both the balance sheet and income statement. When an asset is sold at a gain or loss, the transaction affects both statements. The balance sheet is affected through the removal of the long-term asset and its related depreciation, as well as the recognition of cash received (if any); the income statement records the gain or loss as part of income for the period. If an item is capitalized when it should be expensed or expensed when it should be capitalized, the balance sheet and income statements will be affected for every fiscal period of the asset's life—potentially creating extreme material distortions.

To illustrate the problems that the misrecording of transactions can create, consider the following. In mid-2002, WorldCom (www.worldcom.com) announced that it had capitalized, rather than properly expensing, almost $4 billion of costs during 2001 and 2002; an employee then indicated that he had been required to record another $33.6 million in unjustified expenses in 2000. Such improper accounting "made the company appear profitable when it was not."[4] WorldCom filed for bankruptcy protection in July 2002.

Disclosures

Decision makers demand, and generally accepted accounting principles require, businesses to disclose major classes of depreciable assets by nature or function in their financial statements. Disclosure of PP&E assets by major categories provides decision makers with insights on a company's operating policies and strategies. This information also allows decision makers to draw more meaningful comparisons of different companies' financial data, particularly companies in the same industry.

Similar to the choice of an inventory accounting method, the choice of a depreciation method can significantly influence a company's apparent financial condition and reported profits. To enhance the comparability of financial statement data, accounting standards require that businesses disclose the depreciation method or methods used in their financial statement footnotes. A company does not, however, have to use the same depreciation method for accounting and taxation purposes. Companies often choose to

[4] Christopher Stern, "WorldCom Workers Challenged Books," *The [New Orleans] Times-Picayune* (July 15, 2002, A-1, A-7.

use straight-line depreciation for their income statements and an accelerated method for tax returns. In the early years of asset life, such a choice provides the lowest depreciation and highest income for financial reporting and the highest depreciation and lowest taxable income (and, therefore, lowest taxes payable) for tax preparation.

Given their nature, intangible assets are sometimes discounted in importance by decision makers. However, the financial success of many corporations, especially those in the high-tech and medical fields, stems largely from the intangible assets they have developed or purchased. For example, drug companies often sell a new drug for a very high price because a patent prohibits other drug companies from producing that drug. However, when the patent expires, generic equivalents of the drug can be produced and sold for significantly less than the original. Investors should pay close attention to the age of patents, as a patent that is near the end of its useful life might signal a reduction in future product revenues.

Businesses should disclose in their financial statements any restrictions on the use of long-term assets. For example, if long-term assets are pledged as collateral for loans, this fact needs to be disclosed in the financial statements because the assets cannot be disposed of without the prior approval of the lender.

Ratio Analysis

Two ratios can be used to assess the age and useful life of PP&E assets. The average useful life of PP&E assets is calculated in the following manner.

Average Useful life = Average Investment in PP&E ÷ Depreciation Expense

This ratio estimates the useful life by assuming that this year's depreciation expense is a consistent proportion of the cost. The useful life provided by this ratio should be used with care, however, because different depreciation methods can have different effects on the result.

The average age of plant assets can be estimated using the following ratio.

Average Asset Age = Accumulated Depreciation ÷ Depreciation Expense

This ratio estimates how many years of depreciation have been accumulated for a particular class of assets. As with the average useful life ratio, average asset age is affected differently by the different depreciation methods. Another drawback to this ratio is its inability to account for assets that have been completely depreciated (that is, no additional depreciation is being taken) but remain on the books.

Delta Air Lines (www.delta.com) reported flight and ground equipment costing $24,221 million in 2001 and $22,226 million in 2000. The 2001 accumulated depreciation was $8,347 million and the 2001 depreciation expense on that equipment was $1,283 million.[5] Using the ratio calculation, the average useful life of Delta's equipment is approximately 18 years {[($24,221 + $22,226) ÷ 2] ÷ $1,283}, while the average age of the flight equipment is 6.5 years ($8,347 ÷ $1,283). Delta lists the average age of each type of plane in the footnotes to the financial statements—approximately 9.1 years, but does not include ground equipment, which may account for part of the difference in the ratio calculation and the age presented by Delta.

Another calculation that can be made provides an indicator of whether a company is making sufficient capital expenditures in its business. The ratio of capital spending to depreciation is computed as capital expenditures (found on the statement of cash flows under investing activities) divided by depreciation expense. A rule-of-thumb for the ratio is 1:1.2; "a lower number implies the company is cutting back on expenditures, perhaps to cut costs—a situation that may indicate future financial difficulties."[6]

---

[5] The depreciation amount includes amortization.

[6] Jacqueline Doherty, "Scrutinize This!" *Barron's* (April 1, 2002), p. 17.

SUMMARY

The starting point in accounting for long-term assets is determining their acquisition cost. Only those costs that are reasonable and necessary to acquire these assets and ready them for use should be capitalized. The depreciable cost (cost minus salvage value) of most long-term assets should be allocated to the accounting periods to which those assets provide economic benefits to a business. Three major depreciation methods are straight-line method, units-of-production, and double-declining-balance. Land is not depreciated; natural resources are depleted; intangibles are amortized.

When long-term assets are retired or sold, depreciation, depletion, or amortization must be taken through the date of the disposal. The disposal of a long-term asset usually results in a gain or loss being recorded.

Except for land that is not depreciated, PP&E and natural resources are generally reported at original purchase amounts less, respectively, accumulated depreciation and depletion. Intangibles are normally shown on the balance sheet at original cost less all

VISUAL RECAP 6.2

Long-term Assets: Acquisition and Use

	Property, Plant & Equipment	Natural Resources	Intangible Assets
Cost	Reasonable and necessary costs to acquire the asset	Cost of land and resources minus value of land after natural resources removed	Reasonable and necessary costs to acquire the asset; will not include any research and development costs because these are expensed when incurred
Salvage Value	Estimated value of the asset at the end of its useful life		Usually zero
Useful Life	Expected years of service or units of activity	Units of extractable resources	Shortest of legal life, useful life, or 40 years except for goodwill which is assumed to have an indefinite life
Cost Allocation Method	*Depreciation* 3 Common Methods ■ Straight-Line ■ Double-Declining-Balance ■ Units-of-Production (except for land which is not depreciated)	*Depletion* (Similar to units-of-production depreciation)	*Amortization* (Similar to straight-line depreciation except for goodwill which is not amoritized
Impairment (or loss of value)	Immediate write down in year of impairment		

amortization taken to date. Two exceptions exist. First, if an asset significantly declines in value and is considered "impaired," a write–off of the difference between the asset's unamortized cost and its fair value is recorded. Second, goodwill (an intangible asset) is not amortized and is only written off when it is impaired.

Some major points from this chapter are summarized in Visual Recap 6.2.

Besides valuation issues related to a business's PP&E assets, decision makers should be informed of the specific types of these assets that a business owns, depreciation /depletion/amortization methods applied to these assets, and any restrictions on the use of the assets.

KEY TERMS

amortization
copyright
depletion
depreciable cost
double-declining-balance method
goodwill
impairment
leasehold improvement
natural resource
patent
salvage value
straight-line method
trademark
units-of-production method

QUESTIONS

1. Identify the major types of long-term assets. Provide at least two examples of each type. *(LO 6.1 & 6.4)*
2. Why is depreciation expense recorded each accounting period on depreciable assets? *(LO 6.2)*
3. Discuss how depreciation is calculated under the straight-line, units-of-production, and double-declining-balance methods. Provide a brief numerical example that would indicate why a company might use straight-line depreciation for income statement purposes and double-declining-balance depreciation for tax purposes. *(LO 6.2)*
4. How is the book value of a depreciable asset computed? How does a depreciable asset's book value change from one accounting period to the next? Discuss the difference between the terms book value and fair value. *(LO 6.2)*
5. Explain how a gain or loss on the disposal of a long-term asset is calculated. *(LO 6.2 & 6.4)*
6. On January 1, 2003, Straud Co. sold a piece of equipment with a book value of $29,000 for $24,600. The equipment had cost $89,000 when it was purchased. Explain why the following journal entry is incorrect.

Cash	24,600	
Loss on Sale of Equipment	4,400	
Equipment		29,000

7. Explain the difference between depreciation, depletion, and amortization. What general rules dictate how long an item is depreciated, depleted, or amortized? *(LO 6.3)*
8. Explain why you think goodwill is referred to as an "unidentifiable intangible asset." What types of items would be considered "identifiable intangible assets?" *(LO 6.4)*
9. Identify advantages and disadvantages of using historical costs as the primary valuation basis for PP&E. *(LO 6.5)*

10. What types of expenditures are included in the acquisition cost of a PP&E asset? What types of expenditures are excluded from the acquisition cost of a PP&E asset? *(LO 6.5)*

11. Under what circumstances can businesses depart from the historical cost principle for PP&E assets? *(LO 6.5)*

12. Identify key information needs of financial decision makers regarding a business's long-term assets. How would you prioritize these needs? Explain why you chose your priorities. *(LO 6.5)*

EXERCISES

13. **True or False** *(All LOs)*

Following are a series of statements regarding topics discussed in this chapter.

Required:

Indicate whether each statement is true (T) or false (F).

(1) Most intangible assets should be amortized over their legal life, their useful life, or forty years, whichever is longer.

(2) Businesses are allowed to record gains realized on sales of PP&E assets.

(3) The terms "depreciable cost" and "acquisition cost" for a PP&E asset are interchangeable.

(4) The salvage value of a PP&E asset is not relevant when a company applies the double-declining-balance depreciation method.

(5) Intangible assets are presented on the balance sheet at historical cost.

(6) If a company can prove that the market value of a long-term asset increased during a given accounting period, no depreciation expense should be recorded for the asset during that period.

(7) Land is generally classified as a long-term asset, a PP&E asset, and a depreciable asset.

(8) Depreciation expense is a nonoperating expense.

14. **Acquisition Cost of PP&E Assets** *(LO 6.1)*

Fain Enterprises recently purchased new computer equipment for its company headquarters. Following is information regarding the various cash expenditures related to the acquisition of this equipment.

(a) The original invoice price of the computer equipment was $400,000; however, Fain's owner negotiated a 15 percent price reduction.

(b) The delivery cost for the equipment was $2,300 and was paid by Fain.

(c) Three computer consultants were retained by Fain to install and test the new equipment at a cost of $1,500.

(d) Supplies costing $200 were used in installing and testing the equipment.

(e) The day following the installation of the equipment, Fain's owner decided to move the equipment to the floor on which her office was located. A $600 cost was incurred in moving the equipment.

Required:

(1) Determine the acquisition cost of the computer equipment for accounting purposes.

(2) Prepare an appropriate journal entry to record the acquisition of the computer equipment and the incurrence of the related costs.

(3) A computer purchased for several thousand dollars may have little resale value one year later because of technological changes in the computer industry. Given that the resale value of computers and computer equipment can decline rapidly, is historical cost the proper valuation basis to use for such assets? Defend your answer.

15. **Depreciation Methods** *(LO 6.2)*

Florida Box Co. purchased a bundling machine on January 1, 2003, for a cost of $36,000. The machine is expected to last 5 years, or bundle 660,000 items, at which time it should have a salvage value of $3,000. A counter on the machine revealed that the machine was used at the following levels: 2003, 110,000 bundles; 2004, 140,000 bundles; 2005, 150,000 bundles; 2006, 141,800 bundles; and 2007, 152,000 bundles.

Required:

(1) How much depreciation will be taken each year if the straight-line method of depreciation is used? Show calculations.

(2) What depreciation method is Florida Box using if the depreciation expense in 2004 is $7,000? Show calculations.

(3) What depreciation method is Florida Box using if the depreciation expense in 2003 is $14,400? Show calculations.

(4) At the end of the five-year useful life, what will be the (a) ending book value and (b) the balance of accumulated depreciation?

(5) Assume that Florida Box uses the double-declining-balance method of depreciation. At the end of four years, the book value is $4,665.60 and the accumulated depreciation is $31,334.40. What is the depreciation expense in year 5?

(6) Assume that Florida Box uses the units-of-production method of depreciation. At the end of four years, the book value is $8,910 and the accumulated depreciation is $27,090. What is the depreciation expense in year 5?

16. **Computing Depreciation Expense** *(LO 6.2)*

Michelman Manufacturing purchased a piece of production equipment on January 1, 2003. The equipment cost $6,500 and was estimated to have a salvage value of $500 at the end of its six-year life or 12,000 hours of use.

Required:

(1) Compute depreciation expense on the production equipment for both 2003 and 2004 and prepare the appropriate journal entries using the:

   (a) straight-line depreciation method

   (b) double-declining-balance depreciation method

(2) Assume that Michelman uses the units-of-production method. Compute depreciation expense for 2003 and 2004 and prepare the appropriate journal entries, if the equipment were used 2,500 hours in 2003 and 1,900 hours in 2004.

17. **Sale of a PP&E Asset** *(LO 6.3)*

On June 30, 2002, Newsom Company sold a computer for $1,250 that had been acquired for $2,500 on January 1, 2000. Newsom had originally estimated that the computer would have a five-year useful life and a $500 salvage value. Newsom uses straight-line depreciation. The company's fiscal year ends on December 31 and takes its depreciation expense on its depreciable assets at the end of each fiscal year.

Required:

(1) Determine the book value of the computer on December 31, 2001.

(2) Prepare all entries needed on June 30, 2002, to properly account for the disposal of the computer.

18. **Disposal of PP&E Assets** *(LO 6.3)*

On January 1, 1999, Landers Company purchased ten washing machines to be used in its coin-operated laundry. Each washer cost $400 and was expected to have a $40 salvage value at the end of its eight-year useful life. On September 30, 2002, Landers decided to purchase more efficient machines and sold the ten washers for $2,200. Landers uses straight-line depreciation for PP&E assets and records depreciation expense at the end of each year.

Required:

(1) Prepare the appropriate journal entry to record depreciation expense on the washers prior to their disposal. What is the book value of the washers following the posting of this journal entry?

(2) Determine the gain or loss on the sale of the washers. Prepare the journal entry to record the sale of the washers.

(3) Suppose that, rather than being sold, the washers were simply hauled off to the junkyard. Prepare the journal entry to record the disposal of the washers.

19. **Natural Resources** *(LO 6.4)*

Webster Corporation paid $5 million for 1,500 acres of land. Webster plans to sell the trees that cover the 1,500 acres to a lumber company. After the land is cleared, Webster believes the land will have a value of $500,000.

Required:

(1) What journal entry is made when Webster acquires the land for cash?

(2) When the trees are cleared, the balance sheet account for this land should be $500,000. What accounting method will Webster use to accomplish this? Explain why this method is appropriate.

(3) What average cost should Webster assign to an acre of lumber? Are there any conditions that you believe would make an average cost per acre an unacceptable cost method?

(4) Assume that Webster sells the trees immediately upon clearing the land. What journal entry would Webster make to account for the clearing of 100 acres?

20. **Intangibles** *(LO 6.4)*

On January 1, 2003, Kennedy MedCo acquired an existing patent to produce a pain-reliever from Lincoln Pharmaceuticals for a cost of $1,855,000. The patent offers exclusive rights to produce this medication for another seven years. Kennedy's fiscal year ends on December 31.

Required:

(1) What journal entry is made on January 1, 2003, to record the purchase of the patent?

(2) What will be the salvage value of this patent after seven years? Explain the rationale for your answer.

(3) After seven years, the balance sheet account for this patent should be equal to the salvage value. What accounting method will Kennedy use to accomplish this?

(4) Prepare a schedule for the method you gave in part (3).

(5) Prepare the December 31, 2003 journal entry related to this patent.

21. **Long-Term Asset Analysis** *(LO 6.5)*

The following information is available from the 2002 financial statements of Trebade Corp.:

Income statement: Depreciation Expense		$ 250,000
Statement of cash flows: Equipment investments		978,000
Balance sheet:	Year-end balance of Equipment	3,670,000
	Year-end balance of Acc. Depr.—Equipment	1,058,700

Required:

(1) What is the average investment in equipment for 2002?

(2) What is the average age of the equipment?

(3) What is the average useful life of the equipment?

(4) Would any of your answers to parts (1), (2), and (3) change if you knew the equipment investments had been made on December 31, 2002? If so, why? What would your answers now be to those parts?

PROBLEMS

22. **Acquisition of PP&E Assets** *(LO 6.1)*

In 2002, Kare Corporation acquired several PP&E assets for its manufacturing operations. Following are descriptions of costs incurred by Kare during 2002 related to these assets. All amounts were paid in cash.

(a) On January 1, Kare purchased land with a warehouse for $2,600,000. The land's appraised value was $700,000, while the warehouse had an appraised value of $2,100,000. The estimated useful life of the warehouse is twenty years and its estimated salvage value is $200,000.

(b) On January 3, Kare purchased production equipment for $1,000,000 that had an estimated useful life of five years and an estimated salvage value of $60,000. The equipment seller paid delivery costs of $4,200. Costs to repair the equipment after it was damaged during installation totaled $2,700.

(c) On April 2, Kare purchased office furniture and fixtures for $400,000. These assets have an estimated useful life of ten years and an estimated salvage value of $30,000.

(d) On July 1, Kare purchased four used delivery trucks at a cost of $12,000 each. Each truck had an estimated remaining useful life of four years and an estimated salvage value of $2,400. Expenses paid to deliver the trucks to Kare's business location totaled $900, while insurance paid on the trucks while they were in transit amounted to $300. Kare immediately installed an alarm system on each truck at a cost of $600 per truck.

Required:

(1) Prepare the journal entries to record the acquisitions of PP&E assets by Kare Corporation during 2002.

(2) Kare records depreciation on its PP&E assets each December 31. Assuming that the company uses the straight-line method, prepare the December 31, 2002 adjusting entries for depreciation expense on the assets acquired during 2002.

23. **Alternative Depreciation Methods** *(LO 6.2, ethics)*

Roslyn and Jimmy recently decided to open a restaurant specializing in Georgian cuisine. They purchased an existing restaurant on January 1, 2002, at a cost of $650,000, paying ten percent of the purchase price in cash and signing a note for the balance. The restaurant has an estimated useful life of 25 years and an estimated salvage value of $150,000. Also on January 1, 2002, Roslyn and Jimmy paid cash of $80,000 for used kitchen equipment with an estimated four-year useful life and $8,000 salvage value.

Required:

(1) Compute depreciation expense for 2002 and 2003 on the restaurant using the following methods:
  (a) straight-line
  (b) double-declining-balance

(2) Prepare year-end adjusting journal entries to record the depreciation expense amounts computed in part (1).

(3) Compute depreciation expense on the kitchen equipment for year 2002 through 2005, assuming that the following depreciation methods are used:
  (a) straight-line
  (b) double-declining-balance

(4) Prepare year-end adjusting journal entries to record the depreciation expense amounts computed in part (3).

(5) Suppose that the owners believe that the double-declining-balance method most accurately reflects the true depreciation pattern of their firm's depreciable assets. Would it be unethical for the owners to apply the straight-line depreciation method to these assets? Why or why not?

(6) Provide at least two positive and negative financial implications of buying used kitchen equipment.

24. **Alternative Depreciation Methods** *(LO 6.2, Excel)*

Midori Airlines is a small charter airline company that operates between San Francisco and Los Angeles. On January 1, 2002, Midori purchased a jet costing $1,600,000 with an estimated salvage value of $100,000 at the end of its five-year life. Midori expects that the jet will be flown the following number of miles over its life:

2002	100,000 miles
2003	120,000 miles
2004	130,000 miles
2005	90,000 miles
2006	60,000 miles

Required:

(1) Prepare a depreciation schedule for the jet assuming that Midori uses the following depreciation methods:
  (a) straight-line
  (b) double-declining-balance
  (c) units-of-production

(2) In your opinion, which of these three depreciation methods is most consistent with the matching principle? Defend your answer.

(3) Suppose that, at the time the jet was purchased, Midori had a large loan outstanding from a local bank. Which of the three depreciation methods might Midori's bank loan officer prefer the company use? Defend your answer.

(4) Suppose that, at the time the jet was purchased, Midori had a large loan outstanding from a local bank. How, if at all, would the choice of a depreciation method affect Midori's ability to repay the bank loan? Discuss the rationale for your answer.

25. **Disposal of PP&E Assets** *(LO 6.3)*

On January 1, 2002, Lein Phan Vending purchased five vending machines to place in a high school. Each vending machine cost $3,100 and had an estimated six-year useful life and $400 salvage value. Lein Phan uses the straight-line depreciation method. On April 1, 2005, the company decided to replace the vending machines and sold all of them to a single buyer.

Required:

(1) Prepare the journal entry to record the depreciation expense on the vending machines for the first three months of 2005.

(2) Determine the book value of the vending machines following the posting of the journal entry prepared in part (1).

(3) Prepare the journal entry to record the sale of the vending machines for $8,200.

(4) Prepare the journal entry to record the sale of the vending machines for $11,300.

26. **Accounting for Intangible Assets** *(LO 6.4)*

Coleman, Inc. is a leading manufacturer of pharmaceutical products. Following are transactions or events involving Coleman's intangible assets during 2003.

January 4	Purchased a patent on the drug Zorcerin for $1,500,000. The patent had a legal life of 12 years; Coleman estimated the useful life of the patent at five years.
February 9	Sold a patent with a book value of $753,000 to a competitor for $800,000.
June 30	A competitor introduced a new drug that made a patent held by Coleman obsolete; the book value of the patent was $607,000 at the time.
December 31	Recorded amortization expense on the Zorcerin patent.
December 31	During the year, Coleman, Inc. had incurred $876,800 in research and development costs.

Required:

Prepare the appropriate journal entries for Coleman, Inc.'s 2003 transactions.

27. **Reporting and Analysis of PP&E Assets** *(LO 6.6)*

Wiggins Corporation is a manufacturing firm that has acquired long-term assets used in its operations with a collective cost of $3,600,000. Listed in the following schedule is the acquisition cost of each of these assets and the total depreciation expense recorded on them through the end of 2003.

Description	Acquisition Cost	Accumulated Depreciation through 2003	Depreciation Expense for 2003
Office building	$1,400,000	$230,000	$34,000
Production equipment	1,200,000	112,000	16,400
Office furniture	250,000	61,000	10,000
Land	350,000	0	0
Delivery trucks	400,000	125,000	40,000

Required:

(1) Prepare the PP&E section of Wiggins Corporation's balance sheet at the end of 2003.

(2) Why has no depreciation expense been recorded on the land owned by Wiggins?

(3) Assuming that no PP&E assets have been acquired by Wiggins during the year, what is the average useful life of each category of assets other than land?

(4) Assume that Wiggins had acquired $150,000 of office furniture and $10,000 of delivery trucks during 2003. What is the capital spending to depreciation ratio for each of these two categories of assets? Discuss your assessment of this ratio.

(5) Besides the information you developed in parts (1) through (5), what other information regarding Wiggins' PP&E assets is needed by decision makers who use the company's financial statements?

28. **Comprehensive Problem** *(LOs 6.1–6.5)*

A partial balance sheet is presented for Rufus Industries.

Rufus Industries
Partial Balance Sheet
December 31, 2002

Property, Plant, & Equipment		
Delivery Truck	$ 35,000	
Less: Accumulated Deprecation	(18,750)	$16,250
Office Equipment	$ 45,000	
Less: Accumulated Deprecation	(35,280)	$9,720
Factory Machinery	$100,000	
Less: Accumulated Depreciation	(36,800)	63,200
Total Property, Plant, & Equipment		$85,420
Intangible Assets		
Patents		7,000

Notes:

(a) The delivery truck was purchased on June 30, 2000, and is being depreciated over four years using the straight-line method. Salvage value was estimated at $5,000.

(b) The office equipment was purchased on January 1, 2000, and is being depreciated over five years using the double-declining-balance method. Salvage value was estimated at $4,000.

(c) The factory machinery was purchased on January 1, 1999, and is being depreciated over ten years using the straight-line method. Salvage value was estimated at $8,000.

(d) The remaining useful life on the patent is seven years.

Required:

(1) On July 31, 2003, Rufus sold the delivery truck for $9,000 cash. Prepare any necessary journal entries to record this sale.

(2) On December 1, 2003, Rufus purchased land and a building for a combined cost of $400,000 by paying $100,000 cash and signing a note for the balance. An appraiser estimates the values of the building and land are, respectively, $302,500 and $247,500. Rufus plans to use the building and land for ten years, at which time the building will probably be worth $100,000. Rufus plans to use straight–line depreciation on the building. Journalize this purchase.

(3) Record all necessary depreciation and amortization entries on December 31, 2003.

(4) Prepare a partial balance sheet for Rufus on December 31, 2003.

(5) How did the 2003 transactions affect Rufus' Income Statement?

(6) What are the average useful life and the average age of each category of long-term asset, with the exception of land?

CASES

29. **Choosing a Depreciation Method** *(LO 6.2)*

Albuquerque Stairs, which manufactures stairway railings, purchased a $15,000 lathe on January 1, 2003. The lathe was estimated to have a salvage value of $1,000 at the end of its five-year useful life. The company's owner is trying to decide on a depreciation method to use for this new asset.

Required:

(1) Compute depreciation expense on the new lathe for 2003 and 2004 assuming that Albuquerque Stairs uses the:

(a) straight-line method

(b) double-declining-balance method

(2) Suppose that the company decides to apply the units-of-production depreciation method to the new lathe. The lathe will be used to produce approximately 3,500 units of product over its useful life. Compute the depreciation expense on the lathe for 2003 and 2004 if 550 and 670 units of product are made, respectively, in 2003 and 2004.

(3) Which of the three major depreciation methods best satisfies the matching principle? Defend your choice.

(4) Under which of the three depreciation methods will Albuquerque Stairs have the highest net income for 2003? For 2004? Show your calculations.

(5) If Albuquerque Stairs wants to minimize its tax liability, which depreciation method should the company use for 2003 and 2004? Explain your answer.

(6) Why do you think the government allows a company to use different depreciation methods for accounting and tax purposes? Do you think that using different methods for accounting and tax purposes is ethical? Explain your answer.

30. **Accounting for Fully Depreciated Assets** *(LO 6.3, writing, ethics)*

Jim's Bike Shop purchased a $2,400 air compressor four years ago. The compressor was estimated to have a four-year useful life and no salvage value. The compressor is now fully depreciated with a zero book value. Surprisingly to the business's owner, the air compressor "works like new" and he has no plans to replace it.

Required:

(1) Should this business continue to record depreciation expense on the air compressor each year? Why or why not?

(2) Should a business keep a fully depreciated asset on its books indefinitely as long as the asset is being used in the business? Why or why not?

(3) Explain how the matching principle was violated by Jim's Bike Shop and how this violation affected the financial statements of the business. Was this violation intentional? How might a company use depreciation to mislead users of the financial statements?

(4) Write a memo to Jim explaining the importance of the assumptions made at the assets acquisition (useful life and salvage value). Include in your memo at least one suggestion of how to estimate each number.

31. **Goodwill Impairment** *(LO 6.5, Internet)*

Use the Internet or library resources to find four examples of companies that wrote off impaired goodwill within the past year.

Required:

(1) What companies did you find and how much goodwill did each write off?

(2) How did the write-offs affect each company's financial statements?

(3) What do you think that a write-off of goodwill indicates about company management? Provide at least one positive indicator and one negative. Assume that the same managers were at the company when the goodwill was created. (Hint: Remember what needs to occur for a company to record goodwill.)

32. **Analysis of PP&E** *(LO 6.6, Internet, Excel)*

Use the annual report of Carnival Corporation (www.carnival.com) for the 2001 fiscal year to answer the following questions.

Required:

(1) Calculate and interpret the following ratios for Carnival for the fiscal year ending November 30, 2001.

(a) Average age of assets

(b) Average useful life of assets

(2) What is the capital spending to depreciation ratio? Given the information provided (and not provided) in the annual report, what types of questions might you have about the calculation of this ratio?

(3) Does Carnival discuss the age of its assets? Is it similar to the numbers you calculated? List some possible reasons for any differences.

(4) What depreciation method does Carnival use?

33. **Comparing Companies** *(LO 6.5, group, Internet)*

Identifying the similarities and differences between companies is as crucial to making investment decisions as understanding a single company's financial statements. Form groups of at least four students. Each group should select a single industry. Each group member should locate a different annual report within that industry. (The industry and individual company may be assigned by your instructor.)

Required—individual group members:

(1) Did your company acquire any new property, plant and equipment assets in the most recent fiscal year? If yes, is there a discussion in the financial statements about what was acquired, and where is this discussion included?

(2) Do the financial statements or notes indicate that any PPE assets were sold? Where did you find this information?

(3) Calculate the following ratios for the company you selected for the two most recent fiscal years.

(a) Average age of PPE assets

(b) Average useful life of PPE assets

(4) What depreciation method (or methods) does your company use?

(5) What is the depreciation expense for the most recent three years?

Required—groups:

(6) Compile the ratio calculations for each company prepared by the individual group members into one table. Compare the results from company to company in the same fiscal year. Include in your comparison a graphical analysis.

(7) Compile the depreciation information for each company into one table. Compare the results from company to company in the same fiscal year and across fiscal years. Include in your comparison a graphical analysis.

(8) Discuss reasons why the results from parts (6) and (7) might be similar or different within an industry.

Required—class:

(9) Compare the ratios from each industry. Discuss reasons why these ratios might be similar or different between industries.

(10) Compare the depreciation methods and trends between industries. Discuss reasons for similarities and differences between industries.

SUPPLEMENTAL PROBLEMS

34. **Acquisition of PP&E Assets** *(LO 6.1)* [Compare to Problem 22]

In 2003, Buster, Inc. acquired the following PP&E assets. All amounts were paid in cash.

(a) On January 1, Buster acquired a super-computer for $49,000. Delivery and insurance during shipping was $1,200. Buster had to install, at a cost of $3,000, an anti-static raised floor in the computer room before the computer could be used. Testing the computer cost $1,800, and the insurance was $900 for the first year. Buster expects to use the computer for 10 years. The expected salvage value of the computer is $1,000.

(b) On March 27, Buster bought a $25,000 delivery van. License and registration fees, respectively, were $1,500 and $70. Buster's logo was painted on the van was painted at a cost of $1,300. Buster expects to use the van for 5 years. The expected salvage value of the van is $1,800.

(c) On August 8, Buster bought land on which it intends to build an office building. The land cost was $80,000, which included an $8,000 real estate commission fee. Property taxes paid by Buster included $2,200 of delinquent taxes from the prior owner and $950 for 2003. Buster paid $5,000 to raze a building on the property and to grade the land. Buster expects to begin construction next year and use the building for the next 20 years.

Required:

(1) Prepare the journal entries to record the acquisitions of PP&E assets by Buster, Inc. during 2003.

(2) Buster records depreciation on its PP&E assets each December 31. If Buster uses the straight-line method, prepare the December 31, 2003 adjusting entries for depreciation expense on the assets acquired in 2003.

35. **Depreciation Methods and Disposal of Assets** *(LO 6.2)* [Compare to Problems 24 & 25]

In Style Arrival (ISA) operates a limousine and car service. On March 31, 2002, ISA purchased a car costing $52,000 with an estimated salvage value of $7,000 at the end of its four-year life. ISA expects that the car will be driven the following number of miles each year:

2002	30,000 miles
2003	32,000 miles
2004	36,000 miles
2005	40,000 miles
2006	6,000 miles

Required:

(1) Prepare a depreciation schedule for ISA using the following depreciation methods:
   (a) straight-line
   (b) double-declining-balance
   (c) units-of-production.

(2) On September 30, 2004, ISA stopped using the car. Prepare journal entries to record the sale or disposal under each of the following four assumptions. Assume that ISA used the double-declining-balance method of depreciation.
   (a) Sold for $15,000.00
   (b) Sold for $10,156.25
   (c) Sold for $9,000.00
   (d) Junked the car because it was totaled by a company employee. No other cars were involved and ISA carried no collision insurance.

PART III

ACCOUNTING FOR LIABILITIES AND OWNERSHIP INTERESTS

Chapter 7: Liabilities

Chapter 8: Stockholders' Equity

CHAPTER 7

Liabilities

LEARNING OBJECTIVES

1. Account for the major types of transactions and events affecting current liabilities.
2. Define the key characteristics of, and account for, contingent liabilities.
3. Account for the major types of transactions and events affecting bonds payable.
4. Distinguish between operating leases and capital leases.
5. Discuss accounting issues for long-term liabilities stemming from pension and other postretirement employee benefit plans.
6. Define the key information needs of decision makers regarding liabilities.
7. Compute and interpret the current, long-term debt to equity, and times interest earned ratios, as well as the amount of working capital.
8. (Appendix) Compute the issue price of bonds and prepare journal entries related to discount and premium amortization.

Cutting Back on Plane Payments

September 11, 2001 is a date that no one will ever forget. The devastation created that day by the terrorist attacks continues to impact numerous businesses in all industries. The financial impacts on the airline industry were tremendous and, because of its routes in the East Coast and through Washington's Ronald Reagan National Airport, US Airways (www.usairways.com) was deeply affected.

In its 2001 annual report, US Airways reported total current and long-term liabilities of, respectively, $3,026 million and $7,614 million. After posting losses of over $1.4 billion, the airline, in late June 2002, instituted a restructuring plan to postpone payments on some debts related to aircraft lessors and lenders. In addition, the company wants approximately $200 million in voluntary concessions from debt-holders. The company said that, at that time, all day-to-day financial obligations were being met.

US Airways realized that its credit situation could have resulted in default notices and a possible increase in payment demands by the company's creditors. Having to accelerate liability payments could have forced the company to file for Chapter 11 bankruptcy reorganization.

SOURCE: US Airways, Inc. press release, *Airways Announces Strategic Payment Deferrals Linked to Proposed Consensual Restructuring Plan,* 24 June 2002.

INTRODUCTION

The focus of this chapter is liabilities, both current and long-term. Since contingent liabilities pose unique accounting issues, they are considered independently of other liabilities. The key information needs of decision makers regarding current and long-term liabilities are identified, as well as some ratios that reflect a company's debt status.

CURRENT LIABILITIES

As discussed in Chapter 2, liabilities are amounts owed by a company to other parties. Such amounts require a company to transfer assets or provide services to another because of a past or present transaction. Liabilities that must be paid by a business within one year or its operating cycle, whichever is longer, are classified as current liabilities.

Although specific current liabilities vary from company to company, there are two general types of current liabilities: (1) those whose dollar amounts are defined by a contractual agreement, and (2) those whose dollar amounts must be estimated. An example of the first type is an account payable. When an account payable is recorded, the actual dollar amount due is known. An example of the second type is a quarterly estimate of the income tax payable that will be due at the end of the company's fiscal year.

Accounts Payable

One of the most common current liabilities is an **account payable,** which is an amount owed by a business to its suppliers, generally for purchases of inventory. In a business-to-business relationship, accounts payable typically do not require the payment of interest, and, as discussed in Chapter 5, sellers will often grant discount terms to encourage the prompt payment of these debts.

Notes Payable

Notes payable are debts documented by a legally binding written commitment known as a promissory note. Notes payable can be either current or long-term depending upon their maturity or payment date. Accounting for both types of notes is the same; only the balance sheet classification differs.

No standard format exists for promissory notes. Occasionally, a promissory note is literally nothing more than a scribbled "IOU" on a piece of paper. The person signing the note and promising to pay the **principal** (or face) amount plus interest is called the **maker.** The **payee** is the party to whom payment will be made. The **maturity value** of a note is the total amount the maker must pay the payee on the maturity date, and that value is equal to the sum of the principal and any interest that accrues or accumulates on the note over its term.[1]

The **term of a note** reflects its duration. It is the number of days, months, or years from the date a note is signed until the **maturity date** which is when the note is due for payment. For example, a 60-day note that is signed on July 15 would mature on September 13: 16 days in July (31 – 15), 31 days in August, and 13 days in September. A three-month note dated April 5 would mature on July 5.

The computation for interest expense on a promissory note (or any type of interest-bearing financial instrument) is as follows:

$$\text{Interest} = \text{Principal} \times \text{Rate} \times \text{Time}$$

The principal is the amount for which the note was originally made. The rate refers to the annual interest rate stated in the note; interest rates are always annual unless otherwise specifically stated. The time component is expressed as a fraction, with the term of the note as the numerator and 360 days as the denominator.[2]

To illustrate the accounting for notes payable, suppose that Bonney's Dress Shop borrows $5,000 from a local bank on October 2, 2002, and signs a 120-day, 12 percent note payable. The note's maturity date is January 30 of the following year; this date is calculated as 29 days in October (31-2), 30 days in November, 31 days in December, and 30 days in January. Bonney's Dress Shop would record the receipt of the $5,000 loan as follows.

General Journal				
Date		Description	Debit	Credit
Oct.	2	Cash	5,000	
		Notes Payable		5,000
		Borrowed $5,000 and signed a 120-day, 12% note		

If Bonney's Dress Shop has a calendar year-end, the company must record an adjusting entry for the interest expense since the money was borrowed, but will not be paid until the note matures. This note payable will have been outstanding for 90 days by December 31 (October 2 through December 31); therefore, $150 of interest will have

[1] There are "non–interest-bearing notes," however, this term is slightly misleading. When a non–interest-bearing note is issued, the interest is "taken out" before the payment is received. Thus, at the maturity date, the total payment for a non–interest-bearing note is the face amount of the note; no additional interest is paid at maturity.

[2] The 360-day year is used here for simplicity of computations. Interest is actually calculated in the business world on the basis of a 365- (or 366-) day year.

accrued on the note by that date ($5,000 × 0.12 × 90/360). The adjusting entry to record this accrual on December 31 follows.

General Journal				
Date		**Description**	**Debit**	**Credit**
Dec.	31	Interest Expense	150	
		Interest Payable		150
		Accrued interest on the $5,000, 12% note signed on Oct. 2		

On January 30, Bonney's Dress Shop will repay the bank the $5,000 principal amount plus 12% interest for the note's 120-day term. The total interest due the bank will be $200 (or $5,000 × 12% × 120/360). However, only $50 of interest expense will be recorded on the note's maturity date, which is the interest for the 30-day period January 1 through January 30. The remaining $150 of interest was recorded as an expense in the previous year, and, thus, a debit will be made to Bonney's current liability account Interest Payable, as follows:

General Journal				
Date		**Description**	**Debit**	**Credit**
Jan.	30	Notes Payable	5,000	
		Interest Payable	150	
		Interest Expense	50	
		Cash		5,200
		Recorded interest on the $5,000, 120-day, 12% note from 1/1–1/30 and repaid the note		

Installment Notes Payable

Many notes, like bank loans for automobiles and mortgages, are due in installments, in which each periodic payment includes some interest and some principal. The amount of interest included in each payment modifies the formula shown previously as follows.

Interest Expense = Remaining Principal × Rate × Time

Assume that Ryan Co. purchases a $25,000 truck on January 31, 2003. The company signs a five-year note payable and payments of $483 are to be made at the end of each month at an annual interest rate of six percent (or 0.06 ÷ 12 = 0.005 per month). Exhibit 7-1 shows the computations for the first six months of principal and interest payments (rounded to the nearest dollar), as well as the journal entries for the first two months. Note that the interest amounts are calculated as 0.005 times the remaining principal balance on the previous line. As each payment is made, the principal is reduced and, therefore, the interest expense on the outstanding debt is also reduced in the following payment.

In this example, the amount of the monthly truck payment was given. A variety of Web sites are available that can calculate such payments, given changes in principal amounts, interest rates, and length of borrowing time. The www.home-mortgage-auto-loan-calculator.com Web site provides several different calculators, one of which shows a graph of the interest expense reductions over the life of the loan.

If an installment loan matures over multiple accounting periods, the full amount of the note payable will not be shown as a current liability. The amount that comes due in the next year or operating cycle, whichever is longer, is shown as the "current portion of long-term debt," and the remainder is shown as a long-term liability.

EXHIBIT 7-1

Installment Note Payable

Date	Payment	.005 Interest	Principal	Remaining Principal
January 31				$25,000
February 28	$483	$125	$358	24,642
March 31	483	123	360	24,282
April 30	483	121	362	23,920
May 31	483	120	363	23,557
June 30	483	118	365	23,192
July 31	483	116	367	22,825

Date	Description	Debit	Credit
Feb. 28	Note Payable	358	
	Interest Expense	125	
	Cash		483
	Recorded interest expense and principal reduction on the $25,000, 5-year, 6% truck note payable		
Mar. 31	Note Payable	360	
	Interest Expense	123	
	Cash		483
	Recorded interest expense and principal reduction on the $25,000, 5-year, 6% truck note payable		

Accrued Liabilities

As illustrated by the interest accrual on the Bonney's Dress Shop note payable example and as discussed in Chapter 3, a business must record its expenses in the appropriate accounting periods. Expenses may be accrued at the end of an accounting period because of the passage of time (such as interest expense) or because the related revenue is recognized (such as commissions expense on sales). When such an accrual is recorded, an expense account is debited and a liability account is credited. Recall that an accrued liability was defined as a liability stemming from an expense that has been incurred but not yet paid.

Some accrued liabilities, such as wages payable, interest payable, and income taxes payable, have been discussed previously in the text. Several additional accrued liabilities are considered in the following discussion.

Product Warranty Liability

Many companies provide a product or service warranty. Because warranties help sell products, the company must match warranty costs with sales revenue each accounting period. However, warranty work is oftentimes performed in a period (or periods) after the sale. To properly match the sales revenue with the related warranty expense, businesses estimate total expected warranty costs for products sold during an accounting period and record that amount as an expense in the period of the sale. The offsetting credit to this expense is typically entered in an account entitled Warranty Liability.

Suppose a high-quality ballpoint pen manufacturer has a "repair or replace forever" product warranty. The company expects that 2 percent of the pens sold will need to be repaired or replaced and the average cost of doing so is $15 per pen. If 200,000 pens are sold in 2002, the firm can expect to eventually repair or replace 4,000 (200,000 × 0.02) pens at a cost of $60,000 (4,000 × $15). Given these facts, the adjusting entry to record warranty expense for 2002 follows.

General Journal				
Date		Description	Debit	Credit
Dec.	31	Warranty Expense	60,000	
		Warranty Liability		60,000
		Record estimated warranty expense for year		

During 2003, the company incurs $15,100 of warranty costs. Of these costs, $10,000 was for parts and $5,100 was paid to repair personnel. The following entry would be made to recognize these costs.

General Journal				
Date		Description	Debit	Credit
XXX		Warranty Liability	15,100	
		Parts Inventory		10,000
		Cash		5,100
		Record actual warranty costs for year		

The same type of expense and liability estimation must take place for certain other types of business activities. For example, when restaurants issue "free meal" coupons that extend over the end of an accounting period, the number of coupons that will be redeemed needs to be estimated. Similarly, estimates of potential liabilities must be made when a hotel offers clients a "free stay" after a certain number of check-ins or an airline offers free trips after a given number of flight segments. A footnote in the 2000 annual report of AMR Corporation, the company that owns American Airlines, states that, "the estimated incremental cost of providing free travel awards is accrued when such award levels are reached."[3]

Vacation Pay Liability

Besides earning their base salary or wages, most employees also accumulate vacation pay each payroll period. For example, consider an employee who is paid $400 each week for 52 weeks; annually, she earns $20,800 ($400 × 52). If she is entitled to an annual two-week paid vacation, $800 ($400 × 2 weeks) of the $20,800 qualifies as vacation pay. Expressed another way, this employee accumulates $16 of vacation pay ($800 ÷ 50 weeks) for each week worked. Because of the matching principle, businesses recognize the cost of vacation pay earned by their employees each payroll period as a current liability. However, since some vacation pay accumulated by a company's workforce is usually forfeited because of employee turnover, a company usually does not record the entire estimated vacation pay cost.

Assume that Linton & Co. provides each employee an annual two-week paid vacation. Each payroll period, the vacation pay accumulated by company employees equals 4 percent (2 weeks ÷ 50 weeks) of that week's payroll. If the two-week payroll is $350,000, vacation pay earned by employees is $14,000 (0.04 × $350,000). In a typical year, 10 percent of all vacation pay accumulated by company employees is forfeited. Given this fact, the company would make the following entry for each payroll period.

[3] AMR Corp., *2000 Annual Report*, p. 20.

General Journal			
Date	**Description**	**Debit**	**Credit**
XXX	Vacation Pay Expense	12,600	
	Vacation Pay Liability		12,600
	Record estimated vacation pay expense for the payroll period		

The $12,600 represents 90 percent of the expected $14,000 of vacation pay expense for its most recent payroll period. When Linton & Co.'s employees take vacations, Vacation Pay Liability will be debited for the vacation pay cost and Cash will be credited.

Accrued Payroll Liabilities

Typically, the end of a business's accounting period does not coincide with the end of a payroll period. Therefore, as discussed in Chapter 3, a company will generally have to accrue employee wages at the end of the month or year.

In addition, though it was ignored to this point, there is often a significant difference between a worker's gross pay and his or her net (or take-home) pay because of various payroll deductions. These deductions include the employee's portion of the Social Security tax[4], federal and state income tax withholdings, union dues, and health insurance premiums. When accruing payroll expenses at the end of an accounting period, a business must also consider these employee payroll deductions.

Suppose that as of December 31 of a given year, employees of Rachael's Restaurant have worked one week for which they have not been paid. The gross pay earned by these employees for this week is $4,240. However, of this amount, only net pay of $2,720 is payable to the employees. The remainder, as shown in Exhibit 7-2, is payable to government tax agencies and the insurance company.

In addition to paying employee wages and salaries, employers must contribute an amount equal to the FICA taxes paid by their employees to the Social Security program. Likewise, employers must generally pay state and federal unemployment taxes on

[4] Social Security is officially known as the Federal Insurance Contributions Act (FICA) tax.

EXHIBIT 7-2

Computation of Net Pay and Payroll Accrual

Gross Pay		$4,240
Less Payroll Deductions:		
FICA Taxes	$325	
Federal Income Tax Withholdings	810	
State Income Tax Withholdings	205	
Health Insurance Premiums	180	(1,520)
Net Pay		$2,720

Date	Description	Debit	Credit
Dec. 31	Wages Expense	4,240	
	FICA Taxes Payable		325
	Empl. Fed. Inc. Tax Payable		810
	Empl. State Inc. Tax Payable		205
	Health Ins. Premiums Payable		180
	Wages Payable		2,720
	Record accrued wages and payroll deductions		

employees' earnings. A final component of payroll-related expenses is employee fringe benefits. Fringe benefits include items such as employer contributions to an employee pension fund and payments toward employee health or other insurance premiums. At the end of each accounting period, businesses will generally need to accrue these additional payroll-related expenses in an adjusting entry.

Deferred Liabilities

Deferred liabilities are obligations to provide a product, service, or cash at a later date. A business may receive payments from customers prior to providing them products or services. For example, magazine subscriptions are paid before individual issues are sent. Such amounts have not been earned when they are received; thus they are initially recorded as liabilities. Typically, these deferral amounts are debited to Cash and credited to a deferred revenue account such as Deferred Subscription Revenue or Unearned Rental Revenue. These advance payments are usually classified as current liabilities because the products or services will be delivered to customers within twelve months. For example, when airlines sell mileage credits to customers participating in their frequent flyer programs, the receipts related to the sale of mileage credits are deferred and recognized during the period in which the mileage credits are used.

Contingent Liabilities

Companies face a variety of **contingent** (or potential) **liabilities** that may become actual liabilities if an event occurs or fails to occur. For example, when a product with a warranty is sold, a company may have to incur repair costs if the product breaks. Such a potential cost is recognized as an estimated expense and estimated liability. Other types of contingencies, such as lawsuits or environmental problems, will result in losses rather than expenses because payments related to such situations are not considered normal costs of doing business.

Large corporations regularly face nuisance lawsuits that pose no more than a minimal likelihood of resulting in actual losses. If a contingent liability has only a *remote* chance of resulting in an actual loss, that liability is ignored for accounting and financial reporting purposes. However, almost all legitimate loss contingencies are recorded, at a minimum, in the footnotes to the financial statements.

If a loss contingency meets the following two criteria, a journal entry must be recorded: it is *probable* that an actual cost will result from the contingency, and the amount of the potential cost can be *reasonably estimated.* When a loss contingency is recorded, an appropriate expense or loss account is debited with an offsetting credit to a liability account. Visual Recap 7.1 summarizes the alternative accounting treatments for loss contingencies and the related contingent liabilities.

Interpreting the meanings of the terms "probable," "reasonably possible," "remote," and "subject to reasonable estimation" is the key to accounting properly for loss contingencies. Accounting standards do not provide definitive guidelines regarding how those expressions should be interpreted, and, thus, personal expertise and judgment must be used in deciding the applicability of those terms.

Contingent liabilities, if shown on the balance sheet, may be current or long-term. If, for example, settlement is to be made soon (such as sending out the next year's magazine subscription), the amount is current. However, if a lawsuit has been recorded and settlement on that suit is not expected for several years, the amount will be shown as a long-term liability.

LONG-TERM LIABILITIES

Long-term liabilities include the debts and obligations of a business other than those classified as current. Common long-term debt items include bonds payable, notes payable due

VISUAL RECAP 7.1

Contingent Losses and Related Contingent Liabilities

Likelihood of Actual Loss	Potential Loss Subject to Reasonable Estimation	Accounting Treatment
Probable	Yes	Recorded by debiting an expense or loss account and crediting a liability account. Also disclosed in financial statement footnotes.
Probable	No	Disclosed in financial statement footnotes.
Reasonably Possible	Yes or No	Disclosed in financial statement footnotes.
Remote	Yes or No	Ignored.

more than one year from a firm's balance sheet date, mortgages payable, and many leases. Long-term accrued liabilities include obligations created by pension and other postretirement benefit plans that many companies have established for their employees.

The types and dollar amounts of long-term liabilities reported by large corporations vary considerably from firm to firm. For example, as of July 29, 2001, Campbell Soup Company (www.campbellsoup.com) had $5.9 billion of assets and $2.2 billion of long-term debt. Alternatively, as of June 30, 2001, Microsoft Corporation (www.microsoft.com) had $52.2 billion of assets and no long-term debt.[5] Microsoft is one of the very few fortunate companies that has not needed to borrow money on a long-term basis.

Bonds Payable

A **bond** is a long-term, interest-bearing loan between parties that is represented by a legal document known as a bond certificate. Bonds payable represents the collective amount owed to the parties who have purchased a company's bonds. Bonds are often identified by one or more distinctive features or characteristics. **Secured** (or mortgage) **bonds** are collateralized by specific assets, such as a building, of the issuing company. Unsecured bonds, or **debentures,** are backed only by the issuing firm's legal commitment to make all required principal and interest payments.

Bonds payable are among the most common long-term liabilities of many large public companies. Bonds may be sold to finance the construction of new production facilities, purchase other companies, or retire existing debt. In the first quarter of 2002, new issues in the U.S. bond market totaled $1.3 trillion, up over 30 percent from the same period in 2001.[6] In recent years, the sale of bonds by corporations has been a particularly popular way to obtain long-term funds because interest rates have been considered very low by historical standards.

Prior to selling a bond, a company prepares a **bond indenture** or a legal contract that identifies the rights and obligations of both the buyer and seller of the bond. A bond indenture identifies the following terms:

1. The **maturity date** at which the bond will be repaid. The term of the bond reflects the time between when the bonds are first available for sale and when they mature.
2. The **face value,** or the amount the bondholder will receive when the bond matures.

[5] The long-term debt amount for Campbell Soup ignores pension and other liabilities and, for Microsoft, ignores deferred income taxes.

[6] The Bond Market Association (www.investinginbonds.com), *The Economic Outlook: The Recovery is Underway, but Significant Risks Remain,* accessed July 31, 2002.

3. The **stated** (or contract) **interest rate** that will be paid in cash to bondholders based upon the bond's face value. A $1,000 bond with a stated interest rate of 8 percent pays $80 of interest each year ($1,000 × 0.08 × 12/12). However, if the bond pays interest semiannually, the holder of the $1,000, 8 percent bond will receive $40 of interest (or 4 percent) every six months.

Bond indentures also generally include a call option and may occasionally include a convertibility option. **Callable bonds** can be retired or redeemed by the issuing company when one or more conditions are met, the most common of which is simply the passage of time. For instance, a bond issue may be callable by the issuing company at any point after the bonds have been outstanding for five years. If a bond issue is called, the bond indenture usually requires that the bondholders be paid a call premium (or an amount over face value). Bondholders may also be able to exchange **convertible bonds** for stock in the issuing company. For example, a convertible option may let bondholders exchange each $1,000 bond for 25 shares of the issuing company's common stock.

Bond Trading

The initial sale of a bond occurs in what is called the primary market. This sale generally occurs between the corporation and investment bankers or underwriting firms, such as Morgan Stanley (www.morganstanley.com) and Goldman Sachs (www.gs.com). At this time, the corporation determines the issue price of the bond and prepares journal entries related to the issuance.

After the initial sale, corporate bonds trade on major securities exchanges, such as the New York Stock Exchange (www.nyse.com), known as secondary markets (or after markets). In the secondary market, transactions occur between the original purchaser and a new buyer. Unless repurchasing its bonds, the issuing corporation has no involvement in trading on a secondary market, and therefore makes no journal entries for such trades.

Corporations typically issue bonds in $1,000 face value (or principal) denominations and selling prices are quoted as a percentage of face value. For example, a $1,000 bond that is quoted at 102 is selling for 102 percent of face value or $1,020. Most corporate bonds sell for slightly more or less than their face value; that is, the bonds generally sell at a premium or a discount from face value.

Numerous factors influence the market price of a company's bonds, including the firm's financial condition, level of interest rates in the economy, length of time to the bonds' maturity date, and investors' preferences. Several investment advisory firms, including Moody's Investors Service (www.moodys.com) and Standard & Poor's (www.standardandpoors.com), monitor hundreds of bond issues and assign each a risk assessment rating. Risk refers to the likelihood that a company will eventually default, or fail to make required interest or principal payments, on its bonds. As the factors affecting the default risk associated with individual bond issues change, investment advisory firms update their risk assessment ratings. The market price of a bond issue fluctuates as investors react to changes in these factors; however, day-to-day changes in the market price of a company's bonds do not have accounting implications for that firm after the bond is initially sold.

Determining the Issue Price of Bonds

The original issue price of a bond reflects a combination of all the factors mentioned previously. The relationship of the stated interest rate on the bonds to the interest rates being paid in the market is one of the primary determinants of issue price. Consider the following example. Hardin Manufacturing Company plans to sell five-year bonds with a face value of $1,000 and a stated interest rate of 10%. If 100 bonds were sold at $1,000 each (at face value), Hardin would make the following journal entry:

General Journal				
Date		**Description**	**Debit**	**Credit**
XXX		Cash	100,000	
		Bonds Payable		100,000
		Record sale of 100, $1,000 bonds at face value		

Investors who consider buying Hardin's bonds will also consider other market investments. Suppose another five-year bond was available but it paid 11% interest. Potential investors might consider this bond to be the better investment because the interest payment would be higher. If Hardin wants to attract investors, the company could lower the selling price of the bond to less than the face value, or sell the bond at a discount. In this case, Hardin would sell the bonds for less than $1,000 each, pay 10% interest on each bond's $1,000 face value, and pay the investor $1,000 at maturity. Hardin's entry to record the sale of all the bonds for $950 each follows:

General Journal				
Date		**Description**	**Debit**	**Credit**
XXX		Cash	95,000	
		Discount on Bonds Payable	5,000	
		Bonds Payable		100,000
		Record sale of 100, $1,000 bonds at a $50 discount per bond		

Alternatively, suppose the best alternative to Hardin's bonds was a bond that paid only 9%. In this case, investors might be anxious to purchase Hardin's bonds. Because there is only a limited supply ($100,000) of Hardin's bonds, investors will attempt to acquire Hardin's bonds by bidding up the price. Thus, Hardin is able to sell the bonds for more than face value, or at a premium. In this case, Hardin would sell the bonds for more than $1,000 each, pay 10% interest on the each $1,000 bond's face value, and pay the investor $1,000 at maturity. Hardin's entry to record the sale of all of the bonds for $1,040 each is as follows.

General Journal				
Date		**Description**	**Debit**	**Credit**
XXX		Cash	104,000	
		Bonds Payable		100,000
		Premium on Bonds Payable		4,000
		Record sale of 100, $1000 bonds at $40 premium per bond		

The actual issue price of a bond is a complex determination. A detailed discussion of this process is given in the chapter appendix. The appendix also includes a discussion of accounting for interest payments and how to amortize (write-off) bond discounts and premiums.

A company may decide to retire bonds before their actual maturity date. In doing so, the company will generally experience a gain or loss on the retirement. Assume that Hardin Manufacturing decided to retire its $100,000 bonds three years after their issuance. At the time, because of amortization, the premium related to these bonds was shown at $1,600 in the accounting records. The company paid $100,700 to buy the bonds in the market. The following entry is appropriate.

General Journal			
Date	**Description**	**Debit**	**Credit**
XXX	Bonds Payable	100,000	
	Premium on Bonds Payable	1,600	
	Cash		100,700
	Gain on Bond Retirement		900
	Record retirement of bonds payable and the related extraordinary gain		

Any gain or loss on early bond retirement is considered extraordinary. The amount is calculated as the difference between the carrying value of bonds retired and the amount paid to retire them. Extraordinary gains and losses are unusual and infrequently occurring items that companies must report separately in their income statements.

Long-term Liabilities Other Than Bonds

Many accounting issues presented by bonds payable are relevant to other long-term liabilities. Thus, long-term liabilities such as long-term mortgages payable, long-term lease obligations, pension liabilities, and other postretirement benefit liabilities are only briefly addressed.

Long-term Mortgages Payable

Many long-term notes payable are actually mortgage notes payable, or more commonly "mortgages payable." A lender may require a company that borrows $10 million to purchase a new building to sign a mortgage note that will pledge the building as collateral, or security, for the loan. If the company defaults on the mortgage note, the lender can obtain legal title to the building or force the sale of the building to satisfy the unpaid balance of the mortgage. Mortgages payable usually require equal monthly payments consisting of both principal and interest. The portion of any mortgage payable that becomes due in the upcoming year is shown as a current liability in the balance sheet.

Long-term Lease Obligations

A leasehold is a legal right to use a leased asset for a specified period, subject to any restrictions in the lease agreement. The two parties to a lease agreement are the lessor, or the owner of the asset being leased, and the lessee, or the party leasing the asset.

Accounting standards distinguish between operating leases and capital leases. An **operating lease** is cancelable by the lessee, has a relatively short term, and does not transfer ownership rights or risks to the lessee. A **capital lease** is noncancelable, long-term, and transfers at least some ownership rights or risks to the lessee. Capital leases are a very popular method for businesses to finance the acquisition of a wide range of assets including buildings, equipment, and automobile or airplane fleets. For instance, US Airways reported $64 million of capital lease obligations on its balance sheet at December 31, 2001.

Noncancelable leases that meet at least one of the following criteria qualify as capital leases, while all other leases are classified as operating leases.

1. The lease agreement transfers legal title to the leased asset to the lessee at the end of the lease term.
2. A "bargain purchase option" that can be exercised by the lessee is included in the lease agreement.
3. The term of the lease covers 75 percent or more of the economic life of the leased asset.

4. The present value of the lease payments is equal to 90 percent or more of the market value of the leased asset, or put more simply, the sum of the lease payments approximate the cost of purchase.

When a company leases an asset in a manner that is similar to buying that asset with borrowed funds, both the leased asset and long-term lease liability are reported in the company's balance sheet. This accounting treatment is justified because the lease, in essence, is equivalent to a purchase using debt. Many companies report a significant amount of long-term liabilities related to lease agreements in their balance sheets.

Like other liabilities, a long-term lease obligation must be separated into its current and long-term portions for balance sheet purposes. Additionally, for both operating and capital leases, lessees must disclose in their financial statements future minimum lease payments over the next five years.

Postretirement Benefit Liabilities

Many companies have established pension plans to provide retirement income for their employees. These pension plans are either defined contribution or defined benefit plans.

Under a defined contribution plan, employers make specific periodic *contributions* to a pension fund (typically a percentage of each employee's gross earnings). The journal entry is a debit to Pension Expense and a credit to Cash or to a payable account when the full amounts owed are not funded immediately. An individual pension account is established for each employee. Following retirement, employees receive a monthly, quarterly, or annual benefit based upon the size of their individual pension accounts. In this situation, the input (contribution) to the plan is known; the output (benefit) to the employee depends on how well the contributions are managed.

Under a defined benefit plan, employees are promised specific periodic pension *benefits* based on factors such as length of employment, age at retirement, and average salary level over the last several years. In this situation, the benefit to the employee is known, at least as to formula computation; the contribution must be adjusted each period to "correct for" changes in salary and market conditions. A journal entry is still made to debit Pension Expense and a credit to Cash or a payable account.

A simple example can be used to illustrate the difference between the two types of plans. Ms. Dierk will retire at the end of 2004. She has just begun her pension plan with RightWay Corp. on January 1, 2003. Assume that the company has a defined contribution plan that says it will deposit $1,000 at the end of each year for her plan. At the end of each of the two years, a deposit is made of $1,000. This amount is generally invested in stocks or bonds of RightWay or other companies. If the investment does well, the pension fund will increase. If the investment does poorly, the fund could decline dramatically. There is no way to know how much money will be in Ms. Dierk's pension account when she retires. That amount will depend on the investments made by the pension fund manager.

Alternately, if RightWay Corp. has a defined benefit plan, the company makes a promise to Ms. Dierk that she will receive a specified amount of pension benefit when she retires. For simplicity, the assumption is made that Dierk is promised a lump sum (benefit) of $2,100 upon retirement. The company estimates that all pension investments will earn a 10 percent rate of return. Thus, the following schedule indicates the company needs to make a pension contribution of $1,000 each year to achieve the promised benefit:

12/31/03	Pension contribution	$1,000
12/31/04	Assumed interest at 10% for year	100
12/31/04	Pension contribution	1,000
	Promised pension benefit	$2,100

If, however, the company miscalculated the rate of return that will be earned by the pension assets, the contribution of $1,000 each year will not generate the necessary pension benefit. In such a case, an adjustment will need to be made at the end of 2004 to obtain the required pension benefit amount as follows.

	Promised pension benefit		$2,100
12/31/03	Pension contribution	$1,000	
12/31/04	Actual interest at 6% for year	60	(1,060)
	Needed amount of 2004 contribution		$1,040

Had the pension contribution earned at a rate of 13 percent during 2004 (or $130), RightWay would have only needed to make a contribution of $970 ($2,100 – $1,130) at the end of 2004.

The actual computations for necessary pension contributions are extremely complex, in part because of the large number of years and employees involved. The calculations require use of time value of money concepts, which are discussed in the chapter appendix. Additionally, companies generally employ an actuary who specializes in the mathematics of risk, especially as it relates to insurance and pension calculations, to help determine pension plan benefit estimates.[7]

The type of pension plan offered by an organization and the types of investments in which pension plan assets are placed are extremely important to employees. In 2001–2002, employees in Enron's (www.enron.com) defined contribution plan lost more than $1 billion in value because many of the pension's assets were invested in Enron shares, which went from $80 to less than $1. The company's pension plan managers were part of an Enron administrative committee. In contrast, when US Airways began experiencing financial difficulties, the company appointed an independent corporation to manage the employee's defined contribution plan investments so that any perceived conflict of interest would be avoided.[8]

Many businesses also provide their employees with postretirement benefits other than pensions. The most common type of such benefits is healthcare. Similar to pension benefits, these benefits generally create long-term liabilities. Postretirement benefit liabilities are often enormous and have dramatically affected the reported financial condition of many large companies.

ACCOUNTING INFORMATION FOR DECISION MAKING

Decision makers' primary information needs related to liabilities include access to information concerning all of an entity's long-term obligations and valuation methods, as well as disclosure of any unusual and material circumstances involving long-term liabilities.

Completeness

Investors, creditors, and other decision makers rely on businesses to provide comprehensive disclosure of their liabilities. Decision makers must have confidence that a company's balance sheet reflects all of the firm's outstanding, or unpaid, liabilities. To illustrate, in September 2000, Hilton Hotels Corporation (www.hilton.com) borrowed $500 million for ten years at 7.95 percent; five of the company's hotels were used as collateral for that agreement and that information was disclosed in the company's annual report.

However, some businesses do not include certain long-term obligations in their periodic financial statements. Such **off-balance sheet financing** involves obtaining assets or services by incurring long-term obligations that are not reported in an entity's

[7] Additional information on the term *actuary* and other terms can be found at www.investorwords.com.

[8] Jerry Geisel, "Airline Taps Fiduciary for Pension Plans," *Business Insurance* (July 8, 2002), p. 2.

balance sheet. For example, certain long-term leases qualify as off-balance sheet financing arrangements. Fortunately, the accounting profession has taken steps in recent years to reduce the number of off-balance sheet long-term obligations and the disclosures related to these items have increased.

Valuation Methods

Financial statement users need to be aware of the methods businesses use to assign dollar amounts to individual current liabilities. The reported values of most current liabilities, such as accounts payable, are equal to the amount of cash that must be paid when those liabilities become due. Occasionally, however, businesses eliminate their current liabilities, generally unearned revenue items, through the delivery of goods or services. In regard to estimated liabilities, adequate disclosures should be provided in financial statement footnotes to help decision makers assess whether the estimates are valid.

Proper valuation is a concern to decision makers for most financial statement items. Valuation issues are particularly important for long-term liabilities that must be estimated using time value of money concepts. For example, companies with employee-defined benefit pension plans annually face complex computations in determining long-term, pension-related obligations. Projections must be made about employees' future salaries and pension plan rates of return. A company wanting to minimize pension-related obligations might intentionally underestimate future pay raises of its employees or overestimate the rate of return expected from pension investments. To guard against these possibilities, businesses must disclose key assumptions underlying their pension-related expense and liability computations. Comparable financial statement disclosures are required for other estimated long-term liabilities.

Unusual Circumstances

Unusual and significant circumstances that affect a major account balance should be disclosed in a firm's financial statements. An example of such a circumstance is an inability, or potential inability, by a company to pay its current liabilities as they become due. Companies involved in bankruptcy proceedings face a significant risk of defaulting on their current liabilities.

Long-term debt agreements often include restrictive debt covenants or conditions. Violations of these covenants may cause the entire amount of the long-term debt to become immediately due. Any covenants affecting a company's future operations should be disclosed in the financial statement footnotes. Probably one of the most common restrictive debt covenants is a limitation on the payment of dividends; for example, Applebee's International, Inc. (www.applebees.com) had debt agreements that limited the company to $5,000,000 in dividends through fiscal 1999.[9] Maintenance of certain financial statement ratios is another covenant often included in debt arrangements. In its 2000 annual report, Aaron Rents (www.aaronrentshome.com) disclosed that the company could

> not permit its consolidated net worth as of the last day of any fiscal quarter to be less than the sum of (a) $105,000,000 plus (b) 50% of the Company's consolidated net income (but not loss) for the period beginning July 1, 1997 and ending on the last day of such fiscal quarter. [Restrictions have also been placed] on additional borrowings and [require] the maintenance of certain financial ratios.[10]

When a company violates a restrictive debt covenant, or faces a high risk of doing so, external decision makers should be informed.

---

[9] Applebee's International Inc., 2000 10-K filing with the SEC.

[10] Aaron Rents Inc., *2000 Annual Report.*

Analyzing Liabilities

Liquidity refers to a business's ability to finance its day-to-day operations and to pay its liabilities as they become due. One measure of liquidity, the quick ratio, was discussed in Chapter 4. Another widely used measure of liquidity is the **current ratio,** which expresses the relationship between a business's current assets and its current liabilities at a given time.

Current Ratio = Current Assets ÷ Current Liabilities

Because a company should have more current assets than current liabilities, the current ratio should be greater than one. Although current ratios vary considerably from industry to industry, a common benchmark is a current ratio of at least 2.0.

Another financial measure of liquidity in which current liabilities figure prominently is **working capital,** which is the difference between an entity's current assets and current liabilities.

Working Capital = Current Assets – Current Liabilities

A company that has a minimal amount of working capital, or, worse yet, a negative working capital, generally faces a high risk of defaulting on its current liabilities as they come due. Larger current ratios, quick ratios, and amounts of working capital are generally better than small ones. However, when current assets far exceed current liabilities, the company may have missed an opportunity for investments or may be experiencing other asset-management problems.

External decision makers also monitor a firm's long-term liabilities and related financial data to gain insight on whether the firm can pay off those liabilities as they become due, known as solvency. The most basic solvency ratio is the **debt to total asset ratio,** which is computed using the following formula.

Debt to Total Asset Ratio = Total Liabilities ÷ Total Assets

Smaller values of this ratio indicate that a company is better able to meet its obligations in the long-term.

A company that makes extensive use of long-term debt to meet its financing needs is said to be highly leveraged. Such companies generally face more risk of financially failing than firms that have little or no long-term debt on their balance sheets. Decision makers commonly use the **long-term debt to equity ratio** to measure financial leverage.

Long-term Debt to Equity Ratio = Long-term Debt ÷ Stockholders' Equity

As this ratio increases, a company is perceived as being more risky and will probably have to pay higher interest rates for borrowings.

The **times interest earned ratio** helps decision makers evaluate the ability of companies, particularly highly leveraged companies, to make interest payments on long-term debt as they come due.

Times Interest Earned Ratio = (Net Income + Interest Expense + Income Tax Expense) ÷ Interest Expense

This ratio indicates the number of times that profits earned prior to deducting interest expense and income tax expense "cover" a company's interest expense during a given period. The lower this ratio, the more risk a company generally faces of defaulting on interest payments on its long-term debt. As is true for most financial ratios, there is not complete agreement on what represents a reasonable level for the times interest earned ratio. Typically, this ratio is considered "comfortable" when it is 4.0 and higher.

SUMMARY

Current liabilities are obligations that must be paid, or otherwise extinguished, by a business within one year or its operating cycle, whichever is longer. The most common types of current liabilities are accounts and notes payable, accrued liabilities, deferred revenues, and the current portion of long-term debt.

A contingent liability is a potential liability that may become an actual liability if a particular event occurs or fails to occur. Contingent liabilities that are probable and subject to reasonable estimation must be recorded by journal entries. Other contingent liabilities are merely disclosed in a firm's financial statement footnotes.

Long-term liabilities are debts and obligations other than those classified as current. The more common long-term liabilities are bonds payable, capital lease obligations, and debts associated with employee pension or health benefit plans. Newly-issued bonds payable usually sell for more or less than their face value because their stated interest rate is either higher or lower than the market interest rate on the date they are sold. A capital lease (as compared to an operating lease) is noncancelable and meets one of four established criteria. Such leases and the assets to which they relate are recorded, respectively, as long-term debt and property, plant, and equipment.

Decision makers need to be assured that a business has recorded and, when necessary, made reasonable estimates of all liabilities in its financial statements. Any unusual and material circumstances related to a firm's liabilities, such as potential violations of restrictive debt covenants, also need to be disclosed.

Decision makers use the current ratio (current assets divided by current liabilities) to evaluate a business's liquidity. Working capital (current assets minus current liabilities) is also a good measure of liquidity. When analyzing long-term liabilities, decision makers typically focus on the firm's degree of financial leverage and its ability to make periodic interest payments on long-term debt. A common measure of financial leverage is the long-term debt to equity ratio. A firm's ability to make periodic interest payments on long-term debt is commonly evaluated by referring to its times interest earned ratio.

APPENDIX: ACCOUNTING FOR BONDS

As mentioned in the chapter, the relationship between stated and market interest rates is a major determinant of bond issue price. Suppose that Hardin Manufacturing Company plans to sell $100,000 of bonds, paying interest at 10 percent semiannually on September 30 and March 31. On each interest payment date, Hardin will pay $5,000 ($100,000 × 0.05 × 12/12) of interest to bondholders. The bonds have a five-year term that runs from April 1, 2003, through April 1, 2008.

On April 1, 2003, when the market interest rate is 11 percent, Hardin sells its bonds. The market interest rate is also known as the **effective interest rate** and refers to the annual rate of return that investors can earn by purchasing any of a number of different corporate bonds that pose the same general level of default risk. The market interest rate represents the "yield to maturity" for a given bond or the actual interest rate that will be earned considering both the bond interest paid in cash each year *and* the impact of any bond discount or premium over the life of the bond.

Companies try to set a stated bond interest rate that approximates the market interest rate. However, several weeks or months may pass from the time a decision to issue a bond is made to the actual sale of the bond. Thus, the stated interest rate can be quite different from the market interest rate when the bonds are actually sold. If, at the date of the sale, the stated interest rate is equal to the market interest rate, the bonds would sell at face value.[11] In the

[11] This statement is proved as follows, using present value amounts for a 10%, semiannual interest payments for five years (or factors in the present value tables for 5% and 10 periods):

PV of principal	($100,000 × 0.61391)	$ 61,391
PV of interest	($5,000 × 7.72173)	38,609
PV of bond		$100,000

If a bond is sold at face value, interest expense each period will be equal to the cash interest paid.

case of Hardin's bonds, however, the market interest rate is 11 percent at the issue date and Hardin's bonds only pay 10 percent. Therefore, the bonds will sell for less than their face value or at a discount that will be sufficiently large to allow the purchasers of Hardin's bonds to effectively earn an 11 percent yield to maturity on their investment.

To determine the selling price of Hardin's bonds, the **time value of money concept** must be applied. The concept reflects the fact that a dollar received (or paid) currently is worth more than dollar received (or paid) in the future because the current dollar can be invested to earn interest and, thus, will be larger in the future than it is now. The two key variables in a time value of money problem are the number of time periods and the effective interest rate. Because bonds will pay periodic interest in the future and their principal will be repaid in the future, these two future cash amounts can be discounted to their **present value** (worth at the current time) using the market interest rate. **Discounting** refers to the process of removing interest from future receipts (payments).

The bonds' selling price will be the present value of Hardin's future cash payments over the bonds' five-year term. The cash payments consist of ten $5,000 semiannual interest payments and a $100,000 principal payment at the end of the bond term. In this example, there are ten time periods because there are two semiannual interest periods in each year of the bond's five-year life. The 11 percent market interest rate is divided by two, so as to reflect the two semiannual interest periods; thus, the effective interest rate is 5.5 percent. *The key point to remember is that the market interest rate, not the stated interest rate, determines the present value of the future cash outflows related to a bond issue.*

Using the present value of 1 table in the appendix at the end of the text, the factor for ten periods and a 5.5 percent interest rate is found to be 0.58543. Using the present value of an annuity of 1, the factor for ten periods and a 5.5 percent interest rate is 7.53763. (An **annuity** is a series of payments of a specified size and frequency.) These factors are multiplied, respectively, by the bond principal and interest amounts as follows.

PV of principal	($100,000 × 0.58543)	$58,543
PV of interest	($5,000 × 7.53763)	37,688
PV of principal and interest		$96,231

This computation indicates that, if $58,543 were put in a bank that paid 11 percent interest semiannually, at the end of five years (ten interest periods), the balance in the bank would be $100,000. Thus, the present value of the principal amount is $58,543. If $37,688 were put in a bank that paid 11 percent interest semiannually, one could withdraw $5,000 every six months for five years and, at the end of that period, the balance in the bank would be zero. Thus, the present value of the $5,000 of semiannual interest payments for five years is $37,688. The total of the two cash flows from the bonds is $96,231, which reflects the bonds' selling price. Regardless of the selling price, Hardin must pay the bondholders $100,000 at the bonds' maturity date. In essence, Hardin is being penalized for selling bonds with a stated interest rate that is less than the market interest rate. The discount on the bonds allows the initial purchasers to earn a yield to maturity of exactly 11 percent, the market interest rate on the date the bonds are sold.

Accounting for Bonds Issued at a Discount

Hardin's $100,000 bond issue is used to illustrate the accounting for bonds that are issued at a discount. Journal entries related to the transaction are shown in Exhibit 7A-1 and are discussed in the following information.

On April 1, 2003, the bonds are sold for $96,231. The bond liability is recorded at the principal amount of $100,000, but only $96,231 is received in cash. The $3,769 difference

EXHIBIT 7A-1

Journal Entries for a Bond Issued at a Discount

General Journal				
Date		**Description**	**Debit**	**Credit**
2003				
April	1	Cash	96,231	
		Discount on Bonds Payable	3,769	
		Bonds Payable		100,000
		To record issuance of $100,000, 10%, 5-year bonds at a market rate of 11%		
Sept.	30	Interest Expense	5,377	
		Cash		5,000
		Discount on Bonds Payable		377
		To record payment of semiannual interest and amortization of discount		
Dec.	31	Interest Expense	2,689	
		Interest Payable		2,500
		Discount Bonds Payable		189
		To record accrual of 3 months of interest and amortization of discount		
2004				
Mar.	31	Interest Expense	2,688	
		Interest Payable	2,500	
		Cash		5,000
		Discount on Bonds Payable		188
		To record payment of semiannual interest and amortization of discount		

is recorded in a discount on the bonds payable account, which is a contra-liability account. If a balance sheet were prepared at this time, Hardin Manufacturing would report the bonds payable at a net carrying value of $96,231, or the difference between their $100,000 face value and the $3,769 balance of the bond discount account.

The semiannual interest payment dates for Hardin's bonds are March 31 and September 30. On September 30, 2003, cash interest of $5,000 is paid to bondholders. However, when bonds are sold at a discount, the interest expense recorded each interest payment date is greater than the amount of cash interest that is paid. The $3,769 discount is essentially additional interest expense on the bonds over their five-year term. The matching principle requires this additional interest expense to be recognized over the bonds' life rather than when the principal is repaid. The Discount on Bonds Payable will be amortized, or written off, each interest period as an adjustment to interest expense using the straight-line method of amortization.[12]

Under the straight-line method, an equal amount of bond discount is amortized each interest payment period. The $3,769 discount is divided by the ten semiannual

[12] An alternative method, the effective interest method, should be used to amortize discounts (and premiums) when principal amounts are large and time to maturity is long.

interest periods, resulting in an amortization amount of $377 each period. (The small rounding error would be corrected during the final interest payment period.) Thus, total interest expense for the first interest period is the $5,000 cash payment plus the $377 discount amortization.

On December 31, an adjusting entry is necessary to recognize interest expense for the three-month period October 1 through December 31. The accrued interest amount is $2,500 ($100,000 × 0.10 × 3/12). The discount must also be amortized at this time. The six-month amortization was $377; thus, three-months of amortization would be half that amount or $189 (rounded). Interest expense for the three months is $2,689, or the sum of interest payable and discount amortization.

The next interest payment date is March 31, 2004. At that time, cash interest of $5,000 is paid to the bondholders. The discount on bonds payable is amortized at $188 for the other half of the six-month period. Interest expense is $2,688 ($2,500 + $188). The interest payable accrued at December 31, 2003, is paid on March 31, 2004.

As the bond discount is amortized, the bonds' carrying value gradually increases. After the last interest payment on March 31, 2008, Hardin's bond discount account would be zero and the carrying value of the bonds would be $100,000. The journal entry on April 1, 2008, would include a debit of $100,000 to Bonds Payable with an offsetting credit in the same amount to Cash.

Accounting for Bonds Issued at a Premium

To illustrate the journal entries for a bond selling at a premium, assume that on April 1, 2003, when Hardin sold its bonds, the market rate of interest was 9 percent. When the stated interest rate is higher than the market interest rate on the date the bonds are sold, bonds will sell at a premium. To determine the selling price, the semiannual market interest rate of 4.5 percent is used to discount the bond principal and interest to their present values, given ten interest periods as follows.

PV of principal	($100,000 × 0.64393)	$ 64,393
PV of interest	($5,000 × 7.91272)	39,564
PV of principal and interest		$103,957

Although Hardin sells the bonds for $103,957, the company will be required to pay its bondholders only $100,000 at maturity. A bond premium compensates the company for paying a higher interest rate on its bonds than is available in the market. Bonds sold at a premium are reported on a company's balance sheet at their net carrying value, which is the face value plus the credit balance of Premium on Bonds Payable. Premium on Bonds Payable is not a contra-liability because it has the same type of balance as its related account, Bonds Payable.

Like bond discounts, bond premiums are amortized over the bond term. Premium amortization reduces the interest expense recorded each accounting period. Using straight-line amortization, $396 ($3,957 ÷ 10) of premium is amortized each semiannual interest period.

As the bond premium is amortized, the carrying value gradually decreases. After the interest payment on March 31, 2008, the bond premium account will have a zero balance and the carrying value of the bonds payable will be $100,000. The journal entry to record the payment to the bondholders on April 1, 2008, will include a debit of $100,000 to Bonds Payable and a credit to Cash. Exhibit 7A-2 provides the entries from the date of sale through the second interest period for Hardin's bonds when issued at a premium.

Visual Recap 7.2 provides a summary of the relationships involved in accounting for bonds payable.

EXHIBIT 7A-2

Journal Entries for a Bond Issued at a Premium

General Journal				
Date		Description	Debit	Credit
2003				
April	1	Cash	103,957	
		Bonds Payable		100,000
		Premium on Bonds Payable		3,957
		To record issuance of $100,000, 10%, 5-year bonds at a market rate of 9%		
Sept.	30	Interest Expense	4,604	
		Premium on Bonds Payable	396	
		Cash		5,000
		To record payment of semiannual interest and amortization of premium		
Dec.	31	Interest Expense	2,302	
		Premium on Bonds Payable	198	
		Interest Payable		2,500
		To record accrual of 3 months of interest and amortization of premium		
2004				
Mar.	31	Interest Expense	2,302	
		Interest Payable	2,500	
		Premium on Bonds Payable	198	
		Cash		5,000
		To record payment of semiannual interest and amortization of premium		

VISUAL RECAP 7.2

Effect of Market Interest Rate on Bond Accounting

	Stated Rate = Market Rate	Stated Rate < Market Rate	Stated Rate > Market Rate
Bond Selling Price	Face Value	Discount (< Face Value)	Premium (> Face Value)
Interest Expense	= Interest Paid	> Interest Paid (Difference equal to amortization of bond discount)	< Interest Paid (Difference equal to amortization of bond premium)
Carrying Value of Bond	= Face Value	Carrying value increases to face value over time as discount is amortized	Carrying value decreases to face value over time as premium is amortized

KEY TERMS

account payable
annuity
bond
bond indenture
callable bond
capital lease
contingent liability
convertible bond
current ratio
debenture
debt to total asset ratio
discounting
effective interest rate
long-term debt to equity ratio
maker
maturity date
maturity value
note payable
off-balance sheet financing
operating lease
payee
present value
principal
secured bond
stated interest rate
term of a note
times interest earned ratio
time value of money concept
working capital

QUESTIONS

1. Define (a) liabilities, (b) current liabilities, and (c) long-term liabilities. List several examples of (b) and (c). *(LO 7.1 and 7.5)*
2. What is the difference between an account payable and a note payable? When is a note payable more likely to be used than an account payable? *(LO 7.1)*
3. Define "accrued liability" and list four examples. *(LO 7.1)*
4. Select two large companies that are likely to have a product warranty liability included in their balance sheets. Go to their Web sites and access their financial statements and related footnotes. Does the expected liability appear? Is it disclosed in the footnotes? If nothing about the liability is provided, discuss your thoughts as to why such a presentation is, or is not, appropriate. *(LO 7.1)*
5. What items do employers commonly deduct from employees' paychecks? To whom are these deductions remitted? *(LO 7.1)*
6. Define a "contingent liability." An article in mid-2002 stated that lawsuits were going to be filed against Wendy's, McDonald's, Burger King, and KFC relative to research indicating that starchy foods, when fried, contain acrylamide, a potential carcinogen. (Source: Marian Burros, "How Big Is the Acrylamide Risk?" *The New York Times,* 31 July 2002.) What information, if any, might you expect to see in the future annual reports of these companies related to this situation? *(LO 7.2)*
7. What is a bond issue? What is the advantage to a corporation of including a call option in a bond indenture? *(LO 7.5)*
8. Identify the advantages and disadvantages of leasing, rather than purchasing, assets. What is the difference between the accounting procedures for operating and capital leases? List the distinguishing characteristics of a capital lease. *(LO 7.3)*
9. How do defined contribution and defined benefit pension plans differ? Which would you prefer to be part of? Explain the rationale for your answer. *(LO 7.4)*
10. What key information needs do decision makers have regarding current liabilities and long-term liabilities? *(LO 7.6)*
11. How are the current ratio and working capital calculated? What information is provided by, and how do decision makers typically use, these ratios? *(LO 7.7)*
12. (Appendix) How does the amortization of a bond discount or premium affect bond interest expense but not the amount of bond interest paid by the issuing company? *(LO 7.8)*

EXERCISES

13. **True or False** *(all LOs)*

Following are a series of statements regarding topics discussed in this chapter.

Required:

Indicate whether each statement is true (T) or false (F).

(1) A note payable is an obligation documented by a legally binding written commitment known as a promissory note.

(2) Current liabilities must be paid by a business within one year or its operating cycle, whichever is shorter.

(3) A deferred liability is created when a customer requests a product or service but will not pay for it until the product or service is complete.

(4) Product warranty liability and vacation pay liability are examples of accrued liabilities.

(5) A loss contingency that has a remote chance of resulting in an actual loss should be disclosed in a company's financial statement footnotes.

(6) Because the liability is already recorded, no journal entries are needed when a long-term debt becomes due within one year.

(7) Specific assets of the issuing company are used as collateral for secured bonds.

(8) When a business leases an asset under conditions that are comparable to purchasing that asset with borrowed funds, both the leased asset and the long-term lease obligation must be reported on the firm's balance sheet.

(9) A common restrictive debt covenant is a limitation on the payment of dividends.

(10) Financial decision makers generally do not consider the possibility that a company has intentionally overstated its current liabilities.

(11) A common measure of financial leverage is the long-term debt to current liability ratio.

(12) Defined contribution retirement plans specify the amounts to be paid to employees after retirement.

14. **Liability Classification** *(LO 7.1, ethics)*

Hamilton's Bakery borrowed $50,000 on January 1, 1999. Hamilton's is required to repay $5,000 of the loan principal on December 31 of each year, beginning in 1999. In addition, 10 percent interest on the unpaid principal must be paid on January 1 of each year, beginning in 2000.

Required:

(1) How will this debt be reported in Hamilton's December 31, 2003, balance sheet? How much interest expense related to this debt will be reported in Hamilton's income statement for the year ended December 31, 2003?

(2) How will this debt be reported in Hamilton's December 31, 2004, balance sheet?

(3) If Hamilton's fails to classify any portion of the loan as a current liability in its December 31, 2004, balance sheet, how might decision makers' analysis of the company's financial statements be affected? Explain.

15. **Liabilities on the Balance Sheet** *(LO 7.1)*

The liabilities of Weist Co. are listed below.

(a) Accounts Payable, $298,000

(b) Accrued Expenses, $510,000

(c) Bonds Payable, $700,000

(d) Income Taxes Payable, $272,000

(e) Notes Payable: $78,000 is due within 12 months; $400,000 is due $100,000 per year for the following 4 years.

(f) Salaries Payable, $145,000

(g) Vacation Earned, $208,000

Required:

Prepare the liabilities section of the balance sheet for Weist Co.

16. **Accounting for Current Liabilities** *(LO 7.1, writing)*

FreeWheelers is a bike shop located near the campus of the University of Tennessee. FreeWheelers rents bikes on a nine-month basis. When a bike is rented, the student pays a security deposit equal to 50 percent of the bike's value. Typically, a bike is returned damaged in some way, causing some portion of the security deposit to be forfeited. When a security deposit is received, FreeWheelers' accountant debits Cash and credits Miscellaneous Revenue. If a bike is returned damaged, the accountant debits Repairs Expense and credits Cash or another appropriate account when the bike is repaired. Any portion of the deposit that is not required to repair the bike is returned to the student. Deposit amounts returned to students are recorded with a debit to Miscellaneous Expense and a credit to Cash.

Required:

Write a brief memo to FreeWheelers' accountant regarding the accounting treatment given security deposits on bike rentals. Explain why the current accounting treatment is incorrect and how it may introduce errors into the business's financial statements. Also recommend a more appropriate method of accounting for security deposits.

17. **Notes Payable** *(LO 7.1)*

Three notes payable are listed below. Each note requires that the principal and all of the interest will be repaid on the maturity date. All companies have a December 31 fiscal year end.

(a) On January 1, 2004, Alpha, Inc. borrowed $3,600 on a six-month, 10% note.

(b) On March 31, 2004, Beta Co. borrowed $12,000 on a one-year, 12% note.

(c) On August 1, 2004, Gamma Industries borrowed $3,000 on a two-year, 9% note.

(d) On November 30, 2004, Sigma, Inc. borrowed $2,000 on a six-month, 9% note.

Required:

(1) For each note, determine the following:

(a) Maturity date

(b) Maturity value

(c) Interest accrued on December 31, 2004

(d) Interest accrued on December 31, 2005

(2) Which notes will be listed on the 2004 balance sheet as

(a) current liabilities?

(b) long-term liabilities?

18. **Installment Notes Payable** *(LO 7.1)*

You are planning to purchase a new car as your graduation present to yourself. The car you want can be purchased for $26,500 plus tax, title, and license, which will total

$2,500. You plan to finance the car over five years. Use a loan calculator to determine your car payments under the following assumptions.

Required:

(1) You make a $4,000 down payment and can obtain a loan rate for the balance at
   (a) 6.5 percent.
   (b) 5.8 percent.
   (c) 5.0 percent.

(2) You make a $1,500 down payment and can obtain a loan rate for the balance at
   (a) 6.5 percent.
   (b) 5.8 percent.
   (c) 5.0 percent.

(3) Assume instead that you decide to finance the car over four years and can make a $4,000 down payment. What are your car payments if you can obtain a loan rate for the balance at
   (a) 6.5 percent?
   (b) 5.8 percent?
   (c) 5.0 percent?

19. **Payroll Accounting** *(LO 7.1)*

Khalid Company pays its employees every two weeks. The firm last paid its employees on September 20. For the last ten days of the fiscal year ending September 30, company employees earned gross salaries of $8,200. Following is a list of employee payroll deductions for the period September 21–30:

	Employee Payroll Deductions
FICA Taxes	$ 627
Federal Income Taxes	2,010
State Income Taxes	311
Health Insurance Premiums	225

Required:

(1) Prepare the adjusting journal entry required on September 30 related to employee salaries and payroll deductions.

(2) What payroll-related expenses do businesses incur besides employee wages and salaries?

(3) If a person works as an "independent contractor," employers are not required to deduct income taxes from wages. If you had your choice, would you prefer to work for a company that did or did not deduct income taxes from periodic paychecks? Explain the reasons for your answer.

20. **Recording Warranty Expense** *(LO 7.1)*

The bikes sold by Cross Country Bikes carry a one-year warranty on parts and labor. However, the company expects very few warranty claims. Last year, the company sold 200 bikes and made warranty repairs on three bikes at a total cost of approximately $500.

Required:

(1) If Cross Country Bikes does not record a product warranty liability at the end of each fiscal year, how will the business's financial statements be affected? What accounting concepts or principles will be violated?

(2) Under what condition or conditions could Cross Country Bikes reasonably argue that no product warranty liability needs to be recorded at year-end?

(3) Would the argument you made in part (2) be appropriate for Ford Motor Company? Why or why not?

21. **Accounting for Contingent Liabilities** *(LO 7.2)*

Saddleback Sporting Goods, Inc. manufactures and sells a unique recreational footwear product, a convertible ice skate/roller blade. Periodically, the company is sued because someone using this product is injured. Saddleback is currently the defendant in one such lawsuit. Damages requested by the plaintiff in this lawsuit total $2,400,000. The company's net income for its fiscal year just ended was $460,000 and year-end total assets were $1,232,000.

Required:

(1) What factors should Saddleback consider in determining the accounting and financial statement treatment of this lawsuit?

(2) In reference to the pending lawsuit against Saddleback, identify the conditions under which:

   (a) Saddleback would record an expense and a liability in its accounting records.

   (b) Saddleback would disclose the lawsuit in the footnotes to its financial statements.

   (c) Saddleback would ignore the lawsuit for accounting and financial reporting purposes.

22. **Bond Terminology** *(LO 7.3)*

Following are definitions or descriptions of terms relating to corporate bonds.

   (a) A bond that may be exchanged for stock in the issuing company.

   (b) A long-term loan made by one party to another.

   (c) The legal instrument documenting a bond.

   (d) The typical amount for corporate bonds is $1,000.

   (e) A bond backed only by the legal commitment of the issuing company to make all required principal and interest payments.

   (f) The point at which the bond principal is repaid.

   (g) A bond collateralized by specific assets of the issuing company.

   (h) The legal contract between a bond purchaser and the issuing company.

   (i) The period between the date bonds are first available for sale and the date they mature.

   (j) The rate of interest to be paid to bondholders based on the face value of the bonds.

Required:

Match each definition or description listed with the appropriate term from the following list.

(1) Bond

(2) Face value

(3) Maturity date

(4) Bond indenture

(5) Stated interest rate

(6) Bond term

(7) Bond certificate

(8) Secured bonds

(9) Convertible bond
(10) Debenture

23. **Stated Interest Rate and the Market Interest Rate** *(LO 7.3)*

A $1,000 corporate bond has a stated interest rate of 8 percent. Interest on the bond is paid semiannually.

Required:

(1) How much interest will be paid on each interest payment date?
(2) Suppose this bond was sold when the quoted market price was 98. How much did the company receive for the bond? If a bond is sold for more or less than its face value of a bond, will the amount of interest the company must pay each semiannual period be affected? Explain.
(3) If this bond was sold at a quoted market price of 98, was the market interest rate on the purchase date higher or lower than the bond's stated interest rate? Explain.
(4) How much will the purchaser of this bond receive on the maturity day as repayment of his or her principal?

24. **Selected Long-term Liabilities in Corporate Balance Sheets** *(LO 7.5, writing)*

You have been asked to write a term paper on the nature of large corporations. One aspect you are supposed to cover is how corporations finance their operations. You have found the following long-term liabilities, and related information, in recent corporate balance sheets.

(a) Eight-percent Convertible Debentures Due April 15, 2011—$19,975,000: These debentures were included in a balance sheet of Quixote Corporation, a firm in the computer industry.
(b) Accrued Pension Costs—$12,265,000: Hormel Foods Corporation, which reported this long-term liability, manufactures and markets prepared food products.
(c) Unearned Portion of Paid Subscriptions—$2,700,000,000: This item was a long-term liability of AOL Time Warner, which, among other lines of business, publishes Time, People, and Sports Illustrated.
(d) Mortgages on Property, Plant & Equipment—$4,952,000: This item is a long-term liability of Tuesday Morning Corporation, a discount retailer.

Required:

Begin your report with a brief overview of the nature of liabilities and the general types of long-term liabilities. Next, provide a brief description of the nature and source of each of the long-term liabilities identified. Include in these descriptions how each liability is related, or likely related if you are unsure, to the given company's profit-oriented activities.

25. **Defined Benefit Pension Plan** *(LO 7.5)*

You will be retiring in three years and the company has just instituted a pension plan. Because of your long history with the firm, you have been promised a lump-sum payment of $75,000 on December 31, 2005. The company will make payments to the plan December 31, 2003 through 2005. Pension plan assets are expected to earn 8 percent during 2004 and 2005.

Required:

(1) Assume the company is correct in its assumed rate of return and it wants to make equal pension contributions each year. Rounded to the nearest dollar, how much will the company need to contribute to the plan at the end of each year? Show your calculations.

(2) The company makes the contribution determined in part (1) on December 31, 2003. If the actual rate of return on the plan assets during 2004 is 5 percent, how much in total 2004 and 2005 contributions and interest will be needed for you to receive your promised pension plan benefit at the end of 2005? Projected return is still 8%.

26. **Analyzing Corporate Liabilities** *(LO 7.7, Excel)*

Listed in the following schedule are the current assets and current liabilities of the Laoretti Company for the firm's fiscal years ending December 31, 2002 and 2003.

	December 31	
	2002	2003
Cash and Cash Equivalents	$ 54,817	$ 48,902
Accounts Receivable	63,295	59,748
Inventories	116,528	121,277
Other Current Assets	18,605	15,691
Total Current Assets	$253,245	$245,618
Accounts Payable	$ 71,430	$ 73,819
Accrued Payroll Liabilities	26,608	28,456
Income Taxes Payable	12,089	11,572
Total Current Liabilities	$110,127	$113,847

Required:

(1) Determine this company's working capital and current ratio as of December 31, 2002 and 2003.

(2) Did the company's liquidity improve or weaken between the end of 2002 and the end of 2003? Explain.

27. **(Appendix) Accounting for Bonds** *(LO 7.8)*

Emmerling, Inc. is planning a $1,000,000 bond issue. The bonds will carry an 8 percent interest, pay interest semiannually, and mature in 10 years.

Required:

(1) If the market rate of interest at the date of issue is 6 percent, what will be the bond issue price?

(2) If the market rate of interest at the date of issue is 10 percent, what will be the bond issue price? Does the bond sell at a premium or a discount?

(3) Using your answer from part (2), how much premium or discount will be amortized each interest period?

PROBLEMS

28. **Accounting for an Interest-Bearing Note Payable** *(LO 7.1)*

On April 1, the Canadian River Racing Club (CRRC) purchased ten racing bikes with a cash price of $750 each. CRRC offered to pay for the bikes by making a $2,000 down payment and by signing a $5,500, 8 percent interest-bearing note. The interest and principal on this note would be due in one year.

Required:

(1) Prepare the appropriate journal entries in the accounting records of CRRC on the following dates:

(a) April 1, the date the sales agreement is finalized.

(b) December 31, the final day of CRRC's fiscal year.

(c) April 1 of the following year, when the note matures.

(2) Suppose that CRRC does not make an entry pertaining to this note payable in its accounting records on December 31. How will this oversight affect CRRC's financial statements for the year ending December 31? For the following year?

29. **Accounting for a Product Warranty Liability** *(LO 7.1)*

Cool Air, Inc. sells products with a one-year warranty covering parts and labor. The following table lists the company's three major product lines, the percentage of the products sold in each product line that are returned while under warranty, and the average warranty-related cost incurred on each returned item.

Product Line	Air Conditioners	Air Compressors	Fans
Percentage of products returned while under warranty	8%	6%	3%
Warranty cost per returned item	$120	$50	$18
Unit sales during April	2,400	1,650	1,500

Required:

(1) Compute the estimated product warranty expense that should be recorded by Cool Air at the end of April and prepare the appropriate adjusting entry.

(2) During the first week in May, Cool Air pays warranty-related costs of $7,100. Prepare the entry to record these payments.

30. **Employee Liabilities** *(LO 7.1)*

Weston Smith, Inc.'s hourly employees normally work eight hours a day, five days a week. Employees who work this schedule every week for 50 weeks earn two weeks of paid vacation. The company's four hourly employees are listed below along with information about the two-week pay period that ended on Friday, April 30. Employees will be paid on the following Monday. April 30 is Weston Smith's fiscal year end.

Employee	Hours Worked	Hourly Wage	Gross Pay	Federal Income Tax	State Income Tax	FICA	Insurance Premium
Adams	80	$10.00	$ 800	$196	$56	$61.20	$ 0
Beatty	72	12.00	864	188	42	66.10	58
Collins	80	12.50	1,000	240	75	6.50	116
Donnovan	80	12.75	1,020	211	70	78.03	58

Required:

(1) Calculate net pay for each employee.

(2) Prepare the journal entry to record this payroll.

(3) Regarding Weston Smith's vacation plan,

(a) How many hours do Weston Smith's employees work during a year?

(b) How many hours of vacation do the employees earn if they work the full 50 weeks?

(c) How many hours does an employee have to work to earn one hour of vacation?

(d) What is the value of the vacation earned during the pay-period ending April 30?

(e) Prepare the journal entry to record the accrual of the vacation pay.

31. **Deferred Liabilities** *(LO 7.1)*

Steel Tip Monthly is a magazine for dart enthusiasts. The magazine currently has 500 subscribers who have paid $36 per year for the publication. During the week ending July 3, the magazine sold 30 annual subscriptions at a cost of $36 each. The magazine is mailed on the first of each month.

Required:

(1) Prepare the journal entry to record the subscriptions for the week of July 3.

(2) What journal entry should the magazine make on August 1?

(3) On December 31, *Steel Tip Monthly* went out of business. At that time, the magazine owed 2,134 magazines to its customers. Prepare the journal entry necessary to refund the subscriber's payments.

32. **Bonds** *(LO 7.3)*

Velmar Production Company is issuing 10-year bonds with a $1,000 face value with a 10 percent interest rate, paid annually.

Required:

(1) How much cash interest will an investor receive in a year?

(2) Prepare the journal entry to issue the bonds if they are issued at

  (a) 100.

  (b) 98.

  (c) 101.

(3) For items (a), (b), and (c) in part (2), indicate whether the bonds were sold at a premium, discount, or face value and what that means about the relationship between the stated rate of interest and the market rate or interest.

(4) For items (a), (b), and (c) in part (2), how much will an investor receive at maturity?

33. **Mortgage Payable** *(LO 7.4, Internet)*

Portland College is planning to purchase a home for its president in downtown Albuquerque. One property, with a selling price of $280,000 has been found and the college treasurer is debating on the following purchase options:

Option A: Make a 20 percent down payment and finance the balance over 15 years at 8 percent.

Option B: Make a 20 percent down payment and finance the balance over 30 years at 8 percent.

Option C: Make a 30 percent down payment and finance the balance over 15 years at 6.5 percent.

Option D: Make a 30 percent down payment and finance the balance over 30 years at 6.5 percent.

Required:

(1) Use a mortgage calculator (such as www.mortgage-calc.com) to find the monthly payments for each option.

(2) What is the total interest paid for the mortgage under each of the options?

(3) If either of the 20 percent down options is chosen, the college can invest the other 10% ($28,000) in a certificate of deposit for either 15 or 30 years at an annual rate of 7 percent. Which of the options should the college choose to minimize the total cost of the house?

34. **Analyzing Current Liabilities** *(LO 7.7)*

Listed in the following schedule are the current assets and current liabilities of Ray Department Stores Company for the firm's fiscal years ending in February for two recent years. Dollars are presented in millions.

	December 31	
	Year 1	**Year 2**
Cash	$ 20	$ 17
Cash equivalents	32	139
Accounts receivable, net	1,938	2,081
Merchandise inventories	60	95
Total Current Assets	$4,925	$5,270
Short-term debt	$ 78	$ 0
Current maturities of long-term debt	255	85
Accounts payable	1,023	965
Accrued expenses	910	871
Income taxes payable	119	93
Total Current Liabilities	$2,538	$2,214

Required:

(1) Determine Ray's working capital and current ratio as of the year-end for Year 1 and Year 2.

(2) Did the company's liquidity improve or weaken between the end of Year 1 and the end of Year 2? Explain.

35. **Analyzing Long-term Liabilities** *(LO 7.7, Excel)*

Listed in the following schedule are selected financial data for 2002 and 2003 for Onken Company, a leading firm in the packaging industry. Amounts are expressed in millions.

	2002	**2003**
Total Assets	$4,781.3	$5,051.7
Current Assets	1,605.6	1,708.9
Current Liabilities	1,483.0	1,279.0
Long-Term Debt	1,089.5	1,490.1
Stockholders' Equity	1,365.2	1,461.2
Interest Expense	98.8	148.6
Income Taxes Expense	55.6	24.9
Net Income	31.0	74.9

Required:

(1) Compute Onken's long-term debt to equity and times interest earned ratios for Year 1 and Year 2.

(2) How did the company's interest coverage change over this two-year period?

36. Analyzing Long-term Liabilities *(LO 7.7)*

Randazzo Casinos is a Las Vegas–based firm that owns and operates casinos and other gaming operations. The following financial information was obtained from the company's 2002 and 2003 financial statements. Amounts are expressed in thousands.

	2002	**2003**
Total Assets	$185,110	$301,486
Long-Term Debt	121,792	161,302
Stockholders' Equity	37,153	95,791
Interest Expense	8,949	9,179
Income Taxes Expense	4,806	6,100
Net Income	9,417	11,840

In the company's annual report, executives discussed aggressive future expansion plans. Following are specific comments addressing the issue of how and whether the company would be able to finance these plans.

> *The company's plans to develop new gaming opportunities and expand existing operations will require substantial amounts of additional capital. There is no assurance at this time that such financing is or will be available to the company or, if available, that the financing would be on favorable payment terms.*

Required:

(1) Compute Randazzo Casinos' long-term debt to equity and times interest earned ratios for 2002 and 2003. Did these ratios improve or weaken between the end of 2002 and the end of 2003?

(2) Considering the financial data presented for the company, what factor was apparently most responsible for the significant change in the company's long-term debt to equity ratio between the end of 2002 and the end of 2003? Explain.

(3) Suppose that the average long-term debt to equity ratio for the gaming industry is 50 percent and that the average times interest earned ratio is 4.5. Evaluate Randazzo Casinos' ratios in reference to these industry norms.

(4) What purpose is served by the narrative disclosures in the company's annual report regarding the potential need for additional capital and related information?

37. (Appendix) Accounting for Bonds Payable *(LO 7.8)*

Edmonton Corporation issued $20,000,000 of five-year, 8 percent bonds on May 1, 2002. Interest payment dates are May 1 and November 1 of each year. Edmonton uses straight-line amortization for any bond premium or discount and has a December 31 fiscal year-end.

Required:

(1) Determine the total proceeds Edmonton received from the sale of these bonds, assuming that the market interest rate for similar bonds on May 1, 2002, was

  (a) 6%.

  (b) 10%.

(2) Prepare the appropriate journal entries on the following dates for each assumption listed in part (1).

  (a) May 1, 2002

(b) November 1, 2002
(c) December 31, 2002
(d May 1, 2003

(3) For each assumption listed in part (1), determine the carrying value of the bonds as of December 31, 2002.

CASES

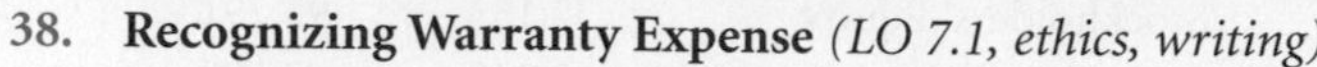

38. **Recognizing Warranty Expense** *(LO 7.1, ethics, writing)*

Warsaw Technologies, Inc. manufactures modems and disk drives. Warsaw's current year's revenues are nearly 20 percent below those of last year. As year-end approaches, the company president has instructed the accounting department not to record a December 31 adjusting entry for warranty expense on products sold during the year. "We can recognize that expense next year when we actually pay those costs. That makes more sense anyway. Why go to the trouble of estimating additional expenses at year-end? We have more than enough of the real thing."

Required:

Write a memo to Warsaw's president explaining why it is necessary to recognize estimated warranty expense at the end of an accounting period. In your memo, point out how the company's financial statements will be misleading if this expense is not recorded.

39. **Accounting for Contingent Liabilities** *(LO 7.2)*

Consider the following three scenarios involving publicly owned companies in the United States.

(a) One of the four wholly-owned subsidiaries of Option Plastics, Inc., is located in a small South American country. Recent elections in the country have brought to power a political party that intends to nationalize all major businesses. The new president has indicated that the government will pay a "reasonable price" for these businesses. The manager of the South American subsidiary estimates that Option Plastics will suffer a loss of between \$4 million and \$6 million when the government buys out the subsidiary sometime in the next two years.

(b) Charles Ironworks has just been slapped with a \$5.5 million fine by the Environmental Protection Agency (EPA). The company's legal counsel intends to contest the fine. When asked to evaluate the likelihood of overturning the EPA fine, the company's chief legal counsel responded, "I think there's a 50-50 chance that we can get the fine reduced. But I have no idea if we can reduce the fine by \$2 or by \$2 million."

(c) Joy's Toys manufactures a wide range of toys designed for children one-to-four years of age. This past week, a competitor, Gaver Corporation, sued Joy's Toys for \$17.2 million. The suit alleges that Joy's Toys infringed on a patent that Gaver holds on a popular toy. In a press release, the chief executive of Joy's Toys observed, "This suit is complete nonsense. Gaver knows that we haven't infringed on its patent. All this company is trying to do is harass us and damage our reputation."

Required:

(1) Evaluate each of the three scenarios in reference to the accounting and financial reporting guidelines for contingent liabilities. How would you recommend that

these items be accounted for and/or reported in each firm's financial statements? Support your recommendation for each scenario.

(2) Do companies have an incentive to intentionally downplay the significance of contingent liabilities and thus exclude them from their financial statements? Explain. If such an exclusion occurs, how are decision makers who rely on financial statement data affected?

40. Retirement of Bonds Payable *(LO 7.3, writing)*

CookieTown Industries has a $10 million bond payable outstanding. The bonds were sold on February 1, 1995 with a ten-year term and a stated interest rate of 12 percent. Bond interest is paid semiannually on February 1 and August 1. The bonds have a current carrying value of $9,877,000.

If CookieTown sold bonds in today's market, the company would be required to pay annual interest of only 9 percent. Consequently, the company's management wants to retire its outstanding bonds and sell new bonds. The current market price of CookieTown's bonds is 122 1/4.

Required:

(1) At the present market price, how much will it cost CookieTown to purchase all of its outstanding bonds? What factor or factors may account for the difference between the collective market price and carrying value of CookieTown's bonds?

(2) Suppose that CookieTown purchases and immediately retires the bonds. Prepare the appropriate journal entry to record this transaction.

(3) What stipulation could have been included in the bond indenture that would have allowed the company to retire the bonds without being forced to purchase them in the open market?

41. Current Ratio and Working Capital *(LO 7.7)*

Charlotte Foods Corporation manufactures and distributes prepared foods. Slidell, Inc. operates more than 300 restaurants located in 19 states. The following schedule lists the year-end current assets and current liabilities of these two firms for 2002 and 2003. Dollars are presented in thousands.

Charlotte Foods Corporation	**2002**	**2003**
Cash and Cash Equivalents	$157,558	$248,599
Short-term Marketable Securities	14,862	11,360
Accounts Receivable	218,487	228,369
Inventories	220,494	213,456
Prepaid Expenses	8,503	6,431
Total Current Assets	$619,904	$708,215
Accounts Payable	$ 98,357	$112,851
Accrued Liabilities	30,212	29,320
Accrued Advertising	24,587	31,863
Employee Compensation	40,195	41,989
State and Local Taxes	14,011	17,606
Dividends Payable	8,434	9,585
Federal Income Taxes	11,262	21,303
Current Portion of Long-term Debt	0	400
Total Current Liabilities	$227,058	$264,917

Slidell Inc.	**2002**	**2003**
Cash	$ 8,241	$ 6,699
Investments	1,947	1,399
Accounts Receivable	12,545	15,445
Inventories	19,063	20,384
Prepaid Expenses	3,371	3,514
Total Current Assets	$45,167	$47,441
Line of Credit	0	9,500
Accounts Payable	9,530	12,200
Dividends Payable	2,618	2,839
Federal and State Taxes	7,597	6,160
Accrued Wages and Fringe Benefits	10,163	10,830
Other Accrued Liabilities	17,185	18,023
Total Current Liabilities	$47,093	$59,552

Required:

(1) Compute the following items for both companies for 2002 and 2003:
   (a) Working capital
   (b) Current ratio
   (c) Quick ratio

(2) Given the data computed in part (1), which of these two companies had the stronger liquidity at the end of 2002 and at the end of 2003? Why?

(3) In your opinion, which of the three measures that you computed in part (1) is the best measure of liquidity? Explain.

(4) Review the data presented for each company. Are there any unusual items or unusual relationships in either company's data that a decision maker might want to investigate further? If so, identify these items and the issues or questions that decision makers would likely raise.

42. **Analyzing Liabilities** *(LO 7.7, Internet, Excel)*

Use the annual report of Carnival Corporation (www.carnival.com) for the 2001 fiscal year to answer the following questions.

Required:

(1) Calculate the following ratios and measurements for Carnival for the years 2000 and 2001. Comment on changes from year to year and what each ratio means for Carnival.
   (a) Current ratio
   (b) Working capital
   (c) Debt to total assets
   (d) Long-term debt to equity
   (e) Times interest earned

(2) Does Carnival have any contingent liabilities? If so, how does the company handle the accounting of such liabilities? Where did you find this information?

(3) What kind of retirement plan does Carnival have for its employees?

(4) What portion of Carnival's long-term debt is due in the next fiscal year?

(5) Does Carnival lease any assets? If so, how does the company account for such leases?

(6) Is Carnival currently financing its operations through the use of bonds? If so, to what extent? If not, what other methods might the company use to finance operations?

43. **Comparing Companies** *(LO 7.7, group, Internet)*

Identifying the similarities and differences between companies is as crucial to making investment decisions as understanding a single company's financial statements. Form groups of at least four students. Each group should select a single industry. Each group member should locate a different annual report within that industry. (The industry and individual company may be assigned by your instructor.)

Required—individual group members:

(1) Calculate the following ratios/measures for the company you selected for the two most recent fiscal years.
   (a) Current ratio
   (b) Working capital
   (c) Debt to total assets
   (d) Long-term debt to equity
   (e) Times interest earned

(2) What percentage of total assets is accounted for by each of the following:
   (a) Current liabilities
   (b) Long-term liabilities
   (c) Stockholders' equity (not including retained earnings)
   (d) Retained earnings

   Create a pie chart to depict these proportions (should total 100%). In one or two sentences, explain what is meant by each portion of the pie.

Required—groups:

(3) Compile the ratio calculations from part (1) for each company prepared by the individual group members into one table. Compare the results from company to company in the same fiscal year. Include in your comparison a graphical analysis. Discuss reasons why these ratios might be similar or different within an industry.

(4) Calculate an average for the five ratios that depicts the industry you are examining.

(5) Compare your pie charts from part (2) and develop a pie chart for the industry average. How do the industry average ratios calculated in part (4) compare to the industry average pie chart?

Required—class:

(6) Compare the ratios from each industry. Discuss reasons why these ratios might be similar or different between industries.

(7) Does one industry seem to be a better investment than another? Do you think this situation is constant over time? Why or why not?

SUPPLEMENTAL PROBLEMS

44. **Accounting for Interest-Bearing Note Payable** *(LO 7.1)* [Compare to Problem 28]

Regier Homebuilders, which has a calendar year-end, borrowed $10,000 from a local bank on October 2. On that date, Regier's chief executive signed a 10 percent, 180-day interest-bearing promissory note.

Required:

Prepare the appropriate journal entries in Regier's accounting records on the following dates:

(a) October 2
(b) December 31
(c) March 31 of the next year

45. **Accounting for a Product Warranty Liability** *(LO 7.1)* [Compare to Problem 29]

Lawn Ranger Manufacturing makes lawn care products that are sold with a one-year warranty covering parts and labor. The following table lists the percentage of products that are returned while under warranty, average warranty-related cost incurred on each returned item, and sales per product line for March.

Product Line	Edgers	Push Mowers	Riding Mowers
Percentage of products returned while under warranty	1%	4%	3%
Warranty cost per returned item	$40	$90	$170
Unit sales during March	3,400	2,820	1,900

Required:

(1) Compute the estimated product warranty expense that should be recorded by Lawn Ranger at the end of March and prepare the appropriate March 31 adjusting entry.

(2) Suppose that during the first week of June, the company incurs warranty-related costs of $1,800 in inventory parts and $400 for labor. The labor costs will be paid on June 15. Prepare the entry to record the warranty costs.

46. **Payroll and Vacation** *(LO 7.1)* [Compare to Problem 30]

McDeal Corporation has six salaried employees who are paid every two weeks and are given two weeks of paid vacation per year. The following payroll information is available for the two-week period ended October 31, 2004.

Gross Pay	$30,000
FICA Taxes	2,295
Federal Income Taxes	7,353
State Income Taxes	1,138
Health Insurance Premiums	1,000

Required:

(1) Prepare the October 31 journal entry to record this payroll.
(2) Prepare the October 31 journal entry to record the accrual of vacation pay.
(3) Prepare the journal entry to pay the employees on November 3.

47. **Deferred Liabilities** *(LO 7.1)* [Compare to Problem 31]

During May 2004, its first month of operation, Pizza Palace sold 200 coupon books for $20 each. The books contain 4 coupons, each of which can be exchanged for a large pizza.

Required:

(1) What journal entry would Pizza Palace make for the sale of the 200 coupon books?

(2) During the week of June 8, 27 coupons were redeemed. Prepare the journal entry to account for the exchange of the coupons for pizzas.

(3) Pizza Palace prepares quarterly financial statements. At the end of the third quarter on January 31, 2005, 67 coupons remained unredeemed. How should these coupon books be presented on Pizza Palace's financial statements?

48. Analyzing Long-Term Liabilities *(LO 7.7)* [Compare to Problem 35]

The following information for Kirsten Corp. has been obtained from the company's 2002 and 2003 financial statements.

	2002	2003
Total Assets	$1,218,302	$1,328,496
Current Assets	666,135	753,580
Total Stockholders' Equity	604,215	675,322
Long-term Debt	226,279	287,837
Net Income	81,584	99,586
Interest Expense	10,203	13,985
Income Taxes Expense	28,578	42,680

Required:

(1) Kirsten Corp. has applied for a $50 million long-term loan from Lowell Bank. Thomas Manufacturing is considering purchasing 10,000 shares of Kirsten's common stock. Would Lowell Bank or Thomas Manufacturing be more likely to be interested in evaluating Kirsten's financial leverage? Explain your choice.

(2) Compute Kirsten's long-term debt to equity ratio in 2002 and 2003. Did the company become more or less leveraged between the end of 2002 and the end of 2003?

(3) Compute Kirsten's times interest earned ratio in both 2002 and 2003. Did this ratio improve or deteriorate between the end of 2002 and the end of 2003? Explain.

49. (Appendix) Accounting for Bonds Payable *(LO 7.8)* [Compare to Problem 37]

When Paris, Inc. issued $5,000,000 of ten-year, 12 percent bonds on September 1, 2002; the market interest rate was 9 percent. The bonds pay interest semiannually on March 1 and September 1. Paris, Inc. has a calendar year-end and amortizes bond discounts or premiums using the straight-line method.

Required:

(1) Determine the present value (or issue price) of these bonds.

(2) Prepare the journal entries related to the bonds on the following dates:

(a) September 1, 2002

(b) December 31, 2002

(c) March 1, 2003

(d) September 1, 2003

(3) What is the carrying value of the bonds as of September 2, 2002?

(4) Claude Wood had originally purchased $1,200,000 of the Paris, Inc. bonds on September 1, 2002. Use present value calculations to determine what Claude paid for his portion of the bonds. If Claude sells his bonds to Lily Putian on February 16, 2006, what journal entry will Paris, Inc. make at that time? Explain your answer.

(5) Assume the market rate of interest at the date of issue had been 14 percent. What would the bond-selling price have been?

CHAPTER 8

Stockholders' Equity

LEARNING OBJECTIVES

1. Describe the important characteristics, advantages, and disadvantages of a corporation.
2. Identify the key rights and privileges of common and preferred stockholders.
3. Account for the issuance of corporate stock.
4. Account for treasury stock transactions, cash and stock dividends, and stock splits.
5. Understand how Retained Earnings is affected by net income (loss), dividends, and prior period adjustments.
6. Prepare a statement of stockholders' equity.
7. Define the key information needs of decision makers regarding stockholders' equity, including dividend yield and return on equity.

Darden Restaurants

Darden Restaurants, Inc. (www.darden.com) operates under four concept names: Red Lobster, Olive Garden, Bahama Breeze, and Smokey Bones BBQ Sports Bar. The company, headquartered in Orlando and listed on the New York Stock Exchange, has restaurants in 49 states and in Canada.

As of year-end 2001, Darden Restaurants had 25,000 shares of authorized no-par value preferred stock and 500,000 shares of no-par value common stock. At that time, the company had issued none of the preferred stock and only 169,000+ shares of its common stock. Almost 52,000 shares of Darden's common stock had been repurchased by the company and was being held as treasury stock. During fiscal year 2001, Darden paid approximately $9.5 million in dividends to its stockholders. On March 21, 2002, the company declared a $0.04 per share dividend to be paid on May 1, 2002, to shareholders of record on April 10, 2002. Darden also reported that its Board of Directors approved a 3-for-2 stock split to shareholders of record as of the close of business on April 10, 2002, with a payable date of May 1, 2002.

SOURCE: Darden Restaurants, *2001 Annual Report* and press releases.

INTRODUCTION

Businesses needing to raise substantial funds to build a factory, buy another company, or establish a foreign subsidiary have two principal financing alternatives. The companies can raise debt capital by borrowing funds (resulting in increased liabilities), or they can raise equity capital by selling ownership interest to outside parties (resulting in increased stockholders' equity). Corporations raise equity capital by selling common or preferred stock. This chapter focuses on the accounting issues and rules related to the stockholders' equity of corporations, and begins with an overview of the corporate form of business organization. Next, the accounting procedures for common stockholders' equity transactions are provided along with a discussion of the Retained Earnings account. The end of the chapter addresses the information needs of decision makers regarding stockholders' equity, followed by illustrations of three key financial ratios related to stockholders' equity.

THE CORPORATION

Most corporations are not large entities such as Darden Restaurants, Inc. or Marriott International, Inc. (www.marriott.com). Many corporations are small and closely-held, with the ownership often retained by members of the same family and with the stock not traded on a public exchange. This text, however, focuses on the large, publicly traded corporations.

Chapter 1 defines a corporation as an association of individuals, created by law and having an existence apart from that of its owners. In the United States, when business owners decide to incorporate, they should first investigate the different corporate laws and taxes in the various states. Once a state of incorporation is selected, the company files articles of incorporation that identify, among other things, the business's purpose, its principal operating units, and the type and quantity of stock that it plans to issue. If all legal requirements are met, the state agency grants the business a **corporate charter** or a contract between a corporation and the state in which it was created and identifies the corporation's principal rights and obligations.

Some corporations choose not to incorporate in the United States or to reincorporate out of the United States (oftentimes to Bermuda and the Cayman Islands) after years of being in business.[1] The primary reason for such choices or moves focuses on minimizing income tax liabilities. However, in mid-2002, the United States Congress began drafting new legislation to eliminate tax benefits of "sham" relocations and to possibly deny "federal contracts to American multinationals that relocate offshore to avoid U.S. taxes."[2] Some of the legislation has been referred to as REPO (Reversing the Expatriation of Profits Offshore), which would treat "tax inverted U.S. companies as if they were still incorporated in the States."[3]

The proposed legislation is getting corporate reaction. On May 9, 2002, The Stanley Works (www.stanleyworks.com), a Connecticut manufacturer of tools and hardware products, stated that shareholders had overwhelmingly approved a plan to reincorporate in Bermuda. However, a revote was taken by shareholders and, on August 1, 2002, the company withdrew the relocation proposal.[4] The corporate Internet site indicated "there are no plans to move any business operations there."[5]

Key Advantages of the Corporation

Corporations have several advantages over sole proprietorships and partnerships. One important advantage is the limited liability of corporate stockholders. In practically all cases, the maximum amount a stockholder may lose if a corporation becomes bankrupt is his or her original investment amount. The firm's unpaid debts cannot be recovered from stockholders' personal assets. In contrast, if a sole proprietorship or partnership goes out of business without paying all of its debts, the owner or each partner is *individually* responsible for those debts.

Unlike sole proprietorships and partnerships, the legal existence of a corporation is unaffected by the death or withdrawal of individual owners. The ownership interest of corporate stockholders who die passes directly to their estate or heirs. A partnership must be dissolved when one partner leaves the firm—although the remaining partners have the option of immediately forming a new partnership without any cessation of business.

Transferring ownership interest in a publicly held corporation is easy because stockholders can generally sell their shares to anyone without the prior approval of the other owners. In a partnership, the other firm members must approve of ownership transfers.

Corporations can usually raise debt and equity capital more readily and in larger amounts than unincorporated businesses. Even small corporations can raise large amounts of capital very quickly by selling stock on a nationwide basis through an IPO (initial public offering).

---

[1] The process of reincorporating in a tax haven is called inversion.

[2] David Rogers, "Bill Gains to Ban U.S. Contracts to Firms Moving to Tax Havens," *Wall Street Journal* (July 10, 2002), p. A4.

[3] Tim Reason," Love it and Leave It?" *CFO* (July 2002), pp. 39ff.

[4] The Stanley Works press release, "Stanley Works Withdraws Re-incorporation Plans," August 1, 2002.

[5] Curt Anderson, "'Shell' Corporations Facing Scrutiny," *The [New Orleans] Times-Picayune* (March 14, 2002), p. C-8.

Key Disadvantages of the Corporation

There are also disadvantages to incorporating a business. The key disadvantage posed by the corporate form of business is the double taxation of corporate profits. Corporations are considered taxable entities, meaning that they must pay income taxes on their annual earnings. These profits are taxed again when corporations distribute earnings as cash dividends to stockholders who must report the dividends as income on personal tax returns. Incomes of sole proprietorships, partnerships, and closely-held corporations are not taxed; instead, owners report their firm's profits, or their proportionate share of their firm's profits, in their individual tax returns, regardless of whether the profits have been distributed.

All businesses are subject to some degree of local, state, and federal oversight. However, corporations are generally subject to more regulations than other businesses. For example, corporations that publicly sell their stock must comply with the extensive accounting and financial reporting requirements of the Securities and Exchange Commission (SEC). Firms listing their stock on a securities exchange, such as the New York Stock Exchange, are also subject to the rules and regulations of that organization. For example, after a year of corporate management and accounting problems, a law was passed in June 2002 that the chief executives and chief financial officers of all corporations with annual revenue over $1.2 billion must now submit sworn statements "certifying the accuracy of recent financial reports."[6] The SEC has a web site (www.sec.gov /rules/extra/ceocfo.htm) listing all corporations that need to, and already have, completed the filing process.

Occasionally, some items listed earlier as advantages of corporations can become disadvantages. For example, a small corporation may be rejected for a bank loan because of the limited liability feature. Bank loan officers realize that only corporate assets, not the personal assets of stockholders, can be seized to satisfy unpaid principal or interest payments if the corporation defaults on a loan. As a result, small corporations pose a higher level of credit risk than sole proprietorships and partnerships of comparable size. To gain approval of a loan application, one or more individual stockholders of a small corporation may agree to personally guarantee the loan.

CORPORATE STOCK

The charter indicates the amount of **authorized stock** or maximum number of shares that the corporation may issue of each designated class of stock. If the charter identifies only one class of stock, that stock is automatically considered the corporation's **common stock** or the residual ownership interest. If a corporate charter identifies a second class of stock, it is usually **preferred stock,** which has certain preferences or privileges compared to common stock.

Issued stock refers to the number of shares that have been sold or otherwise distributed to organization owners, while **outstanding stock** is the number of shares currently owned by a company's stockholders. When no treasury stock exists, issued stock equals outstanding stock. When these quantities differ, the difference is **treasury stock** or the shares that the company has reacquired from owners. For example, assume that Multimart, Inc. has one million shares of authorized stock. Of these shares, 400,000 shares have been sold to investors. Of the 400,000 issued shares, 30,000 shares have been reacquired by Multimart over the last year. Exhibit 8-1 depicts the stock quantities associated with Multimart.

[6] Securities and Exchange Commission Press Release, "SEC Publishes List of Companies Whose Officers Are Ordered to Certify Accuracy and Completeness of Recent Annual Reports," June 28, 2002.

EXHIBIT 8-1
Relationships among Stock Categories

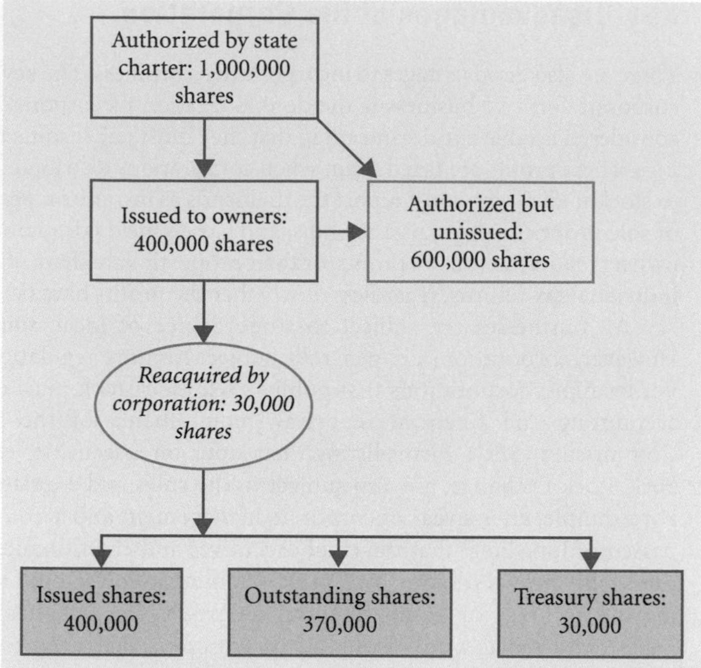

Rights and Privileges of Common Stockholders

The most important legal privilege of common stockholders is the right to vote on key corporate matters, including the election of a board of directors. The board of directors establishes a corporation's long-range objectives and operating policies. A corporation's officers, who are selected by the board of directors, have the responsibility for carrying out the board's policies. Typically, the top corporate executives, such as the chief executive officer and one or more senior vice presidents, serve on the firm's board of directors.

In most states, common stockholders have a **preemptive right** to purchase enough shares to retain their proportional ownership interest in a corporation when the company issues additional common stock. For example, assume that you own 1,000 of 10,000 shares (or 10%) of issued and outstanding common stock in Sleepy Time Hotels Incorporated. If the corporation issued 2,000 additional shares, the preemptive right would allow you the first option to purchase 200 of those shares to retain your 10% ownership interest (1,200 of 12,000 shares). Stockholders may decide to exercise or forfeit their preemptive right.

Common stockholders also have the right to share proportionately in any dividends or distribution of earnings. For example, assume the board of directors of Sleepy Time Hotels, Inc. decides to distribute a cash dividend of $50,000 to its common stockholders. If there were 10,000 shares of outstanding common stock, each common stockholder would be entitled to a $5 dividend ($50,000 ÷ 10,000 shares) for each share he or she owns. The dividend could not be allocated exclusively to a few stockholders.

Finally, if a corporation goes out of business and its assets are liquidated (or sold), common stockholders are entitled to share proportionately in the assets that remain after all other obligations have been satisfied. These obligations include current and long-term liabilities and any amounts that must be paid to other preferred classes of stockholders.

Rights and Privileges of Preferred Stockholders

Preferred stockholders have some preferences relative to a corporation's common stockholders. The most important of these preferences involves the payment of dividends. Preferred stockholders are usually entitled to receive a specified annual rate or amount of cash dividend per share each year. The corporation is not obligated to pay these dividends, but must do so before common stockholders can receive a dividend. In addition, a common feature of preferred stock is that it is cumulative relative to dividends. If a corporation fails to pay a dividend in a given year on a **cumulative preferred stock,** that dividend accumulates and must be paid in future years before common stockholders can receive a dividend.

Additionally, if a corporation is liquidated, creditors are paid and then, if funds are available, preferred stockholders are paid the par value of their stock, or another specified amount, before common stockholders receive any distribution of cash or other assets. While the liquidation preference is considered an advantage in most cases, the preferred shareholders are only entitled to a specific amount, while common shareholders divide the remaining assets on a per share basis. If the remaining assets are significant, the common shareholders may still retain a final monetary advantage.

Most preferred stocks are also **callable,** which means they can be reacquired, or called in, at the option of the issuing corporation. Some preferred stock is **convertible** and may be exchanged by the stockholder for the issuing corporation's common stock.

Besides preferences to dividends, and unless stated otherwise in the corporate charter, preferred stockholders have almost the same rights as those identified for common stockholders. However, one important stockholder right that corporate charters typically withhold from preferred stockholders is the voting privilege.

Par Value and No-Par Value Stock

Most corporate charters designate par values for the different classes of stock that a company is permitted to issue. Par value represents a nominal dollar value assigned to each share of a given class of stock and is typically set at a very low amount. For example, the par value of UPS' common stock (www.ups.com) is $0.01 per share; the par value is $0.50 per common share for Corning, Inc. (www.corning.com). Some corporate charters, such as that of Darden Restaurants, do not designate a par value for a company's stock. Such stock is known as no-par stock.[7] Although the par value has limited, if any, economic significance relative to the selling price of the stock, this value does influence how the sale of the stock is recorded.

STOCK ISSUANCES

Corporations issue stock in many different transactions and for many different amounts per share. However, if the stock has a par value, the balance of the stock account (either common or preferred) may only contain the collective par value of the number of shares issued. Because corporations cannot recognize gains or losses on the sale of their own stock, any proceeds above par value are credited to Additional Paid-In Capital (PIC) on Common Stock, which is a stockholders' equity account. For example, Moonbeam Corporation's issue 100 shares of $10 par-value common stock for $18 per share follows:

General Journal				
Date		Description	Debit	Credit
XXX		Cash	1,800	
		Common Stock		1,000
		Add'l. PIC on Common Stock		800
		Issued 100 shares of $10 par-value common stock for $18 per share		

[7] A company's board of directors may assign a dollar value to a no-par common stock; this value, called a stated value, is essentially equivalent to a par value.

If the stock is no-par value stock (such as that of Darden Restaurants), all proceeds from the issue of the shares is credited to the stock account.

If common stock is issued in exchange for equipment, buildings, or other assets, the issuance is recorded at either the fair market value of the stock issued or the asset acquired, whichever value is more evident. If the company stock is traded on an ongoing basis on a stock exchange, the fair market value of the stock is readily determinable. However, if the stock is not traded very often, is a new issue that has never been traded, or is closely held, then it will probably be more appropriate to use the fair market value of the asset received in the exchange to record the transaction.

Exhibit 8-2 provides a variety of stock issuance transactions and their respective journal entries. Assume that the company's stock trades on the New York Stock Exchange.

TREASURY STOCK

Stock buyback plans are not unusual for large public corporations. If corporate executives believe their company's common stock is selling for less than its actual value, the firm may purchase large blocks of the stock. Corporations typically resell such shares at a later date when the stock's market price has risen. For instance, in July 2002, Home Depot (www.homedepot.com) announced plans to repurchase $2 billion of its shares because the price had dropped to "the lowest point in more than three years."[8] Another reason for companies to buy back their own shares is to sell them to company employees as part of stock option or incentive compensation plans. A company does not have to be concerned with the preemptive right of existing shareholders when treasury stock is distributed because new shares of stock are not being issued.

The easiest way to account for treasury stock transactions is to use the cost method. When the company purchases the stock, the price paid is debited to the Treasury Stock account and credited to Cash. Treasury stock is *not* an asset because a company cannot be an owner of itself; it is a debit-balanced, contra-stockholders' equity account.

When the treasury shares are sold, Cash is debited for the increase and the cost of the shares is removed from the Treasury Stock account. Remember that a company cannot recognize gains or losses on the sale of its own stock, including treasury stock. Thus, if the cash received is greater than the original cost of the shares, Additional Paid-In Capital on Treasury Stock is also credited. If the cash received is less than the original cost of the shares, Additional Paid-In Capital on Treasury Stock is debited.[9]

Exhibit 8-3 continues the Catlin Corp. example and provides the journal entries for several treasury stock transactions. Notice that treasury stock transactions do not affect the Common Stock or Preferred Stock accounts. The balances in those accounts reflect the total amount of shares originally issued rather than those outstanding.

The account Additional Paid-In Capital on Treasury Stock is usually an insignificant amount. For reporting purposes, it is often combined with Additional Paid-In Capital on Common or Preferred Stock, as appropriate.

The transactions associated with issuing common stock and repurchasing common treasury stock are summarized in Visual Recap 8.1. Preferred stock transactions are handled in a manner similar to those of common stock.

---

[8] Barbara Durr, "Home Depot Plans $2bn Share Buy-Back," *Financial Times* (July 16, 2002), p. 30.

[9] If no, or an insufficient amount, Additional Paid-In Capital-Treasury Stock exists, the debit to balance the journal entry is made to Retained Earnings.

EXHIBIT 8-2

Stock Issuance Transactions

Catlin Corp. has the following information prior to the transactions below:

- Preferred stock (PS), no par value; authorized, 10,000 shares; no shares have ever been issued
- Common stock (CS), $1 par value; authorized, 350,000 shares; 145,000 shares issued and outstanding.
- Additional Paid-In Capital on CS has an assumed balance (from the issuances of the 145,000 shares) of $1,468,000.

Date		Description	Debit	Credit
April	1	Cash	27,000	
		Common Stock		1,000
		Additional PIC on CS		26,000
		Issued 1,000 shares of $1 par value common stock for $27,000.		
	4	Equipment	4,700	
		Preferred Stock		4,700
		Issued 200 shares of preferred stock for equipment with a fair market value of $4,700. This is the first issue of the PS; use the equipment's FMV to record.		
	12	Building	224,000	
		Common Stock		8,000
		Additional PIC on CS		216,000
		Issued 8,000 shares of $1 par value CS for a building with a list price of $229,600. Assume the CS traded on 4/11 for $28 per share; use the stock's FMV to record.		
	19	Cash	12,500	
		Preferred Stock		12,500
		Issued 500 shares of no-par PS for $25 per share or $12,500.		
	20	Automobile	30,000	
		Preferred Stock		30,000
		Issued 1,200 shares of no-par PS for an automobile listed at $34,600. Because the PS sold on 4/19 for $25 per share, the stock should be used to FMV to record the acquisition.		

After these transactions, the company has

- Preferred stock (PS), no par value; authorized, 10,000 shares; 1,900 shares issued and outstanding. Preferred Stock has a credit balance of $47,200.
- Common stock (CS), $1 par value; 350,000 shares authorized; 154,000 shares issued and outstanding. Common Stock has a credit balance of $154,000.
- Additional Paid-In Capital—CS has a credit balance of ($1,468,000 + $26,000 + $216,000) or $1,710,000.

EXHIBIT 8-3
Treasury Stock Transactions

Date		Description	Debit	Credit
April	21	Treasury Stock—Common	2,800	
		Cash		2,800
		Purchased 100 shares of the company's own $1 par value common stock in the market for $28 per share		
May	14	Cash	930	
		Treasury Stock—Common		840
		Additional PIC on TS—Common		90
		Sold 30 shares of the treasury stock for $31 per share. Selling price was $3 per share above original cost		
	20	Cash	240	
		Additional PIC on TS—Common	40	
		Treasury Stock—Common		280
		Sold 10 shares of TS to employees for $24 per share. Issue price was $4 less per share than original cost		

After these transactions, the company has

- Preferred stock (PS), no par value; authorized, 10,000 shares; 1,900 shares issued. Preferred Stock has a credit balance of $47,200.
- Common stock (CS), $1 par value; 350,000 shares authorized; 154,000 shares issued; (154,000 – 100 + 30 + 10) or 153,940 shares outstanding. Common Stock has a credit balance of $154,000.
- Treasury stock—There are 60 shares of treasury stock (100 purchased – 40 resold). Treasury Stock—Common has a debit balance of (60 shares x $28) or $1,680.
- Additional Paid-In Capital on TS – Common has a credit balance of ($90 – $40) or $50.

DIVIDENDS

Most companies choose to share their profits in the form of dividends with their stockholders. Dividends may be distributed as cash or additional shares of stock. A **cash dividend** is a monetary, proportionate distribution of a company's earnings to its stockholders. Companies that pay cash dividends typically do so on a regular basis. Although some companies pay semiannual or annual dividends, the most common approach is to pay quarterly cash dividends.

There has been a decrease in the number of companies paying cash dividends. "In 1970 some 98% of S&P 500 stocks paid dividends; [in 2001] only 70% did."[10] Many high-tech companies, such as Microsoft (www.microsoft.com), have never paid dividends and have no plans to do so in the future. In comparison, in 2002, FedEx (www.fedex.com) paid its first dividend of $0.05 per share in the company's 31-year history—a decision that will cost the company about $60 million a year.

[10] Kenneth Klee, "Paying Dividends," *Inc. Magazine* (June 2002), p. 52.

VISUAL RECAP 8.1

Stock Transactions

Common stock transactions are shown.
Preferred stock transactions are similar.
Calculations are shown in parentheses.

Abbreviations:

#S =	Number of Shares (purchased or sold)
PV =	Par Value per Share
SP =	Selling Price or Reissue Price
PP =	Purchase Price
APIC =	Additional Paid-In Capital

	Selling Price = Par Value	Selling Price < Par Value	Selling Price > Par Value
Issuing Common Stock	Cash (#S × SP) CS (#S × PV)	Cannot occur in most states	Cash (#S × SP) CS (#S × PV) APIC [(SP – PV) × #S]

	For any Purchase Price
Repurchasing Common Stock	TS (#S × PP) Cash (#S × PP)

	Reissue (Selling) Price = Purchase Price	Reissue (Selling) Price < Purchase Price	Reissue (Selling) Price > Purchase Price
Reissuing Treasury Stock	Cash (#S × SP) TS (#S × PP)	Cash (#S × SP) TS (#S × PP) APIC [(PP – SP) × #S]*	Cash (#S × SP) TS (#S × PP) APIC [(SP – PP) × #S]

*To the extent available; debit Retained Earnings for any additional needs.

A **stock dividend** is a proportionate distribution of a corporation's own stock to its stockholders. Stock dividends are often given so that the company can conserve its cash but, at the same time, remit something to its stockholders.

Generally, before a company can distribute a dividend to its stockholders, two requirements must be met. First, there must be a credit balance in the Retained Earnings account. Second, there must be a formal dividend declaration, or authorization, by a company's board of directors. If a cash dividend is declared, there is a third requirement: the company must have sufficient cash available to pay the dividend. Remember that having Retained Earnings is not the same thing as having cash. Retained Earnings is a stockholders' equity account that represents the total of profits earned by the business, less the dividends distributed, since incorporation. Cash is an asset that represents actual funds available for use by the company. However, regardless of the amount of Retained Earnings or Cash available, a company may be prohibited from declaring dividends due to a restrictive covenant in a bond indenture.

Three dates are important relative to dividend transactions. In chronological order, these dates are the declaration date, date of record, and payment (or distribution) date. On the dividend declaration date, a company's board of directors authorizes the dividend. On the date of record, a list of the individuals who own the company's stock is prepared. This list becomes the official record of the stockholders entitled to receive the dividend. People who purchase a stock after the date of record are not entitled to receive the dividend. The dividend is paid or distributed on the payment (distribution) date.

When dividends are declared, a debit-balanced temporary account called Dividends is created. This account is closed to Retained Earnings at the end of each accounting period. The Dividends account does not appear on the balance sheet or income statement, but is shown on the Statement of Stockholders' Equity.

Cash Dividends

When declared, a cash dividend becomes a legal liability of the corporation. The amount of the distribution is determined as the dividend amount per share multiplied by the number of shares outstanding (rather than issued). Dividends are not paid on treasury stock because the owner of those shares is the corporation. The company would not pay dividends to itself.

Assume that the board of directors of Catlin Corp. (from the previous examples) decided to declare an annual dividend on May 31. Given the information in Exhibits 8-2 and 8-3, and assuming no additional issuances of stock, the company had 1,900 shares of preferred stock outstanding and 153,940 shares of common stock on May 31. The preferred stock had been issued with a $2 per share annual dividend amount and the board decided to declare a $0.25 per share dividend on the common stock. The dividend is to be paid on June 25 to stockholders of record on June 10. The date of declaration is May 31; the date of record is June 10; and the date of payment is June 25. The entries shown in Exhibit 8-4 would be made on May 31 and June 25; no entry is required on the date of record.

Stock Dividends

Generally accepted accounting principles classify stock dividends as either small or large based on the percentage of the dividend declaration. When a company declares a stock dividend, the percentage specified reflects the percentage increase in the number of shares that will be outstanding. A small stock dividend generally involves a distribution of up to 20 percent additional stock to existing stockholders. All other stock dividends qualify as large stock dividends. Because most stock dividends are small, only the accounting treatment for these dividends is discussed in this text.

Assume that on October 5, 2002, the board of directors of Melbourne, Inc. declares a 10 percent stock dividend. The company has 1,000,000 shares of $3 par value common stock outstanding. Thus, the company will issue 100,000 additional shares (0.10 × 1,000,000) and have 1,100,000 shares outstanding after the dividend. Market value per share of the Melbourne, Inc. stock at the date of declaration is $16. The date of record is October 25 and the distribution date is November 21.

EXHIBIT 8-4

Cash Dividend Transaction

Date		Description	Debit	Credit
May	31	Dividends—PS	3,800	
		Dividends—CS	38,485	
		Dividends Payable		42,285
		Declared the annual $2 per share dividend on PS and a $0.25 per share dividend on CS *PS: $2 × 1,900 shares = $3,800* *CS: $0.25 × 153,940 = $38,485*		
June	25	Dividends Payable	42,285	
		Cash		42,285
		Paid the dividends declared on May 31 to stockholders of record on June 10		

On the declaration date of a stock dividend, the collective market value of the shares to be issued is debited to the Stock Dividends account, a temporary account similar to Dividends. The offsetting credit in this entry consists of two amounts. First, the total par value of the shares to be issued is credited to Common Stock Dividend Distributable. This account is not a liability because no cash or other current assets will have to be used to satisfy it. Common Stock Dividend Distributable is a credit-balanced stockholders' equity account. Second, the difference between the market value of the stock to be distributed and its total par value is credited to Additional Paid-In Capital—Common Stock. The journal entry for Melbourne, Inc.'s stock dividend declaration is shown in the following entry.

General Journal				
Date		**Description**	**Debit**	**Credit**
Oct.	5	Stock Dividends—CS	1,600,000	
		Stock Dividend Distributable—CS		300,000
		Additional Paid-In Capital—CS		1,300,000
		Declared a 10% stock dividend on the $3 par value CS. At this date, there were 1,000,000 shares of CS outstanding and the market value per share was $16. 1,000,000 × 0.10 = 100,000 add'l. shares; 100,000 × $16 = $1,600,000		

On the October 25 record date, a list of stockholders entitled to receive the dividend would be prepared. No accounting entry is necessary on the record date. On the stock distribution date of November 21, Stock Dividend Distributable—CS would be debited and Common Stock would be credited, as follows.

General Journal				
Date		**Description**	**Debit**	**Credit**
Nov.	21	Stock Dividends Distributable—CS	300,000	
		Common Stock		300,000
		Issued the 10% stock dividend to stockholders of record on Oct. 25		

On December 31, the $1,600,000 balance of Melbourne, Inc.'s Stock Dividends account would be closed to Retained Earnings.

The entries for cash and stock dividends are summarized in Visual Recap 8.2.

Oftentimes when a stock dividend is declared, an even number of shares cannot be distributed. For example, if you owned 155 shares of Melbourne when the ten percent stock dividend was declared, you should receive 15.5 additional shares (155 × 0.10). However, Melbourne cannot send you half a share of stock. In this case, Melbourne would send you 15 new shares and the cash equivalent of one-half a share.

STOCK SPLITS

A **stock split** increases the number of shares of a company's stock through a proportionate reduction in the stock's par value. After a stock split, the company issues new shares to stockholders and cancels the old shares. Assume that the board of directors of Melbourne, Inc. declares a 2-for-1 stock split on December 5, after the 10 percent stock dividend had been issued. Prior to the stock split, 1,100,000 shares are outstanding, each

VISUAL RECAP 8.2

Dividends

Abbreviations: Number of Shares Outstanding (#SO)
Dividend Amount per Share ($D)
Number of Shares to be Issued (#SI)
Market Price per Share ($MP)
Par Value per Share ($PV)
Additional Paid-In Captial (APIC)

Date	Cash Dividend	Stock Dividend
Date of Declaration	Dividends (#SO × $D) Dividends Payable (#SO × $D)	Dividends (#SI × $MP) Stock Div. to be Distributed (#SI × $PV) APIC [(#SI × $MP) – (#SI × $PV)]
Date of Record	no entry	no entry
Date of Payment/ Distribution	Dividends Payable (#SO × $D) Cash (#SO × $D)	Stock Div. to be Distributed (#SI × $PV) Common Stock (#SI × $PV)

with a par value of $3. Thus, the balance in the Common Stock account is $3,300,000 (1,100,000 × $3). After the 2-for-1 split, Melbourne would have 2,200,000 shares of common stock outstanding and each share would have a $1.50 par value. The balance in Common Stock is still $3,300,000 (2,200,000 shares × $1.50 par value). The quantity of shares authorized, issued, outstanding, never issued, and in the treasury, all double as a result of the 2-for-1 split.

When Darden Restaurants declared its 3-for-2 stock split, the number of shares increased by 50 percent. One additional share was distributed for every two shares already issued. Since the stock had no par value, there would be no change in that amount. If, however, the stock had had an original par value of $3 par value, it would have had a $2 par value after the split. Because a stock split does not affect the balance of any account, a formal journal entry is not necessary to record the announcement of a stock split.

The effects of dividends and splits on the stockholders' equity accounts and share data are summarized in Visual Recap 8.3.

RETAINED EARNINGS

Financial statement users often erroneously assume that the Retained Earnings figure reported in a corporate balance sheet represents a cash fund accumulated by a company over its existence. Retained Earnings is simply a general ledger account in which certain types of entries, predominantly those related to profits and dividends, are made each accounting period. Retained Earnings is increased for net income and is decreased for a net loss and for cash or stock dividends declared.

If a significant error was made in accounting for a transaction in a prior period, another type of entry will be made to Retained Earnings. A **prior period adjustment** is a restatement of the balance of Retained Earnings because of the correction of an error in a past accounting period. For example, assume that in 1999, a company purchased a piece of land for $125,000. The land was incorrectly recorded as a debit to Land Expense (instead of Land, an asset) and a credit to Cash. When the "Land Expense" account was closed at the end of 1999, it caused Retained Earnings to be too small by $125,000. In 2003, when

VISUAL RECAP 8.3

Effects of Dividends and Splits

	Cash Dividends	Stock Dividends	Stock Splits
ACCOUNTS:			
Stock account—total amount	no effect	increase	no effect
Stock account—# of shares	no effect	increase	increase or decrease[1]
Additional Paid-In Capital	no effect	increase, if small dividend	no effect
Dividends (or Stock Dividends)	increase	increase	no effect
Retained Earnings[2]	decrease	decrease	no effect
Total Stockholders' Equity	decrease	no effect[3]	no effect
SHARES:			
Authorized	no effect	no effect	increase
Issued	no effect	increased	increase
Outstanding	no effect	increased	increase
Treasury Stock	no effect	no effect	increase
Par Value	no effect	no effect	decrease or increase[1]

[1] The increase or decrease depends on the type of split occurring. For example, a 2-for-1 split increases the number of shares and decreases par value; a 1-for-2 split decreases the number of shares and increases par value.

[2] When Dividends (or Stock Dividends) is closed, Retained Earnings is decreased.

[3] The increase to the Stock and APIC-CS accounts offset the decrease to Retained Earnings.

this error is found, a correction must be made to put the land on the books as an asset and to increase Retained Earnings. This entry is:

General Journal				
Date		**Description**	**Debit**	**Credit**
XXX		Land	125,000	
		Retained Earnings		125,000
		Correct the RE balance because of a prior period error that recorded land purchase as an expense		

At the end of each period, a Statement of Retained Earnings may be prepared to show the beginning balance of RE, any prior period adjustments for the period, the net income (or loss) for the period, and the dividends declared during the period. More often, however, the Statement of RE is prepared as part of a Statement of Changes in Stockholders' Equity. An example of a Statement of Changes in Stockholders' Equity is shown in Exhibit 8-5 using assumed amounts (in thousands of dollars), in which the Statement of Retained Earnings is the fourth labeled column. The Additional PIC for Common and Treasury stock accounts have been combined.

ACCOUNTING INFORMATION FOR DECISION MAKING

Together, stockholders and potential stockholders represent a large and important class of financial decision makers. These parties need a wide range of financial information to make wise investment decisions regarding corporate equity securities.

EXHIBIT 8-5
Statement of Changes in Stockholders' Equity

	Preferred Stock no-par	Common Stock $1 par	Additional PIC (Common)	Retained Earnings	Treasury Stock (Common)
Balances, 1/1/03	$1,200	$5,400	$10,690	$14,350	$146
Prior period adjustment				125	
Issuance of stock					
2,000 shares of PS	270				
10,000 shares of CS		10	117		
Net income				5,210	
Cash dividend				(112)	
Stock dividend (10%)		541	6,492	(7,033)	
Purchase of TS					42
Sale of TS			1		(14)
Balances, 12/31/03	$1,470	$5,951	$17,300	$12,540	$174

Dividend Payouts

One principal concern of most investors is the amount of cash that an investment will produce in the future. To predict future cash flows from corporate investments, investors need information concerning dividend policies and the factors that may affect those policies. Retirees, for example, often rely heavily on dividend income.

Changes in dividend amounts or rates may also influence a company's stock price. Announcements of dividend increases often result in an increase in the market price of a stock, while dividend reductions generally result in a market price decline. An exception to this general rule may occur when a firm is in financial difficulty. For instance, in July 2002 when CMS Energy (www.cmsenergy.com) cut its dividend rate by 50 percent to $0.72 per share as part of a refinancing deal with bank creditors, the company's stock price increased by $0.59 per share.[11]

The SEC recognizes the importance of dividend information for decision makers. Companies subject to SEC regulations must disclose the cash dividends paid over the five most recent fiscal years as well as any significant restrictions on dividend payments, such as those that might be included in a bond indenture. The SEC also encourages companies to discuss their dividend policies in their annual reports.

Preferred stocks typically have a predetermined annual dividend rate or amount. However, most corporate charters do not require preferred stock dividends to be paid in any given year. When a dividend is not paid on a cumulative preferred stock, a corporation must maintain a record of these **dividends in arrears.** As indicated earlier, before a company can pay a common stock dividend, any dividends in arrears, as well as current year dividends on cumulative preferred stock, must be paid.

Dividends in arrears are not liabilities of the corporation because the board of directors has not formally declared the dividend. Because they affect a company's ability to pay future dividends, particularly to common stockholders, dividends in arrears should be disclosed in the footnotes to a company's financial statements.

[11] Mitchel Benson, "CMS Energy Cuts Dividend as Part of New Financing Deal," *Wall Street Journal* (July 16, 2002), B9.

Ratios

Many companies disclose **book value per share** for their common stock. This ratio is computed as follows:

$$\text{BV per share} = \frac{\text{Total Common Stockholders' Equity}}{\text{Total Shares of Common Stock Outstanding}}$$

Using the fiscal 2001 year-end information for Darden Restaurants, the company's book value per share is $1,035,242,000 ÷ 169,299,000 or $6.11. Although this rate is widely quoted, it is not a very useful figure in determining a company's value. Remember that the majority of assets are carried in the accounting records at historical, or depreciated historical, cost. Thus, even in the event of a company's liquidation, selling assets and paying off liabilities will not generate the amount of stockholders' equity shown in the balance sheet. However, the book value per share is often considered as a measure of the lowest a company's market price per share could fall without significant investor concern about the financial stability of the company.

Investors may also want to compute a stock's **dividend yield** or the annual dividend divided by its current market price. Preferred stocks typically have a dividend yield comparable to the current yield on high-quality corporate bonds. For fiscal 2001 year-end for Darden Restaurants, the dividend yield can be computed as follows: $0.08 per share ÷ $25.08 average market price for the last quarter or 0.003. Thus, at 3/10ths of 1 percent, the company's dividend yield is quite low.

Investors also continually monitor and assess the corporate profitability of their investments or potential investments. A key financial measure used to evaluate corporate profitability is **return on equity.** This ratio measures the rate of return earned on the capital invested in a firm by its common stockholders. Return on equity is computed as:

$$\text{Return on Equity} = \frac{(\text{Net Income} - \text{Preferred Stock Dividends})}{\text{Average Common Stockholders' Equity}}$$

Preferred stock dividends are subtracted from net income when computing return on equity because those dividends reduce a corporation's earnings available to common stockholders.

Using the fiscal 2001 information for Darden Restaurants, an example of ROE follows.

$$\begin{aligned}\text{ROE} &= \$197{,}000{,}000 \div [(\$1{,}035{,}242{,}000 + \$960{,}470{,}000) \div 2] \\ &= \$197{,}000{,}000 \div \$997{,}856{,}000 \\ &= 19.7\%\end{aligned}$$

This return on equity indicates that the company is generating an impressive rate of return on the funds that stockholders have invested and on the profits that the company has retained. Note that no preferred stock dividends were subtracted in this computation because Darden Restaurants has yet to issue any of its authorized preferred shares.

SUMMARY

Corporations have several advantages over sole proprietorships and partnerships. One primary advantage is limited liability for corporate stockholders so that the maximum financial loss a stockholder faces is the amount of his or her investment. The key disadvantage of the corporate organization is the double taxation of corporate profits. Corporate profits are taxed by the federal, and possibly state, governments and then taxed again when those earnings are distributed as cash dividends to stockholders.

When business owners decide to incorporate, articles of incorporation are filed in the locale in which the company selects to be domiciled. The company is then granted a corporate charter that authorizes the issuance of a maximum number of shares of one or more classes of stock. Common stock represents the residual ownership interests in a corporation. If a corporation is liquidated, its common stockholders are entitled to share proportionately in the firm's remaining assets after all other claims have been satisfied.

Preferred stockholders are granted certain preferences relative to the firm's common stockholders. For example, before common stockholders can be paid any dividends in a given year, preferred stockholders must receive the full amount of dividends to which they are entitled. Preferred stock often has one or more distinctive features, such as a cumulative dividend or convertibility into common stock.

Major types of stockholders' equity transactions include stock issuance, cash or stock dividend declaration and payment/distribution, and stock splits. When stock is sold for more than its par value, the difference between the proceeds and the total par value should be credited to an Additional Paid-In Capital account. To account properly for a dividend, accountants must be aware of three relevant dates: declaration, record, and payment/distribution. A stock split merely changes the number of shares and par value of a company's stock.

Stockholders and potential stockholders must have access to key information regarding the stockholders' equity of individual corporations, including data on organizational dividend policies and dividend yield. Return on equity is a key measure of a corporation's profitability and is computed by dividing net income, less any preferred stock dividends, by a corporation's average common stockholders' equity for a given period.

KEY TERMS

authorized stock
book value per share
callable preferred stock
cash dividend
common stock
convertible preferred stock
corporate charter
cumulative preferred stock
dividend in arrears
dividend yield
issued stock
outstanding stock
preemptive right
preferred stock
prior period adjustment
return on equity
stock dividend
stock split
treasury stock

QUESTIONS

1. Define a "corporation" and a "closely-held corporation"? Why would owners choose one of these forms of business over the other? *(LO 8.1)*
2. Identify the significance of the (a) articles of incorporation and (b) corporate charter to a corporate entity. Which would be more important to a stockholder and why? *(LO 8.1)*
3. Identify key advantages and disadvantages of the corporate form of business organization. *(LO 8.1)*
4. Explain what is meant by "double taxation" of a corporation's income. Why does this double taxation not occur in sole proprietorships or partnerships? *(LO 8.1)*
5. How are common stock and preferred stock the same? How do they differ? *(LO 8.2)*
6. What are the primary rights and privileges of common stockholders and of preferred stockholders? Would you prefer to be a common stockholder or a preferred stockholder? In your explanation, be certain to address the issue of age and how that might affect your answer. *(LO 8.2)*

7. Why might a corporation decide to repurchase some of its outstanding common stock? Other than the one in the text, provide three recent examples of companies that have repurchased their own shares of stock. *(LO 8.4)*
8. What is the difference between a cash dividend and a stock dividend? Discuss how each type of dividend affects stockholders' equity. *(LO 8.4)*
9. What is a stock split and how does it affect stockholders' equity? *(LO 8.4)*
10. Does a corporation with a positive retained earnings balance have an equivalent amount of cash on hand? Explain. *(LO 8.5)*
11. What is a prior period adjustment and where would it be presented in the financial statements? *(LO 8.6)*
12. How is the return on equity ratio computed? Why is this ratio important? *(LO 8.8)*

EXERCISES

13. **True or False** *(All LOs)*

Following are a series of statements regarding topics discussed in this chapter.

Required:

Indicate whether each statement is true (T) or false (F).

(1) Book value per share is computed by dividing Retained Earnings by the number of common shares outstanding.

(2) An important legal privilege of common stockholders is the right to vote on key corporate matters.

(3) Among other items, the articles of incorporation identify the given business's purpose, its principal operating units, and the type and quantity of stock that it plans to issue.

(4) If a corporate charter identifies only one class of stock, that stock is automatically considered the corporation's preferred stock.

(5) Companies that pay cash dividends typically do so on a regular basis.

(6) "Authorized stock" refers to the number of shares of a corporate stock that have been sold or otherwise distributed.

(7) The stock of closely-held corporations is owned by a few individuals, often members of the same family, and is not publicly traded on a securities exchange.

(8) Companies subject to the regulations of the Securities and Exchange Commission must disclose the cash dividends they have paid over their five most recent fiscal years.

(9) Return on equity is computed by dividing a corporation's net income, less preferred stock dividends, by average common stockholders' equity for a given period.

(10) If common shares outstanding are less than common shares authorized, the company must have treasury stock.

14. **Terms** *(LO 8.1 & 8.2)*

Following are definitions or descriptions of terms relating to corporations and corporate stockholders' equity.

(a) The first-time sale of a corporation's stock to the general public

(b) A dollar value that has been assigned to each share of stock

(c) A "legal" being

(d) The maximum number of shares of stock that a corporation is permitted to sell
(e) The class of stock that normally has voting rights
(f) A document describing the basic nature of the corporate entity
(g) The number of shares of stock that has been sold by a corporation
(h) The ability of stockholders to maintain their proportionate ownership interest in a company when new issues of stock are made
(i) The number of shares of stock currently held by company's shareholders
(j) The stock that has been issued and reacquired by a corporation
(k) A contract between a corporation and the locale in which it is domiciled

Required:

Match each definition or description with the appropriate term from the following list.

(1) Corporation
(2) Corporate charter
(3) Initial public offering
(4) Authorized stock
(5) Issued stock
(6) Outstanding stock
(7) Treasury stock
(8) Preferred stock
(9) Common stock
(10) Preemptive right
(11) Par value

15. **Corporate Form of Business Organization** *(LO 8.1, writing)*

Your friends, Steven Anderson and Jason Martinkus are partners in Videos Unlimited, a small but rapidly growing business. Anderson and Martinkus have been told by their attorney that they should consider incorporating their business.

Required:

Anderson and Martinkus have asked your advice about incorporating their business. To help them put things in perspective, write a memo that summarizes the key advantages and disadvantages of the corporate form of business. Be sure to discuss future implications if the business is extremely successful.

16. **Common Stock Issuances** *(LO 8.3)*

On January 15, 2003, Longvue Co. incorporated in Georgia and was authorized to issue 3,500,000 shares of common stock. In an initial public offering, Longvue sold 367,000 shares of common stock for $18 per share.

Required:

(1) Prepare the journal entry to record the sale of the stock if Longvue's common stock
   (a) has a $1.50 par value.
   (b) has a $10.00 par value.
   (c) is no-par value.
(2) Explain why selling common stock at more than par value does not increase net income for the period.

17. **Number of Shares** *(LO 8.3)*

The number of shares of common stock for three companies is given below.

	Number of Shares			
Company	**Authorized**	**Issued**	**Outstanding**	**Treasury**
Adams Corp.	100,000	40,000	(a)	0
Brady, Inc.	1,000,000	600,000	540,000	(b)
Costanza Corp.	500,000	(c)	200,000	50,000

Required:

(1) What is the distinction between issued and outstanding shares of stock?

(2) Determine the number of shares that corresponds to each omitted value.

(3) If Adams Corp. sells 10,000 more shares of stock, how many shares will be authorized, issued, outstanding, and in treasury?

18. **Common Stockholders' Rights** *(LOs 8.2, 8.4, & 8.7)*

You own 500 shares of $40 par value common stock of Cohen & Cohen Securities Brokers. The company has 50,000 shares of common stock outstanding. Cohen & Cohen does not have any other classes of stock outstanding.

Required:

(1) If Cohen & Cohen declares a cash dividend of $30,000, how much of this dividend can you expect to receive? What is the amount of dividend per share?

(2) If Cohen & Cohen decides to sell an additional 14,000 shares of common stock, how many of these shares will you be entitled to purchase? Explain.

(3) Presently, Cohen & Cohen's total stockholders' equity is $3,200,000 and the company's common stock is trading for $71 per share on a major stock exchange. What is the total "value" of the Cohen & Cohen shares that you own? Explain.

19. **Stock Split and Stock Dividend** *(LOs 8.3 & 8.4)*

Marigold Enterprises is authorized to issue 1,000,000 shares of $6 par value common stock. Since incorporation, 550,000 shares have been issued. Currently, Marigold holds 40,000 of its own shares in treasury and has $3,500,000 in Retained Earnings. Marigold is considering the following two options:

(a) declaring a 2:1 stock split

(b) declaring a 15 percent stock dividend

Required:

(1) What is the current balance in the Common Stock account?

(2) How many shares of common stock are currently outstanding?

(3) For each of the two options Marigold is considering, determine the number of shares authorized, issued, outstanding, and in treasury after the declaration. Each option should be executed on the original information.

(4) What would be the balance in Retained Earnings if the (a) split and (b) dividend were chosen?

(5) Determine the par value per share and the balance in the Common Stock account if the (a) split and (b) dividend were chosen.

(6) What would you expect to happen to the market price per share of Marigold common stock if the (a) split and (b) dividend were chosen? Explain the rationale for your answer.

20. **Stock Dividends** *(LO 8.4)*

Denim Industries has 100,000 shares of $10 par value common stock authorized, of which 40,000 shares have been issued and 38,000 are currently outstanding. On November 30, 2003, when the stock is trading at $40 per share, Denim declares a 10 percent stock dividend of stockholders of record on December 24, 2003. The stock dividend will be distributed on January 10, 2004.

Required:

(1) How many shares are in treasury on November 30?

(2) How many shares will be distributed on January 10, 2004?

(3) Prepare any necessary journal entries related to this stock dividend on the following dates:
   (a) date of declaration
   (b) date of record
   (c) date of distribution

(4) On Denim's December 31, 2003 balance sheet, will Denim show a liability for the value of the undistributed stock? Why or why not?

21. **Cumulative Dividends** *(LO 8.4, ethics)*

Eddy Appliance Manufacturers (EAM) has two classes of stock: common stock with a par value of $3 (500,000 shares authorized; 100,000 shares outstanding) and preferred stock with a par value of $100 (25,000 shares authorized; 10,000 shares outstanding). The preferred stock has an annual stated dividend rate of $5 per share. EAM declared the following dividends over a five-year period, during which no additional shares of stock are issued.

Year	Dividend Amount
2001	$150,000
2002	0
2003	150,000
2004	30,000
2005	200,000

Required:

(1) What is the total dollar amount of cash dividend to which preferred stockholders are entitled to in one year?

(2) Assume that EAM's preferred stock is noncumulative. Determine the amount of dividends for preferred and common shareholders in each of the five years.

(3) Assume that EAM's preferred stock is cumulative.
   (a) Determine the amount of dividends for preferred and common shareholders in each of the five years.
   (b) Explain how dividends in arrears, if they exist, should be noted in the financial statements.
   (c) At the end of 2002, EAM's management does not want to list the dividends in arrears in the financial statements as required because there is no legal liability to pay that amount as of December 31, 2002. Is EAM's management right about there being no legal obligation? Explain. Explain why this omission might mislead investors.

22. **Retained Earnings** *(LO 8.5 and 8.6)*

Following are several items that may have an effect on the Retained Earnings account.

(a) Cash dividend
(b) Stock dividend
(c) Stock split
(d) Issuing common stock
(e) Net income
(f) Net loss
(g) Prior period error that overstated revenues
(h) Prior period error that overstated expenses

Required:

(1) For each item, indicate whether it increases, decreases, or has no effect on Retained Earnings.
(2) For each item, indicate whether the effect on Retained Earnings is immediate (that is, initial recording of the item would include a debit or credit to Retained Earnings in the journal entry) or occurs during closing entries.
(3) For each item, indicate whether it increases, decreases, or has no effect on total stockholders' equity.

23. **Book Value per Share and Return on Equity** *(LO 8.7 & 8.8)*

TransAmerica is an interstate railroad cargo transportation company. The following table presents key financial data for TransAmerica over a recent five-year period. Amounts are expressed in millions of dollars.

	1998	1999	2000	2001	2002
Revenues	$549.7	$547.4	$564.7	$593.9	$643.8
Net income	65.4	95.9	68.2	113.9	118.4
Common stockholders' equity (year-end)	260.3	338.8	377.4	454.1	470.1
Common shares outstanding (year-end)	59.7	63.9	64.0	64.1	62.9

Note: At the beginning of 1998, TransAmerica had $128.4 million of common stockholders' equity.

Required:

(1) Compute TransAmerica's book value per share at the end of each year listed.
(2) Compute the company's return on equity for each year.
(3) Is there a definite trend apparent in either book value per share or ROE? If so, indicate whether that trend is favorable or unfavorable.
(4) Suppose that you are a potential investor in TransAmerica common stock. Identify three questions related to the company's financial data that you would want to ask the company's top executives.

PROBLEMS

24. **Issuance of Common Stock** *(LO 8.3)*

On April 21, Pincus Enterprises acquired a large tract of land from Mock Corporation. Pincus issued 500 shares of its $2 par value common stock to Mock in exchange for the land.

Required:

(1) Prepare the journal entry to record this transaction by Pincus Enterprises, if the company's stock is not publicly traded and the land has an appraised value of $41,200.

(2) Assume that on April 20, the Pincus stock traded on the New York Stock Exchange for $77 per share. The land has an appraised value of $41,200. Prepare the appropriate journal entry to record this exchange transaction by Pincus Enterprises.

(3) Suppose, instead, that Pincus sold 500 shares of stock on April 20 for $77 cash per share. The company then acquired the land from Mock Corporation on April 21 for its appraised value. Prepare the journal entries for these two transactions by Pincus Enterprises.

(4) Determine the differences between the financial statement results in parts (2) and (3). Explain why these differences occurred.

25. **Accounting for Treasury Stock Transactions** *(LO 8.4)*

Quick & Reilly is a large discount brokerage firm. On December 31, 2002, the stockholders' equity section of the company's balance sheet indicated that 69,400 shares of the company's common stock were being held as treasury stock. This treasury stock had been acquired for $1,943,200 in a single transaction. The company's common stock has a par value of $0.10 per share.

Required:

(1) Why do companies sometimes reacquire stock that they have previously issued?

(2) Prepare the journal entry to record the purchase of the treasury stock.

(3) Assume that Quick & Reilly sold 2,000 shares of its treasury stock on April 3, 2003, for $35 per share. Prepare the journal entry to record the sale of the treasury stock.

(4) Assume that on May 31, 2003, Quick & Reilly sold another 3,000 shares of its treasury stock for $27 per share. Prepare the journal entry to record the sale of the treasury stock.

(5) Why is treasury stock not classified as an asset?

26. **Accounting for Cash Dividends** *(LOs 8.1 & 8.4)*

Karlinsky Distributors has 1,000,000 shares of common stock outstanding. On January 11 of the current year, Karlinsky declared a cash dividend of $0.20 per share, payable on March 9 to stockholders of record on February 12.

Required:

(1) When did this dividend become a liability to Karlinsky?

(2) Prepare any journal entries required in Karlinsky's accounting records relating to this cash dividend on the following dates in the current year:

(a) January 11

(b) February 12

(c) March 9

(d) December 31

(3) What group of individuals authorized the declaration of this dividend?

(4) What general types of information must public companies regulated by the SEC disclose in their annual reports regarding their dividend policies? Why is this information important to potential investors?

27. **Dividends to Preferred Shareholders** *(LO 8.4, 8.6 & 8.7)*

As of December 31, 2002, Biloxi Corporation has 10,000 shares of cumulative preferred stock outstanding. This stock has a $100 par value and an annual dividend rate of $8 per share. Biloxi has not paid any dividends to its stockholders during the past three years.

Required:

(1) What disclosure is Biloxi required to make in its annual report regarding the unpaid dividends on its preferred stock? What specific amount will be included in the disclosure and how was that amount calculated?

(2) Where in Biloxi's financial statements this disclosure be found?

(3) Why is this disclosure of interest to Biloxi's preferred and common stockholders?

(4) Assume that in February 2003, Biloxi declares a $500,000 cash dividend. How much will be received by Biloxi's common stockholders? If Biloxi has 250,000 shares of common stock outstanding, what is the dividend amount per common share?

(5) Use the information in part (4). If the market price per common share is $22, what is the dividend yield per common share? How would an investor determine if this yield is "good" or "bad"?

28. **Stock Dividends** *(LO 8.4 & 8.5)*

Hodges, Inc. has five million shares of $5 par value common stock authorized. Of that amount, 2.3 million have been issued and 2.1 million are outstanding. On July 2, Hodges declared a five percent stock dividend to shareholders of record on July 31, distributable on August 8. On July 2, Hodges stock was trading at $30 per share.

Required:

(1) Related to this stock dividend, will the balance in any of the following accounts be affected? Explain.
   (a) Cash
   (b) Retained Earnings
   (c) Treasury Stock

(2) How many shares are held by Hodges in the treasury? Will those shares receive the dividend? Why or why not?

(3) How many shares will be distributed in the stock dividend?

(4) Record the journal entries related to this stock dividend on the following dates:
   (a) July 2
   (b) July 31
   (c) August 8

29. **Accounting for Stockholders' Equity Transactions** *(LOs 8.3, 8.4, & 8.6)*

Arnold Manufacturing was granted a corporate charter on January 3, 2002, and began operations shortly thereafter. Arnold's charter authorizes the firm to issue up to 100,000 shares of $3 par value common stock and 20,000 shares of $100 par value preferred stock. The preferred stock carries an annual dividend rate of $8, is cumulative, and can be converted into Arnold common stock through December 31, 2011. Each share of preferred stock can be converted into 2 shares of Arnold common stock. During 2002, the following events or transactions affected the stockholders' equity of Arnold.

January 10	Sold 22,000 shares of common stock for $11 per share.
March 30	Sold 5,000 shares of preferred stock for $101 per share.
June 12	Exchanged 3,000 shares of common stock for a building with an appraised value of $37,000. On this date, Arnold's common stock was trading at $12 per share on a regional stock exchange.
October 3	Sold 7,000 shares of common stock for $13 per share.
November 4	Declared a cash dividend of $8 per share on outstanding preferred stock, payable on December 6, to stockholders of record on November 21.
December 6	Paid the preferred stock dividend.
December 31	Net income for 2002 was $389,000.

Required:

(1) Prepare the journal entries for the events listed.

(2) Prepare all year-end closing entries for which data are available.

(3) Prepare the stockholders' equity section of Arnold's balance sheet as of December 31, 2002.

(4) Assume instead that Arnold's common stock has no par value. Prepare the journal entries for the January 10, June 12, and October 3 transactions.

(5) Refer to the transaction on June 12. Assume that Arnold's common stock is not publicly traded. Prepare the appropriate journal entry for this transaction given this assumption.

(6) What accounting principle dictates that Arnold include information in its financial statement footnotes regarding the specific features or stipulations attached to its preferred stock?

30. Analyzing Stockholders' Equity *(LOs 8.6, 8.7 & 8.8, Excel)*

O'Brien Productions, Inc. produces and distributes several popular television shows. O'Brien's common stockholders' equity at the beginning of 2002 was $2,416,550. Following is information about stockholders' equity for the company's 2002 and 2003 balance sheets. Also listed for each year is O'Brien's net income.

(a) **Preferred Stock:** $10 par value; 5,000,000 shares authorized; 1,200,000 shares were issued in 2002 and were outstanding all of 2003; each share of preferred has a $0.60 per share annual dividend amount.

(b) **Common Stock:** $0.10 par value; 7,500,000 shares authorized; 4,955,000 shares and 4,973,000 shares had been sold to stockholders by the end of 2002 and 2003, respectively.

(c) **Additional Paid-In Capital on Common Stock:** the 4,955,000 common shares were sold for $15.50 each; the common shares sold during 2003 were sold for $19.40 each.

(d) **Treasury Stock:** accounted for at cost; there 920,800 shares held in the treasury at the end of 2002, each having been purchased for $16.20 per share; during 2003, 20,000 shares of treasury stock were sold for $18.00 per share and an additional 15,000 shares were purchased for $21.00 per share.

(e) **Retained Earnings:** there were $2,600,080 and $2,889,300 of Retained Earnings at the ends of 2002 and 2003, respectively.

(f) **Net Income:** O'Brien had $1,019,360 and $883,000 of net income for 2002 and 2003, respectively.

Required:

(1) Prepare a Statement of Stockholders' Equity for O'Brien at the end of 2002 and at the end of 2003.

(2) Compute the book value per share of O'Brien's common stock at the end of 2002 and 2003.

(3) The only transactions that affected O'Brien's Retained Earnings during 2003 were net income and dividends. What amount of cash dividends did O'Brien declare during 2003? How much of this was paid to preferred stockholders? Explain.

(4) Compute O'Brien's return on equity for 2002 and 2003. Did this ratio improve or deteriorate in 2003 compared with the previous year?

(5) For this requirement, assume that O'Brien does not have any preferred stock. Thus, all dividends would be paid to common stockholders. If the market price per common share in 2003 were $20, what would be the dividend yield on common stock in 2003?

(6) Identify one reason that may explain why O'Brien's common stock has such a low par value.

CASES

31. Investor Interpretations *(LO 8.4 & 8.7, writing)*

Jubilee Publishers has been in operation for more than 30 years and went public in the early 1980s. Jubilee has generated a net income every year except for one since it went public. The majority of Jubilee's cash flows are generated from its operations, and Jubilee only resorted to significant borrowing when it has expanded its operations.

Since it became a publicly traded company, Jubilee Publishers has tried to declare a cash dividend every fiscal year, but always declares a cash dividend at least every other year. Last year Jubilee did not declare a dividend. This year, a significant portion of Jubilee's long-term debt is maturing, and declaring a cash dividend this year could lead to a cash flow problem. Jubilee is gaining market share and sales are up, so management believes that this problem is unique to this operating year.

To satisfy its shareholders without declaring a cash dividend this year, Jubilee is considering the following options:

(a) a stock dividend
(b) a stock split
(c) no dividend this year, but a mid-year dividend next year

Required:

Discuss how an investor would interpret each of the three options. Include in your discussion, the benefits and drawbacks to each choice both from Jubilee's standpoint and the investor's standpoint.

32. Annual Reports *(LO 8.8, Internet)*

Use the annual report of Carnival Corporation (www.carnival.com) for the 2001 fiscal year to answer the following questions.

Required:

(1) How many shares of common stock does Carnival have authorized, issued, outstanding, and in treasury for 2000 and 2001?

(2) Has Carnival authorized the issue of preferred stock? If so, why is it not listed on the balance sheet?

(3) What kinds of dividends has Carnival declared, if any, in 2000 and 2001?

(4) Calculate the following ratios for Carnival for the years 2001. [Hint: Use the weighted average number of shares given in the footnotes for each year's calculations.]

(a) Book value per share
(b) Dividend yield
(c) Return on equity

(5) Comment on how an investor would interpret each of the measurements calculated in part (4). Based on the results, would you invest in Carnival? Explain the rationale of your answer.

33. **Comparing Companies** *(LO 8.7 & 8.8, group, Internet)*

Identifying the similarities and differences in companies is as crucial to making investment decisions as understanding a single company's financial statements. Form groups of at least four students. Each group should select a single industry. Each group member should locate a different annual report within that industry. (The industry and individual company may be assigned by your instructor.)

Required—individual group members:

(1) Calculate the following ratios for the company you selected for the two most recent fiscal years.
  (a) Book value per share
  (b) Dividend yield
  (c) Return on equity

(2) Comment on the changes from year to year.

(3) Does this company seem to be a good investment based on these four ratios? Explain your answer.

Required—groups:

(4) Compile the ratio calculations for each company prepared by the individual group members into one table.

(5) Compare the results from company to company in the same fiscal years. Include in your comparison, a graphical analysis. Discuss reasons why these ratios might be similar or different within an industry.

(6) Based on these four ratios across companies, which company is the best investment in the industry you have chosen? Explain your answer.

Required—class:

(7) Compare the ratios from each industry. Discuss reasons why these ratios might be similar or different between industries.

(8) Does one industry seem to be a better investment than another? Do you think this is constant over time? Explain your answers.

SUPPLEMENTAL PROBLEMS

34. **Issuing Stock** *(LO 8.3)* [Compare to Problem 24]

Donnovan, Inc. was established in 2003 and is authorized to issue 1,000,000 shares of common stock with a par value of $1. On August 27, 2003, before the stock was publicly traded, the founders were given stock in exchange for investments in the company.

  (a) Jones invested $200,000 in exchange for 100,000 shares of stock.
  (b) Smith donated a piece of land and a building with an appraised value of $225,000 in exchange for 100,000 shares of stock.

On February 4, 2005, Donnovan issued 10,000 shares at $10 per share in an initial public offering. On February 7, 2005, Smith sold 20,000 of her shares to another investor for $12 per share.

Required:

Prepare all necessary journal entries for Donnovan, Inc. on the following dates:

(1) August 27, 2003
(2) February 4, 2005
(3) February 7, 2005

35. **Accounting for Treasury Stock Transactions** *(LO 8.2 & 8.4)* [Compare to Problem 25]

Refer to the information regarding Donnovan, Inc. in problem 34. By December 2006, Donnovan had 300,000 shares of issued and outstanding common stock. As a year-end bonus for Donnovan's CEO, the company will give him 10,000 shares of Donnovan stock which will be reacquired from the shares that are currently outstanding.

Required:

(1) Donnovan has one million shares authorized and only 300,000 issued. Provide an explanation why Donnovan cannot give its CEO 10,000 shares from the shares that have not been issued.
(2) Suppose that Donnovan reacquires 12,000 shares of its own stock on December 3, 2006 when the stock is trading at $40 per share. Prepare the journal entry to record this repurchase.

36. **Accounting for Dividends and Splits** *(LO 8.4)* [Compare to Problems 26 & 28]

Marley United has authorized 1,000,000 shares of $1 par value common stock, of which 475,000 are currently issued and 425,000 are outstanding. The following events are related to Marley United's common stock.

- On November 1, 2002, Marley United declared a five percent stock dividend to all shareholders of record on November 30, distributable on December 30. At the time of the declaration, the stock was trading at $50 per share.
- On October 8, 2003, Marley United declared a 2:1 stock split. At the time of the split, the stock was trading at $90 per share.
- On November 1, 2004, Marley United declared a $1 per share cash dividend to all shareholders of record on November 30, payable on December 30. At the time of the declaration, the stock was trading at $48 per share.

Required:

(1) Calculate the following amounts after each event took place:
    (a) number of shares authorized
    (b) number of shares issued
    (c) number of shares outstanding
    (d) number of shares in treasury
    (e) par value per share
    (f) balance in the common stock account.
(2) Prepare the journal entries associated with each event.
(3) Why might Marley United have declared a stock dividend in 2002 rather than a cash dividend?
(4) Why might Marley United have split its stock in 2003?
(5) Use library and Internet resources to find three companies that have recently declared a stock dividend or a stock split. How have these declarations affected the companies' stock prices?

37. **Dividends to Preferred Shareholders** *(LOs 8.4 & 8.6)* [Compare to Problem 27]

Connelly Industries has two classes of stock, common and preferred. Information about each class of stock is give below.

(a) The $100 par value preferred stock is cumulative and pays an annual dividend of $8 per share. During 2003 and 2004, 10,000 shares were outstanding.

(b) The common stock has a par value of $0.01. During 2003 and 2004, 250,000 shares were outstanding.

(c) In 2003, no dividends were paid by Connelly. On August 8, 2004, Connelly declared a $1 per share cash dividend for common shareholders of record September 8, payable on September 15.

Required:

(1) What type of disclosure should Connelly have had in its 2003 annual report regarding dividends?

(2) Given the information on the common stock dividend, what is the total amount of cash dividends that had to have been declared by Connelly in 2004? Explain.

(3) How would your answer to part (2) have differed if the preferred stock had been noncumulative?

(4) Record the journal entries related to the 2004 dividends.

(5) What type of disclosure should Connelly have in its 2004 annual report regarding dividends?

38. **Analyzing Stockholders' Equity** *(LO 8.8, Excel)* [Compare to Problem 30]

Following is the stockholders' equity information for a major restaurant corporation for 2001 through 2003. Except for the market price, which is presented in actual dollars, all amounts information is shown in millions.

Stockholders' Equity	**2003**	**2002**	**2001**
Common Stock	$ 9,920	$ 9,234	$ 8,995
Retained Earnings	12,739	12,256	10,994
Treasury Stock	729	605	601
Additional Information			
Net Income	$ 920	$ 1,300	$ 1,850
Common stock dividends	434	0	412
Average common shares outstanding during year	2,074	2,056	2,060
Common shares outstanding at the fiscal year end	2,068	2,071	2,070
Market price of stock at fiscal year end	$ 28.94	$ 27.88	$ 32.19

Required:

(1) Calculate the following ratios for 2001, 2002 and 2003.
   (a) Book value per share
   (b) Dividend yield
   (c) Return on equity (2002 and 2003 only)

(2) Comment on the changes from year to year.

(3) Use library or Internet resources to find averages for dividend yield and return on equity for a company in the restaurant business. How does this company compare to the industry average?

PART IV

ANALYSIS OF ACCOUNTING DATA

CHAPTER 9

The Corporate Income Statement and Financial Statement Analysis

LEARNING OBJECTIVES

1. Account for investments in stocks and bonds.
2. Identify the key elements of the corporate income statement.
3. Compute earnings per share.
4. Account for corporate income taxes.
5. Discuss the objectives of, and sources for, information for financial statement analysis for different types of decision makers.
6. Prepare trend analyses of financial statement data and common-sized financial statements.
7. Compute key financial ratios including liquidity, leverage, activity, profitability, and market strength ratios.
8. Assess earnings quality.

Outback Steakhouse, Inc.

Founded in 1988, Outback Steakhouse, Inc. (www.outback.com) had its initial public offering of stock in 1991 under the NYSE ticker symbol OSI. In addition to its well-known Australian steakhouse concept restaurants, the company operates Carrabba's Italian Grill and Fleming's Prime Steakhouse & Wine Bar, as well as some additional joint ventures. As of year-end 2000, the company had issued less than half of its authorized common shares.

There are over 600 Outback steakhouses in 49 states, and the company has locations in Korea, Brazil, Singapore, and Japan. Outback has engaged in partnerships with venues such as sports arenas. This "bonzer" organization also sponsors youth athletics, charitable events, and the annual Outback Bowl.

Financial statement information for Outback Steakhouse is provided throughout the chapter for financial analysis purposes.

SOURCE: Company History, http://www.outback.com.

INTRODUCTION

The previous chapter focused on accounting for stockholders' equity. This chapter first addresses components, other than normal operations, that impact corporate income, as well as related taxation issues. The second part of the chapter considers an array of financial statement analysis techniques used to gain insights into the financial performance and financial condition of a business as reflected by its financial statements. The final part of the chapter identifies factors that influence earnings quality.

INCOME STATEMENT

An income statement may also be referred to as a "statement of earnings" or "statement of operations." Components of the income statements discussed to this point in the text have been the traditional revenues and expenses of most business enterprises. **Income from operations** represents the earnings produced by a corporation's principal profit-oriented activities. The most simplistic computation for income from operations is operating revenues minus both cost of goods sold and operating expenses.

Many corporations have items appearing on their income statements in addition to operating revenues and expenses. This section addresses the following items: earnings (or losses) from stock or bond investments; discontinued operations; extraordinary items; cumulative effects of accounting changes; and deferred income taxes. Most corporate income statements do not contain all of these elements, as is the case with Outback Steakhouse, Inc. However, these items are common enough that each should be discussed.

As seen in Exhibit 9-1, Outback Steakhouse had $1,906,006,000 in operating revenues and $1,658,136,000 in operating and cost of goods sold expenses in 2000, resulting in income from continuing operations of $247,870,000. This figure is often used as the starting point in developing profit forecasts for the firm. A company's expected growth rate in sales, competitive conditions in its industry, and general health of the

EXHIBIT 9-1

Outback Steakhouse, Inc. Consolidated Statements of Income

	Years Ended December 31	
	2000	1999
Revenues	$1,906,006	$1,646,013
Costs and Expenses		
Cost of sales	$ 715,224	$ 620,249
Labor and other operating expenses	809,393	686,835
Depreciation and amortization	58,109	50,709
General and administrative	75,410	66,666
Total Costs and Expenses	$1,658,136	$1,424,459
Income from Operations	$ 247,870	$ 221,554
Other Income (Expense)		
Interest expense*	(2,058)	(3,042)
Income from operations of unconsolidated affiliates	2,457	1,089
Interest revenue	4,617	1,416
Income before Minority Interest and Taxes	$ 252,886	$ 221,017
Minority Interest Income	(33,884)	(29,770)
Income before Income Taxes	$ 219,002	$ 191,247
Provision for Income Taxes		
Current	(68,149)	(54,019)
Deferred	(9,723)	(12,905)
Net Income	$ 141,130	$ 124,323
Basic Earnings per Share (EPS)	$1.82	$0.61

*In the company's 2000 income statement, this amount was called "Other Expenses." For purposes of computing ratios later in the chapter, it was arbitrarily changed to Interest Expense.

Note: Some amounts have been combined from the company's 2000 Annual Report. Dollars in thousands (except for EPS).

national economy are factors that decision makers can use to project the firm's future earnings, given its current year's income from continuing operations as a base amount.

Earnings from Investments

Corporations often purchase the stocks or bonds of other entities. If such purchases are made simply to invest cash for the short-run, the investments are shown as current assets. Alternatively, some investments by corporations are made for the long-run, usually because the investing corporation wants to establish a working relationship with the other entity. For example, Outback Steakhouse, Inc. owns some Carrabba's Italian Grills and has made long-term investments in others.

Investments in Stocks

Depending on the percentage of ownership, a company may use one of two accounting methods to account for a stock investment: cost or equity. These two methods create important differences on the income statement.

If a company owns less than 20 percent of the outstanding stock of another company, the investing company uses the cost method to account for the investment. Under the **cost method,** the investing company debits the Investment account (an asset) and credits Cash for the cost of the stock purchased. When cash dividends are received by the investing company, it records a debit to Cash and a credit to Dividend Revenue (or Other Revenue, a nonoperating revenue). At the end of each year, the cost and the fair market value of the investment are compared, and the investment account will be written up or down as necessary to fair market. Such gains and losses, however, do not affect the income statement; they are included as credits and debits, respectively, to stockholders' equity.

If a company owns 20 percent or more of the outstanding stock of another company, the investing company uses the equity method to account for the investment. Under the **equity method,** the investing company debits the Investment account and credits Cash for the cost of the stock purchased. When the company in which the investment was made earns profits, the investing company records its share of those profits in its Investment account and on its income statement. This result was listed as the "Income from operations of unconsolidated affiliates" on Outback's income statement. When cash dividends are received by the investing company, it records a debit to Cash and a credit to its Investment account.

If a company owns more than 50 percent of the outstanding shares of stock, the owning company is referred to as the **parent** and the owned company is referred to as the **subsidiary.** When such a relationship exists, the financial statements of the two companies are consolidated at the end of the year. **Consolidation** refers to the process of combining financial statements of a parent and subsidiary. Transactions that took place between the two companies are eliminated during consolidation. However, as in the case of Outback, if the parent company does not own all the stock of the other company, a **minority interest** ownership exists.

Assume that Outback owned 80 percent of the stock of Christine's Crumpets and that company earned revenues of $500,000 and incurred expenses of $350,000 during the year, creating a profit of $150,000. The entire revenue and expense amounts are included in Outback's revenues and expenses. However, the minority interest ownership is entitled to its 20 percent of Christine's Crumpets profits. Thus, on the income statement, a subtraction would be made for "Minority Interest Income." The total minority interest (stock and earnings) is shown on the balance sheet as a separate section between liabilities and stockholders' equity. This presentation may change in the near future.

The relationships between the cost and the equity methods are shown in Visual Recap 9.1.

VISUAL RECAP 9.1

Accounting Methods for Long-term Investments in Other Companies

Method	Cost	Equity	
Ownership	< 20%	20%–50%	> 50%
Initial Investment	Investment Cash	Investment Cash	Investment Cash
Receipt of Dividends	Cash Dividend Revenue	Cash Investment	Cash Investment
Year-end Procedures	Debit (or credit) the Investment account to adjust it to FMV. The offsetting credit (or debit) is to a Stockholders' Equity account.	Investment Income from Unconsolidated Affiliates	Consolidate the financial statements of both companies; remove the effects of transactions between the two companies; subtract minority interest on the income statement.

Investments in Bonds

Investments in another company's bonds payable are another way that corporations often generate additional revenue. If bond investments are to be held to maturity, the accounting for the investment in bonds payable is essentially the mirror image of the accounting performed by the issuer of the bonds payable.

The $100,000, 10%, 5-year bonds payable issued by Hardin Manufacturing Company on April 1, 2003 are used to illustrate the accounting for an investment in corporate bonds. The liability side of this transaction is shown in Chapter 7, Exhibit 7A-1. Assume that Outback Steakhouse, Inc. purchased all of Hardin's bonds at issue date when the market rate of interest was 11 percent. The company intends to hold the bonds to maturity as a long-term investment. Exhibit 9-2 provides the journal entries for the first year relative to this investment.

One important difference in the "mirror image" accounting is that the buyer of corporate bonds does not have a discount or premium account related to the Investment account. Discounts and premiums are amortized directly within the Investment asset account. The interest revenue appearing on the income statement of the investor (like the

EXHIBIT 9-2

Journal Entries for a Bond Investment Purchased at a Discount

General Journal

Date		Description	Debit	Credit
2003				
Apr.	1	Investment in Bonds	96,231	
		Cash		96,231
		To record purchase of $100,000, 10%, 5-year bonds at a market rate of 11%		
Sept.	30	Cash	5,000	
		Investment in Bonds	377	
		Interest Revenue		5,377
		To record receipt of semiannual interest and amortization of discount to the Investment account		
Dec.	31	Interest Receivable	2,500	
		Investment in Bonds	189	
		Interest Payable		2,689
		To record accrual of 3 months of interest and amortization of discount to the Investment account		
2004				
Mar.	31	Cash	5,000	
		Investment in Bonds	188	
		Interest Revenue		2,688
		Interest Receivable		2,500
		To record receipt of semiannual interest and amortization of discount to the Investment account		

related interest expense on the income statement of the issuer) reflects the market rate of interest rather than the stated rate. At the bond maturity date, Outback's Investment in Bonds account will have a balance of $100,000 or the face value of the bonds.

Corporate Income Taxes

Congress historically has imposed graduated, or progressive, tax rates on corporations. As corporations earn more taxable income, the percentage of that income that must be paid to the federal government generally increases. For instance, corporate tax rates for 2002 were:

Taxable income over	But not over	Tax rate
$ 0	$ 50,000	15%
50,000	75,000	25%
75,000	100,000	34%
100,000	335,000	39%
335,000	10,000,000	34%
10,000,000	15,000,000	35%
15,000,000	18,333,333	38%
18,333,333		35%

Thus, a corporation having $150,000 of taxable income would owe federal income taxes of $41,750, calculated as:

0.15 × ($ 50,000)	$ 7,500
+ 0.25 × ($ 75,000 – $ 50,000)	6,250
+ 0.34 × ($100,000 – $ 75,000)	8,500
+ 0.39 × ($150,000 – $100,000)	19,500
	$41,750

Corporations compute *tax expense,* an accounting amount, based on "income before income taxes" as shown on the income statement. But corporations compute *tax payable* based upon the "taxable income" shown on their tax returns. Typically, the amounts for "income before income taxes" and "taxable income" are not equal. The tax code allows corporations to treat certain items differently for tax purposes from the way those items are treated for accounting purposes. However, in most instances, the tax and accounting treatments will "level out" over time and equalize.

Temporary differences refer to such inconsistencies between an entity's pretax accounting income and its taxable income.[1] Temporary differences generally work to the benefit of corporations. Corporations tend, for tax purposes, to use allowable ways to postpone the recognition of revenues or accelerate the recognition of expenses. For example, a company may use the double-declining balance method of depreciation on equipment for tax return purposes and the straight-line method of depreciation for financial accounting purposes. This treatment allows more depreciation to be taken on the tax return early in the asset's life than is taken on the income statement. However, over the entire asset life, the total asset depreciation that can be taken on either the tax return or the income statement is a depreciable cost.[2]

By using temporary differences to their advantage, corporations can defer (postpone) income taxes to be paid to the government. The two-line reference to income taxes in Exhibit 9-1 indicates that Outback Steakhouse had some temporary differences between

[1] There are also "permanent" differences between taxable and financial accounting income amounts. These items will not "level out" over time and are beyond the scope of this text.

[2] This statement ignores the fact that tax law generally allows a company to depreciate an asset to zero, as opposed to financial accounting, which only allows depreciation to salvage value.

its taxable and accounting income amounts. Footnotes to the company's income statement indicate that the majority of those differences were created by the use of different depreciation methods for tax and financial accounting.

In making its entry for year-end tax expense and tax obligation, Outback Steakhouse would need to recognize that these two amounts are not equal because of the temporary differences. A balancing amount will be made to either Deferred Income Tax Liability or Deferred Income Tax Asset.[3] Using the information in Exhibit 9-1, recognition of the taxes for year-end 2000 would necessitate the following entry (amounts are in thousands).

General Journal				
Date		**Description**	**Debit**	**Credit**
Dec.	31	Income Tax Expense	77,872	
		Income Tax Payable		68,149
		Deferred Income Tax Liability		9,723
		To record federal income tax expense and the currently payable and deferred tax amounts		

The Deferred Income Tax Liability represents income tax payments that the firm has postponed until a later period. This account is typically classified on the balance sheet as a long-term liability. Many large corporations report huge deferred tax liabilities in their balance sheets. For example, as will be shown in a later exhibit, Outback Steakhouse, Inc. had $14,382,000 of Deferred Income Taxes on its December 31, 2000 balance sheet.

Nonrecurring Items

Income from continuing operations represents the earnings produced by a corporation's principal profit-oriented activities. This figure is often considered the best indicator of how a company performed in a given period and is generally used as the starting point to predict a firm's future profits. Income from continuing operations does not include income or losses produced by other, nonrecurring items: (1) discontinued operations, (2) extraordinary items, and (3) cumulative effect of a change in accounting principle. If any of these other items exist, a line item called "Income from Continuing Operations" will appear on the income statement prior to these items.

Listing the "nonrecurring operations" components of the income statement separately and at the bottom of the income statement clearly indicates that they should not be considered when making future profit projections. In 2000, Outback Steakhouse, Inc. did not have any of these income statement components. Therefore, the company's income statement is complete at "Net Income," which for this company is essentially its income from continuing operations.

Visual Recap 9.2 depicts the corporate form of the income statement. The various noncontinuing income statement items are discussed in the following sections.

Discontinued Operations

Most large corporations have more than one line of business. For example, Gannett Corporation (www.gannett.com), whose principal lines of business are print newspapers (including *USA Today)* and broadcasting, also owned a cable business. In 2000, the corporation sold its cable business, and a section entitled *discontinued operations* was included

[3] For purposes of simplicity, it is assumed that if Tax Expense is greater than Tax Payable, the account Deferred Tax Liability is credited. If Tax Payable is greater than Tax Expense, the account Deferred Tax Asset is debited. Such an assumption is not technically correct, but discussion of the underlying reasons is beyond the scope of this text.

VISUAL RECAP 9.2

Corporate Income Statement Format

Corporation Name
Income Statement
For the Year Ended XX/XX/XX

\+ Operating Revenues [Net Sales]
– Cost of Goods Sold
= Gross Profit
– Operating Expenses [Selling and Administrative Expenses]
= Income from Operations

± Other Income (Expenses)
= Income from Continuing Operations before Income Taxes
– Provision for Income Taxes
= Income from Continuing Operations

Discontinued Operations
± Income (Loss) from Operations (net of tax)
± Gain (Loss) from Disposal (net of tax)
= Income before Extraordinary Items

± Gain (Loss) on Extraordinary Items (net of tax)
± Cumulative Effect of Change in Accounting Principle (net of tax)
= Net Income

EARNINGS PER SHARE
Continuing operations
± Discontinued operations
± Extraordinary items
± Cumulative effects of a change in accounting principle
= Net Income

Note: Mathematical relationships are shown with +, –, ±, and =, but do not appear on an actual income statement. [Alternative names are shown in brackets.]

in the company's income statement. Because Gannett owned the cable business for a portion of the year, the operations of the cable business affected Gannett's revenues and expenses and should have been included on the income statement. However, those revenues and expenses should not have been included with income from continuing operations because, as of the end of 2000, the cable business was no longer a part of Gannett.

A **discontinued operations** section normally contains two items: the operating income (or loss) for that business segment, and the gain (or loss) resulting from the disposal of the segment. In the case of Gannett, the income for the year 2000 was $2,437,000 (net of income taxes of $1,598,000) and the gain was $744,700,000 (net of income taxes of $889,300,000). Important line items after income from continuing operations in a corporate income statement are shown "net of tax" so as to reveal the effect of such items on an entity's net income.

When a company's income statement reports discontinued operations, an accompanying financial statement footnote typically describes the nature of those operations. That footnote provides additional details, as well as the operating results and gains or losses attributable to the discontinued business segment.

Extraordinary Items

Occasionally, companies incur large gains or losses due to rare events. These items should be shown separately in a corporate income statement because they should not be considered as indicators of future profit potential. Both of the following criteria must be met before a gain or loss qualifies as an **extraordinary item.**

- *Unusual in nature:* The event should be highly abnormal, taking into account the environment in which the entity operates.
- *Infrequent in occurrence:* The event should not reasonably be expected to recur in the foreseeable future, taking into account the environment in which the entity operates.

Extraordinary items follow the discontinued operations section of its income statement.

Only a small percentage of publicly owned companies each year report extraordinary items in income statements. One item that may meet these conditions is an "act of nature." Assume that, in 2003, a freak act of nature caused the Dallas-Fort Worth area of Texas to be hit by hurricane-related winds and that 14 of the Outback Steakhouses in that metropolitan area were severely damaged, creating a loss related to this incident of $2,500,000. Outback's 2003 income statement would include an extraordinary loss of $2,500,000 less the related income taxes (assumed to be $875,000) or a net extraordinary loss of $1,625,000.

Businesses often incur gains or losses that meet one, but not both, of the criteria for extraordinary items. For example, a company that grows agricultural products in a flood-prone area may suffer material losses every five to ten years because of a flood. Since the floods occur periodically, the resulting losses do not meet the "infrequency of occurrence" requirement for extraordinary items. On the other hand, these losses may qualify as unusual in nature. Typically, gains or losses that meet only one of the two criteria for extraordinary items are reported as separate components of an entity's income from continuing operations. Unlike an extraordinary item, an unusual or infrequently occurring gain or loss is *not* presented net of taxes.

Cumulative Effect of a Change in Accounting Principle

A company that changes from one accounting principle to another must often report a **cumulative effect of a change in accounting principle** in its income statement for the year in which the accounting change is made. Such an item can be briefly defined as the monetary impact that the item would have had on prior years' net incomes had the newly adopted accounting principle been used during those years. Cumulative effect components of an income statement are shown "net of tax" after extraordinary items.

Many changes in accounting principles result from companies implementing new accounting standards adopted by the Financial Accounting Standards Board. Examples of other accounting changes include changing from one inventory accounting method to another or from one depreciation method to another. When a company changes an accounting principle, it must justify the change in the footnotes to its financial statements. That justification should explain why the new accounting principle is preferable to the principle that was formerly used.

Earnings per Share

Earnings per share (EPS) is probably the most closely watched financial disclosure each year for publicly owned companies. In its simplest form, **earnings per share** is computed by dividing a company's net income by the weighted-average number of shares of common stock outstanding during the year.[4] In addition, separate EPS amounts are reported for income from continuing operations, discontinued operations, extraordinary items, and the cumulative effect of a change in accounting principle. Presenting earnings per share by its various components allows decision makers to interpret earnings data more quickly and accurately. A lower than expected earnings per share typically causes a company's stock price to decline, while a positive earnings surprise may trigger an increase in stock price.

In computing EPS, common stock shares are "weighted" as to how long they have been outstanding during the year. To illustrate, suppose that a company had 80,000 shares of common stock outstanding for the first six months of 2002. On July 1, the company issued an additional 20,000 shares, resulting in 100,000 shares being outstanding during the final six months of the year. The weighted-average number of shares outstanding for 2002, using this set of assumptions, is 90,000, computed as [(80,000 shares × 6/12) + (100,000 shares × 6/12)].

MAKING INFORMED ECONOMIC DECISIONS

Accounting is principally a service activity developed to provide information useful to financial decision makers. Decision makers need both access to financial data and the skills to analyze that financial data to make informed economic decisions. This section of the chapter focuses on the objectives of financial statement analysis and identifies the information sources used by decision makers to obtain and analyze financial statement data.

Objectives of Financial Statement Analysis

A wide range of decision makers rely on the information found in corporate income statements. The objectives of financial statement analysis vary across different types of decision makers. Suppliers are often concerned about liquidity and profitability so that they can decide whether to continue extending credit to business customers. Prospective employees are concerned with profitability and market share to identify companies that can offer secure, long-term employment opportunities. Bank loan officers, bondholders, and other long-term creditors are concerned with a firm's ability to generate sufficient profits and cash flows to pay its debts over an extended number of years. An organization's customer base typically analyzes financial statements to determine which businesses will provide a reliable source of products or services or will be in existence in the event of the need for warranty work. Finally, executives of charitable organizations may study corporate income statements to identify companies that can afford to donate funds to good causes.

Investors are the decision makers who must take the most comprehensive approach to financial statement analysis. Investors should be concerned with a company's liquidity because if a company encounters short-term cash-flow problems and cannot pay its suppliers, an investment will likely disappear. Investors also want to be reassured that a firm can retire its long-term debt as it matures. Bondholders and other long-term creditors, if not paid on a timely basis, can seize a company's assets and force the firm out of business. A business's profitability is of obvious concern to investors because they want to be assured that a company will generate sufficient profits to provide a reasonable rate of return on owners' equity.

[4] If a company has preferred stock outstanding, dividends on preferred stock are subtracted from net income when computing earnings per share.

Information Sources for Financial Statement Analysis

The corporate income statement is just one source of data regarding corporations. Decision makers must analyze each financial statement in an annual report and the accompanying footnotes and other relevant information to reliably evaluate the firm's financial status and future prospects.

Typically, a public company's annual report is a condensed version of the 10–K registration statement that must be filed each year with the Securities and Exchange Commission (SEC). Investors can request a 10-K for a public company directly from the firm or, for many large companies, access recent 10-Ks at the SEC's EDGAR (electronic data gathering and retrieval) Web site (www.sec.gov/edgar.shtml). Most large companies now include annual reports on their Web sites under the heading "Investor Relations."

Content of annual reports may vary from company to company, but most annual reports contain the following items: the management's discussion and analysis (MD&A) section, a financial highlights table, the financial statements and accompanying footnotes, and an independent auditor's report. The MD&A section contains a summary discussion of factors that have recently affected the company's financial status, as well as a general overview of management's key plans for the future. The financial highlights table tracks important financial items over multiple periods. The company's audit report expresses the opinion by an independent accounting firm as to the "fairness" of presentation of the financial statements relative to generally accepted accounting principles. The audit report is generally "unqualified," which means that there is nothing out-of-the ordinary to report about the financial statements or the company. However, the audit report could include qualifications or discussions of items such as departures from generally accepted accounting principles (GAAP), inconsistent application of GAAP, or conditions that may threaten the firm's survival or its ability to continue as a going concern.

In addition to information provided by the company itself, an assortment of reference materials are published by investment advisory firms, such as Value Line, Standard & Poor's (S&P), Moody's, and Dun & Bradstreet (D&B). The *Value Line Investment Survey,* for example, provides a detailed analysis of key financial statistics and the future prospects of approximately 1,600 public companies. Financial and nonfinancial information for individual companies can also be obtained from business periodicals such as *Barron's, Business Week, Forbes,* and *The Wall Street Journal.*

Industry norms for a wide range of financial ratios and other financial measures are also available. Two popular sources of such information are *Industry Norms and Key Business Ratios* published by Dun & Bradstreet and *RMA Annual Statement Studies* published by Robert Morris Associates. By having access to current industry norms, decision makers can better interpret an individual company's financial statement ratios.

ANALYTICAL TECHNIQUES

This section discusses and illustrates three general analytical techniques for financial statements: trend analysis, common-sized financial statements, and ratio analysis. Each of these methods can be a powerful tool for analyzing and interpreting financial statements.

Decision makers analyze a company's financial statements to identify relationships—expected and unexpected—in the firm's financial data. Further investigation, though, is usually required to determine whether these relationships indicate whether a company's financial health is improving or deteriorating. Analytical techniques can also be used to make predictions about future financial performance and financial condition based upon a company's past data. Analysts must realize, however, that changes in a company's operations, its industry, and the overall economic environment can cause historical data to be a less than reliable indicator of future prospects.

Additionally, financial statement analysis is more difficult for companies that have two or more major lines of business. For such companies, analytical techniques are most useful if they are applied independently to the financial data of each major business segment of the firm. The data in this section are for Outback Steakhouses, Inc., which is in one major line of business used for analysis: retail food sales.

Trend Analysis

A great deal of information can be learned about a company's financial condition and financial performance by simply studying changes in key financial statement items over a set time. To track the proportionate changes in items from period to period, financial statement dollar amounts are converted into percentages and **trend analysis** is used to analyze the percentage changes over time. These percentage trends are then used to predict future dollar amounts for given financial statement items. Trend analysis allows comparisons to be made from year to year without regard for the magnitude of the numbers. Instead, relationships between and among the numbers are observed.

To apply trend analysis, a base year is selected and each amount on the financial statements is expressed as a percentage of the base-year figure. Typically, the first or earliest year for which data are available is selected as the base year. Using the income statement information given earlier in the chapter in Exhibit 9-1, 1999 is selected as the base year for Outback's trend analysis. Exhibit 9-3 shows each amount for 2000 expressed as a percentage of its related 1999 amount. Thus, revenues are 116 ($1,906,006 ÷ $1,646,013) percent of what they were in 1999.

EXHIBIT 9-3

Outback Steakhouse, Inc. Trend Analysis of Income Statements

	Years Ended December 31			
	2000	Trend %	1999	Trend %
Revenues	$ 1,906,006	116%	$ 1,646,013	100%
Costs and Expenses				
Cost of sales	$ 715,224	115%	$ 620,249	100%
Labor and other operating	809,393	118%	686,835	100%
Depreciation and amortization	58,109	115%	50,709	100%
General and administrative	75,410	113%	66,666	100%
Total Costs and Expenses	$ 1,658,136	116%	$ 1,424,459	100%
Income from Operations	$ 247,870	112%	$ 221,554	100%
Other Income (Expense)				
Interest expense*	(2,058)	68%	(3,042)	100%
Income from operations of unconsolidated affiliates	2,457	226%	1,089	100%
Interest revenue	4,617	326%	1,416	100%
Income before MI and Taxes	$ 252,886	114%	$ 221,017	100%
Minority Interest Income	(33,884)	114%	(29,770)	100%
Income before Income Taxes	$ 219,002	115%	$ 191,247	100%
Provision for Income Taxes				
Current and Deferred	(77,872)	116%	(66,924)	100%
Net Income	$ 141,130	114%	$ 124,323	100%
Basic Earnings per Share	$1.82	298%	$0.61	100%

*See notes in Exhibit 9-1.

Reviewing the information in Exhibit 9-3 indicates that Outback Steakhouse had approximately the same relationship between each of its revenues and expenses for the two years. A 16 percent increase in revenues generated almost an equal percentage change in all of the primary cost and expense line items. The major differences between the two years were in the "Other Income (Expense)." The significant increase in "Income from operatiions of unconsolidated subsidiaries" reflects the numerous acquisitions made by the company during 2000; these acquisitions were discussed in the MD&A and the financial statement footnotes. Earnings per share was raised primarily by the increased profitability, but also because there were fewer common shares outstanding at the end of 2000 than there were at the end of 1999, due to the purchase of treasury stock.

Trend analysis (and other analytical techniques) can be enhanced by using computer-based graphics. Computer software packages such as *PowerPoint, Excel, Freelance Graphics,* and *Harvard Graphics* allow decision makers to more easily analyze and interpret financial data. As an example, Exhibit 9-4 depicts a graphical representation of the first five lines of Outback's income statement as both raw numbers and as trend analysis.

EXHIBIT 9-4 Year-to-Year Analysis: Raw Numbers and Trend Analysis

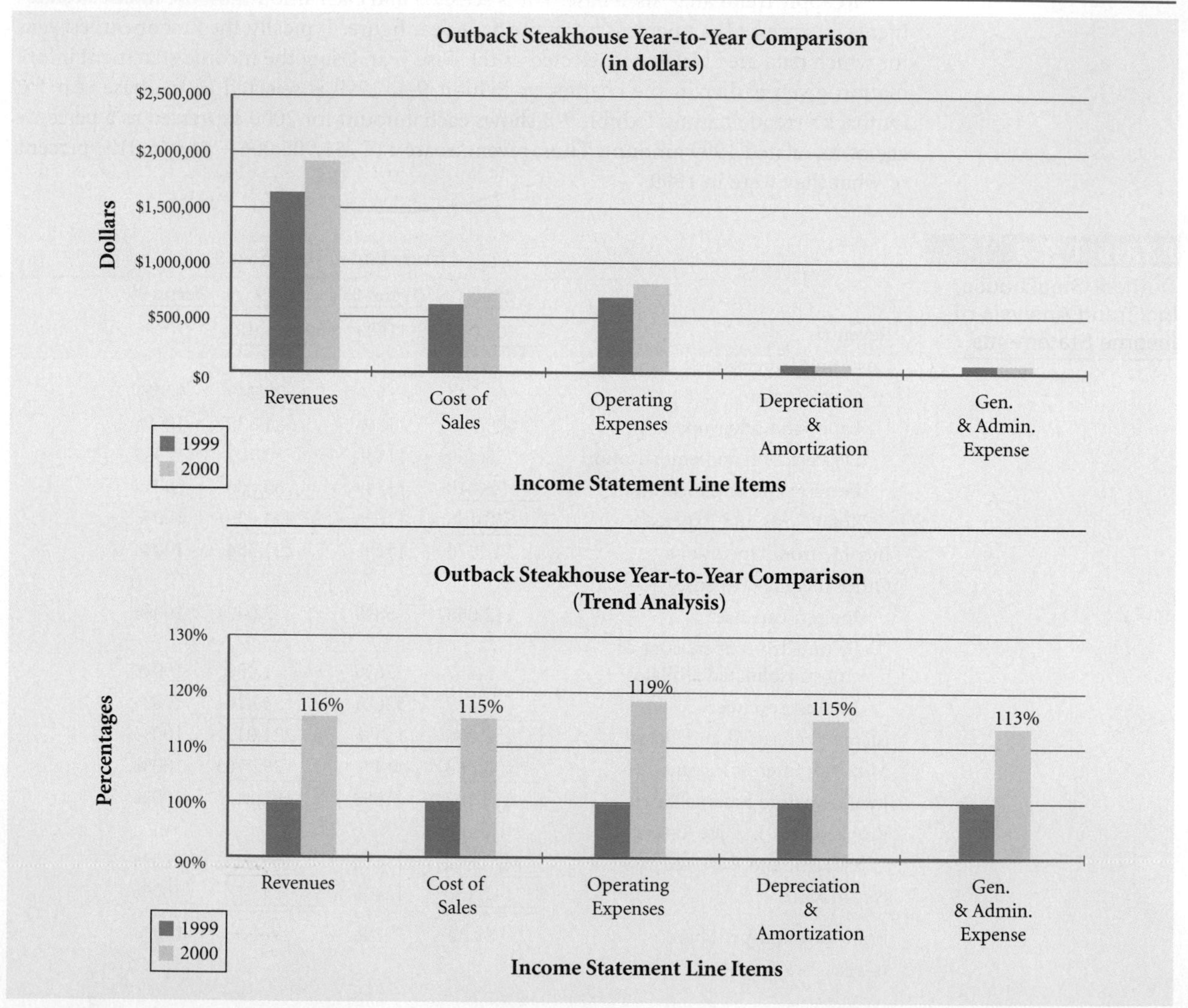

Common-Sized Financial Statements

As opposed to trend analysis which compares year-to-year information, decision makers use common-sized financial statements to better understand relationships among items within a financial statement or series of financial statements. The intra-year relationships are then compared across years to determine if they are maintained. In **common-sized financial statements,** each line item is expressed as a percentage of a major financial statement component. For example, in a common-sized income statement each line item is expressed as a percentage of revenue (or net revenue). In a common-sized balance sheet, each line item is expressed as a percentage of total assets (or total liabilities and stockholders' equity).

Exhibit 9-5 presents Outback's common-sized income statements for 2000 and 1999. Percentages were found by dividing each amount on the 2000 and 1999 income statement by $1,906,006 and $1,646,013, respectively. Note the consistency between the years for the percentage of the various expenses as to revenue amounts. Each year indicates a net income figure of approximately 7 percent on revenues generated. (Some percentages in the exhibits have been rounded for consistency with other amounts.)

Outback Steakhouse, Inc.'s 2000 and 1999 balance sheets are presented in Exhibit 9-6 on page 265 with the common-sized balance sheets. Percentages for the common-sized statement were derived by dividing each 2000 and 1999 balance sheet amount by $1,022,535,000 and $852,282,000, respectively, total assets at year-end.

The common-sized balance sheets indicate that the company's largest financial asset is its property, fixtures, and equipment (PF&E). The common-sized statements also indicate that, in both years, the Common Stock account represents a zero percentage of the total amount of stockholders' equity. From this information, it is easy to tell that Outback Steakhouse, Inc.'s common stock par value is extremely small. By reviewing the actual financial statements on

EXHIBIT 9-5

Outback Steakhouse, Inc. Common-Sized Income Statements

	Years Ended December 31			
	2000	%	1999	%
Revenues	$ 1,906,006	100.0%	$ 1,646,013	100.0%
Costs and Expenses				
Cost of sales	$ 715,224	37.5%	$ 620,249	37.7%
Labor and other operating	809,393	42.5%	686,835	41.7%
Depreciation and amortization	58,109	3.0%	50,709	3.1%
General and administrative	75,410	4.0%	66,666	4.1%
Total Costs and Expenses	$ 1,658,136	87.0%	$ 1,424,459	86.5%
Income from Operations	$ 247,870	13.0%	$ 221,554	13.5%
Other Income (Expense)				
Interest expense*	(2,058)	0.1%	(3,042)	0.2%
Income from operations of unconsolidated affiliates	2,457	0.1%	1,089	0.1%
Interest revenue	4,617	0.2%	1,416	0.1%
Income before MI and Taxes	$ 252,886	13.3%	$ 221,017	13.4%
Minority Interest Income	(33,884)	(1.8)%	(29,770)	(1.8)%
Income before Income Taxes	$ 219,002	11.5%	$ 191,247	11.6%
Provision for Income Taxes				
Current and Deferred	(77,872)	(4.1)%	(66,924)	(4.1)%
Net Income	$ 141,130	7.4%	$ 124,323	7.6%
Basic Earnings per Share	$1.82	298.0	$0.61	100.0

*See notes in Exhibit 9-1.

the company's Web site, it is found that the par value per share is $0.01. At year-end 2000, 78,514,000 shares were issued and 76,632,000 shares were outstanding.

Any unexpected changes or unusual relationships within a single year, or between years, of a company's common-sized financial statements should be investigated to assess whether these items point to developing financial problems for the firm. There are no such apparent changes in the relationships for Outback Steakhouse, Inc.

Common-sized financial statements also allow decision makers to more easily compare and contrast the financial data of two or more companies. Suppose that companies A and B are the two leading firms in an industry. However, Company A is much larger than Company B. This size difference makes it difficult to compare the companies' financial data. Common-sized financial statements for the two firms can be prepared to minimize this problem.

Decision makers can also use common-sized financial statements to compare a company's financial data to industry norms. Dun & Bradstreet's annual publication *Industry Norms and Key Business Ratios* provides industry averages for common-sized balance sheets in several hundred industries. Exhibit 9-7 provides selected items from a recent common-sized balance sheet and income statement for the restaurant industry. Corresponding percentages from the 2000 common-sized balance sheet of Outback Steakhouse, Inc. are presented for comparison purposes.

The statistics in Exhibit 9-7 indicate that Outback Steakhouse had much more cash and PF&E, on a proportional basis, than the average restaurant, as well as significantly less long-term debt. All three of these indicators provide favorable investment indicators for Outback's common stock. Relative to the income statement, Outback's cost of sales and labor costs are relatively high, but depreciation and amortization and income tax percentages are relatively low.

Ratio Analysis

The most widely used method to analyze financial data is **ratio analysis** or the study of relationships between two financial statement items. Decision makers use financial ratios on both a cross-sectional and longitudinal basis. **Cross-sectional ratio analysis** involves comparing a company's financial ratios with those of competing companies and/or with industry norms. **Longitudinal ratio analysis** focuses on changes in a firm's financial ratios over time, generally several years.

Exhibits 9-8 through 9-12 present equations for a variety of financial ratios (some of which were discussed in earlier chapters), along with a brief explanation of their purpose. These ratios are classified into five categories: liquidity, leverage, activity, profitability, and market strength. Ratio computations for Outback Steakhouse, Inc. for the year 2000 are also presented in the exhibits using income statement and balance sheet data from Exhibits 9-1 and 9-6. In some cases, information for Outback's ratio computation is not available. An industry norm is also included, if available.

Liquidity ratios (Exhibit 9-8 on page 266) are used to evaluate whether a firm has the available current assets to pay its upcoming debts. The quick ratio is often a better indicator of liquidity because it omits inventory, which would need to be sold in order to be used to pay debts, and other often nonliquid assets (such as supplies and prepaid items) from the calculation.

Financial leverage ratios (Exhibit 9-9 on page 266) focus on the relationship between creditor and ownership equity in a firm. A company's stockholders benefit if the rate of return earned on borrowed funds exceeds the interest rate paid on those funds; stockholders are placed at a disadvantage if the opposite holds true. The long-term debt to equity ratio is a key measure of the benefit (or detriment) of a company's financial leverage. The times interest earned ratio provides a margin of safety measure that is particularly useful when

EXHIBIT 9-6

Outback Steakhouse, Inc. Common-Sized Balance Sheets

	December 31			
	2000	**%**	**1999**	**%**
ASSETS				
Current Assets				
Cash	$ 131,604	12.9%	$ 92,623	10.9%
Inventories	27,871	2.7%	26,088	3.1%
Other CA	22,572	2.2%	24,500	2.9%
Total CA	$ 182,047	17.8%	$ 143,211	16.8%
PF&E (net)	693,975	67.9%	607,028	71.2%
Investments in Subsidiaries	29,655	2.9%	21,272	2.5%
Other Assets	116,858	11.4%	80,771	9.5%
Total Assets	$ 1,022,535	100.0%	$ 852,282	100.0%
LIABILITIES AND SE				
Current Liabilities	$ 168,045	16.4%	$ 130,935	15.4%
Deferred Income Taxes	14,382	1.4%	4,659	0.5%
Long-term Debt	11,678	1.1%	1,519	0.2%
Other LT Liabilities	4,000	0.4%	4,500	0.5%
Total Liabilities	$ 198,105	19.4%	$ 141,613	16.6%
Minority Interest	$ 16,840	1.6%	$ 17,704	2.1%
STOCKHOLDERS' EQUITY				
Common Stock	$ 785	0.1%	$ 775	0.1%
Additional Paid-in Capital	214,541	21.0%	194,251	22.8%
Retained Earnings	638,383	62.4%	501,384	58.9%
	$ 853,709	83.5%	$ 696,410	81.7%
Treasury Stock	(46,119)	(4.5)%	(3,445)	(0.4)%
Total SE	$ 807,590	79.0%	$ 692,965	81.3%
Total L & SE	$ 1,022,535	100.0%	$ 852,282	100.0%

Note: dollars in thousands

EXHIBIT 9-7

Comparison of Industry and Outback Steakhouse Common-Sized Items

	Industry Norm	**Outback Steakhouse**
Cash	12.8%	12.9%
Total current assets	31.1%	17.8%
Property, fixtures & equipment	54.4%	67.9%
Current liabilities	39.5%	16.4%
Long-term debt	26.9%	1.1%
Gross profit	57.7%	62.5%
Net profit after tax	3.3%	7.4%

analyzing highly leveraged companies. The lower this ratio, the more risk a company faces of defaulting on its periodic interest payments.

Activity ratios (Exhibit 9-10 on page 267) reveal how quickly a company is converting receivables into cash and how quickly it is selling inventory. The longer receivables go uncollected, the more susceptible they are to bad debt losses. Similarly, the longer the time required to sell inventory, the higher the risk that inventory items will become obsolete, damaged, or stolen. Total asset turnover ratio can be used to gauge success in generating revenues relative to the organization's total asset base.

EXHIBIT 9-8
Key Financial Liquidity Ratios

Liquidity Ratios

Measure a firm's ability to finance its day-to-day operations and to pay its liabilities as they mature.

Current ratio = Current Assets ÷ Current Liabilities

Measures a firm's ability to pay its current liabilities from its current assets

Outback Steakhouse:
= $182,047,000 ÷ $168,045,000
= 1.08

Restaurant industry norm:
= 1.0

Quick ratio = $\frac{\text{(Cash + Cash Equivalents + Net Current Receivables + Short-term Investments)}}{\text{Current Liabilities}}$

Measures a firm's ability to pay its current liabilities without relying on the sale of its inventory

Outback Steakhouse:
= $131,604,000 ÷ $168,045,000
= 0.78

Restaurant industry norm:
= 0.5

EXHIBIT 9-9
Key Financial Leverage Ratios

Leverage Ratios

Measure how a firm uses debt capital relative to equity capital; also known as debt utilization ratios.

Debt to total assets ratio = Total Liabilities ÷ Total Assets

Measures the proportion of total assets in a firm financed by debt rather than equity

Outback Steakhouse:
= $198,105,000 ÷ $1,022,535
= 19.4%

Long-term debt to equity ratio = Long-term Debt ÷ Total Stockholders' Equity

Measures the proportion of long-term debt in a firm relative to the total firm capitalization

Outback Steakhouse:
= $30,060,000 ÷ $807,590,000
= 3.7%

Times interest earned =
(Net Income + Interest Expense + Income Tax Expense) ÷ Interest Expense

Measures the number of times that a firm's interest expense is covered by earnings

Outback Steakhouse:
= ($141,130,000 + $2,058,000 + $77,872,000) ÷ $2,058,000
= $221,060,000 ÷ $2,058,000
= 107.4 times

The most common benchmarks against which to evaluate a firm's profitability (Exhibit 9-11 on page 268) are its sales, assets, and stockholders' equity. The first of these measures can help to evaluate how effectively costs have been controlled relative to revenues; and the others provide an indication of how effectively organizational resources have been used to generate profits.

The first four categories of financial ratios focus on a company's financial condition or operating results. Market strength ratios (Exhibit 9-12 on page 268), on the other hand, focus on market perception of the company. Market strength ratios tend to be more volatile than other financial ratios because they are influenced by investors' perceptions and expectations, both of which can change rapidly. Security analysts suggest that investors often overreact to quarterly earnings data, changes in management, and news reports regarding a company's future prospects or those of its industry. The result is volatile stock prices.

A company's P/E ratio reveals how much investors are willing to pay for each $1 of the firm's earnings. And, despite impressive operating results and a strong financial condition, a

EXHIBIT 9-10

Key Financial Activity Ratios

Activity Ratios

Measure how well a firm is managing its assets; also known as asset utilization ratios.

Accounts receivable turnover ratio = Net Credit Sales ÷ Average Accounts Receivable*

Measures the number of times a firm collects its accounts receivable each year

Outback Steakhouse:
Outback does not sell on "house" credit (i.e., have its own credit cards) and has no accounts receivable.

Age of receivables = 360 Days ÷ Accounts Receivable Turnover Ratio

Measures the length of time normally required to collect a receivable resulting from a credit sale

Outback Steakhouse:
Outback has no accounts receivable.

Inventory turnover ratio = Cost of Goods Sold ÷ Average Inventory*

Measures the number of times that a firm sells its inventory each year

Outback Steakhouse:
= $715,224,000 ÷ [($26,088,000 + $27,871,000) ÷ 2]
= $715,224,000 ÷ $26,979,500
= 26.5 times

Age of inventory = 360 ÷ Inventory Turnover Ratio

Measures the length of time normally required to sell inventory

Outback Steakhouse:
= 360 ÷ 26.5
= 13.6 days

Total asset turnover ratio = Net Sales ÷ Average Total Assets*

Measures a firm's ability to generate sales relative to its investment in assets

Outback Steakhouse:
= $1,906,006,000 ÷ [($1,022,535,000 + $852,282,000) ÷ 2]
= $1,906,006,000 ÷ $937,408,500
= 2.03

*Average = (Beginning + Ending) ÷ 2

company's common stock may fare poorly in the capital markets when the P/E ratio is extremely high because the market believes the company's stock is overpriced. If a common stock is selling for an abnormally low P/E ratio, investors will likely view the stock as a bargain. P/E ratios are particularly insightful when analyzed on a comparative basis.

Like most financial statistics, market strength ratios may be unreliable when used independently of other available information. For example, regardless of profitability, a company's market price changes may reflect industry conditions, personnel changes (such as the retirement of key executives), and many other factors. Likewise, a company's P/E ratio can be significantly distorted in any one year by extraordinary losses and other "special" income statement items discussed earlier in this chapter.

A company's market price to book value ratio indicates how much investors are willing to pay for each $1 of the firm's net assets. The market price of a common stock often differs considerably from its book value per share because the accounting-based book value does not necessarily reflect the "true" economic value of a corporation's common stock. Recall that, for accounting purposes, historical cost (rather than market value) is the primary valuation basis used for most assets.

No single ratio or collection of ratios can reveal which stocks' market prices will definitely increase or decrease in the future. Nevertheless, these ratios may provide clues about the stock market's perception of the investment potential of a common stock. Decision makers must understand how to compute financial ratios, as well as recognize

EXHIBIT 9-11

Key Financial Profitability Ratios

Profitability Ratios

Measure a firm's earnings performance.

Profit margin percentage = Net Income ÷ Net Sales

Measures the percentage of each sales dollar that contributes to net income

Outback Steakhouse:
= $141,130,000 ÷ $1,906,006,000
= 7.4%

Gross profit percentage = Gross Profit ÷ Net Sales

Measures the percentage of each sales dollar not absorbed by cost of goods sold. Gross profit = Sales – Cost of Goods Sold

Outback Steakhouse:
= ($1,906,006,000 – $715,224,000) ÷ 1,906,006,000
= $1,190,782,000 ÷ $1,906,006,000
= 62.5%**

Return on assets = (Net Income + Interest Expense) ÷ Average Total Assets*

Measures the rate of return a firm realizes on its investment in assets

Outback Steakhouse:
= ($141,130,000 + $2,058,000) ÷ $937,408,500
= $143,188,000 ÷ $937,408,500
= 15.3%

Return on Equity
= (Net Income – Preferred Stock Dividends) ÷ Average Common Stockholders' Equity*

Measures the rate of return on a firm's common stockholders' equity

Outback Steakhouse:
= ($141,130,000 – $0) ÷ [($692,965,000 + $807,590,000) ÷ 2]
= $141,130,000 ÷ $750,277,500
= 18.8%

Restaurant industry norm:
= 15.7%

*Average = (Beginning + Ending) ÷ 2

** This percentage is not precise because it is unknown how much of the labor and other operating expenses should actually be considered a part of Cost of Goods Sold. However, the amounts are a rough approximation.

EXHIBIT 9-12

Key Financial Market Strength Ratios

Market Strength Ratios

Measure how the capital markets, as a whole, perceive the firm's common stock.

Price-earnings ratio = Current Market Price ÷ Earnings per Share

Measures the amount that investors are willing to pay for each dollar of a firm's earnings for most recent 12-month period

Outback Steakhouse:
= $25.88 ÷ $1.82
= 14.22:1

Market price from *The Wall Street Journal* average price on 12/29/00, the last trading day of 2000.

Market price to book value ratio = Current Market Price ÷ Book Value per Share

Measures the amount that investors are willing to pay for each dollar of a firm's net assets. Book Value per Share = Total common stockholders' equity ÷ Number of Common Shares Outstanding

Outback Steakhouse:
= $25.88 ÷ ($807,590,000 ÷ 76,632,000)
= $25.88 ÷ $10.54
= 2.5

that common sense must be exercised in interpreting those ratios. The final part of this chapter expands upon this intuitive approach to financial statement analysis by discussing the concept of earnings quality and pro forma financial statements.

ASSESSING EARNINGS QUALITY

In recent years, financial statement users have become increasingly concerned about the concept of earnings quality. Although not rigidly defined, **earnings quality** generally refers to the degree of correlation between a firm's economic income and its reported earnings determined by generally accepted accounting principles or GAAP. Economic income is traditionally defined as the change in the total value of a business between two periods. The analytical techniques illustrated in the previous section do not allow a comprehensive assessment of the quality of a firm's reported earnings for several reasons.

Analyzing the quality of a company's reported accounting earnings requires the exercise of considerable judgment on the part of financial decision makers. An understanding of the economic factors that influence given companies' operations, knowledge of accounting rules and concepts, simple intuition, and common sense are the principal tools used in analyzing earnings quality. Exhibit 9-13 provides a list of several ways decision makers can assess the quality of a firm's reported earnings.

First and foremost, financial fraud obviously diminishes the correlation between a company's economic income and its reported accounting earnings. The last few years have been fraught with cases of management or accounting fraud including, but not limited to, Enron, Waste Management, Sunbeam, Leslie Faye, and WorldCom.

When analyzing a firm's reported earnings, decision makers usually focus on the income generated by its continuing operations. Extraordinary gains and losses are generally not given much weight in assessing future profit potential since those items involve nonrecurring and unusual events or transactions that are unlikely to affect a company's future earnings.

Business executives or their accountants can, however, manipulate a firm's reported earnings without ever engaging in financial fraud. For instance, several alternative methods often exist that can be used to account for a specific type of transaction or event. Depreciation expense and cost of goods sold are two examples of income statement items that may be materially affected by a firm's choice of accounting methods. Thus, a good place to gain informa-

EXHIBIT 9-13

Ways to Assess the Quality of a Firm's Reported Earnings

- Compare accounting principles employed by a firm to those used by competitors. Does the set of accounting principles used by the firm tend to inflate its reported earnings?
- Analyze any recent changes in accounting principles or accounting estimates to determine whether they inflated reported earnings.
- Read the footnotes to the financial statements to identify any unusual events that may have affected reported earnings.
- Read the footnotes to the financial statements to determine whether any major loss contingencies exist that could negatively affect future earnings.
- Review extraordinary losses included in the income statement to determine that they are actually nonoperating items.
- Attempt to determine whether there are any significant expenses not reflected in the income statement, such as warranty expense on products sold.
- Attempt to determine whether discretionary expenditures, such as advertising and maintenance expenses, have been reduced or delayed.

tion for analyzing the quality of a company's earnings is the initial financial statement footnote in a company's annual report. This footnote is generally called "Summary of Significant Accounting Policies" and provides information on the accounting methods used by the company. This footnote may reveal whether a company uses income-inflating accounting methods. For example, the use of the FIFO cost-flow assumption for inventory generally results in a higher net income than does LIFO during a period of steadily rising prices.

Other information provided by financial statement footnotes include whether a company has recently changed accounting methods and the impact of such changes on its reported earnings. Footnotes will also identify unusual items that affected the firm's past earnings or have the potential to affect it future earnings. For example, most large companies are involved in some type of litigation that may have the potential to significantly influence the future earnings of a business. A company's financial statement footnotes will provide a summary of the major litigation cases in which it is involved, as well as the likely financial statement impact of these cases. Decision makers should review these disclosures and determine whether they agree with management's assessment (often included in the MD&A section) of how pending legal matters may affect a company's financial status.

Business executives can also influence their firms' reported earnings by modifying operating decisions. Such information can often be gained by reviewing the company's financial statements over several years, especially using common-sized statements. For example, if a company is having a poor year profit-wise, management may purposefully delay expenditures for advertising or maintenance or may decline to fill a job position that has become vacant. Such tactics may improve a company's reported accounting earnings for a given year, but actually diminish the overall economic value of the business. For instance, postponing maintenance expenses could result in a higher rate of equipment breakdowns, higher repair bills, and a decline in production efficiency in future years.

A company's reported profits may not be closely correlated with its economic income even if there have been no explicit efforts to distort those profits. Many financial statement items are estimates, such as warranty and bad debts expense. These estimates may be materially in error although they are made honestly and objectively. Additionally, generally accepted accounting principles do not capture, or quantify, all events that affect the change in the economic value of a business during a given period. In fact, GAAP are not intended to capture all of these variables; for example, increases in the current or market value of most assets are not recorded under GAAP, nor are values of intellectual capital.

SUMMARY

Corporate income statements are an important source of information for financial decision makers. Of particular interest to investors is a corporation's income from continuing operations, which represents the earnings of a company's principal profit-oriented activities. Investors often use this figure as the starting point for predicting a corporation's future profits. Discontinued operations, extraordinary items, and cumulative effects of changes in accounting principles are "special" income statement items that may influence a corporation's net income for any given year but should have little, if any, impact on future years' profitability. These "special" items are reported on the income statement net of the income taxes caused or saved.

Income taxes are a large expense for most corporations and pose complex accounting issues. Corporations often use different methods of determining the items that appear on the income statement and tax return. As a result, a corporation's income tax expense and tax payable for a given year are typically not equal. The difference between these two amounts is recorded in a Deferred Income Tax account. Deferred income tax is usually a long-term liability, although occasionally it may be a current liability or even an asset.

To make informed economic decisions, financial statement users must be able to analyze financial data and draw proper conclusions from such analyses. Different types of decision makers have different financial statement analysis objectives, but investors typically must take the most comprehensive analysis approach.

Annual reports are the principal source of information used in analyzing financial statement data. Several sections of an annual report that are particularly useful are the management discussion and analysis, financial highlights table, financial statement footnotes, and the independent auditor's report. Other sources of information include the publications of investment advisory firms such as Standard & Poor's and Dun & Bradstreet.

Common approaches to analyzing financial statements include trend analysis, preparation of common-sized financial statements, and ratio analysis. Trend analysis studies percentage changes in financial statement items over time and is often used to predict the future value of a financial statement item. Common-sized financial statements illustrate the relationships among items within a financial statement or series of financial statements. Ratio analysis involves a comparison of the relationship between two financial statement items. A company's financial ratios are often compared to its historical amounts and to industry norms. The five general types of financial ratios are liquidity, leverage, activity, profitability, and market strength.

In recent years, financial statement users have focused increasing attention on assessing earnings quality, which refers to the degree of correlation between a business's economic income and its reported accounting earnings. Factors influencing earnings quality include financial fraud, concerted efforts to manipulate or distort financial data, the need to estimate many financial statement amounts, and the ability to choose alternative accounting methods.

KEY TERMS

- common-sized financial statement
- consolidation
- cost method (of accounting for a stock investment)
- cross-sectional ratio analysis
- cumulative effect of a change in accounting principle
- discontinued operation
- earnings per share
- earnings quality
- equity method (of accounting for a stock investment)
- extraordinary item
- income from continuing operations
- longitudinal ratio analysis
- minority interest
- parent company
- ratio analysis
- subsidiary
- temporary difference
- trend analysis

QUESTIONS

1. Explain how a long-term investment by Paolo Company in Sanri Company affects the income statement and balance sheet of Paolo Company if: (a) Paolo owns less than 20% of Sanri; (b) Paolo owns between 20% and 50% of Sanri; and (c) Paolo owns more than 50% of Sanri. *(LO 9.1)*
2. Why is a firm's income from continuing operations of interest to decision makers? *(LO 9.2)*
3. How is earnings per share computed? *(LO 9.3)*
4. Distinguish between "taxable income" and "income before income taxes." How does each item affect the balance sheet and income statement? *(LO 9.4)*
5. Define the term *temporary difference* in reference to corporate income taxes. How does a temporary difference affect the balance sheet? *(LO 9.4)*

6. Is the Deferred Income Tax account typically a liability or an asset account? Is the Deferred Income Tax account typically classified as current or long-term? Explain the rationale for your answers. *(LO 9.4)*
7. What financial data are presented on a corporate income statement for a discontinued line of business? Why are these data reported separately in the income statement? *(LO 9.2)*
8. Briefly explain why the objectives of financial statement analysis vary among different types of financial decision makers. *(LO 9.5)*
9. Identify three analytical techniques used to analyze financial statements. Define each technique and explain how each is used by decision makers. *(LO 9.6, 9.7, 9.8)*
10. What is earnings per share? Why is EPS presented on the income statement as opposed to all other financial statement ratios? *(LO 9.8)*
11. Define the following terms in relationship to ratio analysis: (a) liquidity, (b) leverage, (c) activity, (d) profitability, and (e) market strength. What ratios are used to measure each category? *(LO 9.8)*
12. Define earnings quality. Identify several factors that influence the quality of a company's reported earnings. *(LO 9.9)*
13. Many companies have been said to "manage earnings." Use library or Internet resources to find out what is meant by earnings management and discuss how it could affect earnings quality. *(LO 9.9)*

EXERCISES

14. **True or False** *(All LOs)*

Following are a series of statements regarding topics discussed in this chapter.

Required:

Indicate whether each statement is true (T) or false (F).

(1) Corporations pay taxes based upon their taxable income, rather than on income before income taxes.

(2) A company that changes from one accounting principle to another generally must report a "catch-up" effect in its income statement in the year of the change.

(3) The market price to book value ratio indicates how much investors are willing to pay for each $1 of a company's net assets.

(4) If a corporation's common stock has a much higher price-earnings ratio than its historical norm, sophisticated investors will typically view that stock as "bargain" priced.

(5) A price-earnings ratio reveals how much investors are willing to pay for each $1 of earnings reported by a company over the previous twelve months.

(6) Decision makers commonly use activity ratios to evaluate a company's liquidity.

(7) Common-sized financial statements can be used to identify important structural changes in a company's operating results and financial condition over a period of time.

(8) Financial leverage works to the advantage of company owners when the interest rate paid on borrowed funds exceeds the rate of return earned on those funds.

(9) The study of percentage changes in financial statement items over a period of time is known as trend analysis.

(10) Earnings quality generally refers to the degree of correlation between a firm's economic income and its reported earnings determined by generally accepted accounting principles.

(11) In a common-sized balance sheet, each line item is expressed as a percentage of current assets.

15. **Elements of a Corporate Income Statement** *(LO 9.2)*

Following are some items often reported in corporate income statements.

(a) Operating Income
(b) Cumulative Effect of a Change in Accounting Principle
(c) Gross Profit
(d) Discontinued Operations
(e) Net Income
(f) Extraordinary Loss
(g) Income from Continuing Operations

Required:

(1) List these items in their proper order in a corporate income statement.

(2) Why are extraordinary items included as separate components of a corporate income statement?

(3) If you were going to make a judgment about a company's future financial performance, on which income statement line would you base that judgment? Explain the reason for your answer.

16. **Income Statement Terms** *(LO 9.2)*

Following are definitions or descriptions of terms relating to corporate income statements or income measurement.

(a) The change in an entity's collective net income for prior years assuming a newly adopted accounting principle has been implemented

(b) A difference between an entity's taxable income and pretax accounting income that arises from applying different accounting methods for taxation and financial reporting purposes

(c) An account in which a corporation records the difference between its income tax expense and income tax payable each year; typically a long-term liability account

(d) Generally, net income divided by the weighted-average number of shares of common stock outstanding during a given year

(e) A material gain or loss that is both unusual in nature and infrequent in occurrence

(f) The amount that represents the earnings produced by a corporation's principal profit-oriented activities

(g) A correction of a material error occurring in a previous accounting period that involves a revenue or expense

(h) A section of a corporate income statement devoted to a business segment that is not part of the company at year-end

Required:

Match each definition or description with the appropriate term from the following list.

(1) Discontinued operation
(2) Temporary difference

(3) Earnings per share
(4) Income from continuing operations
(5) Deferred income tax
(6) Prior period adjustment
(7) Cumulative effect of a change in accounting principle
(8) Extraordinary item

17. **Preparing a Corporate Income Statement** *(LO 9.2)*

Derinda Bentz is a business major at Southern Missouri University. Derinda is struggling with an accounting homework assignment to prepare an income statement for an imaginary firm, Harsha Corporation. Derinda has decided that the following items should be included in this income statement.

(a) Cost of Goods Sold
(b) Income Taxes Payable
(c) Accounts Receivable
(d) Income Tax Expense
(e) Earnings per Share
(f) Loss from Discontinued Operations (net of taxes)
(g) Net Sales
(h) Possible Loss from Lawsuit
(i) Accounts Payable
(j) Dividends (declared by the Board of Directors)
(k) Gain on Sale of Equipment
(l) Salaries Payable
(m) Selling and Administrative Expenses
(n) Stock Dividends (declared but not yet distributed to stockholders)

Required:

Help Derinda complete her homework assignment. Which of the items listed should be included in Harsha Corporation's income statement? In what order should these items appear in the income statement? Explain where all items that do not appear in the income statement will appear in the financial statements.

18. **Computation of Earnings Per Share** *(LO 9.3)*

Jericho Corporation had 100,000 shares of common stock outstanding for the first three months of the year. The company issued 20,000 additional shares on April 1, and another 30,000 shares on September 1. Jericho reported net income of $371,250 for the year ended December 31. Jericho has no preferred stock.

Required:

(1) Compute Jericho's weighted-average number of shares of common stock outstanding during the year.
(2) Compute Jericho's earnings per share for the year.
(3) Why is the weighted-average number of shares of common stock outstanding during a year used for earnings per share rather than the number of shares outstanding at the end of the year?

19. **Analysis Terminology** *(LO 9.6, 9.7, & 9.8)*

Following are definitions or descriptions of terms relating to ratio analysis.

(a) Involves studying the relationship between two or more financial statement items

(b) Indicates the amount that investors are willing to pay for each $1 of a company's earnings over the past twelve months
(c) Involves a comparison of a company's financial ratios with those of competing companies or industry norms
(d) Measures a firm's ability to generate sales relative to its investment in assets
(e) Focuses on changes in a firm's ratios over a period of time
(f) Indicates how the capital markets as a whole perceive a company's common stock
(g) Indicates the percentage of each sales dollar that contributes to net income
(h) Measures a firm's ability to pay its current liabilities without relying on the sale of its inventory
(i) Indicates how well a company is managing its assets
(j) Indicates the number of times that a firm sells or turns over its inventory each year
(k) Measures a firm's ability to pay its current liabilities from its current assets

Required:

Match each definition or description listed with an appropriate term from the following list:

(1) Ratio analysis
(2) Inventory turnover ratio
(3) Cross-sectional ratio analysis
(4) Current ratio
(5) Total asset turnover ratio
(6) Longitudinal ratio analysis
(7) Liquidity ratio
(8) Gross profit percentage
(9) Leverage ratio
(10) Activity ratio
(11) Market strength ratio
(12) Age of inventory
(13) Quick ratio
(14) Price-earnings ratio
(15) Accounts receivable turnover ratio
(16) Profit margin percentage

20. **Objectives of Financial Statement Analysis** *(LO 9.5)*

La Quinta Corporation (www.laquinta.com) is one of the leading limited service hotel companies in the United States. Founded in San Antonio, Texas in 1968, the La Quinta hotel chain has grown to over 300 La Quinta Inns and La Quinta Inn & Suites in over 30 states. In its 2000 annual report, La Quinta reported net income of approximately $89,825,000 on revenues of nearly $911,981,000.

Required:

(1) Indicate what objective or objectives the following decision makers would likely have in mind when reviewing the financial statements of La Quinta.
   (a) potential investors in the company's common stock
   (b) an individual applying for a management position with the company
   (c) a banker reviewing a loan application submitted by the firm

(d) businesses that supply goods or services to the company

(2) Identify information sources that the parties listed in part (1) could use to analyze the financial statement data of La Quinta.

21. **Trend Analysis** *(LO 9.6)*

Access the most recent annual report for La Quinta Corporation (www .laquinta.com).

Required:

Prepare a trend analysis for the most current and past year, using the past year as the base year.

22. **Common-Sized Financial Statements** *(LO 9.6)*

Access the most recent annual report for La Quinta Corporation (www .laquinta.com).

Required:

(1) Prepare a common-sized balance sheet for the most recent year for La Quinta.

(2) Prepare a common-sized income statement for the most recent year for La Quinta.

23. **Ratio Analysis** *(LO 9.8)*

Access the most recent annual report for La Quinta Corporation (www .laquinta.com).

Required:

(1) Compute the following ratios for La Quinta:

(a) current ratio

(b) debt to total assets

(c) long-term debt to equity

(d) total asset turnover

(e) return on assets

(2) What are La Quinta's significant accounting policies?

24. **Earnings Quality** *(LO 9.9, writing)*

Charlie Turner wants invest in the stock market but knows very little about accounting and financial reporting practices. Recently, he read an article in *The Wall Street Journal* that focused on the subject of "earnings quality." After reading the article, Charlie was baffled and asked one of his friends, "How can there be a difference in the quality of earnings across companies? Corporate earnings are hard, cold facts, right? Accountants just add numbers here and subtract numbers there to arrive at a company's net income, right? Any way you cut it, two plus two equals four . . . right?"

Required:

Write a memo to Charlie that explains the concept of earnings quality and discusses several factors that influence earnings quality. Since Charlie is unfamiliar with accounting and financial reporting practices, include numerical examples in the memo to clarify how these factors influence earnings quality. Conclude your memo with a few suggestions to Charlie regarding how he can evaluate the quality of reported earnings data.

PROBLEMS

25. **Accounting for Investments in Stocks and Bonds** *(LO 9.1)*

Selected transactions for Gleason Co. are presented below.

(a) Gleason invested $100,000 in Lifetime, Inc.

(b) Gleason received a $1,000 dividend from Lifetime.

(c) Gleason invested in the bonds of Bellmont Enterprises by purchasing ten $1,000, 10% bonds at face value.

(d) Bellmont paid semiannual interest to bondholders.

Required:

(1) Record the investment entries (transactions a & b) assuming that:
  (a) Gleason owns 15% of Lifetime.
  (b) Gleason owns 60% of Lifetime.
  (c) Gleason owns 85% of Lifetime.

(2) Describe Gleason's year-end procedures related to Lifetime under each assumption from part (1).

(3) Record the entries for Gleason's investment in Bellmont (transactions c & d).

26. **Corporate Income Statement** *(LO 9.2 & 9.3, Excel)*

Following is information taken from the accounting records of Tankersley Company at the end of 2002.

(a) Net Sales, $220,000
(b) Operating Income (discontinued operations), $12,000
(c) Cost of Goods Sold, $120,000
(d) Gain on Sale of Assets (discontinued operations), $20,000
(e) Operating Expenses, $60,000
(f) Flood Loss, $25,000
(g) Cumulative Effect of a Change in Depreciation Methods, $12,000 (credit amount)
(h) Tankersley had 10,000 shares of common stock issued and outstanding throughout the year.

Tankersley's effective tax rate is 40 percent and is based in an area that does not normally experience floods.

Required:

Prepare an income statement for Tankersley for 2002 including an earnings-per-share section.

27. **Earnings per Share Computations** *(LO 9.3)*

Following are income statement data for Ellis & Reddings Corporation for the company's most recent fiscal year:

Income from Continuing Operations Before Tax			$ 800,000
Income Tax Expense			(320,000)
Income from Continuing Operations			$ 480,000
Discontinued Operations			
Operating Income	$ 40,000		
Less Income Tax	(16,000)	$ 24,000	
Loss on Disposal	$ (50,000)		
Less Income Tax Savings	20,000	(30,000)	(6,000)
Income before Extraordinary Item			$ 474,000
Extraordinary Loss due to Meteor Crash		$ (100,000)	
Less Income Tax Savings		40,000	(60,000)
Net Income			$ 414,000

At the beginning of the year, Ellis & Reddings had 100,000 shares of common stock outstanding. On October 1, Ellis & Reddings sold an additional 80,000 shares of common stock.

Required:

(1) Compute the weighted-average number of shares of common stock that Ellis & Reddings had outstanding during the year.

(2) Compute and clearly label the earnings per share figures for Ellis & Reddings' income statement.

28. **Temporary Differences for Tax Purposes** *(LO 9.4)*

Over a recent three-year period, Timber Country Enterprises (TCE) had the following pretax accounting income and taxable income amounts.

	Pretax Accounting Income	Taxable Income
Year 1	$440,000	$380,000
Year 2	470,000	410,000
Year 3	370,000	490,000

For each year, the difference between TCE's pretax accounting income and its taxable income was due to its use of different depreciation methods for financial accounting and taxation purposes. Recently, a local attorney, who is a new member of TCE's board of directors, reviewed the company's financial records. At the next board meeting, this individual suggested that the use of different accounting methods for financial accounting and taxation purposes was, in her opinion, unethical.

Required:

(1) Is it unethical to use different accounting methods for financial accounting and taxation purposes? Why or why not?

(2) TCE's effective tax rate in recent years has been 40 percent for both financial accounting and taxation purposes. Compute the company's income tax expense and income taxes payable for Year 1.

(3) Prepare an appropriate journal entry to record TCE's income tax expense for Year 1.

29. **Trend Analysis** *(LO 9.6)*

Following are selected financial data for a recent five-year period for Walters & Cruz, Inc. (Amounts are expressed in thousands except for per share data.)

	Year 1	Year 2	Year 3	Year 4	Year 5
Sales	$144,267	$173,164	$205,348	$322,308	$401,685
Operating Income	3,546	5,023	5,842	8,343	14,666
Earnings per Share	0.26	0.31	0.37	0.29	0.61
Book Value per Share	0.99	1.16	4.02	5.77	6.87

Required:

(1) Prepare a trend analysis for each listed financial item of Walters & Cruz using Year 1 as the base year.

(2) Why are the trend percentages computed in part (1) not consistent across each financial statement item?

(3) How is trend analysis used by financial decision makers? What are the limitations of trend analysis?

30. **Common-Sized Financial Statements** *(LO 9.7)*

P. R. Williamson Company operates two small clothing stores in southeastern Idaho. Following are this company's income statements for the years ended December 31, 2000 through 2002, and year-end balance sheets for 2000 through 2002.

Williamson Company
Income Statements
For the Years Ended December 31, 2000-2002

	2000	2001	2002
Sales*	$ 641,900	$ 652,000	$ 654,500
Cost of Goods Sold	(304,500)	(323,700)	(339,200)
Gross Profit	$ 337,400	$ 328,300	$ 315,300
Operating Expenses	(154,200)	(155,800)	(161,900)
Operating Income	$ 183,200	$ 172,500	$ 153,400
Other Revenue (Expense)**	13,400	(6,400)	(1,200)
Income Before Income Tax	$ 196,600	$ 166,100	$ 152,200
Income Tax Expense	(78,600)	(66,400)	(60,900)
Net Income	$ 118,000	$ 99,700	$ 91,300

* All of the company's sales are on a credit basis.
** Includes interest expense of the following amounts: $9,900 (2000), $7,400 (2001), and $7,100 (2002)

Williamson Company
Balance Sheets
December 31, 2000-2002

	2000	2001	2002
ASSETS			
Cash	$ 22,000	$ 9,100	$ 3,700
Accounts Receivable (net)	72,500	103,300	116,900
Inventory	109,800	102,000	89,000
Prepaid Expenses	2,500	1,400	1,700
Total Current Assets	$ 206,800	$215,800	$ 211,300
Property & Equipment (net)	212,000	201,500	189,400
Other Assets	3,200	2,600	1,500
Total Assets	$ 422,000	$419,900	$ 402,200
LIABILITIES			
Accounts Payable	$ 51,900	$ 57,200	$ 64,900
Notes Payable	25,000	15,000	12,000
Accrued Liabilities	41,100	35,800	7,400
Total Current Liabilities	$ 118,000	$108,000	$ 84,300
Bonds Payable	100,000	80,000	80,000
Total Liabilities	$ 218,000	$188,000	$ 164,300
STOCKHOLDERS' EQUITY			
Common Stock	$ 50,000	$ 50,000	$ 50,000
Additional Paid-in Capital	130,000	130,000	130,000
Retained Earnings	24,000	51,900	57,900
Total Stockholders' Equity	$ 204,000	$231,900	$ 237,900
Total Liabilities & Equity	$ 422,000	$419,900	$ 402,200

Note: Following are the market prices of Williamson's common stock at the end of each year 2000 through 2002: $8.50 (2000); $7.75 (2001); and $6.50 (2002).

Required:

(1) Prepare common-sized income statements for Williamson Company for 2000 through 2002.

(2) What major structural changes occurred over this three-year period in Williamson's income statement data? Are these changes apparently favorable or unfavorable? Explain.

31. **Liquidity and Leverage Ratios** *(LO 9.8)*

Refer to the financial statements of Williamson Company in the previous problem.

Required:

(1) Compute the liquidity and leverage ratios discussed in this chapter for Williamson Company for 2000 through 2002.

  (a) Overall, did the company's liquidity improve or deteriorate between 2000 and 2002? Explain.

  (b) Did this company become more or less leveraged between 2000 and 2002?

(2) Compute the activity ratios discussed in this chapter for Williamson Company for 2001 and 2002.

  (a) Indicate which of these ratios improved and which deteriorated between 2000 and 2002.

  (b) Overall, did the company do a better job of managing its accounts receivable, inventory, and total assets in 2002 compared with 2001? Explain.

(3) Compute the profitability and market strength ratios discussed in this chapter for Williamson Company for 2000 through 2002. (Note: The company had total assets on January 1, 2000, of $425,000, while the company's total stockholders' equity on that date was $186,000.)

  (a) Evaluate the company's profitability ratios for the period 2000–2002. Did the company become more or less profitable over this time period? Explain.

  (b) Evaluate the company's market strength ratios for the period 2000–2002. What do the changes in these ratios over this period indicate?

32. **Market Price to Book Value Ratio** *(LO 9.8)*

Rent 'N Drive, Inc. is a publicly-owned company based in Kansas. The company's principal line of business is truck leasing. Presented in the following schedule are selected financial data for Rent 'N Drive's common stock over a recent five-year period.

	1998	1999	2000	2001	2002
Earnings per share	$ 0.05	$ 1.51	$ (0.84)	$ 1.95	$ 1.86
Dividends per share	0.60	0.60	0.60	0.60	0.60
Book value per share	17.50	18.26	12.81	14.33	15.64
Market price per share	21.63	28.87	26.63	28.00	26.13

Required:

(1) Compute Rent 'N Drive's market price to book value ratio for 1998 through 2002.

(2) Given the industry in which it operates, what factors may have contributed to the decline in Rent 'N Drive's book value per share in 2000?

(3) Would you consider investing in Rent 'N Drive? Discuss the reasons for your answer.

33. **Comparative Analysis of Financial Data** *(LO 9.5 & 9.8)*

The following schedule provides key financial ratios for three companies in the same industry and the industry norm for each of these ratios.

	Industry Norm	Alonso Co.	Buckley, Inc.	Cosgrove Corp.
Current ratio	2.4	1.6	2.3	2.5
Quick ratio	1.0	0.4	1.3	1.2
Long-term debt to equity ratio	0.5	0.6	0.4	0.2
Times interest earned ratio	4.5	2.4	5.6	14.9
Age of receivables	89 days	101 days	77 days	80 days
Age of inventory	97 days	99 days	92 days	76 days
Profit margin percentage	3.4%	2.3%	3.6%	4.7%
Return on assets	4.9%	3.4%	5.6%	6.0%
Return on equity	7.1%	4.9%	7.1%	8.9%
Price-earnings ratio	10.2	7.5	7.7	12.7
Market price to book value ratio	1.8	1.3	1.2	3.2

Required:

(1) Evaluate the overall financial health of these three firms. Given the information provided, which firm do you believe is in the strongest financial condition? Explain.

(2) Again, based only upon the data provided, which firm's common stock do you believe would be the most attractive investment alternative? Why?

(3) List three other items of financial or nonfinancial information that you would want to review before making an investment decision regarding the common stocks of these companies.

34. **Market Price to Book Value Ratio** *(LO 9.5 & 9.8)*

The ratio of a stock's market price to its book value per share reveals how much investors are willing to pay for each $1 of a company's net assets per share. The following information is available for companies A, B, and C.

	Company A	Company B	Company C
Total Assets	$1,000,000	$750,000	$2,000,000
Total Liabilities	250,000	400,000	1,500,000
Number of Common Shares Outstanding	100,000	200,000	125,000
Year-end Stock Price	$8.00	$7.00	$24.00

Required:

(1) For each of the companies listed, compute the book value per share and the market price to book value ratio. (Note: None of the companies have preferred stock outstanding.)

(2) How is it possible for a company's market price to book value ratio to differ significantly from 1.0?

35. **Price-Earnings Ratio** *(LO 9.5 & 9.8)*

Following are recent price-earnings (P/E) ratios of several prominent companies:

	P/E Ratio
Abbott Laboratories	23
The Home Depot, Inc.	29
Maytag Corporation	17
Merrill Lynch & Co., Inc.	11
Texas Instruments Incorporated	33
Union Carbide Corporation	9

Required:

(1) What factors may account for the large variance in the P/E ratios of the companies listed?

(2) Explain the difference between a company's P/E ratio and its market price to book value ratio. Which of these two ratios do you believe is more relevant to potential investors? Defend your answer.

36. **Impact of Accounting Errors on Financial Ratios** *(LO 9.8)*

Following are examples of errors that can be made in processing accounting data. Listed next to each error is a financial ratio.

(a) Recording a sales transaction twice (Gross profit percentage)

(b) Overstating ending inventory (Quick ratio)

(c) Debiting a payment of a long-term payable to a short-term payable account (Return on assets)

(d) Understating the estimated useful life of a depreciable asset (Return on equity)

(e) Failing to prepare a year-end adjusting entry to record interest revenue (Price-earnings ratio)

(f) Failing to record the declaration of a cash dividend shortly before year-end (Profit margin percentage)

(g) Recording a purchase of a long-term asset in a current asset account (Market price to book value ratio)

Required:

(1) In general, indicate the effect on any ratio when the following happens:

(a) numerator increases

(b) numerator decreases

(c) denominator increases

(d) denominator decreases

(2) Indicate whether each error listed increases (overstates), decreases (understates), or has no impact on the financial ratio with which it is coupled.

37. **Earnings Quality** *(LO 9.9)*

Pickard Corporation and Jenkins Company are two firms in the same industry. These two firms have approximately the same annual revenues and total assets. Following is the most recent income statement of each firm.

	Pickard Corporation	Jenkins Company
Sales	$ 1,324,900	$ 1,337,300
Cost of Goods Sold	(690,200)	(640,900)
Gross Profit	$ 634,700	$ 696,400
Operating Expenses		
Selling	(90,000)	(86,400)
General & Administrative	(72,000)	(87,000)
Depreciation	(102,000)	(71,000)
Operating Income	$ 370,700	$ 452,000
Other Revenue (Expense)	5,200	3,700
Income before Income Tax	$ 375,900	$ 455,700
Income Tax Expense	(150,400)	(182,300)
Net Income	$ 225,500	$ 273,400

Pickard Corporation uses the LIFO inventory costing method and an accelerated depreciation method, while Jenkins Company uses FIFO inventory costing and the straight-line depreciation method.

Required:

(1) Define earnings quality.

(2) Why is earnings quality an important consideration for financial decision makers when evaluating financial statement data?

(3) Suppose that a friend of yours is considering investing in the common stock of either Pickard Corporation or Jenkins Company. Write a memo to your friend explaining the concept of earnings quality and comment on how the quality of these firms' reported earnings might be affected by their use of different accounting methods.

CASES

38. **Trend Analysis** *(LO 9.6, Internet)*

Use the annual report of Carnival Corporation (www.carnival.com) for the 2001 and 1999 fiscal years.

Required:

(1) Prepare a trend analysis using 1998 as the base year to compare Carnival's balance sheets and income statements for 1998, 1999, 2000, and 2001. [Hint: Though no template is provided, this task is simplified by using Excel.]

(2) Interpret the trend analysis. For at least three accounts that show reasonable differences, depict the trend using a bar or line graph.

39. **Common-Size Financial Statements** *(LO 9.7, Internet)*

Use the annual report of Carnival Corporation (www.carnival.com) for the 2001 fiscal year.

Required:

(1) Prepare a common-sized balance sheet and income statement for Carnival for 2001 and 2000. [Hint: Though no template is provided, this task is simplified by using Excel.]

(2) Were there any significant changes from 2000 to 2001? If so, discuss those changes.

(3) Were the changes noted in part (2) as obvious by examining raw numbers as they were by examining the common-sized statements? Discuss.

40. **Comparative Ratio Analysis** *(LO 9.5 & 9.8, Internet, group, Excel)*

Identifying the similarities and differences in companies is as crucial to making investment decisions as understanding a single company's financial statements. Form groups of at least four students. Each group should select a single industry. Each group member should locate a different annual report within that industry. (The industry and individual company may be assigned by your instructor.) Note: Additional references may be needed for some data (such as stock trading price and beginning balance of certain accounts for Year 1).

Required—individual group members:

(1) Calculate the following ratios for the company you selected for the two most recent fiscal years.

(a) Current ratio

(b) Quick ratio
(c) Debt to total asset ratio
(d) Long-term debt to equity ratio
(e) Times interest earned
(f) Accounts receivable turnover ratio
(g) Age of receivables
(h) Inventory turnover
(i) Age of inventory
(j) Total asset turnover
(k) Profit margin ratio
(l) Gross profit percentage
(m) Return on assets
(n) Return on equity

(2) Comment on the changes from year to year.
(3) Does this company seem to be a good investment based on these ratios?

Required—groups:

(1) Compile the ratio calculations for each company prepared by the individual group members into one table.
(2) Compare the results from company to company in the same fiscal years. Include in your comparison a graphical analysis. Discuss reasons why these ratios might be similar or different within an industry.
(3) Based on these four ratios across companies, which company is the best investment in the industry you have chosen? Explain the rationale for your choice.

Required—class:

(1) Compare the ratios from each industry. Discuss reasons why these ratios might be similar or different between industries.
(2) Does one industry seem to be a better investment than another? Explain. Do you think this judgment would be constant over time? Explain.

41. **Accounting Errors and the Impact on Financial Statement Data** *(LO 9.2 & 9.8, ethics)*

Following is a condensed version of the 2002 income statement of Linton Supply Company.

Sales	$ 725,400
Cost of Goods Sold	(404,300)
Gross Profit	$ 321,100
Operating Expenses	(111,300)
Operating Income	$ 209,800
Other Revenues (Expenses)	10,200
Income Before Income Tax	$ 220,000
Income Tax Expense	(88,000)
Net Income	$ 132,000

Linton's accountant overlooked a $3,200 utility bill at the end of 2002. This bill should have been recorded with a debit to Utilities Expense and a credit to Accrued Liabilities. The company's year-end Inventory account balance was also incorrect. Because of errors made during the counting of inventory, Linton's year-end inventory was listed as $174,300 in its accounting records instead of the correct figure of

$151,200. This overstatement of year-end inventory caused Linton's Cost of Goods Sold for the year to be understated by an equal amount.

Following is other information regarding Linton Supply.

Average total assets during 2002	$820,500*
Interest expense for 2002 (included in Other Revenues and Expenses)	34,000
Average common stockholders' equity	380,000*
Average income tax rate	40%

*These averages were computed by adding the beginning-of-the-year and end-of-the-year amounts and dividing by two.

Required:

(1) Ignoring the two errors discovered in Linton's accounting records, compute the company's profitability ratios for 2002.

(2) Compute Linton's profitability ratios for 2002 after adjusting the company's financial data for the two errors.

(3) Did the two errors have a material effect on Linton's profitability ratios? Defend your answer.

(4) Do you believe that companies manipulate numbers intentionally to mislead investors? List an example.

SUPPLEMENTAL PROBLEMS

42. **Corporate Income Statement** *(LO 9.2 & 9.3)* [Compare to Problem 26]

Following are income statement data for Shaw Corporation for the year ended December 31, 2002. These items are presented in random order.

Cost of Goods Sold	$360,000
General Expenses	18,000
Gain on Sale of Machinery	22,000
Income Tax Expense on Income from Continuing Operations	?
Operating Income from Discontinued Operations	10,000
Selling Expenses	23,000
Extraordinary Loss due to Fire	25,000
Net Sales	520,000
Loss on Disposal of Discontinued Operations	20,000
Administrative Expenses	19,000
Cumulative Effect of a Change in AccountingPrinciple	5,000

Shaw's average income tax rate is 40 percent on all taxable income items. Throughout 2002, Shaw had 50,000 shares of common stock outstanding.

Required:

Prepare an income statement for Shaw Corporation, including an earnings per share section. [Hint: Remember that certain items on the income statement must be shown with their related tax amounts.]

43. **Deferred Income Taxes** *(LO 9.4)* [Compare to Problem 28]

For the current year, College Station Corporation (CSC) has a $10,000 difference between its pretax accounting income and its taxable income, as indicated in the following schedule.

	Pretax Accounting Income	Taxable Income
Income Before Depreciation Expense	$ 100,000	$ 100,000
Depreciation Expense	(20,000)	(30,000)

Required:

(1) Define "temporary difference" as it applies to the pretax accounting income and taxable income of a corporation. What is the dollar amount of the temporary difference in this situation?

(2) Prepare CSC's year-end adjusting entry to record income tax expense for the current year. Assume that CSC's effective income tax rate is 40 percent for both financial accounting and taxation purposes.

(3) Suppose that CSC pays the amount of tax due for the current year on January 15 of the following year. Record this payment.

(4) How much less income tax did CSC pay in the entry recorded in part (3) due to the temporary difference related to depreciation expense?

(5) Will CSC eventually pay the dollar amount you computed in part (4)? If so, what advantage does CSC realize as a result of the depreciation-related temporary difference?

44. Trend Analysis *(LO 9.6)* [Compare to Problem 29]

LogiComm, Inc. provides communication systems and support to large businesses. Presented in the following schedule are selected financial data reported recently by LogiComm. Amounts are expressed in millions of dollars except for dividends per share.

	Total Revenues	Dividends per Share	Total Assets
1999	$258.5	$0.180	$102.8
2000	260.0	0.180	98.4
2001	299.1	0.195	113.8
2002	325.1	0.240	119.8

Required:

(1) Prepare a trend analysis for each of the three financial statement items listed for Logicomm using 1999 as the base year.

(2) Predict the 2003 figure for each financial statement item. In which of these predicted amounts do you have the most confidence? Why?

(3) During 2003, Logicomm actually had total revenues of $320.2 million, paid dividends of $0.28 per share, and had total assets at year-end of $129.3 million. Compute the percentage error between each of these actual amounts and the corresponding prediction you made in part (2). Comment on any additional insight these results provide you regarding trend analysis.

45. Common-Sized Financial Statements *(LO 9.7)* [Compare to Problem 30]

Following are balance sheets for Gabe's Shoe Repair Shop as of December 31, 2001 and 2002.

Gabe's Shoe Repair Shop
Balance Sheets
December 31, 2001 and 2002

	2001	2002
ASSETS		
Cash	$ 9,200	$ 18,700
Accounts Receivable (net)	8,300	14,400
Inventory	12,500	14,700
Prepaid Expenses	800	300
Total Current Assets	$ 30,800	$ 48,100
Equipment (net)	31,200	27,800
Total Assets	$ 62,000	$ 75,900
LIABILITIES		
Accounts Payable	$ 7,100	$ 2,700
Accrued Liabilities	3,300	3,600
Total Current Liabilities	$ 10,400	$ 6,300
Long-term Bank Loan	10,000	10,000
Total Liabilities	$ 20,400	$ 16,300
STOCKHOLDERS' EQUITY		
Common Stock	$ 12,000	$ 12,000
Additional Paid-in Capital	24,000	24,000
Retained Earnings	5,600	23,600
Total Stockholders' Equity	$ 41,600	$ 59,600
Total Liabilities & Equity	$ 62,000	$ 75,900

Required:

(1) How are common-sized financial statements used by decision makers?

(2) Prepare common-sized balance sheets for Gabe's Shoe Repair Shop as of December 31, 2001, and 2002.

(3) What major structural changes occurred in this business's balance sheet during 2002? What factors may have accounted for these changes?

46. **Ratio Analysis** *(LO 9.8)* [Compare to Problem 42]

Locate the consolidated income statements of Wal-Mart, Inc. (http://www.walmart.com/) for the two most recent fiscal years.

Required:

(1) Calculate the 16 ratios discussed in this chapter for Wal-Mart for the two most recent fiscal years.

(2) Comment on any changes from year to year.

CHAPTER 10

Statement of Cash Flows

LEARNING OBJECTIVES

1. Identify and distinguish among operating, investing, and financing activities.
2. Prepare a statement of cash flows using the indirect method.
3. Interpret cash flow data by comparatively analyzing the three components of an entity's cash flows.
4. Identify the principal uses of the statement of cash flows for financial decision makers.
5. Compute and interpret cash ratios, cash flow per share, and free cash flow.

UAL Corporation

UAL Corporation, the parent company of United Air Lines, had a terrible year in 2001. The terrorist attacks, weakened U.S. economy, reduced business travel, changed business travel behavior, and created a significant revenue decline. The company ended 2001 with a loss from operations of $3.8 billion, compared to operating earnings of $654 million in 2000. In the last year, UAL dramatically reduced its operating cash outflows. For example, in October 2001, the company's cash "burn rate" was about $15 million per day; for the last quarter of the 2001, it was cut to an average of approximately $10 million per day.

Operating activities during 2001 consumed $160 million, including the effects of a federal government grant. Investing activities included $2.0 billion of funds spent on additions to property, plant, and equipment, as well as $178 million of proceeds from PP&E dispositions. Financing activities included cash outflows of $176 million and $289 million, respectively, for principal payments under debt and capital lease obligations. Additionally, UAL issued $1.0 billion in long-term debt during fiscal 2001. In total, over the 2001 year, UAL added a mere $9 million to its beginning cash balance.

In August 2002, UAL reported $2.7 billion in cash reserves were being used up at the rate of almost $1 million per day and $875 million in debt was due in the Fall of 2002. The dwindling funds caused the airline to warn that it might file for bankruptcy if labor groups and suppliers did not grant concessions.

SOURCE: UAL Corporation. *2001 Annual Report,* 2001; Edward Wong, "United Air Lines Warns It May Go Bankrupt," *The (New Orleans) Times–Picayune,* 15 August 2002, sec A, p. 1 and 7.

INTRODUCTION

Business managers must be concerned with both generating revenues and properly managing their firms' cash resources. Some companies with long histories of reporting profits eventually fail because their owners or managers did not pay sufficient attention to cash flows. Thus, businesses are required to include a **statement of cash flows** (SCF) within the annual financial report. This statement summarizes cash receipts and disbursements information and, thereby, indicates the causes of the net change in the cash balance for a specific time period.

The statement of cash flows is not intended to replace either the balance sheet or income statement. Decision makers use these three major financial statements in combination to analyze the financial condition, operating results, and future prospects of business entities.

The opening part of this chapter introduces the statement of cash flows. The indirect and direct methods for preparing a statement of cash flows are discussed next. The chapter concludes with a discussion of three approaches that can be used to analyze and interpret cash-flow data.

THREE PRIMARY TYPES OF BUSINESS ACTIVITIES AND CASH FLOWS

From a technical standpoint, a statement of cash flows has one primary objective: to account for the change in an organization's cash balance during a given accounting period. To achieve this objective, all transactions that affected cash during that period must be identified. For statement of cash flows purposes, "cash" includes both cash and cash equivalents. Recall from Chapter 4 that cash equivalents are investments in short-term securities that have 90 days or less to maturity when purchased.

A statement of cash flows consists of four sections. The first three sections summarize the cash inflows (receipts) and cash outflows (disbursements) from a business's activities during the year as related to the following three categories: operating activities, investing activities, and financing activities. The final section reconciles a business's cash balance at the beginning and end of an accounting period. This reconciliation involves adding the net cash provided or used by operating, investing, and financing activities to the beginning cash balance to arrive at the period-ending cash balance.

Operating activities are generally those transactions and events related to the production and delivery of goods and services by businesses. In other words, operating activities reflect the day-to-day profit-oriented activities of a business. The principal cash inflows from operating activities are cash receipts from customers from both cash sales and collections of accounts receivable. Other cash inflows from operating activities include receipts of interest revenue and cash provided by the sale of investments in trading securities. Major sources of cash outflows from operating activities include payments to suppliers, employees, and taxing authorities. Financial statement users tend to focus on cash flows related to operating activities because, over the long run, a business must generate positive cash flows from its profit-oriented activities to be economically viable.

Investing activities typically involve long-term asset accounts. Thus, **investing activities** include the lending and collecting of loans receivable, acquisition and disposal of property, plant, and equipment, and purchase and sale of long-term investments in debt and equity securities.

The majority of financing activities involve long-term liability and stockholders' equity contributed capital (common and preferred stock) accounts. However, short-term borrowings using notes payable are also included in financing activities. **Financing activities** involve borrowing cash through short-term or long-term notes, selling bonds, repaying debts, selling stock to investors for cash, repurchasing stock from investors (obtaining treasury stock) for cash, and providing stockholders with a return on their investments in the form of cash dividends.

Exhibit 10-1 provides a listing of the primary cash inflows and outflows from operating, investing, and financing activities. Note two important items: (1) the classification of cash flows from the sale or purchase of investments in debt and equity securities depends upon whether the investment is classified as short-term or long-term and (2) the payment of bond principal is a financing activity but the payment of bond interest is an operating activity.

DIRECT VERSUS INDIRECT METHOD OF PREPARING A STATEMENT OF CASH FLOWS

There are two acceptable methods of preparing a statement of cash flows: the direct method and the indirect method. The difference between the two methods reflects the way in which net cash flow from operating activities is reported. In preparing a statement of cash flows using the **direct method,** the operating section lists specific cash inflows and outflows from operating activities, such as those indicated in Exhibit 10-1. Exhibit 10-2

EXHIBIT 10-1

Summary of Transactions Classifications for the SCF

Operating Activities

Cash Inflows	Cash Outflows
Receipts from customers	Payments to suppliers
Receipts of interest and dividends	Payments to employees
Receipts from the sale of debt and equity securities classified as short-term investments	Payments of interest on any type of debt (short-term or long-term)
Miscellaneous receipts related to operating activities	Miscellaneous payments related to operating activities
	Payments for purchasing debt and equity securities classified as short-term investments
	Payments of taxes

Investing Activities

Cash Inflows	Cash Outflows
Receipts from the sale of property, plant, and equipment (PP&E)	Payments to acquire property, plant, and equipment (PP&E)
Receipts from the sale of long-term investments in debt and equity securities	Payments to acquire long-term investments in debt and equity securities
Receipts from the repayment of long-term loans receivable	Payments for long-term loans receivable made to other companies or to business officers

Financing Activities

Cash Inflows	Cash Outflows
Receipts from the issuance of common stock and preferred stock	Payments for dividends
Receipts from the issuance of bonds payable	Payments to acquire treasury stock
Receipts from short or long-term borrowings from banks and other parties	Payments to retire bonds payable and to repay short- or long-term bank loans

shows Howard Restaurant Supply, Inc.'s statement of cash flows prepared using the direct method. Notice the use of specific cash receipt and payment terminology.

The statement of cash flows shown in Exhibit 10-3 for Howard Restaurant Supply, Inc. is prepared using the indirect method. In this case, specific cash flows from operating activities, such as cash received from customers, are not listed in the operating section of the statement of cash flows. When the **indirect method** is used to prepare a statement of cash flows, the net cash flow from operating activities is determined by making certain adjustments to net income. Net income is determined using the accrual basis and includes some items that are not actual cash flows. For example, sales revenue includes some credit sales that have not been collected in cash by year-end; salaries expense may include some salaries that have been accrued but not paid at year-end. Cash flows from investing and financing activities are determined and reported in the same manner under both the direct and indirect methods.

The information needed to determine the specific net income adjustments for Howard Restaurant Supply's SCF is provided in the next section. Determining the amount of these adjustments requires information from the income statement for the year as well as the beginning and ending balance sheets.

EXHIBIT 10-2

Howard Restaurant Supply, Inc.'s SCF—Direct Method

Howard Restaurant Supply, Inc.
Statement of Cash Flows
For the Year Ended December 31, 2002

Cash flows from operating activities:		
Receipts from customers	$ 575,043	
Payments to suppliers	(449,245)	
Payments to employees	(79,866)	
Payments for insurance	(2,635)	
Receipt of interest on bank savings	3,454	
Payments of interest on capital leases	(7,273)	
Payments of income taxes	(21,950)	
Net cash provided by operating activities		$ 17,528
Cash flows from investing activities:		
Proceeds from sale of PP&E	$ 1,228	
Purchases of PP&E	(11,853)	
Purchases of LT equity investments	(10,009)	
Net cash used by investing activities		(20,634)
Cash flows from financing activities:		
Proceeds from long-term borrowings	$ 6,245	
Principal payments on capital leases	(4,994)	
Proceeds from issuance of common stock	4,058	
Purchases of treasury stock	(520)	
Payments of cash dividends	(1,736)	
Net cash provided by financing activities		3,053
Net decrease in cash and cash equivalents		$ (53)
Cash and cash equivalents, beginning of year		3,485
Cash and cash equivalents, end of year		$ 3,432

Companies using the direct method of preparing a statement of cash flows must include a schedule reconciling net cash flow from operating activities with net income in their annual reports. Thus, these companies must essentially prepare the operating section of the statement of cash flows twice. This duplication feature causes the direct method of SCF preparation to be less popular than the indirect method. Although the direct method discloses specific types of operating cash flows and is thereby more informative than the indirect method for financial statement users, the indirect method is more widely used by businesses.

PREPARING A STATEMENT OF CASH FLOWS: INDIRECT METHOD

The initial issues to address when preparing a statement of cash flows are where to obtain and how to organize the data needed for this financial statement. Unlike the preparation of a balance sheet and income statement, which requires general ledger account balances, few cash flow statement items are general ledger account balances. Cash flow amounts must be determined from analyzing the information contained in a business's accounting records and in other financial statements. A streamlined approach to collecting and organizing the cash flow data is used to introduce the accumulation of data for a statement of cash flows prepared on the indirect method.

EXHIBIT 10-3

Howard Restaurant Supply, Inc.'s SCF—Indirect Method

Howard Restaurant Supply, Inc.
Statement of Cash Flows
For the Year Ended December 31, 2002

Cash flows from operating activities:		
Net Income	$ 58,601	
Adjustments to reconcile net income to net cash provided by operating activities:		
Depreciation expense	29,738	
Loss on sale of equipment	460	
Increase in Accounts Receivable	(24,957)	
Increase in Inventory	(12,684)	
Decrease in Prepaid Insurance	2,575	
Decrease in Accounts Payable	(38,405)	
Increase in Income Taxes Payable	2,200	
Net cash provided by operating activities		$17,528
Cash flows from investing activities:		
Proceeds from sale of PP&E	$ 1,228	
Purchases of PP&E	(11,853)	
Purchases of LT equity investments	(10,009)	
Net cash used by investing activities		(20,634)
Cash flows from financing activities:		
Proceeds from long-term borrowings	$ 6,245	
Principal payments on capital leases	(4,994)	
Proceeds from issuance of common stock	4,058	
Purchases of treasury stock	(520)	
Payments of cash dividends	(1,736)	
Net cash provided by financing activities		3,053
Net decrease in cash and cash equivalents		$ (53)
Cash and cash equivalents, beginning of year		3,485
Cash and cash equivalents, end of year		$ 3,432

Analyzing Transactions for a SCF—Operating Activities

The starting point for determining net cash flow from operating activities on an indirect basis is a business's net income. Exhibit 10-4 presents a schedule of the general types of adjustments necessary to convert net income to net cash flow from operating activities.

As mentioned earlier, a company's net income for a given period seldom equals the net cash flow generated by its operating activities. There are two reasons for the difference. First, certain noncash, nonoperating items, such as gains and losses on the sale of PP&E, are considered in computing net income. Second, the revenue and expense amounts included in net income are determined on an accrual, rather than cash, basis. For example, assume that a company accrues $2,000 of interest revenue on a note receivable during the year-end adjusting process. However, the interest is not to be paid to the company until the following year. If the company had no other revenues or expenses during the year in question, its net income was $2,000, while its net cash flow from operating activities was $0.

EXHIBIT 10-4

Standard Format for Determining Net Cash Flow from Operating Activities under the Indirect Method

Net Income		$ XXXX
Plus:	Depreciation and amortization expenses	XXX
	Losses from sale of PP&E and other losses	XXX
	Decreases in current assets (other than cash)	XXX
	Increases in current liabilities	XXX
Minus:	Gains from sale of PP&E and other gains	(XXX)
	Increases in current assets (other than cash)	(XXX)
	Decreases in current liabilities	(XXX)
Net Cash Flow from Operating Activities		$ YYYY

Depreciation and Amortization Expenses

Depreciation and amortization are noncash expenses. Neither results in cash outflows but both decrease net income. To reconcile net income to net cash flow from operating activities, depreciation and amortization expenses must be added to net income. Depreciation is generally included first in the adjustments to net income because it is often one of the largest adjustment amounts. The depreciation and amortization amounts are generally found on the income statement, but they can also be calculated using the beginning and ending balances of related accounts on the balance sheet and other investment and disposal information.

Gains and Losses

Several examples of gains and losses have been discussed in earlier chapters, including gains and losses on the disposal of property, plant, and equipment. As shown in the above schedule, losses must be added to net income when computing net cash flow from operating activities, while gains must be subtracted from net income.

To illustrate the rationale for this treatment of gains and losses, consider the loss on equipment disposal incurred by Howard Restaurant Supply. Assume that the company sold equipment for $1,228 cash. The equipment had originally cost $35,000 and, at the time of the sale, had a book value of $1,688. Thus, Howard had recorded $33,312 ($35,000 – $1,688) of depreciation over the useful life of the equipment. The journal entry for the sale follows:

General Journal				
Date		Description	Debit	Credit
Apr.	9	Cash	1,228	
		Accumulated Depreciation—Equipment	33,312	
		Loss on Disposal of Asset	460	
		Equipment		35,000
		To record the sale of equipment at less than book value		

In the statement of cash flows, transactions involving the purchase or sale of property, plant, and equipment qualify as investing activities. The actual $1,228 cash inflow from Howard's equipment sale is reported as a component of "net cash flow from investing activities." However, the $460 loss on this transaction was included in calculating the firm's net income, which is the starting point for determining net cash flow from operating activities under the indirect method. Without an appropriate adjustment, the total cash flow from this transaction would be reported as a net $768 in Howard's statement of cash flows:

$(460) in cash flows from operating activities through inclusion in net income and $1,228 included in cash flows from investing activities. To remedy this problem, the $460 loss must be added back to net income in Howard's statement of cash flows to determine net cash flow from operating activities.

If the equipment had been sold for $2,100, a $412 gain would have been included in determining net income. On the SCF, the gain would be subtracted from net income when computing Howard's net cash flow from operating activities and the full $2,100 would be shown as the proceeds from sale in the investing section of the statement.

Determination of adjustments for gains and losses requires a review of the income statement for the existence of such amounts and of changes in (often long-term) asset account balances and, if necessary, any related contra accounts (such as Accumulated Depreciation or Accumulated Amortization).

Current Assets

Most of the adjustments required to convert net income to net cash flow from operating activities involve noncash current asset and current liability accounts. As indicated in Exhibit 10-4, changes in these accounts must be added to, or subtracted from, net income when computing net cash flow from operating activities. Determinations of these adjustments require the use of income statement revenue and expense information in conjunction with beginning and ending account balances on the balance sheet.

Accounts Receivable is used to illustrate the logic underlying the adjustments to net income for changes in current assets. For simplicity, assume that Howard Restaurant Supply began the year 2002 with a balance of $0 in Accounts Receivable. At the end of the year, the company's income statement showed total sales of $600,000 and the balance sheet showed Accounts Receivable of $24,957. As a result, Howard's sales for the year produced cash flows from operating activities of only $575,043 ($600,000 – $24,957). When computing the firm's net cash flow from operating activities, the $24,957 not yet collected from sales must be deducted from its net income because it has not been realized in the form of cash.[1] On the SCF prepared using the direct method, the $575,043 is shown as cash receipts from customers.

Thus, if Accounts Receivable increase during a year, the increase is deducted from net income when computing net cash flow from operating activities. This adjustment gives recognition to the fact that the cash inflows from customers were less than the sales recorded during the year. Conversely, if Accounts Receivable decrease during a year, the decrease is added to net income when computing net cash flow from operating activities. This adjustment gives recognition to the fact that the cash inflows from customers exceeded the sales recorded during the year.

Similar reasoning can be applied to other noncash current assets. Increases in noncash current assets are deducted from net income and decreases in these assets are added to net income when computing net cash flow from operating activities under the indirect method.

Current Liabilities

To illustrate the rationale for the treatment of current liabilities, Income Taxes Payable is used. Remember that credits to this account would commonly reflect the accrual of income tax expense, and debits to this account would reflect the payment of taxes. Tax expense is the amount shown on the income statement in the determination of net income but, for purposes of the statement of cash flows, the important piece of information is the amount of taxes paid in cash during the year. Assume that at the beginning of 2002, Howard Restaurant

[1] To simplify the examples in this chapter, the assumption is made that there are no uncollectible accounts receivable and, thus, no allowance for uncollectible accounts.

Supply owed $100 of taxes payable. During 2002, Howard Restaurant Supply recorded $24,150 in tax expense. If the balance at year-end 2002 in Income Taxes Payable is $2,300 (an increase of $2,200), then the company only paid $21,950 ($100 + $24,150 – $2,300) in cash for taxes during 2002. The remaining taxes will be paid in the following year. The $2,200 increase is added to net income on the SCF prepared using the indirect basis to determine cash flow from operating activities. On the SCF prepared using the direct basis, the $21,950 is shown as cash payments of income taxes.

Alternatively, assume that Howard's Income Tax Payable account had a credit balance of $3,000 at the beginning of 2002. If the company recorded $24,150 of income tax expense for 2002 and reported a balance of $800 (a decrease of $2,200) at the end of the year, the actual amount of cash payments for taxes would be $26,350.

Beginning balance of Income Taxes Payable	$ 3,000
+ Income tax expense for year	24,150
Total income taxes owed	$ 27,150
– Ending balance of Income Taxes Payable	(800)
Total income taxes paid	$ 26,350

In this case, the amount of the cash flows is greater than the amount of the expense used in determining net income. The $2,200 decrease in the liability account balance would be deducted from net income on the SCF to arrive at net cash flow provided by operating activities.

Other current liabilities can be analyzed in the same manner. Increases in current liabilities are added to net income and decreases in current liabilities are deducted from net income when computing net cash flow from operating activities under the indirect method.

Analyzing Transactions for a SCF—Investing and Financing Activities

Most businesses have only a few transactions or events each year that qualify as investing or financing activities. These items may be identified by reviewing the company's beginning and ending balances of short-term notes receivable and payable, long-term assets and liabilities, and stockholders' equity accounts. The statement of changes in stockholders' equity can be used to obtain necessary details about the causes of changes in stockholders' equity account balances. Income statement information relative to gains and losses may also be necessary.

Investing Activities

The most common investing activities generating cash inflows are sales of PP&E items or of security investments owned by the company. The most common cash outflow investing activities are purchases of these same items. An earlier section discussed the sale of a piece of equipment by Howard Restaurant Supply and its impacts on the statement of cash flows. This section will discuss the purchase of another PP&E item.

Assume that Howard had a $198,500 beginning and a $175,353 ending balance in its PP&E account. Without any other information, it could be estimated that Howard sold PP&E costing $23,147 ($198,500 – $175,353) during the year. However, it was previously indicated that the cost of equipment sold by Howard during the year was $35,000. If that had been the only PP&E purchase or sale transaction, the PP&E account would have had an ending balance of $163,500 ($198,500 – $35,000). The ending balance is, instead, given at $175,353. Thus, Howard Restaurant Supply must have purchased $11,853 of equipment in addition to selling some equipment.

Ending balance of PP&E		$175,353
Beginning balance of PP&E	$ 198,500	
– Cost of equipment (sold at a $460 loss)	(35,000)	
Balance after equipment sale		(163,500)
Equipment purchased		$ 11,853

Financing Activities

The most common financing activities generating cash inflows are issuances of notes and bonds payable as well as sales of common, preferred, or treasury stock. The most common cash outflow financing activities are principal payments on notes, capital leases and bonds, purchases of treasury stock, and payment of cash dividends on common and preferred stock.

Completing the Analysis

Howard Restaurant Supply's 2002 income satement and comparative balance sheets are given in, respectively, Exhibits 10-5 and 10-6. Assume the following information about the remaining amounts in Howard's SCF.

- Inventory increased by $12,684; this amount is subtracted from net income in the operating section of the SCF prepared on an indirect basis.
- Prepaid Insurance decreased by $2,575; this amount is added to net income in the operating section of the SCF prepared on an indirect basis.
- Long-Term Investments increased by $10,009; this amount represents a purchase of investments and is shown as a cash outflow in the investing section of the SCF.
- Accounts Payable decreased by $38,405; this amount is subtracted from net income in the operating section of the SCF prepared on an indirect basis.

EXHIBIT 10-5

Howard Restaurant Supply, Inc. 2002 Income Statement

Howard Restaurant Supply, Inc.
Income Statement
For Year Ended December 31, 2002

Sales Revenue		$ 600,000
Cost of Goods Sold		(398,156)
Gross Profit		$ 201,844
Expenses:		
Depreciation	$ 29,738	
Wages and Salaries	79,866	
Insurance	5,210	(114,814)
Other Revenues and Expenses:		
Interest Revenue (on bank savings)	$ 3,454	
Interest Expense (on capital leases)	(7,273)	(3,819)
Loss on Sale of Equipment		(460)
Income Before Income Tax		$ 82,751
Income Tax Expense		(24,150)
Net Income		$ 58,601

EXHIBIT 10-6

Howard Restaurant Supply, Inc. Comparative Balance Sheets

Howard Restaurant Supply, Inc.
Balance Sheets
For Years Ended December 31, 2002 and 2001

	12/31/02	12/31/01
ASSETS		
Current Assets:		
Cash and Cash Equivalents	$ 3,432	$ 3,485
Accounts Receivable	24,957	0
Inventory	30,638	17,954
Prepaid Insurance	2,425	5,000
Long-Term Investments	13,809	3,800
PP&E	175,353	198,500
Less Accumulated Depreciation	(86,113)	(89,687)
Total Assets	$164,501	$139,052
LIABILITIES		
Current Liabilities:		
Accounts Payable	$ 13,695	$ 52,100
Income Taxes Payable	2,300	100
Long-Term Liabilities:		
Capital Lease Payable	14,506	19,500
Notes Payable	7,245	1,000
Stockholders' Equity:		
Common Stock (no-par value)	64,058	60,000
Retained Earnings	63,217	6,352
Treasury Stock	(520)	(0)
Total Liabilities and Stockholders' Equity	$164,501	$139,052

- Capital Lease Payable decreased by $4,994; this amount represents a principal payment on the lease obligation and is shown as a cash outflow in the financing section of the SCF.
- Notes Payable increased by $6,245; this amount represents borrowings and is shown as a cash inflow in the financing section of the SCF.
- Common Stock increased by $4,058; this amount represents the issuance of stock and is shown as a cash inflow in the financing section of the SCF.
- Retained Earnings increased by $56,865; this change represents two items: (1) income of $58,601, which is shown as the starting point in the operating section of the SCF prepared on an indirect basis and (2) dividends of $1,736, which are shown as a cash outflow in the financing section of the SCF. The dividends are calculated in the following manner.

  Beginning balance + NI – Dividends = Ending balance
  $6,352 + $58,601 – X = $63,217
  X = $1,736

- Treasury Stock increased by $520; this amount represents stock repurchased by Howard Restaurant Supply and is shown as a cash outflow in the financing section of the SCF.

In the SCF in which the operating section is prepared on a direct basis, some additional calculations are necessary.

- Payments to employees, receipt of interest on bank savings, and payments of interest on capital leases are amounts taken directly from the income statement. There were no asset or liability accounts related to these amounts on Howard's balance sheet; therefore, these revenues and expenses represent actual cash amounts.
- Payments to suppliers represent the effects of transactions related to both Inventory and Accounts Payable. It is assumed that all inventory is purchased on credit. First, the amount of inventory purchased on account must be calculated.

  Beginning inventory + Purchases – CGS = Ending inventory
  $17,954 + Purchases – $398,156 = $30,638
  Purchases = $410,840

  Second, the amount of payments to suppliers of inventory is calculated.

  Beginning A/P + Purchases – Payments = Ending A/P
  $52,100 + $410,840 – Payments = $13,695
  Payments = $449,245

  This amount equals the total effect related to Inventory and Accounts Payable shown in the operating section when the SCF is prepared using the indirect method.

  Cost of Goods Sold (shown as part of NI) ± Change in Inventory ± Change in A/P = –$398,156 – $12,684 increase in Inventory – $38,405 decrease in A/P = –$449,245. The CGS amount is negative because CGS is an expense that causes net income to decrease.
- Payments for insurance are calculated using the Prepaid Insurance account and Insurance Expense information.

Beginning balance of Prepaid Insurance	$ 5,000	debit
+Payments made for insurance	?	debit
–Insurance Expense	(5,210)	credit
=Ending balance of Prepaid Insurance	$ 2,425	debit

  Solving for the unknown indicates that $2,635 was paid for insurance during the year.

Noncash Investing and Financing Activities

Companies occasionally engage in significant noncash investing or financing activities. For example, a company might acquire a building by issuing a long-term promissory note to the seller. Although these types of transactions do not involve cash, they must be disclosed by a firm. Such disclosure is required whether the indirect or direct method of preparing a statement of cash flows is used. Typically, noncash investing and financing activities are included in a schedule that follows the statement of cash flows.

ACCOUNTING INFORMATION FOR DECISION MAKING

A statement of cash flows helps decision makers evaluate a company's ability to generate positive net future cash flows. Economists define the true value of an asset, or entire business, as the present value of its future cash flows. Although a SCF reports historical cash-flow data, a strong correlation usually exists between a company's historical and future cash flows.

The second use of cash-flow data focuses on the information needs of specific types of financial statement users. For example, suppliers want to be reassured that business customers can generate sufficient cash to pay their bills when they come due. Stockholders, on the other hand, should be familiar with a business's ability to generate sufficient excess cash each accounting period to pay dividends. Employees are concerned with whether their employer will have sufficient cash to pay earned salaries and wages.

A statement of cash flows also allows decision makers to reconcile a business's net income with the cash receipts and disbursements produced by its principal operating activities. Profitable companies do not necessarily generate sufficient cash to finance their day-to-day operations. However, if a company's net income significantly exceeds the cash generated by its principal business operations, decision makers will want to investigate this difference. Consider a company that reports a large increase in net income but a negative cash flow from its operating activities in a given year. Further investigation may reveal that the firm increased its net income by adopting a more liberal credit policy that resulted in increased sales to high-risk customers. If many of these new customers are unable to pay their bills, this company essentially inflated its reported profit over the short-term by "giving away" inventory.

Finally, a SCF can help decision makers assess the impact of investing and financing transactions on a business's financial position. A large increase in cash during a recent year from profitable operations is a positive signal of a company's financial health. However, a company that finances its cost of operations—inventory purchases, payroll costs, and so forth—by selling property, plant, and equipment projects a substantially different image. Companies that intend to remain in business cannot continuously sell off productive assets to raise cash; such financing sources are very short-lived.

There is a limit to the amount of cash a company can raise by selling stocks or bonds or by taking out long-term loans—examples of financing activities. Likewise, a company cannot survive for long if it must sell equipment or other productive assets—an investing activity—to generate needed cash. To be economically viable over the long term, a company must eventually generate positive net cash flows from its principal operating activities.

Much can be learned about a company's financial status and future prospects by analyzing the three components of its cash flows. For example, Howard Restaurant Supply's statements of cash flow indicate that the company produced a positive net cash flow from operating activities. Additionally, the cash flow statements reveal that a large proportion of the company's investing cash outflows were for the purchase of property, plant, and equipment. Here again is a positive indication of the company's future prospects: the company is investing cash produced by operating activities in additional productive assets to expand the scope of those activities. Finally, dividend payments were included in Howard's financing cash outflows for 2002 and few stockholders (or potential stockholders) will complain regarding that use of a company's cash resources.

Cash Flow Ratios

Rather than using specific balance sheet or income statement information to make solvency and liquidity ratio computations, some financial statement users prefer to partially assess corporate performance based on cash flows. For example, the operating cash flow ratio can be calculated instead of a current or quick ratio. This measurement of cash flow from operating activities divided by current liabilities provides an indication of a company's ability to meet near-term obligations. The cash interest coverage ratio (cash flow from operating activities plus interest and tax expense divided by interest expense) can be used rather than that times interest earned ratio. A capital expenditure ratio (cash flow from operating activities divided by capital expenditures) measures a company's ability to finance growth.

As with all ratios, "appropriate" values for cash flow ratios depend on the industry in which a company operates. Businesses in the gaming industry, for example, will generate substantially greater operating cash flows than companies in telecommunications or heavy manufacturing.

Cash Flow per Share

One financial measure often tracked by decision makers is cash flow per share. Businesses, however, are prohibited from reporting cash flow per share in annual reports because the FASB believes that reporting both earnings per share and cash flow per share would confuse financial statement users. Cash flow per share information is often provided by investment advisory firms.

One problem relative to cash flow per share disclosures, is a lack of consistency in how this financial measure is computed. The following equation provides one of the more widely accepted approaches to computing **cash flow per share** for an accounting period.

$$\text{Cash Flow per Share} = \frac{\text{Net Cash Flow from Operating Activities} - \text{Preferred Stock Dividends}}{\text{Weighted Average Number of Shares of Common Stock Outstanding}}$$

When a company's earnings per share and cash flow per share are significantly different in a given year, decision makers may be concerned and need additional information. Quite often, a company's operating cash flows begin declining in advance of a decrease in earnings. For example, during the early stages of an economic recession, a company's sales may remain stable. However, the collection period on those sales may lengthen if the recession continues, causing cash flows from operating activities to decline. If economic conditions fail to improve, a company's earnings will likely begin to decline because of falling sales, increases in bad debt expense, and write-offs (or write-downs) of slow-moving inventory.

What decision makers really want is information about a business's future, rather than historical, cash flows and earnings. Although the Securities and Exchange Commission (SEC) encourages public companies to release financial forecasts, projections of cash flows, revenues, and earnings are rarely included in annual reports. To promote the issuance of forecasted financial data, the SEC established a "safe harbor" rule under which the SEC will help protect a company from lawsuits if a financial forecast prepared in good faith by the firm proves to be a poor predictor of future operating results. However, business executives are still reluctant to include financial forecasts in their companies' annual reports because of the risk of being sued if their projections are not achieved.

Free Cash Flow

One computation often made by bankers, financial analysts, and other financial statement users is **free cash flow** (FCF). As with other financial tools, there are a variety of definitions for FCF but, in general, it can be approximated as the net amount of cash provided by operating activities minus capital investments for property, plant, and equipment. Another definition of FCF also allows for the subtraction of dividends and mandatory debt interest and principal repayments.

Although not required, companies such as Coca-Cola (www.coca-cola.com) and Mandalay Resort Group (www.mandalayresortgroup.com) report FCF information in their annual reports; other companies provide this information in press releases, along with definitions of how FCF was computed. FCF is considered by users to provide an indication of a company's ability to maintain its current level of productive capacity. Companies with high levels of FCF may not be engaging in a sufficient amount of capital expenditures. Market valuations of companies are also often assessed on the basis of whether those valuations can be supported by free cash flows. Some regulatory agencies, such as the New Jersey Gaming Commission, use FCF in assessing financial viability analysis.[2] Users may also want to use FCF to calculate some liquidity measurements: FCF to sales and FCF to total interest on debt. One analyst indicates that FCF is "the most transparent metric to gauge company performance" and indicate true earnings quality.[3] However, until a consistent definition is adopted, comparisons of corporate-reported FCFs will not necessarily provide consistent and reliable information for analysis.

SUMMARY

Businesses engage in three principal activities that result in cash inflows and outflows: operating, investing, and financing activities. Operating activities involve transactions and events related to the production and delivery of goods and services. Receipts from customers are the primary cash inflows from operating activities for most businesses, while payments to suppliers and employees are typically among the largest operating cash outflows. Acquisition and disposal of property, plant, and equipment as well as long-term investments in debt and equity securities are important sources of cash flows from investing activities. Finally, cash flows from financing activities include proceeds from the sale of a firm's common and preferred stock, payments of dividends, and principal payments on long-term loans.

Businesses may use either the direct or indirect method of preparing statements of cash flows. The difference between these two methods appears in the operating activities section. Under the direct method, net cash flow from operating activities is the sum of specific cash flows, such as cash received from customers and cash paid to suppliers. Under the indirect method, net cash flow from operating activities is computed by making adjustments to net income for gains and losses, noncash expenses such as depreciation and amortization, and changes in noncash current assets and liabilities.

One common method decision makers apply in analyzing cash-flow data is a comparison of the three components of a firm's cash flows over a period of several years. Such analysis may reveal trends in those cash flows that yield insights on the company's financial condition and future prospects. Although businesses are prohibited from reporting cash flow per share, that amount may be calculated by investment analysts. A common formula for this computation is: (net cash flow from operating activities minus preferred stock dividends) divided by the weighted average number of shares of common stock outstanding. Cash-flow per share can be compared to the company's earnings per share and any significant divergence from the normal relationship between these two key financial measures should be investigated.

Users may also calculate solvency and liquidity ratios using cash flow rather than net income. One measure of a company's ability to continue is its free cash flow (FCF), which can be computed as cash flow from operating activities minus expenditures for capital investments.

[2] John Mills, Lynn Bible, and Richard Mason, "Defining Free Cash Flow," *The CPA Journal* (January 2002), pp. 36–41.

[3] Joseph Chang, "Investors Sharpen Focus on Free Cash Flow," *Chemical Market Reporter* (July 22–29, 2002), pp. 1, 18.

KEY TERMS

cash flow per share
direct method (of preparing a statement of cash flows)
financing activity
free cash flow
indirect method (of preparing a statement of cash flows)
investing activity
operating activity
statement of cash flows

QUESTIONS

1. What is the principal use of a statement of cash flows from the perspective of financial decision makers? *(LO 10.1)*
2. What is the primary accounting objective of a statement of cash flows? *(LO 10.1)*
3. Define and provide two examples of each of the following: (a) operating activities, (b) investing activities, and (c) financing activities. *(LO 10.2)*
4. What are the principal cash inflows and cash outflows from operating activities for most businesses? *(LO 10.2)*
5. Why does the FASB prefer the direct method of preparing a statement of cash flows to the indirect method? Which method is more commonly used? Why? *(LO 10.3)*
6. What is the starting point for determining a business's net cash flow from its operating activities under the indirect method? Why is this figure used? *(LO 10.3)*
7. Under the indirect method of preparing a statement of cash flows, why is depreciation expense added to net income when determining net cash flow from operating activities? *(LO 10.3)*
8. How are significant noncash investing and financing activities typically reported in a set of financial statements? *(LO 10.3)*
9. What can an investor learn from looking at the relationship between operating, financing, and investing cash flows from year to year? *(LO 10.4)*
10. Why might investors use cash flow information to compute solvency and liquidity ratios? Why would an operating cash flow ratio be more informative than a current or quick ratio? *(LO 10.5)*
11. How is cash flow per share typically computed? *(LO 10.5)*
12. Which amount is typically larger each year for a business, cash flow per share or earnings per share? Why? *(LO 10.5)*
13. What items are needed to adjust cash flow from operating activities to free cash flow? Why are investors interested in free cash flow? *(LO 10.5)*

EXERCISES

14. **True or False** *(All LOs)*

Following are a series of statements regarding topics discussed in this chapter.

Required:

Indicate whether each statement is true (T) or false (F).

(1) Increases in noncash current assets are added to net income when computing net cash flow from operating activities under the indirect method.

(2) Profitable companies do not necessarily generate sufficient cash to finance their day-to-day operations.

(3) Financing activities are generally those transactions and events related to the production and delivery of goods and services by businesses.

(4) The Financial Accounting Standards Board permits businesses to report cash flow per share in their financial statement footnotes.

(5) Decision makers use a free cash flow to evaluate a business's ability to sustain future growth.

(6) Decision makers prefer companies to generate most of their cash inflows from investing and financing activities.

(7) The acquisition and disposal of property, plant, and equipment are examples of operating activities.

(8) The indirect method of preparing a statement of cash flows requires that certain adjustments be made to net income to determine the net cash flow from operating activities.

(9) Similar to the balance sheet and income statement, the statement of cash flows is prepared for a specific time.

(10) Cash flows from investing and financing activities are reported in the same manner under the indirect and direct methods of preparing a statement of cash flows.

15. **Classification of Cash Flows** *(LO 10.2)*

Cash flows can be categorized as one of the following:

(a) Cash inflow from operating activities
(b) Cash outflow from operating activities
(c) Cash inflow from investing activities
(d) Cash outflow from investing activities
(e) Cash inflow from financing activities
(f) Cash outflow from financing activities

Required:

Classify each of the following transactions into one of the six categories:

(1) Payments to employees
(2) Loans made to other firms
(3) Payments to acquire trading securities
(4) Receipts from customers
(5) Receipts from the sale of property, plant, and equipment
(6) Payments of interest
(7) Payments made to acquire controlling interests in other firms
(8) Receipts of interest and dividends
(9) Payments to retire outstanding bonds
(10) Payments to suppliers
(11) Purchases of treasury stock
(12) Issuance of preferred stock at more than par value

16. **Net Income and Net Cash Flow from Operating Activities** *(LO 10.4)*

Dugan Technology manufactures computer disk drives and related computer products. The company suffered a loss of nearly $450 million in 2003. However, the company's statement of cash flows for that year reported a net cash flow from operating activities of approximately $20 million.

Required:

How could Dugan incur a large loss in a given year but still have a positive cash flow from operating activities in 2003?

17. **Completing a Statement of Cash Flows** *(LO 10.3)*

Following is a partially completed statement of cash flows for Brigham Company.

Cash flows from operating activities:		
Net income		$ 1,433
Adjustments to reconcile net income to net cash provided by operating activities:		
Depreciation expense		?
Gain on sale of land		(115)
Changes in current assets and liabilities:		
Increase in accounts receivable		(863)
Decrease in inventories		350
Decrease in prepaid expenses		667
Decrease in short-term notes payable		(400)
Decrease in accrued liabilities		(1,004)
Net cash provided by operating activities		$?
Cash flows from investing activities:		
Sale of land	$?	
Purchase of property, plant & equipment	(7,639)	
Net cash used by investing activities		(1,113)
Cash flows from financing activities:		
Sale of common stock	$ 6,329	
Dividend payments	?	
Net cash provided by financing activities		4,072
Net increase in cash		$ 4,115
Cash balance, December 31, 2002		?
Cash balance, December 31, 2003		$11,332

Required:

(1) What method does Brigham Company use to prepare its statement of cash flows? How does the method used differ from the alternative?

(2) Complete Brigham's statement of cash flows.

(3) What was Brigham's largest source of cash during the year in question?

(4) Based on the SCF, how would you assess Brigham's performance during 2003?

18. **Analyzing Cash-Flow Effects** *(LO 10.4)*

Motta Storage Company had the following balances in its Equipment and Accumulated Depreciation, Equipment accounts at the beginning and end of 2003.

	January 1	December 31
Equipment	$100,000	$120,000
Accumulated Depreciation, Equipment	25,000	18,000

During 2003, Motta engaged in the following transactions involving equipment:

March 9 Purchased new equipment for $40,000.

July 16 Sold equipment that originally cost $20,000 and had a current book value of $8,000 for $16,500.

Required:

(1) How much depreciation expense did Motta Storage Company record on its equipment during 2003?

(2) Indicate how Motta's depreciation expense and its transactions involving equipment would appear in the company's 2003 statement of cash flows, assuming the company uses the indirect method of preparing a statement of cash flows.

19. **Analyzing Cash-Flow Effects** *(LO 10.4)*

Barr Corp. had beginning and ending balances in Salaries Payable of, respectively, $3,560 and $2,986. Barr's income statement for 2003 showed Salaries Expense of $79,890.

Required:

(1) Why would Barr Corp. have a balance in Salaries Payable at the beginning of its fiscal year?

(2) How much was paid to employees for salaries during 2003?

(3) Indicate how the information for salaries would appear in Barr's 2003 statement of cash flows, assuming the company uses the indirect method of preparing a statement of cash flows.

(4) Indicate how the information for salaries would appear in Barr's 2003 statement of cash flows, assuming the company uses the direct method of preparing a statement of cash flows.

20. **Comparative Analysis of Cash Flows** *(LO 10.4)*

The following data were included in a recent annual report of Warehouse Foods, a wholesaler of grocery products.

	Year 1	Year 2	Year 3
Net Income	$ 3,716,084	$ 3,818,190	$ 8,638,658
Net Cash Flow from Operating Activities	7,460,501	12,556,072	15,390,336
Net Cash Flow from Investing Activities	(7,792,408)	(41,527,077)	(32,850,636)
Net Cash Flow from Financing Activities	15,113,487	17,478,816	14,982,854

Required:

(1) Why is a company's net income typically less than its net cash flow from operating activities?

(2) Why do most companies, including Warehouse Foods, typically have negative cash flows from investing activities?

(3) Over the three-year period, what type of activities was the largest source of funds for Warehouse Foods? Do business executives want these activities to be their firm's principal source of funds? Explain.

21. **Cash Flow Ratios and Free Cash Flow** *(LO 10.5)*

The following information is available from various financial statements for Imagining, Inc.:

Net cash inflow from operating activities	$350,000
Net cash outflow from investing activities	463,000
Cash purchases of property, plant and equipment	290,000
Interest expense	57,000
Tax expense	128,000
Net income	234,000
Current assets	179,600
Current liabilities	92,100

Required:

(1) Compute the current ratio and the operating cash flow ratio. Discuss any significant differences between the two ratios.

(2) Calculate the times interest earned ratio and the cash interest coverage ratio. Discuss any significant differences between the two ratios.

(3) Calculate free cash flow for Imagining, Inc. Discuss any significant differences between FCF and net income.

22. **Cash Flow Share** *(LO 10.5, Excel)*

The following data are available for Paul's Discount Emporium, a large discount retailer.

	2001	2002	2003
Net Income	$35,574,000	$48,557,000	$73,634,000
Net Cash Flow from Operating Activities	42,713,000	36,196,000	43,257,000
Weighted-average Number of Common Shares Outstanding	66,306,000	67,281,000	69,009,000
Preferred Stock Dividends Paid	—	—	772,000

Required:

(1) Compute Paul's earnings per share and cash flow per share for each year.

(2) For each year, express Paul's earnings per share as a percentage of its cash flow per share.

(3) What factors possibly accounted for Paul's net cash flow from operating activities being less than the firm's net income in 2002 and 2003? Why would a potential investor in this firm want to identify these factors?

PROBLEMS

23. **Classification of Cash Flows** *(LO 10.2)*

Following are line items that could be found in a statement of cash flows.

(a) Repurchase of common stock

(b) Interest received

(c) Refund of income taxes

(d) Principal payment on long-term notes payable
(e) Cash paid to suppliers and employees
(f) Increase in accounts payable
(g) Purchase of property and equipment
(h) Proceeds from issuing long-term note payable
(i) Cash paid for taxes
(j) Principal payments under capital lease obligations
(k) Depreciation expense
(l) Payment of dividends on preferred stock
(m) Principal payments on mortgages
(n) Increase in accounts receivable
(o) Gain on sale of equipment
(p) Proceeds from issuing common stock
(q) Decrease in wages payable
(r) Declaration of a stock dividend
(s) Cash paid to suppliers for inventory
(t) Issuance of treasury stock for cash
(u) Loans to officers
(v) Issuance of common stock for land
(w) Proceeds from the sale of property, plant, and equipment
(x) Cash received from customers
(y) Decrease in prepaid insurance

Required:

Classify each of the items as one of the following, assuming that the SCF is prepared on an indirect basis.

(1) Cash inflow from operating activities
(2) Cash outflow from operating activities
(3) Cash inflow from investing activities
(4) Cash outflow from investing activities
(5) Cash inflow from financing activities
(6) Cash outflow from financing activities
(7) Positive noncash adjustment to net income
(8) Negative noncash adjustment to net income
(9) Does not appear on the statement of cash flows prepared on an indirect basis

24. **Classification of Cash Flows** *(LO 10.2)*

Use the items (a) through (y) listed in problem 23.

Required:

Classify each of the items as one of the following, assuming that the SCF is prepared on a direct basis:

(1) Cash inflow from operating activities
(2) Cash outflow from operating activities
(3) Cash inflow from investing activities
(4) Cash outflow from investing activities

(5) Cash inflow from financing activities
(6) Cash outflow from financing activities
(7) Does not appear on the statement of cash flows prepared on a direct basis

25. **Statement of Cash Flows** *(LO 10.3, Excel)*

Following are the line items included in the 2003 statement of cash flows prepared by Goodly's Clothing Corporation.

Proceeds from sale of long-term investments	$ 8,077
Depreciation expense	5,285
Increase in miscellaneous current assets	(1,396)
Increase in accounts payable	12,590
Purchase of long-term investments	(34,959)
Net income	16,214
Increase in accrued salaries	4,072
Proceeds from sale of property and equipment	192
Increase in inventories	(11,320)
Issuance of long-term notes	500
Reductions of long-term debt	(172)
Gain on disposal of long-term assets	(135)
Issuance of common stock	126
Cash and cash equivalents, beginning of the year	31,350
Increase in income taxes payable	2,108
Acquisitions of property and equipment	(11,043)
Net increase (decrease) in cash and cash equivalents	?
Cash and cash equivalents, end of year	?

Required:

Prepare Goodly's statement of cash flows using the indirect method.

26. **Statement of Cash Flows** *(LO 10.3)*

Use the information in problem 25 for Goodly's Clothing Corporation and assume the following 2003 account balance information is also available.

Credit sales	$1,756,000
Cost of goods sold	810,000
Tax expense	134,000
Salaries expense	235,000

Required:

Determine the following items that would appear on a statement of cash flows prepared on a direct basis.

(1) cash collected from customers
(2) cash paid to suppliers (assuming that all inventory purchases are made on account payable)
(3) cash paid for taxes
(4) cash paid for salaries

27. **Determining Net Cash Flow from Operating Activities, Indirect and Direct Methods** *(LO 10.3)*

Following is an income statement for Claims Corporation for the year ended December 31, 2002, and a schedule listing the company's current assets and current liabilities at the end of 2001 and 2002.

Claims Corporation
Income Statement
For the Year Ended December 31, 2002

Sales		$ 77,600
Cost of Goods Sold		(44,400)
Gross Profit		$ 33,200
Operating Expenses:		
Selling & General Expenses	$8,800	
Depreciation Expense	1,900	(10,700)
Operating Income		$ 22,500
Gain on Sale of Land		5,500
Income before Income Tax		$ 28,000
Income Tax Expense		(11,200)
Net Income		$ 16,800

	2001	2002
Cash	$11,700	$ 4,100
Accounts Receivable	4,500	9,800
Inventory	6,700	11,300
Prepaid Expenses	3,500	800
Accounts Payable	2,900	5,600
Accrued Liabilities	1,600	2,800

Required:

(1) Prepare a schedule documenting Claims Corporation's net cash flow from operating activities for the year ended December 31, 2002, using the indirect method.

(2) Prepare a schedule documenting Claims Corporation's net cash flow from operating activities for the year ended December 31, 2002, using the direct method.

(3) Briefly evaluate the schedule you prepared in part (1). Does this schedule provide any clues regarding the financial health of Claims Pacific? Explain.

28. **Interpreting Cash-Flow Data** *(LO 10.4)*

Over a recent three-year period, General Cereal's statements of cash flows revealed cumulative increases in the company's accounts receivable of $145 million.

Required:

(1) How does an increase in accounts receivable affect a company's net cash flow from operating activities?

(2) If a company's accounts receivable balance is continually increasing from one year to the next, does that indicate, necessarily, that the firm is doing a poor job of "managing" or collecting its accounts receivable? Explain.

29. **Using Cash Flow Data** *(LO 10.4)*

The statement of cash flows for May Department Stores Company (www.maycompany.com) for the fiscal years 1999 through 2001 follow. Dollars are in millions.

	2001	2000	1999
Operating Activities			
Net earnings	$ 703	$ 858	$ 927
Adjustment for non-cash times included in earnings:			
Depreciation and other amortization	559	511	469
Deferred income taxes	63	59	75
Working capital changes:			
Accounts receivable, net	180	97	13
Merchandise inventories	103	(77)	(137)
Other current assets	34	(9)	(22)
Accounts payable	51	(77)	57
Accrued expenses	(10)	(70)	57
Income taxes payable	(19)	65	46
Other assets and liabilities, net	(20)	(11)	45
Cash flows from operations	$ 1,644	$ 1,346	$1,530
Investing Activities			
Capital expenditures	$ (797)	$ (598)	$ (703)
Proceeds from dispositions of property and equipment	41	48	25
Business combinations	(425)	(420)	(40)
Cash flows used for investing activities	$(1,181)	$ (970)	$ (718)
Financing Activities			
Issuances of long-term debt	$ 250	$ 1,076	$ 0
Repayment of long-term debt	(178)	(241)	(135)
Net issuance of short-term debt	78	0	0
Purchases of common stock	(474)	(828)	(468)
Issuance of common stock	54	36	34
Dividend payouts	(297)	(304)	(314)
Cash flows used for financing activities	$ (567)	$ (261)	$ (883)
Increase (decrease) in cash and cash equivalents	$ (104)	$ 115	$ (71)
Cash and cash equivalents, beginning of year	156	41	112
Cash and cash equivalents, end of year	$ 52	$ 156	$ 41

Required:

(1) How would a supplier interpret this data?
(2) How would a current investor interpret this data?
(3) How would a potential investor interpret this data?
(4) How would an employee interpret this data?
(5) Suppliers and employees both want to ensure that May will have enough money to pay them. Is the interpretation different for the two?

30. **Cash Ratios, Cash Flow Share, and Free Cash Flow** *(LO 10.5, Excel)*

In addition to the May Department Stores Company information provided in problem 29, the following information is available.

(a) Weighted average common shares outstanding were:

Year	Shares
1999	339,560,439
2000	313,138,686
2001	304,329,004

(b) May has no preferred stock.

Required:

(1) Using only the information presented, calculate May's cash interest coverage.
(2) Calculate May's capital expenditure ratio.
(3) Calculate May's cash flow per share.
(4) Calculate May's basic earnings per share.
(5) Interpret your calculations from year to year.
(6) Compare cash flow and earnings per share in each year and the change in the relationship between years. Comment on significant relationships.
(7) Calculate May's free cash flow.

CASES

31. **Annual Report** *(LO 10.4 & 10.5, Internet)*

Use the annual report of Carnival Corporation (www.carnival.com) for the 2001 fiscal year to answer the following questions.

Required:

(1) Does Carnival use the direct or indirect method to prepare a statement of cash flows?
(2) List the major cash inflows from each of the three operating activities for 2001.
(3) List the major cash outflows from each of the three operating activities for 2001.
(4) Compare Carnival's net income and cash flows from operations for 2001, 2000, and 1999. Comment on the relationship each year and the change from year to year.
(5) Calculate cash flows per share for 2001, 2000, and 1999. How does cash flow per share compare to basic earnings per share?
(6) In part (4), you compare cash flows from operations and net income. In part (5), you compare cash flows per share and earnings per share. Is one of these techniques better than another?
(7) Assume the viewpoint of a supplier, an investor, and an employee. Comment on the cash flow data from each perspective.
(8) Does Carnival raise a significant portion of money through financing activities or investing activities? List any significant inflows.
(9) Does the industry in which Carnival operates and/or the economy affect how much cash is provided or used by each business activity?
(10) Calculate all cash flow ratios that are possible using the data available.
(11) What is Carnival's free cash flow? Did Carnival spend a significant amount of money on purchasing PPE assets? What does that indicate from an investor's perspective?

32. **Comparing Cash Flows** *(LO 10.4 & 10.5, Internet, group)*

Identifying the similarities and differences in companies is as crucial to making investment decisions as understanding a single company's financial statements. Form groups of at least four students. Each group should select a single industry. Each group member should locate a different annual report within that industry. (The industry and individual company may be assigned by your instructor.) *Note:*

Additional references may be needed for some data, such as stock trading price and the beginning balance of certain accounts for the first year.

Required—individual group members:

(1) Calculate cash flow per share for the most recent two years. Comment on the changes from year to year.

(2) Calculate or locate basic earnings per share for the most recent two years.

(3) Calculate free cash flow for the most recent two years. Comment on the changes from year to year.

(4) Compare net income and cash flows from operations for the most recent two years. Comment on the relationships.

(5) Does the company use the direct or indirect method to prepare their statement of cash flows. If it uses the direct method, locate the reconciliation of net income to operating cash flows.

(6) For each of the following items, indicate how they affected the cash flows of the company you selected, and interpret the effect.

  (a) Change in accounts receivable

  (b) Change in taxes payable

  (c) Change in short-term investments

  (d) Change in accounts payable

  (e) Change in accrued liabilities

Required—groups:

(7) Compare the cash flow per share, earnings per share, cash flow from operations, net income, and free cash flow from company to company in the same fiscal years. Include in your comparison a graphical analysis. Discuss reasons why these figures might be similar or different within an industry.

(8) Based on a comparison of these five items, which company is the best investment in the industry you have chosen?

Required—class:

(9) Compare the cash flow per share, earnings per share, cash flow from operations, net income, and free cash flow from each industry. Discuss reasons why these items might be similar or different between industries.

(10) Does one industry seem to be a better investment than another? Do you think this judgment would necessarily be constant over time?

SUPPLEMENTAL PROBLEMS

33. **Classification of Cash Flows** *(LO 10.2)* [Compare to Problem 23.]

Following are line items included in recent statements of cash flows prepared by a national retailer.

  (a) Accounts payable, increase

  (b) Accounts receivable, decrease

  (c) Accrued expenses, decrease

  (d) Capital expenditures

(e) Deferred income taxes (long-term), increase
(f) Depreciation and amortization expense
(g) Dividend payouts
(h) Income taxes payable, decrease
(i) Issuance of common stock
(j) Issuance of long-term debt
(k) Issuance of short-term debt
(l) Merchandise inventories, decrease
(m) Other current assets, increase
(n) Proceeds from disposals of property and equipment
(o) Purchase common stock in other companies
(p) Purchase of treasury stock
(q) Repayment of long-term debt

Required:

(1) For each of the items, indicate in which section of the statement of cash flows it would appear.
   (a) operating activities
   (b) financing activities
   (c) investing activities

(2) For each item, indicate whether it is a cash inflow or outflow or a non–cash adjustment.

34. **Statement of Indirect Method** *(LO 10.3)* [Compare to Problem 25.]

Following is an income statement for Boulder Hill, Inc., for the year ended December 31, 2004, and the company's balance sheets as of December 31, 2003 and 2004 appear at the top of the next page.

The prepaid expenses and accrued liabilities included in Boulder Hill's balance sheets involve selling or general (operating) expenses. All of Boulder Hill's sales and merchandise purchases are made on a credit basis. Following is additional financial information that was obtained from Boulder Hill's accounting records for 2004.

(a)	Collections of accounts receivable	$90,800
(b)	Purchases of merchandise	35,100
(c)	Payments of accrued (operating) liabilities	3,300
(d)	Payments of operating expenses	9,600
(e)	Prepayments of operating expenses	700
(f)	Expiration of prepaid (operating) expenses	1,300
(g)	Payments to suppliers	37,000
(h)	Proceeds from sale of land	2,600
(i)	Sale of 300 shares of $1 par value common stock for $8 per share	2,400
(j)	Declaration and payment of cash dividends on common stock	7,500
(k)	Payments of 2004 income taxes	13,300
(l)	Accrual of unpaid operating expenses at year-end	3,700
(m)	Year-end adjusting entry to record depreciation expense on equipment	5,700

Boulder Hill, Inc.
Income Statement
For the Year Ended December 31, 2004

Sales		$ 92,900
Cost of Goods Sold		(36,800)
Gross Profit		$ 56,100
Operating Expenses:		
Selling & General Expenses	$14,600	
Depreciation Expense	5,700	(20,300)
Operating Income		$ 35,800
Loss on Sale of Land		(2,500)
Income before Income Tax		$ 33,300
Income Tax Expense		(13,300)
Net Income		$ 20,000

Boulder Hill, Inc.
Balance Sheets
December 31, 2003 and 2004

	2003		2004	
ASSETS				
Cash		$ 12,100		$ 36,500
Accounts Receivable		10,600		12,700
Inventory		14,700		13,000
Prepaid Expenses		1,300		700
Total Current Assets		$ 38,700		$ 62,900
Equipment	$ 52,000		$ 52,000	
Less: Acc. Depreciation	(16,300)	35,700	(22,000)	30,000
Investment in Land		5,100		0
Total Assets		$ 79,500		$ 92,900
LIABILITIES				
Accounts Payable	$ 7,100		$ 5,200	
Accrued Liabilities	3,300		3,700	
Total Current Liab.		$ 10,400		$ 8,900
STOCKHOLDERS' EQUITY				
Common Stock	$ 4,500		$ 4,800	
Additional PIC	18,200		20,300	
Retained Earnings	46,400		58,900	
Total SE		69,100		84,000
Total Liabilities and SE		$ 79,500		$ 92,900

Required:
Prepare a statement of cash flows for Boulder Hill for the year ended December 31, 2004, using the indirect method.

PART V

MANAGERIAL ACCOUNTING

CHAPTER 11

Fundamental Managerial Accounting Concepts

LEARNING OBJECTIVES

1. Differentiate between financial and managerial accounting.
2. Distinguish between product and period costs; direct and indirect costs; controllable and noncontrollable costs; and variable, fixed, and mixed costs.
3. Discuss the different costing systems and valuation methods used by organizations.
4. Calculate and use a predetermined overhead rate.
5. Classify product costs as direct material, direct labor, and overhead.
6. Record the flow of costs through the accounting system.
7. Prepare a statement of cost of goods manufactured.
8. Identify cost flows in a service company.

Rogar International Corporation

Rogar International Corporation (RIC), located in Midlothian, Virginia, produces pot racks, wine openers, and corkscrews. The company has changed dramatically from its 1975 beginnings in Abilene, Texas, as a manufacturer of parts for the Department of Defense. Economic downturns and a failed bank demanding immediate payment created a situation that necessitated owner Bob Crist to adapt. He took three employees and some worn-out equipment to Virginia, and obtained a critical $350,000 line of credit from the firm's major supplier, Mr. C. T. Fung of Hong Kong.

Knowledge gained in his MBA classes made Crist profoundly aware that the direct materials used to produce goods, as well as good wages and solid training given to direct labor employees, are critical to high-quality output. Overhead costs, although essential to production activity, are often the easiest place to control spending. In today's market, value is key. For consumer goods, such as those produced by Rogar, product prices cannot be raised simply to cover increased costs; there is an upper limit to what customers will pay. Good business sense requires that management understand cost behavior and control costs without sacrificing quality.

SOURCE: Information provided by Bob Crist of Rogar International Corporation, 2002.

INTRODUCTION

This chapter defines and discusses the concepts and terminology related to managerial accounting, and distinguishes this field of accounting from financial accounting. Different methods of accumulating and presenting costs in manufacturing and service organizations are discussed; and the preparation of a statement of cost of goods manufactured (or cost of services rendered) is illustrated.

COMPARISON OF FINANCIAL AND MANAGERIAL ACCOUNTING

Accounting exists for three primary purposes: (1) to provide information to external parties (stockholders, creditors, and various regulatory bodies) for investment and credit decisions; (2) to provide information to internal parties for planning and controlling operations; and (3) to estimate an organization's product or service cost. The financial accounting concepts presented earlier in this text were designed to meet the first purpose. **Managerial accounting** attempts to satisfy the second two purposes. The primary differences between these two accounting disciplines are given in Exhibit 11-1.

Although the objectives of financial and managerial accounting differ, accounting information relies on the same underlying details, same recording system, and same set of accounts. Financial accounting information is generally focused on the past, and specified in monetary terms. It is verifiable because of the use of generally accepted accounting principles and the need for consistency in external financial statements. Financial accounts reports are usually summarized and relate to the organization as a whole.

EXHIBIT 11-1

Primary Differences between Financial and Managerial Accounting

	Financial	Managerial
Primary users	External	Internal
Organizational focus	Whole	Parts
Time focus	Past	Present and future
Required	Yes	No
Frequency of reports	Monthly and annually	When necessary
Precision of information	High; use GAAP to determine requirements	Reasonable; use cost-benefit to determine usefulness

Alternatively, managerial accounting is not required, but should provide information for internal management needs. Thus, managerial accounting is more likely to be concerned with specific organizational units and to be less precise than financial accounting because timely information is needed to make internal decisions. Managerial accounting information should be based on factual data and valid estimates, not "wild guesses." One important use of managerial accounting information is to determine an organization's product or service cost. Managerial accounting information should only be developed and provided if its benefit is greater than the cost of producing it.

TYPES OF COSTS

Because the term *cost* has many meanings, an adjective is usually attached to indicate what information is being provided. For example, the term *historical cost* is used in financial accounting to indicate the amount for which an asset was purchased and first recorded in the accounting records. However, the historical cost of an asset is not very important in managerial accounting because that type of cost lacks of relevance to the present. Thus, managerial accounting often focuses on an asset's **replacement cost** or the amount that would need to be paid currently to buy the asset. A discussion of four distinct pairings of cost terms follows.

Product and Period Costs

Companies often distinguish between product and period costs. A **product cost** relates to the items that generate organizational revenues. In a retail company, product costs are the costs of buying inventory to sell to customers; these costs reflect the inventory costs discussed in Chapter 5. Before being sold, these costs appear in the balance sheet as a current asset called Merchandise Inventory; after sale, they are transferred to the income statement as an expense called Cost of Goods Sold.

In a manufacturing organization, product costs include the costs of making the goods that will be sold to wholesalers or retailers. These costs include amounts paid for direct material, direct labor, and overhead; each of these items is discussed in depth later in this chapter. Product costs of a manufacturing company appear in the balance sheet in the current asset section. Depending on the degree of completion of the product, these costs may be included in Raw Material Inventory (materials purchased but not yet used in production), Work in Process Inventory (uncompleted products), or Finished Goods Inventory (products that are ready for sale). When the goods are sold, product costs are transferred to the income statement's Cost of Goods Sold expense.

In a service organization, product costs also include direct material (or supplies), direct labor, and overhead. Service companies may or may not have a Services in Process Inventory account, depending on how long it takes to complete the service and how many dollars of costs are being incurred to complete the service. For example, a restaurant would not have an In Process account because the time to prepare a meal is short, and the meal is served immediately. However, a hospital would have such an account because a patient may be in a hospital for several days or more. Additionally, service companies generally do not have a Finished Services Inventory account. Immediately upon completion of the services, the total service cost is transferred either directly from the Raw Material (or Supply) Inventory account or the Services in Process Inventory to the income statement as a Cost of Services Rendered expense.

Period costs relate to an organization's selling and administrative functions. These costs are closely associated with a specific time period or with the passage of time. Period costs that have future benefits are classified as assets (such as Prepaid Insurance); period costs having no future benefits are expensed (such as Insurance Expense).

Direct and Indirect Costs

Costs can also be described as being direct or indirect. This distinction reflects whether a cost can be related to a particular **cost object,** such as an organizational product, service, department, or territory. A **direct cost** is one that is clearly and easily traceable to, and a monetarily important part of, a specified cost object. An **indirect cost** is one that is not clearly and easily traceable, or is not a monetarily important part of, a specified cost object. However, indirect costs may be assigned, if desired, to cost objects using a variety of techniques.

To illustrate the difference between direct and indirect costs, assume an organization has two sales territories (Northwest and Southwest). Each territory has three salespeople and one manager oversees both territories. Salaries of the salespeople who work solely in one territory would be considered a direct cost of that territory. However, the manager's salary would be considered an indirect cost to both the Northwest and Southwest territories. One way the manager's $80,000 salary could be assigned to the two territories would be to use each territory's proportion of total sales dollars. If Northwest territory sales were $1,500,000 and Southwest territory sales were $500,000, then 75 percent ($1,500,000 ÷ $2,000,000) of the manager's salary could be assigned to the Northwest territory and 25 percent ($500,000 ÷ $2,000,000) could be assigned to the Southwest territory. The appropriate amounts ($60,000 and $20,000, respectively) of the manager's salary could be added to the Northwest and Southwest salespeople's salaries to determine the total estimated salary cost for each territory.

Controllable and Noncontrollable Costs

Organizations may also differentiate between controllable and noncontrollable costs. Any cost that a manager can authorize or directly influence in terms of dollar size is a **controllable cost.** Costs that are not under the control of a specific manager are called **noncontrollable costs.** These cost categories may overlap with, but are not the same as, direct and indirect costs. For example, if the manager in the previous example can set salespersons' salaries within the Northwest and Southwest territories, then those salary costs are direct and controllable costs of the territory. The manager's salary is direct to both territories (although not to the separate territories), but is not controllable because the manager cannot set his or her own salary. However, the manager's salary is a controllable cost to the manager's supervisor. It is important to distinguish between controllable and noncontrollable costs because a manager should only be held responsible for costs that he or she can control.

Variable and Fixed Costs

Costs can be distinguished by how they behave *in total* as activity changes. Activity can be measured in many ways: sales or service volume, production volume, machine time, labor time, number of suppliers used, number of purchase orders sent, number of different products manufactured, or number of services performed.

A **variable cost** changes *in total* in direct proportion to changes in activity. For example, in a furniture manufacturing company, the more tables that are made, the more wood costs will be incurred. In a casino, the more square footage of floor space there is, the more security cost will be necessary. In a steak restaurant, the more meals that are sold, the more pounds of steak will be purchased and used. Suppose that for every steak meal that is sold, $4 will be incurred for meat costs. The total cost of meat varies in direct proportion with number of meals sold, an activity measure. Therefore, a variable cost is constant per unit of activity. Once the per-unit variable cost is known, cost estimates can be made for any expected activity.

Alternatively, a **fixed cost** remains constant *in total* with changes in activity. For example, the cost of annual straight-line depreciation is a fixed cost, as are the costs of monthly rent and the monthly pay of salaried employees. The constant total amount is the cost formula for the fixed cost. Using the steak restaurant example again, suppose that the chef is paid $200 per night in salary regardless of how many steak dinners he prepares. On a night when 20 meals are prepared, the chef is paid $10 to prepare each meal ($200 salary ÷ 20 meals); on a night when 200 dinners are prepared, he is paid $1 per meal ($200 ÷ 200 meals). On a per-unit basis, a fixed cost varies inversely with levels of activity; thus, the higher the activity, the lower the cost per unit.

Given enough time and shift in underlying activity, variable costs will change on a per-unit basis and fixed costs will change in total. Thus, to estimate variable and fixed costs, a **relevant range** of activity must be specified. This range can be viewed as the organization's normal annual operating range. For example, assume that a theater has 250 seats, has four showings per day, and is open 360 days per year. The relevant range of activity is zero to 360,000 people (250 × 4 × 360). If the theater wants to serve more people, additional fixed costs would have to be incurred to obtain more square footage; or additional variable costs would have to be incurred to hire additional ticket sellers, ticket takers, and/or concession workers.

A third category of costs, as defined by behavior, is a **mixed cost.** This type of cost has both a variable and a fixed element. Thus, the total cost changes with changes in activity, but not in direct proportion to those activity changes. One common mixed cost is electricity. An organization pays a flat rate just to have electrical service and then pays an additional fee for usage in kilowatt-hours. For accounting purposes, mixed costs are divided into their variable and fixed components and treated separately for cost analysis.[1]

A summary of all costs discussed in this section is presented in Visual Recap 11.1. In addition, assuming that mixed costs have been properly separated, the following formulas are helpful:

$$\text{Total Cost} = \text{Total Variable Cost} + \text{Total Fixed Cost}$$

$$\text{Total Variable Cost} = \begin{matrix}\text{Variable Cost per}\\ \text{Unit of Activity}\end{matrix} \times \begin{matrix}\text{Number of Units}\\ \text{of Activity}\end{matrix}$$

[1] One easy way to separate a mixed cost into its variable and fixed components is the high-low method. This method uses the costs at the highest and lowest levels of activity (assuming they are within the relevant range) to compute a cost formula. A description of this method can be found in many managerial or cost accounting textbooks.

VISUAL RECAP 11.1

Summary of Costs

Product Cost	Period Cost
A cost associated with making a product or providing a service (such as labor, material, and overhead)	A cost associated with the sales or administrative functions of a business (such as sales commissions, headquarters insurance, and legal fees)

Direct Cost	Indirect Cost
A cost that is easily traceable and monetarily significant to a cost object (such as lumber for a table and sales salary for a sales territory)	A cost that is not easily traceable or is not monetarily significant to a cost object (such as the vice president's salary to units of production or cost of electricity to number of pizzas sold)

Controllable Cost	Noncontrollable Cost
A cost that a manager has the authority to change (such as the salary of a subordinate)	A cost that a manger cannot change (such as his/her own salary or a government mandated cost)

Variable Cost	Fixed Cost	Mixed Cost
A cost that changes by a constant amount with each unit change in activity (such as the cost of hamburger patties at a fast-food restaurant)	A cost that does not change with each unit change in activity (such as the monthly building rental cost for a restaurant)	A cost that has both a variable and fixed portion (such as a car rental agreement that has a fixed daily rate plus a specific amount for each mile driven)

COMPONENTS OF PRODUCT COST FOR MANUFACTURING COMPANIES

As discussed in the previous section, product costs are related to the products that generate an organization's primary revenues. In a manufacturing company, there are three components of product cost: material, labor, and overhead. Some material and labor costs are considered direct or specifically related to a cost object; indirect material and labor costs are included in overhead. When discussing product cost, the cost object is defined as the inventory being manufactured. Direct labor and overhead are necessary to convert raw material (or purchased parts) into a finished product. Thus, the total cost of direct labor and overhead is referred to as **conversion cost.**

Direct Material Cost

A **direct material** is any clearly identifiable and conveniently traceable item that becomes a part of a manufactured product. The cost of a direct material must be monetarily significant to the total product cost. Direct material costs are variable with production volume. For example, lumber is a direct material of wooden tables; as a company manufacturers more tables, more lumber is needed and the direct material cost increases. The cost of any product part that is not identifiable, traceable, or monetarily significant is classified and accounted for as an **indirect material** and included in overhead.

Direct Labor Cost

The people who manufacture company products are called **direct labor.** In a factory setting, direct labor would include seamstresses, bakers, and machine operators. Direct labor cost includes the ordinary wages (usually hourly) earned by direct labor employees, as well as the taxes (such as Social Security and Medicare) paid on behalf of the employee. Direct labor costs are generally variable with production volume.

Employees who do not work directly on production but are part of the production "team" (such as janitorial staff and supervisors) are considered **indirect labor.** These costs are included in overhead. The costs of indirect labor outside the production area (such as company administrators) are period costs, not product cost.

Overhead Cost

Overhead is any product cost incurred in the manufacturing area that cannot be, or is not, directly traced to the making of a product. Overhead consists of indirect material, indirect labor, and other indirect costs that cannot be associated with a specific product. For example, the cost of electricity to run production machinery cannot be directly attributed to an individual product.

Some labor costs that would appear to be direct are treated as indirect. Two specific examples are overtime bonuses and premiums paid to late-shift workers. Generally, to treat these costs as direct to production would provide inappropriate information on product costs. Assume that day-shift workers are paid $8 per hour, late-shift workers are paid a shift premium of $0.50 per hour, and three hours are needed to make one unit of product. If a product were manufactured during only day-shift hours, it would have a direct labor cost of $24. If it were manufactured during the late shift and shift premiums were included in direct labor, that same product would have a direct labor cost of $25.50. The same type of result would occur if the product were manufactured in "regular" time rather than overtime. Because production scheduling is random, a product's direct cost should not depend on when it was manufactured; thus, overtime and shift premiums are generally considered part of overhead.

Overhead can be thought of as a "holding bin" for indirect costs. These costs are waiting to be associated with a particular product. The method of associating them with products is discussed later in this chapter.

Overhead costs may be variable or fixed. Variable overhead includes the costs of indirect material, indirect labor paid on an hourly basis, depreciation on a unit-of-production basis, and the variable portion of any type of mixed factory charges (such as maintenance and utilities). Fixed overhead includes the costs of indirect labor paid on a salary basis, depreciation on a straight-line basis, factory insurance and property taxes, and the fixed portion of mixed factory costs.

INVENTORY COSTING SYSTEMS

A manufacturing company must have a system to accumulate direct material, direct labor, and overhead costs and associate those costs with its products. Inventory costing systems (such as perpetual or periodic) for retail companies are discussed in Chapter 5. The two most common inventory costing systems in a manufacturing company are job order costing and process costing. The organization's choice of costing system typically depends on the type of product that is being manufactured.

Job Order Costing

Job order costing systems are used by manufacturers who produce goods in relatively small quantities, often to customer specifications. Costs are accumulated by **job,** which is a cost object related to a specific order or customer. At any time, the total cost of any job can be found in detailed information that supports the Work in Process Inventory account. An easy way to visualize a job order costing system is to think of the production of airplanes. When Boeing manufacturers airplanes, the exact costs of the planes must be accumulated for each airline's order. Delta and United will want different interior and exterior colors on the planes, as well as different cabin layouts, colors, and fabrics. Boeing will need to keep the costs for Delta's planes separate and distinct from the costs of United planes. The flow of costs in a job order costing system is illustrated in depth later in the chapter.

Processing Costing and Equivalent Units of Production

Manufacturers that produce mass quantities of similar goods (such as breakfast cereals, gasoline, or dog food) use a **process costing system** to accumulate costs. Because the goods are all the same and may flow through many production departments, costs are accumulated by batches of goods rather than by "job." At any time, total accumulated costs relate to a large number of units, some of which may have been completed and some of which are still in production. To assign costs to each of these categories of goods requires the use of **equivalent units of production** (EUP). EUP is an estimate of the number of fully completed units that could have been made during a period if all production efforts had resulted in completed units.

To illustrate, assume that PicNics, Inc., a wooden picnic table manufacturer, started operations in January with no beginning inventory. During January, the company placed enough wood into production to make 1,000 tables and workers began manufacturing tables. January's costs for wood and labor were $10,000 and $5,950, respectively. At the end of January, the company had completed 800 tables and had 200 tables that were one-fourth complete. Because 100 percent of the wood necessary for the tables was placed into production, the cost per table for wood is $10,000 ÷ 1,000 tables or $10. All labor activity, however, did not result in completed tables. The EUP for labor would be stated as [800 tables + (200 tables × 0.25 complete)] or 850 EUPs; thus, the labor cost per table is $5,950 ÷ 850 or $7. Additional processing activity and costs in February will result in the completion of the ending inventory of 200 tables.

VALUING INVENTORY

After determining the appropriate costing system to use, a manufacturing or service company needs to decide on a valuation method. The costing system (job order or process) identifies *which* costs to attach to the cost object and how to attach them. A valuation method determines the dollar amount of the costs to attach. Such a method is similar to the cost flow choice of FIFO or LIFO for merchandise inventory.

Inventory Valuation Methods

The three valuation methods that can be used are actual cost, normal cost, and standard cost. In an **actual cost system,** the actual costs of direct material, direct labor, and overhead are used to compute product cost. Although tracing actual direct material and direct labor costs to products can be fairly easy, tracing overhead costs to products is generally quite tedious; additionally, the information needed is often time delayed. For example, assume a product is manufactured on January 3rd; the cost of electricity used to manufacture that product is uncertain. While the January electric bill can be divided among all units produced, the electric bill may not arrive until January 31—possibly long after the product has been sold.

In a **normal cost system,** the actual costs of direct material and direct labor, as well as an *estimated* cost for overhead, are used to compute product cost. Normal cost systems overcome the problems with attempting to attach actual overhead cost to products. In a **standard cost system,** estimated "norms" for materials, labor, and overhead are used to compute product costs.[2]

Predetermined Overhead Rate

The estimated overhead cost used in normal and standard cost systems to assign overhead to products or services is called a **predetermined overhead rate.** This rate is an expected cost per unit of activity. For example, a company might assign $5 of overhead for every one hour of direct labor associated with a product.

To calculate a predetermined overhead rate, the company divides an estimate of future overhead costs at a specified activity level by that activity level. Predetermined overhead rates are always computed in advance of the period of use and are often computed separately for variable and fixed costs.

Estimating future overhead costs requires that a measure of activity be selected. Assume that the majority of overhead costs are created by the hours of factory machine time. Machine hours would then be viewed as the "driver" or responsible cause for overhead costs. A **flexible budget** can be prepared that reflects the expected overhead costs for the upcoming period (year) based on various levels of activity.

Near the end of 2003, PicNics (the company discussed earlier in the chapter) decides to estimate predetermined production overhead rates for 2004. Using machine hours as the activity measure and assumed information on electricity costs, a flexible budget for overhead costs is developed (Exhibit 11-2). The budget depicts all components of overhead in the left-most column and the associated cost in the next column. In the remaining three columns, estimated overhead is calculated for three levels of activity: 20,000 machine hours, 30,000 machine hours, and 40,000 machine hours. Note that the variable cost remains constant per machine hour regardless of the level of activity, but the fixed cost per machine hour declines as the level of activity increases.

If PicNics expects to work 40,000 machine hours in 2004, its predetermined variable overhead rate will be $1.82 per machine hour and its predetermined fixed overhead rate will be $1.625 per machine hour. For each hour of machine time worked in 2004, PicNics will apply (add) $1.82 for variable overhead costs and $1.625 for fixed overhead costs to the actual costs of direct material and direct labor in a normal cost system or to expected norms for direct material and direct labor in a standard cost system. Assume that, by the end of 2004, 43,000 total machine hours were actually used. The total overhead applied to products, based on the predetermined rate, will be $148,135: variable overhead of $78,260

---

[2] Standard cost systems are discussed more in Chapter 13.

EXHIBIT 11-2

PicNics' Flexible Budget for Production Overhead Costs

	Variable cost per MH	Number of Machine Hours (MH) 20,000	30,000	40,000
Variable costs:				
Indirect labor	$1.20	$24,000	$36,000	$48,000
Indirect material	.60	12,000	18,000	24,000
Variable portion of electricity	.02	400	600	800
Total variable cost		$36,400	$54,600	$72,800
Variable cost per MH	$1.82	$1.82	$1.82	$1.82
	Total fixed cost per year			
Fixed costs:				
Rent	$ 12,000	$12,000	$12,000	$12,000
Depreciation	8,000	8,000	8,000	8,000
Manager salaries	36,000	36,000	36,000	36,000
Insurance	600	600	600	600
Taxes	2,400	2,300	2,300	2,300
Fixed portion of electricity	6,000	6,000	6,000	6,000
Total fixed cost	$65,000	$65,000	$65,000	$65,000
Fixed cost per MH		$3.25	$2.17	$1.625

($1.82 × 43,000) and fixed overhead of $69,875 ($1.625 × 43,000). The applied overhead is added to direct material and direct labor in Work in Process Inventory.

Total predetermined variable and fixed overhead costs for the year can be compared, respectively, to actual variable and fixed overhead costs to determine how accurate the expected flexible budget amounts were. If the overhead added to production costs using the predetermined rates is less than the actual overhead costs incurred for a period, the difference is called **underapplied overhead.** If using the predetermined rate leads to an addition of more costs than were actually incurred, the difference is called **overapplied overhead.**

FLOW OF PRODUCT COSTS

The production process of a job order costing manufacturer is used to illustrate the flow of product costs through the accounting system. The company is assumed to use a perpetual inventory system (as discussed in Chapter 5) and a normal costing system (actual direct material and direct labor costs, as well as a predetermined overhead rate).

In a manufacturing company, the cost of a completed unit of product (finished good) must contain the costs of direct material, direct labor, and overhead. To develop this cost, a manufacturer must track these costs through the production process using three inventory accounts: Raw Material Inventory, Work in Process Inventory, and Finished Goods Inventory. The Raw Material Inventory account may be used for both direct and indirect materials. When direct materials are issued to production, their cost is transferred from Raw Material Inventory to Work in Process Inventory; the cost of indirect materials are transferred to an overhead account.

The PicNics, Inc. example is continued to illustrate the flow of manufacturing costs. The January 1, 2004, inventory account balances for PicNics were as follows: Raw

Material Inventory, $15,000; Work in Process Inventory, $36,200; and Finished Goods Inventory, $55,700.

PicNics uses separate variable and fixed overhead accounts. Each overhead account shows actual overhead costs on the debit side and **applied overhead** (the amount added to Work in Process Inventory using the predetermined rates) on the credit side. Overhead accounts are closed at the end of an accounting period. The predetermined variable and fixed overhead rates, respectively, were shown in Exhibit 11-2 as $1.82 and $1.625 per machine hour at a 40,000 expected level of activity. The following transactions represent PicNics' activity for the year 2004. Effects on the three inventory accounts, variable and fixed overhead, and Cost of Goods Sold are shown in parentheses.

(1) During 2004, PicNics, Inc. bought $530,000 of raw material on account (an increase to Raw Material).

(2) Direct material costing $500,000 and indirect material costing $25,000 were transferred to the production area (a decrease to Raw Material and increases to Work in Process and Variable Overhead).

(3) Direct and indirect labor wages for the year totaled $625,000 and $93,000, respectively. Of the indirect wages, $54,000 was a variable cost and the remainder was for fixed costs such as supervisory and management salaries (increases to Work in Process, Variable Overhead, and Fixed Overhead).

(4) Electricity cost of $7,000 was paid; of this cost, $900 of this amount was variable and $6,100 was fixed (increases to Variable Overhead and Fixed Overhead).

(5) PicNics also paid $12,700 for factory rent, $2,550 for property taxes on the factory, depreciated the factory assets $8,100, and recorded the expiration of $600 of prepaid insurance on the factory assets (increases to Fixed Overhead).

(6) During 2004, 43,000 machine hours were used; this activity level is used to assign overhead cost (based on the predetermined rates) to Work in Process Inventory (decreases to Variable Overhead and Fixed Overhead and an increase to Work in Process).

(7) During 2004, $1,290,000 of goods were completed and transferred to Finished Goods Inventory (a decrease to Work in Process and an increase to Finished Goods).

(8) Sales on account in the amount of $1,850,000 were recorded during the year; the goods that were sold had a total cost of $1,267,000 (a decrease to Finished Goods and an increase to Cost of Goods Sold).

These transactions are summarized in Exhibit 11-3. Selected T-accounts are shown in Exhibit 11-4. The flow of costs is summarized in Visual Recap 11.2.

Cost of Goods Manufactured and Sold

The perpetual inventory system used in Exhibits 11-3 and 11-4 provides detailed information about production costs incurred, costs transferred from work in process, and cost of goods sold (CGS). However, this detail is not readily available in a company using a periodic inventory system. A schedule of **cost of goods manufactured** (CGM) can be prepared to help determine cost of goods sold in a periodic inventory system or to confirm the CGS calculated in a perpetual inventory system. The CGM represents the total production cost of the goods that were completed and transferred to Finished Goods Inventory during the period.

EXHIBIT 11-3

PicNics, Inc. 2004 Production Journal Entries

	Description	Debit	Credit
(1)	Raw Material Inventory	530,000	
	Accounts Payable		530,000
	To record cost of raw materials purchased on account		
(2)	Work in Process Inventory	500,000	
	Variable Overhead	25,000	
	Raw Material Inventory		525,000
	To record direct and indirect materials transferred to production		
(3)	Work in Process Inventory	625,000	
	Variable Overhead	54,000	
	Fixed Overhead	39,000	
	Salaries and Wages Payable		718,000
	To accrue wages and salaries for direct and indirect labor		
(4)	Variable Overhead	900	
	Fixed Overhead	6,100	
	Cash		7,000
	To record payment of electricity cost		
(5)	Fixed Overhead	23,950	
	Cash		15,250
	Accumulated Depreciation		8,100
	Prepaid Insurance		600
	To record payment for factory rent, payment of factory property taxes, accrue depreciation, and expiration of prepaid insurance for the period		
(6)	Work in Process Inventory	148,135	
	Variable Overhead		78,260
	Fixed Overhead		69,875
	To apply predetermined overhead to Work in Process; ($1.82 × 43,000 MHs) and ($1.625 × 43,000 MHs)		
(7)	Finished Goods Inventory	1,290,000	
	Work in Process Inventory		1,290,000
	To record the transfer of work completed during the period		
(8a)	Accounts Receivable	1,850,000	
	Sales		1,850,000
	To record the selling price of goods sold on account during the period		
(8b)	Cost of Goods Sold	1,267,000	
	Finished Goods Inventory		1,267,000
	To record cost of goods sold for the period		

EXHIBIT 11-4

PicNics, Inc. (selected) T-accounts for 2004

Raw Material Inventory

Debit		Credit	
Beg. bal.	15,000	(2)	525,000
(1)	530,000		
End bal.	20,000		

Variable Overhead

Debit		Credit	
(2)	25,000	(6)	78,260
(3)	54,000		
(4)	900		
Underapp.	1,640		

Work in Process Inventory

Debit		Credit	
Beg. bal.	36,200	(7)	1,290,000
(2) DM	500,000		
(3) DL	625,000		
(6) OH	148,135		
End bal.	19,335		

Fixed Overhead

Debit		Credit	
(3)	39,000	(6)	69,875
(4)	6,100		
(5)	23,950		
		Overapp.	825

Finished Goods Inventory

Debit		Credit	
Beg. bal.	55,700	(9)	1,267,000
(7)	1,290,000		
End bal.	78,700		

Cost of Goods Sold

Debit		Credit	
(9)	1,267,000		

VISUAL RECAP 11.2

Flow of Product Costs

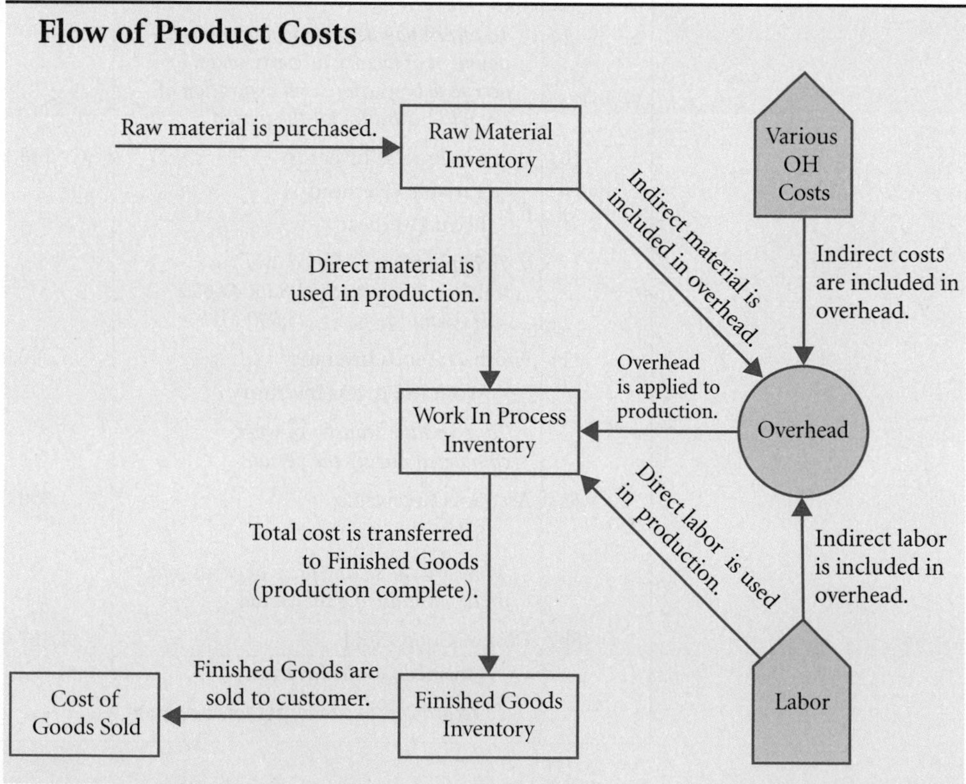

EXHIBIT 11-5

Cost of Goods Manufactured and Cost of Goods Sold Schedules

PicNics Inc.
Schedule of Cost of Goods Manufactured
For Year Ended December 31, 2004

Beginning balance of Work in Process, 1/1/04			$ 36,200
Manufacturing costs for the period:			
Raw Material (direct and indirect):			
Beginning balance	$ 15,000		
Purchases of raw materials	530,000		
Raw material available for use	$545,000		
Ending balance	(20,000)		
Total raw material used	$525,000		
Indirect material used	(25,000)		
Direct material used		$500,000	
Direct labor		625,000	
Variable overhead applied		78,260	
Fixed overhead applied		69,875	
Total manufacturing costs			1,273,135
Total costs to account for			$1,309,335
Ending balance of Work in Process, 12/31/04			(19,335)
Cost of goods manufactured			$1,290,000

Schedule of Cost of Goods Sold
For Year Ended December 31, 2004

Beginning balance of Finished Goods, 1/1/04	$ 55,700
Cost of Goods Manufactured	1,290,000
Cost of Goods Available for Sale	$1,345,700
Ending balance of Finished Goods, 12/31/04	(78,700)
Cost of Goods Sold	$1,267,000

The schedule of CGM starts with the beginning balance of Work in Process (WIP) Inventory and adds all product costs (direct material, direct labor, and overhead) incurred for the period. The summation is called "total costs to account for" and represents all costs that were in WIP during the period. Some of these costs will remain in WIP Inventory because the goods to which they relate are not yet complete. The rest of the costs will be transferred, as cost of goods manufactured, to Finished Goods (FG) Inventory along with the completed goods.[3]

The CGM is added to the beginning balance of FG Inventory to find the cost of goods available for sale by the manufacturer during the period. Ending FG Inventory is calculated by multiplying a physical unit count times a unit cost. Subtracting the cost of the ending finished goods inventory from the cost of goods available for sale provides a figure for cost of goods sold. Formal schedules of cost of goods manufactured and cost of goods sold are presented in Exhibit 11-5, using the information from Exhibits 11-3 and 11-4.

Note that CGM was calculated using normal costing: actual direct material cost, actual direct labor cost, and overhead applied using predetermined rates. As shown in Exhibit 11-4, the Variable and Fixed Overhead T-accounts have balances at the end of 2004. Debits in the Overhead accounts represent actual overhead costs incurred during the period; credits represent overhead applied using the predetermined rates. The underapplied and overapplied overhead calculations for PicNics, Inc. are shown in Exhibit 11-6.

[3] This statement assumes that no goods are lost, stolen, or spoiled during the period.

EXHIBIT 11-6
Underapplied and Overapplied Overhead Calculations for PicNics, Inc.

Actual Variable Overhead		
Indirect material	$ 25,000	
Indirect labor	54,000	
Electricity	900	$ 79,900
Applied Variable Overhead		
($1.82 VOH rate × 43,000 actual MHs)		(78,260)
Underapplied VOH (will cause CGS to increase)		$ 1,640
Actual Fixed Overhead		
Electricity	$ 6,100	
Salaries	39,000	
Factory rent	12,700	
Factory property taxes	2,550	
Factory asset depreciation	8,100	
Factory insurance	600	$ 69,050
Applied Fixed Overhead		
($1.625 FOH rate × 43,000 actual MHs)		(69,875)
Overapplied FOH (will cause CGS to decrease)		$ (825)

When the difference between actual and applied overhead is not a significant amount, underapplied or overapplied overhead is closed at the end of the period to Cost of Goods Sold. Underapplied overhead, because fewer dollars of cost were sent to WIP Inventory than actually were incurred, will cause CGS to increase. The opposite is true of overapplied overhead. Thus, the net adjustment to the CGS shown in Exhibit 11-6 would be an increase of $815 ($1,640 – $825).

COSTS IN SERVICE COMPANIES

Service companies do not manufacture a product, but there is still a cost associated with the service they provide. For example, when a lawyer works on your case or represents you in court, a portion of her salary is associated with the service provided to you. Instead of product cost, service companies track performance costs.

Like manufacturers, service companies use direct labor and overhead to perform a service. However, in many service companies (such as firms of professionals like accountants or lawyers), the amount of raw or direct materials used may be almost negligible and, often, may not be easily traced to a designated cost object (the service performed). Thus, most service companies will not have a Raw Material Inventory account. These companies commonly use a Supplies Inventory because the majority of materials used in performing services are indirect, rather than direct, to the job.

Service companies generally use a job order costing system to keep track of work in process (incomplete jobs). For example, job order costing is essential for patient accounts at a hospital. When each patient checks into a hospital, a separate account is created for him or her. At any time during the hospital stay, the total cost associated with the patient can be obtained by adding up the accumulated costs in his or her account. Upon discharge from the hospital, the patient will receive a bill for all costs related to his or her hospital stay.

Service companies are normally very labor intensive. Individuals who work specifically on performing services are called direct labor and their pay is a direct labor cost. For instance, in a restaurant, the cooks, wait-staff, and bartenders would be classified as direct labor; shift managers, hosts/hostesses, and bus-staff would be classified as indirect labor.

Overhead costs are often quite high in service organizations. Any service-related cost that cannot or is not directly traced to performing a service for sale to others is considered overhead. These costs may be variable or fixed, depending on how they react in total to changes in some designated measure of activity.

Because most services cannot be warehoused, the costs of finished jobs are usually transferred directly from WIP Inventory to a Cost of Services Rendered (CSR) account on the income statement to be matched against job revenues. Thus, the need for a Finished Goods Inventory account is eliminated.

SUMMARY

Accounting has two primary variations: financial and managerial. Managerial accounting is designed to provide information to internal organizational personnel for use in planning and controlling operations and making decisions. Both financial and managerial accounting use the same accounting system and set of accounts, but may process information differently. Managerial accounting information tends to be more flexible and future-oriented, as well as less aggregated, than financial accounting.

The term *cost* is generally preceded by an adjective that helps define that term. Product cost, period cost, direct cost, indirect cost, controllable cost, and noncontrollable cost are just some of the types of costs. Costs that are defined by their reaction in total to changes in activity are called variable, fixed, and mixed costs. Within the relevant range of activity for an organization, total variable costs change in direct proportion to activity changes, while total fixed costs remain constant. A mixed cost has both a variable and a fixed component.

A manufacturer will typically use either a job order or a process costing system to accumulate product costs (direct material, direct labor, and production overhead). Service companies typically use a job order system. In a job order system, costs are totaled by cost component per job and assigned to units produced at the end of the job. In a process costing system, products are undistinguishable and costs are accumulated and assigned to goods upon leaving each department. At the end of the period in a manufacturing company, a cost of goods manufactured schedule will be prepared to support the company's cost of goods sold computation.

Companies may assign values to production units (or services) using an actual, normal, or standard costing system. Only actual costs are used in an actual costing system. In a normal costing system, actual costs are accumulated for direct material and direct labor, but a predetermined overhead rate is used to assign overhead to products (or services). A standard costing system uses expected norms for all types of costs.

KEY TERMS

actual cost system
applied overhead
controllable cost
conversion cost
cost object
direct cost
direct labor
direct material
equivalent units of production
fixed cost
flexible budget
indirect cost
indirect labor
indirect material
job
job order costing system
managerial accounting
noncontrollable cost
normal cost system
overapplied overhead
overhead
period cost
predetermined overhead rate
process costing system
relevant range
replacement cost
standard cost system
underapplied overhead
variable cost

QUESTIONS

1. Define each item in the following sets and discuss the primary differences between the items in each set. *(LO 11.1, 11.2, & 11.3)*
   (a) financial and managerial accounting
   (b) product and period costs
   (c) direct and indirect costs
   (d) variable, fixed, and mixed costs
   (e) job order and process costing
   (f) actual, normal, and standard costing
2. Whether a company uses job order costing or process costing is a decision made by management. Describe the rationale behind using each method and provide examples of three types of companies that would use each. *(LO 11.3)*
3. Why does a company use equivalent units of production? Explain the calculation for equivalent units of production. *(LO 11.3)*
4. What is a predetermined overhead rate? How is it calculated? Why is it used? *(LO 11.4)*
5. What is meant by (a) underapplied and (b) overapplied overhead? Why does underapplied or overapplied overhead exist at year-end? How are underapplied and overapplied overhead treated in the financial statements at year-end? *(LO 11.4)*

6. Could a managerial accountant have a motivation to misrepresent data such as direct or indirect material, labor, or other overhead costs? Explain your answer with an example. Compare the motivation to misrepresent data between managerial and financial accounting. *(LO 11.5 & 11.6, ethics)*
7. Why might the buttons used to make a shirt not be classified as a direct material? Give an instance in which buttons would be classified as a direct material. *(LO 11.5)*
8. For each of the companies listed below, select one product manufactured or service provided, and identify a direct material cost, a source of direct labor, a variable overhead cost, and a fixed overhead cost. *(LO 11.5)*
   (a) General Motors
   (b) Gateway Computers
   (c) H&R Block
   (d) Applebee's Restaurant
9. What is meant by the term "cost of goods manufactured?" How is CGM calculated? Is there any equivalent cost in a service company? If so, what is it called and how would its calculation differ from CGM? If not, discuss why there is no equivalent cost. *(LO 11.7 & 11.8)*

EXERCISES

10. **True or False** *(All LOs)*

    Following are a series of statements regarding topics discussed in this chapter.

    Required:

    Indicate whether each statement is true (T) or false (F).

    (1) Within an organization, a cost is defined as controllable or noncontrollable.
    (2) A cost is either variable or fixed.
    (3) A cost can be a product cost, direct cost, and controllable cost.

(4) Raw materials can be direct or indirect.

(5) Job order costing is typically used in companies that manufacture products to a customer's specifications.

(6) In standard costing, overhead is applied to Work in Process Inventory at a standard rate, but actual direct costs are accumulated in Work in Process Inventory.

(7) When overhead is overapplied at year-end, the "driver" (or basis for application) chosen is inappropriate.

(8) As the number of units manufactured increases, the fixed cost per unit decreases.

(9) Variable and fixed costs are defined by a relevant range and may change when the business operates outside that range.

(10) Service organizations typically have a higher portion of overhead than manufacturing companies.

11. Roles of Accountants *(LO 11.1)*

Following are several duties performed by accountants.

(a) Income statement preparation

(b) Cost of goods manufactured preparation

(c) Reporting historical data

(d) Budgeting future production costs

(e) Valuation of investments

(f) Valuation of work in process inventory

(g) Production of monthly, quarterly, and annual financial data for external users

(h) Production of intermittent reports for internal users

Required:

For each duty, indicate whether it would be performed by a financial or managerial accountant.

12. Types of Costs *(LO 11.2)*

World Class Trophies (WCT) manufactures and sells custom wooden trophies. The company is headed by a CEO, and each of the two divisions, Production and Sales, is headed by a manager. The managers are responsible for all costs in their division. Below are selected costs from WCT.

(a) Wood

(b) Brass ornamentation

(c) Engraving materials

(d) Engraving machine

(e) Salary of sales staff

(f) Rent and insurance on building

(g) Depreciation of equipment

(h) Salary of trophy manufacturers

(i) Salary of machine operators

(j) Maintenance on engraving machines

(k) Electricity

(l) Adhesive for trophy production

Required:

(1) For each cost listed above, identify whether it is a product or period cost. If a definite distinction cannot be made, indicate why and what additional information would be needed before classification can be made.

(2) For each cost listed above, identify whether it is a direct or indirect cost. If a definite distinction cannot be made, indicate why and what additional information would be needed before classification can be made.

(3) For each cost listed above, identify whether it is a variable, fixed, or mixed cost. If a definite distinction cannot be made, indicate why and what additional information would be needed before classification can be made.

(4) For each cost listed above, identify whether it is a controllable or noncontrollable cost from the viewpoint of the Production Manager.

13. **Variable, Fixed, and Mixed Costs** *(LO 11.2)*

Wayside Corp. manufactures desk clocks. The company incurred the following costs to produce 5,000 clocks in May 2003.

Clocks	$ 5,000
Resin bases	8,750
Direct labor	3,250
Machinery depreciation (calculated on a straight-line basis)	1,200
Supervisory salaries	3,400
Utilities	1,600
Total	$23,200

Required:

(1) Considering behavior in relationship to activity changes, how would each of these costs be classified?

(2) What did each clock cost?

(3) If Wayside increases production in June 2003 to 6,000 units, what will be the total cost of each cost component? If you cannot determine the total cost of a cost component, discuss the reason.

14. **Inventory Costing** *(LO 11.3)*

Below are several businesses that produce a product or provide a service.

(a) Auto manufacturer
(b) Custom furniture manufacturer
(c) Interior decorator
(d) Restaurant
(e) Manufacturer of household cleaning products
(f) Producer of a weekly television drama

Required:

(1) For each of the business listed above, indicate whether it probably use job order costing or process costing.

(2) Explain how a company that uses process costing assigns a cost to the inventory that is in process.

(3) In each of the above businesses, do you believe that cost is the primary determinant of the selling price for the product or service? Explain your answer for each business.

15. **Predetermined Overhead** *(LO 11.4)*

L-Jay Co. estimated that, in the year 2003, $455,000 of overhead costs would be incurred at 175,000 machine hours. During 2003, the company incurs 180,000 machine hours and has actual overhead costs of $471,300.

Required:

(1) What is L-Jay's predetermined overhead rate per machine hour for 2003?

(2) How much overhead was applied to production in 2003?

(3) Is overhead underapplied or overapplied at the end of 2003? By what amount?

(4) What is the disposition of the underapplied or overapplied overhead determined in part (3)? How, if at all, will this disposition affect the income statement?

16. **Direct Labor** *(LO 11.5)*

Ultra Manufacturing Company operates two shifts of workers. Day workers are paid $10 per hour; evening workers are paid a shift premium of 20 percent. Overtime premiums are 50 percent above day or evening wages. In August 2003, the following factory payroll information is available:

Total hours worked during the month (60% by day; 40% by evening)	15,000
Overtime hours worked during the month (only by day workers)	1,000

Required:

(1) What were the total wages paid to employees during the month?

(2) Of the amount in part (1), how much would be considered direct labor cost?

(3) Of the indirect labor cost, how much is for shift premiums and how much is for overtime premiums?

17. **Cost Components and Flows** *(LO 11.5 & 11.6)*

The following costs are associated with a furniture manufacturer.

(a) Purchased unfinished wood, nails, and stain.
(b) Purchased machine oil.
(c) Used stain to varnish a desk.
(d) Used machinery to cut wood to specifications for a desk.
(e) Oiled the woodworking machinery.
(f) Used cut wood and nails to assemble a desk.
(g) Completed a desk, which is ready to be sold.
(h) Sold a desk.
(i) Paid a woodworker to build a desk.
(j) Paid a machine operator who oils and maintains the machinery.
(k) Paid insurance on the factory and equipment.
(l) Used direct labor hours to determine the overhead to be applied.

Required:

(1) Identify the costs of the above activities as one of the following:

(a) Direct material
(b) Direct labor
(c) Indirect material
(d) Indirect labor

(2) In a normal costing system, costs are accumulated in one of four categories: raw material, work in process, finished goods, or overhead (fixed or variable). During production, costs flow from one category to another. For each activity cost listed above, indicate which category it would flow from and to. [Hint: When costs originate, they only flow into a category.] The costs are presented in random order.

18. Cost of Goods Manufactured *(LO 11.7)*

The cost of goods manufactured schedule for BritSpan Industries is presented below with numbers omitted.

BritSpan Industries
Cost of Goods Manufactured Schedule
For the Month Ended June 30, 2003

Beginning Inventory—Work in Process			$?
Manufacturing costs for the period:			
Raw Material (direct and indirect)			
Beginning Balance	$120,000		
Purchases	?		
Raw Materials Available	$?		
Ending Balance	140,000		
Total Raw Materials Used	$330,000		
Indirect Materials	40,000		
Direct Material Used		$?	
Direct Labor Used		310,000	
Variable Overhead Applied		95,000	
Fixed Overhead Applied		145,000	
Total Manufacturing Costs			840,000
Total Costs to Account for			$1,240,000
Ending Balance—Work In Process			?
Cost of Goods Manufactured			$ 735,000

Additional information:

Beginning balance of Cost of Goods Sold	$ 0
Beginning balance of Finished Goods	485,750
Beginning units in Finished Goods	67,000
Sales during June	98,000 units

Required:

(1) Calculate the missing numbers.

(2) If 100,000 units were produced during June, what is the cost of manufacturing per item?

(3) What is the Cost of Goods Sold during June? BritSpan uses the FIFO cost flow assumption.

(4) What is the ending balance in Finished Goods Inventory (in dollars and units) on June 30?

19. Cost of Services Rendered *(LO 11.8)*

Waguespack Medical had the following costs for October 2003.

Nurses' salaries	$ 8,300
Doctors' salaries	36,000
Electricity (75% related to patient care)	800
Building rental (75% related to patient care)	1,900
Depreciation on office equipment	670
Depreciation on medical equipment	2,400
Medical supplies used	4,500
Medical supplies purchased	5,800
Medical supplies on hand, October 1	150
Office salaries (35% related to patient care)	1,300

Required:

Prepare a Schedule of Cost of Services Rendered for October 2003.

PROBLEMS

20. **Determining Total Cost** *(LO 11.2)*

Peterson's Eats pays EH, Inc. $680 for an annual service contract on its kitchen equipment. In addition, Peterson's pays $35 each time a technician is called to work on any of the equipment. No other costs (material or labor) are incurred for the service calls under the service contract.

Required:

(1) Prepare a flexible budget for Peterson's service contract costs if technicians are called 12, 18, and 24 times per year.

(2) Determine the cost per service call for each level of service listed in part (1). Why does the cost per service call change?

(3) The average price of a service call without the contract is $75. At what number of service calls is Peterson's saving money by having the service contract?

(4) Why would Peterson's enter into this service contract if the company only expects to have 15 service calls per year?

21. **Predetermined Overhead Rates** *(LO 11.4)*

Companies often set predetermined overhead rates to assign overhead costs to products and services. In such cases, a set amount is applied to product cost for each actual unit of "predictor" or "driver" activity incurred. Following are some overhead costs that would be incurred in an all-inclusive hotel (includes a restaurant, pool, spa, fitness facility, meeting rooms, ballroom, and business center).

(a) Cleaning supplies
(b) Salary of concierge
(c) Electricity
(d) Wages for table cleaners (bus staff)
(e) Unemployment taxes
(f) City property taxes
(g) Liquor license fee
(h) Laundry services
(i) Insurance policy
(j) Internet provider cost

Required:

(1) For each of the above items, indicate three items that could be considered causal factors of the overhead cost. For instance, one predictor of cleaning supplies could be the number of rooms cleaned.

(2) Each hotel room has a phone. The monthly cost of phone service to the hotel is $2,400 plus long-distance charges; this rate has not changed in three years. Why might the hotel charge customers an "access" fee of $2 per call for every call made to outside the hotel? Why might this fee have increased from the $1 charged three years ago?

22. **Predetermined Overhead Rates** *(LO 11.4)*

Gregor Co. has the following estimated 2002 information for its two departments: Production and Assembly.

	Production	Assembly
Estimated overhead costs	$201,000	$22,200
Estimated direct labor hours	1,500	10,000
Estimated machine hours	15,000	3,000

The production department is highly automated and the assembly department is highly labor intensive.

Product N, made by the company, requires the following quantities of machine and direct labor hours in each department.

	Production	Assembly
Direct labor hours	0.15	1.20
Machine hours	8.00	0.30

Required:

(1) Assume that Gregor Co. chooses to use direct labor hours to apply all overhead costs to products. What is the predetermined overhead rate for 2002? How much overhead would be assigned to each unit of Product N in 2002? (Round all calculations to the nearest penny.)

(2) Assume that Gregor Co. chooses to use machine hours to apply all overhead costs to products. What is the predetermined overhead rate for 2002? How much overhead would be assigned to each unit of Product N in 2002? (Round all calculations to the nearest penny.)

(3) If Gregor Co. decides to use the most appropriate base in each department to apply overhead to products, what would be the predetermined overhead rate in each department? How much overhead would be assigned to each unit of Product N in 2002? (Round all calculations to the nearest penny.)

(4) Why do the overhead amounts applied to Product N differ among parts (1), (2), and (3)?

23. **Flow of Product Costs** *(LO 11.6)*

Selected transactions regarding North Point's manufacturing process are listed below.

(a) Purchased raw material on account, $43,000.

(b) Used raw material in production, $22,000.

(c) Incurred labor costs: 1,700 direct labor hours at $20,000, and 400 indirect labor hours at $6,000.

(d) Recorded depreciation on factory equipment, $2,200.

(e) Recorded the expiration of one month of prepaid insurance, $1,000.

(f) Received and paid an electricity bill, $850.

(g) Repaired factory equipment, $250.

(h) Applied overhead to goods in process at a rate of $4 per direct labor hour.

(i) Transferred completed goods to finished goods, $53,600.

(j) Sold goods costing $50,000 to credit customers for $89,000.

Required:

Prepare journal entries to record the North Point's transactions. Use a single account for both variable and fixed overhead.

24. **Cost of Goods Manufactured and Cost of Goods Sold** *(LO 11.7, Excel)*

Blanchard Products had the following beginning and ending inventory balances for April 2004.

	April 1, 2004	April 30, 2004
Raw Material Inventory	$ 4,500	$ 5,200
Work in Process Inventory	21,300	12,700
Finished Goods Inventory	10,800	4,900

All raw materials are considered direct to the manufacturing process. During April, the company purchased $65,000 of raw materials. Direct labor cost for the month was $54,000; workers are paid $6 per hour. Overhead is applied at the rate of $5.50 for each direct labor hour.

Required:

(1) Prepare the Schedule of Cost of Goods Manufactured.

(2) Calculate Cost of Goods Sold for April 2004.

25. **Cost of Services Rendered** *(LO 11.3, 11.5, & 11.8)*

Peter's Pet Place is a veterinary clinic. At the beginning of July, the clinic had $360 of veterinary supplies on hand. The following information is available for July 2002.

Salaries for veterinary staff	$16,000
Salaries for veterinary assistants	6,000
Wages for office workers	3,000
Veterinary supplies purchased in July	4,800
Veterinary supplies on hand on July 31	575
Depreciation on hospital and lab equipment	4,300
Depreciation on office equipment	1,500
Building rent (60% related to treatment)	1,800
Utilities (80% related to treatment)	900

Required:

(1) What is the overhead amount related to the cost of services rendered?

(2) Compute Cost of Services Rendered.

(3) Peter's Pet Palace collected $44,000 in treatment fees. What was Peter's gross profit and net income? [Hint: Gross profit is revenues minus cost of services provided.]

CASES

26. **Cost Classifications** *(LO 11.2)*

Jan Jeffers is a house painter. She incurred the following costs during August 2002 when she painted four houses. In the first week of August, Jan placed a $60 classified ad for her business in the newspaper. She also bought two pairs of coveralls for $35 each to wear while working. Jan spent $25 for a day-planner book in which she records hours spent at each job, mileage to and from jobs (at a rate of $0.32 per mile), information on referral work, and bids submitted for other jobs. Toll road charges for driving to various job locations were $0.75 for each section of toll road traveled. Cell phone charges for the month were $60; Jan has a cell phone plan that allows up to 2,000 minutes of nation-wide calling, a time frame that she has never exceeded. Jan does use the cell phone for both business and personal calls. In August, approximately 40% of her calls were business-related. Materials costs for the month were $500 for paint, $40 for mineral spirits, and $155 for brushes. Jan hired a helper who worked 15 hours at $18 per hour on one of Jan's jobs. The insurance on Jan's work truck is $50 per month.

Required:

Using the following headings, indicate how each of the August costs incurred by Jan would be classified. Assume that the cost object is a house-painting job.

Type of Cost Variable Fixed Direct Indirect Period Product

27. **Controllable and Noncontrollable Costs** *(LO 11.2, writing, ethics)*

You are Manager of Special Events at a large hotel in Dallas. The meeting rooms and ballroom take up one floor of the 12-story building. The other managers at the hotel have responsibilities for Accommodations, Restaurant, and Guest Facilities (pool, fitness club, business center, tennis courts, parking garages, etc.). Each manager, except Guest Facilities, is evaluated on how profitable his or her area of operation was during the period. The Guest Facilities manager is evaluated on the basis of cost control because no fees are charged for many of the services under her control.

Required:

(1) How will you determine what costs incurred at the hotel are controllable or noncontrollable? Be sure to discuss the selection of a cost object.

(2) One month you notice that the Restaurant Manager had decided to charge you "fees" for the following items: laundering linens used in special events; overtime premiums for the cooking and wait-staff for special events; and hourly wages of room service personnel who helped out during special events (when not delivering room service items). The Accommodations Manager had decided to charge you "fees" for one-twelfth of the property taxes, electricity, and building depreciation. The Guest Facilities manager had decided to charge you a "fee" per parking space for every person expected at all special events held during the month. Write a memo to the company president discussing these fees and how they could affect your performance evaluation.

28. **Cost Flow** *(LO 11.6, writing)*

Micro Laser Systems (MLS) produces small electronics parts for other companies. MLS uses process costing because the items manufactured by the company are produced to customer specifications. Currently, MLS is having difficulty identifying the difference between direct and indirect material and labor. As a result, MLS is adding almost all labor and a large portion of material cost to overhead. The rationale of MLS's production management is that the overhead eventually gets applied to the job anyway.

Required:

Write a memo to MLS's management to explain problems that might be encountered by misclassifying things as overhead as opposed to direct material or labor.

29. **Using Cost Information** *(LO 11.7)*

A massive fire began in the production building of Pedro Co. in the early morning of September 18, 2003. The fire destroyed all the company's work in process. To determine the amount of the loss, Pedro Co. has gathered the following information:

(a) Sales for the period September 1 through September 17 were $110,000. The gross margin on product sales has typically been 30%.

(b) At the beginning of September, Work in Process Inventory contained $27,000 of goods.

(c) The finished goods warehouse was not affected by the fire. The Finished Goods Inventory account balance was $3,600 at the beginning of the month and $2,900 after an inventory count on the day of the fire.

(d) Records indicated that the company used $64,000 of direct material during the first 17 days of September.

(e) Wages paid to direct labor employees for the first 17 days of September totaled $8,750; direct labor employees are paid $7 per hour.

(f) The predetermined overhead rate was set using an expected total overhead of $176,400 and expected annual direct labor hours of 18,000.

Required:

(1) Determine the value of the lost work in process inventory for Pedro Co.

(2) What other information might Pedro Co. need to submit to the insurance company to substantiate its loss claim?

30. **Comparing Costs** *(LO 11.2, Internet, group)*

Identifying the similarities and differences among companies is crucial to understanding the nature of operations. Form groups of at least four students. Each group should select a single industry. Each group member should locate a different annual report within that industry. (The industry and individual company may be assigned by your instructor.)

Required—individual group members:

(1) For your business, scan the annual report to gain an understanding of its primary line of business, which should relate to the industry in which the company operates.

(2) List five types (or as many as you can) of the following costs your company probably incurs.

(a) Direct material

(b) Indirect material

(c) Direct labor

(d) Indirect labor

(e) Overhead (other than indirect material and labor)

(3) For each cost you listed, indicate whether it is a product or period cost.

(4) For each cost you listed, indicate whether it is fixed, variable, or mixed.

Required—groups:

(5) Compare the costs you listed with the other members of your group.

(6) The companies you are comparing operate in the same industry. How similar were the costs you listed?

(7) Compile a list of costs in each category that represents the industry you are investigating.

Required—class:

(8) Compare the costs each group listed across industries.

(9) The industries you are comparing are varied. Does the industry in which a company operates affect the lists of costs in each category? Which categories of costs are most different and which are most similar across industry?

SUPPLEMENTAL PROBLEMS

31. **Predetermined Overhead Rates** *(LO 11.4, writing)* [Compare to Problem 21.]

LaHarpe, Inc. manufactures two products, X and Y. For 2003, LaHarpe estimates overhead costs will be $2,400,000, direct labor will be 96,000 hours, and there will be 480,000 machine hours.

At the end of October 2003, each product used the following machine and direct labor hours.

	Product X	Product Y
Direct labor hours per unit	1.0	1.6
Machine hours per unit	11.5	3.0
Number of units produced	2500	3500

Required:

(1) Assume that LaHarpe chooses to use direct labor hours to apply all overhead costs to products. What is the predetermined overhead rate? How much overhead would be assigned to each unit of Product X and Product Y?

(2) Using your calculations from part (1), calculate the underapplied or overapplied overhead based on October's portion of the annual estimate.

(3) Assume that LaHarpe chooses to use machine hours to apply all overhead costs to products. What is the predetermined overhead rate? How much overhead would be assigned to each unit of Product X and Product Y?

(4) Using your calculation from part (3), calculate the underapplied or overapplied overhead based on October's portion of the annual estimate.

(5) The manager of Product X argues that direct labor hours should be used to apply overhead, while the manager of Product Y argues that machine hours should be used. Why are they arguing?

(6) Write a memo to LaHarpe's management explaining some of the items that should be considered when deciding how to apply overhead.

32. **Flow of Product Costs** *(LO 11.6 & 11.7)* [Compare to Problem 23.]

Marcus, Inc. has the following balances in its inventory accounts at May 1.

Raw Material (all direct to production)	$10,000
Work in Process	16,000
Finished Goods	2,500

The following transactions occurred in the company for May.

(a) Purchased raw material on account, $31,000.

(b) Issued raw material to production, $38,000.

(c) Accrued direct labor wages for 2,200 hours, $19,000.

(d) Recorded depreciation on factory equipment, $1,900.

(e) Paid indirect labor wages, $3,600.

(f) Recorded the expiration of prepaid insurance on the factory building, $800.

(g) Received, but did not pay, the utility bill, $700.

(h) Paid maintenance costs of the factory and factory equipment, $250.

(i) Applied overhead to goods in process. Marcus, Inc. applies overhead to production at a rate of $3.50 per direct labor hour.

(j) Transferred completed goods to finished goods, $53,600.

(k) Sold goods costing $50,000 to credit customers for $89,000.

Required:

(1) Prepare journal entries to record the May transactions for Marcus, Inc. Use a single account for both variable and fixed overhead.

(2) Compute the balances in the three inventory accounts at May 31.

(3) Prepare a Schedule of Cost of Goods Manufactured.

(4) Is overhead underapplied or overapplied for May, and by how much? If this overhead were to be closed, would closing cause Cost of Goods Sold to increase or decrease? Explain.

(5) Prepare a Statement of Cost of Goods Sold. Because this is not the end of the year, do not include the underapplied or overapplied overhead in the statement.

CHAPTER 12

Cost-Volume-Profit Analysis

LEARNING OBJECTIVES

1. Define break-even point (BEP) and cost-volume-profit (CVP) analysis, and recognize their limiting underlying assumptions.
2. Use CVP analysis in both single-product and multiproduct companies.
3. Develop a break-even chart and profit-volume graph.
4. Use the margin of safety and operating leverage concepts.

Rosedown Plantation

Built in 1835, Rosedown Plantation, an antebellum home, is located in St. Francisville, Louisiana, not far from Baton Rouge. The site is located on 317 acres of land and has 15 buildings and 20 acres of formal gardens. Rosedown was purchased by the State of Louisiana in 2000 for $5.7 million; at which time officials projected a total of 70,000 visitors per year would generate $560,000 of revenues and $425,300 of expenses. As of mid-2001, the average monthly attendance was about 45% of what was expected. However, even at that rate, the Department of Culture, Recreation and Tourism was not terribly concerned. New estimates indicated that donations of time and money, as well as the use of prison inmates to perform some of the maintenance and repair costs, allowed costs to be reduced to about $250,000 per year. Even with the incurrence of new fixed advertising costs, the property is expected to break even or possibly make a little money at the rate of about 2,600 visitors per month.

SOURCE: Ed Anderson, "Rosedown Attendance Low, But So Are Operating Costs," (New Orleans) *Times–Picayune,* 23 August 2001, sec. A, p. 3.

INTRODUCTION

Many companies and organizations use the break-even point (BEP) concept and cost-volume-profit analysis to understand how income will be affected by changes in selling prices, sales volumes, fixed costs, or variable costs. The **break-even point** is the level of sales at which no profits are generated and no losses are incurred; in other words, total revenues are equal to total costs. Although companies do not want to operate at this sales level, the BEP provides a reference point to managers who can use this information to set sales targets that should generate operating income for the organization. The cost-volume-profit (CVP) model allows managers to integrate desired profitability into the BEP model.

This chapter discussed the BEP and CVP models using income statements, formulas, and graphs. The last part of the chapter addresses two other models, the margin of safety and degree of operating leverage, which are similar to BEP and CVP in the information they provide and their use.

ASSUMPTIONS OF BREAK-EVEN AND CVP ANALYSIS

Break-even and CVP analysis are used in all organizations. **Cost-volume-profit analysis** expands on the break-even point by allowing managers to assess the relationships among, and the profitability impacts of, selling prices, costs, and volumes. CVP analysis is applicable to both single-product and multiproduct organizations.

Before attempting to determine the break-even point or use CVP analysis, the organizational cost structure must first be understood. The following important assumptions form the foundation for BE and CVP analysis.

1. The company is operating within its relevant range of activity (as defined in Chapter 11).
2. All costs are categorized as either variable or fixed.

3. All revenues and variable costs are constant per unit and, thus, will change in total in direct proportion to level of activity or volume.
4. Because revenue and variable cost are constant per unit, the contribution margin per unit is also constant. Per-unit **contribution margin** is the difference between the selling price per unit and the total variable cost per unit. (Total contribution margin is total revenues minus total variable costs for all units sold.) The contribution margin indicates the amount of revenue available to cover fixed costs and generate profits.
5. Total fixed cost is constant per period and, thus, fixed cost per unit decreases as volume increases.

Because they are so strictly stated, these assumptions severely limit the model's ability to reflect business reality and restrict use of the model to the short-run because assumptions generally will not hold true for the long term. For example, the relevant range is likely to change as businesses expand; and revenues, variable, and fixed costs change with some regularity over time. However, the model is useful in assessing the profitability impacts of changes in the organization's cost structure or sales volume.

BREAK-EVEN POINT

Profit equals the excess of total revenues over total costs. A company is said to "break even" when profit is exactly equal to zero. Therefore, the starting point of CVP analysis is the break-even point, which can be expressed either in units or dollars of revenue.

Income statement information for Alana Company (Exhibit 12-1) is used to demonstrate computations for the break-even point and CVP analysis. The company produces a single product: a high quality glass paperweight. All units produced are sold.

Break-even and CVP analysis are based on the income statement formula: Total Revenues – Total Expenses = Profit. Total revenues are calculated as selling price per unit multiplied by number of units sold. As discussed in Chapter 11, accountants separate expenses into two types: variable and fixed. Total variable expenses reflect the variable cost per unit multiplied by the number of units sold. Total fixed expenses are a constant amount and do not depend on the number of units sold. Thus, the following equation reflects the income statement information:

$$\text{Total Revenues} - \text{Total Costs} = \text{Profit}$$
$$R(X) - [VC(X) + FC] = P$$
$$R(X) - VC(X) - FC = P$$

where
R = revenue (selling price) per unit
X = number of units sold (volume)
$R(X)$ = total revenues

EXHIBIT 12-1
Income Statement Information for Alana Company

Sales (25,000 units @ $50)		$1,250,000
Variable expenses:		
Product (25,000 units @ $9)	$225,000	
Selling (25,000 units @ $6)	150,000	(375,000)
Contribution margin (25,000 units @ $35)		$ 875,000
Fixed expenses:		
Product	$495,000	
Selling and administrative	152,500	(647,500)
Pretax profit		$ 227,500

$$VC = \text{variable cost per unit}$$
$$VC(X) = \text{total variable costs}$$
$$FC = \text{total fixed costs}$$
$$P = \text{pretax profit}$$

At BEP, there is no profit, so the formula can also be expressed as Total Revenues – Total Costs = \$0 by substituting \$0 for P in the equation.

Using the known information from Exhibit 12-1, the equation can be solved for Alana Company's break-even point as follows:

$$\$50X - (\$9X + \$6X) - \$647{,}500 = \$0$$
$$\$50X - \$15X - \$647{,}500 = \$0$$
$$\$35X = \$647{,}500$$
$$X = \$647{,}500 \div \$35$$
$$X = 18{,}500 \text{ units}$$

Alana Company receives \$50 for each paperweight, but must spend \$15 per paperweight (variable cost) to produce and sell it. Each paperweight provides a \$35 (\$50 – \$15) contribution margin toward Alana's profits. Before Alana can generate profits, fixed costs of \$647,500 must first be covered. It takes the contribution of 18,500 units at \$35 each to pay the fixed costs. By selling 18,500 units, Alana earns revenues of \$925,000 (18,500 × \$50) and incurs variable costs of \$277,500 and fixed costs of \$647,500. Revenues minus costs equals zero.

As shown in the formula, the break-even point in units (BEP_u) equals the total fixed expenses divided by the contribution margin per unit or:

$$BEP_u = FC \div CM_u$$

where CM_u = contribution margin per unit (R – VC)

The break-even point in units can be converted into break-even revenues ($BEP_\$$), also called break-even dollars of sales, by multiplying the units by the selling price per unit. Alana Company's $BEP_\$$ is \$925,000 (18,500 units × \$50 per unit).

The contribution margin ratio can also be used to compute the break even point in sales dollars. The formula for the CM ratio is:

$$\text{CM ratio} = (R - VC) \div R$$
$$= CM \div R$$

The **contribution margin ratio** indicates the percentage of revenue that remains after variable costs are covered. This calculation can be made either on a per-unit basis when the amounts represent revenue and contribution margin for one unit, or on a total dollar basis when total revenues and contribution margin are used. For Alana Company, the CM ratio is 70 percent (\$35 ÷ \$50). To use the CM ratio to calculate BEP\$, divide fixed costs by the CM ratio; for Alana Company the calculation would be \$647,500 ÷ 0.70, which is equal to \$925,000.

Subtracting the CM ratio from 100 percent gives the **variable cost** (VC) **ratio** or the variable cost percentage of each revenue dollar. For Alana Company, the VC ratio is 30 percent (100% – 70%).

Managers want their organizations to earn profits rather than merely break-even (or incur losses). Thus, a desired amount of profit can be substituted into the formula to convert break-even analysis into cost-volume-profit analysis.

CVP ANALYSIS

Because the BEP and CVP formulas reflect income statement information, managers can use the formulas to analyze a variety of considerations. One common and important use is to determine the sales volume necessary to achieve a desired amount of organizational profit. Profits may be stated on either a before-tax or after-tax basis. The Alana Company example is continued in the following situations.

Before-Tax Profit

Variable costs are incurred each time a product is made or sold. Thus, selling prices should first cover those variable expenses. After variable costs are covered, the remainder (or contribution margin) goes to cover fixed expenses and then to generate profits. After covering all fixed expenses (that is, reaching the break-even point), each dollar of contribution margin is a dollar of profit.

Assume that Alana Company's managers want to generate a pretax profit of $472,500. As shown in the following calculation, substituting this amount in the CVP formula indicates that 32,000 units must be sold.

$$\begin{aligned} R(X) - VC(X) - FC &= P \\ \$50X - \$15X - \$647{,}500 &= \$472{,}500 \\ \$35X &= \$1{,}120{,}000 \\ X &= 32{,}000 \text{ units} \end{aligned}$$

Alana Company must have $1,600,000 of revenues (32,000 units × $50 selling price per unit) to generate the desired $472,500 of profit. Using an income statement format, this amount can be confirmed.

Sales (32,000 units × $50)	$1,600,000
Variable costs (32,000 × $15)	(480,000)
Contribution margin (32,000 × $35)	$1,120,000
Fixed costs	(647,500)
Pretax profit	$ 472,500

After-Tax Profit

Because income taxes represent an important element in business decision-making, managers must understand that choosing a desired profit amount will cause income tax effects. Thus, earning a desired profit before income taxes will not generate a similar amount of organizational profitability. Most managers are more concerned about the "bottom line" (income after taxes or net income) than the pretax profitability. Determining the sales volume needed to achieve a desired net income requires that managers first determine the pretax income to be earned, given the applicable tax rate.

Pretax income minus income taxes equals net income. It is assumed, for simplicity, that the income tax rate is a flat rate (rather than one that increases at various levels of pretax income). If the tax rate is 35 percent, pretax earnings of $100,000 will cause a tax expense of $35,000 (0.35 × $100,000) and result in a net income of $65,000. Therefore, to convert a net income amount to a pretax amount, divide net income by 1 minus the tax rate. Once the pretax amount has been obtained, it can be inserted into the same formula as was used in the previous example.

Assume that Alana Company's tax rate is 35 percent and managers want to earn $325,000 in after-tax profits. The necessary pretax profit desired is ($325,000 ÷ 0.65) or $500,000. Inserting this amount into the CVP formula gives

$$\begin{aligned} R(X) - VC(X) - FC &= P \\ \$50X - \$15X - \$647{,}500 &= \$500{,}000 \\ \$35X &= \$1{,}147{,}500 \\ X &= 32{,}786 \text{ units (rounded)} \end{aligned}$$

Proof of this result is shown in the income statement shown in Exhibit 12-2.

EXHIBIT 12-2

Proof of Alana Company's Net Income Profitability

Sales (32,786 units @ \$50)		\$1,639,300
Variable expenses:		
Product (32,786 units @ \$9)	\$ 295,074	
Selling (32,786 units @ \$6)	196,716	(491,790)
Contribution margin (32,786 units @ \$35)		\$1,147,510
Fixed expenses:		
Product	\$ 495,000	
Selling and administrative	152,500	(647,500)
Pretax profit		\$ 500,010
Tax expense (35%)		(175,004)
Net income (off due to rounding)		\$ 325,006

Other Considerations

Variables other than profit may also be the focal point of CVP analysis. In some companies, selling prices are set by market competition and each company has a fairly well defined market volume (or market share). In such cases, managers may use CVP to determine an "allowable" variable cost per unit: a variable cost amount that will allow the company to make a desired contribution margin per unit.

For example, assume that the paperweight market is 300,000 units annually. Alana Company holds approximately a nine percent market share (or 27,000 units) and cannot significantly affect the \$50 market selling price. The company's fixed costs are still assumed to be \$647,500 and its tax rate is 35 percent. Alana Company management wants to earn \$234,000 of after-tax net income in the upcoming year. What amount can the company spend on variable cost per unit in order to earn the desired net income?

First, the company's income objective must be restated as pretax profit: \$234,000 ÷ 0.65 = \$360,000. This amount is used in the CVP formula for profit. Note, however, that the unknown is no longer units, but variable cost per unit.

$$\begin{aligned} R(X) - VC(X) - FC &= P \\ \$50(27{,}000) - VC(27{,}000) - \$647{,}500 &= \$360{,}000 \\ \$1{,}350{,}000 - VC(27{,}000) - \$647{,}500 &= \$360{,}000 \\ \$702{,}500 - VC(27{,}000) &= \$360{,}000 \\ VC(27{,}000) &= \$342{,}500 \\ VC &= \$12.69 \text{ (rounded)} \end{aligned}$$

Given these circumstances, Alana Company can spend a maximum of \$12.69 on variable cost per unit if the company wants to achieve its desired after-tax profit. The results are shown in Exhibit 12-3.

Note that the answer was given in terms of total variable cost per unit. If Alana Company cannot reduce its product cost of \$9 per unit and still retain the quality of its paperweights, company management will have to concentrate on reducing the variable selling cost per unit from its current level of \$6 per unit to a maximum of \$3.69. If neither of these situations can occur, company management will need to raise its market share or find ways to reduce its fixed costs if the desired level of profitability is to be obtained.

Variable expenses may be decreased or increased by changing product manufacturing specifications, direct material quality, direct labor inputs, or distribution costs. Fixed costs may be modified through investments in, or sales of, capital facilities or changes in managerial salaries or other contract items (such as rent or lease agreements).

The CVP formulas are summarized in Visual Recap 12.1.

EXHIBIT 12-3

Proof of Alana Company's Net Income Profitability

Sales (27,000 units @ $50)		$1,350,000
Variable expenses:		
Product and selling (27,000 units @ $12.69)		(342,630)
Contribution margin		$1,007,370
Fixed expenses:		
Product	$ 495,000	
Selling and administrative	152,500	(647,500)
Pretax profit		$ 359,870
Tax expense (35%)		(125,955)
Net income (off due to rounding)		$ 233,915

VISUAL RECAP 12.1

Summary of BEP and CVP Relationships

$R(X) - VC(X) - FC = P$

$R - VC = CM$

$CM(X) - FC = P$

$BEP_u = FC \div CM_u$

$BEP_\$ = FC \div CM$ ratio

After-tax profits = Pre-tax profits ÷ (1 – tax rate)

USING INCREMENTAL ANALYSIS

Answers from break-even or cost-volume-profit computations are valid only if the assumptions given at the beginning of the chapter are valid. Any change in selling price or cost relationships will cause a change in the BEP and the sales volume needed to obtain a desired profit. All else being equal, the following mathematical relationships can be stated:

- BEP_u and $BEP_\$$ increase (decrease) if total fixed expenses increase (decrease)
- BEP_u and $BEP_\$$ increase (decrease) if CM per unit or the CM ratio decreases (increases).
- Contribution margin will decrease (increase) if the company has a decrease (increase) in unit selling price.
- Contribution margin will decrease (increase) if the company has an increase (decrease) in unit variable cost.

Changes in any of these revenue or cost factors will also cause changes in total profits or losses at any level of activity.

Focusing on factors that change from one course of action to another is called **incremental analysis.** Examples of some potential organizational changes and the incremental analysis that would be used to determine the BEP or profitability effects follow. For simplicity, all profits are stated on a pretax basis; after-tax analysis would apply the 1 – tax rate factor to profits. The original information (Exhibit 12-1) for Alana Company is used in each example. Each of the following four incremental analyses is considered independently.

Increase in Fixed Cost

Alana Company believes that 3,000 more paperweights can be sold if advertising is increased by $125,000. Before profits can be obtained from these sales, the additional fixed cost must first be covered by the increased total contribution margin. *Should the company incur this additional fixed cost?*

	Increase in CM generated (3,000 paperweights × $35)	$ 105,000
–	Increase in fixed cost	(125,000)
=	Net incremental loss	$ (20,000)

The advertising campaign would increase cash inflows by $105,000 but increase costs by $125,000, generating a reduction in profits of $20,000. The campaign should not be undertaken.

Decrease in Selling Price

Alana Company estimates that lowering the paperweight's selling price to $45 will generate additional sales of 10,000 units annually. Sales volume will increase from 25,000 units to 35,000 units, but the unit contribution margin will fall from $35 to $30. *Should the company reduce the selling price?*

	Total CM generated (35,000 paperweights × $30)	$1,050,000
–	Total fixed costs (unchanged)	(647,500)
=	New pretax profit	$ 402,500
–	Current pretax profit (from Exhibit 12-1)	(227,500)
=	Net incremental benefit	$ 175,000

Alana Company will increase its pretax profit and, thus, should reduce its selling price.

Increase in Sales Volume and Costs (1)

Alana Company believes that increasing paperweight quality will cause sales volume to increase by 1,500 units. Quality could be improved by: (1) purchasing a higher grade of raw material that would raise variable cost per unit by $1.50 and (2) buying an automated glass blowing machine to reduce "bubbles" in the paperweights. *Should the company make these efforts to raise quality?*

Variable cost will increase from $15 per unit to $16.50, reducing the contribution margin per unit from $35 to $33.50. Thus, the total CM from the sales of the original 25,000 will decrease. Machine depreciation would raise annual fixed costs by $8,000. Fixed expenses will increase from $647,500 to $655,500.

	Decrease in CM on old paperweight sales (25,000 paperweights × $1.50)	$(37,500)
+	Increase in CM from new paperweight sales (1,500 × $33.50)	50,250
–	Increase in annual fixed cost	(8,000)
=	Net incremental benefit	$ 4,750

There is an incremental benefit in this situation, so Alana Company should make the quality enhancement efforts and, thereby, increase sales volume.

Increase in Sales Volume and Cost (2)

Alana Company has been approached by a foreign company that wants to purchase, for resale, 3,000 paperweights at $30 per unit. Additional packaging and shipping will cause variable cost per unit to increase by $3 for the units produced for the foreign company. Additionally, the fixed cost will increase by $30,000 because of the depreciation on a new labeling machine that will need to be purchased. Alana Company's current sales will not be affected by this opportunity and the additional units fall within the company's relevant range of activity. *Should the company make this sale?*

The total variable cost per "foreign" paperweight is \$18 (\$15 current + \$3 additional shipping and packaging). The contribution margin per "foreign" unit is \$12 (\$30 selling price – \$18 total variable cost). Alana Company is already making profits, so all current fixed costs are covered. However, the new \$30,000 of fixed cost will need to be covered by the additional sales.

Total contribution margin (3,000 paperweights × \$12)	\$ 36,000
– Additional fixed cost (depreciation)	(30,000)
= Net incremental benefit	\$ 6,000

Total contribution margin provided from the sale is greater than the additional fixed cost. Thus, Alana Company's total income would increase by accepting this opportunity and the sale should be made.

All the examples given have been evaluated solely on a monetary basis. However, these types of decisions should be analyzed using both monetary and nonmonetary factors, as well as considering short-term and long-term implications. How close to reality are the increased sales projections? What if cost increases are greater than projected? Will increased workloads create stress for employees who may begin to exhibit fatigue that generates quality problems? Have all future costs truly been considered? (For example, when new equipment is to be purchased, might there be additional costs for maintenance and employee training that have not been estimated?) Or might increased advertising benefit sales for years beyond the time frame considered? Additional considerations include future production capacity, quality control, raw material and other resource availability, and possible legal implications of different sales prices to different customers.

CVP ANALYSIS IN A MULTIPRODUCT ENVIRONMENT

All of the previous situations are based on a single-product company, but most companies produce and sell a variety of items. Some companies sell related products (such as golf clubs and bags or tablecloths and napkins); other companies are quite diversified and sell unrelated products.

Performing CVP analysis in a multiproduct company requires an additional assumption to the ones stated at the beginning of the chapter: a constant product sales mix. The **constant mix** (or "basket") **assumption** reflects the notion that the company sells a consistent set of goods as a package. For example, a furniture company could assume that, for every dining room table sold, four chairs will also be sold. Without the constant sales mix assumption, a break-even point could not be calculated and CVP analysis could not be used. The constant mix assumption allows a weighted average contribution margin (or CM ratio) to be computed for the basket of products being sold. Thus, the CM (or CM ratio) is affected by the quantity of each product in the "basket."

To continue the Alana Company example, assume that management has decided to also produce glass bookends. It is estimated that, for every five paperweights sold, the company will sell two sets of bookends. Therefore, the products have a 5:2 ratio within the "basket." Alana Company will need to purchase additional machinery to make the bookends; this purchase will result in \$34,190 of additional fixed costs for depreciation on the machine. Exhibit 12-4 provides relevant company information and shows the break-even computations.

Any difference in the product sales mix from the stated 5:2 relationship at a sales level of 3,665 "baskets" will cause Alana Company to either incur a loss or generate a profit. If the proportion of bookends sold within the "baskets" increases, Alana Company will incur

EXHIBIT 12-4

Multiple Product Cost Information for Alana Company

	Paperweight		Bookends		"Basket"	
	Per unit	Per basket	Per set	Per basket	Total	%
Number in basket		5		2		
Selling price	$50	$250	$30.00	$60	$310	100%
Variable expenses	(15)	(75)	(24.50)	(49)	(124)	40%
Contribution margin	$35	$175	$ 5.50	$11	$186	60%

New fixed costs: $647,500 + $34,190 = $681,690

$$R(X) - VC(X) - FC = P$$
$$\$310X - \$124X - \$681{,}690 = \$0$$
$$\$186X = \$681{,}690$$
$$X = 3{,}665 \text{ "baskets"}$$

Because products are sold in a 5:2 ratio, the "basket" result requires that Alana Company sell 18,325 (3,665 × 5) paperweights and 7,330 (3,665 × 2) sets of bookends to break even.

a loss because the contribution margin of that product (18.3%) is lower than that of the paperweights (70%). If the proportion of paperweights sold increases, Alana Company will earn a profit.

Assume that Alana Company sells 3,665 "baskets" but the actual sales mix is four paperweights for every two sets of bookends sold. Thus, the proportion has shifted toward the product with the lower contribution margin ratio. The results of such a sales mix are shown in Exhibit 12-5.

GRAPHIC APPROACHES TO BEP AND CVP PROBLEMS

Solving break-even and CVP problems using the algebraic or income statement approach provides a specific numerical answer (although that answer may need to be rounded). However, solutions may also be presented in a pictorial, or graphic, form. Two depictions, the break-even graph and the profit-volume graph, are provided in the following sections with a related discussion.

EXHIBIT 12-5

Change in Sales Mix for Alana Company

	Paperweight		Bookends		"Basket"	
	Per unit	Per basket	Per set	Per basket	Total	%
Number in basket		4		2		
Selling price	$50	$200	$30.00	$60	$260	100.0%
Variable expenses	(15)	(60)	(24.50)	(49)	(149)	57.3%
Contribution margin	$35	$140	$ 5.50	$11	$111	42.7%

New fixed costs: $647,500 + $34,190 = $681,690

$$R(\text{Baskets Sold}) - VC(\text{Baskets Sold}) - FC = \text{Profit (or Loss)}$$
$$\$260(3{,}665) - \$149(3{,}665) - \$681{,}690 = \text{Profit (or Loss)}$$
$$\$111(3{,}665) - \$681{,}690 = \text{Profit (or Loss)}$$
$$\$406{,}815 - \$681{,}690 = \text{Profit (or Loss)}$$
$$-\$274{,}875 = \text{Loss}$$

Break-Even Graph

The **break-even graph** plots the relationships among revenue, volume, and the various costs. The x-axis (horizontal) represents volume in units while the y-axis (vertical) represents dollars earned or spent by the company. Each line on the graph represents revenues or costs. The graph is created as follows.

1. Total fixed cost is a line drawn horizontal to the x-axis. The line is parallel to the x-axis because at any volume, the total fixed costs do not change. The fixed-cost line crosses the y-axis at the dollar value of fixed costs.
2. Total cost is shown as a line that originates at the point where the total fixed cost line intersects the y-axis because when zero units are produced, no variable costs are incurred and therefore total costs are equal to fixed costs. Per-unit variable cost is represented by the slope of the total-cost line. For every additional unit produced and sold, total costs increase by the variable cost per unit.
3. At each volume level, the distance between the fixed cost and the total cost lines represents total variable cost.
4. Total revenue is plotted from zero, using a slope that represents the selling price per unit. For each additional unit sold, revenue increases by the selling price per unit.
5. The break-even point is at the intersection of the revenue and total cost lines. At that point total revenues and total costs are equal.
6. Beyond the BEP (to the right), profit is represented as the distance between the total revenue and total cost lines for any number of units. To the left of BEP is the loss area.

Exhibit 12-6 shows the break-even graph for Alana Company. Notice that at 18,500 units both costs and revenues are equal to $925,000 as calculated earlier in the chapter.

Profit-Volume Graph

A **profit-volume** (PV) **graph** provides the same information as a BEP graph, but shows profit or loss amounts at each level of volume. As in the BEP graph, volume in units is represented

EXHIBIT 12-6

Break-Even Graph for Alana Company

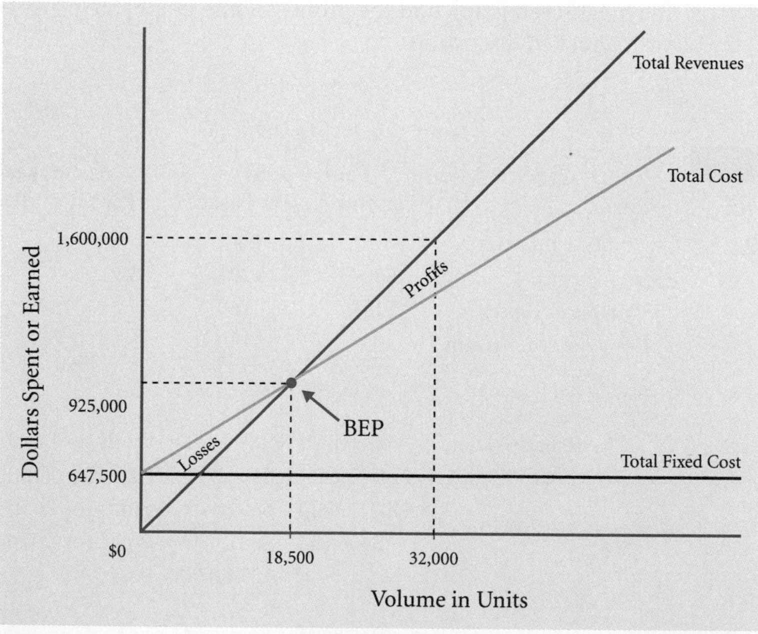

on the PV graph's horizontal axis and dollars are represented on the vertical axis. However, in this graph, the dollars represent the differences between revenue and cost amounts or the profit (loss) amounts. Amounts above the horizontal axis are positive and indicate profits; amounts below the horizontal axis are negative and indicate losses.

Total fixed costs are shown on the vertical axis under the sales volume line as a negative amount. If a company were to sell no units of product, a loss in the amount of total fixed costs would occur. The horizontal axis of zero profitability is placed at the break-even point, which is determined using the algebraic formula. A profit line is drawn between the total fixed costs and the break-even point and extended at the same slope. This line allows the profit or loss amount for any sales volume to be read from the vertical axis. The PV graph for Alana Company is shown in Exhibit 12-7.

Graphic representations of break-even are visually appealing, but they do not provide exact solutions to problems because of the inability to read precise points on a graph. Therefore, accurate computations of profit and loss figures must still be made using the algebraic formula.

OPERATING ABOVE BREAK-EVEN

Managers are often concerned with how close the current level of operations is to the break-even point. Two tools are commonly used to analyze the relationship between current operations and BEP: the margin of safety and the degree of operating leverage.

Margin of Safety

Managers presented with new opportunities often consider the organization's **margin of safety** (MS), or the excess of sales over break-even point. The MS represents the level by which sales can fall before the BEP is reached and, thus, indicates a loss "cushion" measure. The MS can be calculated in units or dollars.[1]

$$MS_u = \text{Actual units} - \text{Break-even units}$$
$$MS_\$ = \text{Actual sales in \$s} - \text{Break-even sales in \$s}$$

Alana Company's break-even point is 18,500 units or \$925,000 of sales. Exhibit 12-1 indicates that Alana Company is currently selling 25,000 paperweights, providing

[1] The margin of safety can also be expressed as a percentage: (MS in units or \$) ÷ (Actual sales in units or \$).

EXHIBIT 12-7

Profit-Volume Graph for Alana Company

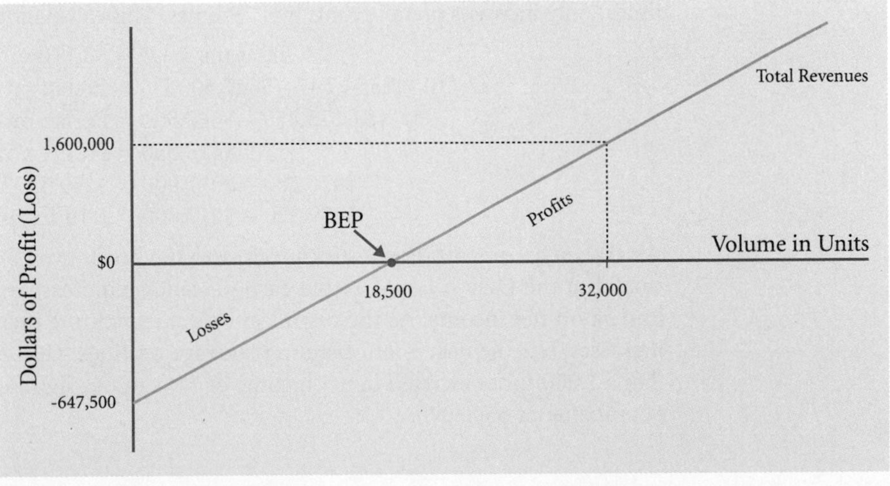

$1,250,000 of total revenue. Alana Company's margin of safety is calculated in the following equations.

$$MS_u = 25{,}000 - 18{,}500 = 6{,}500 \text{ paperweights}$$
$$MS_\$ = \$1{,}250{,}000 - \$925{,}000 = \$325{,}000$$

Because the company is operating above its break-even point, Alana Company's margin of safety is fairly high.

The margin of safety provides an indication of organizational risk. As the MS gets smaller, managers must become more aware of sales levels and cost control so that the company will not fall into a loss situation.

Degree of Operating Leverage

The **degree of operating leverage** (DOL) is closely related to the margin of safety. The DOL reflects an organization's variable and fixed cost relationship and measures how a percentage change in sales from the current level will impact profits. Thus, it indicates an organization's sensitivity to sales volume changes. The formula for the degree of operating leverage factor is given below.

$$\text{DOL} = \text{Total Contribution Margin} \div \text{Pretax Profit}$$

Organizations with high variable costs (and often high direct labor costs) and low fixed costs have low contribution margins and low degrees of operating leverage. These organizations have high break-even points. Alternately, organizations (often those that are highly automated) with high fixed costs and low variable costs have high contribution margins and high degrees of operating leverage. These organizations have low break-even points. As organizations become more automated, they will need higher sales volumes to cover their fixed costs. However, once fixed costs are covered, each unit sold above the BEP provides a generous contribution to profits. Thus, a small sales volume increase can dramatically influence a company's profits.

The Alana Company example is continued with one change from the original information. Assume that Alana Company is currently selling only 19,000 paperweights (rather than the original 25,000). Exhibit 12-8 provides the income statement and degree of operating leverage at the 19,000 sales volume and at two other sales volumes.

When a company experiences a specified percentage increase (or decrease) in sales volume, the profit change equals the DOL times the percentage change in sales. The DOL decreases as an organization moves away from its break-even point. For example, at 24,700 units, Alana Company's DOL is 3.98 (rounded). An additional 30 percent increase in sales (1.3 times) only increases pretax profits by 1.19 times. This calculation is proved as follows:

$$24{,}700 \text{ units} \times 1.3 = 32{,}110 \text{ units of sales}$$
$$(32{,}110 \times \$35 \text{ CM}) - \$647{,}500 \text{ FC} = \text{Pretax profit}$$
$$\$1{,}123{,}850 - \$647{,}500 = \text{Pretax profit}$$
$$\$476{,}350 = \text{Pretax profit}$$
$$\$476{,}350 - \$217{,}000 = \$259{,}350 \text{ increase}$$
$$\$259{,}350 \div \$217{,}000 = 1.19 \text{ times (rounded)}$$

When an organization's sales are close to the break-even point, the margin of safety is small but the DOL is large, so that each percentage increase in sales can make a dramatic impact on net income. As the organization's sales volume increases, the margin of safety increases, but the degree of operating leverage declines. However, it is important to note that a 1,000 times increase in net income of $1 is not as significant as a 3 times increase in net income of $500,000.

EXHIBIT 12-8
Degree of Operating Leverage for Alana Company

	Current Level 19,000 units	Decrease of 20% 15,200 units	Increase of 30% 24,700 units
Sales (@ $50)	$ 950,000	$ 760,000	$1,235,000
VC (@ $15)	(285,000)	(228,000)	(370,500)
CM (@ $35)	$ 665,000	$ 532,000	$ 864,500
FC (total)	(647,500)	(647,500)	(647,500)
Pretax profit	$ 17,500	$(115,500)	$ 217,000

DOL at 19,000 units = $665,000 ÷ $17,500 = 38

At 15,200 units, pretax profits decline by $133,000 (or $17,500 + $115,500) or 7.6 times, which is equal to the DOL of 38 times the 20 percent volume reduction.

At 22,800 units, pretax profits increase by $199,500 (or $217,000 – $17,500) or 11.4 times, which is equal to the DOL of 38 times the 30 percent volume increase.

SUMMARY

In contemplating future activities, management must consider selling prices, volume levels, and variable and fixed costs. These monetary elements will affect the contribution margin, break-even point (BEP), and profits (or losses). The relationships among these elements are examined in break-even and cost-volume-profit (CVP) analysis.

At BEP, total revenues are equal to total costs and the organization neither incurs a loss nor generates a profit. The CVP model adds a desired profit into the income statement equation. An important amount in the BEP or CVP model is contribution margin, which is equal to selling price per unit minus variable cost per unit. Dividing total fixed costs by contribution margin per unit provides the BEP in units. After total fixed costs are covered, each dollar of contribution margin will generate a dollar of pretax profit.

The BEP and CVP models require that certain underlying assumptions about the income statement elements be made. These assumptions limit the ability of the models to reflect reality, but are necessary for the models to be usable. If any assumptions are violated, the information resulting from the model will be less than reasonable.

When an organization sells a variety of products, break-even and cost-volume-profit analyses must be performed using an assumed constant product sales mix (or "basket") assumption. A weighted average contribution margin (or contribution margin ratio) is computed for the organization's "basket" of products. Results of BEP or CVP computations are in "baskets" of products; the sales mix ratio is used to convert these "basket" amount to amounts of individual products.

The margin of safety (MS) can be calculated in units or sales dollars. The MS shows how far an organization is operating from its BEP. The degree of operating leverage (DOL) shows how many times profit would change from its current level given a specified percentage change in sales volume.

KEY TERMS

break-even graph
break-even point
contribution margin
contribution margin ratio
cost-volume-profit analysis
degree of operating leverage
incremental analysis
margin of safety
profit-volume graph
variable cost ratio

QUESTIONS

1. What is the break-even point? Why is calculating break-even point the starting point for cost-volume-profit analysis? *(LO 12.1)*
2. What is a "relevant range?" Why is that assumption necessary for break-even analysis and cost-volume-profit analysis? *(LO 12.1)*
3. Discuss the realism of the underlying assumptions of break-even analysis (that is, how likely it is that the assumptions will hold in reality). *(LO 12.1)*
4. In discussing BEP or CVP analysis, why is it necessary to assume that all units produced by the company are also sold? What difficulties would be caused in the BEP or CVP calculations if units were produced but not sold?
5. What is contribution margin and why does it fluctuate in direct proportion with sales volume? *(LO 12.2)*
6. What is the formula for the contribution margin ratio? What information does the ratio provide? *(LO 12.2)*
7. Why is the constant mix assumption necessary to use CVP in a multiproduct firm? *(LO 12.2)*
8. Describe the difference between the break-even graph and the profit-volume graph. Which graph do you think provides better information? Explain the reason for your answer. *(LO 12.3)*
9. How do the margin of safety and degree of operating leverage apply to CVP analysis? *(LO 12.4)*
10. Explain the benefits and drawbacks of using the margin of safety and degree of operating leverage to determine how well-positioned an organization is in the marketplace. *(LO 12.4)*

EXERCISES

11. **True or False** *(All LOs)*

Following are a series of statements regarding topics discussed in this chapter.

Required:

Indicate whether each statement is true (T) or false (F).

(1) At the break-even point, total revenue dollars equal zero.
(2) The break-even graph depicts fixed costs, total costs, and revenues for any level of output, not just at the break-even point.
(3) After-tax income should be used in CVP analysis if the tax rate is known.
(4) The profit-volume graph does not depict revenues separately from costs.
(5) Variable cost per unit may not be the same for every unit produced if the company operates beyond the relevant range.
(6) Margin of safety and degree of operating leverage must be expressed in dollars.
(7) Contribution margin is the amount the sale of one unit contributes to profit after fixed costs.
(8) Fixed costs divided by the contribution margin ratio equals the break-even point in dollars.

(9) To perform CVP analysis for a multiproduct company, an assumption is made that the product mix is constant.

(10) Degree of operating leverage can be misleading because it is expressed in percentages instead of dollars.

12. **Break-Even Point** *(LO 12.2)*

Selected information for four different companies is listed below.

Company	Revenue Per Unit	Variable Cost Per Unit	Fixed Cost	Units
A	(1)	$ 8.00	$120,000.00	10,000
B	$40.00	(2)	360,000.00	20,000
C	8.00	3.50	59,994.00	(3)
D	59.00	40.00	(4)	42,700

Required:

Find the missing amounts, assuming each company is operating at the break-even point.

13. **Pretax and After-tax Profits** *(LO 12.2)*

Selected information for three companies is provided below.

Company	Pretax Profit	Tax Rate	After-Tax Profit
A	(1)	0.35	$ 650,000.00
B	$2,500,000.00	(2)	1,600,000.00
C	950,000.00	0.29	(3)

Required:

Find the missing amounts.

14. **Break-Even Point** *(LO 12.2)*

Conroe Corp. has a contribution margin ratio of 45 percent. Product selling price per unit is $130 and total fixed costs per year are $2,385,000.

Required:

(1) Using the contribution margin ratio, what is the break-even point for Conroe Corp.?

(2) What is the product's variable cost ratio? What is the product's total variable cost per unit?

(3) Use two different ways to calculate how many units Conroe Corp. needs to sell to break even.

15. **CVP Analysis** *(LO 12.2)*

Cost-volume-profit analysis is used to analyze the relationship between revenues, variable costs, fixed costs, profits, and units produced.

Required:

For each of the following situations, calculate the missing items.

(1) Acme, Inc. sells its product for $30. The variable cost per unit is $16 and fixed costs are $1,115,000. What profit will Acme make if 150,000 units are produced and sold?

(2) Beta Co. can sell 70,000 units in one year. Variable costs are $65 per unit and fixed costs are $2,020,000. How much should Beta sell its product for per unit if the company wants to make a pretax profit of $1,130,000?

(3) Capitol Enterprises sells 85,400 units in one year. The product has a contribution margin of $44 and fixed costs are $1,907,600. What is Capitol Enterprises' pretax profit?

(4) Denson, Inc. sells its product for $45. The product has a variable cost of $35 and fixed costs of $12,000,000. How many units should the company sell if it wants to earn pretax profits of $9,000,000?

(5) Edgar Co. has a tax rate of 35 percent. The company sells a product with a $37 contribution margin; fixed costs of $18,000,000 are incurred by the company annually. How many units should the company sell if it wants to earn after-tax profits of $6,650,000?

16. **Incremental Analysis** *(LO 12.2)*

Use the information from Exercise 14. Conroe Corp. is currently selling 50,000 units per year and has a 30% tax rate.

Required:

(1) What is Conroe Corp.'s current annual income after taxes?

(2) Management believes that increasing advertising costs by $150,000 will increase unit sales by 20 percent. What will be Conroe Corp.'s new annual income if this change is made? Should the company make the change?

(3) Management believes that increasing the quality of the material used in the production process will increase the attractiveness of the product to purchasers. The higher quality material will cost an additional $3 per unit. Conroe's marketing department believes that using this material will not allow an increase in unit selling price but, by spending $45,000 on advertising to inform the public of the higher quality, sales volume should increase by five percent. What will be Conroe Corp.'s new annual income if this change is made? Should the company make the change?

17. **Multiproduct CVP** *(LO 12.2)*

Lillian's Linens sells kitchen towels and potholders. The company generally sells two potholders for every three towels. Each potholder has a $0.25 contribution margin and each towel has a $0.75 contribution margin. Fixed costs for the company are $4,400 per month. The company has a tax rate of 25 percent.

Required:

(1) How much revenue is needed to break even each month? How many potholders and towels would this represent?

(2) How much revenue is needed to earn an annual after-tax profit of $20,250? How many "baskets" of potholders and towels is this?

(3) If the company sells the number of "baskets" determined in part (2), but did so by selling four towels for every two potholders, what would be the company's pretax profit (or loss)? Why is this amount not the desired $20,250?

(4) If the company sells the number of "baskets" determined in part (2), but did so by selling two towels for every three potholders, what would be the company's pretax profit (or loss)? Why is this amount not the desired $20,250?

18. **Graphical Approaches** *(LO 12.3)*

The break-even graph for Barker Enterprises is shown below.

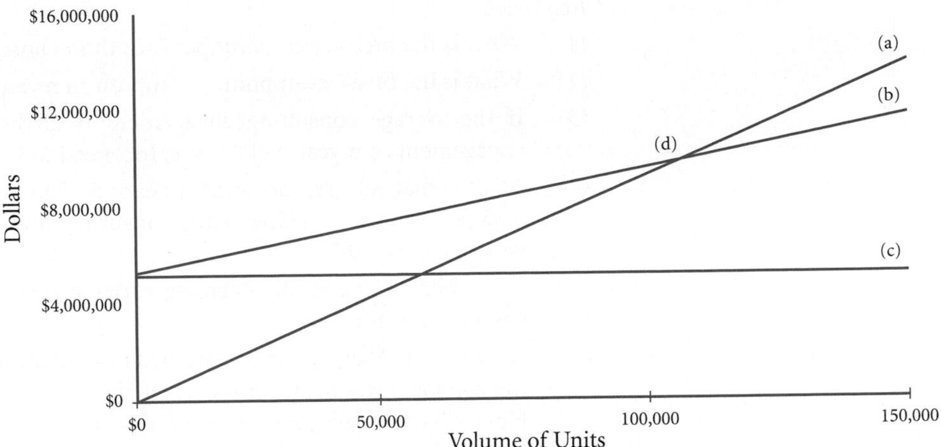

Required:

(1) What do the numbers on the x-axis (horizontal axis) represent?

(2) What do the lines (a), (b), and (c) represent?

(3) What is represented by point (d)?

(4) In approximate dollars, what is the value of the following?

   (a) Fixed costs

   (b) Variable cost per unit

   (c) Revenue per unit

   (d) Break-even point in units

   (e) Break-even point in dollars

   (f) Profit if 150,000 units are produced and sold

   (g) Total revenues if 50,000 units are produced and sold

   (h) Total variable costs if 100,000 units are produced and sold

19. **Margin of Safety; Degree of Operating Leverage** *(LO 12.4)*

Arizona Beverages sells 210,000 bottles of Tempe Tingler each year. The product sells for $6.50 per bottle and variable cost per unit is $2.75. Total annual fixed costs are $750,000.

Required:

(1) What is the margin of safety in units? In dollars?

(2) What is the degree of operating leverage?

(3) If the company can increase unit sales by 30 percent, what percentage increase will it experience in income? Prove your answer using an income statement.

(4) Use original data. If the company increases advertising by $22,500, sales in units will increase by 15 percent. What will be the new break-even point? The new degree of operating leverage?

PROBLEMS

20. **Break-Even Point** *(LO 12.2)*

Allegre, Inc. has the following revenue and cost information.

Revenue: $150 per consulting hour

Variable costs: $85 per consulting hour

Fixed costs: $46,800 per month

Required:

(1) What is the break-even point per month in consulting hours?

(2) What is the break-even point per month in revenue dollars?

(3) If the average consulting engagement is 28 hours, how many consulting engagements per year will Allegre, Inc. need to break even?

(4) Assume that Allegre, Inc. wants to earn $7,800 in profits each month and has a 25 percent tax rate. How many consulting hours does the company need to work each month?

(5) How might Allegre, Inc. decrease variable costs per consulting hour? Fixed costs per month?

(6) Assume that Allegre, Inc. has decided to limit air travel by consultants. Instead the company will invest in a state-of-the-art satellite teleconferencing system. How will these decisions affect variable and fixed costs? What are the potential drawbacks of this decision?

21. **CVP Analysis** *(LO 12.2)*

S'No'Kones has the following cost structure.

Selling price per unit	$1.50
Variable cost per unit	$0.45
Fixed costs per month	$1,260.00

Required:

(1) What is the break-even point for S'No'Kones?

(2) If the owner wants to earn a monthly pretax profit of $400, how many units would need to be sold each month?

(3) The owner wants to earn a pretax profit of $6,090 annually. The snow cone stand is only open five months of the year. How many snow cones would need to be sold in total during those five months? If three months of the five generate 75 percent of the company sales, how many snow cones would need to be sold during those three months?

(4) Recalculate your answer to part (3) assuming a tax rate of 20% and a desired after-tax profit of $6,090.

(5) S'No'Kones is located in the panhandle of Florida. Discuss circumstances that might cause the BEP and CVP assumptions to be inaccurate.

22. **CVP Analysis** *(LO 12.2, Excel)*

Rona's Ribs has the following sales and cost information.

Average number of pounds sold per year	26,500
Average selling price per pound of ribs	$7.50
Variable expenses per pound:	
Raw material	$2.50
Variable labor and overhead	2.80
Annual fixed costs:	
Production expenses	$38,000.00
Selling & administrative expenses	$17,000.00

The company's tax rate is 30 percent. The company's costs have slowly been rising and profits rapidly falling. Rona Maris, company president, has asked your help in answering the following questions.

Required:

(1) What is the contribution margin per pound of ribs? The contribution margin ratio?

(2) What is the break-even point in pounds of ribs? In dollars?

(3) How much revenue must be generated to produce $19,800 of pretax income? How many pounds of ribs would this level of revenue represent?

(4) How much revenue must be generated to produce $29,995 of after-tax income? How many pounds of ribs would this represent?

(5) A restaurant has contacted Rona about buying 15,000 pounds of ribs per year. Rona has the capacity to do this and is interested in taking advantage of this opportunity and wants to generate an after-tax profit on her total sales of $9,800. To make this profit, how much should she charge the restaurant per pound of ribs? (Round to the nearest penny.)

(6) Use original data. Rona believes that she can raise the selling price per pound of ribs by $3 but she expects this would cause a 5,000-pound decline in ribs sold. Should she make this change?

(7) Rona wants to lease a new heavy-duty smoker; this action will cause her fixed costs to increase by $12,000 per year. If she makes this change, as well as the price change discussed in part (6), what will be her new break-even point in pounds of ribs and dollars of sales?

23. **CVP and Incremental Analysis** *(LO 12.2 & 12.4)*

Each unit of product made by TRH, Inc. sells for $40. The company has an annual production and sales volume of 35,000 units. Costs per unit are as follows:

Direct material	$ 9.00
Direct labor	3.00
Variable overhead	1.20
Variable selling expenses	4.20
Total variable cost	$17.40

Additionally, total fixed overhead is $610,200 per year.

Required:

(1) Calculate the contribution margin and contribution margin ratio for the product.

(2) Determine the break-even point in units.

(3) Calculate the break-even point in dollars using the contribution margin ratio.

(4) Determine TRH, Inc.'s margin of safety in units and sales dollars as well as a percentage.

(5) Compute TRH, Inc.'s degree of operating leverage. If sales increase by 20 percent, by what percentage would pretax income increase?

(6) Use original data. How many units would TRH need to sell to break even if fixed costs increase by $31,640?

(7) Use original data. How many units must be sold for TRH, Inc. to earn $339,000 after-tax if the company has a 25 percent tax rate?

(8) Quanta Corp. has offered to buy 5,000 units from TRH, Inc. The variable cost per unit in this sale would increase by $1.50 because of special shipping and packaging. Fixed costs for this sale would be $3,000. Additionally, TRH, Inc. will need to pay a 10 percent commission on selling price to the manager who brought in the offer. This sale would not affect other sales or their costs. If TRH, Inc. wants pretax income from this sale to be $3,750, at what price should the units be sold? Prove your answer using an income statement for these 5,000 units.

24. **Multiproduct CVP** *(LO 12.3)*

Trinidad LLP provides two kinds of services to clients: telephone answering and billing. Because Trinidad's clients for each type of service are approximately the same size, the company has standardized fees for its services: $1,800 per month for telephone answering and $2,500 per month for billing. The company has three telephone clients for every two billing clients. Variable costs of the services are $1,080 for telephone clients and $1,905 for billing clients. Fixed costs are $1,172,500 per year.

Required:

(1) How many telephone clients and billing clients are needed to break even each year?

(2) If Trinidad LLP has a tax rate of 35 percent, how many telephone clients and billing clients are needed to earn an after-tax income of $108,875?

(3) Trinidad LLP currently has 1,230 telephone answering clients and 820 billing clients. What is Trinidad's pretax income? The company is considering lowering fees for telephone answering and billing clients to $1,600 and $2,200, respectively. If this change is made and no new clients are added, how many dollars of fixed costs can the company incur and still maintain the same pretax income as is currently being generated?

(4) Use original data. Trinidad LLP is considering raising the fee for billing clients to $3,175. If this increase were made, the telephone answering to billing client ratio would decline to 3:1. How many telephone clients and billing clients would be needed to break even each year if fixed costs do not change?

(5) What circumstances might affect Trinidad's ability to use the current financial data to calculate BEP or other CVP factors over the next three years?

25. **Graphic Approaches** *(LO 12.4)*

The Phoenix Phunsters has given you the following fee and cost information for the club: monthly membership fee per person, $35; monthly variable cost per person, $22; monthly fixed cost, $1,235. Members provide the majority of services and supplies for the club. The club currently has 80 members and its cash balance has been declining for the past year.

Required:

(1) Prepare a break-even graph for Phoenix Phunsters.

(2) Prepare a profit-volume graph for Phoenix Phunsters.

(3) If you were giving a talk to the membership to get members to understand the need for an increase in membership fees, which of the two graphs would you want to show and why?

CASES

26. **Relevant Range** *(LO 12.1, writing)*

Galileo Publishers sells sets of encyclopedias. In 2002, Galileo sold 50,000 sets at a price of $300 per set. In 2002, the costs to manufacture those sets included the following:

Variable Cost per Set:	
Paper	$30
Cover Material	25
Ink	10
Direct Labor	50
Variable Overhead	70
Fixed Overhead	$4,500,000

In 2002, Galileo received a 10 percent discount on paper, cover material, and ink because of the volume of those items that were purchased. Because of the increased use of encyclopedias on CD-ROM, the sales of encyclopedias are expected to decrease in future years. The decrease in sales will require a decrease in production.

Required:

(1) Calculate Galileo's pretax profit in 2002 using CVP analysis.

(2) Write a memo to Galileo's management explaining how the profit calculation might change as production decreases.

27. **Contribution Margin** *(LO 12.1 & 12.2, group)*

Identifying the similarities and differences in companies is crucial to understanding the nature of operations. Form groups of at least four students. Your group (or your instructor) should decide on a product that you could reasonably produce. [Don't try to be innovative; select something simple like a birdhouse or a cake.]

Required—individual group members:

(1) Identify the costs associated with producing the product your group selected. Separate your list into variable and fixed costs.

(2) Go shopping. Try to find valid prices for the costs to manufacture one item.

(3) Can you find better prices if you produce 50 items? How about 100? Explain.

(4) Assuming that the contribution margin is $10 and labor is paid at a rate of $6 per hour, complete the following table.

	1 unit	**50 units**	**100 units**
Revenue per item			
Variable costs per unit			
List variable costs here			
Contribution Margin	$10	$500	$1,000

Required—groups:

(5) Compare your results with your group members. Identify a complete list of variable costs.

(6) Prepare the table again, as in part (4), using the lowest costs found by each group member.

(7) Are there significant savings per unit if you can produce 50 or 100 as compared to one item? How would such savings impact the assumptions underlying BEP and CVP analysis?

SUPPLEMENTAL PROBLEMS

28. **CVP Analysis** *(LO 12.2)* [Compare to Problems 21 and 22.]

Terry Cook owns the Rest-Well Kennel that has a capacity of 50 animals and is open 360 days per year. Operating costs of the kennel are as follows:

Annual depreciation on the building: $18,000
Labor: $35,000 per year plus $2.00 per animal per day
Food: $3.00 per animal per day
Utilities: $15,000 per year plus $0.25 per animal per day
Other (including advertising): $22,000 per year plus $0.50 per animal per day

Required:

(1) The kennel has an average annual occupancy rate of 80 percent. Determine the minimum daily charge that must be assessed per animal per day to break even.

(2) Terry's tax rate is 25 percent. What must he charge per pet per day to earn an after-tax income of $18,000? (Round to the nearest dollar.)

(3) Terry has found that cat owners will pay a higher rate per day than dog owners will for the services provided by his kennel. The kennel typically has a 1:9 cat-to-dog proportional occupancy. If Terry decides to charge cat owners $15 per day, what does he need to charge per day per dog to earn an annual after-tax income of $21,000? (Round to the nearest dollar.)

(4) Terry is considering renovating the kennel area to provide more spacious private rooms for his dog "guests." The renovation will cost approximately $12,000 and will decrease the number of possible occupants to 30 per day. Cats will still make up 10% of the kennel's clientele and will be charged $15 per day. What will Terry now need to charge per dog per day to cover the cost of renovations and still earn an after-tax income of $21,000? (Round to the nearest dollar.) (Ignore depreciation on renovations.)

(5) Terry is considering adding a dog obedience school to his kennel services. Costs of the school have been estimated at $3,680 per year for the trainer plus $8 per dog. Terry plans to charge $40 per dog to attend obedience school and he wants to earn a pretax profit of $4,000 on the school. How many dogs need to attend the school for Terry to earn his desired profit?

29. **Multiproduct CVP** *(LO 12.2)* [Compare to Problem 24.]

Hernandez, Inc. makes three types of products: ties, blouses, and shirts. The following selling prices and variable costs are expected for 2004.

	Ties	**Blouses**	**Shirts**
Selling price	$18.50	$43.00	$40.00
Direct material	$5.20	$8.95	$11.80
Direct labor	2.80	5.40	7.80
Variable overhead	2.00	4.15	5.75
Variable selling expenses	1.50	3.25	5.00
Variable administrative expenses	1.20	2.10	3.30

In addition, fixed costs are as follows:

Fixed overhead	$920,000
Fixed selling expenses	150,000
Fixed administrative expenses	174,100

The company expects to have the following sales mix: two ties, three blouses, and one shirt.

Required:

(1) Which product is the most profitable? Which is the least profitable? Does this make sense to you? Explain.

(2) What is the expected break-even point for 2004?

(3) How many units of each product are expected to be sold at the break-even point?

(4) Assume that the company desires a pretax profit of $505,180. How many units of each product would need to be sold to generate this profit level? How much revenue in total would be required?

(5) Hernandez, Inc. wants to earn $403,000 after-tax, with a tax rate of 35 percent. Use the contribution margin ratio to determine the revenue needed (round to the nearest dollar).

(6) If Hernandez, Inc. earns the revenue determined in part (4) above, what is the company's margin of safety in dollars and as a percentage?

30. **Graphic Approaches** *(LO 12.3)* [Compare to Problem 25.]

Gunther Ltd. had the following income statement for 2004.

Sales (30,000 gallons @ $14)		$420,000
Variable Costs		
Production (30,000 gallons @ $6)	$180,000	
Selling (30,000 gallons @ $.50)	15,000	(195,000)
Contribution Margin		$225,000
Fixed Costs		
Production	$ 52,250	
Selling and Administrative	64,000	(116,250)
Income before Taxes		$109,000

Required:

(1) Prepare a break-even graph for Gunther Ltd.

(2) Prepare a profit-volume graph for Gunther Ltd.

(3) Prepare a short explanation for company management about each of the graphs.

CHAPTER 13

The Master Budget

LEARNING OBJECTIVES

1. Assess the importance of budgeting.
2. Prepare a master budget.
3. Discuss the uses of a rolling budget.
4. Explain how standard costs are used in preparing budgets and assessing responsibility.
5. Calculate material and labor variances for purposes of control and performance evaluation.

Chicago White Sox

Professional sports teams are big business and, like other businesses, these teams need to have a reliable budgeting system in place. The Chicago White Sox baseball team uses a participative budgeting system that helps the team to be "fiscally responsible." The primary starting point for a sports team's budget is expected attendance (the equivalent of sales). Unlike in the majority of production or retail environments, however, this estimate is highly variable depending on the team's win-lose record and fan loyalty. A second primary budget amount is player salaries, which often run between $10 million and $70 million annually.

All department managers are responsible for their own budgets. Standards are used to estimate revenues from concessions (average purchase per attendee) and expenses, such as the number of security people that needed per game based on expected attendance and pay rates for security personnel. Budget-to-actual comparisons are made periodically and explanations for variances are developed.

SOURCE: Anita Dennis, "Budgeting for Curve Balls," *Journal of Accountancy* (September 1998): 89–92.

INTRODUCTION

Organizations must plan for the future and the plans should include both narrative descriptions and monetary indications of organizational goals. The process of **budgeting** is the interpretation of future plans into monetary amounts so that progress toward organizational goals can be determined. The end result of the budgeting process is a **budget** or financial plan for the future. At specified times during the budget period, budgeted (standard) and actual amounts are compared to determine differences **(variances),** which indicate a positive or negative goal achievement and can help pinpoint responsibility, relative to those goals, to organizational units and managers.

THE BUDGETING PROCESS

Budgeting is a critical activity for all organizations, but no single budgeting process is appropriate for all organizations. In small organizations, good budgeting can mean the difference between staying in business or going bankrupt. In large organizations, budgeting is important to allocate resources to the many available projects and operating activities.

The budgeting process requires that information and assumptions about the organization's operating environment be considered when planning future activities. Additionally, the budgeting process should involve people and ideas from throughout the organization.

At one extreme of the budgeting process, top management prepares the budget with little or no input from subordinates. Budgets are imposed on lower-level personnel who must perform their operating activities in conformity with the budgets. At the other extreme, there is total coordination and cooperation between top management and lower level employees, with employees participating fully in budget development. Most commonly, the budgeting process falls somewhere between these extremes. It is common for organizational budgets to be prepared using a coordinated approach of gathering input from subordinates and having revisions made by top management.

Regardless of who is involved or to what extent, the financial budgeting process traditionally converts narrative organizational goals into monetary amounts, beginning with a revenue estimate for sales or, in a service organization, fees. In a not-for-profit entity, the starting point may be contributions or funding levels. From there, the process employs information on all organizational resources, such as materials, personnel, overhead, cash, and plant assets. The result is called a **master budget,** which is a comprehensive set of budgets, budgetary schedules, and **pro forma** (projected) financial statements.

The Master Budget

The master budget is generally prepared for the company's fiscal year and is based on a single revenue level. Although budgeting software has made it easier for master budgets to be prepared at numerous revenue levels, a single level must be selected so that actual operating activities can be compared against it to assess organizational performance.

The master budget begins annual sales estimates of the types, quantities, and timing of demand for products; this information is then subdivided into quarterly and monthly periods. The sales level chosen affects all other organizational components. For example, the number of units to be sold directly impacts the number of units to be produced which, in turn, directly impacts the quantity of material to be purchased, labor force to be provided, and space. Sales estimates and estimated accounts receivable collection patterns are used to determine the amounts and timing of cash receipts. Sales information also allows the types, quantities, and timing of product production to be specified. Coordinating this information with estimated cash payment patterns for material and labor indicates the amount and timing of some large cash outflows. Thus, because of such interrelationships, all master budget components must be coordinated. As indicated in Visual Recap 13.1, one department's budget is often essential to the development of another department's budget.

Preparing a Master Budget

Preparation of a master budget is illustrated using information on Fast-Food Funthings, a small company that has been in business for one year. The company produces small plastic toys as giveaways for fast food restaurants. It is in the process of preparing its 2004 budget and has estimated total annual sales for that year at 900,000 units. For convenience, this illustration will focus only on the budgets for the first quarter of 2004.

Exhibit 13-1 provides the company's December 31, 2003, balance sheet which is needed to begin preparing the master budget. Estimates are used for year-end balances because the 2004 budget process must begin significantly before December 31, 2003. The time needed by an organization to prepare a budget depends on factors such as size and level of employee participation. Larger organizations and higher employee participation translate into longer budget preparation periods.

Sales Budget

The sales budget is prepared in both units and dollars. Estimated sales in units is multiplied by the selling price per item; in the case of Fast-Food Funthings, each toy sells for $2. Exhibit 13-2 shows monthly sales for the first quarter of 2004 (each month and a quarter total); April and May data are included because some parts of the March budget require the following months' information.

VISUAL RECAP 13.1

Flow of Budgeted Information through the Master Budget

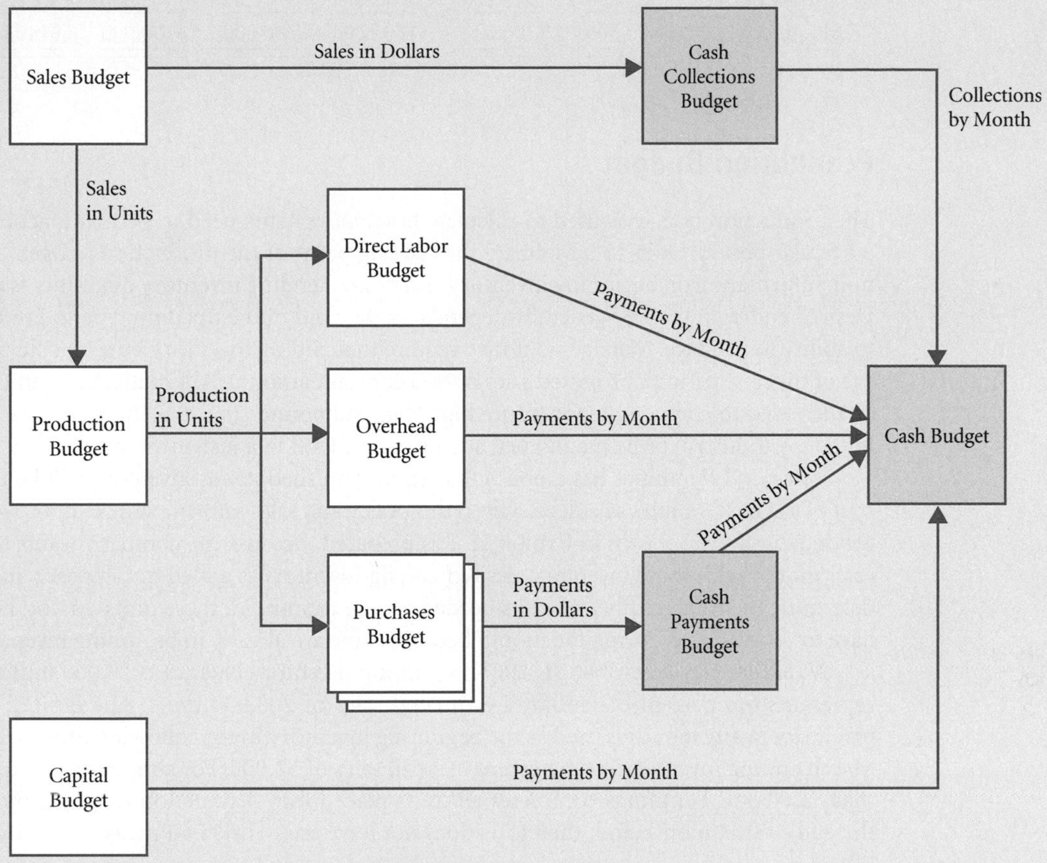

Sales Budget
Sales in Dollars
Cash Collections Budget
Collections by Month
Sales in Units
Direct Labor Budget
Payments by Month
Production Budget
Production in Units
Overhead Budget
Payments by Month
Cash Budget
Payments by Month
Purchases Budget
Payments in Dollars
Cash Payments Budget
Capital Budget
Payments by Month

Note: All budgets are used to prepare pro forma financial statements.

EXHIBIT 13-1

Fast-Food Funthings (Estimated) Balance Sheet December 31, 2003

ASSETS		
Cash		$ 5,000
Accounts Receivable		61,600
Inventories		
Direct Material (87,750 ounces*)	$ 17,550	
Finished Goods (20,000 units)	15,000	32,550
Property, Plant & Equipment	$100,000	
Less Accumulated Depreciation	(30,000)	70,000
Total Assets		$169,150
LIABILITIES AND STOCKHOLDERS' EQUITY		
Accounts Payable		$ 72,000
Common Stock	$ 80,000	
Retained Earnings	17,150	97,150
Total Liabilities and Stockholders' Equity		$169,150

*This quantity of plastic is the amount needed to produce 29,250 units.

EXHIBIT 13-2
Fast-Food Funthings Sales Budget

	January	February	March	Quarter	April	May
Sales in units	200,000	150,000	90,000	440,000	50,000	70,000
Unit sales price	× $2.00	× $2.00	× $2.00	× $2.00	× $2.00	× $2.00
Sales in dollars	$400,000	$300,000	$180,000	$880,000	$100,000	$140,000

Production Budget

The production budget is used to calculate how many items need to be manufactured in a particular period. Units to be sold are the starting point of the production budget. In addition, information on beginning inventory and desired ending inventory quantities is needed. Desired ending inventory generally depends on demand in the upcoming period in relation to ability to produce. Management may require that ending inventory be a specific percentage of the next period's projected sales or be a constant amount. Alternatively, inventory may be increased to compensate for future high-demand periods (such as the Christmas season in the toy industry) or be maintained at a near-zero level in a just-in-time inventory system.

Fast-Food Funthings has a policy that ending finished goods inventory will be ten percent of the next month's sales level. Given this policy and sales information (Exhibit 13-2), the production budget shown in Exhibit 13-3 is prepared. Because the company wants to begin each month with some inventory, desired ending inventory is added to sales each month to determine the total number of units needed for the month. All these units do not, however, have to be produced during the month because some are already in beginning inventory.

Note that the December 31, 2003, beginning inventory balance is 20,000 units, which represents ten percent of January's estimated sales of 200,000 units. The desired ending inventory in any month is used as the beginning inventory in the following month. Desired March ending inventory is ten percent of April sales of 50,000. For simplicity, it is assumed that Fast-Food Funthings completes all units placed into production during a month by the end of that month and, therefore, does not have any Work-In-Process inventory.

Purchases Budget

The purchases budget is prepared to determine quantities of raw material to buy so as to complete the budgeted production, given the quantities of material in the beginning and ending Direct Material Inventory. Fast-Food Funthings must buy enough material each period to meet production needs and be in conformity with the company's desired ending inventory policies. Company policy for direct material is that the ending inventory level be maintained at 15 percent of the quantity needed for the following month's production.

The purchases budget is first stated as units of finished product; then, it is converted to direct material component requirements and dollar amounts. A Fast-Food Funthings toy requires three ounces of plastic that costs $0.20 per ounce. Exhibit 13-4 provides the purchases

EXHIBIT 13-3
Fast-Food Funthings Production Budget

	January	February	March	Quarter	April	May
Sales in units	200,000	150,000	90,000	440,000	50,000	70,000
Desired EI (10%)	15,000	9,000	5,000	5,000	7,000	
Total needed	215,000	159,000	95,000	445,000	57,000	
BI (Exch. 13-1)	(20,000)	(15,000)	(9,000)	(20,000)	(5,000)	
Production in units	195,000	144,000	86,000	425,000	52,000	

budget for Fast-Food Funthings for each month of the first quarter of 2004. Note that beginning and ending inventory quantities are expressed first in terms of finished product (toys), and then converted to the appropriate quantity measure (ounces of plastic). If the product requires more than one raw material, a separate purchase budget is produced for each.

Direct Labor Budget

Given expected production, direct labor requirements are calculated on the direct labor budget. Labor needs are stated in total number of people, specific number of skilled and unskilled laborers, and labor hours needed. Total labor cost is calculated from union labor contracts, minimum wage laws, fringe benefit costs, and payroll taxes.

The direct labor budget begins by converting the number of units to produce (from the production budget) to direct labor hours (DLHs). Direct labor hours are converted to direct labor cost by multiplying by DLHs by the cost per labor hour. Assuming that all direct labor workers are paid the same wage per hour, the direct labor budget is shown in Exhibit 13-5. All compensation is paid in cash in the month in which it is incurred.

Overhead Budget

The overhead budget is used to compute overhead costs for budgeted production levels. Companies typically prepare a production overhead budget and a separate selling and administrative budget; however, Fast-Food Funthings has chosen to combine these two budgets into a single overhead budget (Exhibit 13-6). Variable and fixed costs are determined for all overhead costs at the stated level of production or sales activity.

Assume that Fast-Food Funthings has only variable production overhead costs, which are incurred for hourly-paid indirect labor personnel, electricity on a per-hour basis, and equipment lease rates paid for each hour of use. The variable overhead cost is $0.084 for each unit of production.

EXHIBIT 13-4

Fast-Food Funthings Purchases Budget

	January	February	March	Quarter	April
Finished Units					
Production in units	195,000	144,000	86,000	425,000	52,000
Desired EI in units (15%)	21,600	12,900	7,800	7,800	
Total needed	216,600	156,900	93,800	432,800	
BI units (Exh. 13-1)	(29,250)	(21,600)	(12,900)	(29,250)	
Purchases in units	187,350	135,300	80,900	403,550	
Direct Material					
Ounces per unit	× 3	× 3	× 3	× 3	
Total ounces to purchase	562,050	405,900	242,700	1,210,650	
Cost per ounce	× $0.20	× $0.20	× $0.20	× $0.20	
Total cost of plastic	$112,410	$81,180	$48,540	$242,130	

EXHIBIT 13-5

Fast-Food Funthings Direct labor Budget

	January	February	March	Quarter
Production in units	195,000	144,000	86,000	425,000
DL hours needed per unit	× 0.01	× 0.01	× 0.01	× 0.01
Total DL hours	1,950	1,440	860	4,250
DL wage rate per hour	× $9	× $9	× $9	× $9
Total DL cost (cash)	$17,550	$12,960	$7,740	$38,250

Selling and administrative expenses are budgeted similarly to overhead costs, except that the sales, rather than production, level is the activity driver for this budget. The company has two salespeople who are each paid $1,000 per month plus a 5 percent commission on sales. Administrative salaries total $9,000 per month. Depreciation on selling and administrative equipment totals $1,000 per month. Depreciation is the only noncash cost incurred by Fast-Food Funthings.

Capital Budget

If the company plans to make any purchases of plant assets during the master budget period, those amounts are included in a **capital budget.** Exhibit 13-7 shows that Fast-Food Funthings has decided to buy $300,000 of office equipment in February 2004. Seventy percent of this purchase will be paid for in February and the remainder in March. The company will not begin using the equipment until April 2004, after all workers have completed proper training. Thus, overhead will not change by any additional equipment depreciation in either February or March 2004.

Cash Budget

After all the preceding budgets have been developed, a cash budget can be constructed. However, the sales and purchases budgets must first be converted to a cash basis before the cash budget can be prepared.

Schedule of Cash Collections from Sales

The schedule of cash collections reflects what will be collected in a month as opposed to what was sold. The sales dollars shown in Exhibit 13-2 are stated on an accrual basis and,

EXHIBIT 13-6

Fast-Food Funthings Overhead Budget

	January	February	March	Quarter
Production in units	195,000	144,000	86,000	425,000
Variable cost per unit	× $.084	× $.084	× $.084	× $.084
Total production OH cost	$16,380	$12,096	$7,224	$35,700
Sales in dollars	$400,000	$300,000	$180,000	$880,000
Variable commission rate	× 0.05	× 0.05	× 0.05	× 0.05
Variable commission cost	$20,000	$15,000	$9,000	$44,000
Fixed salesperson salary cost	2,000	2,000	2,000	6,000
Fixed administrative salary cost	9,000	9,000	9,000	27,000
Fixed depreciation expense	1,000	1,000	1,000	3,000
Total S&A cost	$32,000	$27,000	$21,000	$80,000
Total production OH cost	$16,380	$12,096	$7,224	$35,700
Total S&A cost	32,000	27,000	21,000	80,000
Total OH cost	$48,380	$39,096	$28,224	$115,700
Total OH cash cost (no depr.)	$47,380	$38,096	$27,224	$112,700

EXHIBIT 13-7

Fast-Food Funthings Capital Budget

	January	February	March	Quarter
Equipment acquisitions	$0	$300,000	$ 0	$300,000
Cash payments for plant assets	$0	$210,000	$90,000	$300,000

thus, need to be translated into cash information using an expected collection pattern. A collection pattern should be based on recent experiences with customers and, if necessary, can be adjusted for conditions that might change the current collection pattern. For example, changes that could improve current collection patterns include decreases in interest rates or more strict credit granting practices.

All Fast-Food Funthings customers buy on credit and receive no discounts for prompt payment. The company is very careful about granting customers credit and experiences no bad debt problems. Fast-Food Funthings' collection pattern is as follows: 30 percent of sales are collected in the month of sale, 60 percent of sales are collected in the month following the sale, and 10 percent of sales are collected in the second month following the sale. For example, Fast-Food Funthings expects to sell $400,000 in January on credit. Using the expected collection pattern, the company expects to collect cash of $120,000 (0.30 × $400,000) in January, $240,000 (0.60 × $400,000) in February, and $40,000 (0.10 × $400,000) in March.

Because cash collections are expected over a three-month period, there will be some collections in January and February from November and December 2003 sales. Using the sales budget, November and December 2003 sales information, and the collection pattern, management can estimate cash receipts from sales during the first three months of 2004. Assume that November and December sales were $84,000 and $76,000, respectively. Projected monthly first quarter collections are shown in Exhibit 13-8. Note that January and February collections for the remaining balances of November and December equals the $61,600 of Accounts Receivable shown in Exhibit 13-1's December 31, 2003, balance sheet. Additionally, 10 percent of February's sales ($30,000) and 70 percent of March's sales ($126,000), or a total of $156,000, remain in Accounts Receivable to be collected in the second quarter of the year.

The schedule of cash collections may also include provisions for discounts extended to customers for timely payments and provisions for uncollectible accounts receivable.

Schedule of Cash Payments for Purchases

The purchases information from Exhibit 13-3 can be translated into a schedule of cash payments using a cash payments pattern. Fast-Food Funthings buys all direct material on

EXHIBIT 13-8

Fast-Food Funthings Schedule of Cash Collections from Sales

	January	February	March	Quarter
Collection of Nov. sales				
($84,000 × 10%)	$ 8,400			$ 8,400
Collection of Dec. sales				
($76,000 × 60%)	45,600			45,600
($76,000 × 10%)		$ 7,600		7,600
Collection of Jan. sales				
($400,000 × 30%)	120,000			120,000
($400,000 × 60%)		240,000		240,000
($400,000 × 10%)			$ 40,000	40,000
Collection of Feb. sales				
($300,000 × 30%)		90,000		90,000
($300,000 × 60%)			180,000	180,000
Collection of March sales				
($180,000 × 30%)			54,000	54,000
Total collections	$174,000	$337,600	$274,000	$785,600

credit and pays for 20 percent of each month's purchases in the month of purchase and the remainder in the month after purchase. The company receives no cash discounts for prompt payment. Exhibit 13-9 provides the schedule of cash payments for purchases for the first quarter 2004. Note that the payment in January for the remaining balance of December purchases (assumed $90,000) equals the Accounts Payable shown in Exhibit 13-1's December 31, 2003, balance sheet. Additionally, 80 percent of March's purchases ($38,832) remain in Accounts Payable to be collected in the second quarter of the year.

Comprehensive Cash Budget

Using the information shown in Exhibits 13-5 through 13-9, Fast-Food Funthings' cash budget (Exhibit 13-10) can be prepared. This company, like most, maintains a management-specified minimum cash balance in its cash account, which provides a "cushion" to compensate for uncertainty. The budgeting process provides only estimates; actual events of the budget period are not likely to be the same as those estimated. At the end of any monthly period, if Fast-Food Funthings does not have enough cash to meet its minimum balance (assumed to be $5,000), the company will have to borrow the necessary funds.

EXHIBIT 13-9

Fast-Food Funthings Schedule of Cash Payments for Purchases

	January	February	March	Quarter
Payment for Dec. purchases				
($90,000 × 80%)	$ 72,000			$ 72,000
Payment for Jan. purchases				
($112,410 × 20%)	22,482			22,482
($112,410 × 80%)		$ 89,928		89,928
Payment for Feb. purchases				
($81,180 × 20%)		16,236		16,236
($81,180 × 80%)			$ 64,944	64,944
Payment for March purchases				
($48,540 × 20%)			9,708	9,708
Total payments	$ 94,482	$106,164	$ 74,652	$275,298

EXHIBIT 13-10

Fast-Food Funthings Cash Budget

	January	February	March	Quarter
Beginning cash balance	$ 5,000	$ 5,588	$ 5,108	$ 5,000
Cash collections (Exh. 13-8)	174,000	337,600	274,000	785,600
Cash available	$179,000	$343,188	$279,108	$790,600
Cash paid for				
DL (Exh. 13-5)	(17,550)	(12,960)	(7,740)	(38,250)
OH (Exh. 13-6)	(47,380)	(38,096)	(27,224)	(112,700)
PA (Exh. 13-7)	(0)	(210,000)	(90,000)	(300,000)
Purchases (Exh. 13-9)	(94,482)	(106,164)	(74,652)	(275,298)
Balance	$ 19,588	$ (24,032)	$ 79,492	$ 64,352
Borrow (repay)		15,000	(15,000)	0
Sell (acquire) investments	(14,000)	14,000	(59,000)	(59,000)
Interest received (paid)	0	140*	(150)**	(10)
Remainder (minimum $5,000)	$ 5,588	$ 5,108	$ 5,342	$ 5,342

*Interest on investment for one month ($14,000 ˘ 0.01 = $140)

**Interest on borrowing for one month ($15,000 ˘ 0.01 = $150)

Alternatively, if more cash is available than the minimum balance, the company will invest the excess funds so as to earn a reasonable rate of return. For simplicity, it is assumed that any borrowings or investments are made in end-of-month, $1,000 increments. Interest on company borrowing or investments is at a simple annual rate of 12 percent or one percent per month. The interest charged or paid is subtracted from or added to the company's cash account at month end.

Exhibit 13-10 indicates that, in January, Fast-Food Funthings has $19,588 excess cash available over payments. But this amount does not consider the $5,000 minimum balance. Thus, the company can invest $14,000 until the need for that cash arises. In February, Fast-Food Funthings does not have enough funds to meet its obligations. The company will cash in its $14,000 investment and obtain the interest on that amount. However, there still are not enough funds available to make all the necessary payments and retain a $5,000 minimum cash balance. The company then borrows $15,000 on a short-term basis. In March, there is enough excess cash available to pay back the amount borrowed in February and the related interest as well as make a $59,000 cash investment. Companies may also issue stock or sell bonds to raise funds if they are needed on a long-term basis.

Budgeted Financial Statements

The last component of the master budget is the preparation of pro forma financial statements for the period. These statements indicate the financial results that will occur if all budget estimates and assumptions actually happen. If the projected results are not acceptable, management can make necessary changes prior to the start of the budget period. For instance, if pro forma net income is unacceptable, management may (if possible) raise product selling prices or find ways to decrease costs.

Cost of Goods Manufactured Schedule

In a manufacturing company, this schedule must be prepared before Cost of Goods Sold can be determined for the income statement. Using information from previous budgets, the Fast-Food Funthings' budgeted cost of goods manufactured schedule is shown in Exhibit 13-11. Note: The only reason that cost of goods manufactured equals the period's total costs to be accounted for is that, for this example, it was assumed that no beginning or ending work in process inventories existed. Had work in process inventory existed, the computations would be more complex and are beyond the scope of this text.

Income Statement

Exhibit 13-12 presents the pro forma income statement for Fast-Food Funthings for the first quarter of 2004.

Balance Sheet

After completing the income statement, a pro forma balance sheet for March 31, 2004, can be prepared (Exhibit 13-13).

Statement of Cash Flows

The income statement, balance sheet, and cash budget information are used to prepare a Statement of Cash Flows (SCF). This statement (Exhibit 13-14) arranges cash flows into three areas of activity (operating, investing, and financing). On a long-run basis, the majority of a company's cash flows should be provided from its operating activities.

EXHIBIT 13-11

Pro Forma Schedule of Cost of Goods Manufactured

Fast-Food Funthings
Pro Forma Schedule of Cost of Goods Manufactured
For the Quarter Ending March 31, 2004

Beginning work in process inventory (1/1/04)		$ 0
Direct material used:		
Beginning balance of DM (Exh. 13-1)	$ 17,550	
+ Purchases (Exh. 13-4)	242,130	
– Ending balance of DM (Note A)	(4,680)	
= DM used		255,000
Direct labor (Exh. 13-5)		38,250
Production overhead (Exh. 13-6)		35,700
Total costs to be accounted for		$328,950
Ending work in process inventory		(0)
Cost of goods manufactured (Note B)		$328,950

Note A:

Ending balance of direct material in units (Exh. 13-4)	7,800
Number of ounces needed for one unit	× 3
Total number of ounces	23,400
Cost per ounce	× $0.20
Ending balance of direct material in dollars	$ 4,680

Note B:

CGM ÷ Number of units manufactured = Cost per unit
$328,950 ÷ 425,000 = $0.774 per unit

EXHIBIT 13-12

Pro Forma Income Statement

Fast-Food Funthings
Pro Forma Income Statement
For the Quarter Ending March 31, 2004

Sales (Exh. 13-2)		$ 880,000
Cost of goods sold		
Beginning finished goods inventory (Exh. 13-1)	$ 15,000	
Cost of goods manufactured	328,950	
Ending finished goods inventory (Note A)	(3,870)	(340,080)
Gross margin		$ 539,920
Expenses		
Selling and administrative expenses (Exh. 13-6)	$ 80,000	
Interest expense (net) (Exh. 13-10)	10	(80,010)
Income before income taxes		$ 459,910
Income taxes (assumed rate of 30%)		(137,973)
Net income		$ 321,937

Note A:

Units in ending FG (Exh. 13-3) × Cost per unit (Exh. 13-11; Note B)
5,000 × $0.774 = $3,870

EXHIBIT 13-13
Pro Forma Balance Sheet

Fast-Food Funthings
Pro Forma Balance Sheet
March 31, 2004

ASSETS		
Cash (Exh. 13-10)		$ 5,342
Accounts Receivable (10% x $300,000) + (70% × $180,000)		156,000
Inventories		
Direct Material (Exh. 13-4*)	$ 4,680	
Finished Goods (Exh. 13-11)	3,870	8,550
Investment (Exh. 13-10)		59,000
Property, Plant & Equipment (Exh. 13-1 and 13-7)	$ 400,000	
Less Accumulated Depreciation (Exh. 13-1 and 13-6)	(33,000)	367,000
Total Assets		$ 595,892
LIABILITIES AND STOCKHOLDERS' EQUITY		
Accounts Payable (80% × $48,540)		$ 38,832
Taxes Payable (Exh. 13-12)		137,973
Common Stock (Exh. 13-1)	$ 80,000	
Retained Earnings (Exh. 13-1 and 13-12)**	339,087	419,087
Total Liabilities and Stockholders' Equity		$ 595,892

*This amount represents 23,400 ounces of plastic (enough to produce 7,800 units) at a cost per ounce of $0.20.

**Ending RE = Beginning RE + Net Income = $17,150 + $321,937 = $339,087.

EXHIBIT 13-14
Pro Forma Statement of Cash Flows

Fast-Food Funthings
Pro Forma Statement of Cash Flows
For the Quarter Ending March 31, 2004

Operating Activities:		
Net income		$ 321,937
+ Depreciation (Exh. 13-6)		3,000
– Increase in Accounts Receivable ($61,600 – $156,000)		(94,400)
+ Decrease in DM Inventory ($17,550 – $4,680)		12,870
+ Decrease in FG Inventory ($15,000 – $3,870)		11,130
– Decrease in Accounts Payable ($72,000 - $38,832)		(33,168)
+ Increase in Taxes Payable ($0 – $137,973)		137,973
Net cash inflow from operations		$ 359,342
Investing Activities:		
Purchase of plant assets (Exh. 13-7)	$(300,000)	
Short-term cash investment (Exh. 13-10)	(59,000)	
Net cash outflow from investing		(359,000)
Financing Activities:		
Issuance of short-term note (Exh. 13-10)	$ 15,000	
Repayment of short-term note (Exh. 13-10)	(15,000)	
Net cash flow from financing		0
Net increase in cash		$ 342
Beginning cash balance (Exh. 13-1)		5,000
Ending cash balance (Exh. 13-13)		$ 5,342

THE ROLLING BUDGET

Many companies are finding that a static budget has become inappropriate to use in the dynamic business environment. These companies have instituted rolling (or continuous) budgets into their planning process. In general, a **rolling budget** is maintained on a continual 12-month cycle: as one month (or quarter) passes, another month (or quarter) is added to the budget. This process allows the company to continually have a 12-month planning cycle and budgeting becomes an on-going process rather than something that is performed at year-end.

A rolling budget allows a company to adjust its expectations in response to changes in the business environment. Companies often find that their budgets become out-of-date soon after they have been prepared because of new business opportunities. Also, managers often become complacent or frustrated with the budget, depending on whether they have met their budget figures or feel that the budgeted figures will be impossible to obtain in the "remaining" budget period. The rolling budget eliminates the artificial "cut-off" or end of the budget period and allows people to be more focused on goal achievement rather than budget achievement.

STANDARD COSTS

After the budget is adopted, managers must begin exercising control over operations. This phase includes making budget-to-actual comparisons, investigating the causes of differences between the budget and actual figures, determining and taking corrective action in the event of poor performance, and providing feedback to individuals working under the budget figures.

Many of the computations in a budget are based on standard costs, quantities, and times. For example, the estimated quantity of material per unit used in the production budget is a standard. A **standard** is simply a norm or average. Standards are developed for both quantities and costs. A **standard cost** is the budgeted cost to make one unit of product (or perform one unit of service). Standards are developed from historical information and adapted for changed conditions, and internal and external benchmarks.

At the end of the period, standard and actual costs are compared and variances are calculated to indicate how well costs and quantities were controlled during the period. **Variance analysis** is the process of determining the standard-to-actual differences and assessing whether those differences are favorable or unfavorable. Variances are generally calculated for all components of product cost: material, labor, and overhead. The following discussion focuses on material and labor variances; the overhead variances reflect the underapplied or overapplied amounts discussed in Chapter 12.

Material Variances

Material variances indicate how close actual material usage and cost were to expected (standard) material usage and cost. To calculate material variances, three costs are needed.

1. The actual cost of material equals the actual price (AP) paid per unit of material times the actual quantity (AQ) of material used.
2. The standard cost of the actual quantity of material equals the standard price (SP) per unit of material times the actual quantity of material used.
3. The standard cost of material equals the standard price per unit of material times the standard quantity (SQ) of material needed for the production activity that actually took place.

These costs are used to compute the three common material variances illustrated in Exhibit 13-15: material price variance, material quantity variance, and total material variance.

EXHIBIT 13-15

Material Variance Calculations

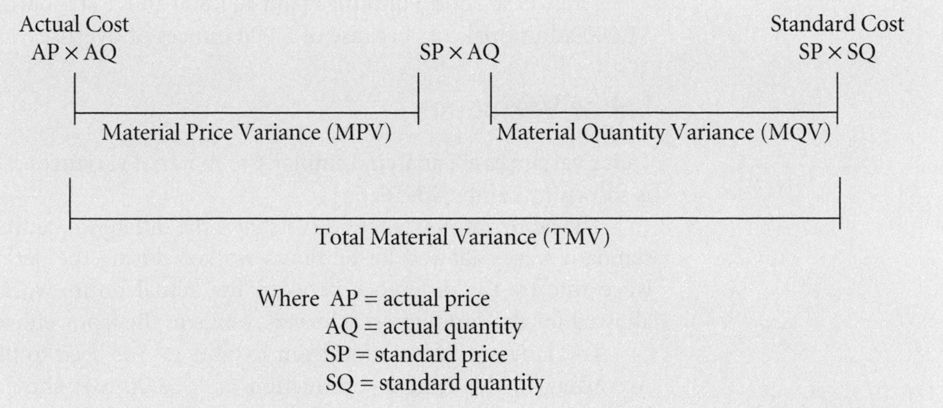

The **material price variance** (MPV) indicates the cost difference that arose because the amount paid for material was below or above the standard price. The MPV is the difference between standard price at actual quantity (SP × AQ) and actual cost at actual quantity (AP × AQ). If the latter is larger, the variance is said to be unfavorable because the materials cost more than expected. If cost is less, the variance is favorable.

The **material quantity variance** (MQV) indicates the cost difference that arose because the actual quantity used was below or above the standard quantity allowed for the actual output. The MQV is calculated as the difference between standard cost at actual quantity (SP × AQ) and standard cost at standard quantity (SP × SQ). If the standard cost at actual quantity is larger than standard cost, the variance is said to be unfavorable because more material was needed than was expected. If less material was needed, the variance is favorable.

The **total material variance** (TMV) is the difference between actual cost and standard cost. If actual is less, the TMV is favorable; if actual is more, the TMV is unfavorable. The TMV can also be calculated as the sum of the material price and quantity variances.

Fast-Food Funthings information is used to illustrate these computations. Exhibit 13-2 indicates that production for January needs to be 195,000 units. Text information also states that each toy requires three ounces of plastic and each ounce costs $0.20. In January 2004, the company produces 195,000 toys, buys and uses 590,000 ounces of plastic (ignoring the purchase requirements given in 13-3), and pays $129,800 (or $0.22 per ounce) for the plastic. The standard cost of January's production is as follows: 195,000 toys × 3 ounces per toy × $0.20 per ounce = $117,000. The total material variance is $12,800 ($129,800 – $117,000). Because the actual cost is greater than the standard cost, the variance is unfavorable.

Two situations combined to cause the $12,800 unfavorable material variance. First, the company paid $0.02 per ounce more than standard for the plastic. Second, the company used more plastic than was required to produce the toys. The **standard quantity allowed** (SQA) translates the actual output of the period (195,000 toys) into the standard quantity of input that should have been needed to achieve that output. The SQA is 195,000 toys times three ounces of plastic or 585,000 ounces needed. Inserting the numbers into the model provides the following:

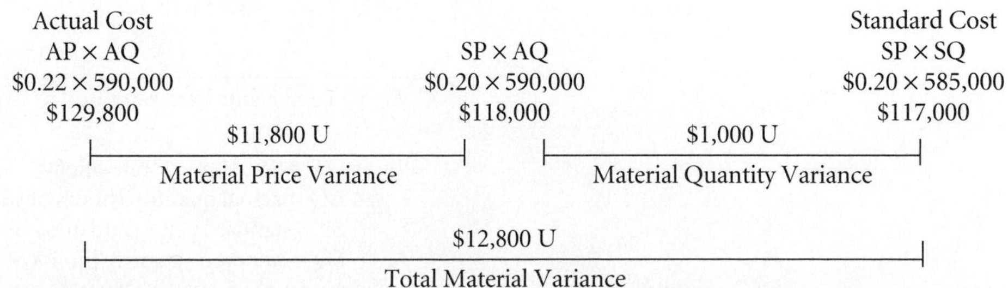

Thus, Fast-Food Funthings paid $11,800 above standard for the plastic and incurred $1,000 additional cost because of 5,000 ounces of overuse.

Labor Variances

Labor variances are analyzed similarly to material variances. The model for labor variances is shown in Exhibit 13-16.

The **labor rate variance** (LRV) shows the difference between actual wages paid and the standard wages allowed for all hours worked during the period. Multiplying the standard wage rate by the difference between the actual hours worked and the standard hours allowed for the production achieved results in the labor efficiency variance (LEV).

The January information from Exhibit 13-5 is used to illustrate these computations. According to this exhibit, production of 195,000 toys should require 1,950 direct labor hours; each worker is paid $9 per hour. Thus, the total standard cost for the production of 195,000 toys is $17,550. Assume that in January, 1,930 direct labor hours were worked and, because of contract renegotiations, hourly pay was raised to $9.10. Inserting these amounts into the model provides the following variance computations:

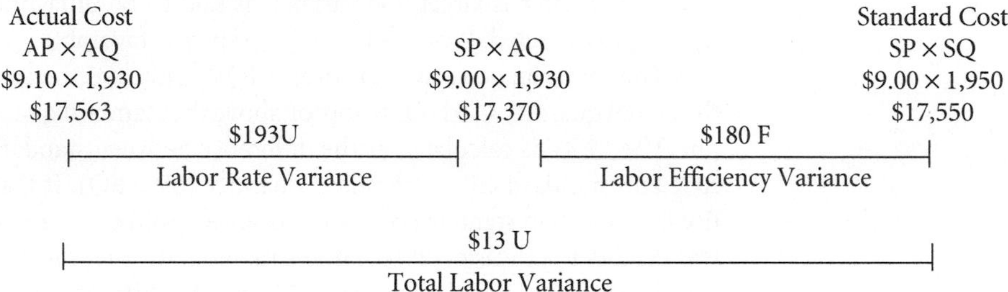

These calculations indicate that the company incurred an additional $193 above what was budgeted in direct labor cost for January because of the difference between the standard and actual pay rates. However, the direct labor workers were very efficient in the production process in January because they produced the toys in 20 hours less than what was expected, thereby saving the company $180 of budgeted costs. The total labor variance is only $13 unfavorable because the favorable and unfavorable variances were almost equal.

Visual Recap 13.2 depicts the relationship between the material and labor subvariances.

Understanding Variances

It is important to note that an extremely large favorable variance is not necessarily a good variance. Such a variance could mean an error was made when the standard was set or that a

EXHIBIT 13-16
Labor Variance Calculations

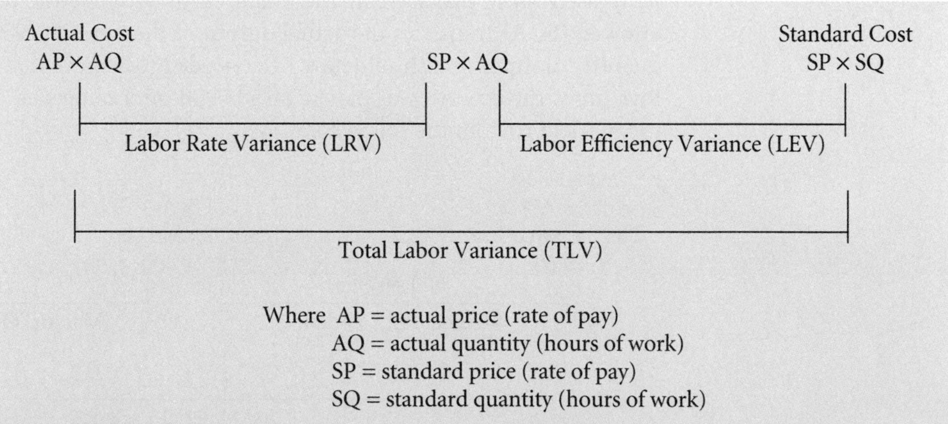

related, offsetting unfavorable variance exists. For example, if low-quality material is purchased, a favorable price variance may result, but additional material may need to be used to overcome defective production. Additionally, an unfavorable labor efficiency variance could result because it took longer to complete a job because many defective units were produced using the inferior materials. Another common "linked" variance situation begins with labor rather than material: the use of less skilled, lower-paid workers will result in a favorable rate variance, but may cause excessive material usage. Managers must constantly be aware that relationships between and among variances exist and, thus, should not analyze variances in isolation.

In implementing control procedures, managers must recognize that their time is a scarce resource, so distinctions must be made between situations to ignore and those to investigate. The establishment of upper and lower limits of acceptable deviations often guides this distinction from standard. These tolerance limits for deviations allow managers to use **management by exception.** This technique lets managers to take no action if a variance is small and within an acceptable range. However, if a variance is large, the manager responsible for the cost should determine why the variance occurred. Finding the cause(s) and taking corrective action (if possible or recommended) will allow future operations to adhere more closely to established standards.

VISUAL RECAP 13.2

Visualizing Variance Calculations

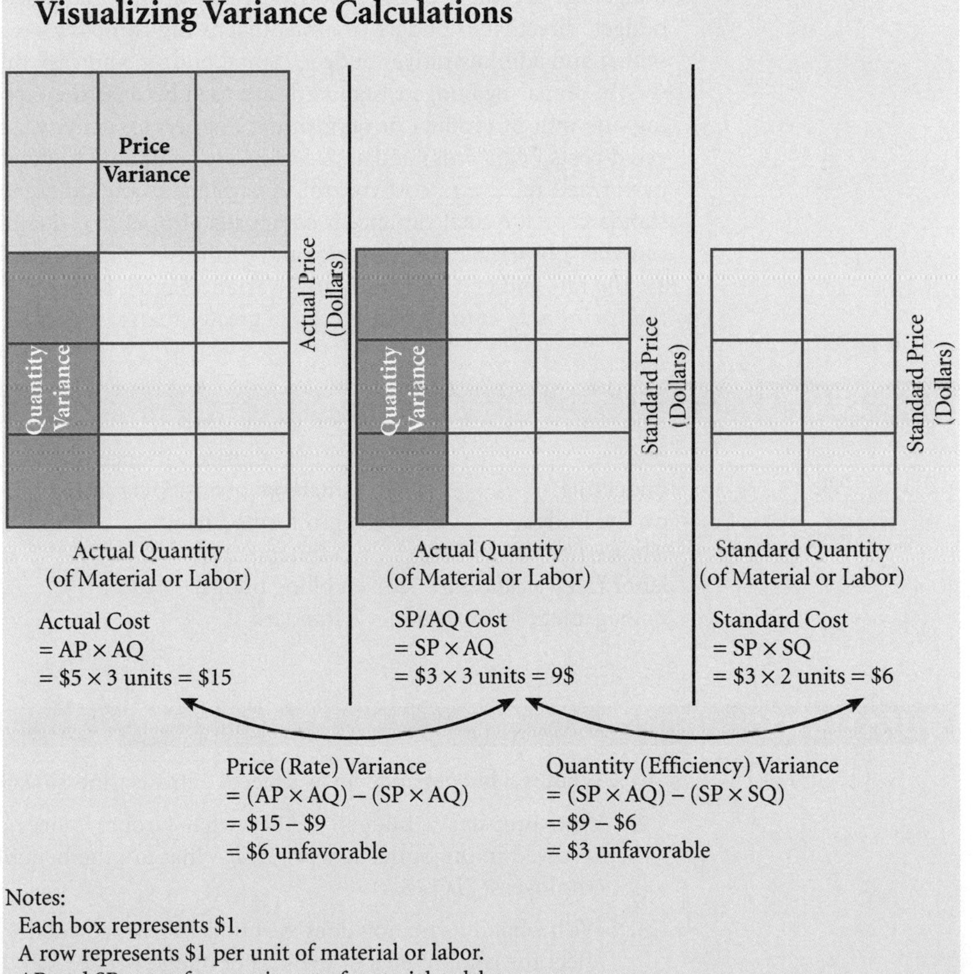

Notes:
Each box represents $1.
A row represents $1 per unit of material or labor.
AP and SP can refer to unit cost of material or labor.
AQ and SQ can refer to unit quantity of material or labor.

Variances large enough to fall outside the management by exception acceptability ranges often indicate trouble. However, calculating a variance does not reveal the variance cause or the person or group responsible. To determine variance causes, managers must investigate significant variances through observation, inspection, and inquiry. Such investigations will involve the time and effort of operating and accounting personnel. Operating personnel should try to spot variances as they occur and record the reasons for the variances to the extent that they are discernable. For example, operating personnel could readily detect and report causes such as machine downtime or material spoilage.

SUMMARY

Budgeting refers to the monetary quantification of a company's plans. Managers may either impose budgets on subordinates or allow subordinate managers to participate in the budgeting process. Such participation is generally useful because organizational departments interact with each other. Thus, one department's budget may be the basis of, or have an effect on, other departmental budgets.

A master budget is a complete set of budgetary projections that begins with a sales budget and ends with pro forma financial statements. The master budget is generally specified by months and quarters within the annual period. The primary budgets in a master budget are the sales budget, production budget (if a manufacturing company), purchases budget, direct labor budget (if a manufacturing company), overhead (production and/or selling and administrative) budget, capital budget, and cash budget.

In preparing budgets, standards are used because they represent the norms for making one unit of product or performing one service activity. At the end of a period, budgeted costs (standards) and actual costs are compared to determine how well a company performed relative to cost control. A variance is any difference between an actual and a standard cost. A total variance is composed of price and quantity subvariances. For material, the subvariances are the price and quantity variances. For labor, the two subvariances are the rate and efficiency variances. Variances must be designated as favorable (actual less than standard) or unfavorable (actual greater than standard).

KEY TERMS

budget
budgeting
capital budget
labor efficiency variance
labor rate variance
management by exception
material price variance
material quantity variance
pro forma financial statement
rolling budget
standard
standard cost
standard quantity allowed
variance
variance analysis

QUESTIONS

1. What is a budget and why is it needed in a business? *(LO 13.1)*
2. Who prepares a budget? Under what circumstances are lower-level employees involved in the budgetary process? What are the benefits of involving lower-level employees? *(LO 13.2)*
3. With what information does the budgeting process start? How does this information affect the components of the master budget? *(LO 13.2)*
4. How are production and purchases budgets similar and how do they differ? What type of organizations will use each of these budgets? *(LO 13.2)*

5. One of the younger workers in your production operations asks you, "Why do we have ending inventory at the end of the month? Why not just produce the exact quantity on the sales budget?" How do you respond to these questions?

6. Explain the purpose of adding desired ending inventory and subtracting beginning inventory to the production budget. How do the desired ending inventory and beginning inventory amounts on a production budget differ from the desired ending inventory and beginning inventory amounts on a purchases budget? *(LO 13.2)*

7. Why do production overhead and selling and administrative expenses need to be separated into their variable and fixed components for budgeting purposes? Why would production overhead costs need to be distinguished from selling and administrative expenses in the budgeting process? *(LO 13.2)*

8. Compare an organization's cash budget to your checking account. Include in your comparison a short discussion of minimum cash balances. What actions can an organization take if a cash shortage is expected to develop? What actions can you take if a cash shortage is expected to develop? What causes any differences in these actions? *(LO 13.1)*

9. Why does the master budget conclude with a presentation of pro forma financial statements? Will the amounts shown on pro forma financial statements be equal to the amounts shown on actual financial statements at the end of the budget period? Why or why not? *(LO 13.2)*

10. What are the benefits of a rolling budget? Will the use of a rolling budget create more or less work for managers? Explain the rationale for your answer. *(LO 13.3)*

11. Why does a company use standard costs? How would standard costs be developed? *(LO 13.4)*

12. What is the difference between a material price variance and a material quantity variance? Can one occur without the other? What are some causes of material price and quantity variances? *(LO 13.5)*

13. You are the manager of a midsize restaurant. In making budget-to-actual comparisons this month, you find that there is a large favorable material price variance and a large unfavorable material quantity variance. Are you pleased with the individual who purchases your food items and disappointed with the chef? Explain. *(LO 13.5)*

14. List at least three reasons why a company might experience (1) a labor rate variance and (2) a labor efficiency variance. Will your explanations result in favorable or unfavorable variances? Explain. *(LO 13.5)*

15. What is management by exception? Why is this process useful? *(LO 13.5)*

EXERCISES

16. **True and False** *(All LOs)*

Following are a series of statements regarding topics discussed in this chapter.

Required:

Indicate whether each statement is true (T) or false (F).

(1) A flexible budget is prepared one month or one quarter at a time.

(2) The cash payments budget is used only for cash disbursements related to purchases of raw material.

(3) The production budget is used to determine how much raw material is needed to manufacture the units that will be sold in a month.

(4) A favorable total material variance is a positive indication that materials are being used efficiently.

(5) A labor efficiency variance is the difference between (actual labor cost multiplied by actual labor quantity) and (actual labor cost multiplied by standard labor quantity).

(6) If a company has no plans to purchase new equipment in the next year, the company should still prepare a capital budget.

(7) The direct labor budget should include the cost of individuals who work in the administrative offices directly for upper-level management.

(8) A budget is the quantitative representation of a company's plans for the future.

(9) The order in which budgets are prepared is based on reverse chronological order.

(10) A company only produces one sales budget, production budget, and purchase budget for a product regardless of the number of units sold, units produced, or diferent raw materials required.

17. **Sales Budget** *(LO 13.2)*

Clubs, Inc. expects to sell one million cases of flexible straws in 2004 for $8 per case. Typically, Clubs has the following selling pattern: 7 percent of annual sales are made in January, February, May, and October; 11 percent in March and June; 12 percent in April and July; 8 percent in August and December, and five percent in September and November.

Required:

Prepare the sales budget for Clubs, Inc. for 2004. Include both a quarterly and yearly total.

18. **Production Budget** *(LO 13.2)*

The production budget for Denton Manufacturers for the second quarter of 2004 follows.

	April	May	June	Quarter
Sales in units	12,000	(a)	15,000	40,000
Desired ending inventory	(b)	2,250	2,100	(c)
Total needed	13,950	15,250	17,100	42,100
Beginning inventory	1,875	1,950	(d)	(e)
Budgeted units to produce	(f)	(g)	(h)	(i)

Required:

(1) Find the missing numbers represented by the letters (a) through (i).

(2) What was the budgeted amount of beginning inventory in March?

(3) What is the budgeted amount of sales in July?

19. **Purchases Budget** *(LO 13.2)*

Denton Manufacturers, from Exercise 18, produces candles that contain four raw materials: wax, dye, scented oil, and a wick. Each candle uses eight ounces of wax and one ounce of dye, which Denton purchases for $0.15 and $0.08 per ounce, respectively. Denton ends each month with enough wax to manufacture 10 percent of the following month's production level; desired ending inventory for dye is 25 percent of the following month's production level. Production for July is 13,925 units.

Required:

Prepare Denton's purchases budgets for wax and dye for each month of the second quarter and the total for the second quarter of 2004.

20. **Direct Labor Budget** *(LO 13.2)*

Denton Manufacturers, from Exercises 18 and 19, estimates that an employee can make 15 candles per hour. Denton's employees are paid $7 per hour.

Required:

Prepare Denton's direct labor budget for each month of the second quarter and the total for the second quarter of 2004.

21. **Cash Collections Budget** *(LO 13.2)*

Clubs, Inc. (from Exercise 17) makes 20 percent of sales for cash and the rest on credit. Of those sales made on credit 70 percent are collected during the month of sale, 20 percent are collected during the following month, and the remaining 10 percent are collected two month after the sale.

Required:

Prepare Clubs, Inc.'s cash collections budget for the second quarter of 2004.

22. **Missing Information for Materials** *(LO 13.4 & 13.5)*

Standard and actual material information is given below for four companies

	Company A	Company B	Company C	Company D
Units produced	?	5,000	7,200	?
Standard quantity/unit	3 lbs.	12 ounces	? pts.	4 units
Standard quantity allowed	? lbs.	? lbs.	1,800 gals.	41,200 units
Standard cost/quantity	$6 per lb.	$12 lb.	$9 gal.	$? unit
Actual quantity used	12,025 lbs.	3,750 lbs.	?	41,210 units
Actual material cost	$70,000	?	$15,000	$125,000
Material price variance	?	$4,000 U	?	?
Material quantity variance	$150 U	?	$225 F	$30 U

Required:

For each company, calculate the missing figures. Assume that the quantity of material purchased is the same as the quantity of material used in each case.

23. **Missing Information for Labor** *(LO 13.4 & 13.5)*

Standard and actual labor information is given below for four companies

	Company A	Company B	Company C	Company D
Units produced	1,000	500	?	1,600
Standard hours per unit	2	?	3.5	1.7
Standard hours allowed	?	?	7,350	?
Standard rate per hour	$9	?	$7.10	$8.50
Actual hours worked	1,850	2,060	?	?
Actual labor cost	?	$14,500	$50,000	$23,900
Labor rate variance	$50U	$286U	$1,049F	?
Labor efficiency variance	?	$414U	?	$170F

Required:

For each company, calculate the missing figures.

PROBLEMS

24. **Production Budget** *(LO 13.2)*

Projected unit sales for Astor Corp. for the last half of 2004 are:

July	15,000	October	18,000
August	30,000	November	27,000
September	24,000	December	28,600

Finished goods inventory on June 30, 2004 is 3,700 units. The company tries to keep an ending inventory of 25 percent of the following month's expected sales.

Required:

Prepare a production budget for the third quarter 2004.

25. **Production and Purchases Budgets** *(LO 13.2)*

Marconi Company has projected the following sales of Product #431 for the first four months of 2004: January, 4,000 units; February, 3,800 units; March, 5,600 units; and April, 2,900 units. Each unit of product requires two-and-a-half gallons of Material X and three pounds of Material Y. Expected beginning of the year inventories for all items follow.

Product #431	840 units
Material X	2,900 gallons
Material Y	3,600 pounds

Marconi desires an ending inventory for Product #431 of 20 percent of the following month's sales and ending inventories for components X and Y of 30 percent of that month's production quantity needs. Material X costs $5.90 per gallon and Material Y costs $3.75 per pound.

Required:

(1) Prepare a production budget for Product #431.

(2) Prepare purchases budgets for Materials X and Y.

26. **Sales, Production, Purchases, and Direct Labor Budgets** *(LO 13.2)*

Delaune's Cookery makes and sells mixers and bread-makers. In November 2003, Delaune's Cookery began the budgetary process. Project sales for 2004 are 30,000 mixers at $25 each and 20,000 bread-makers at $60 each. Management gathered the following data to begin the 2004 budget process:

(a) The following purchased components are needed to produce one unit of product:

Component	Mixer	Bread-maker
Plastic housing	1-#531B @ $4	1-#648C @ $12
Motor	1-#KMU @ $7.50	1-#KBU @ $8.90
Beaters	2-#BU6 @ $1.10	4-#BU6 @ $1.10

All other materials are considered indirect materials and part of overhead.

(b) Expected and desired inventories are as follows:

	Expected Ending Inventory December 31, 2003	Desired Ending Inventory December 31, 2004
Mixers	1,500	1,000
Bread-makers	3,000	1,400
#531B plastic housings	250	350
#648C plastic housings	310	400
#KMU motors	6,000	1,200
#KBU motors	690	600
#BU6 beaters	2,500	2,000

(c) Projected direct labor requirements for 2004 and rates are as follows:

Product	Class A labor ($7/hour)	Class B labor ($9/hour)
Mixer	1.0 hour per unit	1.0 hour per unit
Bread-maker	1.4 hours per unit	2.5 hours per unit

Required:

(1) Prepare sales budget (in dollars) for 2004.

(2) Prepare a production budget (in units) for 2004.

(3) Prepare a components purchases budget (in units and dollars) for 2004.

(4) Prepare a direct labor budget (by class in hours and dollars) for 2004.

(5) What types of items would be included in production overhead for this company?

(6) The company is thinking of manufacturing its plastic housings rather than buying them from suppliers. What types of costs would such insourcing create? What types of costs would such insourcing eliminate? How would you suggest that company management assess such a decision?

27. **Cash Collections** *(LO 13.2)*

Calista Gardens is developing its monthly cash budgets for the first quarter of 2004. The company has been in business since April 2003 and has experienced the following approximate cash flows: sales each month are 30 percent cash and 70 percent credit. Of the credit sales, 50 percent are paid for in the first month after the sale, 40 percent in the second month after sale, and 10 percent in the third month after sale. The company has almost no bad debts and, thus, these can be ignored. Total sales for the last three months of 2003 and expected total sales for the first three months of 2004 are as follows:

October	$36,000	January	$18,900
November	$24,000	February	$27,000
December	$52,000	March	$22,000

Required:

(1) Prepare a monthly schedule of cash collections for Calista Gardens for the first quarter of 2004.

(2) Calculate the expected Accounts Receivable balance at March 31, 2004.

(3) In early February 2004, the company realized that cash inflows from sales and collections for the previous month were only $19,450, which was significantly less than the budgeted amount. What explanation could be offered for this situation? What information did Calista Gardens need to prepare its cash budget that it did not have?

28. **Cash Budget** *(LO 13.2)*

The Accounts Receivable balance at January 1, 2004, for Clive's Computer Repairs was $170,700. Of that balance, $144,000 represents remaining Accounts Receivable from December billings. The normal collection pattern for the firm is 40 percent of billings in the month of service, 45 percent in the month after service, and 14 percent in the second month following service. The remaining one percent of billings is uncollectible. January billings are expected to be $210,000.

Required:

(1) What were November billings for the company?

(2) What amount of December billings is expected to be uncollectible?

(3) What are projected January 2004 cash collections for the company?

(4) How can a company decrease the amount of uncollectible accounts it has? How, if at all, will these techniques impact the company's total dollars of revenue?

29. **Pro Forma Income Statement** *(LO 13.2)*

The income statement for the year ended December 31, 2003, for Chico Co. follows:

Sales (70,000 × $15)		$1,050,000
Cost of goods sold:		
Direct material	$280,000	
Direct labor	175,000	
Overhead	61,250	(516,250)
Gross profit		$ 533,750
Expenses		
Selling	$ 60,000	
Administrative	75,000	(135,000)
Income before taxes		$ 398,750
Income taxes		159,500
Net income		$ 239,250

Sales volume in 2004 is expected to increase by 15 percent because of a 5 percent decrease in selling price. Material costs are expected to increase 7 percent, but labor costs are expected to decrease by 10 percent due to increased automation at the company. Overhead is applied to production based on a percentage of direct labor costs; this percentage will increase by 5 percent because of the newly installed automated equipment. Seventy percent of the selling expenses are variable; the remainder is fixed. All administrative costs are fixed and are expected to increase by 20 percent in 2004.

Required:

(1) Prepare a pro forma income statement for the year ended December 31, 2004.

(2) If management wanted net income to increase to $261,000 in 2004, what would selling price per unit (rounded to the nearest cent) have to be at the new sales volume? Prepare a pro forma income statement to prove your answer.

30. **Comprehensive Master Budget** *(LO 13.2)*

Crystal Corp. produces foam rubber #1 hands to wave at athletic events. The company has asked you to prepare its 2004 master budget and has given you the following information.

(a) Following is the company's estimated December 31, 2004 balance sheet.

Crystal Corp.
Balance Sheet
December 31, 2004

Assets			**Liabilities & Equity**		
CURRENT ASSETS			LIABILITIES		
Cash		$ 10,200	Notes Payable	$ 25,000	
Accounts Receivable		24,300	Accounts Payable	4,200	
Raw Material Inventory		750	Dividends Payable	25,000	
Finished Goods Inventory		1,460	*Total Liabilities*		$ 54,200
Total Current Assets		$ 36,710	**Stockholders' Equity**		
Property & Equipment			Common Stock	$230,000	
Equipment	$425,000		Paid-in Capital	20,000	
Accumulated Depreciation	(90,000)	335,000	Retained Earnings	67,510	317,510
Total Assets		$371,710	*Total Liabilities and SE*		$371,710

(b) The selling price per "hand" is $12. Estimated sales of foam hands follow.

January 2004	8,000
February 2004	10,000
March 2004	15,000
April 2004	12,000
May 2004	11,000

(c) Seventy percent of sales are for cash. Of the remaining sales on credit, 25 percent is collected in the month of sale and the remainder is collected in the month after the sale. Crystal Corp. expects no bad debts.

(d) Each foam hand has the following direct material and direct labor standard quantities and costs:

Foam	$1.25 per sheet
1/10 hour of direct labor	$6.00 per hour

(e) Variable overhead is applied to production at the rate of $12 per machine-hour. It takes five minutes of machine time to make one foam hand. All variable overhead costs are paid in cash. Total annual fixed overhead of $360,000 is applied to production based on an expected annual capacity of 450,000 "hands". Fixed overhead is incurred evenly throughout the year and is paid in cash, except for $48,000 of depreciation.

(f) All work in process is completed during the period.

(g) Accounts Payable is only for raw material purchases. Sixty percent of purchases (rounded to the nearest dollar) are paid in the month of purchase and the remainder are paid in the next month.

(h) The dividend payable will be paid in February 2004.

(i) A new piece of equipment costing $12,000 will be purchased on February 1, 2004. Eighty percent of the cost will be paid in February and 20 percent in March. The equipment will have no salvage value and has a useful life of three years. The equipment will not be put into use, and thus not be depreciated, until April 2004.

(j) The note payable has a nine percent interest rate and interest is paid at the end of each month.

(k) Crystal Corp.'s management has set a minimum cash balance of $10,000. Investments and borrowings are made in even $1,000 amounts at the end of the month. Investments will earn one-half percent per month, deposited to the company's checking account at the end of each month.

(l) The ending inventories of raw material and finished goods should be, respectively, five percent and ten percent of the next month's needs. This situation is not true at the end of 2003, due to sales and production miscalculation.

(m) Selling and administrative costs per month are as follows: salaries, $14,000; rent, $10,000; and utilities, $1,800. These costs are paid in cash as they are incurred.

Required:

(1) What is the standard cost per foam hand? How many foam hands are in the beginning Finished Goods Inventory?

(2) How many sheets of foam are in the beginning Raw Material Inventory?

(3) Prepare a master budget for each month of the first quarter of 2004 and pro forma financial statements for the first quarter of 2004.

31. **Direct Material Variances** *(LO 13.4 & 13.5)*

Dragon Corp. makes sheer wrap-around bathing suit cover-ups. During April 2002, the company purchased and used 3,780 yards of material at $7.50 per yard. Each cover-up requires 1.5 yards of material; the standard material cost is $7.30 per yard. During April, the company produced 2,500 cover-ups.

Required:

(1) What is the standard quantity of material allowed for the actual production?

(2) Compute the material price and quantity variances.

(3) Why might the actual price of a raw material be greater than the standard price set for the material? How might Dragon Corp.'s management try to contain the cost of raw material?

32. **Direct Labor Variances** *(LO 13.4 & 13.5)*

Kisimee Department Store has two employees who wrap packages for customers. The standard time to wrap a package is ten minutes. During November, the employees worked a total of 320 hours and wrapped 2,160 packages. The company's standard hourly wage rate is $7.00 per hour, but these employees were actually paid $7.50 per hour.

Required:

(1) What are the standard hours allowed for the total packages wrapped?

(2) Compute the labor rate and efficiency variances.

(3) Provide some possible explanations for the variances.

33. **Direct Material and Direct Labor Variances** *(LO 13.4 & 13.5)*

Onken Co. manufactures wooden penholders. The following material and labor standards have been set for one holder.

5 ounces of wood at $0.50 per ounce	$2.50
5 minutes of labor time at $9.00 per hour	0.60

During July, the company incurred the following costs to manufacture 15,600 holders.

4,750 pounds of wood at $8.30 per pound	$39,425
1,280 hours of labor time at $9.25 per hour	11,840

Required:

(1) What is the standard quantity of material allowed for the actual production?

(2) Compute the material price and quantity variances.

(3) What are the standard hours of labor time allowed for the actual production?

(4) Compute the labor rate and efficiency variances.

(5) What relationship might exist between the material price variance and the material usage and labor efficiency variances?

(6) What relationship might exist between the labor rate variance and the labor efficiency variance?

CASES

34. **Cash Budget** *(LO 13.2)*

Leroy Landry, the accountant for Louie's Laundry, unfortunately left the company's second quarter budget folded in his shirt pocket when his wife Lola washed his clothes. Finding bits of paper in the bottom of the washer, she tried piecing the scraps together. Some of the figures were still readable; others were blurred; and others just weren't there. All borrowings, repayments, and investments must be made in even $100 amounts and are made at the beginning of a month. Interest is paid on borrowings at 12 percent per year and earned on investments at 8 percent per year. Interest paid or received is directly taken out of, or deposited into, the company's checking account. The company has no investments at the beginning of April 2004; however, an outstanding bank loan of $200 was obtained in February 2004.

	April	May	June	Total
Beginning cash balance	$ 385	$?	$ 346	$?
Cash collections	2,750	?	?	?
Total cash available	$?	$4,548	$?	$11,065
Cash payments for				
Supplies	$890	$?	$ 880	$ 2,430
Labor	?	1,525	1,550	?
Other	970	?	895	?
Total payments	$3,290	$?	$?	$ 9,720
Cash available (short)	$?	$1,443	$ 741	$?
Borrow (repay)	500	(700)	?	?
Sell (buy) investments	$0	?	(400)	?
Interest received (paid)	(7)	3	?	?
Remainder (**minimum $300**)	$?	$?	$?	$ 347

Required:

Complete the missing numbers on the cash budget.

35. **Budgeted Financial Statements** *(LO 13.2, writing, ethics)*

Convey Reynolds is a manufacturing company that produces grooming appliances such as hair dryers and curling irons. The managers of each division prepare a master budget, but Convey Reynolds does not require budgeted financial statements.

Required:

Write a memo to Convey Reynolds' upper management explaining why budgeted financial statements are important. Include in your memo a discussion of the potential for misleading budgets that do not contain pro forma financial statements.

36. **Budget Slack** *(LO 13.2 & 13.5, writing, ethics)*

Many times, allowing employees to participate in the budgeting process creates an unpleasant side effect: budget slack. Budget slack occurs when revenue estimates are understated and expense estimates are overstated so that, when the actual results are known, it appears that employees did a great job in generating sales or controlling costs.

You are the restaurant manager in a medium-size hotel in a city that is extremely popular with tourists. The CEO of the hotel has asked his upper-level managers to prepare budgets for their areas for the upcoming year. Your friend, the manager in charge of group sales, has decided to reduce his expected projections of events and revenues by 15 percent in preparing his budget. His reasoning is that he receives a year-end bonus of $1,000 for every one-percentage point above budget that his actual revenues are.

Required:

(1) Write a memo to your friend explaining how his understatement of expected revenues will affect the budget that you will be preparing.

(2) Write a memo to the CEO addressing some of the problems with the current bonus system. Do not implicate your friend in any way or address his budget behavior in this memo.

(3) For what types of material and labor prices and quantities would you be able to be able to develop standards in preparing your budget for the CEO?

37. **Starting a Business** *(LO 13.2, group)*

Part of starting a business is preparing a budget for the first quarter or year of operations. The budget should help determine if the idea is feasible, how much startup money will be needed, and whether the effort and time is worth it.

Form groups of four students and decide on a small manufacturing business you can start. Try to select a product to manufacture that will not require several different pieces or expensive machinery (such as t-shirts, buttons, or cookies).

Required—Individuals:

(1) Research your idea. Find prices for the raw materials and determine what labor and overhead costs will be associated with manufacturing different amounts of the product.

Required—Groups:

(2) Get together as a group and combine your research. Compile an entire list of raw materials and other costs.

(3) Based on the costs, set a selling price for your product.

(4) Prepare the following budget for the first quarter of operations:

- (a) a sales budget
- (b) a production budget
- (c) a purchases budget for each raw material
- (d) a direct labor budget
- (e) an overhead budget
- (f) a capital budget if you must buy equipment
- (g) a cash collections budget
- (h) a cash payments budget
- (i) a cash budget
- (j) a budgeted cost of goods manufactured schedule
- (k) a budgeted income statement
- (l) a budgeted balance sheet
- (m) a statement of cash flows.

(5) Is this endeavor feasible? Explain.

(6) How much startup money will be needed?

SUPPLEMENTAL PROBLEMS

38. **Production and Related Budgets** *(LO 13.2)* [Compare to Problems 25 and 26.]

Burato, Inc. produces and sells plastic drawers and containers. Standard quantities for one unit of each product follow.

	Plastic ($0.80 per pound)	Dye ($0.10 per ounce)	Direct labor ($7.00 per hour)
Drawers	1/2 pound	1 ounce	0.10 hours
Containers	1.5 pounds	3 ounces	0.20 hours

Overhead is applied to production at the rate of $1.50 per direct labor hour. Burato expects to sell 42,000 drawers and 35,000 containers in 2004. Expected inventories at the beginning and end of the year follow.

	January 1, 2004	December 31, 2004
Drawers	3,500 units	4,100 units
Containers	4,900 units	3,850 units
Plastic	3,900 pounds	5,300 pounds
Dye	12,000 ounces	9,800 ounces

Required:

(1) Prepare the following:

(2) Prepare the production budget for drawers and containers.

(3) Prepare the purchases budget in units and dollars for plastic and dye.

(4) Prepare the direct labor budget in hours and dollars.

(5) Prepare the schedule of overhead to be applied to production.

(6) Assume that total actual overhead at the end of 2004 was $16,500. Burato actually produced 45,000 drawers and 37,000 containers, working a total of 12,200 direct labor hours. Is overhead underapplied or overapplied at the end of 2004 and by how much?

39. **Production and Purchases Budgets** *(LO 13.2)* [Compare to Problems 25 and 26.]

Pedro's Ltd. makes a single type of product and carries no Work in Process Inventory. The company has prepared the following sales forecast for each half of 2004.

January through June	750,000 units
July through December	840,000 units

Estimated ending finished goods inventories are:

December 31, 2003	60,000 units
June 30, 2004	52,000 units
December 31, 2004	30,000 units

Each unit of product requires 2.5 pounds of Material A (cost, $4 per pound) and 1.5 pounds of Material B (cost, $14 per pound). Estimated raw material inventories are:

	Material A	Material B
December 31, 2003	20,000 pounds	5,000 pounds
June 30, 2004	13,000 pounds	9,000 pounds
December 31, 2004	7,600 pounds	22,000 pounds

Required:

(1) Prepare a production budget for each half of 2004.

(2) Prepare purchases budgets for Materials A and B for each half of 2004 (in units and dollars).

(3) Pedro's Ltd. expects to steadily decrease its ending inventory of Material A, but shows a significant increase in its holdings of Material B (the more expensive material). Why would a company want to hold such large quantities of a raw material inventory item? Give an example of an inventory item of which a company might want to increase its holdings. What costs would a company incur for holding large quantities of an inventory item?

40. **Sales, Production, Purchases, and Cash Budgets** *(LO 13.2 & 13.4)* [Compare to Problem 26.]

HoDown Hats makes felt cowboy hats with leather trim that sell for $35 each. Each hat requires three-fourths of a yard of felt and 20 inches of leather. Felt costs $9 per yard; leather costs $3.60 per yard. The company's policy is to have raw materials equal to at least ten percent of the next month's production. HoDown can only buy felt in 100-yard quantities and leather in 5-yard quantities. Thus, if HoDown needs 4,257 yards of felt, it must purchase 4,300 yards. This situation means that there might be more ending inventory than desired at the end of a month for felt and leather. Such a circumstance would affect the quantity of the beginning inventory for the following month.

Another company policy is to have a monthly finished goods ending inventory of 25 percent of the next month's sales.

During the first quarter of 2004, management expects no work in process inventories at the beginning or ending of any month. Additionally, the company expects April's production of hats to be exactly equal to its sales volume for that month.

Sales for the first four months of 2004 follow.

	January	February	March	April
Sales volume	6,200	4,600	5,200	6,000

The company collects 15 percent of its Accounts Receivable in the month of sale and the remainder in the month following the sale. There are no uncollectible accounts.

The December 31, 2003, balance sheet revealed the following selected balances: Cash, $3,500; Accounts Receivable, $163,625; Raw Material Inventory (450 yards of felt and 11,000 inches of leather), $5,150; Finished Goods Inventory (1,600 hats), $32,400; and Accounts Payable, $31,500.

The company pays for 30 percent of a month's purchases of raw material in the month of purchase (rounded to the nearest dollar). The remaining amount is paid in the month after purchase.

Direct labor cost per hat is $7 per hat produced and is paid in the month of production. Total factory overhead is $18,000 per month plus $1.50 per hat produced; of that amount, $3,000 per month is for depreciation. Total nonfactory cash costs are equal to $21,800 per month plus ten percent of sales revenue. All factory and nonfactory cash expenses are paid in the month of incurrence. In addition, the company plans to make an estimated quarterly tax payment of $45,000 and pay executive bonuses of $35,000 in March 2004.

Required:

(1) Prepare a sales budget by month and in total for the first quarter of 2004.

(2) Prepare a schedule of cash collections from customers by month and in total for the first quarter of 2004. The Accounts Receivable balance on December 31, 2003, represents the unpaid amount of December sales.

(3) What were total sales for December 2003? What is the April 1, 2004 balance of Accounts Receivable?

(4) Prepare a production budget by month and in total for the first quarter of 2004.

(5) Prepare purchases budgets for felt and leather by month and in total for the first quarter of 2004. (Hint: Total felt and leather to purchase for the quarter are, respectively, 12,000 and 8,865 yards. Note that the price of leather is quoted per yard rather than per inch.)

(6) Prepare a schedule of cash payments for purchases by month and in total for the first quarter of 2004. The Accounts Payable balance on December 31, 2003, represents the unpaid amount of December purchases.

(7) What were total raw material purchases for December 2003? What is the April 1, 2004 balance of Accounts Payable?

(8) Prepare a combined payments schedule for factory overhead and nonfactory cash costs for each month and in total for the first quarter of 2004.

(9) Prepare a cash budget for each month and in total for the first quarter of 2004.

(10) What is the standard cost per cowboy hat? (Hint: Review the beginning balance information.) How was this cost calculated? Given the cost per hat for fixed production overhead, what is the expected quantity of production each month?

41. **Material Variances** *(LO 13.5, Excel)* [Compare to Problem 31.]

Speedy Suits produces two-piece cotton-knit outfits. Speedy estimates that it will take one yard of fabric and five yards of thread to make one outfit. Typically, one yard of fabric costs $2 and one yard of thread costs $0.25.

At the end of October, Speedy had produced 35,000 two-piece outfits using 34,050 yards of fabric that cost $70,100 and 140,800 yards of thread costing $34,900.

Required:

(1) Calculate the following variances:
(2) Total material variance for fabric
(3) Material price variance for fabric
(4) Material quantity variance for fabric
(5) Total material variance for thread
(6) Material price variance for thread
(7) Material quantity variance for thread

42. **Labor Variances** *(LO 13.5, Excel)* [Compare to Problem 32.]

Speedy Suits, from the previous exercise, uses two types of labor to produce the two-piece suits: workers who cut the fabric are paid $5.25 per hour and can cut ten suits per hour, and workers who sew the fabric are paid $6 per hour and can sew five suits per hour.

At the end of October, Speedy had produced 35,000 two-piece outfits using 3,400 hours of cutting time at a labor cost of $18,190 and 7,150 hours of sewing time at a labor cost of $42,900.

Required:

(1) Calculate the following variances:
(2) Total labor variance for cutting labor
(3) Labor rate variance for cutting labor
(4) Labor efficiency variance for cutting labor
(5) Total labor variance for sewing labor
(6) Labor rate variance for sewing labor
(7) Labor efficiency variance for sewing labor

43. **Material and Labor Variances** *(LO 13.5)* [Compare to Problem 33.]

Sail Away produces boats and uses a standard cost system for material (fiberglass and paint) and labor. Standard costs and quantities for materials and labor for one boat follow.

1,600 pounds of fiberglass at $1.25 per pound	$2,000.00
3 quarts waterproof paint at $75 per gallon	56.25
50 hours of labor at $15 per hour	750.00

In June 2003, Sail Away's actual data for the production of 150 boats was as follows:

Fiberglass:	245,000 pounds purchased and used @ $1.65 per pound
Paint:	115 gallons @ $73.50 per gallon
Direct labor:	7,250 hours @ $16 per hour

Required:

(1) Calculate the material and labor variances for Sail Away for June 2003.
(2) Provide some possible reasons for each of the variances.

CHAPTER 14

Activity-Based Management and Performance Measurement/Reward

LEARNING OBJECTIVES

1. Distinguish between value-added and non-value-added activities as part of activity-based management.
2. Identify cost drivers of activities.
3. Allocate costs using activity-based costing.
4. Identify financial and nonfinancial performance measurements for different responsibility centers.
5. Discuss the use of a balanced scorecard in performance evaluation.
6. Tie the use of rewards to the performance measurement system.

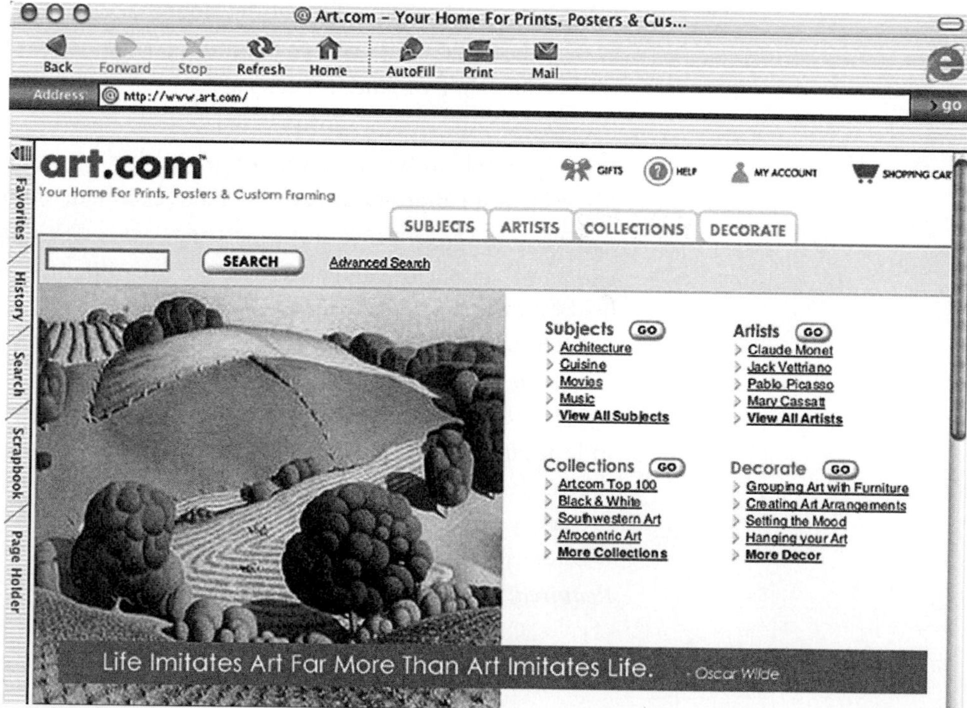

Art.com

The Web site for Art.com, which sells print and framed print artwork, went online in the Spring of 1998. After studying the company for two years, 12 specific activities were identified which consumed organizational resources. One of these, Web site optimization is unique to e-tail businesses, but is comparable to managing a traditional retail sales floor. The primary cost drivers of Web site optimization are complexity (links), number of site pages, and number of changes. Web site changes depend on the nature of the business; storefront life can be as short as two weeks or as long as six months. A second major activity is merchandise inventory selection and management. This task is expensive because items must be scanned, described, classified, and linked to search options. Inventory annotations must be available that indicate new and discontinued items.

Activity-based costing (ABC) information helped Art.com to efficiently and effectively allocate resources by understanding individual product cost and profitability. According to Art.com, "management can't manage what it doesn't know. With ABC, management can be proactive in leading the e-tail business to success."

SOURCE: Thomas Zeller, David Kublank, and Philip Makris, "How art.com Uses ABC to Succeed," *Strategic Finance,* March 2001, pp. 24–31.

INTRODUCTION

This chapter discusses activity-based management and activity-based costing as ways to develop better product or service cost information. Activity-based management identifies business activities as being value-added and non-value-added so that the non-value-added activities can be reduced or eliminated to, in turn, reduce product or service costs. Activity-based costing is used when traditional means of overhead allocation (such as direct labor hours or machine hours) do not generate reasonably accurate product or service costs.

Because control of product or service costs is often used in assessing managerial performance, the topic of performance measurement is also presented in this chapter. Performance may be judged using financial and/or nonfinancial measurements. Regardless of the type(s) of metrics used, performance rewards should be tied to the measurements selected.

ACTIVITY-BASED MANAGEMENT

Product and service costs help managers determine issues such as whether entry into a particular market is appropriate, whether a specific product or service is providing an acceptable rate of return, and which products and services require, or should receive, additional investments. Businesses generally make and sell items only if they produce a "reasonable" profit margin. Customers generally purchase items only when prices are perceived to be "reasonable" for the value received from the items. There are, however, exceptions to these rules. Businesses may sell products or provide services at less than cost if there are opportunities to "make up the difference" elsewhere, such as by selling related products or services. Customers may purchase a product or service, such as gasoline or dry cleaning, because it is essential rather than because it is perceived as being a good value.

Activity-based management (ABM) is concerned with the activities performed during the manufacturing or service process and the related costs of those activities. The goal of ABM is to understand how a production or service process occurs and thereby streamline it, which, in turn, may reduce costs and increase customer value and business profitability. Major components of ABM are discussed in this section.

Analyzing Activities

An **activity** is any repetitive action performed to fulfill a business function. To begin analyzing activities, the organizational processes or functions must be identified. All activities have associated costs, which can be eliminated if the activities are eliminated. However, the decision to eliminate an activity should be based on whether the activity adds value.

An activity or process usually overlaps several functional areas. For example, the production process also affects engineering and design, purchasing, warehousing, accounting, personnel, and marketing. In a hotel, the service process affects (in general) reservations, the front desk, and housekeeping. Several processes should be selected for intense investigation, which begins with the preparation of a process map.

All steps, not just the obvious ones, that are taken in performing an activity should be indicated in **process map.** For example, in the process of checking e-mail, two obvious steps are turning on the computer and accessing the e-mail program. But time is also spent in waiting for the computer to boot up and program to be accessed, waiting for the e-mail to be downloaded and scanned for viruses, opening the e-mail, and so forth. Some e-mail will need to be saved to a file; others may require adjustments for sound volume.

Each process map for each activity will be unique to an organization and its employees. Once a process map is complete, the time necessary to complete each activity and a designation of whether each activity is value-added or non-value-added should be included.

Value-Added and Non-Value-Added Activities

If a "black or white" perspective is adopted, activities are either value-added or non-value-added. **Value-added** (VA) **activities** increase a product or service's worth to a customer who is willing to pay for them. **Non-value-added** (NVA) **activities** increase the time spent making a product or performing a service, but do not increase the product's or service's worth to the customer. Thus, from the customer's perspective, NVA activities are unnecessary and create costs that could be eliminated without affecting the product's or service's market value or quality.

A simple example of value-added and non-value-added activities can be seen in a baseball game. The activities of pitching, batting, running bases, catching, and throwing would certainly be considered value-added by the fans (customers), because these are the activities that the fans came to see. However, the activities of switching teams on the field and discussions between players and coaches might be considered to be non-value-added by the fans. Other NVA activities might include waiting for the game to start or the seventh-inning stretch. Some NVA activities may be necessary for the game to run more smoothly and, as such, cannot be eliminated, but that does not necessarily make them "valuable" to the customer.

NVA activities that are necessary because of the way an organization functions, but would not be seen as desired by customers, are called **business-value-added activities.** For example, a company will usually prepare invoices as documentation for sales and collections. Preparing invoices creates a business cost that must be covered by the selling prices of the company's products or services. However, invoice preparation adds no direct value to a company's products or services, and customers would prefer not to have to pay for this activity.

All activities use up time, either productively (VA) or unproductively (NVA). Time usage can be classified in four ways: processing (or service), transfer, idle, and inspection. Activities necessary to manufacture a product or perform a service require processing or service time; these activities are, and the time taken to perform them is, value-added. Moving products or components from place to place uses transfer time; storage of parts or waiting at a production operation for processing necessitates idle time. Transfer and idle time are non-value-added.

Performing quality control creates inspection time, which is generally considered non-value-added. Customers expect that activities within a process will be performed correctly and it should not be necessary to inspect goods while they are being made or while services are being performed. However, there are some exceptions to this attitude. Customers would generally consider quality control essential in the pharmaceutical, food-processing, and airline industries. In these settings, customers would be willing to have the time taken, and to pay, for quality inspections, making those activities value-added.

Companies should try to eliminate or minimize the activities that, from the customer's perspective, add the most time, most cost, and least value. Although few companies can eliminate all business value-added activities, understanding that these activities are, in fact, non-value-added should encourage managers to minimize such activities to the greatest extent possible.

COST DRIVERS

A cost cannot be eliminated or reduced unless the reason for its incurrence is known. A **cost driver** is the factor that has a direct cause-effect relationship on a cost. Many drivers may be identified for a business or single cost. For example, the drivers for hotel insurance cost could include number of employees, property value, the number of accidents or claims during a specified time period, location of property, and coverage desired. In a restaurant, the primary cost drivers would be items such as square footage (or number of tables), hours of operation, number of employees, availability of alcohol, and meals served per month. A company should attempt to select a reasonable number of cost drivers that would affect the majority of the organization's costs.

Accountants have traditionally accumulated overhead into one or two accounts (such as total or fixed and variable factory overhead) and used one or two drivers (such as direct labor hours or machine hours) to assign overhead costs to products and services. These procedures, although causing no problems for financial statement preparation, may produce inappropriate product or service costs for management's use in complex production or service environments.

Levels of Cost Incurrence

Costs are created by various drivers that reflect different groupings of activities. For example, direct material and direct labor are unit-based and the total cost of these items will increase with each increase in production or service volume. Some overhead costs, such as indirect material or indirect labor, are also unit-based. In each case, the more units that are produced or the more services that are performed, the greater the total cost for the cost element. However, other costs are incurred for broader-based categories of activity such as batch, product or process, and organizational.

Costs that are caused by a group of things being made, handled, or processed at a single time are referred to as batch-level costs. The cost of setting up a machine is an example of a batch-level cost. Assume that a company makes two products: A and B. Setting up a machine to make either one of these products costs $500. During one month, the machine is set up twice: once to manufacture 4,000 units of product A and once to manufacture 1,000 units of product B. Total setup cost for the month is $1,000. If setup cost is viewed as a unit-based cost, the setup cost per unit of A or B will be $0.20 per unit ($1,000 ÷ 5,000 units). However, the actual setup cost per unit is $0.125 ($500 ÷ 4,000 units) per unit of Product A and $0.50 ($500 ÷ 1,000 units) per unit of Product B. Treating setup as a batch-level cost indicates the commonality of the cost to the units within the batch and is more indicative of the relationship between the activity (setup) and the driver (different production runs).

The development, production, or acquisition of different items causes a product-level (or process-level) cost. Assume that a travel agency has the following customers during July: a group of ten senior citizens, a group of six college students, and a family of four. The agency makes five itinerary changes during the month at a cost of $200 per change. Four of these changes related to the group of senior citizens and one change related to the group of college students; no changes were made for the family. If the cost of the changes were viewed as unit-based, the overhead cost per unit for changes would be $50 ($1,000 ÷ 20 people). Use of this method inappropriately assigns $200 of the cost to the family of four, which had no itinerary changes. Using a product/process-level driver (number of changes) for these costs assigns $800 of costs to the senior citizens and $200 to the college students. These costs could then be assigned, on a per-unit basis, to the individual members of the groups at $80 and $33.33, respectively, per senior citizen and college student.

Certain overhead costs are incurred only for the purpose of supporting facility operations. These costs are common to many different activities, products, and services, and can only be allocated to products and services arbitrarily. For example, the driver of building depreciation cost is the passage of time rather than production of units or performance of services. Organizational-level costs should theoretically not be assigned to products at all, but because the amounts are insignificant relative to all other costs, most companies allocate organizational-level costs to goods produced or services rendered using some arbitrary basis such as direct labor or machine hours.

Activity-Based Costing

Activity-based costing (ABC) is an overhead allocation method. Costs are collected by cost driver categories and are then attached to products and services based on the activities performed to make, render, distribute, or support those products and services. Three fundamental components of ABC are: classifying costs into multiple levels of incurrence, accumulating costs by cost drivers, and using multiple cost drivers to assign costs to products and services. Activity-based costing is useful in companies that:

- make (or render) many different kinds of products (or services) in significantly different volumes;
- have high overhead costs, often related to automation, that can be traced to specific products using nontraditional cost drivers; and
- are showing profits for low-volume, hard-to-make (perform) products (services) and losses for high-volume, easy-to-make (perform) products (services).

In activity-based costing, overhead costs are accumulated in the traditional manner (for instance, by variable or fixed cost behavior) in the general ledger. These costs are then regrouped based on two aspects of the cost: level of incurrence (unit, batch or product/process) and primary underlying cost driver (such as kilowatt-hours of electricity, square feet of occupancy, or number of transactions). Depending on whether they are to be allocated to products or services, organizational-level costs may or may not be regrouped by cost drivers. Each group of costs, as opposed to all overhead costs, are assigned to products and services using an overhead allocation similar to that discussed in Chapter 11.

As an example, assume that Hyde, Inc. produces two products: product Q, which sells for $40 per unit and has direct material and direct labor costs of $27, and product R, which sells for $130 and has direct material and labor costs of $89. In 2003, Hyde, Inc. produced and sold 70,000 units of Q and 8,000 units of R. Total overhead for the year was $579,800. Exhibit 14-1 illustrates Hyde, Inc.'s overhead allocation process using the traditional cost driver of direct labor hours (DLHs).

In this situation, total overhead is divided by total direct labor hours (the cost driver) resulting in $2.60 of overhead assigned for every DLH. Each unit of product is assigned overhead based on the number of DLHs required to produce a single unit. As a result, product Q receives $6.50 of overhead per unit while product R receives $15.60.

If Hyde, Inc. used activity-based costing, the overhead would be divided into groups and each group would be applied using a different driver. This concept is illustrated in Visual Recap 14.1.

Assume that the $579,8000 of total overhead consists of $240,000 in material movement costs, $189,000 in utilities, $126,800 in cleanup costs, and $24,000 in setup costs. Exhibit 14-2 indicates the overhead allocations to the two products if ABC were used. In this situation, there are four drivers and allocation bases, one for each overhead category.

Note the significant difference in overhead cost per unit of product Q and product R using activity-based costing. Using the direct labor hour method to allocate overhead cost to products makes product R appear to be the more profitable of the two products. However, when overhead is allocated using activity-based costing, product R becomes unprofitable.

Activity-based costing often indicates that a large number of costs are associated with low-volume products and complex production operations, and that these costs are not properly allocated under traditional overhead allocation systems. ABC tends to reduce the overhead cost attached to high-volume, standard products and increase the overhead costs attached to low-volume, complex specialty product costs.

Activity-based costing is not appropriate for all organizations because it is expensive and time-consuming to implement. Additionally, ABC does not change the total overhead incurred; it merely distributes that overhead cost in a more appropriate manner. Overhead cost can only be minimized by using activity-based management techniques to eliminate or reduce non-value-added activities and their related costs.

EXHIBIT 14-1

Hyde, Inc. Overhead Allocation (Traditional)

Overhead = $579,800

Cost Driver: Direct Labor Hours (DLH)

Product Q:	70,000 units @ 2.5 DLHs =	175,000 DLHs
Product R:	8,000 units @ 6.0 DLHs =	48,000 DLHs
Both Products		223,000 DLHs

Overhead rate per DLH = $579,800 ÷ 223,000 DLH = $2.60 per DLH

Overhead Assigned

Product Q:	2.5 DLH × $2.60 per DLH =	$6.50 per unit of Q
Procuct R:	6.0 DLH × $2.60 per DLH =	$15.60 per unit of R

Profit Analysis Per Unit

	Product Q	Product R
Selling price	$ 40.00	$ 130.00
Less: DM and DL cost	(27.00)	(89.00)
OH cost (assigned on DLHs)	(6.50)	(15.60)
Profit margin	$ 6.50	$ 25.40
Profit as a % of SP (rounded)	16%	20%

VISUAL RECAP 14.1

Allocating Overhead: Traditional versus Activity-Based Costing

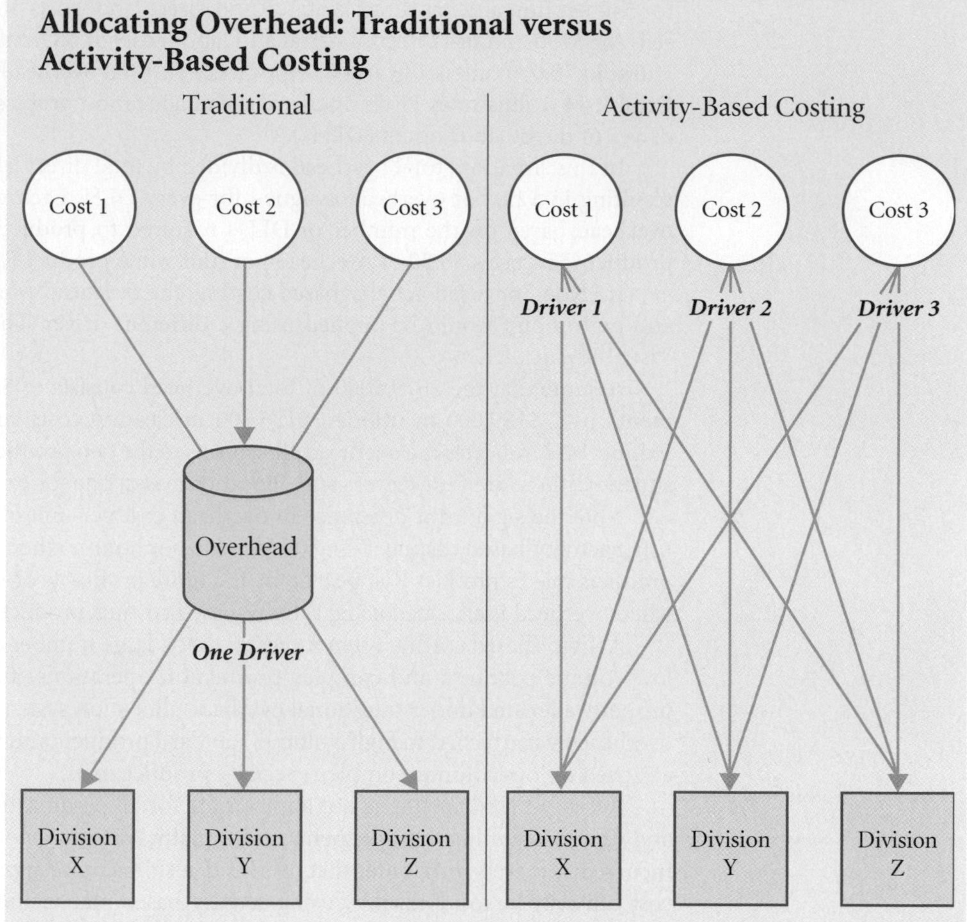

Activity-based costing provides two important benefits from its reallocation of overhead costs. First, decision making is improved because product and service costs are more accurate, and better reflect the resources used by the production or performance process. Second, performance measurement is improved because the enhanced product or service cost information is a more appropriate way to judge how well costs were controlled and how profitable a product or organizational unit was.

MEASURING SHORT-RUN PERFORMANCE

To be successful, organizations must meet many different goals and objectives. First and foremost, a business organization must be profitable to survive. Profitability performance measures are short-run in nature and relate to the type of organizational unit being evaluated.

A **responsibility center** is an organizational subunit that is under the control of a designated manager. Responsibility centers are classified based on the manager's authority and type of financial responsibility. The three most common classifications are cost, profit, and investment centers. In a **cost center,** the manager is responsible only for controlling

EXHIBIT 14-2

Hyde, Inc. Overhead Allocation (Activity-Based Costing)

Overhead

(1)	Material move cost (MMC)	$240,000
(2)	Utility cost (UC)	189,000
(3)	Clean-up cost (CC)	126,800
(4)	Setup cost (SC)	24,000
	Total Overhead	$579,800

Cost Drivers

(1)	Pounds of material moved	800,000
(2)	Number of kilowatt hours used	6,300,000
(3)	Hours of clean-up labor	31,700
(4)	Number of setups	6

Overhead Rates

(1)	MMC	$240,000 ÷ 800,000 lbs.	= $0.30 per lb.
(2)	UC	$189,000 ÷ 6,300,000 kWh	= $0.03 per kWH
(3)	CC	$126,800 ÷ 31,700 hours	= $4 per hour
(4)	SC	$ 24,000 ÷ 6 setups	= $4,000 per setup

Overhead Assigned

		Product Q			Product R		
		Driver Used	× Rate	= Overhead Assigned	Driver Used	× Rate	= Overhead Assigned
(1)	MMC	280,000 lbs.	× $0.30	$ 84,000	520,000 lbs.	× $0.30	$156,000
(2)	UC	1,750,000 kWH	× $0.03	52,500	4,550,000 kWH	× $0.03	136,500
(3)	CC	21,000 hrs.	× $4.00	84,000	10,700 hrs.	× $4.00	42,800
(4)	SC	2 setups	× $4,000	8,000	4 setups	× $4,000	16,000
Total Overhead Assigned				$228,500			$351,300
Divided by units of product				÷ 70,000			÷ 8,000
OH per unit of product (rounded)				$3.26			$43.92

Profit Analysis Per Unit

	Product Q	Product R
Selling price	$ 40.00	$ 130.00
Less: DM and DL cost	(27.00)	(89.00)
OH cost (using ABC)	(3.26)	(43.92)
Profit margin	$ 9.74	($2.92)
Profit as a % of SP (rounded)	24%	n/a

costs in the unit. In a **profit center,** the manager is responsible for both cost control and revenue generation in the unit. In an **investment center,** the manager is responsible for cost control, revenue generation, and the unit's asset base. A manager's performance should be evaluated only on the specific areas under his or her control.

Cost Center

In a cost center, the only means to judge performance is an assessment of whether the center's costs were in line with budgeted amounts. Thus, actual costs are compared to budgeted costs at the same level of activity to determine the variance amount. Consider the following information: Lee Larkind is the manager of the Reservations Department in HLS

Corp. For October, the department's budget was as follows based on an activity level of 480 hours (three people working 40 hours per week for four weeks in the month):

Personnel costs ($12 per hour × 480 hours)	$ 5,760
Supplies ($15 per hour × 480 hours)	7,200
Electricity ($0.50 per hour worked × 480 hours)	240
Depreciation ($2,000 per month)	2,000
Total budgeted costs	$15,200

During October, company management gave reservations employees a $0.50 per hour wage increase. The employees worked a total of 500 hours, and the department reported the following costs:

Personnel costs ($12.50 per hour × 500 hours)	$ 6,250
Supplies ($14.25 per hour × 500 hours)	7,125
Electricity ($0.90 per hour × 500 hours)	450
Depreciation ($2,000 per month)	2,000
Total actual costs	$15,825

At first glance, it appears that Mr. Larkind has not controlled departmental costs well during October. However, the two sets of figures should not be compared directly because they have been calculated using different levels of activity. The original budget first needs to be restated at an activity level of 500 hours before making the comparisons:

	Budget at actual activity level	Actual costs	Difference
Personnel costs ($12 per hour × 500 hours)	$ 6,000	$ 6,250	$250
Supplies ($15 per hour × 500 hours)	7,500	7,125	(375)
Electricity ($0.50 per hour × 500 hours)	250	450	200
Depreciation ($2,000 per month)	2,000	2,000	0
Total budgeted costs at actual activity	$15,750	$15,825	$ (75)

Reviewing this information indicates that the department's costs were only $75 more than what would have been budgeted if the actual activity level had been used in the original budget. Mr. Larkind controlled departmental costs fairly well considering the increase in wage rates and hourly electricity costs—especially when it is realized that neither the wage increase nor the electricity cost increase was under Larkind's control.

Profit Center

In a profit center, performance can be judged on both cost control and revenue generation. A profit center manager's goal is to maximize the center's net income. Profit centers are generally independent organizational units whose managers have the authority to buy goods, obtain resources, and set selling prices.

In addition to the type of cost control comparison shown in the previous section, performance evaluation in a profit center will also include revenue and profit measurements. Price, sales mix, and volume variances from budget are illustrated in the following revenue variance model (assuming the profit center sells only one type of product):

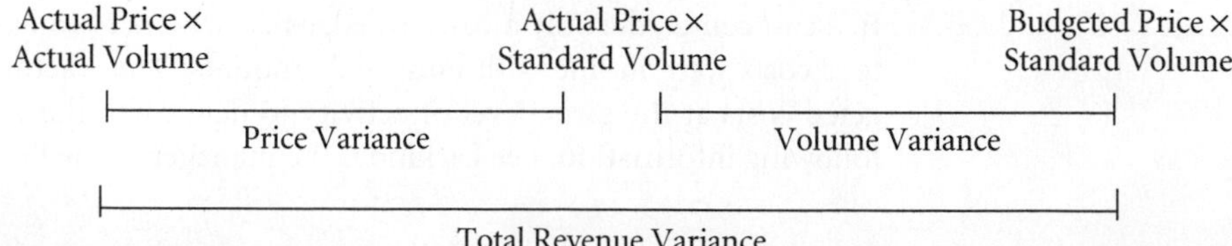

Continuing the previous example, assume that Reservations Department is a profit center rather than a cost center and is allowed to charge hotels $10 for each reservation generated by the department. It was estimated that the department would make 2,000 reservations during October; thus, expected revenue for the department was $20,000. In October, the department actually generated 2,200 reservations. During that month, a new reservation system was implemented that reduced the work involved; therefore, the hotel charge per reservation was lowered to $9.50. The price, volume, and revenue variances for October are as follows:

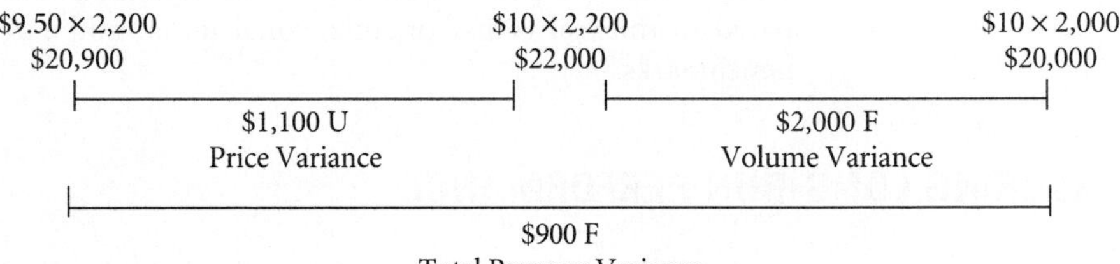

Even though the price charged per reservation was reduced, the increase in volume for the Reservation Department was sufficient to produce more than the total expected revenue for the month.

Budgeted profits for the Reservations Department should also be compared to actual profits in evaluating performance as follows:

Budgeted revenues	$ 20,000	Actual revenues	$ 20,900
Budgeted costs (at actual volume)	(15,750)	Actual costs	(15,825)
Expected profit	$ 4,250	Actual profit	$ 5,075

The Reservations Department and its manager, Mr. Larkind, performed exceptionally well during October by controlling costs, increasing revenues, and increasing profitability.

Investment Center

In an investment center, performance can be judged on the basis of cost control, revenue generation, and return on investment. Most investment centers are independent, freestanding divisions or subsidiaries of an organization. Center managers can acquire, use, and sell plant assets so as to earn the highest rate of return on the center's asset base. Thus, in addition to the measures shown previously for cost and profit centers, an investment center's performance can also be measured by calculating **return on investment** (ROI):

$$\text{ROI} = \text{Income} \div \text{Assets}$$

Assume that Mr. Larkind of the Reservations Department has control over the department's asset base of $50,000. The department's ROI is computed as follows:

$$\begin{aligned}\text{ROI} &= \$5{,}075 \div \$50{,}000\\ &= 10.2\%\end{aligned}$$

The 10.2 percent rate would be compared to the rate desired by the corporate entity to determine whether it was reasonable and acceptable.

The **Du Pont model,** a restatement of the ROI formula, can be used to provide information about two factors that comprise the rate of return: profit margin and asset turnover. **Profit margin** is the ratio of income to sales, and indicates the portion of each sales dollar that is not consumed by expenses. **Asset turnover** reflects the dollars of sales generated by each dollar of asset investment and, as such, indicates asset productivity.

$$\text{Profit Margin} = \text{Income} \div \text{Revenues}$$
$$\text{Asset Turnover} = \text{Revenues} \div \text{Assets}$$

The Du Pont model uses the product of the profit margin and asset turnover to calculate ROI. For the Reservations Department, these calculations are:

$$\begin{aligned} \text{ROI} &= \text{Profit Margin} \times \text{Asset Turnover} \\ &= (\text{Income} \div \text{Revenues}) \times (\text{Revenues} \div \text{Assets}) \\ &= (\$5{,}075 \div \$20{,}900) \times (\$20{,}900 \div \$50{,}000) \\ &= 24.3\% \times 41.8\% \\ &= 10.2\% \end{aligned}$$

To determine acceptability of performance, results of these calculations should be compared to internal (other organizational units) and external (world-class companies) benchmarks.[1]

MEASURING LONG-RUN PERFORMANCE

Companies must be managed to be profitable in the short-run and to exist for the long-run. To this end, mission statements should be developed that reflect management's view of how the organization will uniquely and continuously meet customers' needs with its products or services. A company that makes shoddy products or does not maintain a competitive edge may be profitable this year and next, but probably will not exist in ten years. In addition, managers who make decisions that increase this year's profits at the expense of future profits will "look good" this year but not in the future. Thus, it is necessary for management to have both short-run and long-run objectives that are compatible with the organization's mission statement.

Balanced Scorecard

Short-run objectives generally reflect a predominantly financial focus and, as such, can be measured with the traditional monetary metrics discussed in the previous section. Alternatively, an organization's long-term objectives will involve actions and efforts that will enhance market position. Traditional financial measures cannot indicate progress toward these goals although, in the long run, these goals will definitively impact an organization's profitability. Thus, nonfinancial performance measures are instituted to indicate progress toward the success factors of a global organization. Such measures help assess performance in the areas of customer satisfaction, quality, cycle time, and organizational learning. A "balanced scorecard" can be developed for organizations wanting to measure all aspects of performance.

Each balanced scorecard section should indicate specific measurements that would help assess the organization's process toward its long-run goals and objectives. The measurements should be easy to understand and to compute. Following are some examples of nonmonetary measurements for each scorecard area other than the financial section.

Customer:

- Increase in market share from prior period
- Percentage of customers retained from prior period
- Percentage of new customers out of total customers this period
- Score of at least 90% on all customer satisfaction surveys

Internal Process:

- Defect rate this period vs. defect rate of industry leader

[1] Many other short-term financial performance measurements (such as residual income and cash flows) may also be used to evaluate performance. These measurements are beyond the scope of this text.

- Increase in cycle efficiency (value-added time ÷ total cycle time) from prior period
- New product time-to-market vs. average time-to-market in industry
- Number of patents obtained this period vs. number obtained by primary competitor
- Sales dollars generated from new products vs. total sales dollars

Learning and Growth:

- Percentage of employees retained from prior period vs. goal of 95%
- Number of employee suggestions implemented vs. number submitted
- Hours of training per employee this period vs. goal of 40 hours per employee
- Percentage of employees who are cross-trained in three or more functional areas vs. goal of 100%
- Number of projects worked on by teams of different business units vs. total number of projects

Exhibit 14-3 illustrates the style and use of the balanced scorecard.

Benchmarking

To assess the success of an activity, a measurement should compare a numerator and a denominator, or make a comparison between periods, with an internal or external benchmark. **Benchmarking** means comparing an organization's products, processes, or services against those of organizations who have been proven to be "best in class." These "best in class" organizations may or may not be in competition with the organization doing the benchmarking. For example, if an organization wanted to judge its warehouse "picking" process (selecting goods to ship to customers), one of the best in class organizations is L.L. Bean. To judge the efficiency and effectiveness of its picking process, a company would not have to be in the catalog clothing business to compare picking processes with L.L. Bean.

EXHIBIT 14-3 Balanced Scorecard Illustration

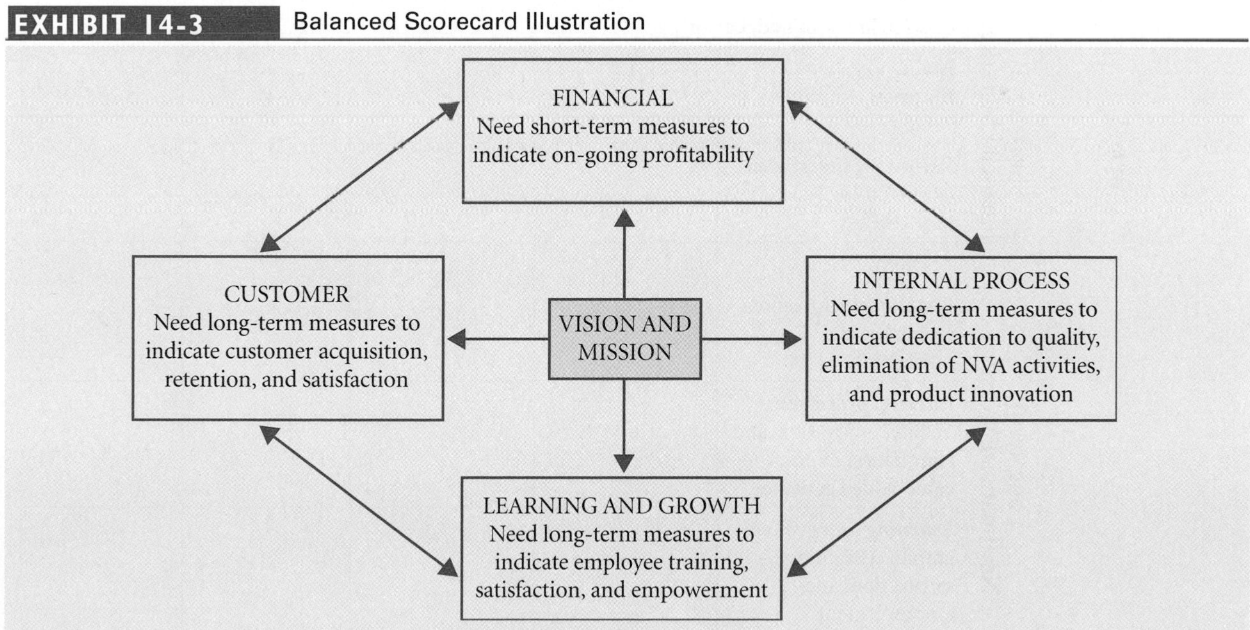

SOURCE: Robert S. Kaplan and David P. Norton, "Using the Balanced Scorecard as a Strategic Management System," *Harvard Business Review* (January–February 1996): 76.

Some organizations may want to use internal goals or other organizational units as benchmarks of performances. If this choice is made, the organization should be certain that those internal goals or units are set to reflect the success criteria shown by market leaders. Otherwise, the organization may find itself the best at doing something that no one wants done or performing significantly better than in the past, but not well enough to compete with the market leaders.

Deciding on Performance Measures

Different balanced scorecards should be created for different levels of managerial responsibility. As the responsibility level goes lower in the organization, the measurements will become more job specific and, generally, more individualized. Specific responsibility for performance should be assigned for each measurement target as well as a monitoring schedule. Monitoring of performance will probably be performed more frequently at lower levels of responsibility.

Performance measurements should reflect an organization's need to concentrate on those factors that provide value to the customer. Probably two of the most important current performance measures of businesses are product or service quality and customer responsiveness. In committing to product or service quality, an organization must adjust how products are designed and manufactured, employees are trained and utilized, and plant assets are justified for purchase. Setting multiple financial and nonfinancial performance measures should cause organizations to implement techniques (such as total quality management) that will help improve the organization, its products, its processes, and its customer and supplier relations, as well as reduce costs to provide better value. Visual Recap 14.2 illustrates some choices of performance measures.

VISUAL RECAP 14.2

Choice of Performance Measures

	Measures of Performance	Cost Center	Revenue Center	Investment Center	Balanced Scorecard
Short-term Financial Measures	Costs in line with **budget**	✓	✓	✓	
	Ability to generate ***revenues*** (Revenue variance)		✓	✓	✓*
	Return on Investment (ROI and DuPont Model)			✓	
Long-term Nonfinancial Measures	***Customer:*** acquisition, retention, and satisfaction				✓
	Internal processes: quality, innovation, and elimination of non-value-added activities				✓
	Learning and growth: employee training, satisfaction, and empowerment				✓

*Indicates that at least one short-run financial measure should be included on a balanced scorecard

Rewarding Performance

For a performance measurement system to be effective, it should be aligned with the performance reward system. The important issues in designing a performance reward system are that the system:

- Reflects the performance measurements that have been set,
- Is tied to individual and, if appropriate, group performance,
- Encourages both a short-run and long-run perspective about the organization, and
- Is balanced between financial and nonfinancial incentives.

Typically, rewards above basic salary and wages have been tied to performance above certain stated objectives—usually a financial accounting measure such as organizational net income or earnings per share. However, because the measurement system is changing from a focus totally on financial aspects of performance to multiple performance measurement characteristics, the compensation system also needs to change. New performance reward plans should be designed to encourage higher levels of employee performance and loyalty for behaviors that lead to achievement of organizational goals.

Like the nonfinancial performance measures, performance rewards should encourage employees to adopt a long-run perspective. For example, some rewards now involve the issuance of common stock to employees because it is believed that employees who are partial owners of their employing company develop the same perspective as other stockholders.

Another consideration in performance reward systems is the use of team as well as individual rewards. In today's business environment, employees often function as teams rather than as individuals. Team incentives are necessary to encourage cooperation among employees. However, if only team incentives are offered, the reward system may be ineffective. As the team grows larger, individual employees may shirk their duties or try to "free-ride" on the team. Balancing individual and team rewards requires a careful assessment of activities and a performance measurement system that can differentiate between individual and team skills and efforts.

An employee's organizational level and current compensation should affect the performance rewards offered. Individuals at different levels in the organization typically view rewards differently because of the relationship of pay to standard of living. At lower employee levels, more incentives should be monetary and short term; at higher levels, more incentives should be nonmonetary and long-term. However, the system should include some nonmonetary and long-term incentives for lower-level employees and some monetary and short-term incentives for top management. Such a compensation system provides lower-level employees with more money to directly enhance their lifestyles, but also provides long-run rewards (such as stock options) to encourage an "ownership" view of the organization. In turn, more rewards (such as stock and stock options) should be given to top managers so that they will be more concerned about the organization's long-run rather than their short-run personal gains.

A **stock option** is a right to buy a company's stock at a future date at a guaranteed price, such as the current market price. In today's business environment, any discussion of the use of stock options as performance rewards for employees has to include this reward's potential for problems. Silicon Valley companies such as Cisco Systems (www.cisco.com) and Sun Microsystems (www.sun.com) were corporate leaders in dispersing stock options to employees. Unfortunately, the downturn in the technology market made a substantial number of employee-would-be-millionaires holding options that have lost all their value. Enron (www.enron.com) executives, on the other hand, managed to convert all their stock options to stock, which was sold for millions of dollars prior to the collapse of the company.

All employees value and require money to satisfy basic human needs, but employees also appreciate other types of "compensation" that satisfy their higher order social needs.

For example, employees are generally more productive in an environment in which their efforts are appreciated. Compliments and small awards can be used to formally recognize employee contributions. Implementing employee empowerment contributes to making a work environment more fulfilling. Other types of perquisites (or "perks") such as additional paid days off, onsite childcare, free parking, and health or recreational club memberships are also frequently used as rewards for performance.

Sometimes, perks can be carried to an extreme. For instance, prior to its major business difficulties, Tyco International (www.tyco.com) made (and later forgave) a $19 million no-interest loan to its CEO Dennis Kozlowski so that he could purchase a 15,000 square foot home in Boca Raton, Florida. Tyco also spent more than $11 million on antiques and other furnishing, including a $6,000 shower curtain, for Kozlowski's $18.5 million New York apartment. And, in 2001, the company spent over $1 million for a birthday party in Sardinia for Kozlowski's wife.[2] In mid-2002, Tyco posted a $2.32 billion loss for the third fiscal quarter.[3] In establishing a performance reward system, management must remember that the primary objective of a business enterprise is to be profitable so that it may meet an underlying accounting assumption—that of a going concern.

SUMMARY

Activity-based management stresses the (1) differentiation between value-added and non-value-added activities and (2) reduction or elimination of the non-value-added activities to the greatest extent possible. A process map can be prepared to indicate all the steps taken in performing a process. Cost drivers of the various activities and the levels (unit, batch, product/process, or organizational) at which those drivers occur should be determined.

Activity-based costing is an alternative method of allocating overhead to products and services based on the activities performed rather than using a single allocation base such as direct labor or machine hours. ABC often shows that the traditional method of allocating overhead assigned too much overhead to high-volume, standard products and not enough to low-volume, specialty products.

Organizations have to meet many goals and objectives to achieve success. Determining progress towards those goals and objectives requires a performance measurement system that considers both the short-run and long-run. Financial measures of performance must reflect a manager's area of responsibility. Thus, each type of responsibility center (cost, profit, or investment) has different types of performance measures that can be used. However, all financial measures are historical in nature and, thus, are more focused on the past than on the future.

The balanced scorecard stresses the need for both financial and nonfinancial performance measures. The nonfinancial categories of the scorecard are customer, internal process, and learning and growth. Measurements should be designed that indicate an organization's ability to meet today's global success factors of customer satisfaction and responsiveness, high quality products or services, and innovation.

The performance reward system should be directly tied to the performance measurement system and include both financial and nonfinancial rewards as well as short-run and long-run rewards. Different levels of employees will need a different balance of these rewards, but the system should reflect the value placed on work activities and should encourage employees to adopt a long-run perspective for their organization.

---

[2] Mark Maremont and Laurie Cohen, "How Tyco's CEO Enriched Himself," *Wall Street Journal* (August 7, 2002), p. A1.

[3] Mark Maremont, "Tyco Posts $2.32 Billion Loss; Cites Downturn, CIT Spinoff," *Wall Street Journal* (July 24, 2002), p. A6.

KEY TERMS

activity
activity-based costing
activity-based management
asset turnover
benchmarking
business-value-added activity
cost center
cost driver
Du Pont model
investment center
non-value-added activity
process map
profit center
profit margin
responsibility center
return on investment
stock option
value-added activity

QUESTIONS

1. Define and give four examples in a business organization of value-added, non-value-added, and business-value-added activities. Why, in the strictest possible definition, should business-value-added activities be classified as non-value-added activities? *(LO 14.1)*

2. Select a reasonably simple activity (similar to the checking e-mail example given in the chapter) that you perform in your daily routine. What activities would be included in a process map for your chosen activity? Classify each of the activities as value-added or non-value-added, as related to the outcome of the activity. *(LO 14.1)*

3. What is a cost driver? Provide one example (other than that given in the text) of a cost being incurred at the batch, product/process, and organizational levels. Why is it important to classify costs as to their level of incurrence? *(LO 14.2)*

4. How does activity-based costing differ from traditional costing methods? On what type of cost does activity-based costing focus? *(LO 14.3)*

5. How does the use of activity-based costing generally affect product costs? Will the use of activity-based costing lower a company's total costs? Why or why not? *(LO 14.3)*

6. Differentiate among the three common classifications of responsibility centers. Choose two different kinds of organizations and provide an example (other than those given in the text) of each type of center.

7. How is the ability to measure performance affected by a responsibility center's classification? Why is it important to only evaluate managers based on the costs that they are able to control? *(LO 14.4)*

8. What two formulas can be used to calculate return on investment? What additional information is provided by the use of the Du Pont model to calculate ROI? *(LO 14.4)*

9. What is a balanced scorecard? Why is each category included in the balanced scorecard important to an organization? *(LO 14.5)*

10. Define benchmarking. Should every process at a company be benchmarked against best practices? When would it be appropriate not to benchmark? *(LO 14.5)*

11. Why should an organization select multiple metrics to measure performance? Why is there a need to measure performance using both short-run and long-run time horizons? *(LO 14.6)*

12. Why does an organization not need to focus solely on industry competitors when determining a benchmark comparison? *(LO 14.6)*

13. Why must an organization's reward system be aligned with its performance measurement system? Why should the reward system not be tied solely to monetary bonuses? *(LO 14.6)*

EXERCISES

14. **True and False** *(All LOs)*

Following are a series of statements regarding topics discussed in this chapter.

Required:

Indicate whether each statement is true (T) or false (F).

(1) The Du Pont model is return on investment measurement.

(2) Quality inspection is a non-value-added activity.

(3) Product-level cost drivers should be used when the company manufactures products to each customer's specification.

(4) As the responsibility level of a manager goes lower in the organization, the measurements of his/her job performance will become more general.

(5) Corporations should eliminate as many non-value-added activities as possible, but should not consider eliminating business-value-added activities.

(6) To assess a firm's ability to pay an annual dividend, short-run performance measures are better than long-run performance measures.

(7) Activity-based costing is useful to companies that have high direct material and direct labor costs and relatively low overhead.

(8) A manager's performance measurements should correspond to the type of responsibility center the manager heads.

(9) Cost drivers should be chosen so that expenses are distributed evenly between divisions.

(10) Long-run performance measures are typically financial.

15. **Value-Added and Non-Value-Added Activities** *(LO 14.1)*

Different types of businesses engage in different types of activities. Three businesses follow.

(a) Dillard's Department Stores

(b) H&R Block Tax Preparation Service

(c) Saturn Automobile Manufacturer

Required:

For each business, list two examples of

(1) A value-added activity.

(2) A non-value-added activity.

(3) A business-value-added activity.

16. **Cost Levels and Cost Drivers** *(LO 14.2)*

Following are ten cost activities that might be incurred in an organization.

(a) Paying a franchise license fee

(b) Transferring a production run to the warehouse

(c) Setting up a printer to run 5,000 copies of a textbook

(d) Maintaining engineering designs for company products

(e) Using wood to manufacture a table

(f) Depreciating a factory building

(g) Delivering meals to hospital patients

(h) Putting a stamp on an envelope

(i) Developing dietary guidelines for special-need meals in a rest home

(j) Drilling a hole in a product

Required:

Classify each of the costs as unit-level, batch-level, product/process level, or organizational level. Identify a cost driver for each item and explain why that driver is appropriate.

17. **Cost, Profit, and Investment Centers** *(LO 14.4)*

Keely Corp., a manufacturing company, has three divisions and each produces a different item: widgets, whatchamacallits, and whosey-whatsits. Each product is distinctly different, so the divisions do not share raw material, labor, or machinery.

Required:

(1) If the Widgets Division were a cost center, list several costs for which the division manager would be responsible.

(2) How would your answer in part (1) change if the Widgets Division were a profit center?

(3) How would your answers from parts (1) and (2) change if the Widgets Division were an investment division?

(4) Would it be possible for the Widgets Division to be an investment center if the three divisions used similar raw material? Explain.

(5) Would it be possible for the Widgets Division to be an investment center if the three divisions shared machinery? Explain.

(6) Assume that the widgets, whatchamacallits, and whosey-whatsits were transferred to a fourth division that puts them together to make a final product. Would it be possible for the Widgets Division to be a profit center? Explain.

18. **Return on Investment** *(LO 14.4)*

Broadway Division has the following information for the year ended December 31, 2003.

Assets invested	$5,120,000
Revenues	3,500,000
Expenses	2,390,000

Required:

(1) Calculate return on investment.

(2) Calculate profit margin.

(3) Calculate asset turnover.

(4) Use the answers from parts (2) and (3) to prove the answer in part (1).

19. **Performance Measurements** *(LO 14.4)*

Consider your enrollment in this class as your job.

Required:

Using each of the four balanced scorecard categories, develop two measurements that would be appropriate to judge your performance in this class.

20. **Performance Rewards** *(LO 14.6)*

You are the new manager of a local health club. You are being paid what you perceive to be a good monthly salary with an annual three-week paid vacation and good health benefits. The club's owner has stated she wants the club to earn a reasonable rate of return, increase membership, and have low employee turnover.

Required:

(1) Provide the answers that might be given by the owner in response to your question of "Can you be more specific about how these goals will be measured?"

(2) What performance rewards might you request under these measurements?

PROBLEMS

21. **Value-Added and Non-Value-Added Activities** *(LO 14.1)*

Several activities related to different businesses follow.

(a) Preparing a purchase order
(b) Storing raw materials
(c) Reworking products
(d) Handling customer complaints
(e) Sewing fabric to make clothing
(f) Inspecting quality of purchased material
(g) Matching receiving reports to purchase orders
(h) Ringing up a customer sale on a register
(i) Printing a customer's airline ticket
(j) Moving products from one area to another
(k) Copying documents in a law office
(l) Inspecting the finished product in a pharmaceutical company
(m) Packing men's dress shirts in cellophane bags
(n) Designing a new product
(o) Filing paid supplier invoices
(p) Issuing engineering change orders for products
(q) Mixing ingredients to make salad dressing
(r) Assembling product parts
(s) Cleaning up spills
(t) Bagging clothing after dry cleaning

Required:

Identify which of the listed items are value-added and which are non-value-added from the standpoint of the end customer for the organization performing the task.

22. **Activity-Based Costing** *(LO 14.2 & 14.3, Excel)*

Kiawanee Corp. manufactures Products X, Y, and Z. These products have the following costs and production operating statistics:

	Product X	Product Y	Product Z
Direct material and labor cost	$180,000	$140,000	$200,000
Direct labor hours required	40,000	30,000	10,000
Machine hours required	15,000	20,000	40,000
Pounds of material required	600,000	300,000	100,000
Number of setups required	20	25	10
Number of units produced	80,000	40,000	8,000

The company's total overhead cost is $1,229,000, which is comprised of costs for the following activities (shown with an appropriate cost driver):

Activity	Cost	Driver
Materials handling	$700,000	Pounds of materials used
Scheduling and setup	132,000	Number of setups
Utilities and depreciation	345,000	Machine hours incurred
Indirect materials used	52,000	Direct labor hours

The competitive market process has set the selling prices of Products X, Y, and Z at $11, $15, and $45, respectively.

Required:

(1) Assume that the company applies overhead on a direct labor hour basis. Determine the overhead cost (round to two decimal points) per direct labor hour. Determine the total cost per unit of Products X, Y, and Z.

(2) Using the information determined in part (1) and the sales prices given, what decision might Kiawanee management make about its products?

(3) Calculate the overhead cost per activity if the designated cost drivers are used.

(4) Determine the cost per unit of Products X, Y, and Z if the company applies overhead on the activity-based costing information developed in part (3).

(5) Using the information determined in part (4) and the sales prices given, what decision might Kiawanee management make about its products? Why does this decision differ from that determined in part (2)?

(6) Is Kiawanee using the appropriate cost drivers? Give an alternate suggestion for each cost driver and explain why that suggestion was made.

23. **Cost Center Performance Measurement** *(LO 14.4)*

The following budgeted and actual costs existed for the Placement Office of Tempe's community college for 2002.

	Budget	Actual
Salaries for professional staff	$150,000	$165,000
Printing and postage	650	910
Job fair events	4,600	6,800
Depreciation on computer equipment	1,200	1,200
Supplies	2,900	3,200

Required:

(1) Determine the variances for each budget item.

(2) Do you think that the Placement Director did a good job in controlling costs? Why or why not?

(3) Would you change your answer to part (2) if you knew that the Placement Office had expected to place 65 percent of the college's graduates in 2002 but, instead, placed 85 percent of the graduates? Why or why not?

24. **Profit Center Performance Measurement** *(LO 14.4)*

Silence is Golden is a division of Tranquility, Inc. The division produces relaxation tapes and is considered a profit center. The following budgeted and actual information is available for August 2003:

Budgeted sales	150,000 tapes at $9.00 per tape
Actual sales	190,000 tapes at $7.50 per tape

Required:

Compute the price, volume, and total revenue variances for the division.

25. Cost and Profit Center Performance Measurement *(LO 14.4, Internet)*

The El Paso Division of the Tejas Fence Co. is currently operated as a cost center. The following standard costs have been determined for the production of one metal gate at the El Paso Division.

Pipe (50 feet at $0.80 per foot)		$40.00
Direct labor (2 hours at $9.00 per hour)		18.00
Overhead:		
Indirect material	$1.20	
Indirect labor	.60	
Depreciation	3.50	
Utilities	.90	
Maintenance	.50	
Other	1.30	8.00
Total		$66.00

These costs have been determined using a normal production quantity of 55,000 gates per month. All gates are transferred to the Amarillo Division where they are hung on posts, painted with rustproof paint, and sold to distributors.

During October 2003, El Paso Division produced 50,000 gates and incurred the following costs.

Pipe (2,590,000 feet purchased and used)	$1,813,000
Direct labor (120,000 hours)	1,086,000
Indirect material	40,000
Indirect labor	25,000
Depreciation	155,000
Utilities	52,500
Maintenance	17,500
Other	55,000

Required:

(1) What is the standard total cost for October's production? What was the total actual cost of production for October? Based on these figures, did the manager of the division do a good job in controlling costs?

(2) Prepare a line-by-line comparison of standard and actual costs for October. Based on these figures, what concerns might be expressed about the manager's ability to control costs?

(3) Assume that top management of Tejas Fence Co. has decided to establish a "selling price" of $85 for the gates from El Paso Division to the Amarillo Division. One of the reasons for the increased usage of pipe during October was that the pipe purchased was of slightly inferior quality than the pipe normally used. Because of this, Amarillo Division refused to "pay" $85 for the gates and established a price of $80 per gate. Calculate the revenue variances for El Paso Division.

(4) A "selling price" between divisions is referred to as a transfer price. Use logic and library or Internet resources to discuss how and why such a price might be set.

26. Return on Investment *(LO 14.4)*

Gary Corp. has three divisions that are classified as investment centers. Selected financial information about the each division follows.

	Division 1	Division 2	Division 3
Net income for year	$ 450,000	$ 980,000	$ 1,340,000
Sales for year	1,569,000	3,986,000	8,231,000
Assets	14,350,000	29,438,000	37,259,000

Required:

(1) Calculate the return on investment for each division. How would you rank the divisions in terms of levels of performance?

(2) Calculate the profit margin and asset turnover for each division. How would you rank the divisions in terms of levels of performance?

(3) Assume that the manager of Division 1 was new to her job. She has found that the previous manager did not dispose of approximately $2,400,000 of assets that were no longer being used by the division to manufacture products. Exclude these assets from the asset base and recalculate the asset turnover and return on investment for Division 1. Does this information affect your rankings of the division's performance? Explain.

27. **Balanced Scorecard and Performance Reward** *(LO 14.5 & 14.6)*

You are the owner of a small movie-rental store run by a full-time manager.

Required:

(1) Develop a brief mission statement for your business.

(2) Prepare a balanced scorecard for the manager, providing at least three measurements in each balanced scorecard category. Make certain that your measurements reflect the business mission.

(3) Prepare a balanced scorecard for the four part-time employees of the business, providing at least two measurements in each balanced scorecard category.

(4) Why are there differences between the scorecards developed in parts (2) and (3)?

(5) Design a reward system that would encourage the store manager to achieve the scorecard metrics.

CASES

28. **Value-Added and Non-Value-Added Activities** *(LO 14.1, writing)*

There is a distinct difference in many organizations between instituting activities that enhance quality production or service and activities that would be considered quality inspection. For example, installing a machine that has an automatic cut-off when a flawed product is detected is considered quality enhancement and is value-added. Having employees inspect each product after production is completed is non-value-added.

Required:

Choose an organization with which you are familiar, such as your school or your workplace. Write a short paper on some of the quality activities that you believe are value-added and some of the quality activities that you believe are non-value-added. Explain the reasons for your classifications.

29. **Benchmarking** *(LO 14.6, group, Internet)*

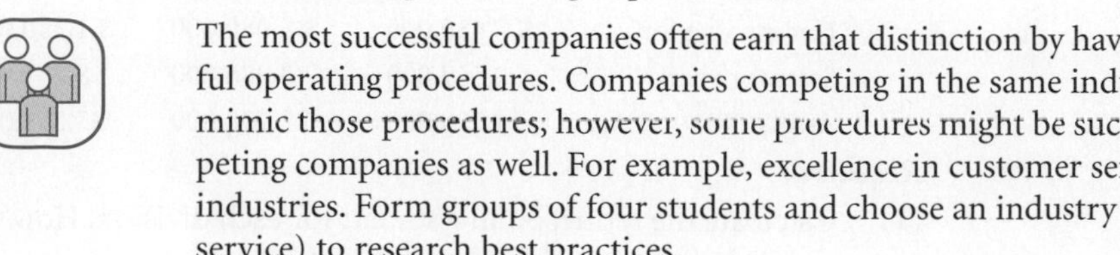

The most successful companies often earn that distinction by have the most successful operating procedures. Companies competing in the same industry often want to mimic those procedures; however, some procedures might be successful in noncompeting companies as well. For example, excellence in customer service is good for all industries. Form groups of four students and choose an industry (manufacturing or service) to research best practices.

Required—Individuals:

(1) Use library and Internet resources to research benchmarking and "best in class" (or "world class") companies.

(2) What organizations did you find that were mentioned as being "best in class"?

(3) What types of criteria were used to make this judgment?

Required—Groups:

(4) Get together as a group and combine your research. How was your research similar and different?

(5) Are the best practices you found specific to the industry in which the organization operates or would they be useful in other industries?

30. **Profit Center and Performance Measures** *(LO 14.4 & 14.6, writing, ethics)*

Icon Film Manufacturers makes film for still and motion picture cameras and other related items. Icon is divided into several divisions, each of which is treated as a profit center. Icon's upper management rewards the manager of the 35mm film division with an annual bonus equal to a percentage of the net income of the division.

Required:

(1) Is net income the best way to evaluate the performance of the manager's performance? Explain your answer.

(2) Should net income be the only method to evaluate the manager's performance? If not, list other measures.

(3) Can the manager of a profit center manipulate net income to increase his/her year-end bonus? Explain your answer.

(4) During a conversation with the Chief Executive Officer (CEO) of Icon, you learn that the manager of the 35 mm Film Division is planning to retire in two years. Write a memo to the CEO of Icon explaining the items discussed in parts (1), (2), and (3) and why these evaluation methods and concerns may be more important given the impending retirement of the manager.

31. **Annual Reports** *(LO 14.3 & 14.4, Internet, Excel)*

Use the annual report of Carnival Corporation (www.carnival.com) for the 2001 fiscal year to answer the following questions.

Required:

(1) Assume that Carnival has two investment centers: cruise and tour. [Hint: See page 18 of the annual report.]

 (a) Calculate the return on investment for 2001, 2000, and 1999 for each center using the Du Pont model.

 (b) Compare year to year for each division and comment on the trend for each division.

 (c) Compare the two divisions and comment on the relationship.

(2) Carnival lists corporate expenses that are not assigned to a particular division. If Carnival plans to treat divisions as investment centers, should the corporate expenses be divided between the divisions? If yes, what is the best method?

32. **Performance Rewards** *(LO 14.6)*

Holland's is a small ladies' clothing store with fourteen employees. On any day, eight or nine employees will be scheduled to work. More than 95 percent of Holland's revenues are from the sale of clothing, and the remainder is from the sale of accessories such as gentle fabric wash, stain remover, padded hangers, and so forth.

Employees are informed of the daily sales projection, but individual employees are not given a sales quota. March is Holland's slowest month. To encourage the sales people to work harder in March, they are given $0.25 for every accessory item they sell, and the top sales person gets a $10 bonus for the month.

Required:

(1) Is the $0.25 incentive a good performance reward? Can it be improved? Explain.

(2) Is the $10 bonus a good performance reward? Can it be improved? Explain.

SUPPLEMENTAL PROBLEMS

33. **Value-Added and Non-Value-Added Activities** *(LO 14.1)* [Compare to Problem 21.]

Ron Serrillo is the Personnel Manager at Emmerling, Inc. He has analyzed his applicant interview process for the last two weeks and has found he consistently performs the following activities.

(a) Reads applicant's resume
(b) Straightens desk prior to interview
(c) Walks from desk to get cup of coffee
(d) Returns to desk and drinks coffee
(e) Scans applicant's resume
(f) Uses intercom to ask receptionist to send in applicant
(g) Stands to greet applicant
(h) Shakes applicant's hand
(i) Sits down
(j) Picks up resume and scans
(k) Interviews applicant
(l) Stands to say goodbye to applicant
(m) Shakes applicant's hand
(n) Sits down
(o) Scans resume
(p) Makes notes on interview
(q) Walks from desk to get cup of coffee
(r) Returns to desk and drinks coffee
(s) Makes decision about whether to hire applicant

Required:

Indicate whether each of these activities is value-added or non-value-added, as related to the outcome of the activity. Provide a brief reason for each of your determinations.

34. **Activity-Based Costing** *(LO 14.3)* [Compare to Problem 22.]

The purchasing department of Xena Co. creates $338,000 of overhead costs each year. The annual cost and quantity of activity involved in each primary task in the department follow.

Activity	**Cost**	**Driver**	**Quantity of Driver**
Finding suppliers	$ 80,000	# of Internet searches	100,000
Issuing purchase orders	190,000	# of purchase orders	10,000
Matching POs and receiving reports	68,000	# of matches	8,000

The number of purchase orders differs from the number of matches required because many suppliers ship multiple orders together. Product #548 required 25 Internet searches, 4 purchase orders, and 1 match.

Required:

(1) Assume that Xena allocates all purchasing department costs to products using number of purchase orders issued only. Calculate the purchasing department cost that would be allocated to Product #548.

(2) Assume that Xena allocates purchasing department costs to products using activity-based costing. Determine the cost per type of activity in the purchasing department. Determine the purchasing department cost that would be allocated to Product #548.

(3) Which of the two allocations do you believe to be a more accurate representation of the cost of Product #548? Explain the reasoning for your answer.

APPENDIX

Table 1: Present Value of $1

Table 2: Present Value of an Ordinary Annuity of $1

Table 1: Present Value of $1

Period	1.00%	2.00%	3.00%	4.00%	5.00%	6.00%	7.00%	8.00%	9.00%	9.50%	10.00%	10.50%	11.00%
1	0.9901	.09804	0.9709	0.9615	0.9524	0.9434	0.9346	0.9259	0.9174	0.9132	0.9091	0.9050	0.9009
2	0.9803	0.9612	0.9426	0.9246	0.9070	0.8900	0.8734	0.8573	0.8417	0.8340	0.8265	0.8190	0.8116
3	0.9706	0.9423	0.9151	0.8890	0.8638	0.8396	0.8163	0.7938	0.7722	0.7617	0.7513	0.7412	0.7312
4	0.9610	0.9239	0.8885	0.8548	0.8227	0.7921	0.7629	0.7350	0.7084	0.6956	0.6830	0.6707	0.6587
5	0.9515	0.9057	0.8626	0.8219	0.7835	0.7473	0.7130	0.6806	0.6499	0.6352	0.6209	0.6070	0.5935
6	0.9421	0.8880	0.8375	0.7903	0.7462	0.7050	0.6663	0.6302	0.5963	0.5801	0.5645	0.5493	0.5346
7	0.9327	0.8706	0.8131	0.7599	0.7107	0.6651	0.6228	0.5835	0.5470	0.5298	0.5132	0.4971	0.4817
8	0.9235	0.8535	0.7894	0.7307	0.6768	0.6274	0.5820	0.5403	0.5019	0.4838	0.4665	0.4499	0.4339
9	0.9143	0.8368	0.7664	0.7026	0.6446	0.5919	0.5439	0.5003	0.4604	0.4419	0.4241	0.4071	0.3909
10	0.9053	0.8204	0.7441	0.6756	0.6139	0.5584	0.5084	0.4632	0.4224	0.4035	0.3855	0.3685	0.3522
11	0.8963	0.8043	0.7224	0.6496	0.5847	0.5268	0.4751	0.4289	0.3875	0.3685	0.3505	0.3334	0.3173
12	0.8875	0.7885	0.7014	0.6246	0.5568	0.4970	0.4440	0.3971	0.3555	0.3365	0.3186	0.3018	0.2858
13	0.8787	0.7730	0.6810	0.6006	0.5303	0.4688	0.4150	0.3677	0.3262	0.3073	0.2897	0.2731	0.2575
14	0.8700	0.7579	0.6611	0.5775	0.5051	0.4423	0.3878	0.3405	0.2993	0.2807	0.2633	0.2471	0.2320
15	0.8614	0.7430	0.6419	0.5553	0.4810	0.4173	0.3625	0.3152	0.2745	0.2563	0.2394	0.2237	0.2090
16	0.8528	0.7285	0.6232	0.5339	0.4581	0.3937	0.3387	0.2919	0.2519	0.2341	0.2176	0.2024	0.1883
17	0.8444	0.7142	0.6050	0.5134	0.4363	0.3714	0.3166	0.2703	0.2311	0.2138	0.1978	0.1832	0.1696
18	0.8360	0.7002	0.5874	0.4936	0.4155	0.3503	0.2959	0.2503	0.2120	0.1952	0.1799	0.1658	0.1528
19	0.8277	0.6864	0.5703	0.4746	0.3957	0.3305	0.2765	0.2317	0.1945	0.1783	0.1635	0.1500	0.1377
20	0.8195	0.6730	0.5537	0.4564	0.3769	0.3118	0.2584	0.2146	0.1784	0.1628	0.1486	0.1358	0.1240
21	0.8114	0.6598	0.5376	0.4388	0.3589	0.2942	0.2415	0.1987	0.1637	0.1487	0.1351	0.1229	0.1117
22	0.8034	0.6468	0.5219	0.4220	0.3419	0.2775	0.2257	0.1839	0.1502	0.1358	0.1229	0.1112	0.1007
23	0.7954	0.6342	0.5067	0.4057	0.3256	0.2618	0.2110	0.1703	0.1378	0.1240	0.1117	0.1006	0.0907
24	0.7876	0.6217	0.4919	0.3901	0.3101	0.2470	0.1972	0.1577	0.1264	0.1133	0.1015	0.0911	0.0817
25	0.7798	0.6095	0.4776	0.3751	0.2953	0.2330	0.1843	0.1460	0.1160	0.1034	0.0923	0.0824	0.0736
26	0.7721	0.5976	0.4637	0.3607	0.2812	0.2198	0.1722	0.1352	0.1064	0.0945	0.0839	0.0746	0.0663
27	0.7644	0.5859	0.4502	0.3468	0.2679	0.2074	0.1609	0.1252	0.0976	0.0863	0.0763	0.0675	0.0597
28	0.7568	0.5744	0.4371	0.3335	0.2551	0.1956	0.1504	0.1159	0.0896	0.0788	0.0693	0.0611	0.0538
29	0.7493	0.5631	0.4244	0.3207	0.2430	0.1846	0.1406	0.1073	0.0822	0.0719	0.0630	0.0553	0.0485
30	0.7419	0.5521	0.4120	0.3083	0.2314	0.1741	0.1314	0.0994	0.0754	0.0657	0.0573	0.0500	0.0437
31	0.7346	0.5413	0.4000	0.2965	0.2204	0.1643	0.1228	0.0920	0.0692	0.0600	0.0521	0.0453	0.0394
32	0.7273	0.5306	0.3883	0.2851	0.2099	0.1550	0.1147	0.0852	0.0634	0.0058	0.0474	0.0410	0.0355
33	0.7201	0.5202	0.3770	0.2741	0.1999	0.1462	0.1072	0.0789	0.0582	0.0500	0.0431	0.0371	0.0319
34	0.7130	0.5100	0.3660	0.2636	0.1904	0.1379	0.1002	0.0731	0.0534	0.0457	0.0391	0.0336	0.0288
35	0.7059	0.5000	0.3554	0.2534	0.1813	0.1301	0.0937	0.0676	0.0490	0.0417	0.0356	0.0304	0.0259
36	0.6989	0.4902	0.3450	0.2437	0.1727	0.1227	0.0875	0.0626	0.0449	0.0381	0.0324	0.0275	0.0234
37	0.6920	0.4806	0.3350	0.2343	0.1644	0.1158	0.0818	0.0580	0.0412	0.0348	0.0294	0.0249	0.0210
38	0.6852	0.4712	0.3252	0.2253	0.1566	0.1092	0.0765	0.0537	0.0378	0.0318	0.0267	0.0225	0.0190
39	0.6784	0.4620	0.3158	0.2166	0.1492	0.1031	0.0715	0.0497	0.0347	0.0290	0.0243	0.0204	0.0171
40	0.6717	0.4529	0.3066	0.2083	0.1421	0.0972	0.0668	0.0460	0.0318	0.0265	0.0221	0.0184	0.0154
41	0.6650	0.4440	0.2976	0.2003	0.1353	0.0917	0.0624	0.0426	0.0292	0.0242	0.0201	0.0167	0.0139
42	0.6584	0.4353	0.2890	0.1926	0.1288	0.0865	0.0583	0.0395	0.0268	0.0221	0.0183	0.0151	0.0125
43	0.6519	0.4268	0.2805	0.1852	0.1227	0.0816	0.0545	0.0365	0.0246	0.0202	0.0166	0.0137	0.0113
44	0.6455	0.4184	0.2724	0.1781	0.1169	0.0770	0.0510	0.0338	0.0226	0.0184	0.0151	0.0124	0.0101
45	0.6391	0.4102	0.2644	0.1712	0.1113	0.0727	0.0476	0.0313	0.0207	0.0168	0.0137	0.0112	0.0091
46	0.6327	0.4022	0.2567	0.1646	0.1060	0.0685	0.0445	0.0290	0.0190	0.0154	0.0125	0.0101	0.0082
47	0.6265	0.3943	0.2493	0.1583	0.1010	0.0647	0.0416	0.0269	0.0174	0.0141	0.0113	0.0092	0.0074
48	0.6203	0.3865	0.2420	0.1522	0.0961	0.0610	0.0389	0.0249	0.0160	0.0128	0.0103	0.0083	0.0067
49	0.6141	0.3790	0.2350	0.1463	0.0916	0.0576	0.0363	0.0230	0.0147	0.0117	0.0094	0.0075	0.0060
50	0.6080	0.3715	0.2281	0.1407	0.0872	0.0543	0.0340	0.0213	0.0135	0.0107	0.0085	0.0068	0.0054

11.50%	12.00%	12.50%	13.00%	13.50%	14.00%	14.50%	15.00%	15.50%	16.00%	17.00%	18.00%	19.00%	20.00%
0.8969	0.8929	0.8889	0.8850	0.8811	0.8772	0.8734	0.8696	0.8658	0.8621	0.8547	0.8475	0.8403	0.8333
0.8044	0.7972	0.7901	0.7832	0.7763	0.7695	0.7628	0.7561	0.7496	0.7432	0.7305	0.7182	0.7062	0.6944
0.7214	0.7118	0.7023	0.6931	0.6839	0.6750	0.6662	0.6575	0.6490	0.6407	0.6244	0.6086	0.5934	0.5787
0.6470	0.6355	0.6243	0.6133	0.6206	0.5921	0.5818	0.5718	0.5619	0.5523	0.5337	0.5158	0.4987	0.4823
0.5803	0.5674	0.5549	0.5428	0.5309	0.5194	0.5081	0.4972	0.4865	0.4761	0.4561	0.4371	0.4191	0.4019
0.5204	0.5066	0.4933	0.4803	0.4678	0.4556	0.4438	0.4323	0.4212	0.4104	0.3898	0.3704	0.3521	0.3349
0.4667	0.4524	0.4385	0.4251	0.4121	0.3996	0.3876	0.3759	0.3647	0.3538	0.3332	0.3139	0.2959	0.2791
0.4186	0.4039	0.3897	0.3762	0.3631	0.3506	0.3385	0.3269	0.3158	0.3050	0.2848	0.2660	0.2487	0.2326
0.3754	0.3606	0.3464	0.3329	0.3199	0.3075	0.2956	0.2843	0.2734	0.2630	0.2434	0.2255	0.2090	0.1938
0.3367	0.3220	0.3080	0.2946	0.2819	0.2697	0.2582	0.2472	0.2367	0.2267	0.2080	0.1911	0.1756	0.1615
0.3020	0.2875	0.2737	0.2607	0.2483	0.2366	0.2255	0.2149	0.2049	0.1954	0.1778	0.1619	0.1476	0.1346
0.2708	0.2567	0.2433	0.2307	0.2188	0.2076	0.1969	0.1869	0.1774	0.1685	0.1520	0.1372	0.1240	0.1122
0.2429	0.2292	0.2163	0.2042	0.1928	0.1821	0.1720	0.1625	0.1536	0.1452	0.1299	0.1163	0.1042	0.0935
0.2179	0.2046	0.1923	0.1807	0.1699	0.1597	0.1502	0.1413	0.1330	0.1252	0.1110	0.0986	0.0876	0.0779
0.1954	0.1827	0.1709	0.1599	0.1496	0.1401	0.1312	0.1229	0.1152	0.1079	0.0949	0.0835	0.0736	0.0649
0.1752	0.1631	0.1519	0.1415	0.1319	0.1229	0.1146	0.1069	0.0997	0.0930	0.0811	0.0708	0.0618	0.0541
0.1572	0.1456	0.1350	0.1252	0.1162	0.1078	0.1001	0.0929	0.0863	0.0802	0.0693	0.0600	0.0520	0.0451
0.1410	0.1300	0.1200	0.1108	0.1024	0.0946	0.0874	0.0808	0.0747	0.0691	0.0593	0.0508	0.0437	0.0376
0.1264	0.1161	0.1067	0.0981	0.0902	0.0830	0.0763	0.0703	0.0647	0.0596	0.0506	0.0431	0.0367	0.0313
0.1134	0.1037	0.0948	0.0868	0.0795	0.0728	0.0667	0.0611	0.0560	0.0514	0.0433	0.0365	0.0308	0.0261
0.1017	0.0926	0.0843	0.0768	0.0700	0.0638	0.0582	0.0531	0.0485	0.0443	0.0370	0.0309	0.0259	0.0217
0.0912	0.0826	0.0749	0.0680	0.0617	0.0560	0.0509	0.0462	0.0420	0.0382	0.0316	0.0262	0.0218	0.0181
0.0818	0.0738	0.0666	0.0601	0.0543	0.0491	0.0444	0.0402	0.0364	0.0329	0.0270	0.0222	0.0183	0.0151
0.0734	0.0659	0.0592	0.0532	0.0479	0.0431	0.0388	0.0349	0.0315	0.0284	0.0231	0.0188	0.0154	0.0126
0.0658	0.0588	0.0526	0.0471	0.0422	0.0378	0.0339	0.0304	0.0273	0.0245	0.0197	0.0160	0.0129	0.0105
0.0590	0.0525	0.0468	0.0417	0.0372	0.0332	0.0296	0.0264	0.0236	0.0211	0.0169	0.0135	0.0109	0.0087
0.0529	0.0469	0.0416	0.0369	0.0327	0.0291	0.0258	0.0230	0.0204	0.0182	0.0144	0.0115	0.0091	0.0073
0.0475	0.0419	0.0370	0.0326	0.0289	0.0255	0.0226	0.0200	0.0177	0.0157	0.0123	0.0097	0.0077	0.0061
0.0426	0.0374	0.0329	0.0289	0.0254	0.0224	0.0197	0.0174	0.0153	0.0135	0.0105	0.0082	0.0064	0.0051
0.0382	0.0334	0.0292	0.0256	0.0224	0.0196	0.0172	0.0151	0.0133	0.0117	0.0090	0.0070	0.0054	0.0042
0.0342	0.0298	0.0260	0.0226	0.0197	0.0172	0.0150	0.0131	0.0115	0.0100	0.0077	0.0059	0.0046	0.0035
0.0307	0.0266	0.0231	0.0200	0.0174	0.0151	0.0131	0.0114	0.0099	0.0087	0.0066	0.0050	0.0038	0.0029
0.0275	0.0238	0.0205	0.0177	0.0153	0.0133	0.0115	0.0099	0.0086	0.0075	0.0056	0.0043	0.0032	0.0024
0.0247	0.0212	0.0182	0.0157	0.0135	0.0116	0.0100	0.0088	0.0075	0.0064	0.0048	0.0036	0.0027	0.0020
0.0222	0.0189	0.0162	0.0139	0.0119	0.0102	0.0088	0.0075	0.0065	0.0056	0.0041	0.0031	0.0023	0.0017
0.0199	0.0169	0.0144	0.0123	0.0105	0.0089	0.0076	0.0065	0.0056	0.0048	0.0035	0.0026	0.0019	0.0014
0.0178	0.0151	0.0128	0.0109	0.0092	0.0078	0.0067	0.0057	0.0048	0.0041	0.0030	0.0022	0.0016	0.0012
0.0160	0.0135	0.0114	0.0096	0.0081	0.0069	0.0058	0.0049	0.0042	0.0036	0.0026	0.0019	0.0014	0.0010
0.0143	0.0120	0.0101	0.0085	0.0072	0.0060	0.0051	0.0043	0.0036	0.0031	0.0022	0.0016	0.0011	0.0008
0.0129	0.0108	0.0090	0.0075	0.0063	0.0053	0.0044	0.0037	0.0031	0.0026	0.0019	0.0013	0.0010	0.0007
0.0115	0.0096	0.0080	0.0067	0.0056	0.0046	0.0039	0.0033	0.0027	0.0023	0.0016	0.0011	0.0008	0.0006
0.0103	0.0086	0.0077	0.0059	0.0049	0.0041	0.0034	0.0028	0.0024	0.0020	0.0014	0.0010	0.0007	0.0005
0.0093	0.0077	0.0063	0.0052	0.0043	0.0036	0.0030	0.0025	0.0020	0.0017	0.0012	0.0008	0.0006	0.0004
0.0083	0.0068	0.0056	0.0046	0.0038	0.0031	0.0026	0.0021	0.0018	0.0015	0.0010	0.0007	0.0005	0.0003
0.0075	0.0061	0.0050	0.0041	0.0034	0.0028	0.0023	0.0019	0.0015	0.0013	0.0009	0.0006	0.0004	0.0003
0.0067	0.0054	0.0044	0.0036	0.0030	0.0024	0.0020	0.0016	0.0013	0.0011	0.0007	0.0005	0.0003	0.0002
0.0060	0.0049	0.0039	0.0032	0.0026	0.0021	0.0017	0.0014	0.0011	0.0009	0.0006	0.0004	0.0003	0.0002
0.0054	0.0043	0.0035	0.0028	0.0023	0.0019	0.0015	0.0012	0.0010	0.0008	0.0005	0.0004	0.0002	0.0002
0.0048	0.0039	0.0031	0.0025	0.0020	0.0016	0.0013	0.0011	0.0009	0.0007	0.0005	0.0003	0.0002	0.0001
0.0043	0.0035	0.0028	0.0022	0.0018	0.0014	0.0012	0.0009	0.0007	0.0006	0.0004	0.0003	0.0002	0.0001

Table 2: Present Value of an Ordinary Annuity of $1

Period	1.00%	2.00%	3.00%	4.00%	5.00%	6.00%	7.00%	8.00%	9.00%	9.50%	10.00%	10.50%	11.00%
1	0.9901	0.9804	0.9709	0.9615	0.0524	0.9434	0.9346	0.9259	0.9174	0.9132	0.9091	0.9050	0.9009
2	1.9704	1.9416	1.9135	1.8861	1.8594	1.8334	1.8080	1.7833	1.7591	1.7473	1.7355	1.7240	1.7125
3	2.9410	2.8839	2.8286	2.7751	2.7233	2.6730	2.6243	2.5771	2.5313	2.5089	2.4869	2.4651	2.4437
4	3.9020	3.8077	3.7171	3.6299	3.5460	3.4651	3.3872	3.3121	3.2397	3.2045	3.1699	3.1359	3.1025
5	4.8534	4.7135	4.5797	4.4518	4.3295	4.2124	4.1002	3.9927	3.8897	3.8397	3.7908	3.7429	3.6959
6	5.7955	5.6014	5.4172	5.2421	5.0757	4.9173	4.7665	4.6229	4.4859	4.4198	4.3553	4.2922	4.2305
7	6.7282	6.4720	6.2303	6.0021	5.7864	5.5824	5.3893	5.2064	5.0330	4.9496	4.8684	4.7893	4.7122
8	7.6517	7.3255	7.0197	6.7327	6.4632	6.2098	5.9713	5.7466	5.5348	5.4334	5.3349	5.2392	5.1461
9	8.5660	8.1622	7.7861	7.4353	7.1078	6.8017	6.5152	6.2469	5.9953	5.8753	5.7590	5.6463	5.5371
10	9.7413	8.9826	8.5302	8.1109	7.7217	7.3601	7.0236	6.7101	6.4177	6.2788	6.1446	6.0148	5.8892
11	10.3676	9.7869	9.2526	8.7605	8.3064	7.8869	7.4987	7.1390	6.8052	6.6473	6.4951	6.3482	6.2065
12	11.2551	10.5753	9.9540	9.3851	8.8633	8.3838	7.9427	7.5361	7.1607	6.9838	6.8137	6.6500	6.4924
13	12.1337	11.3484	10.6350	9.9857	9.3936	8.8527	8.3577	7.9038	7.4869	7.2912	7.1034	6.9230	6.7499
14	13.0037	12.1063	11.2961	10.5631	9.8986	9.2950	8.7455	8.2442	7.7862	7.5719	7.3667	7.1702	6.9819
15	13.8651	12.8493	11.9379	11.1184	10.3797	9.7123	9.1079	8.5595	8.0607	7.8282	7.6061	7.3938	7.1909
16	14.7179	13.5777	12.5611	11.6523	10.8378	10.1059	9.4467	8.8514	8.3126	8.0623	7.8237	7.5962	7.3792
17	15.5623	14.2919	13.1661	12.1657	11.2741	10.4773	9.7632	9.1216	8.5436	8.2760	8.0216	7.7794	7.5488
18	16.3983	14.9920	13.7535	12.6593	11.6896	10.8276	10.0591	9.3719	8.7556	8.4713	8.2014	7.9452	7.7016
19	17.2260	15.6785	14.3238	13.1339	12.0853	11.1581	10.3356	9.6036	8.9501	8.6496	8.3649	8.0952	7.8939
20	18.0456	16.3514	14.8775	13.5903	12.4622	11.4699	10.5940	9.8182	9.1286	8.8124	8.5136	8.2309	7.9633
21	18.8570	17.0112	15.4150	14.0292	12.8212	11.7641	10.8355	10.0168	9.2922	8.9611	8.6487	8.3538	8.0751
22	19.6604	17.6581	15.9369	14.4511	13.1630	12.0416	11.0612	10.2007	9.4424	9.0969	8.7715	8.4649	8.1757
23	20.4558	18.2922	16.4436	14.8568	13.4886	12.3034	11.2722	10.3711	9.5802	9.2209	8.8832	8.5656	8.2664
24	21.2434	18.9139	16.9355	15.2470	13.7986	12.5504	11.4693	10.5288	9.7066	9.3342	8.9847	8.6566	8.3481
25	22.0232	19.5235	17.4132	15.6221	14.0939	12.7834	11.6536	10.6748	9.8226	9.4376	9.0770	8.7390	8.4217
26	22.7952	20.1210	17.8768	15.9828	14.3752	13.0032	11.8258	10.8100	9.9290	9.5320	9.1610	8.8136	8.4881
27	23.5596	20.7069	18.3270	16.3296	14.6430	13.2105	11.9867	10.9352	10.0266	9.6183	9.2372	8.8811	8.5478
28	24.3164	21.2813	18.7641	16.6631	14.8981	13.4062	12.1371	11.0511	10.1161	9.6971	9.3066	8.9422	8.6016
29	25.0658	21.8444	19.1885	16.9837	15.1411	13.5907	12.2777	11.1584	10.1983	9.7690	9.3696	8.9974	8.6501
30	25.8077	22.3965	19.6004	17.2920	15.3725	13.7648	12.4090	11.2578	10.2737	9.8347	9.4269	9.0474	8.6938
31	26.5423	22.9377	20.0004	17.5885	15.5928	13.9291	12.5318	11.3498	10.3428	9.8947	9.4790	9.0927	8.7332
32	27.2696	23.4683	20.3888	17.8736	15.8027	14.0840	12.6466	11.4350	10.4062	9.9495	9.5264	9.1337	8.7686
33	27.9897	23.9886	20.7658	18.1477	16.0026	14.2302	12.7538	11.5139	10.4664	9.9996	9.5694	9.1707	8.8005
34	28.7027	24.4986	21.1318	18.4112	16.1929	14.3681	12.8540	11.5869	10.5178	10.0453	9.6086	9.2043	8.8293
35	29.4086	24.9986	21.4872	18.6646	16.3742	14.4983	12.9477	11.6546	10.5668	10.0870	9.6442	9.2347	8.8552
36	30.1075	25.4888	21.8323	18.9083	16.5469	14.6210	13.0352	11.7172	10.6118	10.1251	9.6765	9.2621	8.8786
37	30.7995	25.9695	22.1672	19.1426	16.7113	14.7368	13.1170	11.7752	10.6530	10.1599	9.7059	9.2870	8.8996
38	31.4847	26.4406	22.4925	19.3679	16.8679	14.8460	13.1935	11.8289	10.6908	10.1917	9.7327	9.3095	8.9186
39	32.1630	26.9026	22.8082	19.5845	17.0170	14.9491	13.2649	11.8786	10.7255	10.2207	9.7570	9.3299	8.9357
40	32.8347	27.3555	23.1148	19.7928	17.1591	15.0463	13.3317	11.9246	10.7574	10.2473	9.7791	9.3483	8.9511
41	33.4997	27.7995	23.4124	19.9931	17.2944	15.1380	13.3941	11.9672	10.7866	10.2715	9.7991	9.3650	8.9649
42	34.1581	28.2348	23.7014	20.1856	17.4232	15.2245	13.4525	12.0067	10.8134	10.2936	9.8174	9.3801	8.9774
43	34.8100	28.6616	23.9819	20.3708	17.5459	15.3062	13.5070	12.0432	10.8380	10.3138	9.8340	9.3937	8.9887
44	35.4555	29.0800	24.2543	20.5488	17.6628	15.3832	13.5579	12.0771	10.8605	10.3322	9.8491	9.4061	8.9988
45	36.0945	29.4902	24.5187	20.7200	17.7741	15.4558	13.6055	12.1084	10.8812	10.3490	9.8628	9.4163	9.0079
46	36.7272	29.8923	24.7755	20.8847	17.8801	15.5244	13.6500	12.1374	10.9002	10.3644	9.8753	9.4274	9.0161
47	37.3537	30.2866	25.0247	21.0429	17.9810	15.5890	13.6916	12.1643	10.9176	10.3785	9.8866	9.4366	9.0236
48	37.9740	30.6731	25.2667	21.1951	18.0772	15.6500	13.7305	12.1891	10.9336	10.3913	9.8969	9.4449	9.0302
49	38.5881	31.0521	25.5017	21.3415	18.1687	15.7076	13.7668	12.2122	10.9482	10.4030	9.9063	9.4524	9.0362
50	39.1961	31.4236	25.7298	21.4822	18.2559	15.7619	13.8008	12.2335	10.9617	10.4137	99.148	9.4591	9.0417

11.50%	12.00%	12.50%	13.00%	13.50%	14.00%	14.50%	15.00%	15.50%	16.00%	17.00%	18.00%	19.00%	20.00%
.08969	0.8929	0.8889	0.8850	0.8811	0.8772	0.8734	0.8696	0.8658	0.8621	0.8547	0.8475	0.8403	0.8333
1.7012	1.6901	1.6790	1.6681	1.6573	1.6467	1.6361	1.6257	1.1654	1.6052	1.5852	1.5656	1.5465	1.5278
2.4226	2.4018	2.3813	2.3612	2.3413	2.3216	2.3023	2.2832	2.2644	2.2459	2.2096	2.1743	2.1399	2.1065
3.0696	3.0374	3.0056	2.9745	2.9438	2.9137	2.8841	2.8550	2.8263	2.7982	2.7432	2.6901	2.6386	2.5887
3.6499	3.6048	3.5606	3.5172	3.4747	3.4331	3.3922	3.3522	3.3129	3.2743	3.1994	3.1272	3.0576	2.9906
4.1703	4.1114	4.0538	3.9976	3.9425	3.8887	3.8360	3.7845	3.7341	3.6847	3.5892	3.4976	3.4098	3.3255
4.6370	4.5638	4.4923	4.4226	4.3546	4.2883	4.2236	4.1604	4.0988	4.0386	3.9224	3.8115	3.7057	3.6046
5.0556	4.9676	4.8821	4.7988	4.7177	4.6389	4.5621	4.4873	4.4145	4.3436	4.2072	4.0776	3.9544	3.8372
5.4311	5.3283	5.2285	5.1317	5.0377	4.9464	4.8577	4.7716	4.6879	4.6065	4.4506	4.3030	4.1633	4.0310
5.7678	5.6502	5.5364	5.4262	5.3195	5.2161	5.1159	5.0188	4.9246	4.8332	4.6586	4.4941	4.3389	4.1925
6.0698	5.9377	5.8102	5.6869	5.5679	5.4527	5.3414	5.2337	5.1295	5.0286	4.8364	4.6560	4.4865	4.3271
6.3406	6.1944	6.0535	5.9177	5.7867	5.6603	5.5383	5.4206	5.3069	5.1971	4.9884	4.7932	4.6105	4.4392
6.5835	6.4236	6.2698	6.1218	5.9794	5.8424	5.7103	5.5832	5.4606	5.3423	5.1183	4.9095	4.7147	4.5327
6.8013	6.6282	6.4620	6.3025	6.1493	6.0021	5.8606	5.7245	5.5936	5.4675	5.2293	5.0081	4.8023	4.6106
6.9967	6.8109	6.6329	6.4624	6.2989	6.1422	8.9918	5.8474	5.7087	5.5755	5.3242	5.0916	4.8759	4.6755
7.1719	6.9740	6.7848	6.6039	6.4308	6.2651	6.1063	5.9542	5.8084	5.6685	5.4053	5.1624	4.9377	4.7296
7.3291	7.1196	6.9198	6.7291	6.5469	6.3729	6.2064	6.0472	5.8974	5.7487	5.4746	5.2223	4.9897	4.7746
7.4700	7.2497	7.0398	6.8399	6.6493	6.4674	6.2938	6.1280	5.9695	5.8179	5.5339	5.2732	5.0333	4.8122
7.5964	7.3658	7.1465	6.9380	6.7395	6.5504	6.3701	6.1982	6.0342	5.8775	5.5845	5.3162	5.0700	4.8435
7.7098	7.4694	7.2414	7.0248	6.8189	6.6231	6.4368	6.2593	6.0902	5.9288	5.6278	5.3528	5.1009	4.8696
7.8115	7.5620	7.3257	7.1016	6.8889	6.6870	6.4950	6.3125	6.1387	5.9731	5.6648	5.3837	5.1268	4.8913
7.9027	7.6447	7.4006	7.1695	6.9506	6.7429	6.5459	6.3587	6.1807	6.0113	5.6964	5.4099	5.1486	4.9094
7.9845	7.7184	7.4672	7.2297	7.0049	6.7921	6.5903	6.3988	3.2170	6.0443	5.7234	5.4321	5.1669	4.9245
8.0578	7.7843	7.5264	7.2829	7.0528	6.8351	6.6291	6.4338	6.2485	6.0726	5.7465	5.4510	5.1822	4.9371
8.1236	7.8431	7.5790	7.3300	7.0950	6.8729	6.6629	6.4642	6.2758	6.0971	5.7662	5.4669	5.1952	4.9476
8.1826	7.8957	7.6258	7.3717	7.1321	6.9061	6.6925	6.4906	6.2294	6.1182	5.7831	5.4804	5.2060	4.9563
8.2355	7.9426	7.6674	7.4086	7.1649	6.9352	6.7184	6.5135	6.3198	6.1364	5.7975	5.4919	5.2151	4.9636
8.2830	7.9844	7.7043	7.4412	7.1937	9.9607	6.7409	6.5335	6.3375	6.1520	5.8099	5.5016	5.2228	4.9697
8.3255	8.0218	7.7372	7.4701	7.1291	6.9830	6.7606	6.5509	6.3528	6.1656	5.8204	5.5098	5.2292	4.9747
8.3637	8.0552	7.7664	7.4957	7.2415	7.0027	6.7779	6.5660	6.3661	6.1772	5.8294	5.5168	5.2347	4.9789
8.3980	8.0850	7.7923	7.5183	7.2613	7.0199	6.7929	6.5791	6.3776	6.1872	5.8371	5.5227	5.2392	4.9825
8.4287	8.1116	7.8154	7.5383	7.2786	7.0350	6.8060	6.5905	6.3875	6.1959	5.8437	5.5277	5.2430	4.9854
8.4562	8.1354	7.8359	7.5560	7.2940	7.0482	6.8175	6.6005	6.3961	6.2034	5.8493	5.5320	5.2463	4.9878
8.4809	8.1566	7.8542	7.5717	7.3075	7.0599	6.8275	6.6091	6.4035	6.2098	5.8541	5.5356	5.2490	4.9898
8.5030	8.1755	7.8704	7.5856	7.3193	7.0701	6.8362	6.6166	4.4100	6.2153	5.8582	5.5386	5.2512	4.9930
8.5229	8.1924	7.8848	7.5979	7.3298	7.0790	6.8439	6.6231	6.4156	6.2201	5.8617	5.5412	5.2531	4.9930
8.5407	8.2075	7.8976	7.6087	7.3390	7.0868	6.8505	6.6288	6.4204	6.2242	5.8647	5.5434	5.2547	4.9941
8.5567	8.2210	7.9090	7.6183	7.3472	7.0937	6.8564	6.6338	6.4246	6.2278	5.8673	5.5453	5.2561	4.9951
8.5710	8.2330	7.9191	7.6268	7.3543	7.0998	6.8615	6.6381	6.4282	6.2309	5.8695	5.5468	5.2572	4.9959
8.5839	8.2438	7.9281	7.6344	7.3607	7.1050	6.8659	6.6418	6.4314	6.2335	5.8713	5.5482	5.2582	4.9966
8.5954	8.2534	7.9361	7.6410	7.3662	7.1097	6.8698	6.6450	6.4341	6.2358	5.8729	5.5493	5.2590	4.9972
8.6058	8.2619	7.9432	7.6469	7.3711	7.1138	6.8732	6.6479	6.4364	6.2377	5.8743	5.5502	5.2596	4.9976
8.6150	8.2696	7.9495	7.6522	7.3754	7.1173	6.8761	6.6503	6.4385	6.2394	5.8755	5.5511	5.2602	4.9980
8.6233	8.2764	7.9951	7.6568	7.3792	7.1205	6.8787	6.6524	6.4402	6.2409	5.8765	5.5517	5.2607	4.9984
8.6308	8.2825	7.9601	7.6609	7.3826	7.1232	6.8810	6.6543	6.4418	6.2421	5.8773	5.5523	5.2611	4.9986
8.6375	8.2880	7.9645	7.6645	7.3855	7.1256	6.8830	6.6559	6.4431	6.2432	5.8781	5.5528	5.2614	4.9989
8.6435	8.2928	7.9685	7.6677	7.3881	7.1277	6.8847	6.6573	6.4442	6.2442	5.8787	5.5532	5.2617	4.9991
8.6489	8.2972	7.9720	7.6705	7.3904	7.1296	6.8862	6.6585	6.4452	6.2450	5.8792	5.5536	5.2619	4.9992
8.6537	8.3010	7.9751	7.6730	7.3925	7.1312	6.8875	6.6596	6.4461	6.2457	5.8797	5.5539	5.2621	4.9993
8.6580	8.3045	7.9779	7.6752	7.3942	7.1327	6.8886	6.6605	6.4468	6.2463	5.8801	5.5541	5.2623	4.9995

GLOSSARY

A

account payable A current liability that represents an amount owed by a business to a supplier (generally for inventory purchases)

account The basic storage unit for financial data in an accounting system; the compilation of all accounts is the general ledger

accounting cycle The set of recurring accounting procedures that must be performed for a business each accounting period

accounting equation The mathematical expression indicating that the sum of an entity's assets must equal the collective sum of its liabilities and owners' or stockholders' equity

accounting period concept An accounting principle that allows accountants to prepare meaningful financial reports for ongoing business enterprises by dividing the lives of these entities into regular reporting intervals of equal length

accounting A service activity designed to provide quantitative information about economic entities that is intended to be useful in making economic decisions

accounts receivable turnover ratio A measure of how often a business collects or "turns over" its accounts receivable each year; calculated as net credit sales divided by average accounts receivable

accrual basis of accounting A method of accounting under which the economic impact of a transaction is recognized (recorded) whether or not the transaction involves cash

accrued asset A receivable resulting from a revenue that has been earned but not yet received

accrued liability An amount that is currently owed by a business that had to be recorded at the end of an accounting period because it had not been recorded previously; often must be estimated

accumulated depreciation The total amount of depreciation that has been recorded on a depreciable asset or group of depreciable assets since their acquisition

activity Any repetitive action performed to fulfill a business function

activity-based costing An alternative method to allocating overhead costs to products and services by collecting costs on the basis of the underlying nature and extent of the activities performed to make, render, distribute, or support those products and services

activity-based management The process of investigating activities performed during product manufacturing or service performance so that the process may be streamlined to increase customer value and business profitability

actual cost system An inventory valuation method in which the company uses the actual costs of materials, labor, and overhead to compute product cost

adjusting entry A journal entry made at the end of an accounting period to ensure that the revenue recognition and expense recognition rules are properly applied that period

age of inventory A measure of how old inventory on hand is, computed as 360 days divided by the inventory turnover ratio

age of receivables A measure of the collectibility of accounts receivable; calculated as the (rounded) number of days in a year (360) divided by the accounts receivable turnover ratio

allowance method An accounting method used to estimate the uncollectible accounts expense each accounting period

amortization The allocation of the cost of an intangible asset to the accounting periods that it provides economic benefits to an entity

annuity A series of payments of a specified size and frequency

applied overhead The amount of predetermined overhead that is added to the Work in Process Inventory account

asset turnover A ratio that indicates the dollars of sales generated by each dollar of asset investment; calculated as (sales ÷ asset investment)

asset A probable future economic benefit obtained or controlled by a particular entity as a result of past transactions or events

authorized stock The maximum number of shares of a given class of stock a company is permitted to issue under the terms of its corporate charter

available-for-sale securities Investments in stocks or bonds that are made for the short-term and in order to generate a rate of return that is greater than what could be earned by investing excess cash in an interest-bearing account

B

balance sheet A financial statement that summarizes the assets, liabilities, and owners' equity of an entity at a specific point in time

bank reconciliation A schedule that presents the differences between the bank statement and the cash account so that an accurate balance of cash can be determined for a specific time

benchmarking The process of comparing an organization's products, processes, or services against those of organizations that have been proven to be "best in class"

bond indenture The legal contract between a bond purchaser and the issuing company; identifies the rights and obligations of each party

bond A long-term loan made by one party to another that is legally documented by a bond certificate

book value (of a PP&E asset) The cost of a depreciable property, plant and equipment asset minus its accumulated depreciation

book value per share Common stockholders' equity per share for a corporation; computed by dividing total common stockholders' equity by the number of outstanding shares of common stock

break-even graph A visual depiction of the relationships among revenue, volume, fixed costs, and variable costs; the point at which the total revenue and total cost lines intersect is the break-even point

break-even point The level of sales at which no profits are generated and no losses are incurred

budget A financial plan for the future

budgeting Planning for the future using monetary amounts

business value-added activity An activity that is essential to operations, but for which customers would not willingly choose to pay

business An organization that attempts to earn a return over the cost of providing services or goods that satisfy the needs or wants of others

C

callable bond A bond that can be retired or redeemed by the issuing company when one or more conditions are met

callable preferred stock Preferred stock that can be reacquired at the option of the issuing corporation

capital budget The plan for long-term expenditures for plant assets

capital lease A lease that is generally non-cancelable, long-term, and transfers at least some ownership rights or risks to the lessee

cash basis of accounting A method of accounting under which revenues are recorded when cash is received and expenses are recorded when cash is disbursed

cash dividend A proportionate distribution of a company's prior earnings to its stockholders made in the form of cash

cash equivalent Any investment in a short-term security, such as certificates of deposit (CDs), money market funds, and United States treasury bills, that has 90 days or less to maturity when purchased

cash flow per share A measure of the net cash flow from operating activities for an accounting period, less preferred stock dividends, divided by the weighted average number of shares of common stock outstanding during that period

chart of accounts A numerical listing, by assigned account number, of a business's accounts

closing entry A journal entry made at the end of an accounting period to close out or transfer the balance of one or more temporary accounts to the appropriate owners' equity account

common stock A class of stock that represents the residual ownership interests of a corporation

common stock The total par or stated value of the number of shares of stock that the corporation has issued

common-sized financial statement A financial statement in which each line item is expressed as a percentage of a major financial statement component

comparability A measure of the degree to which an entity's accounting information can be easily compared with similar information reported for the entity in prior accounting periods and with similar information reported by other entities

compound journal entry A journal entry that affects more than two accounts

conservatism principle An accounting principle dictating that uncertainty regarding an asset's or revenue's valuation should generally be resolved in favor of understating the asset or revenue; for liabilities and expenses, the uncertainty should be resolved in favor of overstatement

consolidation The process of combining the financial statements of a parent and its more-than-50-percent owned subsidiary at the end of a period

contingent liability A potential liability that may become an actual liability if one or more events occur or fail to occur

contra-account An account that is an offset to or reduction of a related account for financial statement purposes; an example is Accumulated Depreciation

contribution margin ratio The percentage of revenue that remains after variable costs are covered; calculated as unit contribution margin divided by unit selling price

contribution margin The difference between the selling price per unit and the total variable cost per unit

controllable cost A cost that a manager can authorize or directly influence in terms of dollar magnitude

conversion cost The cost of direct labor and overhead

convertible bond A bond that may be exchanged for stock in the issuing company at the option of the bondholders

convertible preferred stock Preferred stock that can be exchanged, at the option of preferred stockholders, for common stock of the issuing corporation

copyright An exclusive right granted by the federal government to produce and sell works of art such as songs, books, and films

corporate charter A contract between a corporation and the state in which it was created and identifies the corporation's principal rights and obligations

corporation An entity created by law and having both an existence apart from that of its members as well as distinct and inherent rights and duties

cost center A responsibility center in which the manager is solely responsible for controlling costs

cost driver A factor that has a direct cause-effect relationship with a cost

cost method (of accounting for a stock investment) The method of accounting used when a company owns less than 20 percent of another company; the investing company recognizes Dividend Revenue when cash dividends are received

cost object Anything to which management wants to attach costs, such as an organizational product, service, department, or territory

cost of goods available for sale The sum of beginning inventory and merchandise purchases minus purchase returns for an accounting period

cost-volume-profit analysis A model that expands on the break-even model so as to include the profitability impacts caused by assessing the relationships among selling prices, costs, and volumes

credit term An agreement between a buyer and seller regarding the timing of payment by the buyer and any discount available to the buyer for early payment

credit The right-hand side of a T-account or an entry made on the right-hand side of a T-account (or in the credit column of an account); as a verb, to enter an amount on the right-hand side of a T-account or in the credit column of an account

cross-sectional ratio analysis A comparison of a company's financial ratios with those of competing companies and/or with the industry norms for those ratios

cumulative effect of a change in accounting principle The change in an entity's collective net income for prior years assuming a newly adopted accounting principle has been implemented

cumulative preferred stock Preferred stock on which dividends that are not paid in a given year accumulate and must be paid in the future before common stockholders can receive a dividend

current asset Cash or another asset that will be converted into cash, sold, or consumed during the next fiscal year or the normal operating cycle of a business, whichever is longer

current liability A debt or obligation of a business that will be eliminated by giving up current assets or incurring another current liability

current ratio A measure of liquidity calculated as current assets divided by current liabilities

current replacement cost The per unit cost that a business must pay to replace inventory items sold to customers

D

debenture A bond backed only by the legal commitment of the issuing firm to make all required principal and interest payments; often referred to as debentures

debit The left-hand side of a T-account or an entry made on the left-hand side of a T-account (or in the debit column of an account); as a verb, to enter an amount on the left-hand side of a T-account or in the debit column of an account

debt to total asset ratio A solvency ratio that indicates the ability of a company to meet its long-term debts; calculated as total liabilities divided by total assets

deferred expense An asset representing a prepayment of an expense item

deferred revenue A liability resulting from an amount received by a business for a service or product that it will provide or deliver in the future

degree of operating leverage A measure that reflects an organization's variable and fixed cost relationship and indicates how a percentage change in sales from the current level will impact profits (or losses)

depletion The allocation of the cost of natural resources to the periods these assets provide economic benefits to an entity

depreciable cost The acquisition cost of a depreciable asset less its salvage value

depreciation The accounting process of writing off, as an expense, the cost of a property, plant and equipment asset over its useful life to the business

direct cost A cost that is clearly and conveniently traceable to and a monetarily important part of a specified cost object

direct labor The category of people who work specifically on manufacturing a product

direct material A readily clearly identifiable and conveniently traceable part of a product, the cost of which is monetarily significant to the total product

direct method (of preparing a statement of cash flows) An approach to preparing the statement of cash flows in which specific cash inflows and outflows from a business's operating activities are identified and listed in the initial section of the financial statement

direct write-off method An accounting method under which uncollectible accounts expense is recorded when it is determined that a specific account receivable is unlikely to be collected; this non-GAAP alternative to the allowance method is used for taxation purposes

discontinued operation A business segment that will no longer be a part of the organization; information on the sale of such a segment is shown as a separate section of the income statement

discounting The process of removing the interest portion of future cash receipts (payments) so as to obtain the present value of those future receipts (payments)

dividend in arrears An unpaid dividend on cumulative preferred stock; should be disclosed in a company's financial statement footnotes

dividend yield The annual dividend paid on a stock divided by its current market price

dividend A distribution by a corporation of earnings to stockholders

double-declining-balance method A depreciation method under which annual depreciation expense is computed by multiplying twice the straight-line rate times an asset's book value at the beginning of the year

double-entry bookkeeping A method of maintaining financial records developed more than five hundred years ago that serves as the foundation of modern accounting systems worldwide

Du Pont model A restatement of the ROI formula to provide information about profit margin and asset turnover; calculated as (income ÷ sales) • (sales ÷ asset investment)

E

earnings per share An amount typically calculated as net income divided by the weighted-average number of shares of common stock outstanding during a given year

earnings quality The degree of correlation between a firm's economic income and its reported earnings determined by generally accepted accounting principles (GAAP)

effective interest rate The market interest rate on the date bonds are initially sold; represents the true rate of interest incurred over the term of a bond issue by the issuing company

entity concept An accounting principle dictating that a business enterprise be treated as a distinct unit independent of its owners

equity method (of accounting for a stock investment) The method of accounting used when a company owns 20 percent or more of another company; the investing company recognizes its proportionate share of the investee's profits (or losses) for the period in income and as an increase to the Investment account; the Investment account is reduced when cash dividends are received

equivalent units of production An estimate of the number of fully completed units that could have been manufactured in a process costing production environment during a period if all production efforts had resulted in completed units

expense A cost of doing business; a decrease in assets or an increase in a liability resulting from an entity's profit-oriented activities

extraordinary item A material gain or loss that is both unusual in nature and infrequent in occurrence

F

FIFO (first-in, first-out) method An inventory costing method under which the per unit costs of the most recently acquired goods are used to establish the cost basis of ending inventory

Financial Accounting Standards Board (FASB) The private sector rule-making body that has the primary authority for establishing accounting standards in the United States

financial ratio A measure that express the relationship or interrelationships between, or among, two or more financial statement items

financial statement footnote An inclusion to an annual report that is intended to assist decision makers in interpreting and drawing proper conclusions from an entity's financial statements

financial statement Any one of many reports about monetary information related to a business; the most common financial statements are the income statement, balance sheet, statement of stockholders' equity, and statement of cash flows; collectively, these items are the principal means accountants use to communicate financial information regarding business entities and other organizations to investors, creditors, and other decision makers external to those entities

financing activity Any transaction or event of a business that involves obtaining cash from lenders and/or repaying those amounts as well as obtaining cash from investors and providing them with a return of and a return on their investments

fiscal year The twelve-month period covered by an entity's annual income statement

fixed cost A cost that remains constant in total with changes in activity as long as operations are within the relevant range

flexible budget A series of estimates of expected costs for the upcoming period based on various levels of activity

FOB destination Shipping term in which the seller delivers the goods free on board (FOB) to the destination; thus, the seller incurs the freight charge and retains legal possession of the goods until they reach the destination

FOB shipping point Shipping term in which the seller delivers the goods free on board (FOB) to the shipping point; thus, the buyer incurs the freight charge and obtains legal possession of the goods once they reach the shipping point

free cash flow A measurement of the cash generated by a company's operations in excess of that needed to maintain current organizational productivity; can be calculated as cash flow from operating activities minus capital investments for property, plant and equipment

full disclosure principle An accounting principle dictating that all information needed to obtain a thorough understanding of an entity's financial affairs be included in its financial statements or accompanying narrative disclosures

G

general journal The accounting record in which dollar amounts for transactions and other financial events are initially recorded by businesses; the book of original entry for transactions

general ledger The accounting record that contains each of the individual accounts for a business's assets, liabilities, owners' or stockholders' equity, revenues, and expenses

generally accepted accounting principles (GAAP) The collection of concepts, guidelines, and rules that are used in applying double-entry bookkeeping to the task of recording and reporting financial information

generally accepted accounting principles (GAAP) The concepts, guidelines, and rules that accountants follow in recording and reporting financial information

going concern assumption An accounting principle dictating that an entity should be treated as if it will continue to operate long enough to use its longest-lived asset. This time frame is often assumed to be indefinite, unless there is evidence to the contrary

goodwill The excess of the cost of a group of assets over their collective market value

gross profit percentage Cost of goods sold divided by sales; a measure of the profit margin generated by the sale of a product

gross profit The difference between an entity's net sales and cost of goods sold during an accounting period

H

historical cost principle An accounting principle dictating that the primary valuation basis for most assets is their historical or original cost

horizontal ratio analysis *See trend analysis*

I

impairment The excess of the carrying value of an asset over its current fair market value or the present value of its expected future cash flows

income from continuing operations The earnings produced by a corporation's principal profit-oriented activities

income statement A financial statement summarizing a business's revenues and expenses for a given accounting period

incremental analysis A method of finding solutions to problem by focusing only on the factors that change from one course of action to another

indirect cost A cost that is not clearly and conveniently traceable to a cost object or is not monetarily significant to the total cost of a cost object and, thus, would be assigned to the cost object using some rational base of allocation

indirect labor Factory employees who do not work directly on production (such as janitorial staff or supervisors), but are included as part of overhead

indirect material A product part that is not identifiable, traceable, or monetarily significant to the product; included as part of overhead

indirect method (of preparing a statement of cash flows) An approach to preparing the statement of cash flows in which net cash flow from operating activities is determined by making certain adjustments to a business's net income

intangible asset A long-term asset used in the business that does not have a physical form or substance

inventory turnover ratio A measure of how often a business sells or turns over its inventory each year; computed as cost of goods sold divided by average inventory

inventory Goods that businesses intend to sell to their customers as well as raw materials and in-process items that will be converted into saleable goods

investing activity Any transaction or event of a business that includes the making and collecting of loans, acquisition and disposal of property, plant & equipment, and/or purchase and sale of debt and equity securities other than trading securities and cash equivalents

investment center A responsibility center in which the manager is responsible for controlling costs, generating revenue, and obtaining reasonable returns on the asset base

issued stock The number of shares of a class of stock that has been sold or otherwise distributed by a corporation; these shares may be outstanding or held as treasury stock

J

job order costing system An inventory costing system that is used by manufacturers who are producing goods in relatively small quantities, often to customer specifications, or by service companies that are accumulating costs for a particular customer

job A cost object related to a specific order or customer

journalize The process of recording financial data about a transaction of a business in a journal

L

labor efficiency variance The cost saved (favorable) or lost (unfavorable) because of the difference between the standard wages for the actual hours worked and the standard wages for the standard hours allowed for the actual production

labor rate variance The cost saved (favorable) or lost (unfavorable) because of the difference between the actual wages paid for the actual hours worked and the standard wages for the actual hours worked

leasehold improvement A betterment made to a leased property by a lessee that reverts to the lessor at the end of the lease

liability A probable future sacrifice of economic benefits; an amount owed by an entity to a third party

LIFO (last-in, first-out) method An inventory costing method under which the per unit costs of the earliest acquired goods are used to establish the cost basis of ending inventory

liquidity An entity's ability to finance its day-to-day operations and to pay its liabilities as they mature

longitudinal ratio analysis A variation of ratio analysis that focuses on the changes in a business's ratios over a period of time

long-term debt to equity ratio A common measure of financial leverage; computed by dividing a company's long-term debt by its stockholders' equity

lower-of-cost-or-market (LCM) rule An accounting rule that requires businesses to value their ending inventories at the lower of cost or market value, the latter typically being defined as current replacement cost

M

maker The party who has signed a promissory note and is thus obligated to pay a certain amount to another party by a certain date

management by exception A technique in which managers set upper and lower tolerance limits for deviations and investigate only deviations that fall outside these tolerance ranges

managerial accounting The function of gathering, processing, and analyzing information (both quantitative and qualitative) to (1) provide information to internal parties for planning and controlling operations and (2) estimate an organization's product or service cost

margin of safety The excess of sales over break-even point; can be calculated in units or sales dollars

matching principle An accounting principle requiring that expenses be recorded in the same accounting period as the related revenues

material price variance The cost saved (favorable) or lost (unfavorable) because of the difference between the actual price paid for material and the standard price for material

material quantity variance The cost saved (favorable) or lost (unfavorable) because of the difference between the actual quantity of material used and the standard quantity of material allowed for the goods produced during the period, times the standard price for material

materiality An accounting principle referring to the relative importance of specific items of accounting information as to their influence on a financial statement user's decision

maturity date The date that the maker of a promissory note must pay its maturity value to the payee

maturity value The sum of the principal and interest due on a promissory note on its maturity date

minority interest The portion of ownership interest of a subsidiary not owned by the parent company

mixed cost A cost that is comprised of both a variable and a fixed element

moving-average method An inventory costing method applied in a perpetual inventory system; under this method, the cost basis of ending inventory is determined by multiplying the number of unsold units of each inventory item by its moving-average per unit cost at the end of the accounting period

N

natural resource A long-term asset, such as a coal deposit, oil and gas reservoir, or tract of standing timber, that is extracted or harvested from the earth's surface or from beneath the earth's surface

net income (net loss) The positive (negative) difference between an entity's revenues and expenses during an accounting period

noncontrollable cost A cost that a manager cannot authorize or directly influence in terms of dollar magnitude

nonoperating revenue The inflow of new assets into a business from "sideline" (nonprimary) activities of the company

non-value-added activity An activity that increases the time spent on a product or service but does not increase its worth to the customer

normal cost system An inventory valuation method in which the company uses actual costs of materials and labor and an estimated cost for overhead to compute product cost

note payable An obligation that is documented by a legally binding written commitment known as a promissory note; can be either a current or long-term liability depending upon its maturity date

O

off-balance sheet financing The use of long-term obligations that are not reported in an entity's balance sheet to acquire assets or services

operating activity Any transaction or event related to the production and delivery of goods and services by a business

operating cycle The period of time elapsing from the use of cash in the normal operating activities of an entity to the collection of cash from the entity's customers

operating expense A cost, other than cost of goods sold, that an entity incurs in its principal business operations

operating income An entity's gross profit less its operating expenses; represents the income generated by an entity's principal line or lines of business

operating lease A lease that is usually cancelable by the lessee, covers a short-term, and does not transfer ownership rights or risks to the lessee

operating revenue The inflow of new assets into a business from the sales prices of the products sold or the services performed from the primary operations of the company

outstanding stock The number of shares of a given class of stock owned by a company's stockholders

overapplied overhead The result of applying more overhead to the Work in Process Inventory than the actual amount of overhead incurred

overhead Any cost incurred in the manufacturing area that cannot or is not directly traced to the product, or any service-related cost that cannot or is not directly traced to performing a service for sale to others

P

par value The specific dollar amount per share that is printed on each stock certificate

parent company A company that owns more than 50 percent of another company (the subsidiary)

partnership An unincorporated business with two or more owners patent An exclusive right granted by the United States Patent Office to manufacture a specific product or use a specific process

payee The party to whom the maker of a promissory note must eventually pay the maturity value of that note

period cost Any cost related to the selling and administrative functions of an organization

periodic inventory system An inventory accounting system in which the dollar value of ending inventory is determined by counting the goods on hand at the end of each accounting period and then multiplying the quantity of each item by the appropriate per unit cost

permanent account An account whose period-ending balance is carried forward to the next accounting period

perpetual inventory system An inventory accounting system in which a perpetually updated record of the quantity of individual inventory items and their per unit costs is maintained

petty cash A limited amount of cash that is kept on hand by a business to pay for small items

posting The process of transferring accounting data from a journal to the appropriate general ledger accounts

predetermined overhead rate An expected overhead cost per unit of activity that is used to assign overhead to products or services

preemptive right The right of a stockholder to retain his or her proportional ownership interest in a corporation when additional stock is issued

preferred stock A class of stock that has certain preferences or advantages relative to a company's common stock

present value The current value of one or more future cash receipts (payments) that have been discounted at the market rate of interest rate

principal The amount initially owed by the maker of a promissory note

prior period adjustment A restatement of the balance of Retained Earnings because of a correction of an error in a past accounting period

pro forma financial statement A projected or budgeted balance sheet, income statement, statement of cash flows or statement of changes in stockholders' equity

process costing system An inventory costing system that is used by manufacturers that are producing mass quantities of similar goods

process map A type of flowchart that indicates all steps taken in performing an activity

profit center A responsibility center in which the manager is responsible for controlling costs and generating revenues

profit margin A ratio of income to sales that indicates the portion of each sales dollar that is not consumed by expenses; calculated as (income ÷ sales)

profit-volume graph A visual depiction of the relationships among revenue, volume, fixed costs, and variable costs that shows the profit or loss amounts at each level of volume; the point at which the total cost line insects the volume axis is the break-even point

purchase allowance A price concession granted by a supplier in exchange for keeping damaged or defective goods

purchase discount A discount offered by a supplier to encourage prompt payment of credit purchases made by their customers

purchase return A reduction in an amount owed to a supplier as a result of returned goods

Q

quick asset Cash, a cash equivalent, a short-term investment, and the net amount of current notes or accounts receivable

quick ratio A measure of an entity's liquidity; calculated as quick assets (cash and cash equivalents, short-term investments, and net current receivables) divided by current liabilities

R

ratio analysis An analytical technique that typically involves studying the relationship between two financial statement items

relevant range The normal annual operating range of activity for the organization

replacement cost The cost that would be required at the present time to buy an asset similar to one that is currently in use

responsibility center An organizational subunit that is under the control of a designated manager

retail inventory method A periodic inventory method that requires information to be kept on the retail prices of the goods purchased and a cost-to-retail percentage to be determined so as to estimate the cost of ending inventory; provides better internal control than most periodic systems because the retail value of goods that should be on hand at year-end is known

retained earnings The total amount of profits that have been generated by a company and not distributed to stockholders

return on equity A key measure of a corporation's profitability; computed by dividing net income, less preferred stock dividends, by average common stockholders' equity for a given period

return on investment A ratio that indicates the relationship between the income generated by an organization or organizational subunit to the asset base used to produce that income; calculated as (income ÷ asset investment)

revenue recognition rule An accounting rule requiring revenues to be both realized and earned before they are recognized (recorded)

revenue An increase in assets or decrease in liabilities resulting from an entity's profit-oriented activities

rolling budget A budget that consistently plans for the upcoming 12-month period; when one budget month ends, a new month is added

S

sales allowance A price reduction granted to customers to persuade them to keep damaged or defective merchandise

sales discount A reduction in price offered to customers to entice them to pay their account balances on a timely basis

sales return A refund paid to or a reduction of the amount owed by customers who return damaged or defective merchandise

salvage value The estimated value of an asset at the end of its useful life

secured bond A bond collateralized by specific assets of the issuing company; sometimes referred to as a mortgage bond

Securities and Exchange Commission (SEC) A federal agency that regulates the sale and subsequent trading of securities by publicly owned companies; also oversees the financial reporting and accounting practices of those companies

sole proprietorship An unincorporated business owned by one individual

source document Any supporting item that identifies the key features or parameters of business transactions; examples include invoices, sales slips, legal contracts, and purchase orders

specific identification method An inventory costing method under which actual per unit costs are used to establish the cost basis of ending inventory

standard cost system An inventory valuation method in which the company uses estimates of typical costs for materials, labor, and overhead to develop product cost

standard cost A budgeted cost to manufacture one unit of product or perform a single service

standard quantity allowed A measure of quantity that translates the actual output achieved into the standard input quantity that should have been used to achieve that output

standard A norm or average

stated interest rate The rate of interest paid to bondholders based upon the face value of the bonds; also known as the face interest rate or contract interest rate

statement of cash flows A financial statement revealing how an entity generated and spent cash during an accounting period

statement of cash flows A financial statement that accounts for the net change in a business's cash balance during a given period; this statement summarizes the cash receipts and disbursements from a business's operating, investing, and financing activities

statement of stockholders' equity A financial statement reconciling the dollar amounts of a corporation's stockholders' equity components at the beginning and end of an accounting period

stock dividend A proportionate distribution of a corporation's own stock to its stockholders

stock option A right to buy a company's stock at a future date at a guaranteed price, such as the current market price

stock split An increase in the number of shares of a company's stock accompanied by a proportionate reduction in the stock's par value

stockholder An owner of a corporation

straight-line method A depreciation method that allocates an equal amount of depreciation expense to each year of an asset's estimated useful life

subsidiary A company that has more than 50 percent of its stock owned by another company (the parent)

T

T-account An account typically used for illustrative or analytical purposes whose name is derived from its shape; such accounts are not part of any formal accounting system

temporary account An account whose period-ending balance is transferred or closed to the appropriate owners' equity account in a sole proprietorship or partnership or to Retained Earnings in a corporation

temporary difference A difference between an entity's taxable income and pretax accounting income that arises from applying different accounting methods for taxation and financial accounting purposes

term of a note The number of days from the date a promissory note is signed, not counting the signing date, to the date the note matures

time value of money concept The idea that a dollar received (or paid) currently is worth more than dollar received (or paid) in the future because the current dollar can be invested to earn interest and, thus, will be worth more in the future than it is now

times interest earned ratio A financial ratio used to evaluate a firm's ability to make interest payments on its long-term debt; computed by dividing the sum of net income, interest expense, and income taxes expense by interest expense

trademark A distinctive name, symbol, or logo used to identify a specific business entity or one of its products

treasury stock Common or preferred stock that has been issued by a corporation and then reacquired by that corporation

trend analysis The study of percentage changes in financial statement items over a period of time

trial balance A two-column listing of a business's general ledger account balances, one column for debit balances and one column for credit balances

U

underapplied overhead The result of applying less overhead to Work in Process Inventory than the actual amount of overhead incurred

unearned revenue An amount that has been received in cash by the business but for which the business has not yet provided the product or service that will cause the earnings process to be complete

unit of measurement concept The accounting principle dictating that a common unit of measurement is used to record and report transactions and other financial statement items

units-of-production method A depreciation method under which an asset's useful life is expressed in the number of units of production or use; depreciation expense for any given period is a function of the level of usage of the asset during that period

V

value-added activity An activity that increases a product or service's worth to a customer and for which the customer would be willing to pay

variable cost ratio The variable cost percentage of each revenue dollar; calculated as (100 percent – CM ratio), or total variable cost per unit divided by unit selling price

variable cost A cost that changes in total in direct proportion to changes in activity as long as operations are within the relevant range

variance analysis The process of determining whether a variance is favorable or unfavorable and finding its underlying cause

variance A difference between actual and budgeted prices or quantities

W

working capital The difference between an entity's current assets and current liabilities

INDEX

Q

R

S

PHOTO CREDITS

Page 2: © PhotoDisc, Inc.
Page 20: © PhotoDisc, Inc.
Page 46: © Stone/Mark Segal
Page 94: © PhotoDisc, Inc.
Page 124: © Corbis Digital Stock
Page 154: © PhotoDisc, Inc.
Page 182: © The Image Bank/Philippe AEF.Houze
Page 220: Photo provided courtesy of Darden Restaurants
Page 250: © Taxi/Gary Buss
Page 288: © Corbis Digital Stock
Page 318: Photo provided courtesy of Rogar International
Page 346: Photo provided courtesy of Rosedown Plantation
Page 370: © PhotoDisc, Inc.
Page 400: Screen shot used with permission of Art.com